Constructing Japan

Brill Studies in Architectural and Urban History

Editors-in-Chief

Cor Wagenaar
(*Delft University of Technology and University of Groningen*)

Editorial Board

Carla Keyvanian (*Auburn University*)
Johan Lagai (*Ghent University*)
Ian Morley (*Chinese University of Hongkong*)
Reinout Rutte (*Delft University of Technology*)
Nancy Stieber (*University of Massachusetts, Boston*)
Bohdan Tscherkes (*Lviv Polytechnic National University*)

VOLUME 3

The titles published in this series are listed at *brill.com/auh*

Constructing Japan

*Knowledge Production and Identity Building in Late
Nineteenth-Century Western Architectural Discourses
(1853–1900)*

By

Beate Löffler

BRILL

LEIDEN | BOSTON

Cover illustration: Forms of Japanese gates and entrances, illustration accompanying the essay "Some notes on Japanese architecture" by Francis Taylor Piggott, in *The builder* 64 (8 April 1893), here p. 262 (public domain).

Library of Congress Cataloging-in-Publication Data
Names: Löffler, Beate, 1971– author
Title: Constructing Japan : knowledge production and identity building in late nineteenth-century Western architectural discourses (1853–1900) / by Beate Löffler.
Other titles: Brill studies in architectural and urban history
Description: Leiden ; Boston : Brill, [2025] | Series: Brill studies in architectural and urban history, 2589–4412 ; volume 3 | Includes bibliographical references and index.
Identifiers: LCCN 2025005409 (print) | LCCN 2025005410 (ebook) | ISBN 9789004702332 hardback | ISBN 9789004724174 ebook
Subjects: LCSH: Architecture, Modern–19th century | Architecture, Modern—Western countries—Japanese influences
Classification: LCC NA645 .L64 2025 (print) | LCC NA645 (ebook) | DDC 724/.5—dc23/eng/20250311
LC record available at https://lccn.loc.gov/2025005409
LC ebook record available at https://lccn.loc.gov/2025005410

Typeface for the Latin, Greek, and Cyrillic scripts: "Brill". See and download: brill.com/brill-typeface.

ISSN 2589-4412
ISBN 978-90-04-70233-2 (hardback)
ISBN 978-90-04-72417-4 (e-book)
DOI 10.1163/9789004724174

Copyright 2025 by Beate Löffler. Published by Koninklijke Brill BV, Plantijnstraat 2, 2321 JC Leiden, The Netherlands.
Koninklijke Brill BV incorporates the imprints Brill, Brill Nijhoff, Brill Schöningh, Brill Fink, Brill mentis, Brill Wageningen Academic, Vandenhoeck & Ruprecht, Böhlau and V&R unipress.
Koninklijke Brill BV reserves the right to protect this publication against unauthorized use. Requests for re-use and/or translations must be addressed to Koninklijke Brill BV via brill.com or copyright.com. For more information: info@brill.com.

This book is printed on acid-free paper and produced in a sustainable manner.

Contents

Acknowledgements IX
List of Figures X
Abbreviations XXVII
Timeline XXVIII

1 Introduction 1
  1 Context, Source Materials and Methodological Approach 4
  2 Research Background and Disciplinary Context 6

2 My Perception, Your Perception
  Available Knowledge, Research Questions, Approaches, and Expert Networks in the Late Nineteenth Century 17
  1 Knowledge of Japanese Architecture Available in the West 17
    1.1 *From Marco Polo to Matthew C. Perry* 17
      1.1.1 Encyclopaedias 18
      1.1.2 Architectural Reference Books 27
    1.2 From Matthew C. Perry to the *Exposition Universelle* of 1900 28
      1.2.1 Visual Sources 33
      1.2.2 Architectural Reference Books 34
  2 Diplomats, Experts and Knowledge Mediators' Networks 37
    2.1 *Media* 37
      2.1.1 Cultural Journals and General-Interest Magazines 39
      2.1.2 Art Periodicals 40
      2.1.3 Architectural Journals 41
    2.2 *Contributors and Networks* 42
      2.2.1 Édouard (Edward) Lévi, named Montefiore 43
      2.2.2 Yamamoto Kakuma 46
      2.2.3 Richard Henry Brunton 47
      2.2.4 Ernest Mason Satow 48
      2.2.5 Edward William Godwin 51
      2.2.6 Rutherford Alcock 52
      2.2.7 James Jackson Jarves 53
      2.2.8 Jules Lescasse 54
      2.2.9 Josiah Conder 55
      2.2.10 Thomas Russell Hillier McClatchie 58
      2.2.11 George Cawley 60
      2.2.12 Philippe Burty 61
      2.2.13 Charles James William Pfoundes 63

             2.2.14   Preliminary Observations: Actors and
                      Backgrounds   65
             2.2.15   The Asiatic Society of Japan   67

3 **The Invisible Dwelling House**
   Topics and Non-topics in Architectural Discourses on Japan
   (1853–1900)   69
   EXCURSUS: THE JAPANESE DWELLING   71
   1   Architecture as an Art Form   77
        1.1   *Fine Arts and Architecture*   79
        1.2   *Applied Art and Craftsmanship*   86
              1.2.1   Decorative Details (Carvings, Colours,
                      Metal Fittings)   86
              1.2.2   The Japanese Artisan in General   91
              1.2.3   The Japanese Artisan in a Specific Field:
                      the Carpenter   94
   2   Architecture as a Field of Engineering   97
        2.1   *Building Structure and Earthquake Resistance*   102
              2.1.1   Statements   103
              2.1.2   Dispute   110
              2.1.3   Dead End   113
        2.2   *The Science and Economy of Construction*   115
              2.2.1   (Dis)Avowing the *Ars Mechanicae*: Carpenter
                      or Engineer   116
              2.2.2   Tools, Practices and Material Management   118
   3   Architecture as 'Social' Planning   120
        3.1   *Urban Representation and Development*   121
        3.2   *The City as a Mirror of Social Order*   127
              3.2.1   Sewage Systems and Hygiene as a Technical and
                      Social Issue   128
              3.2.2   Wooden Construction as a Socioeconomic Option   133
   4   Architecture as an Expression of Culture: Observing the Other,
        Defining the Self   136
        4.1   *Landscape, Recreational Travel and Sight-Seeing*   141
        4.2   *Cityscapes and the Impending Disappearance of
              Japaneseness*   145
        4.3   *Essentialised Japaneseness: the Vernacular Dwelling House*   150
   5   Preliminary Observations: Western Knowledge Production on
        Japanese Architecture up to the Turn of the Century and
        Its Canonisation in Handbooks   159
        5.1   *Japan in Western Architectural Handbooks*   162

4 Visiting and Visualising Architecture
Buildings, Models, Images, Exoticism and the 'Esperanto' of Construction Drawing 173
  1   Japanese Architectural Artefacts at the International Exhibitions in the West   173
    1.1   *London International Exhibition on Industry and Art, 1862*   175
    1.2   *Exposition universelle d'art et d'industrie de Paris, 1867*   176
    1.3   *Weltausstellung Wien, 1873*   181
    1.4   *Centennial International Exhibition in Philadelphia, 1876*   196
    1.5   *Exposition universelle de Paris, 1878*   204
  EXCURSUS: THE JAPANESE NATIVE VILLAGE, LONDON, 1885–1887   211
    1.6   *Exposition Universelle de Paris, 1889*   219
    1.7   *World's Columbian Exhibition in Chicago, 1893*   226
    1.8   *Exposition Universelle de Paris, 1900*   242
  2   Japanese Architecture Visualised: Books, Woodblock Prints and Souvenir Photographs   252
    2.1   *Illustrations in Western Books and Periodicals*   253
      2.1.1   Publications on Artistic or Architectural Topics   255
      2.1.2   Edward S. Morse's *Japanese Homes and Their Surroundings*   265
      2.1.3   Publications on Japanese Culture in General   266
  EXCURSUS: TRANSFER ERRORS AND UNINTENDED KNOWLEDGE PRODUCTION   288
    2.2   *Visual Material with Limited Dissemination in the West*   305
      2.2.1   Japanese Woodblock Prints   307
      2.2.2   Souvenir Photographs   318
    2.3   *Visual Material Not Disseminated in the West*   329
      2.3.1   Documentary Photography   329
      2.3.2   *Hinagatabon*   334

5 Conclusions and Further Questions   342

Glossary of Technical Terms   351
Glossary of Persons   357
Bibliography   366
Figures: Colour Section   411
Index   436

Acknowledgements

A meaningful research study depends on more than just valid questions and available literature. It also depends on funding, research libraries and suitable spaces in which to work. Not least, it benefits significantly from a supportive network of colleagues.

I thank the IN-EAST School of Advanced Studies at the University of Duisburg-Essen (funded by the Federal Ministry of Education and Research (BMBF)), for its wide-ranging support and an inspiring multi-disciplinary work environment. I owe the refining and clarification of my approaches and conclusions to the school's research context, which invited me to explain and re-contextualise the research within the broader network of competing concepts of scholarship over and over again for a number of years.

I am indebted to those many colleagues at IN-EAST and beyond who spent time and thought to discuss and comment on my ideas, thus developing them even further over time.

Finally, the work would have been incomplete without Emi Kinoshita Ph.D. (Leipzig), who organised literature from abroad and helped to disentangle *kanji* whenever needed, Prof. Dr. Johanna Blokker (Bamberg/Cottbus), who was the first to proofread the text, and Phil Jackson, who polished the revised manuscript. All remaining errors and 'Germanisms' in sentence structure and wording are entirely my own.

Figures

3.1–3.4	Een Heerenhuis/ein Herrenhaus (Siebold, Nippon, plates II, Tab. VIII–X), cropped	74
3.5–3.6	Two interiors with preparation for a wedding ceremony (Titsingh, Illustrations, after p. 224)	75
3.7	Utagawa Hiroshige: Shimosuwa, form the series Sixty-nine Stations of the Kisokaidō, about 1835–1838 (Boston Museum of Fine Arts, William S. and John T. Spaulding Collection, 21.5182, www.mfa.org, https://collections.mfa.org/download/232861 [last accessed 31 March 2024])	76
3.8	Utagawa Hiroshige: Akasaka, from the series The Fifty-three Stations of the Tōkaidō Road, 1847–1852 (Boston Museum of Fine Arts, William S. and John T. Spaulding Collection, 21.5135, www.mfa.org, https://collections.mfa.org/download/232814 [last accessed 31 March 2024])	76
3.9	Temple at Uyeno: Tokio (Conder, Notes, 2. plate, section)	88
3.10–3.11	Old Nails from Temple-doors in Nara; Diagram of Ornament in Gable (Dresser, Japan, pp. 114, 268)	89
3.12	Sculpture sur bois (Guérineau, Ornements, s.p.)	90
3.13	Pagoda at Nikkō (Dresser, Japan, p. 201)	111
3.14	Pagoda [section] (Conder, Pagodas, p. 529)	111
3.15	Entrance to the British Legation at Takanawa Tōzen-ji Temple in Edo (Hübner, Spaziergang (1882), after p. 323)	124
3.16	Le Tōzen-ji photographié par Felice Beato dans les années 1860 (anonymous via Wikipedia commons, https://commons.wikimedia.org/wiki/File:TozenjiBeato1860s.JPG [last accessed 31 March 2024])	124
3.17	Map of Japan with the exterritorial settlements and the locations for recreational travel and sightseeing discussed in the texts. (Map by the author, omitting all of the smaller islands)	142
3.18	Temple front, Nikkō Tosho-gu, by Ogawa Sashichi, ca. 1895 (Widener Library, Harvard University, https://digitalcollections.library.harvard.edu/catalog/W490875_URN-3:FHCL:4432106 [last accessed 31 March 2024])	411
3.19	Store house for treasure, Nicco, by Tamamura Kozaburo, 1880s? (E.G. Stillman collection, today Fine Arts Library, Special Collections, Harvard University, EGS26.11), cropped	411
3.20	Temple at Nikkō, 1880s? (E.G. Stillman collection, today Widener Library, Harvard University, EGS11.28), cropped	411
3.21	Das Standbild des Dai-Butzu (Heine, Beiträge, p. 313)	149

FIGURES   XI

3.22   The great statue of Buddha at Kamakura (La Farge, Artist's Letters,
          frontispiece)   149
3.23–3.24 Views of Hermann Muthesius' Japanese room, taken from a photo album,
          about 1889 (courtesy of Werkbundarchiv – Museum der Dinge, Nachlass
          Hermann Muthesius, D 7335)   154
3.25   Rooms [in a Japanese house] by Adolfo Farsari, 1886 (Boston Museum of
          Fine Arts, Gift of Jean S. and Frederic A. Sharf, 2004.269.16, www.mfa.org,
          https://collections.mfa.org/objects/417133/ [last accessed 31 March 2024]),
          cropped   154
3.26   Henry Treffry Dunn: Sonnets and Ballads [Gabriel Rossetti and Theodore
          Watts-Dunton at No. 16 Cheyne Walk], 1882 (© National Portrait Gallery,
          London, NPG 3022)   154
3.27   The Tree of Architecture. Showing the main growth or evolution of
          the various styles (Fletcher, History of Architecture, 1905, frontispiece
          recto)   168
4.1   The Japanese Court (The Japanese Court, p. 320)   176
4.2   Japan among other national displays (Petit et al., Exposition universelle,
          plate 90), cropped   177
4.3   Le Kiosque Japonais [with parts of the display from Siam]
          (L'Exposition 1867 Illustré, p. 233), cropped   177
4.4   Japanese Satsuma pavillion at the French expo 1867 [possibly by Pierre
          Petit], 1867 (anonymous via Wikipedia commons, https://de.m
          .wikipedia.org/wiki/Datei:Japanese_Satsuma_pavillion_at_the_French
          _expo_1867.jpg [last accessed 31 March 2024])   179
4.5   Kiosque du Japon (Grand album 1867, pl. 31)   179
4.6   Section Orientale. Vue générale du l'exposition japonaise dans le parc
          ['Japanese farm'] (Le monde illustré 11, 542 (1867), p. 137)   180
4.7   Egyptisches Palais und Garten des Japanesen, Wiener
          Photographen-Association, Wien, 1873 (© MAK – Österreichisches
          Museum für angewandte Kunst)   182
4.8   Map of Japanese Garden, reworked and annotated from original scan
          (Tanaka/Hirayama, Oukoku Hakuran, p. 258)   184
4.9   Japanische Gebäude und Gartenanlagen, Wiener Photographen-
          Association, Wien, 1873 (© MAK – Österreichisches Museum für
          angewandte Kunst)   184
4.10   Japanese Garden and shrine, Wiener Photographen-Association, Wien,
          1873 (© MAK – Österreichisches Museum für angewandte Kunst)   185
4.11   Japanische Gartenanlagen, Michael Frankenstein, Wien, 1873
          (© MAK – Österreichisches Museum für angewandte Kunst)   185
4.12   Jardin japonais (Exposition illustrée 1873, p. 253)   186

4.13	Der Garten der Japanesen und dessen Eröffnung durch das österreichische Kaiser-paar (Über Land und Meer 30, 40 (1873), p. 784)	186
4.14	Japanese Garden [with lantern, shrine and *kagura* stage], stereoscopic photograph (ÖNB/Wien, 63712-STE), cropped	187
4.15	Japanese Garden [View from exit behind the shrine towards the *kagura* stage], stereoscopic photograph (ÖNB/Wien, 63713-STE), cropped and partially retouched	187
4.16	Japanese workmen building a Japanese village (Illustrated London news (10.05.1873), p. 433)	188
4.17	Das japanische Theehaus im Vauxhall [The Japanese Tea-house] (Illustrirte Zeitung (18.10.1873), p. 292)	188
4.18	In der japanesischen Galerie (Illustrirte Zeitung, 19 July 1874, p. 44)	190
4.19	Area where exhibits from Japan were displayed (© MAK – Österreichisches Museum für angewandte Kunst)	190
4.20	The so-called Japanese Gallery, stereoscopic photograph, Wiener Photographen Association ((c) Austrian Archives/brandstaetter images/picturedesk.com), cropped	190
4.21	Architectural model of a pagoda, Michael Moser, 1872 (album with exhibits intended for Vienna) (ÖNB/Wien, Pk 3239,61), cropped	191
4.22	View of the Japanese Gallery (Illustrirte Zeitung, 6 December 1873, p. 424)	191
4.23	Architectural models of rural dwellings, Michael Moser, 1872 (album with exhibits intended for Vienna), (ÖNB/Wien, Pk 3239,49), cropped	193
4.24	architectural models of urban dwellings, Michael Moser, 1872 (album with exhibits intended for Vienna) (ÖNB/Wien, Pk 3239,47), cropped	193
4.25	Architectural models of shrines of the Ise type, Michael Moser, 1982 (album with exhibits intended for Vienna) (ÖNB/Wien, Pk 3239,58), cropped	193
4.26–4.27	Architectural model of a rural outbuilding, belonging to the group of rural building models prepared for the Weltausstellung in Vienna in 1873 during its restoration (2015, Weltmuseum Wien, restoration laboratory, photograph by the author)	412
4.28–4.30	Details of the architectural model of a daimyō residence prepared for the Weltausstellung in Vienna in 1873 during restoration (2015, Weltmuseum Wien, restoration laboratory, photograph by the author, edited)	412
4.31–4.32	View and detail of the architectural model of a daimyō residence prepared for the Weltausstellung in Vienna in 1873 after restoration, Weltmuseum Wien (© KHM-Museumsverband)	413

FIGURES XIII

4.33   Japanese com's dwelling, stereoscopic photograph, 1876 (The Miriam and Ira D. Wallach Division of Art, Prints and Photographs: Photography Collection, New York Public Library Digital Collections, G91F381_009ZF), cropped   197
4.34   Japanese Building, Entrance detail (Centennial Exhibition 1876 Philadelphia Scrapbook, courtesy of the Free Library of Philadelphia, Print and Picture Collection, c180300, https://libwww.freelibrary.org/digital/item/2402 [last accessed 23 April 2024])   197
4.35   Headquarters of the Japanese commission, erected by native workmen (Norton, Historical Register, p. 38)   197
4.36   Japanese dwelling (back view), Benjamin Linfoot, 1876 (courtesy of the Athenaeum of Philadelphia, Linfoot Collection, 70-PR-018) section, margins edited   198
4.37   Interior of the Japanese workmen's temporary quarters (Norton, Historical Register, p. 41)   413
4.38–4.40   Communal fishermen's quarters for 60 men, House Aoyama, Historical Village of Hokkaido (Kaitaku-no Mura) Sapporo (photograph by the author)   414
4.41   Japanese bazaar (Westcott, Portfolio, pl. 50), cropped   199
4.42   The Japanese Bazar, sketch by Charles H. Vanderhoof (Harper's Weekly (26 August 1876), p. 692)   199
4.43   Japan Pavilion (Bazaar) (Norton, Historical Register, p. 271)   201
4.44   Japanese court (Wilson, Masterpieces 1876, p. clxviii), cropped   201
4.45   Japanese mirror (Norton, Historical Register, p. 158)   201
4.46   Japanese Workmen Laying the Foundation of the Japanese Building (Norton, Historical Register, p. 46)   202
4.47   Erection of the Japanese buildings on the centennial grounds (Norton, Historical Register, p. 42)   203
4.48   Rue des nations (section including the neighbouring nations and detail) (Le Monde illustré, 1109, July 1878, supplement)   205
4.49   Pavillon du Japon. Paris 1878 (courtesy of Archives nationales, F/12/SUPPL./618/96775), cropped   206
4.50   Pavillon du Japon, advertising card (courtesy of Collections des musées de France – Mucem, 995.1.16.8; BR4.3.2.1.8, Photo Mucem), cropped   206
4.51   Parc du Trocadéro. Pavillon du Japon avec vue sur le palais du Trocadéro (courtesy of Ville de Paris/Bibliothèque historique) cropped and slightly edited   207
4.52   Japanese Garden, Trocadero (The Illustrated Paris Universal Exhibition, London 1878, p. 33, courtesy of Bridgeman Images, BL 3514505)   207

4.53	Exposition du Japon, advertising card (courtesy of Collections des musées de France – Mucem, 996.40.1258.1; X4.227.1, Photo Mucem), cropped 207	
4.54	La maison japonaise au Trocadéro : vue exterieure (World's Fair (ed.): Exposition de Paris – Journal hebdomadaire, 29 June 1878, p. 97, courtesy of Gallica/BnF), cropped 208	
4.55	La maison japonaise au trocadéro – vue intérieure (World's Fair (ed.): Exposition de Paris – Journal hebdomadaire, 29 June 1878, p. 101, courtesy of Gallica/BnF) 209	
4.56	Intérieure de la ferme japonaise du Trocadéro (M. Kauffmann, Le Monde Illustré, 22 June 1878, p. 401, courtesy of Gallica/BnF), cropped 209	
4.57	Portes de l'exposition japonaise dans le parc du Trocadéro (Burty, Notes sur l'architecture, plate), cropped 210	
4.58	Maison d'été japonaise (courtesy of Archives nationales, F/12/11909) 210	
4.59	Stage set for Gilbert & Sullivan's 'The Mikado' by Hawes Craven (1837–1910), 1885 (courtesy of Victoria and Albert Museum, S.252–1999), cropped 415	
4.60	The Mikado, performed by the Castanet Club, Montreal, QC, composite, 1886 (courtesy of McCord Museum, II-83315, https://collections.musee-mccord-stewart.ca/en/objects/144970/la-piece--the-mikado--interpretee-par-le-club-castanet-m?ctx=30ae7b6d475f7ef9e19d4a6f2d38f198a1669a0a&idx=6 [last accessed 9 April 2024]), cropped 212	
4.61	La Ghesha et le Chevalier, (Acte II), about 1900 (courtesy of Lesley Downer) 213	
4.62	Au theatre Loïe Fuller: La Ghesha et le Chevalier (Baschet, Le Panorama, s.p., courtesy of Gallica/BnF), cropped 213	
4.63	Karamon [at] Iyeyasu temple, Nikkō [The Karamon of Tōshō-gu in Nikkō, with the Haiden beyond] (Gift of E.G. Stillman to Widener Library, Harvard University, EGS08.17 KH 1755), cropped 214	
4.64	Advertisement posters for Tannaker's Japanese Native Village (courtesy of Bridgeman Images, 3298984) 415	
4.65–4.66	The Japanese village at Knightsbridge. The theatre and one of the streets (The illustrated sporting and dramatic news, 17 January 1885, p. 444), cropped and edited 215	
4.67	Afternoon Tea at the Japanese Village (The Graphic, 13 March 1886, p. 285) 216	
4.68	Temple, &c., at the Japanese village, 1885 (in: The Building News and Engineering Journal 48, 23 January 1885), p. 121) 217	

FIGURES　　　　　　　　　　　　　　　　　　　　　　　　　　　　　　　　　XV

4.69　　　　　The new Japanese village at Knightsbridge. The temple and the sleeping quarters (The illustrated sporting and dramatic news, 2 February 1886, p. 404), cropped and edited　　218

4.70　　　　　Façade de la section japonaise (Monod, L'Exposition 1889, 3, p. 59)　　221

4.71　　　　　Porte d'entrée de l'Exposition Japonaise (L'Exposition chez soi 1889, 1, p. 693)　　221

4.72　　　　　Menusiers japonais à l'exposition (Monod, L'Exposition 1889, 3, p. 60)　　221

4.73　　　　　Entrée du jardin japonais au Trocadéro (Andre, Jardin japonais, p. 240)　　222

4.74　　　　　Le Jardin japonais au Trocadéro. – Vue intérieure (Andre, Jardin japonais, p. 241)　　222

4.75　　　　　La section horticole japonaise (M. Dosso, L'Univers illustré 32, 1803, 12 October 1889, p. 641)　　222

4.76–4.77　　Charles Garnier, Histoire de l'habitation humaine, Japon, façade principale [and floorplan], 1889 (courtesy of Archives nationales, CP/F/12/4055/D/B), cropped　　416

4.78　　　　　Japanese house, left, and Chinese house, right, in the History of Habitation exhibit (courtesy of Library of Congress, 92520882, https://www.loc.gov/item/92520882/ [last accessed 9 April 2024])　　225

4.79　　　　　Habitation japonaise (Le petit moniteur illustré, 13.10.1889, p. 645, section)　　225

4.80　　　　　Maison japonaise (Garnier, L'Habitation, p. 852)　　225

4.81　　　　　Le Pavillon Japonais, advertising card (courtesy of Collections des musées de France – Mucem, 995.1.536.20; GC3.15.20, Photo Mucem), cropped　　225

4.82–4.83　　Bird's Eye View Looking Northwest From Liberal Arts Building with the Japanese structure on the island on the left side and with the United States Government Building and Japanese Ho-o-den (Arnold/Higinbotham, Official Views, Plate 4 and 54), cropped　　227

4.84　　　　　Japanese artisans, portrait, World's Columbian Exposition, Chicago, IL, 1891–1893. Daniel Burnham, Director of Works, C. D. Arnold, photographer. World's Columbian Exposition Photographs by C. D. Arnold, Ryerson and Burnham Art and Architecture Archives, Art Institute of Chicago. Digital file #198902.03_069–107)　　229

4.85　　　　　Japanese carpenters and stone masons in distinctive native attire starting to construct Japanese Pavilion, ca. 1892. Dec. 5. Photograph (Library of Congress, 2005675980, https://www.loc.gov/item/2005675980/ [last accessed 20 April 2024])　　229

4.86	At work on the Japanese building, by T. Dart Walker (Harpers Weekly, March 1893, p. 260) 230
4.87	View of the Hō-ō-den (courtesy of Bridgeman Images, SIC743355) 231
4.88	View of the Ho-o-den (Wight, Japanese, 5, p. 49) 231
4.89	Phoenix Hall, Byodo-in [in Uji], 2016 (Martin Falbisoner, via Wikipedia commons, https://de.m.wikivoyage.org/wiki/Datei:Phoenix_Hall,_Byodo-in,_November_2016_-01.jpg [last accessed 20 April 2024], section) 416
4.90	Dedication of the Japanese building, stereoscopic photograph, 1893 (The Miriam and Ira D. Wallach Division of Art, Prints and Photographs: Photography Collection, New York Public Library Digital Collections, G90F186_007F, section) 232
4.91–4.92	Views of the central hall and the north wing of the Hō-ō-den (Avery Architectural & Fine Arts Library, Columbia University, https://dx.doi.org/10.7916/d8-soex-3h41 and https://dx.doi.org/10.7916/d8-zfex-pr96 [last accessed 20 April 2024]), edited and cropped 233
4.93	Construction details of the Hō-ō-den (section) (Wight, Japanese, 5) 234
4.94–4.95	Scale drawings of the Hō-ō-den as they appeared in the Inland Architect in December 1892 (Wight, Japanese, 5) 235
4.96	Interior of left wing [shinden zukuri] (Okakura, Ho-o-den, after p. 14) 237
4.97–4.98	Library in right wing of the Hō-ō-den and tea room in right wing of the Hō-ō-den [shoin zukuri] (Okakura, Ho-o-den, after p. 20) 237
4.99	The Jodan-no-ma, or Central hall of the Ho-o-Den at the World's Columbian Exposition (Okakura, Decoration, pp. 181–182) 237
4.100–4.101	World's Columbian Exhibition, 1893: Japanese tea garden (Arnold/Higinbotham, Official Views, Plate 49 and 50), cropped 239
4.102–4.103	Die Facade der japanischen Sektion [The façade of the Japanese department] and Japan's Pavillon im Gebäude für Forstwesen [Japan's pavilion in the hall for forestry] (Unsere Weltausstellung, pp. 448 and 559), cropped 240
4.104	Japanese exhibit in art hall (Buel, Magic, s.p.) 240
4.105–4.106	Japanese Bazaar – Midway Plaisance (Glimpses of the World's Fair. A Selection of Gems of the White City Seen Through a Camera. Chicago 1893, s.p.) 241
4.107	Der japanische Pavillon [The Japanese pavilion] (Malkowsky, Pariser Weltausstellung, p. 166), cropped 244

FIGURES   XVII

4.108   Palais et pavillons du Japon./(Trocadéro) by Louis Larger (courtesy of
         Musée Carnavalet, Histoire de Paris, G.31715)   244
4.109   Parc du Trocadéro – Section de l'Empire du Japon – Pavillon Central
         by G. Delton (Postcard, Special Collections. Copley Library, University
         of San Diego), cropped   244
4.110   Le Japon (Baschet, Le Panorama, s.p., courtesy of Gallica/BnF),
         cropped   244
4.111   Golden Hall of the Hōryū-ji, north façade, 2006 (photograph by the
         author)   417
4.112   Haupttempel, Kon-do (Goldene Halle), Grundriss [Main temple,
         golden hall, floor plan] (Baltzer, Tempelanlage von Horiuji, 91, p. 559,
         section)   417
4.113   Exhibition Hall of Japanese traditional art (Nōshōmushō, 1900nen
         Pari, 1, past page 830, section, edited)   417
4.114   Pavillon du Japon (Le Petit journal. Supplément du dimanche
         (9 September 1900), p. 285, courtesy of Gallica/BnF), cropped   418
4.115   Japan (courtesy of Collections des musées de France – Mucem,
         995.1.4579.23; SC2.9.29, Photo Mucem), cropped   418
4.116–4.117 Kinkaku-ji (formally: Shari-den of Rokuon-ji, Kyōto), originally
         1398, here reconstruction of 1955 after loss due to arson, 1950) and
         Ginkaku-ji (formally: Kannon-den of Jishō-ji, Kyōto, 1482–1490)
         (photographs by the author)   418
4.118–4.119 Book cover and plate (Kinkaku-ji, Kyōto) of the volume *Histoire de l'art
         du Japon* (Fukuchi, Histoire de l'art du Japon, plate XLVII, courtesy of
         Gallica/BnF), cropped   247
4.120   Le tour du monde, design by Alexandre Marcel, 1900 (Brown Digital
         Repository. Brown University Library, https://repository
         .library.brown.edu/studio/item/bdr:87128/ [last accessed
         20 April 2024])   248
4.121   Le Tour du Monde by Henri Toussaint (Bridgeman Images,
         CHT217203)   249
4.122   Ausstellungspalast des Königreichs Siam [exhibition pavilion of the
         Siamese Kingdom] [at the left side, the pagoda of the Tour du Monde]
         (Malkowsky, Pariser Weltausstellung, p. 176)   249
4.123–4.125 Alexandre Marcel, design for the Japanese Tower in Laeken with
         auxiliary structures (Marcel, Orientalisme, s.p.)   419–420
4.126–4.127 The Pagoda in Laeken, seen from the site of the Chinese pavilion, and
         the entrance pavilion to the pagoda in Laeken, Alexandre Marcel,
         1901–1904 (photographs by the author)   420

4.128–4.129	Compound bracket, and bracketing supporting roof of temple-gate, Chionjin, Kioto [Chion-in] (Dresser, Japan, pp. 239, 240)	421
4.130	Column and tie-beams from the Chion-in (Dresser, Japan, p. 245)	421
4.131	L'architecture polychrome au Japon. Colonne et traverse du temple de Tsousennji [Chūzen-ji, Nikkō] (Daly, Temples japonais, plate 21, distortion due to book curve)	421
4.132	Le Guerrier Tadanobou se precipitant du haut d'un toit (D'après Yosai) (Gonse, L'Art, p. 12, edited)	258
4.133	The water tank at Shiba. With its monolithic columns, on the tops of which festooned drapery in colours and gold is painted are painted with coloured and golden drapery (Dresser, Japan, p. 15)	259
4.134	Cisterne au temple de la Shiba, à Tokio (Gonse, L'Art, p. 27)	259
4.135	Cisterne im Tempel der Shiba zu Tokio (Lützow, Japanische Kunst, p. 45)	259
4.136	Steinernes Brunnenbecken im Tempelhof von Shiba, überdacht von einem Ziegeldache auf zehn Monolithen, mit farbigen und goldenen Draperien bemalten Pfeilern (Brinckmann, Kunst, p. 52)	259
4.137	Cistern in the temple of Shiba, at Tokio (Gonse, art, p. 115)	259
4.138	Cour d'un mausolée de la Shiba (Hübner, Promenade (1881), 1, p. 426)	260
4.139	Der Hof einer Begräbnisstätte in Yedo (Hübner, Spaziergang (1882), p. 207)	260
4.140	Felice Beato: Tombs of Taikuns – At Shiba near Yeddo (courtesy of Nagasaki University Library, Metadata Database of Japanese Old Photographs in Bakumatsu-Meiji Period)	260
4.141	Kusakabe Kinbei: Stone Basines [sic] Shiba Tokio (courtesy of Nagasaki University Library, Metadata Database of Japanese Old Photographs in Bakumatsu-Meiji Period)	260
4.142	System of brackets (Conder, Further notes, p. 190)	261
4.143	Middle-class Japanese dwelling (Conder, Domestic, plate XXVII, trimmed)	262
4.144–4.146	Supports, encorbellements (Guérineau, Ornements, plates 13, 23, 24)	263–264
4.147–4.148	Ridge of thatched roof at Kabutoyama, Musashi; and Bamboo-ridge of thatched roof in Musashi (Morse, Homes, pp. 98, 95)	265
4.149–4.150	Kitchen in old farmhouse at Kabutoyama, and fireplace in country house (Morse, Homes, pp. 186, 193)	266
4.151	Een buddhistische Tempel/ein buddhistischer Tempel (Siebold, Nippon, plates II, Tab. I (plate number identical to other instalments of Siebold's plates))	268

FIGURES   XIX

4.152	Rin-Zoo (Siebold, Nippon, plates v, Tab. IV)	268
4.153–4.154	Elements of a *rinzō* (Hokusai, Manga, 5, s.p.)	269
4.155	Een Heerenhuis/ein Herrenhaus (Siebold, Nippon, plates II, Tab. VIII–X)	270
4.156	Country House (Steinmetz, Japan, p. 155)	270
4.157	Farm Yard, Yokuhama (Wilhelm Heine; Hawks, Narrative, 1856, p. 394)	271
4.158	Farming activities and buildings (Perry, The Americans, p. 258)	273
4.159	Japanese farmyard (Religious Tract Society, Japan, p. 158)	273
4.160	Hof eines japanischen Landguts [farmyard of an estate] (Steger, Nippon-Fahrer, p. 157)	273
4.161	Vue d'un canal dans la cité marchande de Yédo, à l'heure de [sic] midi (E. Thérond; Humbert, Le Japon, 2, p. 19)	276
4.162	River band at Tokio, ca. 1880 (E. G. Stillman collection, today Widener Library, Harvard University, EGS13.23)	277
4.163	A canal in Tokio (Keane, Asia, p. 639)	277
4.164	Scene in the harbour (Menpes, Letter, p. 21)	277
4.165–4.168	Portail d'Atango-yama (D. Lancelot, after a photograph); Légation américaine à Yédo, partie incendiée (E. Thérond, after a photograph); Idole et grotte du Tjoōdji (A. de Bar, after a sketch of A. Humbert), Un maison de thé (Emile Bayard, after a Japanese print) (Humbert, Le Japon, 1, pp. 331, 309, 312 and 292)	278
4.169–4.170	A Fire-Ladder; Finial of a Japanese Temple (from native drawings, Oliphant, Narrative, 2, pp. 133, 82)	280
4.171–4.172	Japanese Astronomers and Japanische Astronomen (from a native drawing, Oliphant, Narrative, 2, p. 218; Steger, Nippon-Fahrer, p. 267)	280
4.173	Interior scene of a dwelling with *tokonoma* (Tamenaga, Ronins, after p. 178)	422
4.174	Interior scene of a dwelling with *tokonoma* (Dening, Japan 1, after p. 42)	422
4.175	Entrance of a business (Takizawa, Okoma, p. 46)	422
4.176	Interior, probably a tea-room (Wertheimber, Muramasa Blade, p. 66)	422
4.177	Daibutsu in Kamakura (Jephson, Life in Japan, after p. 88)	283
4.178	Le daiboudhs, statue colossale du bouddha à Kamakoura (E. Thérond after a photograph of Felice Beato, Humbert, Le Japon, 1, p. 241.)	283
4.179	Diabutsu Kamakura (Gardiner, Japan, p. 32)	284
4.180	Daibutsu ('Great Buddha') at Kamakura (Dixon, Land of the Morning, p. 509)	284

4.181	Image of Daibutz, or Great Buddha (Mortimer, Far off, p. 552)	284
4.182	Felice Beato (1832–1909): Photograph of the pagoda of Tsurugaoka Hachiman-gū, 1867–1868 (The J. Paul Getty Museum, Japanese Landscapes and Other Views, 2007.26.207.5, partial gift from the Wilson Centre for Photography)	285
4.183	Felice Beato (1832–1909): Photograph of the pagoda of Tsurugaoka Hachiman-gū with the finial already missing, 1870s (The Miriam and Ira D. Wallach Division of Art, Prints and Photographs: Photography Collection, New York Public Library Digital Collections, 118912)	285
4.184	The pagoda of Tsurugaoka Hachiman-gū (Jephson, Life in Japan, after p. 84)	286
4.185	The pagoda of Tsurugaoka Hachiman-gū (Humbert, Le Japon, 1, p. 233)	286
4.186	Croquis de Blaireau (Humbert, Le Japon, 1, p. 85)	289
4.187	Sketch of a weasel (Humbert, Japan, p. 227)	289
4.188	Badger on a bamboo (Greey, Young Americans, p. 101)	289
4.189	Mutter und Tochter aus Simoda (Heine, Expedition, 2, after p. 208)	290
4.190	Une dame japonaise et sa fille (Oliphant, Le Japon, after p. 140)	290
4.191	Aussicht auf den Berg Fusi-Jama (Das Kaiserreich Japan, 1860, frontispiece)	291
4.192	Archer japonais (troupes du Siogoun) (E. Thérond after a photograph; Humbert, Le Japon, 1, p. 226)	292
4.193	Kumamoto Castle, 2009 (663highland via Wikipedia commons, https://upload.wikimedia.org/wikipedia/commons/7/7c/Kumamoto_Castle_02n3200.jpg [last accessed 4 May 2024]), cropped	292
4.194	Japanese funeral at Simoda (Hawks, Narrative, 1857, p. 472)	423
4.195	Begräbnis in Simoda (Steger, Nippon-Fahrer, p. 189), cropped	423
4.196	Japanese Funeral (Oliphant, Narrative, 2, pp. 188–189)	423
4.197	Japanisches Begräbnis (Steger, Nippon-Fahrer, p. 271)	423
4.198	Kiyóto. Baron Hübner in den Palast des Mikado eindringend, nach einer Skizze des Verfassers (Hübner, Spaziergang (1882), after p. 248)	293
4.199–4.200	Das Sonnenthor und das Küchenthor, Palast des Mikado, nach einer Skizze des Verfassers (Hübner, Spaziergang (1882), p. 249)	294
4.201	京都御所 建春門 [Kyōto Gosho Kenshunmon; Kenshun Gate, Kyōto Imperial palace] (Saigen Jiro, 2016 via Wikipedia commons, https://de.m.wikipedia.org/wiki/Datei:Kyoto-gosho_Kenshunmon-2.JPG [last accessed 21 April 2024])	294
4.202–4.203	The Tea-Party; Family Worship (Steinmetz, Japan, pp. 180, 255)	295

FIGURES

4.204	Go sannoma. Hall of audience (Kaempfer, History of Japan, 2, plate XXXII), cropped	296
4.205	Living room with bamboo hangings, sudare (courtesy of Kodansha Editorial Ltd.: Brown, Azby: The Japanese Dream House. How technology and tradition are shaping new house design; New York et al. 2001, p. 38)	424
4.206	The Audience Hall of Ninomaru Gōten of the Nijō-jō in Kyōto (courtesy of Bridgeman Images, IBE5348864)	424
4.207	Une dame de la cour de Kioto rentrant dans ses appartements. (A. de Neuville after a Japanese painting; Humbert, Le Japon, 1, p. 163)	298
4.208	Salle Principale du Palais du Prince Satzuma (Paris, Excursion a Kioto, plate 1, section)	298
4.209	Interior of Japanese dwelling (Converse, Notes, p. 63)	299
4.210	The *genkan* of a historic business preserved in the Edo-Tōkyō Open-Air Architectural Museum Garden Tōkyō, 2018 (photograph by the author)	299
4.211	A Japanese dinner (Glass, The World, after p. 489)	300
4.212	Japanese garden (Steinmetz, Japan, p. 31)	301
4.213	Japanese garden (Tronson, Personal Narrative, frontispiece)	301
4.214	Japanese tea gardens (Ainsworth, Around the World, 1, p. 145)	302
4.215	Del af en Japansk trädgård (Bæckström, Ett besök, p. 211)	302
4.216	Tempelgarten in Tokio (Kreitner, Im fernen Osten, p. 273)	425
4.217	Hotta family garden, Tōkyō, by Kusakabe, Kimbei, ca. 1883 (E.G. Stillman Collection, Widener Library, Harvard University, http://id.lib.harvard.edu/via/olvgroup12195/urn-3:FHCL:4420306/catalog [last accessed 4 May 2024])	425
4.218	Hotta family garden, Mukojima, Tōkyō, by Esaki Reiji, ca. 1885 (E.G. Stillman Collection, Widener Library, Harvard University, http://id.lib.harvard.edu/via/olvgroup12195/urn-3:FHCL:4420316/catalog [last accessed 4 May 2024])	425
4.219	Utagawa Hiroshige I: Fireworks in the Cool of the Evening at Ryōgoku Bridge, about 1840 (Boston Museum of Fine Arts, William S. and John T. Spaulding Collection, www.mfa.org, https://collections.mfa.org/objects/237585/ [last accessed 4 May 2024])	426
4.220	Tower of Nagoya castle (Reed, Japan, 2, p. 230)	304
4.221	Ehmidge castle, Kioto (Mossman, Japan, after p. 4)	304
4.222	Tower of Nagoya castle (Greey, City of Tokio, p. 243)	304
4.223	The citadel of Owari castle (Maclay, Budget Letters, after p. 218)	304

4.224	A Japanese dwelling-house (McCabe, Tour Around the World, p. 760), cropped 305
4.225	A Japanese mansion (Butler, Stories, p. 10) 305
4.226	Japanese dwellings (Wilson, Letters, after p. 24) 305
4.227	Utagawa Hiroshige: Ishibe, from the series "Fifty-Three Stations of the Tokaido", 1855 (Art Institute of Chicago, Bruce Goff Archive, gift of Shin'enkan, Inc., 1990.607.153 (see as well Van Gogh Museum Amsterdam, n0493M1986)) 426
4.228	Utagawa Hiroshige: Goyu, no. 35 from the series The Tōkaidō: the Fifty-Three Stations, 1847–1850 (courtesy of Van Gogh Museum Amsterdam, n0096V1962) 426
4.229	Utagawa Hiroshige III: Illustration of Foreign Residences and the Catholic Church in Yokohama (Yokohama shōkan tenshudō no zu), 1870 (New York Metropolitan Museum of Art, Gift of Lincoln Kirstein, JP3349), cropped 310
4.230	Yokohama Catholic church, Prudent Girard, 1862 (Nachrichten aus den Missionen. Japan, p. 106) 310
4.231	Utagawa Kuniteru II: Illustration of Mitsui Group's Western-Style Three-Story House at Surugachō, Tōkyō, 1873 (courtesy of Jordan Schnitzer Museum of Art, University of Oregon, Eugene, Oregon, Utagawa Kuniteru 2, Illustration of Mitsui Group's Western-Style Three-Story House at Surugachō, Tōkyō, 1873, print, 2021:36.412a-c, Gift of Irwin Lavenberg, The Lavenberg Collection of Japanese Prints) 427
4.232	Utagawa Yoshitora: An Accurate Picture of the Mitsui Building at Suruga-chō in Tōkyō, 1874 (Boston Museum of Fine Arts, Jean S. and Frederic A. Sharf Collection, www.mfa.org, https://collections.mfa.org/objects/161368 [last accessed 25 June 2023]) 427
4.233	駿河町三井組 [Suruga-chō Mitsui-gumi; Mitsui House in Suruga-chō, Tōkyō] (Japanese Art No. 446, p. 21 via https://ja.wikipedia.org/wiki/清水喜助#/media/File:Surugatyo_mitsuigumi_left_front_view.jpg [last accessed 4 May 2024]) 428
4.234	Utagawa (Gountei) Sadahide: Revised Yokohama Landscape, 1861 (New York Metropolitan Museum of Art, Bequest of William S. Lieberman, 2005, 2007.49.124a-f, https://www.metmuseum.org/art/collection/search/73410 [last accessed 4 May 2024], section) 429
4.235–4.236	View of the area of Gojō-bashi in Kyōto; Shop selling sweets near Kyōto Daibutsu (Hōkō-ji) (both Akisato, Miyako, 2, s.p.), cropped 314

FIGURES XXIII

4.237–4.238	Houses and fire-watch tower in Edo's Baba-chō; Street scene with businesses in Edo's Sugura-chō (both Saitō, Edo meisho, 1, s.p.), cropped 315	
4.239	Utagawa Hiroshige: View of Suruga-chō, from the series Famous Places in the Eastern Capital, about 1832–38 (Boston Museum of Fine Arts, Gift of Adams Collection, www.mfa.org, https://collections.mfa.org/objects/231323 [last accessed 4 May 2024]) 430	
4.240	Utagawa Hiroshige: Suruga-chō (One Hundred Famous Views of Edo), 1856 (Los Angeles County Museum of Art, Anonymous gift (M.73.75.26), https://collections.lacma.org/node/190735 [last accessed 15 May 2024]) 430	
4.241	Utagawa Hiroshige: Suruga-chō in the Eastern Capital (Thirty-six Views of Mt. Fuji), 1858 (Los Angeles County Museum of Art, Gift of Mr. and Mrs. Joseph M. Cobert (AC1994.188.2), https://collections.lacma.org/node/189641 [last accessed 15 May 2024]) 430	
4.242	昇斎一景: するか町 (東京三十六景) [Shōsai Ikkei: Suruga-chō (Thirty-six Views of Tōkyō), 1871 (Tōkyō Metropolitan Library, 0421-K003, http://archive.library.metro.tokyo.jp/da/detail?tilcod=0000000003-00010149 [last accessed 15 May 2024]) 431	
4.243	Kobayashi Kiyochika: Snow in Suruga-chō, 1879 (National Museum of Asian Art Collection, Robert O. Muller Collection, S2003.8.1141, https://asia.si.edu/explore-art-culture/collections/search/edanmdm:fsg_S2003.8.1141/ [last accessed 15 May 2024]) 431	
4.244	Utagawa Hiroshige III (1842–1894): The Misui store in Suruga-chō (Tōkyō meisho), 1881 (Tōkyō Metropolitan Library, 0421–C37, http://archive.library.metro.tokyo.jp/da/detail?tilcod=0000000003-00055205 [last accessed 15 May 2024]) 431	
4.245	Utagawa Hiroshige (1797–1858): The Pagoda at Zojo Temple and Akabane (Zojoji to, Akabane), from the series "One Hundred Famous Views of Edo (Meisho Edo hyakkei)", 1857 (Art Institute of Chicago, Clarence Buckingham Collection, 1925.3757) 317	
4.246	Utagawa Hiroshige (1797–1858): Kinryūzan Temple in Asakusa (Kaminari-mon, Hōzō-mon and pagoda of Asakusa Sensō-ji), One Hundred Famous Views of Edo, 1856 (Brooklyn Museum, Frank L. Babbott Fund, 39.575, https://www.brooklynmuseum.org/opencollection/objects/49880 [accessed 30 July 2023]) 317	
4.247	Utagawa Sadahide: Nihonbashi no shokei (View of a daimyo procession at Nihonbashi, famous views of Edo), 1863 (courtesy of The Lavenberg Collection of Japanese Prints) 432	

4.248	Utagawa Hiroshige: The Tōkaidō: The Fifty-Three Stations. 39. Okazaki (Yahagi no bashi), ca. 1834 (New York Metropolitan Museum of Art, Rogers Fund, https://www.metmuseum.org/art/collection/search/36960 [last accessed 15 May 2024]) 432
4.249	Katsushika Hokusai: Yahagi Bridge at Okazaki on the Tokaido, ca. 1828–1839 (The Art Institute of Chicago, Clarence Buckingham Collection, 1928.1083) 432
4.250	Die Yahaki-Brücke (Siebold, Nippon, 15. delivery of plates, plate 35), cropped 433
4.251	Utagawa Hiroshige: Okazaki, Yahagi Bridge from 53 Stations of the Tokaido, 1832–1847 (The Art Institute of Chicago, Clarence Buckingham Collection, 1930.68) 433
4.252	Utagawa Hiroshige: Yahagi Bridge on the Yahagi River near Okazaki, 1855 (The Art Institute of Chicago, Gift of Mr. and Mrs. Harold G. Henderson, 1968.348) 433
4.253–4.256	Ogawa Kazumasa: Girls having afternoon tea; Fujigawa river and Mt. Fuji from Iwabuchi, Tokaido; Omizusha, a basin, at Nikkō Toshogu Shrine; A vegetable vendor (courtesy of Nagasaki University Library, Metadata Database of Japanese Old Photographs in Bakumatsu-Meiji Period) 434
4.257–4.258	Tamamura Kozaburo: Woman in rickshaw, with two drivers, and Woman carrying infant on her back, 188–? (Fine Arts Library, Special Collections, Harvard University, https://curiosity.lib.harvard.edu/early-photography-of-japan/catalog/70-W599675_URN-3:FHCL:5142530 and https://curiosity.lib.harvard.edu/early-photography-of-japan/catalog/70-W599681_URN-3:FHCL:5142534 [last accessed 15 May 2024]), cropped 321
4.259	Ogawa, Kazumasa: Japanese women playing go, ca. 1887 (Widener Library, Harvard University, https://curiosity.lib.harvard.edu/early-photography-of-japan/catalog/70-W537828_URN-3:FHCL:4432156 [last accessed 15 May 2024]) 321
4.260–4.262	Recurring architectural details, *shōji*, in genre scenes (Stillfried, Raimund von; Beato, Felice et al.: Japonais, vol. 4, Stillfried & Andersen, s.l. 1878, F 238, F 244, F 240, courtesy of Gallica/BnF) 322
4.263–4.264	Felice Beato: American legation, Yedo; and Yokohama, 1867 (?) (Fine Arts Library, Special Collections, Harvard University, https://curiosity.lib.harvard.edu/early-photography-of-japan/catalog/70-W567950_URN-3:FHCL:5113433 and https://curiosity.lib.harvard.edu/early-photography-of-japan/catalog/70-W569356_URN-3:FHCL:5113438 [last accessed 18 May 2024]) 323

FIGURES   XXV

4.265–4.266   Tamamura Kozaburo: Kintai Bridge on Nishiki River at Iwakuni, 187–?;
              Shinto shrine, somewhere in Japan, ca. 1876 (Fine Arts Library, Special
              Collections, Harvard University, https://curiosity.lib.harvard.edu
              /early-photography-of-japan/catalog/70-W598268_URN-3:FHCL
              :5142514 and https://curiosity.lib.harvard.edu/early-photography
              -of-japan/catalog/70-W598258_URN-3:FHCL:5142507 [last accessed
              18 May 2024])   435

4.267   Uchida Kuichi: Kodaiji temple at Nagasaki, ca. 1870 (Widener Library,
              Harvard University, https://curiosity.lib.harvard.edu/early
              -photography-of-japan/catalog/70-W542250_URN-3:FHCL:8043236
              [last accessed 18 May 2024])   435

4.268   Kusakabe Kimbei: Buddhist temple at Asakusa, Tokio, 1880s? (Widener
              Library, Harvard University, https://curiosity.lib.harvard.edu/early
              -photography-of-japan/catalog/70-W542173_URN-3:FHCL:8043201 [last
              accessed 18 May 2024])   435

4.269   Funeral procession on city street in Japan, ca. 1890 (E.G. Stillman
              collection, today Fine Arts Library, Special Collections, Harvard
              University, https://curiosity.lib.harvard.edu/early-photography
              -of-japan/catalog/70-W577015_URN-3:FHCL:5113395 [last accessed
              18 May 2024])   324

4.270–4.271   Tamamura Kozaburo: Tonosawa Onsen, ca. 1890; and Women relaxing
              on veranda of teahouse, 188–? (Fine Arts Library, Special Collections,
              Harvard University, https://curiosity.lib.harvard.edu/early
              -photography-of-japan/catalog/70-W576566_URN-3:FHCL:5113365
              and https://curiosity.lib.harvard.edu/early-photography-of-japan
              /catalog/70-W577009_URN-3:FHCL:5113390 [last accessed
              18 May 2024])   324

4.272–4.273   Tamamura Kozaburo: Honmachi-dori, Yokohama, ca. 1885; and Fujiya
              Hotel, 188–? (Fine Arts Library, Special Collections, Harvard University,
              https://curiosity.lib.harvard.edu/early-photography-of-japan
              /catalog/70-W598253_URN-3:FHCL:5142503 and https://curiosity.lib
              .harvard.edu/early-photography-of-japan/catalog/70-W576567
              _URN-3:FHCL:5113366 [last accessed 18 May 2024])   326

4.274   Tōkyō Imperial Hotel, Watabe Yuzuru (1855–1930), 1890, ca. 1892
              (Fine Arts Library, Special Collections, Harvard University, https://
              curiosity.lib.harvard.edu/early-photography-of-japan/catalog
              /70-W553622_URN-3:FHCL:4702652 [last accessed 18 May 2024])   327

4.275   View of main street, Tokio, ca. 1860–1899 (The Miriam and Ira D.
              Wallach Division of Art, Prints and Photographs: Photography
              Collection, The New York Public Library, 119002)   328

4.276	Yoshiwara, Tōkyō, ca. 1890 (Fine Arts Library, Special Collections, Harvard University, https://curiosity.lib.harvard.edu/early-photography-of-japan/catalog/70-W553603_URN-3:FHCL:4702694 [last accessed 18 May 2024]) 328
4.277–4.280	Yokoyama Matsusaburo: Kyōto Imperial palace, Tsunegoten; Main Hall of Hōryūji Temple; Nara, Shōshōin; Ise, Naikō, 1872 (courtesy of Tōkyō National Museum, R-1378, R-1427, R-1398, R-1453 via https://colbase.nich.go.jp [last accessed 18 May 2024]), cropped 333
4.281–4.282	Yokoyama Matsusaburo: two views of Katsura Rikyū (Katsura Imperial Villa), stereo photographs, 1872 (courtesy of Tōkyō National Museum, R-1074 and R-1077 via https://colbase.nich.go.jp [last accessed 1 August 2023]), cropped 334
4.283–4.284	Hinagatabon, 1727: View and details of a bracketing system (Kōtan, Shinpu: Shōka Gokuhiden [Secret Volume for the Carpenter], 2 vols., 1727, s.p., via AIJ, *hinagatabon*, https://www.aij.or.jp/da1/hinagata/kizou.html [last accessed 18 May 2024]), partially rotated, slightly edited 336
4.285–4.286	Hinagatabon, 1812: Position of rafters and eave laths regarding the curvature of the roofing (Ishikawa, Ju'uho: Shōka Hinagata Zōho Shoshin Den [Patterns for the Carpenter, Introduction], revised ed., 6 vols., 1812, s.p., via AIJ, hinagatabon, https://www.aij.or.jp/da1/hinagata/kizou.html [last accessed 18 May 2024]), assembled, slightly edited 337
4.287	Hinagatabon, 1851: Section of a dwelling with interior fittings (Shinsen zōho taishō hinagata taizen [Large Encyclopaedia of Patterns for the Carpenter] new, revised ed., 5 vols., 1851, s.p., via AIJ, hinagatabon, https://www.aij.or.jp/da1/hinagata/kizou.html [last accessed 18 May 2024]) 338
4.288–4.289	Hinagatabon, 1866: View, section and floor plan of a very small shrine; View and section of a larger shrine building (Zōho Daishō Hinagata [Augmented Models for the Carpenter], extended ed., 6 vols., 1866, s.p., via AIJ, hinagatabon, https://www.aij.or.jp/da1/hinagata/kizou.html [last accessed 18 May 2024]) 339

Abbreviations

AIJ	The Architectural Institute of Japan
ASJ	Asiatic Society of Japan
JS	Japan Society
OAG	Deutsche Gesellschaft für Natur- und Völkerkunde Ostasiens or Ostasiengesellschaft (German Society for Natural History and Ethnology of East Asia)
RIBA	Royal Institute of British Architects

Timeline

Politics and technology in the West	Events and buildings of Western-Japanese contact	Writing on art, architecture and culture of Japan
		1832–1852 Philipp Franz von Siebold: *Nippon*
1851–1860		
1851 The Great Exhibition, London, ⌂ Crystal Palace		
1852–1870 Second French Empire		
1853–1856 Crimean War		*1855* Richard Hildreth: *Japan: As it was and is*
⌂ 1853–1870 Haussmann's renovation of Paris		*1856* Francis L. Hawks; Matthew C. Perry: *Narrative of the expedition of an American squadron to the China seas and Japan*
1856–1860 Second Opium War		
1858 First Transatlantic Cable		
1861–1865 American Civil War		
1861–1870	1862 London International Exhibition on Industry and Art	
1863 London Underground		1862 Rutherfod Alcock: *Catalogue of works of industry and art, sent from Japan*
⌂ 1863 Completion of dome of Capitol Building, Washington D.C.		
⌂ 1864 Clifton Suspension Bridge (William H. Barlow, 1812–1902); Sir John Hawkshaw, 1811–1891)		
	1867 Exposition universelle d'art et d'industrie de Paris	
⌂ 1868 St Pancras railway station London (William H. Barlow, 1812–1902)		
1869 Opening of the Suez Canal		
1870–1940 Third French Republic		*1870* Aimé Humbert: *Le Japon illustré*

TIMELINE   XXIX

Media and institutions bridging Japan to the Western architectural discourse	Politics and technology in Japan
1815–1878 *Manga* (Hokusai Katsushika, 1760–1849)	1846–1867 Reign of Emperor Kōmei (1831–1867)
	1853–1858 Reign of shōgun Tokugawa Isetada (1824–1858) 1853–1854 Commodore Perry's visits to Japan 1854–1855 Ansei Earthquakes
1856–1859 *One Hundred Famous Views of Edo* (Utagawa Hiroshige, 1797–1858)	1858-1866 Reign of shōgun Tokugawa Iemochi (1846–1866)

1851–1860

	1863 Imperial order to expel barbarians
	1866–1867 Reign of shōgun Tokugawa Yoshinobu (1837–1913) 1868 Boshin War
	1868–1912 Reign of Emperor Meiji (1852–1912) 1869 Edo renamed as Tōkyō becomes Imperial Residence ⌂ 1870 Imperial Mint, Ōsaka (Thomas J. Waters, 1842–1898)

1861–1870

(cont.)

	Politics and technology in the West	Events and buildings of Western-Japanese contact	Writing on art, architecture and culture of Japan
1871–1880	1871–1918 German Empire 1871 Great Chicago Fire ⌂ 1872 Menier factory in Noisiel (Jules Saulnier, 1817–1881) 1876 Battle of Little Bighorn	1873 **Weltausstellung Wien** 1876 **Centennial International Exhibition, Philadelphia** 1878 **Exposition universelle de Paris**	*1872* Alexander Graf von Hübner: Promenade autour du monde *1873* Kakuma Yamamoto: Guide to the celebrated places in Kiyoto *1875* Ernest M. Satow: A Guide Book to Nikkō *1875* Edward W. Godwin: Japanese wood construction *1876* James J. Jarves: A Glimpse at the Art of Japan *1876* William E. Griffis: The Mikado's Empire *1877* Georges H. Bousquet: Le Japan de Nos Jours et les Echelles de l'Extreme Orient *1878* Josiah Conder: Notes on Japanese architecture *1878* Rutherford Alcock: Art and Art Industries in Japan *1879* Philippe Burty: Notes Sur L'architecture Au Japon *1879* Maurice Dubard: Le Japon pittoresque

Media and institutions bridging Japan to the Western architectural discourse	Politics and technology in Japan
1871 Plan for the Preservation of Ancient Artifacts	1872 Railway between Tōkyō-Shimbashi and Yokohama
	⌂ 1872 Tomioka Silk Mill (Edmond Auguste Bastien, 1839–1888; Odaka Atsutada, 1830–1901)
1873 Imperial College of Engineering, Tōkyō	⌂ 1873 First National Bank Building (Shimizu Kisuka II, 1815–1881)
	⌂ 1874 Ginza "Bricktown" (Thomas J. Waters, 1842-1898)
1876–1883 Technical Art School (Kobu Bijutsu Gakko)	⌂ 1876 Kaichi School, Matsumoto (Tateishi Kiyoshige, 1829–1894)
1877 Josiah Conder (1852–1920) at the Imperial College of Engineering, Tōkyō	1877 First National Industrial Exhibition, Tōkyō

(cont.)

Politics and technology in the West	Events and buildings of Western-Japanese contact	Writing on art, architecture and culture of Japan
		1881 Johanes J. Rein: *Japan. Nach Reisen und Studien ...* 1882 Christopher Dresser: *Japan, its Architecture, Art and Art-Manufactures*
⌂ 1883 Brooklyn Bridge, New York (John A. Roebling, 1806–1869) ⌂ 1884 Garabit Viaduct (Gustave Eiffel, 1832–1923) ⌂ 1885 Home Insurance Building Chicago (William L. Jenney, 1832–1907) ⌂ 1886 Statue of Liberty, New York		1883 Louis Gonse: *L'Art Japonais* 1885 Edward S. Morse: *Japanese Homes and Their Surroundings* 1888–1891 Samuel Bing: *Le Japon artistique: documents d'art et d'industrie* 1888 Percival Lowell: *The soul of the Far East*
	1889 Exposition Universelle de Paris and Eiffel Tower ⌂ 1889 Knapp House (Ralph A. Cram, 1863–1942)	1889 Marcus B. Huish: *Japan and its Art* 1890 Basil H. Chamberlain: *Things Japanese*
1890 Wounded Knee Massacre 1890 Forth Bridge, Queensferry		

1881–1890

edia and institutions bridging Japan the Western architectural discourse	Politics and technology in Japan
81 Tokyo Institute of Technology (Tōkyō okkō gakkō)	1881 Second National Industrial Exhibition, Tōkyō
	◊ 1883 Rokumeikan, Tōkyō (Josiah Conder, 1852–1920)
887 Tōkyō Fine Arts School (Tōkyō bijutsu akkō)	
	1889 Meiji Constitution
	1890 Third National Industrial Exhibition, Tōkyō

1881–1890

(*cont.*)

	Politics and technology in the West	Events and buildings of Western-Japanese contact	Writing on art, architecture and culture of Japan
1891–1900			*1891* Eliza R. Scidmore: *Jinrikisha days in Japan*
		1893 **World's Columbian Exhibition, Chicago and the Hō-ō-den**	*1893* Félix Régamey: *Japan in Art and Industry*
	⌂ 1895 Royal Greenhouses in Laeken, Brussels (Alphonse Balat, 1818–1895)		
	⌂ 1897 Boston Subway		*1897* John La Farge: *An Artist's letters from Japan*
			1897 Frank Brinkley; Kakuzō Okakura: *Japan, Described and Illustrated by the Japanese*
	⌂ 1899 Maison du Peuple, Brussels (Victor Horta, 1861–1947)		
	1900 Boxer Rebellion	1900 **Exposition Universelle de Paris** and *Tôkyô Teishitsu Hakubutsukan: Histoire de l'art du Japon*	

...edia and institutions bridging Japan ...the Western architectural discourse	Politics and technology in Japan
	1891 Mino Owari Earthquake
	1894–1895 First Sino-Japanese War
1895 Heian Jingū, Kyōto (Itō Chuta, 1867–1954)	1895 Fourth National Industrial Exhibition, Kyōto
1897 Ancient Temples and Shrines Preservation Law	
	1899 End of Western extraterritoriality

(*cont.*)

	Politics and technology in the West	Events and buildings of Western-Japanese contact	Writing on art, architecture and culture of Japan
1901–1910	1901 Queen Victoria †	1904 **Louisiana Purchase Exposition, St. Louis** ⌂ 1905 Japanese Tower at Laeken (Alexandre Marcel, 1860–1928)	*1901 Banister Fletcher: A history of architecture for the student, craftsman, and amateur (3rd, extended ed.)* *1903 Franz Baltzer: Das Japanische Haus* *1903 Kakuzō Okakura: The Ideals of the East* *1904 Kakuzo Okakura: The Awakening of Japan* *1905 Ralph A. Cram: Impressions of Japanese Architecture and The Allied Arts* *1906 Kakuzo Okakura: The Book of Tea*
	⌂ 1909 AEG Turbine Factory, Berlin (Peter Behrens, 1868–1940) ⌂ 1911 Fagus Factory Alfeld (Walter Gropius, 1883–1969) ⌂ 1913 Woolworth Building, New York (Cass Gilbert, 1859–1934) 1914–1918 World War I	1910 **Japan-British Exhibition, London** and *Japan. Naimushō: Japanese Tamples and their Treasures*	

TIMELINE   XXXVII

...edia and institutions bridging Japan | Politics and technology in Japan
... the Western architectural discourse

                          1903 Fifth National Industrial Exhibition, Ōsaka
                          1904–1905 Russo-Japanese War

1901–1910

...06–1913 Preservation of the *kondō* of
...ōdai-ji, Nara

                          1912–1926 Reign of Emperor Taishō (1879–1926)

                          ◻ 1914 Tōkyō Station (Tatsuno Kingo, 1854–1919)

CHAPTER 1

Introduction

Since Japan was coerced to end its self-imposed isolation in the 1850s, Euro-American architects have not stopped discussing Japanese architecture. Each generation has encountered impressive facets of traditional or modern Japanese buildings: craft skills, clean lines and simplicity, standardisation and prefabrication, the creative use of new materials, or innovative urban development. In addition to this, they have explored the similarities and differences between Japanese approaches, ideas and practices, and established western models. At the same time, Japanese building practitioners have not only adopted, but also adapted western ideas, blending them with traditional Japanese building practices.

There is no doubt that the reciprocal engagement with building-related issues has had a notable influence on architectural development in both regions, as well as the global discourse on architecture. Today, Japan's contributions to architecture – both in terms of historical and contemporary structures – are highly appreciated not only by representatives of the in-field discourse but also by the general public as architectural names and concepts have become a natural part of collective knowledge.

Yet, there are some puzzling incongruities. For example, there is a limited amount of comprehensive western-language literature covering both Japanese architecture as a whole and specific buildings in detail. The available resources focus on a small number of research interests such as tea houses, castles or individual religious buildings, while fundamental topics often covered in western studies in architectural history are notable by their absence. This situation does not align with the professed interest in Japanese architecture, as demonstrated by the richly illustrated publications easily available on the book market, nor with the research available in Japanese that could be translated in some cases. It appears that the aim is not to come to a comprehensive understanding of the entirety of Japanese architecture, but to select specific and often unrelated themes according to a pattern that makes no sense within the (western) architectural knowledge system.

Interested western architects, artists, teachers, designers, professionals, and laypersons alike are all faced with the challenge of compensating for superficiality or deficiencies. This may involve resorting to simplification, myth, imagination, or creative interpretation.

It is possible that architects' creative management of knowledge gaps and divergent interpretations of data might catalyse the emergence of desirable and valuable artistic expressions as part of the design process. In terms of teaching architectural history and global communication of architecture, however, this involves the imperative of avoiding blind spots, even if this means perpetuating an undesirable situation in the long term.

This problematic scenario was originally articulated by William H. Coaldrake in 1986 within his highly commendatory review of the book "What Is Japanese Architecture?" authored by Nishi Kazuo and Hozumi Kazuo.[1] To encapsulate the predicament in succinct terms, Coaldrake wrote:

> Until now the answer to the question posed in the title of this book consisted of the same stereotyped platitudes that have been bandied around since the time of Frank Lloyd Wright and Bruno Taut – 'simplicity', 'functionalism', 'sense of materials', 'open-plan interior', and the like, more recently laced with catchwords such as *ma* ('time-space interval') and *oku* ('inner space') popularized in Western-language writings of Japanese architects. This recent work (...) is refreshingly free of such bland generalizations.[2]

Yet, decades later, these "stereotyped platitudes" paradoxically persist and thrive. Simply conducting research that transcends historic biases is therefore insufficient to break free from these patterns. We also need to understand how they are rooted in general assumptions and common knowledge and why an artistic exchange of inspiration and imagination may inadvertently contribute to their perpetuation.[3]

Another incongruence relates to the phenomenon of Japonisme. During the initial decades of greater exchange of information between Japan and the West in the late nineteenth century in particular, architectural issues were usually discussed within the context of this overarching phenomenon. This aligns with our broader understanding of the arts but disregards a categorical difference between architecture and collectables, such as porcelain or lacquer ware. While the latter soon found their way into European shops and collections,

---

1 Nishi, Kazuo; Hozumi, Kazuo, *What is Japanese architecture?* (Tōkyō: Kodansha, 1983).
2 Coaldrake, William H., "Review of Nishi, Kazuo; Hozumi, Kazuo, *What is Japanese architecture?* (Tōkyō: Kodansha, 1983)," *Monumenta Nipponica* 41.3 (1986): 374–376, here p. 374.
3 For a very instructive presentation of the problem, especially at the interface between architectural historical research and architectural education see Choi, Don, "Non-Western Architecture and the Roles of the History Survey," *Fresh Air. Proceedings of the 95th ACSA Annual Meeting* (2007): 745–750.

triggering an intense preoccupation with Japanese aesthetics, the former remained confined to Japan, and remained unobserved and unexplored by interested westerners, with a few exceptions.

This prompts the following questions: How did these interested western individuals manage to adopt and discuss ideas of Japanese architecture? How could they form an opinion? Who provided them with the pertinent information, and by what means? Moreover, how did they position their evaluations of building-related phenomena against the backdrop of gunboat diplomacy, unequal treaties, claims of hegemony, and racially biased assumptions? These elements invariably moulded the relationships between western nations and non-western cultures well into the twentieth century, defining the framework for cultural experiences and exchanges.

This book addresses these questions by drawing on a range of disciplines, including architectural and intellectual history, Japanese studies, ethnology and East Asian art history. It serves as a bridge between different specialists' interests and perspectives of relevance. Consequently, each reader will encounter content that may feel both familiar and unfamiliar, depending on their own background. Despite being reviewed by colleagues from a wide range of disciplines, certain contexts may still appear either too succinct or excessively detailed.

However, this overarching approach aims to provide a broad overview of the knowledge of architecture in Japan developed among western individuals from many different backgrounds during the latter half of the nineteenth century. The study traces how they gathered and disseminated textual and visual information, evaluating the structures and designs they discovered through the lens of architectural thought rooted in the Vitruvian tradition, Christian ethics, the Enlightenment's penchant for systematisation, and contemporary theories of culture and civilisation, western superiority, and progress. It follows the evolution of the perception of Japanese architecture, which transitioned from being merely different due to the fact that it belonged to another culture, to becoming the 'categorical Other' within the expert-centred Euro-American knowledge system five decades later: classified and even appreciated, but inescapably unequal.

The process of knowledge production is shown to be an intricate interplay between such heterogeneous factors as honest curiosity, the emergence of architecture as a modern profession, the competition for hegemony among Euro-American nation states in an increasingly globalised world, and the attempt to fit an overwhelming influx of new information about the world into existing models of world order. Japan's architecture was both an aesthetic and a constructive challenge that somehow had to fit within this context, for better or worse.

Throughout the exploration of this topic, the considerations analysed here show an often unspoken consensus between expert circles and the broader contributors of architecture's fundamental role in expressing power relations. However, the vast majority of actors were unable to recognise that Euro-American practices and codes in building and planning, when applied to political contexts, were inherently regional and non-universal. As a result, they struggled to recognise and evaluate architectural representations of power that deviated from western paradigms, such as certain aspects of the material and symbolic arrangement of space in Japan.

1 Context, Source Materials and Methodological Approach

The specific case of Japan's history during the second half of the nineteenth century forms a clear spatial and temporal background for this study. The country was forced by western hegemonic powers to end its isolationist policy and to participate in the trial of strength that was then taking place in East Asia. Having seen what had happened with China, the Japanese government tried to avoid colonisation by initiating a complex process of modernisation. With the aim of creating a competitive Japanese nation-state, it introduced administrative systems as well as technological and cultural knowledge from the West, it dispatched students to renowned educational institutions abroad, and it hired experts from Europe and North America as advisers and teachers. So it was that western diplomats, traders, engineers, scientists and missionaries, among many others, visited or took up residence in Japan, explored the country and reported home through letters, newspaper articles and books.

This allows us to understand in an almost exemplary way how, within a few years, a well-developed, largely autonomous culture was researched and categorised by specialists and amateurs from the outside. Similarly, patterns of argumentation and interpretation are becoming visible through the mechanisms and consequences of the increasing institutionalisation of European scholarship which are happening at the same time. The analysis allows for fundamental insights into the modern constitution of scholarly architecture-related subjects (art history and architecture, civil engineering and urban planning), but also into the division of labour with the subjects of ethnology or anthropology. In addition, this study touches on another level of epistemic work: it contributes to an understanding of architectural thought and knowledge production in a global historical context.

During the relevant period, the second half of the nineteenth century, there were many publications that dealt with Japanese art, culture, architecture, urbanism and/or building construction in the narrower or broader sense. This holds true, even if travel reports are not included in detail, but used only to round off the overall picture when referred to in expert contexts. Most of the texts are in English, since the language had already established itself as the *lingua franca* of Japan-related research in the 1870s, while German and French are represented as well.

This study examines the stock of available monographs, essays and journal notes for topics and references. It concentrates for in-depth analysis on those texts that determined the discourse based on their number of editions, the breadth of their influence or the expertise of their authors. The biographical and professional backgrounds of the authors, as well as the publication details, are recorded, in addition to the breakdown of the architectural content according to the usual criteria of architectural history. Furthermore, the western meta-discourses framing information transfer and knowledge production are traced through reviews, newspaper articles and lectures, underlining the perceptions of relevance that lead to the discussion of one topic and the marginalisation of the other.

The focus is on the western state of knowledge at that time, i.e. knowledge that was available and widespread in Europe and North America. It is understood that this includes publications by Japanese writers produced in western languages or dominated by visual material. It is presumed that, above all, releases in English – or for that matter in other European languages – represented a deliberate step toward a transcultural dialogue and recognition. While there was only a small number of Japanese informers and decision-makers who were heard on architectural matters by western audiences during the decades in question, they represent the many known and unknown Japanese actors behind the scenes of western discourses at the time.

Together with the analysis of the texts, both the Japanese architecture presented at international exhibitions and the various visual materials referring to architecture are also examined with regard to motifs, their origins and reception. Since the digitisation of historical visual media and their publication online is a relatively new phenomenon, the available stock might not yet be homogeneous or dense enough to justify its own broad-based study. Used judiciously, however, it is suitable for deepening the insights gained from the texts and the accompanying illustrations, especially in the light of the tremendous importance of visual information in architectural design and discourse.

2 Research Background and Disciplinary Context

While this study poses a highly original set of questions and focus on and addresses a significant research desideratum, it is not the first to look at such issues[4] and would not have been feasible without the extensive work completed by the proverbial giants: the generations of colleagues from different fields who prepared the foundation of data and started the discourses which inspired and enabled this research.

The following overview of the schools of thought involved, including the overlaps and gaps between their works, aims to provide a guide to further reading, especially where impulses inspired specific questions but did not influence the content of the study itself. It aims to show why this book might have been necessary decades earlier but needed the convergence of today's approaches and knowledge to be able to formulate the right questions in the first place and follow these through without adding to existing myths.

The most evident field of relevant research consists of studies of the history of art and architecture as well as urban studies relating to Japan. The impact of Japanese arts on the development of western creative fields and industries since the latter half of the nineteenth century is well known. *Japonisme* in its widest sense was of such relevance that it is impossible today to imagine aesthetic and architectural modernism without it. As a consequence, there are many publications on that topic as well as both western and Japanese actors, ideas and schools.

Against this background it is easy to overlook a gap within the (hi)stories told: while a number of architects were involved in the collection and appreciation of *Japonica*, and many design ideas can be traced back to this interest, architecture was largely missing from the overall discourses on Japanese art until deep into the twentieth century. Neither Edward William Godwin (1833–1886) nor Josiah Conder (1852–1920), and neither Hermann Muthesius (1861–1927) nor Ralph A. Cram (1863–1942) nor Frank L. Wright (1867–1959) spent a significant amount of time writing about Japanese architecture, let alone conducting systematic research on the issue. Even Bruno Taut's (1880–1938) numerous thoughts on Japan, its art and culture, were not so much

---

4 At least two colleagues have addressed similar issues. Kevin Nute's quite recent book *The Constructed Other: Japanese Architecture in the Western Mind*, published by Routledge in 2021 partially overlaps the questions and conclusion in this study. Don Choi has announced a volume to be published by Taylor & Francis in 2024, titled *Architecture and Modern Japan: History, Technology, and Nation, 1850–1920*.

scientific studies but the multifaceted reasoning of a designing architect, interwoven in a net of imagination, attribution, inspiration and observation. While some of Taut's insights were published immediately, many remained largely unknown,[5] leaving his information on Japan and its architecture as haphazardly imbalanced as was the entire field for many years, as we saw already in William Coaldrake's complaint above.

Coaldrake himself made a considerable contribution to counteracting the simplifications and mythologisations that had dominated writings on Japan's architectural past and present for more than a century. His studies *The Way of the Carpenter*, 1990, and *Architecture and Authority in Japan*, 1996, have become classics in the field,[6] as have many of his essays on specific topics such as pre-modern building law and the emergence of the designing architect in early seventeenth-century Japan.

Fortunately, Coaldrake was not alone in his assessment of the situation, nor was he the only one to study the field. There were some older works of value, such as Alexander C. Soper's architectural part of *The Art and Architecture of Japan*, 1955; Michiko Meid's analysis of the introduction of western architecture to Japan, 1977; or Heinrich Engel's *The Japanese House*, 1964.[7] However, while providing a treasure trove of detailed information on construction, the latter was one of those publications that used the unwiedly platitudes of architectural 'Japaneseness' mentioned above to inspire the contemporary designing architect.

In fact, research on Japanese architecture is dominated by two main traditions: the analytical study of the history of Japanese architecture up to the Second World War on the one hand, and grappling with contemporary Japanese architecture and urban design/planning as part of a global negotiation of architectural design on the other. The two fields rarely meet; the epistemic interests of the groups seem too different.

---

5   Manfred Speidel has been working for more than two decades to fill the gaps and to edit all of Taut's writings and notes regarding Japan: *Das japanische Haus und sein Leben* (Berlin, 1997) (= *Houses and People of Japan*, 1938); *Ich liebe die japanische Kultur. Kleine Schriften über Japan* (Berlin, 2003); *Ex Oriente lux. Die Wirklichkeit einer Idee. Eine Sammlung von Schriften 1914–1938* (Berlin, 2007); *Bruno Taut in Japan. Das Tagebuch*, 3 vols. (Berlin, 2016).
6   Coaldrake, William H., *The Way of the Carpenter. Tools and Japanese Architecture* (Tōkyō; New York, 1990); id., *Architecture and Authority in Japan* (New York; London, 1996).
7   Paine, Robert Treat; Soper, Alexander Coburn, *The art and architecture of Japan* (Baltimore, 1955; and two more editions in 1974 and 1981); Meid, Michiko, *Der Einführungsprozeß der europäischen und nordamerikanischen Architektur in Japan seit 1542* (Cologne, 1977); Engel, Heinrich, *The Japanese house. A tradition for contemporary architecture* (Ruthland, VT; Tōkyō, 1964).

This is even more interesting given that the immense western interest in contemporary Japanese developments, which was not least triggered by the metabolist manifesto of 1960, involved both architecture and urban planning and invited reflection on lines of architectural thought beyond the Vitruvian model.[8]

Indeed, the discourses on *metabolism* were accompanied by a broadening of questions and methods brought into the field from the social sciences. This affected the literature on housing and the urban environment in particular.[9] Anthropological and geographical questions began to intermingle with spatial and material issues. These were inspiring developments, even though they complicated matters: the conceptual understanding of 'architecture' had expanded to an extent that challenged communication and made achieving an overview of the entire field nearly impossible. Consequently, western discourses did not go on to study the built environment as a holistic field, but separated that environment into specific work areas such as urban history, contemporary urban development and planning, modern design and architecture, preservation and heritage protection, or traditional construction techniques. This restricted cross-disciplinary exchange for some years.

At the same time as this general development, there were two interesting phenomena. On the one hand, the ongoing fundamental research by Japanese colleagues was communicated in many publications during the 1970s, even if it largely addressed a general audience. However, the translations stopped almost entirely soon thereafter, thus restricting access to building surveys, cross-sectional analyses of specific building types and some trends in architectural theory to a very small audience, especially before the emergence of such helpful tools as digitised library catalogues, OCR and the internet.[10] On

---

8   The manifesto: Kawazoe, Noboru (ed.), *Metaborizumu senkyūhyakurokujū: toshi e no teian/Metabolism: the proposals for new urbanism* (Tōkyō: Bijutu Syuppan Sha, 1960).

9   Gutschow, Niels, *Die japanische Burgstadt* (Paderborn, 1976); Kornhauser, David, *Urban Japan. Its Foundations and Growth* (London et al., 1976); Enders, Siegfried, *Japanische Wohnformen und ihre Veränderung* (Hamburg, 1979); Pezeu-Massabuau, Jacques, *La maison japonaise* (Paris, 1981).

10 The 30 volumes of *The Heibonsha Survey of Japanese Art*, edited during the 1970s, are still indispensable for teaching, given the lack of more recent publications. Merging historical information with technical data such as floor plans and sections, the volumes addressing architectural issues (or including some of them) presented the landmarks of architectural tradition in a concise way, while omitting footnotes. Many other volumes by Japanese authors published in English or even in German during these decades were aimed at a general audience as well. See *The Heibonsha Survey of Japanese Art*, 30 vols. (Tōkyō: Heibonsha, 1972–1979); see also, e.g., Itō, Teiji; Futagawa, Yukio, *Alte Häuser in Japan* (= *Nihon-no-minka*) (Stuttgart, 1984); Kawashima, Chūji, *Minka. Traditional houses*

the other hand, some specific areas gathered momentum and saw ongoing cooperation across language barriers as well as a bridging of the gap between disciplinary expertise and popular editions. This affected knowledge of a few castles such as Himeji, some religious buildings such as Ise Jingū, and – most extensively – the publications on Katsura Rikyū, the Katsura Imperial Villa in Kyōto.[11]

In general, however, it was only towards the end of the twentieth century that a new generation of scholars and publications merged topics across the fields. While based in specific fields themselves, William H. Coaldrake, Dallas Finn, Nicolas Fiévé and others managed to integrate ideas and arguments toward a holistic study of Japanese architecture, its interpretation, historisation and preservation.[12]

---

    of rural Japan (Tōkyō; New York, 1986). In contrast, see Inoue, Mitsuo, *Space in Japanese Architecture* (= *Nihon kenchiku no kūkan*) (New York; Tōkyō, 1985) and some of the volumes which were never translated, e.g., Ōta, Hirotarō (ed.), *Nihon kenchikushi kiso shiryō shūsei* [History of Japanese building basics document collection], 21 vols. (Tōkyō: Chūō Kōron Bijutsu Shuppan, 1971–2006); *Nihonkenchiku koten sōsho*, planned 10 vols., e.g., Kawata, Katsuhiro (ed.), *Kinsei kenchikusho – dōmiya hinagata* [Source books of Japanese temple and shrine design] (Kyōto: Tairyūdō Shoten, 1988); Wakayama, Shigeru; Fumoto, Kazuyoshi (eds.), *Kinsei kenchikusho – kōhō hinagata* [Sourcebooks of Japanese building construction] (Kyōto: Tairyūdō Shoten, 1993); Takahashi, Yasuo, et al. (eds.), *Zushū Nihon toshishi* [An illustrated history of Japanese cities] (Tōkyō: Tōkyō Daigaku Shuppankai, 1993).

11   Without making any claim to comprehensiveness, see e.g. Horiguchi, Sutemi; Harada, Jiro; Sato, Tatsuzo, *The Katsura Imperial Villa* (Tōkyō: Mainichi, 1952); Tange, Kenzo; Gropius, Walter; Ishimoto, Yasuhiro, *Katsura. Tradition and Creation in Japanese Architecture* (New Haven; London, 1960); Naito, Akira; Nishikawa, Takeshi, *Katsura. A Princely Retreat* (New York, 1977); Itoh, Teiji; Arai, Masao; Ogawa, Taisuke, *Katsura: A Quintessential Representative of the Sukiya Style of Architecture* (Tōkyō, 1983); Isozaki, Arata; Ishimoto, Yasuhiro, *Katsura. Raum und Form* (Stuttgart, 1987); Ponciroli, Virginia; Isozaki, Arata, *Katsura. La villa imperiale* (Milan, 2004); Nakamori, Yasufumi, *Katsura. Picturing modernism in Japanese architecture* (New Haven; London, 2010).

12   Among the monographs alone, see e.g. Coaldrake, Carpenter; Nute, Kevin, *Frank Lloyd Wright and Japan: the role of traditional Japanese art and architecture in the work of Frank Lloyd Wright* (London; New York, 1993); Larsen, Knut Einar, *Architectural Preservation in Japan* (Trondheim, 1994); Wendelken-Mortensen, Cherie, *Living with the Past: Preservation and Development in Japanese Architecture and Town Planning* (Ph.D. Thesis, Cambridge: Massachusetts Institute of Technology, 1994); Coaldrake, Authority; Finn, Dallas, *Meiji revisited. The Sites of Victorian Japan* (New York, 1995); Enders, Siegfried; Gutschow, Niels (eds.), *Hozon. Architectural and Urban Conservation in Japan* (Stuttgart; London, 1998); Fiévé, Nicolas, *L'architecture et la ville du Japon ancien: espace architectural de la ville de Kyōto et des résidences shôgunales aux XIVe et XVe siècles* (Paris, 1996); id., *Pratique architecturale et naissance de l'histoire de l'architecture au Japon* (Paris, 1999).

With this basis established, it became possible and necessary to ask even more questions and to look anew at Japanese architecture and the processes of exchange between Japan and the western world, and scholars took this work forwards: Irène Vogel Chevroulet and Ken Tadashi Oshima looked at the architectural discourses between the 1870s and the 1940s, Alice Tseng wrote about architectural nation-building, Gregory Clancy studied the rise of seismology as a new field of building-related research, and Dana Buntrock examined architectural education and the use of building materials.[13] This work was supplemented by studies by colleagues from neighbouring disciplines such as Jordan Sand, Julia Odenthal or Christian Tagsold, who did not actually look at architecture itself but at the circumstances in which it played its social role.[14] Many of them kept and still keep a keen eye on questions of orientalism/occidentalism in the creation of meaning during the transfer processes themselves and in their subsequent narration.

Similar processes went on in urban studies. Here, Japanese authors are much more visible than they are in architectural history, if not as editors of the English publications themselves, then as the authors of chapters and essays within them. However, the two fields of architectural history on the one hand

---

13   Vogel Chevroulet, Irène, *La création d'une japonité moderne (1870–1940) ou le regard des architectes européens sur le Japon: Josiah Conder, Robert Mallet-Stevens, Bruno Taut et Charlotte Perriand* (Saarbrücken, 2010); Oshima, Ken Tadashi, *Constructed natures of modern architecture in Japan, 1920–1940. Yamada Mamoru, Horiguchi Sutemi, and Antonin Raymond* (Ph.D. thesis, New York: Columbia University, 2003); id., *International Architecture in Interwar Japan. Constructing Kokusai Kenchiku* (Seattle, 2009); Tseng, Alice Y., *The Imperial Museums of Meiji Japan. Architecture and the Art of the Nation* (Seattle, WA; London, 2008); Clancey, Gregory, *Earthquake Nation. The cultural politics of Japanese seismicity, 1868–1930* (Berkeley, LA; London, 2006); Buntrock, Dana, *Japanese Architecture as a Collaborative Process. Opportunities in a flexible construction culture* (London et al., 2002); id., *Materials and meaning in contemporary Japanese architecture: tradition and today* (London, 2010).

14   Sand, Jordan, *House and Home in Modern Japan. Architecture, Domestic Space, and Bourgeois Culture, 1880–1930* (Cambridge, MA; London, 2005); Odenthal, Julia, *Andere Räume – Räume der Anderen. Die Rezeptionsgeschichte der japanischen Architektur in der deutschen und japanischen Kunst- und Architekturgeschichte (1850–1950)* (Munich, 2015); Tagsold, Christian, *Spaces in Translation. Japanese Gardens and the West* (Philadelphia, 2017) – see also Lowen, Lenore, *One Foot in the Past, One Foot in the Future: Japanese Cultural Identity and Preservation Law 1868–1950* (Ph.D. thesis, Los Angeles: University of Southern California, 2013); Ganzer, Inga, *Hermann Muthesius und Japan: Die Rezeption und Verarbeitung japanischer Vorbilder in der deutschen Raumkunst nach 1900* (Petersberg, 2016).

and urban (planning) history on the other barely meet, apart from in a handful of authors such as Nicolas Fiévé or Carola Hein.[15]

In addition to the works that influenced the conceptual frame of this study, there was and still is significantly more literature with a more popular or journalistic approach, which provides an overview of the issues discussed with respect to contemporary Japanese architecture as well as of the main topics of Japan's architectural development.[16]

Sadly, some of the stereotyping simplifications about which William Coaldrake complained thirty years ago still survive in some of these publications. They take two different forms which intermingle on occasion: mythologisation in the tradition of *orientalism* on the one hand, and argumentation in the spirit of *nihonjinron*, the discourse about Japanese uniqueness vis-à-vis the West, on the other.

Orientalism, the simplified and often contra-factual imagination of oriental cultures in western cultures, is one of the recurring issues in this study. On the one hand, there is orientalism in art, as in *Chinoiserie* or harem depictions, in which the use of stereotypes is seen – not without reason – as part of the creative processes. On the other hand, there is the understanding of *orientalism* as a means of power relations in the sense of Eduard Said's controversial eponymous book and Homi Bhabha's work.[17] In terms of the production of

---

15 Sorensen, André, *The Making of Urban Japan: Cities and planning from Edo to the twenty-first century* (London, 2002); Fiévé, Nicolas; Waley, Paul (eds.), *Japanese Capitals in Historical Perspective: Place, power and memory in Kyoto, Edo and Tokyo* (London, 2003); Hein, Carola; Diefendorf, Jeffry M.; Ishida, Yorifusa (eds.), *Rebuilding Urban Japan after 1945* (Houndmills, Basingstoke, Hampshire, 2003); Fiévé, Nicolas, *Atlas historique de Kyōto. Analyse spatiale des systèmes de mémoire d'une ville, de son architecture et de son paysage urbain* (Paris, 2008); Brumann, Christoph; Schulz, Evelyn (eds.), *Urban Spaces in Japan. Cultural and Social Perspectives* (London; New York, 2012); Stavros, Matthew, *Kyoto. An Urban History of Japan's Premodern Capital* (Honolulu, 2014).

16 For an introduction to the general issue and a great deal of very helpful information, see, in addition to Nishi, *Japanese Architecture and Naito, Akira: Edo, the City that Became Tokyo. An illustrated history* (Tōkyō: Kodansha, 2003), e.g., Young, Michiko, et al., *Introduction to Japanese architecture* (Hong Kong, 2004); id., *The Art of Japanese Architecture* (Tōkyō; Rutland, VT, 2007); Cluzel, Jean-Sébastien, *Architecture éternelle du Japon. De l'histoire aux mythes* ([Dijon,] 2008); Locher, Mira; Kuma, Kengo; Simmons, Ben, *Traditional Japanese Architecture. An exploration of elements and forms* (Tōkyō, 2010) or Fujitsuka, Mitsumasa; Koshihara, Mikio, *Japan's Wooden Heritage: A Journey Through a Thousand Years of Architecture* (Tōkyō, 2017).

17 Said, Edward, *Orientalism* (New York, 1978); more relevant here is Bhabha, Homi K., *The location of Culture* (London; New York, 1994), here esp. the chapter "The Other Question. Stereotype, discrimination and the discourse of colonialism," pp. 66–84. See also Merida, Tarik, *Japanese Racial Identities within US-Japan Relations, 1853–1919* (Edinburgh, 2023).

knowledge of Japanese architecture in late nineteenth century, both concepts are closely interlinked. While many popular publications focus on the artistic exchange and keep the discussion of such issues to a minimum, more recent academic studies on *Japonisme* often successfully bridge the two readings of the term.[18]

Still, the most helpful approach for understanding the workings of such patterns in this context are studies of visual media that show the practices of staging and contextualising Japan for a western audience. They are often rooted in ethnology and cultural studies and form a crucial conceptual part of this research.[19]

Nihonjinron shows very similar patterns of argumentation but is less relevant to the historical sources, being primarily a characteristic of research literature after the Second World War. The term summarises phenomena of Japanese self-exoticisation in which the western attribution of oriental 'otherness' is used and extended to argue for an exceptionalism of Japanese

---

18   See e.g. Lancaster, Clay, *The Japanese Influence in America* (New York, 1963); Ives, Colta Feller, *The Great Wave: The Influence of Japanese Woodcuts on French Prints* (New York, 1974); Wilkinson, Nancy B., *Edward William Godwin and Japonisme in England* (Ph.D. thesis, University of California at Los Angeles, Los Angeles, 1987); Ministère de la Culture et la Communication (ed.), *Le japonisme, catalogue* (Paris, 1988); Mabuchi, Akiko, *Japanese art and Japonisme. Part 1, Early English writings (John La Farge; James Jackson Jarves; Marcus Bourne Huish; Christopher Dresser)* (Bristol, 1999); Wichmann, Siegfried; Whittall, Mary, *Japonisme: The Japanese Influence on Western Art Since 1858* (London, 1999); Lemoine, Bernadette (ed.), *Regards et discours européens sur le Japon et l'Inde au XIXe siècle* (Limoges, 2000); Lambourne, Lionel, *Japonisme: Cultural Crossings Between Japan and the West* (New York, 2007); Sigur, Hanna, *The Influence of Japanese Art on Design* (Salt Lake City et al., 2008); Mae, Michiko; Scherer, Elisabeth (eds.), *Nipponspiration. Japonismus und japanische Populärkultur im deutschsprachigen Raum* (Cologne, Weimar, Vienna, 2013); Irvine, Gregory, *Japonisme and the Rise of the Modern Art Movement: The Arts of the Meiji Period* (London, 2013); Cluzel, Jean-Sébastien (ed.), *Le japonisme architectural en France, 1550–1930* (Dijon, 2018).

19   Pratt, Mary Louise, *Imperial Eyes: Travel Writing and Transculturation* (London, 1992); Delank, Claudia, *Das imaginäre Japan in der Kunst. „Japanbilder" vom Jugendstil bis zum Bauhaus* (Munich, 1996); Rousmaniere, Nicole C.; Hirayama, Mikiko (eds.), *Reflecting Truth. Japanese Photography in the Nineteenth Century* (Amsterdam, 2004); Bennett, Terry, *Photography in Japan: 1853–1912* (Rutland, Vermont, 2006); Gartlan, Luke; Behdad, Ali, *Photography's Orientalism: New Essays on Colonial Representation* (Los Angeles, 2013). – See also Schulz, Evelyn, *Stadt-Diskurse in den "Aufzeichnungen über das Prosperieren von Tōkyō" (Tōkyō hanjō ki). Eine Gattung der topographischen Literatur Japans und ihre Bilder von Tōkyō (1832–1958)* (Munich, 2004) and the excellent impulses provided by the scholarly team of MIT Visualizing Cultures, https://visualizingcultures.mit.edu/home/index.html [accessed 1 July 2019].

culture. The discourse was largely a Japanese one, but a number of very influential western publications argued in the same vein, such as Ruth Benedict's *The Chrysanthemum and the Sword*, 1947.[20]

The phenomenon lessened towards the end of the twentieth century. Yet, books narrating Japanese exceptionalism remain in use and the ideas are still around. In terms of architecture there are, for example, Werner Blaser's publications, which provide genuinely helpful visual material together with very simplified and exoticising explanations.[21] A very recent and complicated example of this kind is the exhibition *Japan in Architecture*, held at the Mori Art Museum in Tōkyō in summer 2018, and the accompanying catalogue.[22] The exhibition offered a wealth of information on Japanese architecture over the centuries with many large-scale models, plans and photographs. In clear contrast to the painstakingly prepared material, some of the narrative contextualisation positions Japanese architecture as the antithesis of western architectural traditions and therefore the natural advocate of all non-western architectural traditions. Sadly, this replaces one hegemonic claim with another and uses a similarly simplified and polarising argumentation as the western writers it argues against.

These cases of persistent re-emergence of stereotypes underline the utmost relevance of conscious and precise epistemic framing: the largely balanced research of recent decades has not yet been able to overwrite the simple patterns of interpretation that are still embedded in common knowledge which appear in schoolbooks and popular literature and even on the shelves of university libraries. The new research contradicts and complicates the existing knowledge that took more than a century to build and to form into books which might be factually outdated but are plentiful and easily accessible.

Thus, the very phenomena that inspired this research still exist, not only represented by historical sources and desiderata. The contextualisation of research questions needs to take this into account, both in scholarly and in popular/general communication.

---

20 For an extended discussion of these phenomena and their contexts, see Hijiya-Kirschnereit, Irmela, *Das Ende der Exotik* (Frankfurt/M., 1988) and Dale, Peter N., "On Identity as Difference," in *The Myth of Japanese Uniqueness* (London, 1990), pp. 201–227.

21 See e.g. Blaser, Werner, *Tempel und Teehaus in Japan* (Olten, Lausanne, 1955; Engl. 1956 and further editions in 1988). Even more problematic is Blaser, Werner, *West Meets East. Mies van der Rohe* (Basel; Boston; Berlin, 1996).

22 Mori Art Museum (ed.), *Japan in Architecture. Genealogies of its Transformation* (Tōkyō: Echelle, 2018).

Fortunately, work on such less definite areas of knowledge production is nevertheless possible due to two more crucial fields of research: the general study of the history of architecture and construction, and the history of Japan and Japanese-western relations.

During the last few decades, the historiography of architecture and of architectural history gained in importance. Having actually known already for some time now that architecture is not about form, material and spatial disposition alone, but also about ideas of constructing societies, the field can no longer ignore architecture's political agency and architects' social responsibility.

Today there is intense scrutiny of the relevance of institutions, networks, reference books or schools, and career options for architects or engineers, not only for actual planning and design, but also for the conceptual understanding of architecture itself, the professionals creating it and their role in and for society.[23]

So far, the majority of Euro-American studies start from national or institutional frameworks or specific questions such as women architects, the emergence of the architectural history survey texts or the transnational careers of architects.[24] While the findings overlap insofar as showing architectural production as culturally framed on a very essential level, a meta text for such research is still missing and exchange still happens largely at conferences or focuses on projects such as the efforts to de-colonise Banister Fletcher's

---

23 An early forerunner of these studies was Mohamed Scharabi, who was already publishing in 1967: Scharabi, Mohamed, *Einfluss der Pariser École des Beaux-Arts auf die Berliner Architektur in der 2. Hälfte des 19. Jahrhunderts. Nachgewiesen anhand von Entwürfen in d. Plansammlung d. Fakultät f. Architektur an der Technischen Universität Berlin* (Berlin, 1967).

24 Pepchinski, Mary; Budde, Christina (ed.), *Women Architects and Politics. Intersections between Gender, Power Structures and Architecture in the Long 20th Century* (Bielefeld, 2022); *Constructing the Architectural Canon: The Architectural History Survey Text in the Nineteenth Century*, workshop by Petra Brouwer at the Netherlands Institute for Advanced Study in Wassenaar, 2016. For an example for her research about Dutch architectural handbooks, see, for example, Brouwer, Petra, "Das niederländische Architekturhandbuch im 19. Jahrhundert. Motor der Erneuerung," in: Hassler, Uta (ed.), *Der Lehrbuchdiskurs über das Bauen* (Zürich, 2015), pp. 152–167; Hvattum, Mari, *Building the Nation before Nationalism: The Cosmopolitan Historicism of mid-19th-century Europe*, paper at the EAHN conference in Dublin, 03.06.2016; id., "On Durability," lecture during the ISPA conference *The Human in Architecture and Philosophy* (Bamberg 20.07.2016); See in addition the conference *The Historiography of Architectural History. Genesis of a scientific discipline between national perspectives and European models* held in Munich, 3 July 2019 or *The History of Architectural History*, Rome, 8 and 9 November 2022.

History of Architecture.[25] As a result, this research expands awareness of the intrinsic logic of the field in the late nineteenth century considerably, but does not yet reach the complexity of available analyses of mutual relations between Japan and western nations, their biases and imbalances. Older copies of Fletcher's book are still on the shelf and his ideas are still extant; it is still difficult to understand how we need to re-order the perception of relevance beyond the western canon for teaching and future research. It will take time and effort to build on older research judiciously without building on biases as well. The main lines of development, however, are already emerging and allow the strategies of inclusion and exclusion by race, social background or gender that shaped and still shape not only architectural practice, but also the writing about it, to be taken into account.[26]

This research is possible not least due to the extensive material on architectural history accumulated during the last century. It allows us to question former/older assumptions and theories and to detect desiderata. In fact, this very material makes it necessary to do so and to find new concepts of contextualisation for the development of architectural knowledge and teaching, for writing architectural history beyond the famous names and places towards an analysis of building in nuanced contexts. This is not a discussion of the information in older documents, buildings surveys, drawings or excavations, but the patterns of relevance that contextualised and still contextualise the research and thus define which projects are seen as relevant or not. This is about questioning path dependencies of architectural research and discussing why we came to ignore some topics that might have been of interest.

There is a last but no less important body of literature and research that has allowed for the transfer of the aforementioned architectural questions into the context of the Japanese-western knowledge exchange: the extensive amount of information we now have on modern Japanese history and society. Authors

---

25 See the development from older issues to Fletcher, Sir Banister; Cruickshank, Dan (ed.), *Sir Banister Fletcher's a history of architecture* (Oxford, 1996) and Fletcher, Banister; Fraser, Murray; Gregg, Catherine (eds.), *Sir Banister Fletcher's global history of architecture*, 2 vols., 21st ed. (London; New York; Oxford; New Delhi; Sydney, 2020).

26 See e.g. Anderson, Christy, "Writing the Architectural Survey: Collective Authorities and Competing Approaches," *Journal of the Society of Architectural Historians* 58.3 (1999/2000): 350–355; Cheng, Irene, "Structural Racialism in Modern Architectural Theory," in: Cheng, Irene; Davis, Charles L. II; Wilson, Mabel O. (eds.), *Race and modern architecture. A critical history from the enlightenment to the present* (Pittsburgh, 2020), pp. 134–152; Bremner, Alex, *Building Greater Britain: Architecture, Imperialism, and the Edwardian Baroque Revival, c. 1885–1920* (New Haven; London, 2022).

with the most diverse backgrounds have reconstructed historical events and traced actors and institutions. Their works provide the foundation of 'fact' that is needed to question, analyse and display the diverging patterns of perception in architecture beyond the focus on the singular topic alone.[27]

---

27 To name just a few general overviews of Japanese history, some of them classics themselves: Bersihand, Roger, *Geschichte Japans von den Anfängen bis zur Gegenwart* (Stuttgart, 1963); Marius B. Jansen and Gilbert Rozman (eds.), *Japan in Transition. From Tokugawa to Meiji* (Princeton, 1986); Dettmer, Hans A., *Grundzüge der Geschichte Japans* (Darmstadt, 1992); Hardacre, Helen; Kern, Adam Lewis (eds.), *New Directions in the Study of Meiji Japan* (Leiden et al., 1997); Hall, John Whitney (ed.), *Das Japanische Kaiserreich*, 13th ed. (Frankfurt/M., et al., 2002); Pohl, Manfred, *Geschichte Japans* (Munich, 2002); Inoue, Kiyoshi, *Geschichte Japans*, 3rd ed. (Frankfurt; New York, 2003); Zöllner, Reinhard, *Geschichte Japans. Von 1800 bis zur Gegenwart* (Paderborn, 2006).

CHAPTER 2

My Perception, Your Perception

Available Knowledge, Research Questions, Approaches, and Expert Networks in the Late Nineteenth Century

The discussion of Japanese culture, art and architecture became meaningful and relevant in the West during the second half of the nineteenth century. However, it built on older sources and depended on informants and mediators, publication practices and global political developments.

This chapter provides an overview of the prior knowledge available and accessible to the general public and specialised fields and its subsequent extension by new information and new media. It then looks at the informants and mediators, their backgrounds, competences and interests.

It shows that a framework of concepts and expectations concerning Japan was already in place in the mid-nineteenth century. The chapter also shows that the collection, evaluation and dissemination of new information over time was in the hands of specific groups of actors in society and shaped by their interests and perceptions.

1 Knowledge of Japanese Architecture Available in the West

1.1 From Marco Polo to Matthew C. Perry

Before the mid-nineteenth century, the knowledge of Japan available in western languages was limited: it was a distant land and, due to the ensuing isolationist policy of the Tokugawa shōgunate, access was limited. Furthermore, many of the missionaries, traders, and travellers who published their experiences with Japan between 1543 and 1853 had a limited circulation.

The media that conveyed information to a wider audience were encyclopaedias and magazines. They provided access to the general knowledge currently available as well as topics perceived as relevant and occasionally introduced the sources accessible at the time in citations or bibliographic appendices for further reading.

The following pages give a paradigmatic overview of the general knowledge of Japan summed up in encyclopaedias in different European languages up to the 1850s. It demonstrates the treatment and contextualisation of the general information and art-related topics, supplemented by short comments regarding the most relevant textual sources informing the encyclopaedias and a comparison with the entries in architectural reference books of the time.

1.1.1   Encyclopaedias

What is probably the earliest of the modern encyclopaedias, Ephraim Chambers' *Cyclopedia*, did not have a specific entry on Japan in its issues between 1728 and 1788, although it did mention it as an island and people, for example in the entries on *Japan-earth* and *Japanning*.[1] Diderot and d'Alembert's *Encyclópedie* of 1751–1772, however, already provided a wide range of information. In the entry *Japon*, Louis de Jaucourt (1704–1779) mentioned the position and shape of the country, its climate, topography, natural resources and income, its commerce, forms of government and administration, its philosophy,[2] religion and history.[3] He did not discuss arts and crafts separately, but addressed those as part of the history of trade, thus emphasising their exceptional quality:

> The Portuguese purchased the best tea in Asia there, the most beautiful porcelain, those painted, lacquered, and varnished woods like screens, tables, trunks, boxes, tray-top tables, and other similar items, which every day diminish the value of our luxury goods; copper of a superior quality to ours; finally silver and gold, the main object of all the trading industries.[4]

De Jaucourt continued, embedding the artistic virtues of Japan into a story of cultural progress:

---

1   Chambers, Ephraim, *Cyclopaedia, or An Universal Dictionary of Arts and Sciences: Containing the Definitions of the Terms* …, vol. 2 (London, 1728), p. 367; id., *Cyclopaedia, or An Universal Dictionary of Arts and Sciences: Containing the Definitions of the Terms* …, Supplement 1 (London, 1753), n.p.; id.; Rees, Abraham, *Cyclopaedia, or Universal dictionary of arts and sciences* … (London, 1786), s.p.
2   Denis Diderot went into detail with a separate entry about Japanese philosophy. Diderot, Denis, "Japonois, Philosophie des," in: Diderot, Denis; d'Alembert, Jean le Rond (eds.), *Encyclopédie ou Dictionnaire raisonné des sciences, des arts et des métiers* (Paris, 1765), vol. 8, pp. 455–458, accessed via: University of Chicago: ARTFL Encyclopédie Project (Spring 2013 Edition), Robert Morrissey (ed.), http://encyclopedie.uchicago.edu/ (accessed March 9, 2015).
3   Jaucourt, Louis de, "Japan, le," in: Diderot, Denis; d'Alembert, Jean le Rond (eds.), *Encyclopédie ou Dictionnaire raisonné des sciences, des arts et des métiers* (Paris, 1765), vol. 8, pp. 453–455, cited from: *The Encyclopedia of Diderot & d'Alembert Collaborative Translation Project*. Translated by Jennifer Rappaport (Ann Arbor: Michigan Publishing, University of Michigan Library, 2013). http://hdl.handle.net/2027/spo.did2222.0002.634 (accessed March 9, 2015).
4   Jaucourt, "Japan," p. 455.

Japan, as populated as China proportionally, and no less industrious, while the nation is prouder and braver there, possesses almost everything that we have and almost everything that we lack. The peoples of the Orient were once much superior to our western peoples, in all the manual and spiritual arts. But how we have made up for lost time, says M. de Voltaire! The countries where Bramante and Michelangelo built Saint Peter's of Rome, where Raphael painted, or Newton calculated infinity, or Leibnitz shared this glory, or Huyggens applied the cycloid to the pendulum clock, where Jean de Bruges discovered oil painting, where Cinna and Athalie have been written; these countries, I say, became the first countries of the world. The eastern peoples are now in fine art only barbarians or children, despite their antiquity and all that nature did for them.[5]

Even though he referenced Saint Peter's in Rome in his attempt to underline Europe's success in rising to superiority over the older civilisations of the East, de Jaucourt did not comment on Japanese architecture at this point. He wrote, however, an entry on *Temples des Japonois*, which included a number of architectural characteristics of shrines and temples.[6] De Jaucourt characterised a major Shintō shrine as pleasantly positioned amongst the trees, the access granted by a spacious avenue, bordered by cypress trees, which led to a simple gate of stone or wood. He described the shrine building itself as simple and

> without ornament or magnificence, just rectangular, made from wooden beams which are thick and worked with considerable care. The height is barely more than that of two or three men, the width only two or three fathoms. It is about one and a half rods raised from the ground and supported by wooden posts. Around the mia is a small gallery to which one walks up some steps.[7]

---

5   Jaucourt, "Japan," p. 455.
6   Jaucourt, Louis de, "Temples des Japonois," in: Diderot, Denis; d'Alembert, Jean le Rond (eds.), *Encyclopédie ou Dictionnaire raisonné des sciences, des arts et des métiers* (Paris, 1765), vol. 16, pp. 83–84, accessed via: University of Chicago: ARTFL Encyclopédie Project (Spring 2013 Edition), Robert Morrissey (ed.), http://encyclopedie.uchicago.edu/ (accessed March 9, 2015).
7   "(…) sans ornement ni magnificence, communément quarré, fait de bois, & dont les poutres sont grosses & assez propres. La hauteur n'excede guere celle de deux ou trois hommes, & la largeur n'est que de deux ou trois brasses. Il est élevé d'environ une verge & demi au – dessus de la terre, & soutenu par des piliers de bois. Autour du mia il y a une petite galerie où l'on monte par quelques degrés." Jaucourt, "Temples des Japonois," p. 83.

The author remarked on the performance of prayer in front of the building, which always remained closed, before returning to its physical characteristics:

> The roof is covered with tiles, slate or wooden shingles and projects widely in all directions to cover this gallery surrounding the temple. It differs from the roofs of other buildings since it is more elaborately carved and made up of several layers of supports, which, by projecting below, are clearly unique. Sometimes there is an especially strong beam along the ridge with two more straight beams which cross at its ends.
>
> This structure is meant as a reproduction and remembrance of the first temples and while it is very simple, it seems very carefully thought out and nearly inimitable in the way the whole building is stabilised through the weight of the beams and their overlap.[8]

The article provided further information on the ritual use of shrines and continued with a shorter paragraph on Buddhist temples which de Jaucourt believed were similar in many regards to the former and to Chinese pagodas.[9]

A similar mixture of information about temples, deities, and practices of worship in Japan, but again offering no architectural data, was provided by the seventh edition of the *Encyclopædia Britannica* in 1842, under the heading *Deluge*.[10] The entry *Japan* gave a comparatively elaborate description of dwellings, castles, temples, and cities, though from a folkloristic perspective:

---

[8] "Le toit est couvert de tuiles, de pierre ou de coupeaux de bois, & il s'avance beaucoup de chaque côté pour couvrir cette espece de galerie qui regne tout – autour du temple. Il differe de celui des autres bâtimens, en ce qu'il est recourbé avec plus d'art, & composé de plusieurs couches de poutres, qui s'avançant par – dessous, ont quelque chose de fort singulier. A la cime du toit, il y a quelquefois une poutre plus grosse & plus forte que les autres, posée en long, & à ses extrémités deux autres poutres toutes droites qui se croisent. Cette structure est faite à l'imitation, aussi – bien qu'en mémoire de celle du premier temple; & quoiqu'elle soit fort simple, elle est néanmoins très – ingénieuse & presque inimitable, en ce que les poids & la liaison de toutes ces poutres entrelacées, sert à affermir tout l'édifice." Jaucourt, *Temples des Japonois*, p. 83.

[9] "(…) ressemblent beaucoup aux pagodes des Chinois (…)," Jaucourt, *Temples des Japonois*, p. 84.

[10] "Deluge," in: *The Encyclopaedia Britannica, or, Dictionary of arts, sciences, and general literature*, 7: *Clodius – Dialling*, 7th ed., with preliminary dissertations on the history of the sciences, and other extensive improvements and additions; including the late supplement, a general index, and numerous engravings (Edinburgh, 1842), pp. 690–703, esp. pp. 696, 698.

> The dwelling-houses of the Japanese, whether public or private, are by no means to be compared to those in Europe, either for size or magnificence, being commonly low, generally consisting of one story, and built of wood, owing to the danger of earthquakes. Their apartments are small, but uncommonly neat and clean, and for the most part carefully and curiously furnished; the windows, doors, posts, and passages, are finely painted and varnished; and the ceilings neatly covered with gilt or silver-coloured paper, and embellished with flowers. They have few partition walls to divide the rooms from one another; but instead of these they use folding screens made of coloured or gilt paper laid into wooden frames, which they can put on or remove at pleasure; and by this means they enlarge their rooms or make them narrower as best suits their fancy or convenience. These houses are built of cedar wood, of which there is great abundance in the country. (…)
>
> The towns are mostly populous and well built; and the streets run straight forward, crossing at right angles. They have no fortifications. The two chief gates are shut every night. The houses of the country people and husbandmen are small and poor, consisting of four low walls, covered with a thatched or shingled roof: 'They have,' says Kaempfer, 'many children and great poverty, and yet, with some small provision of rice, plants, and roots, they live content and happy.' The temples dedicated to Buddha, or to other foreign idols, are far superior to all other buildings, for their great height, curious roofs, and numberless other beautiful ornaments. They are built of the best cedars and firs, and adorned with carved images of their idols. (…) The best situations in the country are chosen for these temples; those which afford a fine view of the adjacent country, or are in the vicinity of a spring, a rivulet of clear water, or a wood with pleasant walks.[11]

While commenting on materials, volumes, decorations, and appropriateness of the buildings, the entry conveys no specific relevance of the topic and omitted information about art or architecture as understood as a field of professional expertise. Beyond that, the extensive quote demonstrates the way in

---

11   Buchanan, David, "Japan," in: *The Encyclopaedia Britannica, or, Dictionary of arts, sciences, and general literature*, 12: *Hydrodynamics – Kyreeghur*, 7th ed., with preliminary dissertations on the history of the sciences, and other extensive improvements and additions; including the late supplement, a general index, and numerous engravings (Edinburgh, 1842), pp. 510–522, pp. 517–518.

which the information meanders between description, citation and argument without any obvious hierarchy or order of topics.

The German *Brockhaus*, 1843–1848, provided the same overview of the geographical, historical, and cultural characteristics of Japan as the *Encyclopédie* and the *Encyclopaedia Britannica*, while Japanese literature merited additional attention in the entry on oriental literature.[12] Beyond that, it summarised the arts and sciences according to contemporary theories of civilisation:

> The Japanese are very fond of the arts and sciences and have distinguished themselves among the Asians; but they have remained on a low level of development in these areas due to their isolation. In particular in regard to the fine arts, the calendar, astrology and medicine they are the pupils of the Chinese, even though the contact they have had with Europeans has taught them better lessons on some topics.[13]

Meyers Conversations-Lexicon, 1839–1852, shared with *Brockhaus* both its overview of Japan and its assessment of the arts and sciences.[14] The entry added just two crucial sentences, however:

> Architecture is still in its infancy, since building is perceived as a manual trade alone. Beyond this, there are well-constructed canals and ingenious bridges.[15]

---

12 "Orientalische Literatur," in: *Allgemeine Deutsche Real-Encyklopädie für die gebildeten Stände. Conversations-Lexikon*, 10, *Moskau bis Patricier*, 9, Originalaufl. (Leipzig, 1846), pp. 509–511.

13 "Künste und Wissenschaften lieben die Japaner sehr und haben sich in mehren derselben vor allen andern Asiaten hervorgetan; doch sind sie in Folge ihrer Abgeschlossenheit auf einem niedrigen Grade der Ausbildung derselben stehen geblieben und größtentheils in ihnen die Schüler der Chinesen, insbesondere in den schönen Künsten, in der Zeitrechnung, Astrologie und Arzneiwissenschaft, obschon der Umgang, den sie mit den Europäern hatten, sie über manches besser belehrt hat." "Japan," in: *Allgemeine Deutsche Real-Encyklopädie für die gebildeten Stände. Conversations-Lexikon*, 7. *Heim bis Juwelen*, 9, Originalaufl. (Leipzig, 1845), pp. 621–626, here p. 622.

14 "Japan," in: Meyer, Joseph (ed.), *Das große Conversations-Lexicon für die gebildeten Stände: dieser Encyclopädie des menschlichen Wissens sind beigegeben: die Bildnisse der bedeutendsten Menschen aller Zeiten, die Ansichten der merkwürdigsten Orte, die Pläne der größten Städte, 100 Karten für alte und neue Erdbeschreibung, für Statistik, Geschichte und Religion ... / 1,16: Hügel – Johann (Geogr.)* (Hildburghausen, 1850), pp. 1167–1186, here p. 1175.

15 "Die Baukunst ist noch wenig ausgebildet, da man das Bauen noch allgemein als ein bloßes Handwerk betrachtet. Uebrigens hat man gut gebaute Kanäle und sinnreich konstruirte Brücken." "Japan" (Meyer, 1850), here pp. 1175–1176.

This short passage is important since it contained three different concepts of architecture and/or building: architecture as an art form (Baukunst), building as a manual trade (Handwerk), and construction as a mechanical art/engineering. The formulation showed the conscious differentiation between the three concepts and their precise ranking within the contemporary understanding of culture and progress.

Against this background, it is evident that buildings and cities in Japan are described as cultural expressions of Japanese character and custom alone. The entries do not analyse the structures as the results of artistic expression or attempts to solve problems of construction. The building-related information in *Meyers Conversations-Lexicon* resembles the French and British encyclopaedias by listing building types such as houses, temples or castles and specific building projects, such as bridges and roads, with some brief descriptions.[16] They allow the readers to imagine similarities and differences between their own and the Japanese built environments in a very general way.[17]

Essentially, the encyclopaedic information across the countries and languages shared a great deal of common content as far as Japanese culture, art, and architecture were concerned. At this time, the actual information was usually brief and not discussed as a topic of itself. It was either interwoven with other issues such as trade interests or used as an indicator for a level of civilisation.

The encyclopaedias differed occasionally relative to regional interests and contemporary issues. In terms of the latter, they were clearly up to date and reacted swiftly to new publications and shifts in global policies. Some of the encyclopaedias reflected both the rising interest in opening up Japan and subsequently the actual events of the American expedition led by Commodore Matthew Perry 1853–1854 in later editions.

The already relatively extended entry on *Japan* in *Meyers Conversations-Lexicon* became even longer with the supplements, issued 1853–1855, which addressed customs, government, and the Dutch establishment in Nagasaki.[18]

The concurrent edition of *Brockhaus* did not change the scope of its treatment and the Spanish *Enciclopedia Moderna*, 1851–1855, by Francisco de Paula

---

16 "Japan" (Meyer, 1850), here pp. 1172–1173.
17 It might be interesting to compare the descriptions of different countries and building traditions. Preliminary research, however, points to an inverse proportionality of distance and complexity of description. See e.g. Rujivacharakul, Vimalin, "Asia in World Architecture and World Cartography," in: Rujivacharakul, Vimalin; Hahn, H. Hazel; Oshima, Ken Tadashi; Christensen, Peter (eds.), *Architecturalized Asia. Mapping a Continent through History* (Honolulu, 2013), pp. 17–34.
18 "Japan" (Meyer, 1850), here pp. 44–68.

Mellado, likewise provided similar basic information, except for an additional entry about Japanese linguistics.[19]

In contrast, the content regarding *Japan* in the *Encyclopaedia Britannica*, 1852–1860, shifted between the seventh and the eighth editions. The data on the arts in general remained short, the commentary on architecture even shorter:

> Architecture, as an art, can hardly be said to have any existence – their temples, palaces, and private houses being all low and temporary structures, generally of wood; and the frequency of earthquakes leads them to bestow less care on their buildings than in other circumstances they might do.[20]

There were, however, some additional sources. Aside from the usual texts on Japan, which will be discussed briefly in the next section, the 1856 entry also included quite recent data "[on] account of the American expedition (1852–54)"[21] and a number of links to William Adams (1564–1620). The former was a fresh citation from Francis Hawk's (1798–1866) *Narrative of the expedition of an American squadron to the China seas and Japan*, which had just been published that year.[22] The latter was surprising due to the biographical data of Adams, but explicable through the release of Thomas Rundall's *Memorials of the Empire of Japan* in 1850, which edited *The Firste Booke of Relations of Moderne States* from Harleian Mss. 6249 and letters of William Adams from the early seventeenth century.[23]

---

19   C.f. "Japan," in: *Allgemeine Deutsche Real-Encyklopädie für die gebildeten Stände*, 8, Höfken – Kirchenbann, 10, *verb. und verm. Aufl.* (Leipzig, 1853), pp. 418–423; "Japon," in: Mellado, Francisco de Paula, *Enciclopedia Moderna. Diccionario universal de literatura, ciencia, arte, agricultura, industria y comercio* (Madrid; Paris, 1851–1855), 25, cols. 135–141, resp. 141–143.

20   J-N. C., "Japan," in: *The Encyclopaedia Britannica, or Dictionary of Arts, Sciences, and General Literature* / 12: *Hum – Jom*, 8th ed., with extensive improvements and additions, and numerous engravings (Edinburgh, 1856), pp. 688–699, p. 694.

21   J-N. C. "Japan," pp. 688, 692, FN.

22   Hawks, Francis L.; Perry, Matthew Calbraith, *Narrative of the expedition of an American squadron to the China seas and Japan, performed in the years 1852, 1853, and 1854, under the command of Commodore M. C. Perry, United States Navy, by order of the government of the United States. Compiled from the original notes and journals of Commodore Perry and his officers, at his request and under his supervision* (Washington, 1856). C.f. Hawks/Perry, *Narrative*, p. 397 with J-N. C., "Japan," p. 692.

23   Rundall, Thomas, *Memorials of the empire of Japon in the XVI and XVII centuries* (London: Hakluyt society, 1850). Regarding possible authorship and dating of the manuscript see

Other than in the most recent examples, the origin of the information often remained vague or entirely absent, both in terms of general topics and concerning the evaluation of Japanese art and architecture. Some of the encyclopaedias, however, identified the main sources or added abbreviated bibliographical information at the end of an entry that allow a glimpse into the background sources. Engelbert Kaempfer (1651–1716) and Philipp Franz von Siebold (1796–1866) were predominant among the references.

Kaempfer was a German physician and explorer. He was under contract to the Dutch East India Company (*Vereenigde Oostindische Compagnie*, VOC) and served at the Dutch settlement in Nagasaki between 1690 and 1692. During this time, he attended two homages to the shōgunate's court in Edo. Kaempfer's testimony *The history of Japan*[24] was first published in English in 1727–1729, a decade after his death, and was soon translated into French and Dutch. The original text in German was edited in 1777–1779.[25]

Philipp Franz von Siebold, a German physician and naturalist worked for the VOC in Nagasaki between 1823 and 1829 and published his experiences and conclusions in *Nippon* between 1832 and 1852.[26]

The most extensive list was provided by *Meyers Conversations-Lexicon* in 1850, with an annotated report on the sources, starting with Marco Polo and the Jesuits.[27] Beyond Kaempfer and Siebold it included four more individuals in the service of the VOC: Isaac Titsingh (1745–1812), Hendrik Doeff (1764–1837), Germain Felix Meijlan (1785–1831) and Frederik van Overmeer Fisscher (1800–1848). Their observations appeared in print during the 1820s and 1830s. Carl Peter Thunberg (1743–1828) had visited the Nagasaki settlement in the late

---

also: Shimada, Takau, "The authorship and date of Harl. ms. 6249, ff. 106v–110," in: *The British Library journal* 16 (1990), pp. 187–191.

24 Kaempfer, Engelbert, *The history of Japan, giving an account of the ancient and present state and government of that empire: of its temples, palaces, castles and other buildings, of its metals, minerals, trees, plants, animals, birds and fishes, of the chronology and succession of the emperors, ecclesiastical and secular, of the original descent, religions, customs, and manufactures of the natives, and of their trade and commerce with the Dutch and Chinese: together with a description of the kingdom of Siam*, 2 vols. (London, 1727–1729).

25 Meier-Lemgo, Karl, "Kaempfer, Engelbert," in: *Neue Deutsche Biographie* 10 (1974), pp. 729–730 [Onlinefassung]; URL: http://www.deutsche-biographie.de/ppn118559168.html [last accessed 26 April 2024].

26 Siebold, Philipp Franz von, *Nippon. Archiv zur Beschreibung von Japan und dessen Neben- und Schutzländern Jezo mit den südlichen Kurilen, Sachalin, Korea und den Liukiu-Inseln*, 7 vols. (text), 5 vols. (plates) (1832–1852); Gerabek, Werner E., "Siebold, Philipp Franz Balthasar," in: *Neue Deutsche Biographie* 24 (2010), pp. 329–330 [Onlinefassung]; URL: http://www.deutsche-biographie.de/ppn118613960.html [last accessed 26 April 2024].

27 "Japan" (Meyer 1850), p. 1184. – For the corresponding publications see the bibliography.

eighteenth century during his travels as a naturalist; Wassili Michailowitsch Golownin (1776–1831) was detained between 1811 and 1813 by Japanese officials in the course of an exploration of the Kuril Islands; and Peter Parker (1804–1888) visited the Ryukyu Islands in the course of missionary activities and the failed attempt to bring shipwrecked Japanese back into the country in 1837. Two further sources, Arnoldus Montanus (1625–1683) and Heinrich Julius Klaproth (1783–1835) compiled their accounts from secondary material, as did the unknown editor of *Manners and customs of the Japanese*.[28]

While not complete,[29] the list summarised the most important printed sources of knowledge about Japan available in the mid-nineteenth century. Its content mirrors the informational situation at this time as a result of Japan's isolationist policy which narrowed the main access to information about and the actual experience of Japan down to the Dutch trade post on the island of Deshima in Nagasaki and made the residents there the main mediators of knowledge transfer. Their respective competences and interests shaped the publications as did the periods of their residency and their responsibilities within the VOC. It is probably no coincidence that the majority of publications coincided with the rise in interest in Japan and the changing publishing market in Europe at the beginning of the nineteenth century.

The historical critique of the different sources itself is well established and will be omitted in favour of a focus on the content alone, as edited in the encyclopaedias: the entries in all of the texts seemed to have a high level of similarity as far as geographical, economic, and social topics were concerned. Regarding the art(s) and architecture as well as building practices in general, the information available was very limited, serendipitous, and consisted of three main claims: the first stated that there was hardly any architecture in Japan in general; the second described richly decorated temples or shrines in scenic settings, and the third characterised the built environment of cities and villages as being simple and composed of curiously outfitted wooden dwellings.

Beyond that, the information regarding architecture was mostly descriptive. More abstract ideas such as those concerning the profession of builders, planners or architects were entirely absent. The sources agreed, however, that streets were well kept and clean with a functioning infrastructure and bustling with people, thus interlinking the built environment with governmental regulations and action and, indirectly, with theories of culture and civilisation.

---

28   *Manners and customs of the Japanese, in the nineteenth century; from the accounts of Dutch residents in Japan and from the German work of Dr. Philipp Franz von Siebold* (London, 1841).

29   Adolphe Philibert Dubois de Jancigny (1795–1860), Samuel Wells Williams (1812–1884).

1.1.2 Architectural Reference Books

While the architectural reference books relied on the same textual sources as the encyclopaedias, the thematic focus was less on geographical or philosophical matters than practical. Beyond that, both the additional information from centuries of trading luxury goods for Asian porcelains and lacquer ware, and the persistent recurrence of Chinoiserie in European decorative styles influenced the topics of interest.[30]

This was visible in the very early dictionaries on architecture which always noted Japan together with China and only in relation to porcelain.[31] Interestingly enough, this was also true of the *Encyclopédie méthodique*'s volumes regarding architecture, 1788–1825. As a rearranged and extended version of Diderot's *Encyclopédie*, they omitted Louis de Jaucourt's entry on Japanese temples, for example. There was no dedicated entry on Japan, which was only mentioned together with China and India in relation to the development of architectural tastes, as well as in a comment on monumental Buddhist sculpture, and again in a passage on porcelain.[32]

The *Allgemeine Encyclopädie der Wissenschaften und Künste* is a rare example with an extensive entry by Karl Friedrich Neumann (1793–1870) about *Japan*, addressing history, religion and geography but neither art nor architecture.[33] In general, however, Japan is usually absent in the relevant architectural reference books of the time.

An initiative by the newly founded Institute of British Architects showed that this was not due to a lack of interest in global phenomena of architecture. The institute issued a book concerning *Questions upon various subjects connected with architecture* directed at *correspondents and travellers*, underlining

---

30   There is a great deal of scholarly literature on this question: regarding architecture, see for example: Koppelkamm, Stefan, *Der imaginäre Orient. Exotische Bauten des 18. und 19. Jahrhunderts in Europa* (Berlin, 1987) and concerning the accumulative lack of contact see, for example, Castelluccio, Stéphane, "La réception de l'architecture japonaise en France aux XVIIe et XVIIIe siècles. Un rendez-vous impossible," in: Cluzel, Jean-Sébastien (ed.), *Le japonisme architectural en France, 1550–1930* (Dijon, 2018), pp. 89–95.

31   *Dictionnaire D'Architecture ou Explication De Tous Les Termes, dont on se sert dans L'Architecture (etc.)* / 1693 – p. 205; Aviler, Augustin-Charles d', *Dictionnaire d'architecture civile et hydraulique et des arts qui en dépendent: comme la maçonnerie, la charpenterie, la menuiserie …* ([Reprod.] Paris, 1755), p. 301.

32   Quatremère de Quincy, Antoine (1755–1849), *Encyclopédie méthodique. Architecture*, 4 vols. (1788–1825), here 1, p. 111; 2, p. 3; 3, p. 170.

33   Neumann, Karl Friedrich, "Japan," in: Ersch, Johann Samuel; Gruber, Johann Gottfried (eds.), *Allgemeine Encyclopädie der Wissenschaften und Künste: mit Kupfern und Charten* (Leipzig, 1818–1889), here vol. 14 (1937), pp. 366–378.

the interest and need to collect architectural information.[34] It expressed specific interest in Indian and Hindu architecture, as well as Saracenic, Moresque and Siculo-Norman architecture and Mexican and other American antiquities in the second edition of 1842.[35]

James Fergusson's (1808–1886) *Handbook of Architecture* with its claim of *Being a Concise and Popular Account of the Different Styles of Architecture Prevailing in All Ages and All Countries*,[36] 1855, indicated a similar need for further study. He stated that "China possesses scarcely anything worthy of the name of architecture"[37] and included Japan in this evaluation. Fergusson emphasises, however, that this evaluation might undergo modification as soon as more knowledge about China became available.[38]

Overall, the architectural reference books available in the mid-nineteenth century rarely discussed Japan at all. If they did, the information contained philosophical, philological or cultural knowledge in relation to cultural development and/or advancement in terms of civilisation. Since the modern professional fields of construction had not yet fully developed in the West, neither the aesthetic interests of the architect, the practical issues of the client nor the structural questions of the engineer had been quite differentiated and formulated. The publications mirrored both this vagueness and the awareness of the knowledge deficits regarding non-European architectural traditions.

1.2   From Matthew C. Perry to the *Exposition Universelle* of 1900

Matthew C. Perry's American expedition to Japan of 1853–1854 initiated a shift in information transfer. Not only the members of this expedition, but also

---

34 Institute of British Architects, *Questions upon various subjects connected with architecture: suggested for the direction of correspondents and travellers, and for the purpose of eliciting uniformity of observation and intelligence in their communications to the Institute* (London, 1835).

35 Royal Institute of British Architects, *How to observe: architecture: or questions upon various subjects connected therewith, suggested for the direction of correspondents and travellers, and for the purpose of eliciting uniformity of observation and intelligence in their communications to the Institute* (London, 1842).

36 Fergusson, James, *The illustrated handbook of architecture. Being a concise and popular account of the different styles of architecture prevailing in all ages and all countries*, 2 vols. (London, 1855). – See for context as well Brouwer, Petra, "An illustrated comparison of 'true styles'. James Fergusson's The illustrated handbook of architecture (1855)," in: Burioni, Matteo, *Weltgeschichten der Architektur. Ursprünge, Narrative, Bilder 1700–2016* (Passau, 2016), pp. 42–44.

37 Fergusson, *Handbook*, 1, p. 133.

38 Fergusson, *Handbook*, 1, p. 143.

those undertaking similar ventures on behalf of competing western nations came to experience Japan in the ensuing years. Most of the early accounts were written by diplomatic or military personnel, interpreters and missionaries. With the establishment of the extraterritorial settlements and the initiation of the Meiji government's modernisation programme (1868–1912), entrepreneurs and traders, teachers, journalists, artists and globetrotters took up residence and reported home.

The following pages provide a general overview of the shifts in information transfer, both textual and visual, and their consequences for the overall knowledge of Japanese art and architecture.

Longer texts published between 1853 and 1868 are almost exclusively travelogues with a focus on the journey itself and negotiation procedures. The information regarding Japan remained superficial, not least because the time on shore was very limited, or because the information was, in fact, derived from older sources. Handbooks such as Richard Hildreth's highly successful *Japan. As It Was And Is*, 1855, summarised the older accounts by Kaempfer, Siebold et al. and thus provided easy access to information beyond the scope of the encyclopaedias or the sometimes rare original texts.[39]

A good example of the mixture of actual observation and embedded knowledge from other sources in these travelogues was the architectural information in the essay from US Navy Captain Andrew Hull Foote (1806–1863) about his *Visit to Simoda and Hakodai in Japan*, 1858. He wrote regarding Shimoda:

> Simoda was formerly, from its position at the entrance of the bay of Yedo, a large town, where much business was transacted, but has greatly declined and certainly now has the appearance of rather a poverty-stricken place. The streets intersect each other, in most cases, at right angles. Several of the houses are built of stone, others of bamboo, and some are stuccoed with mud; while thatched huts are abundant. The roofs are generally formed of colored tiles, black and white. No chimneys are seen in Simoda; and the smoke from the cooking fires finds its ways out of holes, in the upper part of the walls, left open for the purpose. The slightly-constructed buildings are better adapted to the shocks of earthquakes, so prevalent in this vicinity, than a harder material would prove. The cleanliness of their houses far surpasses anything of the kind I have ever seen, the Quaker settlements in our country not excepted. (...)

---

39   Hildreth, Richard, *Japan: As it was and is* (Boston, 1855).

> The streets of Simoda are fifteen or twenty feet wide and partly paved with stone. At the sides are gutters and sewers for draining the refuse water and filth into the harbor, or into a small stream, running through the outskirts of the town, – another evidence of an advanced state of civilization over the Chinese.[40]

The description was of ethnographical character and contained a range of topics such as history, urban structure, building materials, architectural details, daily chores, matters of earthquake resistance and hygiene. While the absence of chimneys, for example, was clearly an observation that could have been made by any visitor, the comments regarding the earthquake-resistant qualities of Japanese buildings had most probably been learned from older texts. The essay conveyed Foote's thoughts in a pattern of overlapping yet selective impressions, in which gaps presented themselves to be filled with the reader's pre-existing knowledge or imagination.

With more and more westerners taking up permanent residence in Japan, the information available in western printed media changed considerably from the late 1860s onwards: they now included books and essays covering topics from legal matters, trade customs, minerals or woods, to religious practices and musical styles in Japan.

Travelogues also remained a popular text genre but had shifted in character in a way that influenced the perception of Japanese architecture. It was no longer considered exciting simply to reach Japan in general: what counted now was to get to certain places within Japan. Although places of residence for westerners and mobility within the country were subject to legal limitations, tourist travel began in earnest, both by the resident westerners themselves and by visiting globetrotters.[41] Visitors with widely diverse backgrounds repeatedly described and depicted a number of scenic places. Among the most popular were natural sites such as Mount Fuji and man-made places such as the temples of Nikkō and Shiba, which housed gravesites of the recently deposed Tokugawa shōgunate. The rapid publication of these travelogues established and strengthened a reference list of places-to-know and places-to-go in Japan.

---

40 Foote, A[ndrew] H[ull], "Visit to Simoda and Hakodai in Japan," in: *Journal of the North China Branch of the Royal Asiatic Society* 1 (1858), pp. 129–137, here pp. 130–131.

41 On the reasons for the choice of routes, see Hockley, Allen, *Globetrotters' Japan: People. Foreigner on the tourist circuit in Meiji Japan*, Online-Resource, 2008, https://visualizingcultures.mit.edu/gt_japan_people/index.html [last accessed 26 April 2024], and Toyosawa, Nobuko, *The cartography of epistemology: The production of "national" space in late 19th century Japan* (Ph.D. thesis, University of Illinois at Urbana-Champaign, 2008).

While there was a close relationship between the available travel infrastructure and the places visited, the illustrated volumes of sites of Japanese tradition such as *Miyako meisho zue*, 1780, surely influenced the selection of places that became sightseeing locations for westerners during the late nineteenth century. Firstly, because visitors might already have been aware of these destinations through visual media, and secondly because the Japanese hosts might have suggested favoured routes and places.[42] A singular and very early printed sample of this process of mediation was Kakuma Yamamoto's *Guide to the celebrated places in Kiyoto and the surrounding places for the foreign visitors*. This small volume was explicitly "written for the convenience of the foreign visitors to the Kiyoto Exhibition" in 1873.[43]

However, while noteworthy sites were a recurring topic in texts on Japan, only a small number of essays addressing architectural topics focused exclusively on them, such as Ernest M. Satow's descriptions of *The Shin-tau Temples of Ise* and his *Guide Book to Nikkō*, as well as Thomas R. H. McClatchie's *The Castle of Yedo* and Roger T. Conder's *The Mausoleum at Nikko*.[44] Most architectural essays at this time took a more general approach. Henry R. Brunton discussed *Constructive Art in Japan*, Edward W. Godwin *Japanese wood construction* and César D. Daly addressed *Les temples japonais*.[45] Some writers such as

42   Hockley, *Globetrotters', People*, s.p.; Akisato, Ritō, *Miyako meisho zue* [Kyōto, 1780]; Wieczorek, Alfried; Sui, Claude W. (eds.), *Ins Land der Kirschblüte. Japanische Reisefotografie aus dem 19. Jahrhundert* (Heidelberg, 2011). On Japanese travel books, see Goree, Robert Dale Jr., *Fantasies of the Real: Meisho zue in Early Modern Japan* (unpubl. dissertation, Yale University, 2010).
43   Yamamoto, Kakuma, *Guide to the celebrated places in Kiyoto and the surrounding places for the foreign visitors* (Kyōto: Niwa Keisuke, 1873), here the preface.
44   Satow, Ernest Mason, "The Shin-tau Temples of Ise," in: *Transactions of the Asiatic Society of Japan, Vol. II* (1874), pp. 113–139; id., *A Guide Book to Nikkō* (Yokohama, 1875); McClatchie, Thomas R. H., "The Castle of Yedo," in: *Transactions of the Asiatic Society of Japan, Vol. VI, Part 1* (October 1877–January 1878), pp. 119–150; Conder, Roger Thomas, "The Mausoleum at Nikko," in: *Transactions of the Royal Institute of British Architects* 2 (2nd series) (1885/1886), pp. 209–214.
45   Brunton, R. Henry, "Constructive Art in Japan (1)," in: *Transactions of the Asiatic Society of Japan II* (1874), pp. 64–86; id., "Constructive Art in Japan (2)," in: *Transactions of the Asiatic Society of Japan III* (1875), pp. 20–30; Godwin, Edward William, "Japanese wood construction V–VI," in: *Building News and Engineering Journal* (12 February 1875), pp. 173–174; (19 February 1875), pp. 200–201, 214; Daly, César Denis, "Les temples japonais," in: *Revue générale de l'architecture et des travaux publics* 43 (1886), cols. 50–51, plates 16–26; id., "Les temples bouddhistes du Japon," in: *Revue générale de l'architecture et des travaux publics* 43 (1886), cols. 97–107, 193–198, plates 16–26 and 44; (1887), cols. 7–18.

Josiah Conder published repeatedly,[46] but the number and extent of essays remained limited and the texts were widely dispersed in building-related or Asia-related journals. In terms of monographs, there was just a single book entirely dedicated to an aspect of Japanese architecture in the latter half of the nineteenth century: Edward S. Morse's very popular *Japanese Homes and Their Surroundings*, 1885.[47]

The art historical publications of the time either dismissed Japanese architecture as irrelevant, as in James J. Jarves' *A Glimpse at the Art of Japan* or Rutherford Alcock's *Art and Art Industries in Japan*, or treated it only marginally, as in Louis Gonse's *L'Art Japonais*.[48] An exception in certain respects was Christopher Dresser's *Japan, its Architecture, Art and Art Manufactures*, 1882, which even included structural considerations, as we will discuss in the next chapter.[49]

This underlines the fact that fine arts and architecture were separate fields of interest and expertise where Japan was concerned. Art dealers, collectors, connoisseurs, researchers and artists referred back to older experiences and defined a field of expertise regarding Japanese arts and crafts. In addition, art collections were initiated or extended and museum exhibitions established.

The realms of portable, collectible art objects and of immobile, non-collectible architectural artefacts remained disconnected in terms of interest, research methods, and publishing practices. The two fields rarely met, except in the context of the World's Fairs, especially in Vienna in 1873, Chicago in 1893, and Paris in 1900. The Japanese pavilion at the *World's Columbian Exposition* in Chicago was conceived by Okakura Kakuzō (1863–1913) as a total work of art and was publicised accordingly, as we will see later. Okakura's booklet for the Exposition presents the pavilion Hō-ō-den itself, a downsized copy of the Uji Byōdō-in, and the exhibited artefacts in context according to the main periods

---

46 For example Conder, Josiah, "Notes on Japanese architecture," in: *Transactions of the Royal Institute of British Architects* 28 (1877/1878), pp. 179–192, 209–212; id., "Further notes on Japanese architecture," in: *Transactions of the Royal Institute of British Architects* 2 (2nd series) (1885/1886), pp. 185–214; id., "Domestic architecture in Japan," in: *Transactions of the Royal Institute of British Architects* 3 (2nd series) (1886/1887), pp. 103–127.

47 Morse, Edward Sylvester, *Japanese Homes and Their Surroundings* (Boston; New York; London, 1885).

48 Jarves, James Jackson, *A Glimpse at the Art of Japan* (New York, 1876); Alcock, Rutherford, *Art and Art Industries in Japan* (London, 1878); Gonse, Louis, *L'Art Japonais* (Paris, 1883).

49 Dresser, Christopher, *Japan, its Architecture, Art and Art Manufactures* (London; New York, 1882).

of Japanese history.[50] A few years later in Paris, the Commission Impériale du Japon issued the *Histoire de l'art du Japon*, an illustrated volume that outlined the main works of Japanese art and architecture for the first time in the form of a chronologically and thematically organised survey.[51] Beyond its content, the book marks a certain high point in the combination of visual and textual information.

1.2.1 Visual Sources

While several illustrations had already appeared in Kaempfer's *History*, Arnoldus Montanus' *Atlas Japannensis*, or Siebold's *Nippon*, including views of common dwellings and sectional drawings, the number of images remained comparatively small due to the considerable production expenses involved.[52] From the 1860s onwards, the role of visual sources depicting Japan and its architecture increased and became essential for the process of knowledge transfer for two reasons: firstly, because almost no-one was able to actually visit all of the relevant buildings, and secondly, since many of the authors who wrote about Japanese art and architecture remained entirely in the West.

In general, Japanese woodblock prints, line drawings, paintings and photography must be taken into account and were used concertedly as illustrations. While the woodblock prints heavily influenced the renewal of fine art in Europe and illustrated recent events in Japan as well, photography eventually became the dominant medium for visual information regarding Japanese architecture.

---

50 Okakura, Kakudzo [Okakura, Kakuzo], *The Hō-ō-den. An illustrated Description of the Building erected by the Japanese Government at the World's Columbian Exhibition* (Jackson Park, Chicago; Tōkyō, 1893).

51 Fukuchi, Mataichi; Kino, Toshio; Mabuchi, Akiko, *Japan. Rinji Hakurankai Jimukyoku*, Tōkyō Teishitsu Hakubutsukan; [Hayashi, Tadamasa, *Universal Exposition Commission Impériale du Japon*]: *Histoire de l'art du Japon. Ouvrage publié par la Commission Impériale du Japon à l'Exposition universelle de Paris, 1900* (Paris, 1900). – See further discussion in chapter 4.

52 In addition to texts and images, architectural models provided architectural information. However, while their overall number seems to have been substantial, research is still in an early stage. See for example the work done by Shimizu Shigeatsu, Kyōto Institute of Technology (KIT), for an overview Cluzel, Jean-Sébastien; Gautier, Marion; Nishida, Masatugu, "Maquettes d'architecture japonaise. 1840–1937. La collection du musée du Quai Branly," in: Cluzel, Jean-Sébastien (ed.), *Le japonisme architectural en France, 1550–1930* (Dijon, 2018), pp. 138–141 and the context sketched in the sub-chapter about the 1873 Vienna World's Fair.

As early as the 1850s and 1860s, members of various diplomatic expeditions to Japan were already documenting its built environment in photographs.[53] Some of the images were later used to illustrate travelogues. At the same time, professional studios had already been set up in Yokohama, one of the primary Japanese trade ports, by Shimooka Renjo in 1862 (1823–1914) and by Felice Beato (1832–1909) in 1863.[54] These and many other studios distributed souvenir photographs, which were probably the most common and most extensive source of visual information on Japanese architecture at the time. The souvenir photographs focused on local customs and costumes, beautiful women and flowers, and landscapes and sites, including a number of famous temples and shrines, above all those of Tōkyō, Kamakura and Nikkō.[55]

Visitors chose their preferred images, had them arranged in albums and took them back home. Thus, the visual knowledge of Japanese architecture available outside Japan consisted of an eclectic array of impressions in which architectural information was fit for inspiration but had little significance in terms of architectural practice and research.[56]

1.2.2 Architectural Reference Books

The increase in the flow of information, both textual and visual, was nevertheless immense and bound to influence the specialised volumes catering to builders, architects, and art professionals.

Oscar Mothes' *Allgemeines deutsches Bauwörterbuch* of 1858–1859 reacted to the input and included a column on *japanische Baukunst* in the second volume. Pointing out that legal limits impeded architectural development, it mentioned the low height of the houses, their simplicity and cleanliness. It went on to shrines and temples, decoration and building materials.[57] The second

---

53 Such as the Prussian Eulenberg Expedition see Dopson, Sebastian, "Photography and the Prussian Expedition to Japan, 1860–61," in: *History of Photography* 33.2 (May 2009), pp. 112–131.

54 Greater detail is provided by Bennett, Terry, *Early Japanese images* (Rutland, VT et al., 1998).

55 See Hockley, *Globetrotters', People*, s.p.; and Harvard College Library, *Early photography of Japan*, online resource, https://curiosity.lib.harvard.edu/early-photography-of-japan [last accessed 26 April 2024].

56 In recent years, a number of these albums have been digitised and made available by libraries and archives. This has opened an extensive field of visual sources for research and cross-referencing between printed accounts and this informal transfer of visual information, which will be examined in chapter 4.

57 Mothes, Oscar (ed.), *Allgemeines deutsches Bauwörterbuch, das ist Encyclopädie der Baukunst für Alle, die mit dem Hochbau, Flachbau, Bergbau, Maschinenbau zu thun haben* (Leipzig, 1858–1859), 2, pp. 162–163.

edition of 1863–66, titled *Illustrirtes Bau-Lexikon*, included more than five pages on this subject matter. The account was structured typologically, addressing religious edifices, cities and settlements, palaces and dwellings. While more ethnographic than architectural, the text included half a dozen illustrations taken from Siebold's *Nippon*, thus considerably enhancing the information provided.[58]

Mothes' entry was entirely up to date but did not set a precedent within the field. Daniel Ramée's *Dictionnaire général des Termes d'Architecture en français, allemand, anglais et italien*, 1868, continued in the tradition of older books and mentioned Japan only in relation to porcelain.[59] The situation was similar with *Technologisches Wörterbuch: Deutsch-Englisch-Französisch: Gewerbe, Civil- & Militär-Baukunst, Artillerie, Maschinenbau, Eisenbahnwesen, Strassen- und Wasserbau, Schiffbau und Schiffahrt*, 1870: it limited its coverage in English to the same keywords that had been part of older books, such as "Japan-earth" or "Japanning."[60]

In its volume on architecture, the *Encyclopédie historique, archéologique, biographique, chronologique et monogrammatique des Beaux-Arts plastiques, architecture et mosaïque, céramique, sculpture, peinture et gravure* compiled by August Demmin, 1873, addressed China and Japan repeatedly.[61] In many cases, the architectural information was embedded in discussions of history and cultural phenomena.[62] Exceptions were some passages regarding the physical dimensions of Ōsaka Castle, others on architectural style in general, and a section under the heading *L'architecture en Chine et au Japon*, in which the author claimed the absence of any interesting architectural artefacts and the similarity to Chinese structures.[63]

---

58 Mothes, Oscar (ed.), *Illustrirtes Bau-Lexikon: praktisches Hülfs- und Nachschlagebuch im Gebiete des Hoch- und Flachbaues, Land- u. Wasserbaues, Mühlen- u. Bergbaues, der Schiffe- und Kriegsbaukunst, sowie der Mythologie, Ikonographie, Symbolik, Heraldik, Botanik und Mineralogie, so weit solche mit dem Bauwesen in Verbindung kommen; für Architekten und Ingenieure ...* (Leipzig, 1863–), 2, pp. 303–308.

59 Ramée, Daniel, *Dictionnaire général des Termes d'Architecture en français, allemand, anglais et italien* (Paris, 1868), p. 346.

60 *Technologisches Wörterbuch: Deutsch-Englisch-Französisch: Gewerbe, Civil- & Militär-Baukunst, Artillerie, Maschinenbau, Eisenbahnwesen, Strassen- und Wasserbau, Schiffbau und Schiffahrt* [...] (Wiesbaden; Paris; London; 2nd, revised ed., 1869), vol. 1 (German), p. 261, resp. (1870), vol. 2 (English), p. 321.

61 Demmin, August, *Encyclopédie historique, archéologique, biographique, chronologique et monogrammatique des Beaux-Arts plastiques, architecture et mosaïque, céramique, sculpture, peinture et gravure* (Paris, 1873–1874).

62 See e.g. Demmin, *Encyclopédie*, p. 17.

63 Demmin, *Encyclopédie*, pp. 283, 224, 538, 541.

Taken as a whole, the book was more a comparative study of global cultures and their histories, customs, and writings than a handbook on the fine arts, let alone on architecture.

At the same time, James Fergusson's *History of Indian and Eastern Architecture*, 1876, went on to lament the lack of knowledge regarding Japan (and for that matter China as well) as he had already in his earlier *Handbook of Architecture* and stated:

> So far as our knowledge at present extends, there is not a single permanent building in the island of so monumental a character to deserve being dignified by being classed among the true architectural examples of other countries. It may be that the dread of earthquakes has prevented them raising their buildings to more than one or two storeys in height, or constructing them of more solid materials than wood. It may be, however, that the Japanese do not belong to one of the building races of mankind, and have no taste for this mode of magnificence. It is the same story as in China; we shall not know whether it is true that there are no objects worthy to be styled architecture in Japan till the island is more scientifically explored than it has been; nor, if they do not exist, shall we till then be able to say to which of the two above causes their absence is to be ascribed. Such information as we have is very discouraging; and it is to be feared that, though quaint and curious in itself, and so far worthy of attention, it is of little interest beyond the shores of the islands themselves. On the other hand, it is to be feared that the extent of our knowledge is sufficient to make it only too clear that the art, as practiced in Japan, has no title to rank with that already described in the preceding pages, and consequently no claim to a place in a general history of architectural art.[64]

This evaluation was repeated in 1891 and again in 1899 in *A history of architecture in all countries*.[65]

It summed up the main arguments shaping the organisation and presentation of expert knowledge of Japanese architecture at the time. While the writers were aware of the lack of information in general, their tentative assessments dismissed Japanese buildings as architecturally irrelevant due to the use of wood, the lack of longevity and the absence of monumentality. In some cases, this was attributed to the frequency of earthquakes, in others it was seen

---

64   Fergusson, James, *History of Indian and Eastern Architecture* (London, 1876), pp. 709–710.
65   Fergusson, James, *A history of architecture in all countries, from the earliest times to the present day: in five volumes* (London, 1899), 3, 709–710.

as a cultural and/or racial phenomenon and was embedded within discourses regarding global art and civilisation.

I suggest reading the content of the architectural refence books as expressing the basic assumptions concerning Japanese culture and architecture created in the west and as the foundation on which later studies rested. Later authors might have noted and discussed the scarcity of actual information without questioning its reliability to any great extent and accepting it as sufficient common knowledge and a foundation for their own work.

2 Diplomats, Experts and Knowledge Mediators' Networks

The discussion above provides an overview of the general development of western knowledge of Japanese architecture, focusing on the availability of that knowledge to the public via textual and visual media. This section works backwards from the media used to disseminate information to the individuals who provided the knowledge as well as those who evaluated and disseminated it, and the fields of interest involved. It will become apparent that the emerging body of knowledge was somewhat coincidentally shaped by a small number of contributors, their respective areas of expertise and interests, and the social and professional networks in which they acted. To capture this, architecture is defined in its broadest sense. This means including the fields of urban design and urban development as well as all topics related to architecture as an art, architecture as construction, and, last but not least, architecture as cultural practice.

2.1 *Media*
The previous section already sketched the development of topics. It is, however, worth looking at monographs and periodicals from a more statistical perspective as well. The following discussion aims to determine whether monographs and periodicals complemented each other in terms of topics and/or authors and how both developed over time until World War II. In addition, it offers the opportunity to trace the influence of certain authors across fields and to observe the subsequent delineation of fields of expertise.

The bibliography used for this analysis is admittedly biased, since publications regarding particular topics in the arts, such as *Keramic art of Japan* by George A. Audsley and James L. Bowes,[66] 1875, have been omitted as irrelevant to a discussion of architecture, while essays and reviews with similar topics

---

66 Audsley, George Ashdown; Bowes, James, *Keramic art of Japan* (Liverpool, 1875).

have been included. The monographs on the arts are thus limited to overviews and are much fewer in number than they would be in a full bibliography on Japanese arts. The same goes for travelogues and ethnographical reports, which stood in for architectural knowledge during the years in which specialised publications were still completely lacking. Even with these caveats, however, it is interesting to notice the migration of topics through the text genres and fields.

As mentioned above, travelogues and ethnographic reports increased in number during the 1850s, grew further after 1877 and reached a significant peak between 1891 and 1910. After this time, this text genre nearly vanished. Travel guides remained but no longer compensated for regional geography or ethnographic reports. Monographs on the arts appeared from 1874 onwards with peaks in 1886, 1892–1893 and significantly between 1900 and 1904. Numbers subsequently decreased until 1914 and persisted at a low but steady level until World War II. Architectural monographs appeared in the late 1890s and experienced a minor peak in 1905. For more than twenty years thereafter, the number of publications remained at a very low level until it rose again in 1929 and reached a significant peak in 1936.

At first sight, this pattern suggests a succession of topics of interest, which appears valid as far as travelogues and ethnological reports are concerned, which no longer compensated for a lack of specialist publications. In terms of specialist topics in art and architecture, however, the trend more likely delineates an increasing distinction between fields, a division of experts' discourses, and changes in the perceived relevance of different research topics in relation to European discourses, as will be shown later in this book.

Generally speaking, the relevant monographs remained limited in numbers. The bibliography used for this analysis includes approximately 375 books and more than 400 notes and articles from journals, mostly in English, German, and French, between Luís Fróis' *Brevis Iapaniae Insvlae Descriptio* of 1582, and the essay *Der Ursprung des Torii* by Dietrich Seckel and Otto Karow of 1943.[67] The topics range from descriptions of the urban environment, construction, fire protection and earthquake resistance, singular buildings or building types, hygiene and social practices, to sightseeing, decorative detailing or new

---

67   Fróis, Luís, *Brevis Iapaniae Insvlae Descriptio, Ac Rervm Qvarvndam In Ea Mirabilium, à Patribus Societatis Iesv nuper gestarum, succinta narratio: Item, Insigne Qvoddam Martyrium, quod in Aphrica quidam pro Christiana religione Catholica inuicta constantia subijt* (Coloniae Agrippinae, 1582); Seckel, Dietrich; Karow, Otto, "Der Ursprung des Torii," in: *Mitteilungen der deutschen Gesellschaft für Natur- und Völkerkunde Ostasiens XXXIII* (1942–1943), Teil B, pp. B1–B86.

building projects and infrastructural development. While this seems to provide plenty of information, it mostly remained perfunctory and presents difficulties when tracing the discourses, especially when attempting to hear more than just the major voices alone.

The Big Data indexing of periodicals is still in its infancy and currently presents as many obstacles as it does opportunities. To the extent that it is viable, it allows for a broader overview of major and minor topics as well as for references outside specifically Japanese contexts. There are, for example, some text genres and contexts in which Japanese art and architecture were the subject of discussion: these include cultural journals and general-interest magazines, exchanges among art collectors, discourses regarding Japanese culture in general, and architectural journals. The next paragraphs provide a brief overview of this, but name just a few of the periodicals. For a full list and the respective periods of analysis, please refer to the first part of the bibliography.

2.1.1 Cultural Journals and General-Interest Magazines

Cultural journals and general-interest magazines such as the German *Die Gartenlaube* and *Über Land und Meer* provided topical information on current events and public debate.[68] Short excerpts offered entertaining or instructive glimpses into larger publications by renowned authors. The information about Japan, its culture, art, and architecture functioned as items of curiosity, with no context and with little relevance beyond their novelty.[69]

A similarly eclectic range of subjects was addressed in journals dedicated to Asian or Japanese studies.[70] This included building-related topics along with art, culture, economics, or language. The essays provided specialist information in its cultural context, often connected to arguments regarding global theories of civilisation, culture or the arts. The authors were of widely diverse backgrounds and language skills and wrote not only about their fields of professional expertise, but indulged their amateur interests as well, such as the missionary Isaac Dooman who discussed *The Influence of Greco-Persian art on Japanese arts*, 1896.[71]

---

68   *Die Gartenlaube* (1853–1984, analysed 1853–1908), *Über Land und Meer* (1858–1923, analysed 1860–1911).
69   An exception is the Russo-Japanese War 1904–1905 that gained a lot of attention in *Über Land und Meer*.
70   For an overview of the relevant periodicals that were systematically analysed, see the list in the bibliography.
71   Dooman, Isaac, "The influence of Greco-Persian art on Japanese arts," in: *Transactions of the Asiatic society of Japan XXIV* (1896), pp. 137–175.

The sample analysis of digitised periodicals shows a gradual shift of topics in the Asia-related journals. The diversity of the contents decreased considerably during the 1870s and 1880s and led to more specialisation towards the end of the century. The journals became thematically differentiated and eventually narrowed their focus to specific disciplines such as economy and trade, or culture and language. The *Österreichische Monatsschrift für den Orient*, for example, largely abandoned cultural issues and moved towards commercial information. During the 1910s, it then shifted its entire regional focus toward the Balkans. In general, architectural issues became rare or ceased to appear in periodicals related to Asian and Japanese studies.

2.1.2 Art Periodicals

Art periodicals such as *The Art Journal* or the *Gazette des beaux-arts* welcomed the input provided by Japanese art in support of a reform of the struggling system of European art production. They commented on acquisitions, exhibitions, collectors, and on artists who visited Japan, both in snippets and in multi-page essays.[72] The extended essays usually combined the data provided on a specific topic with issues of European culture, western industrialisation, education, global art theory, or the theory of civilisation. Japanese arts and handicrafts became labelled as specifically Japanese and were inscribed with additional cultural values according to the contemporary European discourses. Hence, the Japaneseness of the artefacts did not exist as a quality in itself, but stood in relation to the discourses, as can be seen in the subsequent shift in vocabulary.

While the terms *Japan* or *Japanese* were initially used to signify phenomena in strict relation to Japan, their use diversified and loosened toward the end of the century, until the term *Japanese* became an adjective or adverb primarily used to signify a perceived Japaneseness in the artistic expression of European art works, for better or worse. This Japaneseness ranged from the overall choice of a subject or the division of the available space in a painting, to the ways of depicting plants or a specific use of colours or lines. In some cases, it was even used as a category of non-westernness to express the global relevance of a particular topic.

While Japonisme is often perceived as a phenomenon predominantly associated with French art discourses, the art journals present a somewhat different view. The journals from England, France and Germany paid a similarly low level of attention to issues related to Japan. The only exception was *Studio:*

---

[72] For an overview of the art periodicals that were systematically analysed, see the list in the bibliography.

international art. This journal was edited by Charles Holme (1848–1923) and published between 1893 and 1925. The number of Japan-related essays and notes it published was many times more than any of the other journals. Holme was deeply involved in trade with East Asia, travelled the region, and was one of the founders of the Japan Society in 1892.[73] This close relation to Japan also explains two more peculiarities of *Studio*. The journal had a regular Japanese contributor in Jiro Harada (1878–1963),[74] whose essays began appearing in its pages in 1910. From 1913 onwards, reports from Tōkyō were a regular section of the journal. This shifted the overall use of the terms *Japan* or *Japanese* in *Studio*. While the above-mentioned descriptive use to signify a perceived Japaneseness also occurred, the use of the two keywords decreased significantly during the 1920s. The Japan-related content remained stable, but the information provided by Harada was no longer distinguished by its Japaneseness. He used technical terms without further explanation. As far as *Studio* was concerned, Japanese art had found its autonomous place in (European) art discourse. However, in all of the other art journals it remained ethnically contextualised and thus was not seen as comparable in quality to European art.

2.1.3 Architectural Journals

In other respects, *Studio* is fully representative of art journals: while book reviews on Japanese art appeared in all of them, architectural topics were virtually absent. Interestingly enough, this applies to a number of architectural journals as well. While all of the analysed art journals covered more or less the same topics in relation to Japan, the architectural journals showed significant regional differences.[75] The French journals usually mentioned Japan in connection with the decorative arts due to the dominating role of the *École des Beaux-Arts*'s architectural department. The journals in English had a similar interest in collectibles but went beyond this to report on a broad range of topics such as earthquakes, gardens, or fire prevention. Actual architectural

---

73   Codell, Julie F., "Holme, Charles (1848–1923)," in: *Oxford Dictionary of National Biography* (Oxford University Press, 2004); online edn., May 2008 [http://www.oxforddnb.com/view/article/33950, accessed 14 January 2016] – see also Holme, Charles; Huberman, Toni (eds.), *The diary of Charles Holme's 1889 visit to Japan and North America with Mrs Lasenby Liberty's "Japan: a pictorial record"* (Folkestone, UK, 2008).

74   Rogala, Jozef, *A Collector's Guide to Books on Japan in English: An Annotated List of Over 2500 Titles with Subject Index* (Abingdon, 2004), p. 79. Miyuki Katahira focuses on Harada: see for example Katahira, Miyuki, "Ōbei ni okeru nihon teienzo no keisei to harada jiro no The Gardens of Japan," in: *Nihon kenkyū* 34.3 (2007), pp. 179–208.

75   For an overview of the architectural periodicals that were systematically analysed, see the list in the bibliography.

articles were rare and often limited to book excerpts or summaries of articles published elsewhere. The focus of German-speaking journals was the technology of infrastructure: streets, tunnels, sewers and water mains, and especially railways. The common factor across the languages was a certain interest in earthquake-resistant construction. This topic is the only one that raised debate within the expert groups, as can be seen in the discourse between Josiah Conder (1852–1920) and Christopher Dresser (1834–1904) regarding the construction principles of Japanese pagodas during the late 1880s, to be discussed in detail later on.

Moreover, the architectural information regarding Japan remained limited and arbitrary in topic well into the twentieth century. Japan was scarcely perceived as relevant for European architectural discourses of the time and the terms *Japan* and *Japanese* were used literally up to the late 1920s. By then, some essays in *Das Werk*, the journal of the *Schweizerischer Werkbund*, applied the terms to signify a certain Japaneseness in construction or spatial design. They praised Japanese architecture for its simplicity, concision, and openness or lightness and drew, for example, parallels to Ludwig Mies van der Rohe's design for the German pavilion at the 1929 International Exposition in Barcelona.[76]

2.2   *Contributors and Networks*

The migration of topics from one field to another and the changing interest or disinterest in architectural topics raises the question of knowledge mediators, their background, expertise and exchanges.

Many of the early knowledge mediators regarding Japan had simply fallen into the role. Most of the above-mentioned contributors before 1853, such as Engelbert Kaempfer and Philipp Franz von Siebold, experienced the country in the context of a posting to the Dutch settlement in Nagasaki. An exception was, for example, the Russian Navy officer Wassili Michailowitsch Golownin (1776–1831), who was captured during an exploration of the Kurile Islands and remained in Japan for some time. While severely restricted in their range of movements and social relations due to Japan's isolationist policy starting during the seventeenth century, foreign visitors collected and imparted an extensive if somewhat inconsistent body of knowledge corresponding to their professional and extra-professional needs and interests.

A similar chance alignment of circumstances combining a posting to Japan with restrictions regarding mobility and communication is observable in the

---

76   "Der Pavillon des Deutschen Reiches an der internationalen Ausstellung Barcelona 1929," in: *Das Werk* 16.11 (1929), pp. 350–351.

case of diplomatic and military personnel during the treaty negotiations of the 1850s; mobility and communication were also factors for entrepreneurs, traders, and missionaries who chose to settle in Japan from the 1860s onward. They reported back home, added to the body of travelogues, and recounted cultural interactions within and around the extraterritorial settlements. Some found time to pursue their passions, such as collecting arts and crafts or coins, or studying Japanese history or religion.

When the Japanese government targeted foreign experts from Europe and North America as advisers and teachers in the late 1860s and posted the so-called *o-yatoi gaikokujin* nationwide, the range of long-term foreign residents in Japan broadened and with them the fields of professional and personal interests regarding Japan.[77] Some architectural topics moved from travelogues and ethnographical reports to become distinct threads. Notes, essays, and monographs relating to architectural knowledge in the broadest sense began to appear and increased in number.

The following gives an impression of this and presents all the contributors of essays or books with at least remote architectural topics known by name between 1870 and 1880 in chronological order of their publication. These 13 people are typical of the overall phenomenon of diverse backgrounds and research interests. Their writings set the foundation on which the study of the architecture of Japan was based for decades. A brief look into their personal and professional lives, and their approach to Japanese architecture, aims to provide a general understanding of the contingency of the early studies.

2.2.1   Édouard (Edward) Lévi, named Montefiore

Édouard (Edward) Lévi, named Montefiore (1826–1906/7), belonged to a Jewish family network of businessmen, bankers, artists, and philanthropists expanding between England, Australia, Belgium and France. Although an engineer and amateur etcher, he was employed at the Paris branch of the Belgian finance house Cahen d'Anvers et Compagnie, probably due to his marriage to Emma Cahen in 1855.[78]

---

77   Hazel Jones estimates the number of foreign experts to be about 3,000 with governmental contracts and a similar number in the private sector. Jones, Hazel J., *Live Machines: Hired Foreigners and Meiji Japan* (Tenterden; Kent; Vancouver, 1980), p. xv. For an extended list of such contract experts, see Lepach, Bernd, *Meiji-Portraits*, online resource, http://meiji-portraits.de/ [last accessed 15 May 2024].

78   Draffin, Nicholas, "An Enthusiastic Amateur of the Arts: Eliezer Levi Montefiore In Melbourne 1853–71," in: *Art journal of the National Gallery of Victoria* 28 (1987), online resource, https://www.ngv.vic.gov.au/essay/an-enthusiastic-amateur-of-the-arts-eliezer-levi-montefiore-in-melbourne-1853-71/ [accessed 29 August 2017], s.p.; Hudson, Hugh,

The available biographical information on Montefiore is not sufficient to confirm or deny any residency in Japan. His collection of Japonica, however, was impressive, as a catalogue of 1894 shows.[79] It is probably from this collection too that Montefiore and his brothers, of which he had at least three, lent artefacts to a number of international exhibitions, including the Expositions Universelles in Paris in 1867 and 1878.

As a member of the *Société d'Ethnographie Americaine et Orientale* in Paris, he donated images and artefacts of South East Asian as well as Australian origin to the Société d'Ethnographie and gave two presentations.[80] While the first of these in 1869 referred to a donated boomerang, the second, published as an essay in 1871, addressed *Les temples au Japon* and included one of his own etchings. It shows the *Le temple de Kami-hamayou domine la ville de Simonoseki*, copied from a photograph.[81] The (reversed) photograph was taken by Felice Beato (1832–1909) and titled *Tycoon's temple Simonoseki*. Since Beato took part in the Shimonoseki Campaign of 1864, the image probably dates from the same year.[82]

The information provided in Montefiore's essay is mostly of linguistic character and focuses on the ritual aspects of the three main religions of Shintō, Buddhism, and Confucianism. However, his text states that the most famous and venerated Kami temple in Ise province might also be the humblest, being a small hut built from wood and straw and faithfully kept in its original condition from generation to generation and thus from a purely artistic point of view is inferior compared to other temples in Japan.[83]

"A Jewish Philanthropist in Colonial Australia: Eliezer Levi Montefiore's Papers in the Autograph Collection of the State Library of Victoria," in: *Australian Jewish Historical Society Journal XX*, 3 (2011), pp. 349–394, here 350; Massa-Gille, Geneviève, *Journal d'Hippolyte Fortoul: Ministre de l'instruction publique et des cultes (1811–1856)*, 2, 1er Juillet 1855–4 Juillet 1856 (Genève, 1989), p. 147.

79   Chevallier, Paul; Bing, Samuel, *Objets d'art japonais provenant du cabinet de monsieur E.-L. M*** qui seront vendus a Paris a l'hotel des commissaires-priseurs 9, Rue Drouot, Salle N 7 du Jendi 17 au Samedi 19 et le Lundi 21 Mai 1894 à deux heures précises* [handwritten additional note "Montefiore"]. I am indebted to Dr. Hugh Hudson, University of Melbourne, for his generous support and the reference to this work.

80   *Mémoires de la Société d'ethnographie de Paris. Mémoires et documents originaux Société d'ethnographie de Paris, Section D'ethnographie Descriptive, Séance Du 7 Juin 1869*, pp. 259–260.

81   Montefiore, Edouard Levi, "Les temples au Japon avec une eau-forte," in: Mémoires de l'Athénée oriental fondé en 1864 (1871), pp. 95–100, here p. 99.

82   Yokohama Kaiko Shiryokan (ed.), *Felice Beato shashinshu 1. Bakumatsu Nihon no fūkei to hitobito* (Tōkyō: Akashi Shoten, 2006), p. 121.

83   Montefiore, "temples," pp. 95–96.

Montefiore's discussion of Buddhist monasteries omits architectural details but lists the required buildings, among them the main gate, a belfry, a rotating shelf for sutras, a treasury (of sutras), another hall, the mountain gate symbolising an important threshold on the spiritual path, and the refectory. The number of the buildings and their names points to an ideal description of a Zen monastery as his source of information.[84]

Montefiore's essay references two colleagues from the *Société d'Ethnographie Americaine et Orientale*, namely Charles de Labarthe, author of the *Catalogue des palais des souverains-pontifes japonais*,[85] and Léon de Rosny (1837–1914), who provided expertise in translation. The latter might also have had further involvement, since Montefiore refers to the Wakan Sansai Zue, 和漢三才図会, by Terajima Ryōan, a Japanese encyclopaedia based on an earlier Chinese work, which de Rosny had commented on in an earlier essay.[86] A reference to a Nippon-kō 日本考 in another footnote remains ambiguous. It is to be assumed that Montefiore used more publications than the two mentioned here, since the admittedly much later catalogue of his collection lists a number of Japanese and western publications.[87]

Montefiore plays no role as an informant in later texts about Japanese art or architecture but Philippe Burty referred to his text and etchings in *Notes Sur L'architecture Au Japon. A Propos De L'exposition Universelle De 1878*, published in 1879.[88]

Édouard Lévi Montefiore was a representative of the large group of Japanophile collectors and scholars whose interests benefited from the opening of Japan while contributing to western knowledge of Japan.

---

84 "Un temple complet, suivant les Japonais, doit comprendre: 1 ° la grande porte (daï-mon); 2 ° le clochet (zou-ro); 3 ° le tabernacle (rin-zô); 4 ° la demeure du supérieur (hô-syo); la bibliothèque (kyôsyo); l'escalier du faîte (zan-mon); le réfectoire (ziki-dô)." Montefiore, "temples," p. 98. I am grateful to Dr. Jonas Gerlach, Düsseldorf, for his help in unraveling this.

85 Labarthe, Charles de, "Le Catalogue des palais des souverains-pontifes japonais," in: *Revue orientale et américainee VIII* (1863), suppl., pp. 65–69.

86 May, Ekkehard; Schmitt-Weigand, John; Köhn, Stephan, et al. (eds.), *Edo bunko. Die Edo Bibliothek. Ausführlich annotierte Bibliographie der Blockdruckbücher im Besitz der Japanologie der J. W. Goethe-Universität Frankfurt am Main als kleine Bücherkunde und Einführung in die Verlagskultur der Edo-Zeit* (Wiesbaden, 2003), pp. 285–288; Rosny, Léon de, *Notice ethnographique de l'encyclopédie japonaise Wa-kan-san-saï-dzou-yé* (Paris, 1861).

87 Chevallier, *Objets d'art japonais*.

88 Burty, Philippe, "Notes Sur L'architecture Au Japon. A Propos De L'exposition Universelle De 1878," in: *Revue De L'architecture Et Des Travaux Publics* 35 (1878), cols. 55–63, 103–111, 153–163.

2.2.2 Yamamoto Kakuma

Yamamoto Kakuma (山本覺馬, 1828–1892) was of *samurai* origin and became a scholar of 'Dutch learning', *rangaku*. He was one of the less well-known Japanese scholars who discussed ideas of national reform and advocated western knowledge. Yamamoto converted to Christianity and was instrumental in Niijima Jō's establishment of the Doshisha English School in Kyōto in 1875.[89]

As a member of Kyōto's prefectural administration, Yamamoto initiated the first industrial exhibition in Kyōto in 1872. His *Guide to the celebrated places in Kiyoto and the surrounding places for the foreign visitors* was prepared in 1873 for the second industrial exhibition and had a clear educational aim: "When they come in they perhaps will be anxious to visit the celebrated and splendid places, to bring back with them the seeds of story to their countries. But they will not be able to find out the places all, and thus be obliged to get a guide, and then this book perhaps may prove useful."[90] This was the first publication of its kind in English, conceived by Yamamoto, written by the publisher Niwa Keisuke, and laid out by Yamamoto's sister Niijima Yae (1845–1932) together with one of Niwa Keisuke's younger sisters. Ishida Saijirō designed the illustrative etchings.[91]

The booklet consists mostly of one-page articles with one illustration each introducing 47 different locations, areas, or related topics, and includes two maps of Kyōto itself and its environs. The majority of the locations are temples or shrines, complemented by entries about the Gosho, the former residency of the emperor and venue of the exhibition, the landscape of Maruyama with its gardens, cherry trees and view of the city, the earthenware of Kiyomizu, the silk weaving of Nishijin, and the Mimizuka, a monument of war trophies from the sixteenth century.[92] The mention of the sites at Lake Biwa resonates with the reference to the well-known *Eight Views of Ōmi* 近江八景, depicted by Utagawa Hiroshige (1797–1858) among others.[93]

While the list of sights reads like a best-of of temples and shrines in the city and vicinity, the architectural artefacts are in fact only a reference point for the presentation of historical information and small curiosities. It is very probable that this small guide was fashioned with books such as the *Miyako meisho zue*

---

[89] Nihon Rekishi Gakkai (ed.), *Meiji Ishin Jinmei Jiten* (Tōkyō: Yoshikawa Kōbunkan, 1981), p. 104.

[90] Yamamoto, *Guide*, s.p.

[91] Meyer, Eva-Maria, "The Guide to the Celebrated Places in Kiyoto," blog entry, 02/2014, http://www.meyer-sensei.de/post/77373183755/the-guide-to-the-celebrated-places-in-kiyoto [last accessed 26 April 2024].

[92] Yamamoto, *Guide*, pp. 3, 13, 17, 39, 20.

[93] Yamamoto, *Guide*, p. 44.

都名所図会, 1780, or series of woodblock prints such as Hiroshige's famous *One Hundred Famous Views of Edo* 名所江戸百景, 1856–1859, in mind.[94] However, while 300 copies were issued to guests at the exhibition, its impact was far smaller in comparison and it was never mentioned in contemporary texts.[95]

Yamamoto Kakuma's activities and ideas were exemplary for the many Japanese actors involved in the creation of modern Japan and contributed to the transfer of information to and from Japan, rarely mentioned by their western counterparts.

2.2.3 Richard Henry Brunton

Richard Henry Brunton (1841–1901) was a Scottish civil engineer for David and Thomas Stevenson, Edinburgh. He was hired by the Japanese government as a foreign expert to establish a system of lighthouses along the coast and became involved in other matters of built infrastructure as well.[96] He arrived in Japan in August 1868 and, on his return to Europe in 1876, stated: "On the completion of my service, the Lighthouse Department had established, or had in hand, thirty-seven ocean lights, nine harbour lights, three light vessels, fifteen buoys, and eight beacons."[97] Not all of them were Brunton's, but his contribution was by far the largest.[98]

Brunton was a member of the *Asiatic Society of Japan* at its very beginning in 1872 but was no longer listed as a member in 1876. In 1874 and 1875, however, the *Transactions of the Asiatic Society of Japan* published two essays on *Constructive Art in Japan*, in which he reported his perception and evaluation

---

94 Akisato, Miyako. – For more on this genre see Goree, Fantasies; Fiévé, Nicolas, "Kyoto's Famous Places. Collective Memory and 'Monuments' in Tokugawa Period," in: Fiévé, Nicolas; Waley, Paul (eds.), *Japanese capitals in historical perspective: place, power and memory in Kyoto, Edo and Tokyo* (London, 2003), pp. 153–171.

95 Meyer, "Guide." – There exist at least two versions of the booklet from 1873 as well as 3 editions of a very similar publication decades later: Yoshii, Tsunetaro, *Illustrated guide to Kyoto & its suburbs: with map, an entirely new work* (Osaka, 1890).

96 Kenrick, Douglas Moore, *A century of western studies of Japan: the first hundred years of the Asiatic Society of Japan 1872–1972* (Tōkyō, 1978), p. 79; "List of Members," in: *Transactions of the Asiatic Society of Japan* IV (1875/76) (Reprint 1888), s.p.

97 Beauchamp, Edward R. (ed.); Brunton, Richard Henry (author), *Schoolmaster to an Empire* (New York; Westport, CT; London, 1991), p. 143; Meid, *Einführungsprozeß*, p. 169. – See also his memoir Brunton, Richard Henry, *Building Japan 1868–1876* (Sandgate; Folkestone, 1991); Rohan, Kieran M., "Lighthouses and the Yatoi Experience of R. H. Brunton," in: *Monumenta Nipponica* 20.1–2 (1965), pp. 64–80. Rohan seems to be mistaken with regard to the year of Brunton's arrival in Japan (p. 67).

98 Checkland, Olive, "Richard Henry Brunton and the Japan Lights 1868–1876, a brilliant and abrasive engineer," in: *Transactions of the Newcomen Society* 63.1 (1991), pp. 217–228, here p. 225.

of Japanese architectural tradition and practice.[99] Here he expresses his disappointment with the standards of civilisation in Japan. Dwellings, streets and infrastructure receive a scathing review, while the stately, decorated and substantial religious buildings underwhelm him with their sameness. Brunton recognises the expert carpentry and the neatness of the work on Japanese wooden structures but dismisses their constructive features, which he regards as faulty. He argues for western building practices to prevent earthquake damage. However, the second part of his essay discusses not only the promise but also the pitfalls of western-style building experiments in Japan.[100]

Brunton's essays name neither informants nor textual sources. The first to reference him was Philippe Burty in 1879 in *Notes sur l'architecture au japon*, which will be discussed below. In 1885 Edward Sylvester Morse (1838–1925) mentioned Brunton in his influential book *Japanese Homes and Their Surroundings*.[101] Japanologist Basil Hall Chamberlain (1850–1935) listed him among the texts "more or less concerned with Japanese architecture" which were "scattered through the Asiatic Transactions,"[102] and Edward F. Strange (1862–1929) of the Victoria and Albert Museum referred to him alongside seismologist John Milne (1850–1913) as an expert on earthquake-resistant construction.[103]

Richard Henry Brunton represents the broad range of engineers that entered public discourse during industrialisation and came to claim interpretive authority with their goal-oriented approach to research and their emerging status as experts, both within western societies and as advisors during Japan's modernisation.

2.2.4 Ernest Mason Satow

Ernest Mason Satow (1843–1929) came to Japan as a student interpreter in the consular service and served Rutherford Alcock (1809–1897) and Harry S. Parkes (1828–1885). He was noted for his unusual proficiency in Japanese and quickly rose through the ranks. In 1884 he left Japan to serve in Siam, Uruguay, and Morocco before returning to Japan as minister plenipotentiary in 1895.

---

99   Kenrick, *A century*, p. 79; Brunton, "Constructive Art (1)"; id., "Constructive Art (2)."
100 Brunton, "Constructive Art (1)," pp. 64–65, 73–74, 23. For more detail, see Clancey, *Earthquake*, pp. 43–44.
101 Burty, "Notes," here col. 105; Morse, *Homes*, p. xxix.
102 Chamberlain, Basil H., "Architecture," in: id., *Things Japanese. Being Notes on Various Subjects Connected with Japan* (London, 1890), pp. 22–31, here p. 31.
103 Strange, Edward Fairbrother, "Architecture in Japan," in: *The architectural review for artist and craftsman: a magazine of architecture and decoration* 1 (1896/97), pp. 126–135, here p. 129.

In 1900 Satow transferred to a similar position in China and finally returned to England in 1906.[104]

Satow collected Japanese books and wrote on many aspects of Japanese culture. He became one of the formative personalities in the study of Japan. As a founder of the *Asiatic Society of Japan* (1872, Yokohama) and a member of the *Japan Society, UK* (1891), he was crucial in the transfer of Japanese cultural knowledge to an interested western audience, not least to the inhabitants of the extraterritorial settlements in Japan themselves. This included the dissemination of practical and popular knowledge by way of travel guides to Nikkō, 1875, and to central and northern Japan, 1881.[105]

His essay on *The Shin-tau Temples of Ise*, published in the *Transactions of the Asiatic Society of Japan* in 1874, and the *Guide Book to Nikkō*, 1875, mentioned above, provide readers with information on architectural sights through a combination of (sometimes detailed) phenomenological descriptions and historical background information taken from occasionally-referenced Japanese sources.[106]

Regarding Ise, Satow sketches the form and construction of ancient dwellings and sees the Shintō buildings as derived from these, only with planks for walls instead of woven mats and a raised wooden floor instead of an earthen surface.[107] He expresses his disappointment with the "simplicity and perishable nature"[108] of these buildings and later circles back to the ephemeral character of the shrines, explaining their continued existence as follows: "The perishable nature of the Japanese architecture of course renders it impossible that the original buildings should have lasted [from 478] down to the present

---

104 Brailey, N. J., "Satow, Sir Ernest Mason (1843–1929)," in: *Oxford Dictionary of National Biography* (Oxford University Press, 2004), online edn., Jan. 2008 [http://www.oxforddnb.com/view/article/35955, accessed 12 February 2015] and Kornicki, Peter F., "Ernest Mason Satow (1843–1929)," in: Cortazzi, Hugh; Daniels, Gordon (eds.), *Britain and Japan 1859–1991: themes and personalities* (London, 1991), pp. 76–87 *passim*.

105 Kornicki, "Satow," pp. 80–81; 83–84. See also: "Toyosawa," pp. 131–172; Suleski, Ronald, "Japanese Studies in the East: The Asiatic Society of Japan," in: *Tsūshin* 4.1 (1998), pp. 15–16, here p. 16; more detail is provided by Kenrick, *A century*, pp. 31–62; Satow, *Nikkō*; Satow, Ernest Mason; Hawes, A. G. S., *A handbook for travellers in central & northern Japan, being a guide to Tōkiō, Kiōto, Ōzaka, Hakodate, Nagasaki, and other cities, the most interesting parts of the main island; ascents of the principal mountains; descriptions of temples; and historical notes and legends* (Yokohama, 1881).

106 Satow, "Ise." Satow revised this text in 1882, changing, for example, the transliteration of Japanese names and book titles. This version was reprinted in the 1888 issue of the journal.

107 Satow, "Ise," pp. 119–121.

108 Ibid., p. 121.

day, and in fact it seems to have been the rule from time immemorial to rebuild the temple once every twenty years, alternately on each of two sites which lie close to each other."[109] With regard to Nikkō, and more specifically to the Nikkō Tōshō-gū, he is explicit in his admiration of the beauty of the buildings, colours, and decorations.[110]

While the architectural information remained scarce and never moved beyond description, Satow's texts fostered the knowledge of Japanese architectural sites within the circle of foreign residents and beyond. Aside from his notes from a trip in 1872, his text on Nikkō refers only to "an excellent native guidebook to Nikkō entitled Nikkōzan-shi, in five volumes with illustrations,"[111] while the essay on Ise lists the *Ise Sangu Meisho Zue*, Norinaga Motoori's *Kojiki-den*, or Hirata Atsutane's *Koshi seibun* as sources. His texts made these available to western audiences. The discussion that followed his lecture on Ise is documented in the records of the *Asiatic Society* and shows a focus on and an interest in Shintō in general. The people involved, each of them an active collector of knowledge on Japan in their own right, were Dr. James Curtis Hepburn (1815–1911), Rev. Edward W. Syle (1817–1890), Max von Brandt (1835–1920), Sir Harry S. Parkes (1828–1885), Dr. Samuel R. Brown (1810–1880), and Mori Arinori (1847–1889).[112] This deep involvement with the contemporary discourse explains the extensive acknowledgement that Satow's contributions received from fellow writers in later years and the breadth of their references to topics of his expertise. To name just a few such references relating to architecture: Christopher Dresser mentioned Satow's lecture on Ise with respect to Shintō; Edward Morse cited his translation of the *Kojiki* for its insights on ancient forms of Japanese housing; Basil H. Chamberlain referred to the essay on Ise among others in his discussions of early forms of architecture; Roger Thomas Conder pointed to the *Handbook for travellers* and its account of *The Mausoleum at Nikko*, and Justus Brickmann named Satow as his authority for an assumption, without giving further information about the particular source.[113]

Ernest Mason Satow represents the diplomats who provided information on Japan in the decades immediately after 1854: he was well educated, with

---

109 Ibid., p. 126.
110 Satow, *Nikkō*, pp. 11–12, 14.
111 Ibid., p. 42. Ueda, Mōshin; Watanabe, Kazan, *Nikkōsan shi*, 5 vols. (Edo: Suharaya Ihachi, 1837).
112 Satow, "Ise," pp. 135–139.
113 Dresser, *Japan*, p. 378; Morse, *Japanese Homes*, p. 323; Chamberlain, "Architecture," pp. 26–30; Conder, "Mausoleum"; Brinckmann, Justus, *Kunst und Handwerk in Japan* (Berlin, 1889), p. 78.

a broad range of humanist interests and language competences. He bridged the Japanese traditions of scholarship and culture, and western curiosity and regard concerning East Asia.

2.2.5   Edward William Godwin

Edward William Godwin (1833–1886) was an English architect and a key figure in late nineteenth-century discourses on art and architecture. An early admirer of Japanese art as it came to England via collectors, traders, and later publications in the 1860s, he adopted Japanese aesthetic characteristics into his designs.[114]

Godwin published two articles on *Japanese wood construction* in the *Building News and Engineering Journal* in 1875 and a short text *on Japanese Building* in *The British Architect and Northern Engineer* in 1878.[115]

His main source was an unnamed Japanese book of fifty-six pages, of which about half dealt with wooden construction. Godwin lists the architectural elements – shown here as balustrades, walls, roofs, houses (without roofs), tents, bell towers, lanterns, and gateways – comments on them, and concludes that together with other books on the topic and added photographs, "we may get a fair general idea of the architectural characteristics of Japan."[116] His text describes mostly decorative details and argues for the acceptance of architectural art in wooden construction. He complains about the level of ignorance regarding the values of Japanese architecture among western specialists.[117]

Beyond the 56-page Japanese publication mentioned explicitly, which was most probably the fifth volume of Katsushika Hokusai's *Manga*, 1814–1837, Godwin names Aimé Humbert (1819–1900) as a source, whose travelogue *Le Japon illustré*, was published in French in 1870 and in English in 1874.[118]

---

114   Soros, Susan Weber, "Godwin, Edward William (1833–1886)," in: *Oxford Dictionary of National Biography* (Oxford University Press, 2004) [http://www.oxforddnb.com/view/article/10889, accessed 12 February 2015] and Soros, Susan Weber (ed.), *E. W. Godwin: Aesthetic Movement Architect and Designer* (Yale, 1999), esp. pp. 71–91.

115   Godwin, "Construction"; Godwin, Edward William, "Japanese Building," in: *The British Architect and Northern Engineer* (30.08.1878), p. 85. No author's name was attached to the article, but Juliet Kinchin and Paul Stirton attribute it to Godwin. Kinchin, Juliet; Stirton, Paul, *Is Mr. Ruskin living too long?* (Oxford, 2005).

116   Godwin, "Construction," p. 173.

117   Godwin, "Building," p. 85.

118   Aslin, Elisabeth, *E. W. Godwin. Furniture and Interior decoration* (London, 1986), p. 24; Wilkinson, Nancy B., "E. W. Godwin and Japonisme," in: Soros, Susan Weber; Arbuthnott, Catherine, *E. W. Godwin: Aesthetic Movement Architect and Designer* (Yale, 1999), pp. 71–91, here pp. 79, 85. The essay uses illustrations from Werner Blaser's *Japanese temples and Tea-Houses* (Basle, 1956), to illustrate the Japaneseness of Godwin's designs on pages

The extensive scholarship on Godwin's artistic and architectural work points to additional background information for his evaluation of Japanese architecture. He used the Japanese collection of the British Library and had access to the Japanese Pavilion from the World's Fair in Vienna in 1873, the building having been translocated to Alexandra Park, London, in 1874 on the initiative of Christopher Dresser, another Japan aficionado who will be discussed in detail below.[119]

While Godwin's writings on Japanese architecture were referenced only once, in an essay on *Japanese houses* in *American Architect and Building News* in 1876, his use of Japan-inspired design solutions for furniture and interiors had a significant impact in the field.[120]

Edward William Godwin was one of the mediators of Japonisme by adopting, discussing and transferring aspects of Japanese art into his designs. As such, some of his artistic work represented an immediate transfer of architectural insights from one cultural realm to another.

2.2.6 Rutherford Alcock

Rutherford Alcock (1809–1897) was a trained physician and British diplomat in East Asia. He served as "her Majesty's Minister" in Japan from 1858 to 1865. In part due to his professional position, and in part out of personal interest, he collected and studied Japanese arts and crafts and provided samples for the Great International Exhibition in London of 1862. During a break in his tenure and again after his retirement, he returned to England and published on diverse topics, mostly on diplomatic issues and Japanese art.[121] He was a

---

88–89. This is unfortunate, firstly of all because the images suggest a body of visual sources that did not yet exist for Godwin, and secondly because the reference to Katsura Rikyū suggests a knowledge of places and sights which was only explored by westerners decades later. Finally, Blaser's popular books are only moderately reliable as far as studies on Japanese architecture go. – Godwin, "Construction," p. 201; Humbert, Aimé, *Le Japon illustré* (Paris, 1870); Humbert, Aimé, *Japan and the Japanese illustrated* (London, 1874).

119 Soros, Susan Weber, "The Furniture of E. W. Godwin," in: id.; Arbuthnott, Catherine, *E. W. Godwin: Aesthetic Movement Architect and Designer* (Yale, 1999), pp. 225–261, here p. 259, FN 40; Wilkinson, Nancy B., *Edward William Godwin and Japonisme in England* (unpublished dissertation, Los Angeles: University of California, 1987), p. 147; Wilkinson, Nancy B., "E. W. Godwin and Japonisme," in: Soros, Susan Weber; Arbuthnott, Catherine, *E. W. Godwin: Aesthetic Movement Architect and Designer* (Yale, 1999), pp. 71–91, here p. 74; "Alexandra Palace," in: *British architect* 1 (15 May 1874), p. 315.

120 "Japanese Houses," in: *American Architect and Building News* 1 (1876), pp. 26–27, here 27.

121 Alcock, *Art*, pp. 1–2; id., *Catalogue of works of industry and art, sent from Japan. International Exhibition, 1862* (London, 1862); id., *The capital of the tycoon. A narrative of a three years' residence in Japan*, 2 vols. (London, 1863).

long-time and honorary member of the *Asiatic Society of Japan* and joined the *Japan Society* as well.

As far as Japanese architecture was concerned, Alcock started with a series of essays on Japanese Art in *The Art Journal* in 1875, which was revised and reissued as *Art and Art Industries in Japan* in 1878.[122] His statement on architecture encompasses a single paragraph in which he states that the Japanese created barely anything noteworthy. He describes low wooden structures and sees their characteristics as arising from the seismic instability of the area and the poverty of the Japanese. Alcock reasons that expressions of Japanese art are only to be expected in other media.[123]

In the revised version of 1878, Alcock references a number of sources. Among them are, first of all, peers who worked on similar issues relating to Japanese art, such as James Jackson Jarves, John Leighton, George Ashdown Audsley and James Lord Bowes;[124] also cited, however, are art theoreticians such as William Hogarth, John Ruskin and John Addington Symonds,[125] and (established) authorities on Japanese history and culture such as Kaempfer, Siebold and Hübner.[126] In return, Alcock was referenced by art specialists such as Marcus B. Huish and William Anderson, as well as architectural journals such as *The Builder*.[127]

Rutherford Alcock was another diplomat who used the opportunities of his profession to bring information on Japan to Europe. Other than Satow, his sources were not of philological character but art objects themselves and his interpretation of their cultural role and meaning.

2.2.7   James Jackson Jarves

James Jackson Jarves (1818–1888) was an American art historian and collector. After years of travel in the Americas and to Hawaii, he arrived in Europe in 1851

---

122 Alcock, Rutherford, "Japanese Art," in: *Art Journal* (1875), pp. 101–105, 201–206, 333–334; (1876), pp. 41–44, 113–116; (1877), pp. 41–44, 97–99, 161–163; (1878), pp. 1–3, 137–140; Alcock, *Art*.
123 Alcock, "Japanese art" (1875), p. 101.
124 Jarves, *Glimpse*; Audsley; Bowes, *Keramic*.
125 Hogarth, William, *The Analysis of Beauty* (London, 1753); Ruskin, John, *Laws of Fésole* (Sunnyside; Orpington; Kent, 1877); Symonds, John Addington, *Miscellanies* (London, 1871).
126 Hübner, Alexander Graf von, *Ein Spaziergang um die Welt* (Paris, 1872) (French: *Promenade autour du Monde*, 1877).
127 Huish, Marcus B., *Japan and its Art* (London, 1889), p. 1; Anderson, William, *The pictorial arts of Japan. With a brief historical sketch of the associated arts, and some remarks upon the pictorial art of the Chinese and Koreans* (London, 1886), 1, p. vii; "Japanese architecture (extract from Alcock's essay in *The Art Journal*)," in: *The Builder* 33 (17 April 1875), p. 357.

and settled in Florence. Jarves wrote extensively on European art and culture for an American audience and dealt in art. In 1876, he published *A Glimpse at the Art of Japan*. In the three paragraphs dedicated to architecture, he concludes that architecture, as a fine art, did not exist in Japan, both due to the danger of earthquakes and due to a cultural disinterest, or even a peculiarly Japanese inability to express "human excellence."[128] Jarves's sources remain obscure: he references only Hippolyte Taine's (1828–1893) *The philosophy of art*. His own book was acknowledged by Rutherford Alcock and William Anderson.[129]

James Jackson Jarves represents the propagators within the processes of knowledge production. An armchair scholar as far as Japanese art was concerned, his thoughts remained limited to art circles alone but helped to fuel and distribute existing assessments.

2.2.8 Jules Lescasse

Jules Lescasse (1842–1901) was a French civil engineer and architect on contract to the Japanese government. He moved from China to Japan in 1871 and became involved in infrastructural and architectural projects, such as the works at the Ikuno mine in Hyogo Prefecture, the design of a reception hall for Tsugumichi Saigo's House in Tōkyō, and the construction of the German legation and the German naval hospital in Yokohama. Lescasse returned to France in 1876/1877 and again between 1886 and 1890, but left Japan for good in 1892 when his project for the French consulate in Yokohama failed to proceed.[130]

Lescasse wrote in a very focused way exclusively on reinforcement against earthquakes. In 1877 he published an article on *Earthquakes and Buildings* in

---

128 Jarves, *Glimpse*, pp. 21–22; "Jarves, James Jackson," in: *Dictionary of Art Historians. A Biographical Dictionary of Historic Scholars, Museum Professionals and Academic Historians of Art*, Online resource, https://arthistorians.info/jarvesj/ [last accessed 29 April 2024].

129 Jarves, *Glimpse*, p. 41; Taine, Hippolyte, *The philosophy of art* (New York, 1873); Alcock, *Art*, p. 8; Anderson, *Arts*, 1, p. vii.

130 Lepach, Bernd, "Lescasse, Jules," in: *Meiji-Portraits*, online resource, http://www.meiji-portraits.de/meiji_portraits_l.html [last accessed 26. April 2024]; Nishibori, Akira, "Meiji jidai no kōzan kankei furansuhito ni tsuite (1)," in: *Yokohama keiei kenkyū/Yokohama business review* 12.3 (1991), pp. 61–72; Lagarde-Fouquet, Annie, "Contribution d'ingénieurs et architectes français à la construction de Yokohama (Japon) entre 1860 et 1900," in: Bertoncello, Brigitte, *"Les Acteurs de la composition urbaine (édition électronique)", 137e Congrès national des sociétés historiques et scientifiques, Tours, 2012* (Paris: Éditions du CTHS, 2014), pp. 56–69, here pp. 60, 62–63. "Reception Hall of Marquis Tsugumichi Saigo House," *Meiji-mura architectural museum*, online resource, http://www.meijimura.com/enjoy/sight/building/1-8.html [accessed 3 November 2016].

the *Japan Gazette* and contributed an *Étude sur les Constructions Japonaises, &c* to the *Memoires de la Societé des Ingénieurs Civils*.[131]

In *Étude sur les Constructions Japonaises, &c.* he sketches the constructive features of Japanese houses and examines the Japanese arguments for the form of foundations, the heaviness of roofs and the design of joints. In the end, Lescasse acknowledges the ability of the low buildings to sway in the event of a minor tremor. However, he sees serious weaknesses when it comes to stronger horizontal shocks. He suggests employing a wide-meshed wooden framework with masonry infill reinforced by an iron armature. In his final paragraphs he discusses ways in which to protect these walls from weathering.[132]

Lescasse's ideas received no attention in architectural journals but were recognised by the seismologist John Milne, who included Lescasse's suggestions in his paper *On Construction in Earthquake Countries*, 1885, and in his later publications.[133] The German architects Böckman & Ende adapted the ideas for their Ministry of Justice building in Tōkyō, while the Japanese architect Tsumaki Yorinaka (1859–1916) used it for brick storehouses in Yokohama.[134]

Jules Lescasse was one of the many hired experts whose writings – if there were any at all – never went any further than a specialist's consideration of a specific topic. The focus was on direct communication to achieve applicable problem solving, not on discussing Japan.

2.2.9   Josiah Conder

Josiah Conder (1852–1920) was an English architect. After his training and work with T. Roger Smith (1830–1903) and William Burges (1927–1831), Conder moved to Japan in 1876/77 and took over the Chair of (Western) Architecture at the Imperial College of Engineering in Tōkyō, an institution with a polytechnic curricular structure.[135] At the same time, he designed the *Rokumeikan*

---

131   Clancey, *Earthquake*, p. 252: Lescasse, M. J., "Earthquakes and Buildings" (serialised in four parts), *Japan Gazette* (2 March to 15 March 1877); Lescasse, M. J., "Étude sur les Constructions Japonaises, &c.," in: *Memoires de la Societé des Ingénieurs Civils* (6 April 1877), pp. 211–218 (meeting and discussion), pp. 451–458 (text). A supposedly abstract but in fact updated and much more technical version of his study was 1889 published in *the Transactions of the Seismological Society of Japan* as "Description of a System Intended to Give a Great Security to Buildings in Masonry Against Earthquakes."
132   Lescasse, "Étude."
133   Milne, John, "On Construction in Earthquake Countries," in: *Minutes of the Proceedings of the Institution of Civil Engineers* 83, session 1885–86, part I, paper 2108, pp. 278–295; id., *Earthquakes and other Earth Movements* (New York, 1886); id., *Seismology* (London, 1898).
134   Lagarde-Fouquet, "Contribution," p. 60.
135   In Japanese, the department was called zōka 造家, house building. Meid, *Einführungsprozeß*, p. 194; Finn, Dallas, *Meiji revisited. The Sites of Victorian Japan* (New York, 1995),

guesthouse, opened in 1883, commissioned by the Foreign Ministry of Japan to host foreign visitors. His contract with the government expired in 1882 and his pupil Kingo Tatsuno (1854–1919) took over, while Conder remained an advisor for a few more years.[136] After a trip back to England in 1886/1887, he gave his private practice in Japan an institutional framework and established his own architectural office. Conder remained in Japan until the end of his life.[137]

While Josiah Conder was a member of both the *Asiatic Society of Japan* and the *Japan Society, London*, he published only non-architectural essays in these groups' respective *Transactions*.[138] His essays regarding Japanese architecture were published exclusively in architectural or engineering journals, above all in the *Transactions of the Royal Institute of British Architects* (RIBA), except for some texts on earthquake resistance, which appeared in *The Japan Weekly Mail*.[139]

Conder's texts on architectural topics up to 1880 include *Notes on Japanese Architecture*, 1878, and *Theatres in Japan*, 1879. A *Lecture upon Architecture* to Japanese architectural students was published as a booklet in 1878.[140]

---

p. 106; Crook, J. Mordaunt, "Josiah Conder in England. Education, training and background," in: Conder, Josiah; Kawanabe, Kusumi; Suzuki, Hiroyuki, *Rokumeikan no kenchikuka josaia kondoru ten* (Tōkyō: Higashinihon tetsudō bunkazai dan, 1997), pp. 22–24, here pp. 22–23. – On engineering education in Japan and the establishment of the Imperial College of Engineering, see Duke, Benjamin C., *The History of Modern Japanese Education: Constructing the National School System, 1872–1890* (New Brunswick, NJ, 2009), esp. pp. 172–181 and Wada, Masanori, *Engineering Education and the Spirit of Samurai at the Imperial College of Engineering in Tokyo, 1871–1886* (Master thesis, Blacksburg, VA: Virginia Polytechnic Institute and State University, 2007).

136   Finn, *Meiji*, pp. 106, 167; Fujimori, Terunobu, "Josiah Conder and Japan," in: Conder, Josiah; Suzuki, Hiroyuki; Fujimori, Terunobu; Hara Tokuzo (eds.), *Josiah Conder: A Victorian Architect in Japan, Catalogue/Rokumeikan no kenchikuka josaia kondoru ten*, revised edition ([Tōkyō:] Kenchiku Gahōsha, 2009), pp. 13–17, here p. 13.

137   Meid, *Einführungsprozeß*, p. 203; Finn, Dallas, "Josiah Conder (1852–1920) and Meiji Architecture," in: Cortazzi, Hugh; Daniels, Gordon (eds.), *Britain and Japan 1859–1991: themes and personalities; published on the occasion of the centenary of the Japan Society 1891–1991* (London, 1991), pp. 86–106, here p. 89. – For more about his life see e.g. Tseng, Alice Y., "Styling Japan: The Case of Josiah Conder and the Museum at Ueno, Tokyo," in: *Journal of the Society of Architectural Historians* 63.4 (December 2004), pp. 472–497.

138   Between 1879 and 1889, Conder published articles in the Transactions of the Asiatic Society of Japan on the history of Japanese costume, on landscape gardening in Japan, and on Japanese flower arranging. Kenrick, *A century*, p. 405.

139   For more on this topic, see Clancey, *Earthquake*, p. 117.

140   Conder, "Notes," pp. 179–192, 209–212. The same text, sometimes referred to by the title On some ancient examples of Japanese architecture, was published at the same time in *The British Architect and Northern Engineer* (8 March 1878), pp. 110–114 and in Van Nostrand's *Eclectic Engineering magazine* 18 (1878), pp. 509–519. Abstracts were published in *The*

Conder provides a preliminary survey of building types in the Japanese architectural tradition in his *Notes*, addressing dwellings of different social classes, military fortifications, and religious buildings. He briefly describes significant features, materials, and design solutions and refers to social practices. The essay on theatres follows the same pattern but is far more detailed. His third text from these early years, the *Lecture upon Architecture*, is an interesting counterexample. Its audience, as in the case for the journal articles, is architectural practitioners, but it is aimed not at British colleagues and students, but at Japanese. Conder addresses this by negotiating the normative western experience of architecture and the Japanese quotidian experience within a frame of cultural identity. He perceives wooden construction as being within the tradition of Japanese culture and appreciates the manual expertise involved, but he would like to see its qualities transferred into the reliability of solid (western) constructions, which he perceives as natural and inevitable.

Conder included almost no references to any sources in his architectural texts except for his own essays and – in a later paper – the work of Thomas R. H. McClatchie (1852–1886).[141] While he later became involved in an intense discussion regarding earthquake-resistant construction that spread across the popular media in Japan and the specialist media in Britain, Conder's architectural expertise on Japan was mostly ignored in his primary field; even the influential Edward Morse never mentioned him in his extensive list of references.[142] He was, however, acknowledged by Charles Pfoundes in connection with theatres and by the art historian Louis Gonse (1846–1921) in *L'Art Japonais*, 1883.[143] Japanologist Basil H. Chamberlain offers a blanket recommendation of Conder's publications in the RIBA journals in his handbook *Things Japanese*, 1890.[144] The jurist and world traveller Fernand Levieux (1870–1896) based his *Essai sur l'architecture japonaise*, 1895, on one of Conder's

---

Building news and engineering journal 34, 1878 (8 March 1878), pp. 236–237; (15 March 1878), pp. 262–263 and *The Builder* 36 (9 March 1878), pp. 238–239; (16 March 1878), pp. 263–266; (13 March 1878), pp. 386–387; id., "Theatres in Japan," in: *The Builder* (5 March 1879), pp. 368–376; Conder, Josiah, "A few remarks on architecture/What is architecture? (Lecture upon Architecture. Addressed to the architectural students. Kobudaigakko, Tokei, Japan)," 1878, archival material, Royal Institute of British Architects (RIBA, 72(042) // CON).

141   Conder, *Domestic*, pp. 111–112.
142   His brother, Roger Thomas Conder (†1906), an architect himself, acted as a spokesperson in some cases and likewise published on Japanese topics. He emigrated to Argentina about 1888; Morse, *Homes*.
143   [Pfoundes, Charles,] "Something more about Japanese theatres," in: *The Builder* 37 (24 May 1879), p. 583; Gonse, *L'Art*, p. 99.
144   Chamberlain, "Architecture," p. 31.

later texts – as Irène Vogel Chevroulet points out – but does not refer to him.[145] Conder's papers and monographs within the field of Japanese cultural studies, dealing with flower arranging and gardens, gained much more attention and recognition than did his architectural treatises. However, Banister Fletcher's classic *A history of architecture* came to include Conder in his list of references since 1901, thus firmly canonising Conder's expertise for generations of English-speaking architects to come.

Josiah Conder was one of the very few western architects working in Japan who published on Japan within his specialist field, addressing both aesthetic and practical issues and thus bridging the two architectural spheres of design and engineering. His case, albeit very specific in its failure to gain attention among his fellow architects at this time, shows the growing differentiation between fields of expertise and interest within western academia, the importance of memberships and the role of contemporary published media in the transfer of information.

2.2.10   Thomas Russell Hillier McClatchie

Thomas Russell Hillier McClatchie (1852–1886) was the son of a missionary with the Church Missionary Society. He grew up in England in a hiatus between two of his father's assignments to China and as a young man entered the Consular Service. McClatchie passed his language examination with honours, was sent to Japan in 1870, and worked for his maternal uncle, Harry Smith Parkes (1828–1885). He rose through the ranks of consular personnel to the position of Acting Vice Consul in Yokohama in 1883.[146]

He was an early member of the *Asiatic Society of Japan* and studied various topics relating to Japanese culture. His papers cover Japanese weaponry, heraldry, anthropology, literature, and architecture. At the same time, he was also

---

145 Levieux, Fernand, "Essai sur l'architecture japonaise," in: *Extrait du Bulletin de la Société Royale Belge de Géographie* 19.3 (1895), pp. 229–250; Lacroix, A., "Fernand Levieux," in: l'Institut Royal Colonial Belge (ed.), *Biographie Coloniale Belge*, vol. IV (1955), cols. 520–521. Vogel Chevroulet, Irène, "The Architecture of Japan: Discovery, Assimilation and Creation – Josiah Conder opens the Way," in: Müller, Simone; Itō, Tōru; Rehm, Robin (eds.), *Wort-Bild Assimilationen Japan und die Moderne* (Berlin, 2016), pp. 68–93, esp. p. 90.
146 Abel, Laszlo, "Thomas Russell Hillier McClatchie (1852–1886)," http://www.aikidojournal.com/article?articleID=710 [downloaded 17 July 2013]; Lane-Poole, Stanley; Dickins, Frederick Victor; Parkes, Harry Smith Sir K. C. B., *The Life of Sir Harry Parkes, sometime Her Majesty's Minister to China & Japan*, vol. 2 (London, 1894), pp. 266–267.

a passionate sportsman and studied Japanese martial arts. McClatchie fell sick in 1882 and died on the journey back to England in 1886.[147]

His two papers on architectural topics focus on *The Castle of Yedo*, 1877, and *The Feudal Mansion of Yedo*, 1879, both of which were published in the *Transactions of the Asiatic Society of Japan*.[148] The first essay perceives the partially decaying castle as a formative element of the urban scheme of the city of Edo (by then Tōkyō) and thus as a site of historical and contemporary interest. It reconstructs the history of the castle and describes its features and functions, including its reflection of social strata, its modes of representation, its spatial design beyond fortification, its spaces of worship, and even its ornamentation. The second essay handles the disused residences of the warrior-class families surrounding the castle in a similar manner. The actual built artefacts, which are perceived as ordinary and monotonous, become embedded in a rich history of social order and elaborate state administration.

McClatchie repeatedly references Engelbert Kämpfer's *History of Japan*, 1727, and also mentions William E. Griffis' *The Mikado's Empire*, 1876.[149] Beyond these, he lists an extensive body of Japanese sources. Likely the best known among these is the *Edo meisho zue* 江戸名所図会, the *Pictorial guide to the celebrated localities of Edo*, issued by Saitō Yukinari (1804–1878) in 1834–1836, with illustrations by Hasegawa Settan (1778–1843). Most others addressed codes of conducts, schedules and functions of *bushi* as well as the building schemes of castles.[150] McClatchie's essays were acknowledged by Edward S. Morse in his *Japanese Homes*, 1885, and by Josiah Conder in *Domestic architecture in Japan*, 1886/1887.[151]

Thomas McClatchie was one more diplomat with a broad scope of interests and the language skills necessary to build his studies on Japanese sources. Connecting his data to the works of others with associated interests contributed to the intertwined study of Japanese culture by western residents.

---

147   Abel, McClatchie, "Obituary to Thomas R. H. McClatchie," in: *Japan Weekly Mail* 5.9 (27 February 1886), p. 195; Kenrick, *A century*.
148   McClatchie, *Castle*; McClatchie, Thomas R. H., "The Feudal Mansion of Yedo," in: *Transactions of the Asiatic Society of Japan VII*, 3 (1879), pp. 157–186.
149   Kaempfer, *History*; Griffis, William Elliot, *The Mikado's Empire* (New York, 1876).
150   McClatchie lists Ochiboshiu 落穂集, 1727 or 1728, by military strategist Daidōji Yūzan 大道寺友山 (1639–1730); Ōno Hiroki's 大野広城 (1788–1841) Tonoi-bukuro 殿居嚢, 1837–1839, and his anthology Aobyōshi 青標紙, 1840; Nihon Gu'aishi 日本外史, 1836–1837, by Rai San'yo 賴山陽; Shuzugōketsuki 主図合結記 by Yamagata Daini 山縣大貳; four more volumes, which he transcribes as Kindai geppiō, Kōtei-ki, Wa-ji-shi, and Sansei-roku without further detail.
151   Morse, *Homes*, p. xxix; Conder, *Domestic*, pp. 111–112.

2.2.11 George Cawley

George Cawley (1848–1927), an English civil and mechanical engineer, was hired by the Japanese Ministry of Public Works as an instructor in practical engineering at the Imperial College of Engineering, Tōkyō, in 1873.[152] He left Japan in 1878 but served as a consulting engineer to the Imperial Japanese Railways for two decades in total and remained connected to Japanese topics, as both his membership of the *Japan Society* and his Japan-related publications indicate.[153]

In 1878, Cawley presented a paper giving *Some remarks on Construction in Brick and Wood, and their relative suitability for Japan* to the *Asiatic Society of Japan*. Starting with a reference to the already settled matter of construction in brick and wood in Europe and America, Cawley allows for new considerations due to the differing physical conditions in Japan.[154] He organises his argument along the core principles he has observed in contemporary planning in the "highly-civilized communities"[155] of the world, namely strength, stability, durability, comfort, convenience, hygiene, and beauty. His engineer's view finds almost nothing to recommend, least of all in regard to the principles of wooden construction; this he sees as less developed in Japan than in other regions of the world due to what he describes as the wasteful and unscientific use of materials. Cawley acknowledges the admiration excited by some of the temples but qualifies this gravely by observing a serious lack of durability and proportion. In terms of comfort and convenience, Cawley draws a distinction between the cultural character of the Japanese and of westerners in terms of sensibilities and practices, and concludes that the Japanese will come to appreciate western-style brick dwellings as soon as they have the chance to experience proper specimens of these. To summarise, Cawley expresses his

---

152 Lepach, Bernd, "Cawley, George [Cauley]," in: *Meiji-Portraits*, online resource, http://www.meiji-portraits.de/meiji_portraits_c.html [accessed 29 August 2016]; Dyer, Henry, *Dai Nippon: a study in national evolution* (London, 1904), p. 4; Cawley, George, *Vehicle to be used in electric traction on railways*. Patent US 708462 A, 1902.

153 Lepach, Cawley, "Obituary for George Cawley," in: *Proceedings of the Institution of Mechanical Engineers* 1 (1927), p. 579; *List of Members of the Japan Society, UK, 1894–1920*, courtesy of Alice Caffyn, JS, 2016.

154 Cawley, George, "Some remarks on Construction in Brick and Wood, and their relative suitability for Japan," in: *Transactions of the Asiatic Society of Japan* VI (1878), pp. 291–317, here pp. 292–293. – His second paper related to matters of Japanese building was published much later. Cawley, George, "Wood, and its Application to Japanese Artistic and industrial design," in: *Transactions and proceedings of the Japan Society, London* 2 (1895), pp. 194–232.

155 Cawley, "Remarks," p. 293.

decidedly technical perspective and entirely condemns the building practices observed, while leaving room for favourable comments on Japan in terms of other supposedly national characteristics.

Cawley references a paper on earthquake-related matters by William Edward Ayrton (1847–1908) and John Perry (1850–1920), which is either the essay *On a Neglected Principle that may be Employed in Earthquake Measurement*, 1877, in the *Transactions of the Asiatic Society of Japan,* or the pamphlet *On structures in earthquake countries,* 1878.[156] His text was later referenced by Edward S. Morse in *Japanese Homes*, 1885, and by Basil H. Chamberlain in *Things Japanese*.[157]

George Cawley was another engineering expert applying established specialist knowledge from Europe to the Japanese context. By discussing his observations in the cross-disciplinary network of the *Asiatic Society of Japan*, he enabled the diffusion of the content beyond his own field.

2.2.12   Philippe Burty

Philippe Burty (1830–1890) was a French art critic, art collector, and graphic artist whose literary work is closely related to *Japonisme* – a term he is said to have coined – and to Impressionism.[158] Being a non-resident member of the *Asiatic Society of Japan*, he published broadly across the art journals of the time on matters of Japanese fine art.[159] Except for some sentences on the Japanese pavilion in his article *Exposition universelle de 1878: Le Japon ancien et le Japon moderne*, 1878, in which he described the experience of perceiving

---

156   Cawley, "Remarks," p. 298; Clancey, *Earthquake*, p. 67.
157   Morse, *Homes*, p. xxix; Chamberlain, "Architecture," p. 31.
158   Weisberg, Gabriel P., "Burty, Philippe," in: *Allgemeines Künstlerlexikon – Internationale Künstlerdatenbank – Online*, originale Fundstelle Beyer, Andreas; Savoy, Bénédicte; Tegethoff, Wolf (eds.), *Allgemeines Künstlerlexikon (AKL). Die Bildenden Künstler aller Zeiten und Völker* 15, p. 289; D'Amat, Roman, "Burty (Philippe)," in: Balteau, Jules (ed.), *Dictionnaire de biographie française,* vol. 7, *Bournonville – Cayrol* (Paris: Librairie Letouzey et Ané, 1956), p. 707.
159   Weisberg, Gabriel P., "Burty, Philippe," in: *Allgemeines Künstlerlexikon – Internationale Künstlerdatenbank – Online*, originale Fundstelle Beyer, Andreas; Savoy, Bénédicte; Tegethoff, Wolf (eds.), *Allgemeines Künstlerlexikon (AKL). Die Bildenden Künstler aller Zeiten und Völker* 15, p. 289; D'Amat, "Burty," p. 707. – To name only a few examples of his essays: Burty, Philippe, "Le mobilier modern," in: *Gazette des beaux-arts: la doyenne des revues d'art* 24 (1868), pp. 26–45; id., "Japonisme," in: *L'art: revue hebdomadaire illustrée* 2.2 (1876), pp. 49–58 (les femmes de qualité), pp. 277–282 (yébis et daï-kokou), 3, pp. 150–155 (yébis et daï-kokou) as well as *Japonisme: conférences de M. Burty* 3.2 (1877), p. 116; id., "Exposition universelle de 1878: Le Japon ancien et le Japon moderne," in: *L'art: revue hebdomadaire illustrée* 4.4 (1878), pp. 241–264.

something primitive and refined at the same time, Burty did not write at any length on Japanese architecture.[160]

The single exception to this is the paper *Notes Sur L'architecture Au Japon. A Propos De L'exposition Universelle De 1878*, 1879, which he wrote at the request of César Daly for the *Revue de l'architecture et des travaux publics*. Here Burty gives a summary of the contemporary research literature – which he perceives as narrow for those who do not read Japanese – and the sources available to him, namely illustrated volumes such as "géographies illustrées," the *meisho zue*, Hokusai's *Manga* and photographs.[161] Starting from this basis, he sketches the early history of Japanese architecture, lists building materials such as stone, wood and bamboo, and describes the main features of various building typologies, including castles and (fortified) residences, temples, shrines and graveyards. Burthy argues against aestheticians who propagate the notion that there is no architecture in Japan due to the somewhat pragmatic use of established principles and practices in the Japanese building tradition, and yet he expresses doubts about whether Japan can be said to have any genuine architects.[162] He suggests expanding the understanding of "architecture" to include – once again – the relation between building and landscape, as was done with respect to Greek temples. In doing so, he concludes, it would be possible to do justice to Japanese architecture and to the Japanese sensitivity to the natural landscape.[163]

Burty references many sources beyond the visual, including the travelogues and regional studies of Heinrich Julius Klaproth, Isaac Titsingh, Pierre François-Xavier de Charlevoix (with a reference to Kaempfer), Alexander Graf von Hübner, Georges Bousquet and Théodore Duret.[164] When discussing details he refers to Frederick Victor Dickins, to Henry Brunton's article *Constructive Art in Japan*, to Griffis' *The Mikado's Empire*, to Lieutenant Colonel Goff's *A walk through Japan*, and to Edouard Levi Montefiore's *Les temples au Japon avec une eau-forte*, or rather to another of his illustrations completed after a photograph, this time of Tokugawa Ieyasu's tomb in Nikkō as published in *Far East*, 1874.[165] Additional sources included the catalogue of the *Exposition*

---

160   Burty, "Exposition," p. 243.
161   Burty, "Notes," here cols. 56–57.
162   Ibid., cols. 56–57, 110–111.
163   Ibid., cols. 162–163.
164   For the corresponding publications see the bibliography.
165   Goff, Lieutenant Colonel, *A walk through Japan, 1877* (London, 1878); Montefiore, "temples"; *The Far East. A monthly illustrated journey* 6.3 (September 1874).

Universelle in Paris in 1878 and the Paris collection of Henri Cernuschi.[166] Burty mentions a book "Bou Ki. Dessins de machines militaires," supposedly published in 1846, which remains obscure. While painstakingly compiled, the essay was referenced only once, by William Anderson in *The pictorial arts of Japan*, 1886.[167]

Philippe Burty, with his extended networks of information dissemination, played a crucial role in fostering Japonisme in terms of both the appropriation and the study of Japanese art and culture in Europe. Without experiencing Japan himself, he built his arguments on the texts, images and objects arriving from secondary reports, World's Fairs, and art trade and mediated them further.

2.2.13 Charles James William Pfoundes

Charles James William Pfoundes (1840–1907) was born in Ireland. In 1854 he left his family for Australia, where he joined the navy and rose to the rank of Captain. Upon arriving in Japan in 1863, he began to study the language, customs and arts. Over time, he became a mediator between the western and Japanese cultural realms and was the first to advocate for Buddhism in Europe. Pfoundes travelled repeatedly between the continents: in 1870/71 he accompanied a Japanese delegation to Europe and North America, in 1876 he sailed to Philadelphia to help prepare the *Centennial International Exhibition*, and in 1877/78 he journeyed through Europe.[168] He married and settled in London for a while, where "in his private capacity [he] gained admission to a wide range of London's learned societies and made a considerable name for himself as a prolific speaker on mainly Japanese and Oriental topics."[169] In 1893, Pfoundes moved to Japan for good and became involved in the mission of Buddhism to Europe as a means to "temper the arrogance of the West."[170]

---

166 Commission impériale japonaise à l'Exposition universelle de Paris, 1878 (ed.), *Le Japon à l'Exposition universelle de 1878*, 2 vols. (Paris, 1878).
167 Anderson, *Pictorial arts*.
168 Bocking, Brian; Cox, Laurence; Yoshinaga Shin'ichi, "The First Buddhist Mission to the West: Charles Pfoundes and the London Buddhist mission of 1889–1892," in: *Diskus. The Journal of the British Association for the Study of Religions* 16.3 (2014), pp. 1–33, here pp. 5–6.
169 Bocking, "Buddhist Mission," p. 6.
170 Turner, Alicia; Cox, Laurence; Bocking, Brian, "A Buddhist Crossroads: Pioneer European Buddhists and Globalizing Asian Networks 1860–1960," in: *Contemporary Buddhism* 14.1 (May 2013), pp. 1–14, here p. 4, and Bocking, Brian, "Flagging up Buddhism: Charles Pfoundes (Omoie Tetzunostzuke) among the International Congresses and Expositions, 1893–1905," in: *Contemporary Buddhism* 14.1 (2013), pp. 17–37.

Pfoundes wrote on the most diverse topics and across the full range of media, from newspapers to journals and monographs. He published three texts on Japanese architecture in *The Builder* of 1879: a comment on Josiah Conder's essay on Japanese theatres, thoughts on *The artisan of Japan and his work*, and the essay *Constructive art in Japan*.[171]

In *The artisan of Japan*, Pfoundes introduces the Dai-ku, the (master) carpenter who embodies the architect, builder and joiner in one person, as the beacon of expert craftsmanship, before going on to sketch the building process from design outline to foundation setting, wood processing, measurements and tools. After some notes on plastering and on fireproof structures, he talks about the translocation of whole buildings, the interior fittings of dwellings, and the professional background of the building trade. Pfoundes states that the Japanese workmen undergo systematic training and have numerous and inexpensive handbooks available to them.[172] In *Constructive art in Japan*, he surveys the development of Japanese shrines and their sites in relation to the primaeval hut and later describes the characteristics of Buddhist buildings. While he sees no influence of the early western missionaries on religious or domestic architecture, he identifies similarities between European and Japanese castles. Pfoundes adds thoughts about the changes that private and public life have undergone since westerners once again became active in Japan and ends with some comments on the construction of traditional fireproof buildings and some building details.[173] He does not actually evaluate the observed phenomena, but seems to approve the utilisation of western building patterns as long as they are able to ensure the privacy of the inhabitants and the fire resistance of the buildings.

Pfoundes references only his own publications, except for a nod to civil engineer Colin Alexander McVean (1838–1912) and architect Thomas James Waters (1842–1898), who were among the first to call for the use of western building methods in Japan.[174] Pfoundes' texts on Japanese art and architecture in general excited comment as part of ongoing discussions on art issues within journals, but were not referenced beyond this.

---

171 The attribution of Pfoundes' authorship for some of the articles rests on bibliographies and cross-referencing. [Pfoundes, Charles,] "Something more about Japanese theatres," in: *The Builder* 37 (24 May 1879), p. 583; [Pfoundes, Charles,] "The artisan of Japan and his work," in: *The Builder* 37 (17 May 1879), p. 540; Pfoundes, Charles, "Constructive art in Japan," in: *The Builder* 37 (1879), pp. 1306–1307, 1395.
172 Pfoundes, "Artisan," p. 540.
173 Pfoundes, "Constructive," p. 1395.
174 Ibid. For biographical data on both men, see Lepach, Bernd, *Meiji Portraits*, online resource, http://www.meiji-portraits.de/index.html [accessed 4 November 2016].

Charles Pfoundes was an information broker and mediator who moved beyond the dominant roles of diplomats, hired experts or armchair scholars. While his activities were instrumental in enabling cross-cultural communication between Japanese and western institutions, his contributions on architecture remained largely unacknowledged.

2.2.14   Preliminary Observations: Actors and Backgrounds

This list of contributors provides but a glimpse due to its focus on architectural issues alone, the deliberate disregard of travelogues, and the exclusion of some influential figures who either joined or published just a few years later. However, the short sketches of biographies and opinions offer a reliable picture of the sources and paths of knowledge generation at the time. Moreover, discussing the similarities and differences within this group addresses some issues characteristic of the knowledge mediators at this time.

All members of the group are male and identify as educated individuals. They communicated information they regarded as relevant to their peers and the broader public by presenting papers and submitting essays to periodicals. Thus, their communication was not by chance but intentional, targeting both male and female sections of society. It is known from later sources that these publications influenced female readers; however, as authors, women remained the exception in the context of architectural Japan.[175]

Beyond this, the authors vary in terms of origin, profession, religious self-identification, and their reasons for engaging with Japan and its architecture. Yet, there are patterns. Caucasian Europeans of a middle-class background are predominantly represented, whereas Japanese contributors and non-Christian beliefs are the exception. The distribution among the European nations is indicative of the broader situation, with English being the common language, but French and German participants are also present, albeit in smaller numbers.

The authors were either diplomats or technical experts creating/submitting information or mediators of the incoming data. While the former all resided in Japan for some time, none of the later did except for Yamamoto Kakuma. The four technical experts Brunton, Cawley, Lescasse and Conder all shared building expertise, as did Godwin, one of the mediators.

The mostly coincidental dispatch to or interest in Japan on the part of the individual writers created a fairly holistic pool of approaches and information

---

175   There are some travel reports authored by women, in terms of the architectural discourse, however, they are entirely absent at this time. – For a reference to sources, see Scidmore, Eliza Ruhamah, *Jinrikisha days in Japan* (New York, 1891), "introduction."

on architectural issues. The approaches, which we would today describe as linguistic, ethnological, art-historical or artistic, technical, scientific and so on, framed the field in a manner reminiscent of the Humboldtian ideal of comprehensive general education. The western look at the world mixed a search for universal truths and knowledge order with honest curiosity, self-esteem and a sense of mission. While (or since) the Japanese view shared many of these characteristics and the modernisation process included a similar study of West, the knowledge production was not a cooperative process across the linguistic and cultural realms but was strongly shaped by the respective perceptions of relevance.

This is evident in this context through the low incorporation of Japanese authors and the topics addressed by the diplomatic authors and the technical experts. The former, the learned men with more humanistic leanings, covered anything and everything Japanese and went beyond the often limited perspectives of the more specialised experts among the foreign government advisors – namely the *o-yatoi gaikokujin* from engineering – who aimed to fulfil their task of providing up-to-date and supposedly superior scientific knowledge to Japan.

Against this background, the emerging body of new architectural knowledge mixed original research with superficial knowledge: some deep wells of learning were surrounded by shallower areas due to the small total number of informants and the even smaller number of specialists. The same random pattern is evident in the evaluation of the contributions, by both peers and the general audience.

As the brief biographical profiles suggest, social networks and in-field mechanisms of knowledge dissemination played a key role in the acceptance of new information and the establishment of knowledge. Learned societies were pivotal, connecting actors and facilitating the exchange of information. While several societies with diverse focuses existed at the time, the *Asiatic Society of Japan* stands out as the most important for our discussion. The *German East Asiatic Society (Deutsche Gesellschaft für Natur- und Völkerkunde Ostasiens, OAG)*[176] originated at the same time but did not feature papers about Japanese buildings before the twentieth century, and the *Japan Society* was not chartered until 1891.

It makes sense to look at the structure and activities of the *Asiatic Society of Japan* to highlight the conceptual overlap between individual contributors and their communication networks.

---

176   Spang, Christian W.; Wippich, Rolf-Harald; Saaler, Sven, *Die OAG. Die Geschichte der Deutschen Gesellschaft für Natur- und Völkerkunde Ostasiens 1873–1979* (München, 2024).

2.2.14 The Asiatic Society of Japan

The Asiatic Society of Japan was established in 1872 in Yokohama, serving as a platform for the collection and study of Japan-related topics in the English language. It targeted a general audience, fostering exchange between learned men, rather than aiming for scholarly excellence in a specific field. As such, it was neither a professional body such as the *Royal Institute of British Architects* nor, strictly speaking, a scientific society. The society primarily catered to foreign residents of Euro-American background living in Japan, providing a space to meet, discuss and share information from similar associations.[177]

From the outset, the society's focus was clear. During the first annual meeting, the AJS elaborated on the delay in "our entering into relations with other Societies of similar character; and obtaining their publications in return for our own"[178] and attributing it to a fire that disrupted the publication of the inaugural volume of the *Transactions of the Asiatic Society of Japan*. The report emphasised the upcoming exchange of documents with the *German Asiatic Society* and the Royal Asiatic and Geographical Societies of London as well as plans to establish both a library and a museum.[179] The 1888 catalogue of the library's holdings provides ample testimony to the fruition of these initiatives, featuring approx. 260 books and 130 journals and periodicals covering an eclectic array of scientific topics. The dominant language was English, supplemented by French, German and Spanish. In addition, the catalogue listed around 30 books in Japanese, primarily translations addressing issues of contemporary interest, accompanied by a few manuscripts.[180]

Membership was predominantly composed of native English actors. This aligned with the society's language orientation, the role of British actors in the formation of the exterritorial settlements, the influx of foreign experts aiding Japan's modernisation, and the network structure evident in the library holdings. The member lists from the initial decades read like a Who's Who of Japan-related expertise at this time. As a result, the society's papers blended cultural subjects of interest to diplomats with the field-specific issues of engineering, semiology, geology or medicine.[181]

---

[177] See extensively Kenrick, *A century*; Farrington, Anthony, "The Asiatic Society of Japan – Its Formative Years," in: *Historical English Studies in Japan* 9 (1976), pp. 81–91.

[178] "Asiatic Society of Japan. Report," in: *Transactions of the Asiatic Society of Japan* 1 (1874), Reprint 1882, pp. v–ix, here p. v.

[179] Ibid., p. vi.

[180] Asiatic Society of Japan, *Catalogue of the books and manuscripts in the library of the Asiatic society of Japan* (Tōkyō, 1888); Farrington, "Asiatic Society," p. 84.

[181] "Asiatic Society of Japan. Report (1874); Asiatic Society of Japan. List of members," in: *Transactions of the Asiatic Society of Japan* 8 (1880), pp. xxii–xxv.

Both the catalogue and the membership directory reflect the pattern already observed: the creation, discussion and spread of knowledge occurred within a framework constrained by cultural background, language, race or gender. Japanese contributors were notably sparse, women effectively non-existent. The initial language barrier might explain the former, even though many modern Japanese elites received an English education. One might have assumed that there would have been an effort to integrate as many Japanese scholars as possible into these academic pursuits, but participation was mostly limited to a small group holding positions in government or in education.[182] Similarly, while women were generally admitted and members' families took part in the society's activities, active participation through discussions or lectures by women was rare until the turn of the century.[183]

To summarise, throughout the late nineteenth century, the *Asiatic Society of Japan* facilitated the exploration and dissemination of knowledge related to Japan. It did so by leveraging a vast network of social and institutional connections, albeit within a defined socio-cultural structure. The dominance of diplomats and contracted experts, combined with the limited involvement of Japanese actors and the near-complete exclusion of women from any formal roles, shaped the interpretive standard of the data collection along hegemonial patterns.

While other western-focused societies addressed these linguistic and cultural imbalances, Japanese institutions and societies formulated their viewpoints and gradually adopted English as an additional medium. Nonetheless, I contend that the institutions of knowledge collection, such as the *Asiatic Society of Japan*, played a significant role in shaping scholarly interests and specialisations for many years to follow.

The next chapter transitions from this broader perspective to delve into the processes of evaluation, dissemination, or elimination of information and knowledge, concentrating solely on the architectural aspects related to Japan among western actors.

---

182   Kenrick, *A century*, pp. 84–90, 131–134. See in addition the membership lists in *Transactions* and Farrington, "Asiatic Society," p. 87.
183   Kenrick, *A century*, pp. 107, 158–159.

CHAPTER 3

The Invisible Dwelling House

Topics and Non-topics in Architectural Discourses on Japan (1853–1900)

As discussed above, information gathering and knowledge production regarding Japan in general and Japanese architecture in particular started on a very small scale but widened considerably after 1868. However, the many topics addressed in the approximately 80 notes, essays and monographs that came to feature architecture-related issues in a closer sense in the period ending around 1900 invite overestimation of the actual range and depth of the information provided.[1] This effect is even stronger within the approximately 140 additional texts from the same journals that cover Japanese issues in the wider sense, from World's Fairs and industrial exhibitions to the arts and art education, and further to culture and sightseeing in Japan in general.

This chapter provides an overview of the topics of interest within the publications and discourses on Japanese architecture and built heritage up to the turn of the twentieth century by understanding knowledge production as a negotiation of interest and relevance. It sorts the sources according to their approach to the diverse conceptual understandings of 'architecture' within the wider realm of building and society and analyses the evaluation of incoming data across the fields of emerging modern academia as well as their overspill into popular knowledge. The aim is to give an overview of the topics of interest and to provide a frame within which at least one of the 'non-topics' becomes perceivable: namely, the conspicuous lack of substantial architectural, constructional or functional information on Japanese architectural forms in general, and on Japanese dwellings in particular.

This apparent lack of interest in dwellings is somewhat surprising since whenever and wherever they reached Japan, western travellers had to cope with the local built environment, most closely with the buildings in which they stayed or resided. Hence travelogues and cultural and regional studies mentioned features of dwellings at least *en passant*, just as they mentioned shrines and temples, landscapes, customs and food. However, while there were dedicated guide books for temples and shrines, everyday encounters with dwellings did not lead to closer examination, with the exception Morse's *Japanese*

---

1 For the research background of the bibliography, see the part on media in chapter 2.

Homes.[2] Why was this? One might assume that it was due to the descriptions in older sources such as Kaempfer or Siebold which already existed and which might have been thought comprehensive enough to satisfy curiosity. I argue, however, that the absence of focused study had more to do with perception and contextualisation: the Japanese dwelling was perceived as irrelevant for most contemporary discourses in the West. On close examination, this seems to apply even to religious buildings, which attracted attention as objects of curiosity but were rarely treated as architectonic entities.

In terms of historical analysis, architecture is a moving target. Across the centuries, the conceptual understanding of the term and the field of expertise involved changed, as did the competencies and responsibilities of the actors within the general realm of building. In the course of the subsequent institutionalisation of architectural education in the emerging nation states of the nineteenth century, regional preferences in the division of tasks became apparent, as did overlaps and rivalries with neighbouring disciplines.[3] Incoming information on Japanese architecture was therefore discussed and evaluated against a background of negotiations on competencies, self-descriptions, educational frameworks and economic possibilities.

We will look at the various topics and discourses involved, from the narrowest reading of architecture as an art form, to architecture as a field of engineering and a field of 'social' planning, and on to its most general reading as a cultural expression.[4] In each case, we will look at the approach to the relevant issues with respect to knowledge collection from Japan, the adoption and application of ideas from Japan in the nations of the West, the patterns of evaluation and the overarching systems of conceptions of the world to which the lines of argumentation made reference. We will see that pleasure in and admiration of certain arts does not necessarily coincide with a positive evaluation, but that both processes of assessment instead exist in separate spheres. A similar distinction needs to be made between the pragmatic use of a certain practice of building and its discursive evaluation.

However, before we analyse the perception and evaluation of Japanese dwellings, we need to lay a foundation by summing up basic information. The

---

2 Morse, *Homes*.
3 The overall history of this development is still a work in progress to which many scholars are contributing. An overview is provided by Nerdinger, Winfried (ed.), *Der Architekt – Geschichte und Gegenwart eines Berufsstandes*, 2 vols. (München; London; New York, 2013).
4 See also Löffler, Beate, "Petrified worldviews. Eurocentric legacy in architectural knowledge bases on Japan," in: *InterDisciplines* 8.2 (2017), pp. 69–95; id., "The Perpetual Other. The Japanese architecture in western imagination," in: *International Journal for History, Culture and Modernity* 3.3 (2015), pp. 83–112.

following excursus includes a historical description and some images, both of which convey a general idea of the building type in question before the Meiji reforms muddied the water by implementing western building practices and encouraging hybrid solutions. The aim here is to provide an understanding of what one could have actually known about these buildings at the time of the discussions if one did not live in Japan.

EXCURSUS: THE JAPANESE DWELLING

It is hardly surprising that all travelogues and regional studies mentioned features of dwellings at least *en passant*. While they often reported astonishing observations and experiences, they rarely gave a description that would allow the reader to form a complete picture of the actual buildings in the mind's eye. This observation also applied to essays by specialists such as the architect Josiah Conder or engineer Richard H. Brunton, even though they frequently addressed colleagues, and at times the general public, who had no experience of Japan.

Carl Peter Thunberg's *Travels in Europe, Africa, and Asia, made between the years 1770 and 1779*, in its English version from 1795, contained a structured summary of the general and specific architectural characteristics of the Japanese house.[5] He described the overall structure of the house as a system of wooden beams and uprights that provided an outer shell of infilled and plastered timber-frame walls, unified by a colour scheme encompassing the whole outer surface. He mentioned the elevation of the building above the ground as well as the roof coverings, depending on status. Thunberg focused on the contrast between the compact outer enclosure of the overall building and the modular use of interior partitions:

> There are no partition-walls in their houses, which are merely supported by posts or upright beams, between which again at the cieling [sic] and floor other beams run across, with grooves in them, for partitioning off the apartments. Thus, the whole house at first forms only one room, which, however, may be partitioned off with frames

---

5 Thunberg's travelogue was published in Swedish (1788–1793), German (1792), English (1893) and French (1796). Richard Hildreth reproduced some of it in *Japan. As it was and is* (Boston, 1855).

that slide in the grooves made in these cross-beams, and may be put up, taken away, or slid behind each other at pleasure.[6]

Thunberg continued with some more fundamental details on the living quarters, occasionally distinguishing certain features by social class, such as the size of the house or the effort spent on their aesthetic appearance. He described the system of sliding doors and blinds used to negotiate between the interior and exterior spheres[7] and introduced the handling of interior surfaces without underlining the practice of sitting on the floor that most of the travelogues discussed at length:

> The *floors* are always covered with mats made of a fine species of grass (Juncus) interwoven with rice-straw, from three to four inches thick, and of the same size throughout the whole country, viz. two yards long, and one broad, with a narrow blue or black border. It was only at Jedo, in the imperial palace,[8] that I saw mats larger than these. (...) The insides of the houses, both cieling [sic] and walls, are covered with a handsome thick paper, ornamented with various flowers; these hangings are either green, yellow, or white, and sometimes embellished with silver and gold.[9]

The functional parts of the houses were summed up more briefly and in a slightly fragmented way, bringing together different spheres of household practices, on the one hand, and building parts on the other. This includes, for examples, the separation of the street-side business part of a trader's house and the yard-side orientation of the living quarters, or the elements of the privy and the disposition of the bath or garden.[10]

Thunberg gave no information about the construction of the house or its relation to neighbouring houses or the urban environment and made no overt comparisons to known European models to guide the readers' imagination apart from the observation that the whitewashed outer walls

---

6   Thunberg, Carl Peter, *Travels in Europe, Africa, and Asia, made between the years 1770 and 1779*, vol. 3 (London, 1795), pp. 277–278.
7   Thunberg, *Travels*, 3, pp. 278–279.
8   Thunberg is mistaken here: Edo was the capital of the shōgunal government of the Tokugawa dynasty. The imperial court resided in Kyōto.
9   Thunberg, *Travels*, 3, pp. 279–280, italics by Thunberg.
10   Thunberg, *Travels*, 3, pp. 280–281.

"make a tolerably good appearance."[11] Since Thunberg's books appeared without illustrations of the buildings, his audience was left to deduce the character of the Japanese house from their own experience with their local built environment.

Other publications on Japan (as well as objects from art collections such as Japanese woodblock prints), however, occasionally provided visual information on dwellings. For the purpose of this general introduction, we look to Philipp Franz von Siebold's *Nippon*, 1832–1852, which included the most comprehensive set of images in this regard.[12] Here we find some external views of town- and farmhouses as well as views of a manor, supplemented by floor plans and a sectional drawing (Figs. 3.1–3.4).[13]

Single interior scenes were more frequent, often portraying Japanese or foreigners during household chores or entertaining. They generally convey little about the construction or function of the space. It therefore makes sense to turn to the illustrations from Japanese sources that Isaac Titsingh (1754–1812), long-serving head merchant of the VOC in Nagasaki, provided in *Illustrations of Japan*, 1822,[14] on the one hand and on (coloured) woodblock prints, on the other.

Titsingh provided an axonometric view of interior spaces in use during several stages of an upper-class wedding ceremony (Figs. 3.5 and 3.6). Here, the use of sliding walls to separate the overall interior space, as described by Thunberg, is clearly visible.

---

11   Thunberg, *Travels*, 3, pp. 277–278.
12   Siebold, Philipp Franz von, *Nippon. Archiv zur Beschreibung von Japan und dessen Neben- und Schutzländern Jezo mit den südlichen Kurilen, Sachalin, Korea und den Liukiu-Inseln*, 7 vols. (text), 5 vols. (plates) (Leiden, 1832–1852). The volumes were published as author's editions with inconsistently numbered illustrations; this complicates referencing, since many batches bear identical names.
13   Siebold, *Nippon*, Tafelband II, Tab. XI–XV and Tab. VIII–X.
14   Titsingh, Isaac, *Illustrations of Japan; consisting of Private Memoirs and Anecdotes of the reigning dynasty of The Djogouns, or Sovereigns of Japan; a description of the Feasts and Ceremonies observed throughout the year at their Court; and of the Ceremonies customary at Marriages and Funerals: to which are subjoined, observations on the legal suicide of the Japanese, remarks on their poetry, an explanation of their mode of reckoning time, particulars respecting the Dosia powder, the preface of a work by Confoutzee on filial piety, &c. &c. by M. Titsingh formerly Chief Agent to the Dutch East India Company at Nangasaki. Translated from the French, by Frederic Shoberl with coloured plates, faithfully copied from Japanese original designs* (London, 1822).

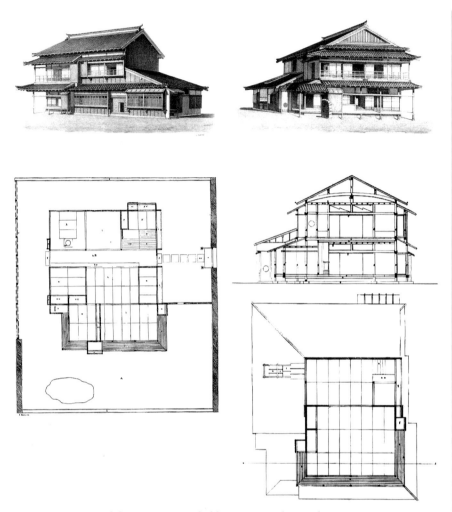

FIGURES 3.1–3.4   Philipp Franz von Siebold: Depictions of manor houses

Japanese woodblock prints often focused on people, seasons and landscapes. Thus, dwellings and interiors with actual architectural information remained comparatively rare. Utagawa Hiroshige's (1797–1858) print *Shimosuwa* from *Sixty-nine Stations of the Kisokaidō* (Fig. 3.7) shows travellers resting in an inn, observed from the garden side of the building. While a traveller in the background takes a bath, a group in the centre has a meal. The woodblock print shows many of the characteristic features of a Japanese dwelling: a raised floor, wraparound veranda, awning and

THE INVISIBLE DWELLING HOUSE 75

FIGURES 3.5–3.6   Isaac Titsingh: Two interiors with preparation for a wedding ceremony

main roof, sliding doors and the use of the floor for seating.[15] The series *The Fifty-three Stations of the Tōkaidō Road* by the same artist includes some more scenes of interest. One of the many versions of *Ishibe* is very similar in composition to that mentioned above,[16] with one of the scenes of Akasaka showing a street with businesses (Fig. 3.8). The building in the centre has two levels and its ground floor room is open to the street – both strong indicators for an inn or similar facility, even in the absence of

---

15   It remains a mystery, why the bathing man in the back is wearing clothing in the tub.
16   Utagawa Hiroshige (Andō, Hiroshige), "Ishibe, from the series *The Fifty-three Stations of the Tōkaidō Road*" [between 1840 and 1848] (Library of congress, https://lccn.loc.gov/2008660896 [last accessed 26 April 2024]).

FIGURE 3.7 Utagawa Hiroshige: Shimosuwa (Sixty-nine Stations of the Kisokaidō), about 1835–1838

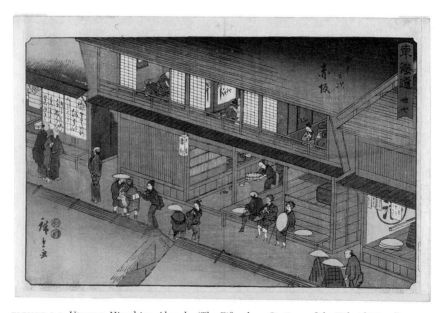

FIGURE 3.8 Utagawa Hiroshige: Akasaka (The Fifty-three Stations of the Tōkaidō Road), 1847–1852

guests sitting out front and peopling the upper storey. Again, some main features of the building's structure can be discerned: the use of wood, the wooden hall and raised guest rooms, and the moveable wall partitions, to name only a few. However, none of the available illustrations from this time showed the 'business end' of the houses, with the kitchens, workshops or stables. Also, as textual and visual sources remained separate, they did not contribute to each other. Consequently, some discussants might have known about the appearance merely from the prints, others from textual descriptions alone.

With this basic information established, we can now turn to the western experts and aficionados and observe and analyse how they perceived Japan's built environment. We will start with the narrowest reading of architecture, that of architecture as an art form, and develop towards the most general understanding, that of architecture as an expression of essential human 'dwelling on earth' and culture.

We will see how different authors addressed specific characteristics of Japanese architecture within a broader or narrower sense and made decisions on the applicability of western norms in an inclusive or exclusive way.

1 Architecture as an Art Form

The impact of Japanese art on European fine and applied arts, usually subsumed under the heading *Japonisme*, is well-published in art historical literature in general and in connection with many artists and schools, among them *Impressionism*, the *Arts and Crafts Movement*, *Jugendstil* and *Art Deco*. The Japanese artefacts coming into Europe, mostly fans, ceramics, lacquerware, scrolls, etc., had an immense influence on the reform of the applied arts, which had been criticised as stuck in meaningless repetition and copying in the mid-nineteenth century, not least due to the rise of mass-produced ornaments and bric-a-brac. The exhilaration that greeted the many pieces exhibited from 1862 onwards and their designs, often seen as balancing between perfection and quirkiness, is omnipresent in the art journals of the time.[17] In 1872, an anonymous author in *The Art Journal* summarised the situation:

---

17   For an introduction to the resonance of the International Exhibition in London in 1862, see e.g. Checkland, Olive, *Japan and Britain after 1859: Creating Cultural Bridges* (New York; London, 2003), pp. 20–21, 90, 112–114.

> The attention of people in this country has of late been increasingly turned to the Art of Japan. Various circumstances have tended to produce this effect. Commerce has sprung up between our shores and that once inaccessible group of islands, which forms a sort of Oriental Great Britain. International exhibitions have displayed objects of Japanese workmanship such as were rarely to be seen in Europe – perhaps nowhere out of Holland – twenty years ago. (…) Thus not only do we find shops and warehouses crowded with Japanese ware – some rich and costly, some wonderfully cheap, and all possessing a certain degree of excellence – but our manufacturers, especially our potters, are turning their attention to the reproduction of some of the most quaint and splendid of these Oriental designs.[18]

In many of the texts on art, however, fascination is mingled with confusion. The European reading of art was deeply shaped by a canonical order of genres, topics, techniques and practices of appreciation which had developed over time and become factually institutionalised since the eighteenth century.[19] Arts in the modern understanding of the word were not created equally – so to speak – and the Japanese impulses did not fit neatly into European patterns of interpretation. While these impulses presented no problem at all as sources of inspiration for creative processes, they caused art critics to stutter as soon as analytical description and/or evaluation of the artefacts was called for.[20]

---

18 C., F. R., "Japanese art," in: *Art Journal* (1872), pp. 293–295, here 293.
19 Shiner, Larry, *The invention of art. A cultural history* (Chicago, 2001). David Clowney sums this up: "In brief, the thesis is this: There was a traditional 'system of the arts' in the West before the eighteenth century. (Other traditional cultures still have a similar system.) In that system, an artist or artisan was a skilled maker or practitioner, a work of art was the useful product of skilled work, and the appreciation of the arts was integrally connected with their role in the rest of life. 'Art,' in other words, meant approximately the same thing as the Greek word *techne*, or in English 'skill,' a sense that has survived in phrases like 'the art of war,' 'the art of love,' and 'the art of medicine.' The usefulness of an art and its products was not limited to the merely utilitarian or decorative (e.g., cooking, clothing, shelter, personal adornment, or warfare), but also included religious worship, cultural instruction and celebration, memorializing rulers, marking rites of passage, entertainment, and many other functions that linked it with intellectual and cultural life." Clowney, David, "A Third System of the Arts? An Exploration of Some Ideas from Larry Shiner's The Invention of Art: A Cultural History," in: *Contemporary Aesthetics* 6 (2008), http://hdl.handle.net/2027/spo.7523862.0006.004 [last accessed 26 April 2024], s.p.
20 For a detailed analysis on the impact of ethnographic material on the use of the ornament in architecture at this time, see Payne, Alina, *From Ornament to Object. Genealogies of Architectural Modernism* (New Haven; London, 2012).

1.1 Fine Arts and Architecture

Against this background, western acknowledgement of Japanese art was not at all unconditional. James Jackson Jarves (1818–1888), Rutherford Alcock (1809–1897) and Louis Gonse (1846–1921), who were among the first to provide comprehensive overviews of Japanese art in the 1870s and 1880s, managed to express their intense appreciation and yet to put Japanese art in its place. They did so primarily by referring to the normative systems of European art, in which applied arts such as ceramics, fans, or lacquerware were subordinate to the high arts of painting, sculpture and architecture, and secondly by linking Japanese art to ethnic character.[21]

Alcock, an avid collector of Japanese art himself,[22] made clear the distinction between high and low art in his book *Art and Art Industries in Japan*, 1878, in just two sentences:[23]

> Of high Art, such as has been cultivated in Europe since the dark ages, the Japanese know nothing. But the range of true artistic work in its application to industrial purposes in Japan is very wide, and more varied than anywhere in Europe.[24]

James Jackson Jarves took the same position and presented his evaluation in *A Glimpse at the Art of Japan*, 1876, transferring Alcock's stance in the realms of art theory:

> Indeed, painting, sculpture, and architecture, in their supreme significance, – the fine arts, with human soul and form as their fundamental motives, and human excellence or spiritual loveliness as their

---

21   Concerning this issue from a broader perspective, see Cheng, Irene, "Structural Racialism in Modern Architectural Theory," in: Cheng, Irene; Davis, Charles L. II; Wilson, Mabel O. (eds.), *Race and modern architecture. A critical history from the enlightenment to the present* (Pittsburgh, 2020), pp. 134–152.

22   In the catalogue of the more than 600 items that Alcock sent to London for the International Exhibition in 1862, nearly all would have been categorised as applied art or folk art or even everyday items. Alcock, *Catalogue*; id., *Art*, p. 221. A member of the Takeuchi Embassy to Europe, Tokuzo Fuchibe, commented on the displayed items "that they had been like old bric-a-brac and that all the Japanese exhibits had been very shabby." "National Diet Library. Japan: Second London International Exposition of 1862. First international exposition seen by Japanese," web presentation, http://www.ndl.go.jp/exposition/e/s1/1862-1.html [accessed 26 April 2018].

23   Alcock actually elaborates briefly on the distinction between fine und applied art. Alcock, *Art*, p. 124.

24   Alcock, *Art*, p. 15.

distinctive aims in expression, – are not found in the aesthetic constitution of the Japanese.[25]

He argued further that since Japanese art did not perceive man as the prime subject of artistic expression, as the Greek tradition did, it was thus to be judged as essentially different from European standards:

> Far narrower in range, unscientific in our meaning, less profound in motives, unambitious in its aims, less fettered by technical rule or transitory fashions, it is more subtile [sic], intense, varied, free, and truthfully artistic in decorative expression; more abounding in unexpectedness and delicious surprises, in aesthetic coquetries and charms of aesthetic speech intelligible to every degree of culture.[26]

These statements are comparatively explicit in drawing a clear line between 'artistic enjoyment' and 'true fine art'. At the same time, the argumentation demonstrates a search for terminology and a category of distinction, the attempt to describe the experience of Japanese art. Many other texts use gentler descriptions and explanations but express the same conviction about the superiority of western fine art.

The authors are equally explicit in their rejection of Japanese architecture. Alcock had stated in *The Art Journal* in April 1875:

> In architecture, the Japanese, like their neighbours the Chinese, have produced scarcely anything – not even as much as the Chinese, for they may claim the pagoda as essentially of their own creation and still peculiar to their country.[27]

The second part of Alcock's sentence is the key to comprehending the reference system informing his overall evaluation. It connects the concept of architecture with originality of design, with the act of (artistic) creation. This links the understanding of architecture with the fine arts along the lines of the leading institution in the field at the time, the École des Beaux-Arts in Paris.

The state-centred French education system had come to divide the field of architecture into four task areas, each with its own training and institution. While the École des Ponts et Chaussées trained military personnel for civil

---

25   Jarves, *Glimpse*, p. 22.
26   Ibid.
27   Alcock, "Japanese Art" (1875), pp. 101–105, here p. 101.

engineering, bridge and fortress construction, the École d'Arts et Métiers qualified architects and engineers for the private sector and the École Polytechnique for government service and all types of public buildings. In result, the education at the École des Beaux-Arts focused on artistic design alone, formed the architect as a pure artist, equal to the painter and sculptor and freed from the toils of the building site. Education at this institution and others of a similar type all over Europe was aimed first and foremost at training artists able to artfully depict and create within a known vocabulary of appropriate form.[28]

Alcock's evaluation denies Japanese architecture an intrinsic spark of creative design and thus the recognition of artistic value in line with the ideals of European fine art.

Jarves added some detail on the philosophical background of Japanese design in 1876:

> Architecture, in its noblest condition, is equally unknown in Japan. There is shown no elaborate attempt to develop it, either in intellectual or spiritual shapes. Instead they erect temporary homes or shrines, tent-like in principle, bizarre in construction, mostly of wood or frailer material, and in nowise responding to that fine instinct of immortality which materializes itself in our finest religious edifices, or even those aspirations which find vent in our ambitious palaces and public buildings.[29]

This resonates with the pragmatic approach of Josiah Conder (1852–1920), when he addressed his students in 1878:

> Upon one thing I insist, and that is, that a building must be substantial, and that in its very essence and nature it is to be a secure protection from the elements, and from all probable destructive forces. Without a certain

---

28 For contemporary positions on the aims of design education, see White, William H., "A Brief Review of the Education and Position of Architects in France Since the Year 1671," in: *Transactions of the Royal Institute of British Architects of London* 5 (1883–84), pp. 93–120 + plates; Spiers, R. Phene, "The French Diplôme d'Architecture and the German System of Architectural Education," in: *Transactions of the Royal Institute of British Architects of London* 5 (1883–84), pp. 121–132. Compared to Conder, Josiah, "Architecture," in: *Imperial College of Engineering (Kobu-dai-gakku), Tokei. Class reports by the professors for the period 1873–77* ([Tōkyō,] 1877), pp. 63–65. See also Pfammatter, Ulrich, *Die Erfindung des modernen Architekten. Ursprung und Entwicklung seiner wissenschaftlich-industriellen Ausbildung* (Basel; Boston; Berlin, 1997) and Lemaistre, Alexis, *L'école des beaux-arts: dessinée et racontée par un élève* (Paris, 1889).

29 Jarves, *Glimpse*, p. 21.

necessary amount of substantial material we can produce only sheds and bungalows which cannot be dignified by the name of Architecture. (...) It seems to me that there is little use of changes in building in your country, if the chief aim is not solidity and strength.[30]

The words of both authors point towards the ruling architectural canon of the time, which attributed notions of architectural art only to representative stone buildings and was bound within a clear European hierarchy of artistic value. At the head of this hierarchy stood the temples of ancient Greece, the archetype being the Acropolis in Athens; these were followed by Renaissance churches such as St. Peter's Basilica in Rome, then the cathedrals of the French Gothic period, and finally the later academic styles. Against this background and the Vitruvian ideals of *firmitas* (solidity), *utilitas* (usefulness), and *venustas* (beauty) in architectural theory, vernacular buildings did not qualify as architecture, nor did wooden or, for that matter, cast-iron constructions, no matter how technically or aesthetically elaborate or monumental.

Edward F. Strange (1862–1929), curator at the Victoria and Albert Museum in London, expressed this bluntly. He pointed out that almost all of the important landmarks in the architectural development of the West were of stone or brick, "wood being – naturally, as we should say – merely an accessory of comparatively trivial importance."[31] The Anglican missionary Isaac Dooman (1857–1931) drew a similar conclusion and made a categorical distinction in 1897, when he underlined the prerogative of interpretation attributed to European tradition: "Greece will stand forever as the consummator and representative of all that is highest and noblest in man."[32]

This did not remove the fact that some of the temples, shrines, castles or residences in Japan were impressive structures, built with obvious technical expertise and embellished with skill and attention to material and detail. It was difficult to ignore this and challenged the authors to find alternative ways of integrating the competence of Japanese builders and the joyful and entertaining experience of visiting such places into their framework of norms and interpretations. Edward William Godwin (1833–1886) did so in 1878 by shifting the frame of reference:

---

30 Conder, "Remarks on architecture," pp. 3–4.
31 Strange, Edward Fairbrother, "Architecture in Japan," in: *Architectural Review* 1 (1897), pp. 126–135, here p. 126.
32 Dooman, "Influence," p. 137.

Japanese architecture is not to be judged downwards from the Tea houses and the inferior Temples any more than we should judge the domestic architecture of the Greeks upwards from the Parthenon or even the Propyleim.[33]

A few sentences later he answered the question of the possibility of a Japanese architectural art:

We are bold to say that there is: that in their wood building there is an art full of refinement and capable of wide adaption: that we may learn much from their arrangement of masses, their shaping of outlines, the combination and the opposition of delicacy and strength, that they exhibit in all their detail: and that nowhere shall we see a simple building purpose fulfilled with greater propriety, more modesty, or a keener sense of beauty.[34]

Godwin thus opened two additional levels of discourse beyond the focus on the European canon alone. First he reminded the visitor of the variety of buildings within a cultural context and the levels of reasonable comparison. Then he broke down the buildings of interest into individual features, omitting those he perceived as irrelevant and admiring those he perceived as exemplary.

The French art historian Louis Gonse (1846–1921) found yet another approach that seems to contradict the canon at first glance. In his book *L'Art Japonaise*, 1883, he admonished:

Our vanity leads us to think that architectural genius belongs exclusively to the Aryan race, and, when a foreign architecture, as that of the Japanese, is spoken of, our first sentiment is one of mistrust. I have known reliable authors to deny a priori the value and even the existence of architectural art in Japan. It is necessary to destroy such a prejudice.[35]

---

33 Godwin, Edward William, "Japanese Building," in: *The British Architect and Northern Engineer* (30 August 1878), p. 85.
34 Ibid.
35 Gonse, *L'Art*, p. 3, cited after id., *Japanese art* (Chicago, 1891), p. 96.

He then lauded the simple elegance of Japanese interiors, describing the temples in Nikkō as the "most wonderful and most splendid curiosity that strangers can see"[36] and concluded: "They have found the rule of art which responds the best to their tastes and their temperament."[37]

It is in terms such as "curiosity" or in statements such as the latter sentence that reveal Gonse's adherence to the conceptual difference between the European and the Japanese traditions of art and architecture. In Gonse's eyes, Japan did not exist in the same architectural realm as Europe. Thus, scholarly discussion of Japanese architecture was neither needed nor desired as part of the general (western) discourse. At the same time, Gonse created an alternative legitimation for the study of Japanese buildings when he evaluated them as a matter of cultural competence of a specific ethnic group, much as had Jarves in his earlier quote on the "aesthetic constitution of the Japanese."[38]

By categorising Japanese culture as specifically 'Japanese' relative to 'normal' (western) culture, however, the authors defined Japan as 'the other', as incomparably outside the assumed universal western norm and thus as ultimately not equal. Occasionally, the distinction was made by referring to race, but other authors used manifold and often subtle means to argue perceived difference and its seemingly natural and irrevocable influence on art, building, behaviour or any other observed phenomena.[39]

Gonse's dualistic differentiation, this additional realm of discourse, made it possible to look at Japanese matters of interest without questioning the overall system of reference provided by the European artistic canon and the assumption of western superiority.[40]

The British Japanologist Basil H. Chamberlain also used this discursive mechanism in his standard reference *Things Japanese*, 1890:

---

36 Ibid., p. 18, resp. p. 107.
37 Gonse, *L'Art*, p. 11, cited after id., *Art*, p. 102.
38 Jarves, *Glimpse*, p. 22.
39 Compare the very similar observations in Bremner, Alex, *Building Greater Britain: Architecture, Imperialism, and the Edwardian Baroque Revival, c.1885–1920* (New Haven; London, 2022), pp. 2–3; and for an analysis of similar intra-Western strategies Cupers, Kenny, "The Invention of Indigenous Architecture," in: Cheng, Irene; Davis, Charles L. II; Wilson, Mabel O. (eds.), *Race and modern architecture. A critical history from the enlightenment to the present* (Pittsburgh, 2020), pp. 187–202.
40 Löffler, *Perpetual Other*.

> The Japanese genius touches perfection in small things. (...) The massive, the spacious, the grand, is less congenial to their mental attitude. Hence they achieve less success in architecture than in the other arts.[41]

In consequence, Chamberlain distinguished between the building itself and its artistic decoration when he addressed the memorial sites of the Tokugawa shōgunate, which were famous for their many decorative details and were considered highlights for sightseeing:

> Nikkō and Shiba are glorious, not as architecture (in the sense in which we Europeans, the inheritors of the Parthenon, of the Doges' Palace, and of Lincoln Cathedral, understand the word architecture), but for the elaborate geometrical figures, the bright flowers and birds and fabulous beasts, with which the sculptor and painter of wood has so lavishly adorned them.[42]

In summary, the western actors sought patterns of argument to relate differing artistic traditions to each other and to integrate new impulses and experiences into an overarching system of evaluation and knowledge. When dealing with Japan, contemporary basic assumptions about art and architecture had to be reformulated. The assessment of critics, art historians and architects is clear: Japanese architecture was perceived as 'not really architecture' since it did not meet the standards of architecture as a fine art in a sense that was strictly European in its origin but claimed an all-encompassing, global validity.

While the observation of difference is a normal tool of comparison, the othering of Japan resulted in specified collections of art and particularised study. As with European folk art, the study of Japanese art and architecture remained in the context of East Asian or non-western art alone, the observations were not integrated into the general (western) understanding of art.

Nevertheless, Japanese culture, however artistically 'limited' and 'local' in character in the eyes of the time, was understood as expressed in the buildings in such an excellent way that there were artistic solutions which could be considered worthwhile to Europeans for inspiration, study or even teaching.[43]

---

41 Chamberlain, "Architecture," pp. 22–23.
42 Chamberlain, "Architecture," p. 23.
43 Around the turn of the twentieth century, American architect Ralph Adams Cram (1863–1942) tried to reconcile the notions of art across the canonic gaps by discussing Velasquez and Korin: "The trouble is, however, that it is almost impossible to say where

1.2 *Applied Art and Craftsmanship*

At this time in Europe, applied art, craftsmanship and formal education in both areas did not so much demand an all-encompassing theory of art as just discussed, but a greater variety of information, models and ideas which could be applied eclectically across all forms of design and decoration. It was in this field that information gathering on Japanese art and the transfer of knowledge to the West were most dynamic. While applied art and craftsmanship ranked lower in the overall scheme of arts, they responded most immediately to the changes and challenges introduced by industrialisation and modern market practices. The impulse provided by Japanese artefacts was perceived as a means of addressing the stagnation in creativity and was as easily applicable in education as in art.

This was not relevant to the curricula of the above-mentioned fine art schools such as the École des Beaux-Arts in Paris but affected another tier of professional qualification, the industrial schools. These were usually local institutions and provided additional artistic and theoretical training for craftsmen. Again, voices expressing general interest in a transfer of artistic knowledge from Japan to Europe were predominant, but acknowledgement of architecture was occasionally heard as well, not least since many architects were involved in interior design and furniture. The topics of interest differed from those in fine art; they revolved around the forms and colours of craft design, the manual skills and the social status of the artisan, the economic environment of art, and so on.

1.2.1 Decorative Details (Carvings, Colours, Metal Fittings)

Information on the decorative details of buildings was common in texts on Japanese art, above all in the descriptions of sights, as we saw in the quote by Basil H. Chamberlain. Such descriptions were usually more an expression of the visitor's emotions than factual data on the detail itself. This was due not least to the size and immobility of the architectural artefacts, which made them uncollectible and made detailed description cumbersome for publication. In addition, many impressions were gained from photographs or other visual media that did not allow for detailed analysis, or were even taken from

---

racial convention merges into racial character, and where this in its turn stops before the universal human, the quality that is one in the Japanese and the European. Art is in so large measure a thing of both character and convention, that it is particularly hard for a man to look through and beyond these things and apprehend the ultimate reality." Cram, Ralph Adams, *Impressions of Japanese Architecture and The Allied Arts* (New York, 1905), pp. 18–19, see also pp. 180–182.

verbal descriptions alone in the absence of appropriate illustration. The British designer Christopher Dresser and many others complained about this situation. We will look more closely at the use and availability of visual media in a later chapter.

Overviews of Japanese art dedicated chapters to carvings and sculpture as well as to metalwork, but did not include carved elements connected to buildings in more than a cursory way. The following sequence from Josiah Conder's essay *Notes on Japanese architecture*, 1878, bridged the two spheres by addressing the buildings of the Kan'ei-ji in Tōkyō-Ueno:

> The shrines of the 4th and 5th Shoguns are of bronze, with their railings, gates and bas reliefs; the bronze has a dull greenish colour, approaching to black. Though the arrangements and general mode of construction of these sacred buildings are so similar that to describe each involves much repetition, yet there is such a variety of details – such different treatment in points of decoration, both carving and colouring – that there is in them an endless study for the artist.
>
> The carving is generally cut in camphor wood and the colour is mixed with a kind of size which seems effectually to resist the action of the weather. The posts, beams and all large surfaces decorated in one colour, are coloured with the medium of lacquer; which is either left of a dead colour, or is polished to a great degree of brightness. The bronze shoes and other ornaments are deeply engraved and filled in with black in the hollows.[44]

This short paragraph is characteristic in its mode of summary description, which presented an inviting account of a general architectural situation without being able to provide information that would allow a reader to make an informed judgement of the building as a whole. The sketch on the accompanying plate, however, showed a gate to the temple in its entirety and various other building parts in different places (Fig. 3.9). This made it possible at least to estimate the use and position of the carvings and metal fittings.

Most other instances of architectural description were even shorter and accompanied by less illustration. Christopher Dresser wrote about Nikkō in 1882:

---

44   Conder, Josiah, "Notes on Japanese architecture," in: *Transactions of the Royal Institute of British Architects* 28 (1878), pp. 179–192, 209–212, here p. 190.

> Across the river, on the sides of a tree-covered hill, are the great shrines – the most important and the most beautiful of all the shrines of Japan – shrines as glorious in colour as the Alhambra in the days of its splendour, and yet with a thousand times the interest of that beautiful building. Here we have birds, flowers, water, clouds, carved in a manner that could not be surpassed.[45]

He later described the buildings of the Tōshō-gū in terms of their decorative appearance and went slightly deeper:

> On some of the buildings which bound this court, and face us as we enter it, are carved panels of great magnificence. The first of these panels on the left consists of the paeony and the sacred bird, or hon – which may be regarded as the Japanese phoenix – with its three young. Another consists of a grand treatment of the fir-tree, another of the kiku flower, the plant of which the Mikado's domestic crest is formed, and on which the hon is supposed to feed, and others of various flowers and birds, all treated with masterly skill.[46]

FIGURE 3.9
Josiah Conder: drawing of a temple gate in Tōkyō-Ueno

---

45 Dresser, *Japan*, p. 198.
46 Dresser, *Japan*, p. 204.

THE INVISIBLE DWELLING HOUSE

FIGURES 3.10–3.11   Christopher Dresser: illustrations of architectural details: nails from temple doors in Nara and diagram of a gable ornament

Such is the level of description that the overviews provided. Dresser illustrated his book with building parts and details which gave the professionally trained designer insight into the basic principles of lines and planes but did not usually create a holistic understanding of the relation between building and ornament (Figs. 3.10 and 3.11). Some of the scenes in Émile Guimet's *Promenades japonaises*, 1878,[47] showed such detailing in function, as did some of the illustrations in Edward Morse's book *Japanese Homes*, 1885.[48] A more systematic if very brief account of the interplay between structural elements and décor was provided by Abel Guérineau in three colour plates for César Daly's *Les temples japonais*, 1886,[49] and in the black-and-white plates of his own volume *Ornements japonais*, 1889 (Fig. 3.12, see also Fig. 4.131 in colour section).[50]

The dominant features in the comments on these architectural details were the rich forms and the skill of the craftsmen, as with Louis Gonse's sub-chapter on the general principles of architecture:

> That which we admire in a tiny netsuke, in a lacquer box, or in any useful object, we find in the ornamentation of a temple; there is the same faithful execution, the same correct handiwork. The smallest details, no matter how hidden from sight, are executed with the same scrupulous care. Like our admirable masters of the 13th century, the Japanese artists of the

---

47   Guimet, Émile, *Promenades Japonaises. Tokio-Nikko* (Paris, 1878).
48   Morse, *Homes*.
49   Daly, César Denis, "Les temples japonais," in: *Revue générale de l'architecture et des travaux publics* 43 (1886), cols. 50–51, plates 16–26.
50   Guérineau, Abel, *Ornements japonais* (s.l., 1889).

best epochs judged that in a work of art, however complicated, nothing was unworthy of careful attention.[51]

The reader therefore gained an overall sense of the appearance of the respective element but nothing regarding its relationship to the architecture; similar to the handbooks of ornaments published at the time in Europe. The overall interest in these architectural carvings did not exceed the level of general curiosity regarding a source of formal inspiration. There were no building surveys, however cursory, even in Nikkō. Nobody initiated a complete collection of drawings or photographs, not even of a single building of special interest. The western occupation with architectural carvings, colours and fittings remained a collection of fragments quite similar to the handling of the collectable art objects that formed the vast majority of the subjects of study in Japanese crafts. It was only admiration of Japanese handiwork that went farther.

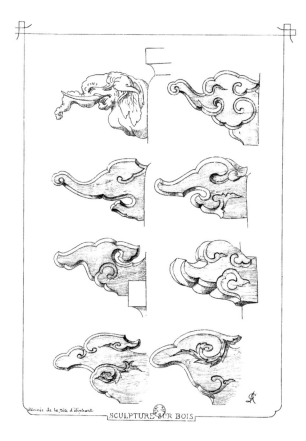

FIGURE 3.12
Abel Guérineau: carved details

---

51   Gonse, *L'Art*, p. 21, cited after id., *Art*, p. 96.

1.2.2 The Japanese Artisan in General

Beyond the acclaimed skills already mentioned above, the Japanese artisan himself became a topic of consideration. Jarves dedicated one of the five sections of his book to *The Conditions of Life of the Japanese Artisan and his Work*. After summing up the overall natural and sociocultural circumstances in which the artisan's work was embedded, he described or rather imagined the situation of the pre-modern artisan:

> The workman was a thorough worker and master of his particular art, content with nothing short of absolute technical perfection, aesthetic and material, in every object he undertook, whether it was cheap or valuable. Usually, he labored by himself, in his own cottage, or else with sympathetic associates on such branches of art as had been slowly perfected by many generations of his ancestors under the fostering care of their feudal lords. Thus he was born both to pride and skill in his work.[52]

He went on to contrast this situation of the Japanese artisan with that of his English counterpart in the nineteenth century, who was "doomed to monotonous uninspiring toil, herded with his fellows in unwholesome factories or the filthy purlieus of crowded cities."[53] This was a point on which Alcock – who otherwise largely concurred with Jarves' views about Japan – disagreed.

> There is something fanciful, I think, and unreal in this contrast. I do not see what there is in the nature of a Japanese artisan's work, in all the different branches of industrial occupation, which should be any more 'akin to his tastes, and a source of happiness to all concerned,' than in the case of the English mechanic.[54]

While Jarves sketched an imagined ideal situation, based in his work on European art, Alcock deconstructed this notion, since his thoughts had an altogether different aim: to foster the development of industrial arts by drawing practical conclusions from Japanese workmanship applicable to Britain.[55] Thus his argumentation (as a servant of the British Empire) did not reject machine work and the exigencies of modernity and economy. At the same time,

---

[52] Jarves, *Glimpse*, pp. 136–137. See a similar passage e.g. in Dresser, *Japan*, p. 417.
[53] Jarves, *Glimpse*, p. 137.
[54] Alcock, *Art*, pp. 244–245.
[55] Alcock, *Art*, p. 9.

however, he commented (as an art collector) on the changes in contemporary Japanese society and the expected decline of its artistic production.

> Japan will undoubtedly be able to supply its machine-made wares in greater numbers and at a cheaper rate; but they will have lost their peculiar cachet, if not all that now constitutes their charm to the artist, and the true lover of work which bears the impress of individual genius and feeling as well as skill.[56]

He drew the obvious conclusion and recommended:

> Let us hasten, before this fate overtakes the Japanese, and their Art in all its pristine qualities is lost, to study what it can teach us.[57]

This approach, the expected decline of Japanese art due to the process of modernisation, was copied by a number of authors and deeply influenced the later development of Japanese art studies, both in Europe and in Japan. It mirrors a more general perception of cultural loss pervading artistic debate in the West. We will come back to it at the end of this chapter.

Another voice in this area of the discourse was Christopher Dresser. His approach differed from that of other observers in that he commented on his own preconceptions and mannerisms and seemed able to tolerate a great deal of ambivalence in his cultural encounters with Japan; his interpretations did not try to resolve conflicting notions at all costs. His account of *Japan, its Architecture, Art and Art Manufactures*, 1882, combines a diary with structured professional observations and makes repeated reference to the role of the artisan. In a chapter in which he addressed the relationship of Japanese art forms to those on the Asian continent, he came to the following conclusion:

> Inspection of the Nara collections also reveals this fact – a fact brought prominently into notice during a long journey in Japan – that while the Japanese are the most subtle and delicate of workmen, the most accomplished of handicraftsmen, the most conscientious of artists, they are yet by no means inventive as a race. There is a good deal of truth in the statement that the Japanese have originated nothing, but have improved upon everything which they have seen.[58]

---

56 Alcock, *Art*, pp. 33–34.
57 Ibid., pp. 246–248.
58 Dresser, *Japan*, p. 111.

What remains unanswered is the question of which system of reference informed this observation. Dresser did not define 'inventiveness' or elaborate on his conceptual understanding any more than the other authors who hinted at similar notions of creativity and originality with respect to Japanese art. This may be a case of a self-referencing, hermetic argumentation: Japanese art was not perceived as art and hence was by definition devoid of intrinsic creativity. It was thus understood as incapable of development, the actors being not artists but merely 'reproducers' of practices and experiences the origins of which were traced to China or were not discussed at all. The significant differences in character and expression between Chinese and Japanese art and the repeated phases of Japanese isolation had no place in this reasoning; neither did the multifaceted character of Japanese schools of art, e.g. ceramics or textiles. All of these would have complicated a system of knowledge and reference in which European norms were the undisputed pinnacle.

To resolve the evident inconsistencies, Dresser resorted to the practice mentioned above of dualistic categorisation; beyond this, however, his ideas of the role of the artist/artisan usually saw them as parallel rather than contrasting phenomena. He reflected for example on the absence of division of labour in the local production of pottery, reaching the following conclusion:

> I have viewed, with no little interest, the satisfaction depicted on the countenance of a manufacturer of this kind when signing the completed work. There is as much pride in Japan manifested by the maker in completing a little cup, a lacquer box, a sheet of leather-paper, or even a pair of chop-sticks, if the work be but excellent, as there is in one of our great artists contemplating an historical painting; and by perfect work any handicraftsman in Japan may attain to the celebrity enjoyed here by a Landseer, a Turner, or an Owen Jones, and the fame supplies a stimulus for the production of work still more excellent.[59]

With the reference to a historical painting, the highest-ranking genre of painting at the time, Dresser draws parallels with the competences shown in fine and applied art, simultaneously adhering to and ignoring the canon.

The matter of professional ethics came up again and again – not only in Dresser's book but in the texts of other authors as well – often in relation to thoughts on marketability and thus linking back to Alcock's initiatives.[60]

---

59 Dresser, *Japan*, pp. 173–174.
60 Ibid., pp. 429–430, 414. See also "Japanese Competition with England," in: *The Builder* 35 (1877), p. 978.

The extent to which this issue was relevant in European art production at the time soon becomes evident, as does the difficulty, which theoreticians experienced in assessing the situation:

> There is a vast difference between toil undergone for the sake of mere money-making, and the production of the most perfect works of which man is capable. No thought of gain enters the mind of the great artist while he is engaged upon his work. Much of the work done by the British workman is positively despicable, because his only thought has been how to make the most money with the least exertion of mind or body. But the loving, painstaking toil which the Japanese bestow upon so many of their productions is actually ennobling; and by such labour the workman rises necessarily far above the mere moneyed man.[61]

The interplay between ideal images of the artisan in Japanese culture and contemporary topics in European artistic discourse produced a range of evaluations, from proposals for the pragmatic exploitation of Japanese art, to arguments for the idolisation of the artisan. They indicate the negotiation of art as a field of professional expertise within the framework of a modern society similar to the processes in architecture.

The American author Percival L. Lowell (1855–1916), to name but one more source, sang the praises of the artisan in his book *The soul of the Far East*, 1888, by characterising their work as an "unconscious mode of thinking," as a universal element of Japanese culture. He saw the competence of the Japanese artisan as a "birthright of the Far East." Lowell balanced this by pointing out that, in turn, such artisans have "not even a speaking acquaintance"[62] with science and thus with the ways of modern technology. This approach of cultural preconditions and the balancing of superiority with failure was close to Gonse's dualistic strategy. The remark on science was especially important for the overall topic of building as a planned, conscious process, as we will see below. It invites us to take a closer look at a certain type of Japanese artisan who is of the utmost importance when it comes to architecture: the carpenter.

1.2.3 The Japanese Artisan in a Specific Field: the Carpenter

The wood-based nature of traditional Japanese building practice meant that the lead carpenter, the *daiku*, was assigned a role similar to that of the European architect: he was the principal designer and coordinator of the

---

61 Dresser, *Japan*, p. 180.
62 Lowell, Percival, *The soul of the Far East* (Boston; New York, 1888), pp. 110–111, 121.

whole process of constructing and equipping the building, interacting with the client, and directing personnel and subcontractors.[63] As we have seen above, however, Japanese building practice was not perceived by western observers as architecture at all. As a consequence, their perception of the actors in the building-related professions and even the *daiku* was split into two areas. Firstly, they were discussed as woodworking craftsmen analogous to other craftsmen in the applied arts, as we will see here. Secondly, the *daiku* was discussed as the actor responsible for construction principles in Japan, as we will see later in this chapter.

In 1876, Japanese carpenters erected two buildings for the *Centennial International Exhibition* in Philadelphia. While the practices involved in the building process became the object of ridicule, the results were widely approved.[64] Thompson Westcott (1820–1888) observed on *The Japanese Dwelling*:

> The woods are of fine grain, carefully planed and finished, and the house, which is the best-built structure on the Centennial grounds, was as nicely put together as a piece of cabinet-work.[65]

Edward Strahan (Earl Shinn, 1838–1886) came to a similar conclusion in his comment on *The Japanese Bazaar*.[66]

While the American observers might have not sported the same disdain for wood as a primary building material as the Europeans, it was in general this kind of competence that was lauded in a similar way to the proficiency of Japanese potters or metalworkers, and that runs as a subtext through many publications on the art as well as the building and construction of Japan.[67] This culminated in 1878, when *The Building News and Engineering Journal* reported that Richard Henry Brunton, a stern critic of the Japanese building tradition, was suggesting that Japanese carpenters be imported to man the strike-bound construction site of the Royal Courts of Justice in London:

---

63   For extensive discussion of the term *daiku* as well as the overall profession and situation at this time, see Clancey, *Earthquake*, pp. 11–12, 28–38. See also the seminal but more general study by Coaldrake, *Carpenter*.
64   "Japanese work at the Centennial grounds," in: *American Architect and Building News* 1 (1876), pp. 55–56.
65   Westcott, Thompson, *Centennial portfolio: a souvenir of the international exhibition at Philadelphia, comprising lithographic views of fifty of its principal buildings* (Philadelphia, 1876), p. 22.
66   Strahan, Edward, *The Masterpieces of the Centennial International Exhibition* (Philadelphia) *1: Fine Art* (Philadelphia, 1876), p. CL.
67   E.g. Gonse, *L'Art*, pp. 24–25.

> [Brunton] declares that he has erected forty public buildings in Japan, and can testify to the diligence and aptitude of the Japanese workmen. Indeed, the efficiency of the native men is such that he was enabled very soon to dispense with the English foremen he had placed over them. The Japanese is the only workman, according to Mr. Brunton, who, while possessing a capacity for neatness and finish all his own, can compete with the English in alacrity.[68]

This echoed the opinion of American zoologist Edward S. Morse, who reported in *Japanese Homes and Their Surroundings*, 1886:

> A somewhat extended experience with the common everyday carpenter at home leads me to say, without fear of contradiction, that in matters pertaining to their craft the Japanese carpenters are superior to American. Not only do they show their superiority in their work, but in their versatile ability in making new things.[69]

He saw the reason for this, much as did commentators on art, in the unbroken family traditions that the Japanese had managed to maintain. From these he drew a lesson for his home country, admonishing that "civilization and modern appliances count as nothing unless accompanied with a moiety of brains and some little taste and wit."[70] With this, Morse casually contradicted the supposed absence of originality and innovation in Japanese art. His intention, however, was different. Again, the situation in Japan, whether observed or imagined, provided suggestions for reforming the social position of the craftsman and the artist in western society according to a romanticised 'medieval' model with guild-like structures and patronage. George Cawley noted in his late essay on *Wood, and its Application to Japanese Artistic and Industrial Design*, 1895:

> [T]he cabinet-maker or carver of a century ago, I can see him, in imagination, in the workroom of his modest home, comfortably employed under the patronage of some art-favouring feudal lord, whose commission would be for work of excellence, and excellence only. No limiting conditions, referring to market price or time of delivery, would arise

---

68 "Proposed importation of Carpenters," in: *The Building News and Engineering Journal* 34 (18 January 1878), p. 73.
69 Morse, *Homes*, p. 35.
70 Morse, *Homes*, pp. 35–36.

to narrow the scope of the artisan's skill. Under circumstances such as I have pictured – now gone for ever – the skilled wood worker could freely allow his long and special training, his deftness of manipulation, and his cultured taste to combine for the accomplishment of work indicative of his highest power as a shaper of wood.[71]

Cawley thus praised the Japanese carpenter, but did so while denying him the skills for "higher branches of carpentry,"[72] pointing instead to a hierarchical distinction among different competencies with respect to woodworking. This differentiation resembles the pattern we already saw in connection with fine art, and points to the struggles to assign a position to Japanese art and architecture within the western system of meaning and knowledge.

To summarise, the art discourses concerning Japan place Japanese architecture at a low level, just enough to remove it from the discourses on western fine art. Building-related crafts and the profession of the carpenter were of interest as a source of formal inspiration and in terms of pedagogical admonishments addressed to a western audience within the intra-western debates in the context of industrialisation alone.

It is important to understand that Japanese art was discussed strictly in terms of aesthetic and economic usefulness, as a resource of creative impulses and potential contractors.[73] The recognition given to the diversity of design and perfection of craftsmanship did not lead to the consideration of Japanese experts as teachers or the inclusion of Japanese art theories in the (western) discourses of the time.

It remains to be seen whether similar phenomena recur in the arguments regarding engineering to which we will now turn.

2 Architecture as a Field of Engineering

Japanese architecture did not fulfil the binding European criteria of the nineteenth century to be understood as fine art and was not discussed in terms of

---

71 Cawley, George, "Wood, and its Application to Japanese Artistic and Industrial Design," in: *Transactions and proceedings of the Japan Society* 2 (1895), pp. 194–223, here pp. 218–219.
72 Cawley, "Wood," p. 221.
73 For similar results observed from a different angle, see Satō, Dōshin, *Modern Japanese Art and the Meiji State: The Politics of Beauty* (Los Angeles, 2011), pp. 133–135.

an applied art. Yet this artistic definition of 'architecture' was (and still is) just one of several possible readings of the term.

At any given time, many buildings failed to be perceived as art, buildings which the field nevertheless came to accept and even to appreciate later on. Besides, as a system of skeleton construction, Japanese building was in fact conceptually closer to the building practices pursued by the civil engineers of the time than to the decorative surfaces created by graduates of the art schools. Even closer were the similarities to the manifold traditions of half-timbered construction all over Europe and the accompanying treatises.[74] As a consequence, it was the structural value of the skeleton, the use of wood in general, as well as the tools and building practices that became the issues most discussed among experts and interested lay persons from the West.

It should be borne in mind that, unlike the usual objects of fine and applied art, building structures are immobile. When it comes to Japan and the western discourses, this means that prime examples of the former soon became part of private and public collections in the West and allowed for close examination, while many more mostly trivial items were on display in the shops of specialised dealers. Yet Japanese buildings were usually impossible to experience outside Japan: transmitted information remained restricted to words and images and the occasional model. World's fairs and similar exhibitions were the sole exception.

Thus, it comes as no surprise that the construction of the Japanese buildings at the *Centennial International Exhibition* in Philadelphia in 1876 mentioned above gained a great deal of public attention. While the architectural journals usually ignored the non-western pavilions at the fairs, *American Architect and Building News* reprinted a short article from the *Philadelphia Times* that described an early stage of the building process. While the description constantly alternates between playful curiosity, ridicule, communication of facts and expressions of disrespect, it gives an impression of the basic unfamiliarity of what the observers were experiencing, Neither the driving of the piles for the sub-construction using a hand-operated ram, nor the procedures for measuring, and neither the use of tools, nor the overall habits of the Japanese team conformed to expectations. The crudeness of the critique – even if essentially meant to entertain the reader – underlines that the encounter with Japanese

---

74 See, for example, Lippert, Hans-Georg, "Die Kunst des guten Bauens. Architekturtraktate als Handreichung für den Wohnhausbau," in: Onnen, Elke; Spohn, Thomas (eds.), *Die neuen Häuser in den neuen Städten und Dörfern. Neuerungen im Hausbau unter dem Einfluss der Landesherren und ihrer Baumeister zwischen 1650 und 1830* (Petersberg, 2019), pp. 59–66.

culture was not perceived as happening on an equal footing at all; rather, there was an assumption of western superiority. While the article is relatively long, it is worth quoting in full to convey an understanding of how information was interwoven with caricature and critique:

> The most curious part of the day's work was the driving of a number of piles, each six feet long and ten inches in diameter, upon which is to rest, like a corn-crib, a rectangular structure eighty-four by forty-four feet, and in general appearance like the pictures of Japanese houses that children see in their primers. The way in which the Japs managed the pile-driving brought many a burst of laughter from the bystanders. They had a portable tripod about twenty feet high, with two fixed pulleys under the apex, from which was suspended by a grass rope a cylindrical iron hammer weighing three hundred pounds. Six Japs on each side of the machine seize a grass rope which passes over one of the pulleys; the foreman stands at one side, holds up his forefinger, closes one eye, and then, apparently not satisfied with this, picks up a short stick, holds it in a vertical position between his two forefingers, sights the pile with it, and at last winks with both eyes as a signal to the workman that the ceremony of Japanese plumb-bobbing is concluded; whereupon the hammer moves up and down very rapidly, driving the pile an inch into the earth at every descent, until it is time for the foreman to do a little more plumb-bobbing. One pile struck a rock; and, while everybody was wondering how things were to be managed, one of the gang ran off and brought back something that had teeth like a saw, but which was shaped like a butcher's cleaver; but the panting Jap had severed the stick in about half the time required for a saw of American make to do the same work.
>
> The Japs draw their planes towards them, instead of pushing them from them, and use an ink line instead of a chalk line. It resembles a tape-line case, and contains a sponge which may be saturated with ink of any color; through this sponge the cord may be drawn and then wound up, dispensing with the tedious process of chalking. The holes for the piles were marked out in this odd way: two posts, one at each end of the foundation, were connected at the top by a tightly-drawn cord; from end to end of this, the mandarin foreman walked with his rule, measuring off spaces, which he marked by tying bits of string in bow-knots to the main cord, and then standing off to go through his delicate operation of plumb-bobbing, which he repeated every time that his men removed the tripod to drive a new pile. Their adze is a remarkable tool, chiefly on account of its handle, which is shaped as Hogarth's line of beauty might

be if warped by torrid weather. The wielder of this tool stands over his timber, and hacks away, driving the steel far underneath his foot at every blow. When the ropes of the pile-drivers were too long, the foreman fastened blocks of wood in slip-knots to shorten them; but one of these slipped and dropped on the head of a young Jap, causing him to let go the rope, fall backward, and roll over to a big log, upon which he sat down to rest himself and laugh.

The Japanese square is eighteen and a half inches long, and nine and a quarter wide; and is graduated, like the rule, by the decimal system, nine and a quarter of their inches being equal to eight of ours.

In the bamboo building not a nail will be used; all the material is there, dovetailed, bevelled, and mortised, ready to be fastened together with wooden pins. The artisans live in a frame structure within the enclosure, do their own cooking and laundry work, and live on soup, rice, and dried meats, which they brought with them in hermetically sealed cans. The officials having charge of Japanese operations in the park refuse to give the slightest information as to what they are doing. When asked about their building and intended exhibition, the questioner is invariably put off with, "Wait till comes time; you then see." It displeases them when spectators laugh at the uncouth mechanical operations of the flat-nosed and tawny-featured Orientals.[75]

This media coverage that evokes the zoo-like situation of some ethnological expositions of the time[76] is exceptional among the sources on Japanese architecture in that it allows a glimpse into levels of perception which were pertinent but usually obscured by technical language and habitual restraint.

About ten weeks later, another note in *American Architect and Building News* provided information on the state of construction work in a much more pragmatic tone:

The Japanese are giving the finishing touches to a most extraordinary structure. It is a two-story house, built mainly of cedar, and without a nail or pane of glass in it. The sides may all be opened by shoving back the

---

75 "Japanese work at the Centennial grounds," pp. 55–56.
76 On this topic, see e.g. Maxwell, Anne, *Colonial Photography and Exhibitions. Representations of the 'Native' and the Making of European Identities* (London et al., 1999); Rothfels, Nigel, *Savages and Beasts. The Birth of the Modern Zoo* (Baltimore, 2002); Dreesbach, Anne, "Colonial Exhibitions, 'Völkerschauen' and the Display of the 'Other'," *European History Online* (Mainz: Institute of European History, 2012), http://www.ieg-ego.eu/dreesbacha-2012-en [accessed 30 May 2023].

walls, which are really shutters. A lattice of lath-work covers the lower story, so that the inmates may open all the shutters within, and yet not be exposed to public gaze. A bird is handsomely carved in bas-relief on the wooden panel between the top of the front door and the overhanging porch. The roof is made of dark "tiles," with lighter ones at the angles and borders, and fierce dragons' heads at various important points. The "tiles" are said to be of wood. They have been varnished if this is the case, and have a lustre not unlike that made by first-class stove polish. This roof is as innocent of nails as the lower part of the building. It is kept in place by numerous long poles, which lie against its edges, and are kept in place by being lashed together as well as inserted firmly in the ground.[77]

This is a typical example – both in length and content – of the notes on Japanese architecture that appeared in field-related journals up to the early twentieth century: a collection of details, barely related to each other, which conveyed an impression of interesting 'otherness' but did not allow readers to form a virtual image of the described building in their minds. While material and size were mentioned, most of the information pertained to decorative features, while none was given on the underlying construction principles. Yet it is evident that this was not at all due to lack of comprehension on the part of the western observer. The Japanese buildings 'functioned' well as buildings. Their intrinsic logic was as comprehensible to western observers as the tools and building practices were, despite the decidedly non-western way in which the Japanese actors handled technical and constructive issues; there was no question that these buildings were in fact buildings. Rather, the discussions revolved around the question of whether Japanese approaches were capable of resulting in *satisfactorily* constructed buildings. However, this question did not require real attention in the West since it was not perceived as being relevant here: the established practices of massive construction as employed in western representative buildings were understood as the most advanced practices available to Man. Against this background, wooden constructions did not merit attention on an equal footing. As a sole exception, local phenomena of historic vernacular buildings were studied as a means of constructing national cultural heritage.[78] This was an important and consequential endeavour in terms of

---

77 "Japanese Architecture," in: *American Architect and Building News* 1 (1876), pp. 136.
78 E.g. Landau, Georg, "Der Hausbau," in: *Beilagen z. Correspondenz-Blatt des Gesangvereins der deutschen Geschichts- und Alterthumsvereine*, 1857–1862; Schaefer, Carl, *Die Holzarchitektur Deutschlands vom XIV. bis XVII. Jahrhundert* (Berlin, 1883–1888); Schäfer, Dietrich, *Das Bauernhaus im deutschen Reich und seinen Grenzgebieten* (Dresden, 1906)

architectural study but remained largely separate from debates among planners and practitioners.

As a result, the contributions which were published in building-related journals – such as the essays of Josiah Conder – received friendly interest but little more than that. Thus, the greater part of the discussion of the construction principles of Japanese houses occurred not as part of the in-field evaluations by engineering experts of whatever national background; rather, it occurred in the meetings and through the publications of the *Asiatic Society of Japan*, as in-field evaluations in the context of Japanese studies. In contrast to questions concerning Japanese art, evaluations of architecture were not exchanged through a circle of collectors and traders located across the globe, but were more site-related, comprising 'local' discussions conducted by practitioners from many backgrounds as well as lay persons with knowledge of Japan, and based on everyday experiences. Most of these individuals being hired experts, they strove to find solutions to innovate Japanese building technologies, or to replace them entirely.

2.1 *Building Structure and Earthquake Resistance*

The engineers used their own observations and expert knowledge to evaluate Japanese phenomena. In doing so, they often contradicted older, received interpretations of Japanese construction.[79] Engelbert Kaempfer had described the main features of Japanese houses and remarked along the way:

> The reason of their building their houses so very low, is the frequency of earthquakes this country is subject to, and which prove much more fatal to lofty and massy buildings of stone, than to low and small houses of wood. (…) I took notice, that the roof (…) rests upon thick, strong, heavy beams, as large as they can get them, and that the second story is generally built stronger and more substantial than the first. This they do by reason

---

and Viollet-le-Duc, Eugène, "Maison," in: *Dictionnaire raisonné de l'architecture française du XIᵉ au XVIᵉ siècle* (Paris, 1854–1868), vol. 6, pp. 214–300. – On the historical context see: Lippert, Hans-Georg, "Systematik und Sehnsuchtsbild. Der Beitrag der frühen Hausforschung zum traditionellen Bauen im 20. Jahrhundert," in: Krauskopf, Kai, Lippert, Hans-Georg, Zaschke, Kerstin (eds.), *Neue Tradition. Vorbilder, Mechanismen und Ideen* (Dresden, 2012), pp. 13–40 und Cupers, "Invention."

[79] This sub-chapter merely scratches the surface of the larger issue. For an extensive and immensely insightful study, see Clancey, *Earthquake*. For the context of architectural discourses in the West, see Löffler, Beate, "Thwarted Innovation: The discourse on earthquake resistance in Japanese architecture – a historical review," in: *Construction History* 34.2 (2019), pp. 35–52.

of the frequent earthquakes, which happen in this country, because, they observe, that in case of a violent shock, the pressure of the upper part of the house upon the lower, which is built much lighter, keeps the whole from being overthrown.[80]

This information was reprinted together with other older sources in the handbook *Japan: As it was and is* by American journalist and historian Richard Hildreth (1807–1865), a book that reached a broad audience due to its consideration of numerous issues.[81] It is reasonable to assume that other authors broaching this issue at this time such as Andrew H. Foote and French naval officer Maurice Dubard (1845–1929) gained their knowledge primarily from Kaempfer;[82] it is doubtful that their limited time on shore during the missions in Japan allowed for independent data collection. Dubard wrote in 1879:

> Houses in Japan are constructed with precautions against anticipated earthquakes. As light as wicker baskets, they quiver and oscillate, but rarely collapse.[83]

2.1.1 Statements

With the arrival of modern western engineers, these evaluations began to be questioned. Many foreigners were now faced with frequent tremors and earthquakes and showed little confidence in Japanese building solutions, given their apparent frailty in comparison to the structures usual in the westerners' home countries. While research and publication on seismic and geological issues was intense,[84] the question of how these building solutions related to earthquake resistance remained initially unsolved. The German geographer Johannes

---

80 Kaempfer, *History*, 2, pp. 411–412.
81 Hildreth, Richard, *Japan. As it was and is* (Boston, 1855). Further issues in 1860, 1861 (extended), 1902, 1905, 1906, 1907 …
82 Foote, "Visit"; Dubard, Maurice, *Le Japon pittoresque* (Paris, 1879). For biographical information see "Dubard, Louis François Maurice," in: *Archives Biographiques Françaises (ABF)* via http://db.saur.de/WBIS/basicSearch.jsf [accessed 30 May 2023].
83 Dubard, *Japon pittoresque*, p. 139, quoted after id., *Japanese Life, Love, and Legend: A Visit to the Empire of the 'Rising Sun'* (London, 1886), p. 133.
84 For example, no less than four of the 23 essays on various topics published in the *Transactions of the Asiatic Society of Japan* in 1878 focused on seismic or geological issues: Ichizo Hattori's *Destructive Earthquakes in Japan* (pp. 249–275), Winfield S. Chaplin's *An Examination of the Earthquakes Recorded at the Meteorological Observatory, Tôkiyô* (pp. 352–356), David H. Marshall's *Notes on some of the Volcanic Mountains in Japan* (pp. 321–345), and Edward Divers' *Notes on the Amount of Sulphuretted Hydrogen in the Hot Springs of Kusatsu* (pp. 346–348).

Justus Rein (1835–1918), who gave the issue extended space in his publications, summarised the situation when he wrote in his comments on Japanese dwellings in 1881:

> How far this Japanese style of building has been determined and limited by the frequent occurrence of violent earthquakes, it is difficult to say.[85]

French artist Félix Régamey (1844–1907), while inclined to fascinated appreciation of most things Japanese, used a simple but convincing argument in 1892 to express his position on this matter when he pointed towards the continued existence of old wooden structures in Japan and the evidently conscious preference of wood over stone.[86] This, however, was a line of thought ignored by the western engineering experts at this time.

While non-expert foreigners seemed to accept existing patterns of explanation, engineers like Richard Henry Brunton rejected notions such as Kaempfer's and Dubard's outright and instead established a new paradigm, which would come to characterise the ensuing discussion:

> [W]ith its unnecessarily heavy roof and weak framework, it is a structure of all others the worst adapted to withstand a heavy earthquake shock.[87]

He supported this evaluation with arguments taken from ongoing discussions of the cultural parameters of Japanese development during modernisation:

> That earthquakes are prevalent throughout the whole of Japan is a fact which, in the minds of many, has affected the whole system of building in Japan, and has prevented the development of the native talent for construction. This is looked upon as sufficient reason for the absence of stone erections or buildings of solidity and durability. But if earthquakes have exercised this influence over the Japanese mind, the people have been influenced by false premises; as I think that to imagine that slight

---

[85] Rein, Johannes Justus, *Japan. Nach Reisen und Studien im Auftrage der Königlich Preussischen Regierung*, 2 vols. (Leipzig, 1881–1886), 1, p. 480, FN; English quote from id., *Japan. Travels and Researches. Undertaken at the cost of the Prussian Government*, 2nd ed. (London, 1888), p. 414, FN.

[86] Régamey, Félix, *Le Japon pratique* (Paris, 1891), p. 232, quoted after id., *Japan in Art and Industry with a Glance at Japanese Manners and Customs* (New York, 1892), p. 236. Régamey went on to speak about the earthquake resilience, but it can be assumed that his stance was influenced by Dresser.

[87] Brunton, "Constructive (1)," p. 72.

buildings, such as are seen here, are the best calculated to withstand an earthquake shock is an error of the most palpable kind. Now that foreigners have introduced a different system of building, the present Japanese have no hesitation in adopting it, and edifices of any size or material are now erected with their approval. No objection is ever made on account of earthquakes, and on these grounds I am of opinion that at all events the present race have not that dread of earthquakes which would lead them to eschew solid constructions, and we must seek at some other source the reasons for the want of progress in the art of building.[88]

Brunton went to underline that this was not due to a lack of intelligence but only knowledge among the Japanese and was easily remedied through education.[89]

Brunton's paper listed significant earthquakes in Japan and summarised his convictions regarding heavy and rigid constructions as the most sensible solution for earthquake-prone regions. He relied for this on bracing principle developed during centuries of European wooden construction summed up in the German rhyme *Dreieck besteht, Viereck vergeht* (Triangle persists, square fails). The traditional Japanese house, in contrast, was a top-heavy but generally slight construction without bracing – a structural preference which Brunton did not see as reflecting any particular 'cultural condition'. He thus saw no valid reason not to change Japanese building practices to basically follow the norms of European statics.

For a second paper the following year, he had initially planned to present the results of applying western building techniques in Japan. However, he found himself unable to do so since, he claimed, the number of buildings was too small and the quality of their execution too poor to make it worthwhile for the audience.[90] Instead, he returned to the need for earthquake-resistant construction in Japan. He pointed to the lack of knowledge regarding the cause and localisation of earthquake shocks and expressed his hope that innovative research methods would soon provide more information. He then sketched the features of a structural system developed by an anonymous English engineer, in which the foundations and the main volume of a building were separated by ball-like resting points:

---

88 Ibid., p. 65.
89 Ibid., p. 86.
90 Brunton, Richard Henry, "Constructive Art in Japan (2)," in: *Transactions of the Asiatic Society of Japan III* (1875), pp. 20–30, here pp. 20–21.

He procured this idea from seeing in Japanese drawings the uprights of their houses resting on round stones, imagining this to be done in order to give them as slight a hold of the earth as possible. But from enquiries I have made this does not seem to have entered the minds of the Japanese, and the only way they can account for the uprights being placed on round stones is to keep the wood away from the moisture of the ground and because round boulders are more easily and cheaply procured than square stones.[91]

Brunton expressed his doubt regarding the practicability of a 'flexible' house and repeated his argument in favour of solid, rigid constructions. The French civil engineer Jules Lescasse and his British colleague George Cawley added their observations,[92] the latter with reference to the seismological studies of William Edward Ayrton and John Perry.[93]

It is interesting to note the discrepancy between the titles of Brunton's essays and their content: *Constructive Art in Japan* conveyed very little beyond the information already provided by older sources. While less obvious in other texts, the situation was the same with nearly all of the other authors in the ensuing years: they provided information on details without ever mentioning the overall construction principles of the building or providing sufficient technical drawings. The reader was merely informed in a few sentences about the general use of wood, the mobility of the walls and the heaviness of the roofs.

This invites speculation about the possible reasons for these significant shortcomings. One might assume that the European experts looked at the Japanese buildings with the structural body of the Victorian house and its continental counterparts in mind,[94] as we already saw above with Conder's insistence on substance and protection "from all probable destructive forces."[95]

This would mean that the essayists felt they needed only to look at those details which deviated from the known and accepted model. However, while this assumption might have played a role, it would point towards a significant

---

91 Brunton, "Constructive (2)," p. 29.
92 See e.g. Cawley, "Construction," pp. 295–296.
93 Lescasse, Jules, *Étude sur les constructions japonaises et sur les constructions en général, au point de vue des tremblements de terre, et description d'un système destiné à donner une grande sécurité aux constructions en maçonnerie* (Paris, 1877); Cawley, "Construction."
94 See for an introduction Tegethoff, Wolf, "Vom Landhaus zur ‚Wohnmaschine'. Der Wandel des Lebensumfeldes im Spiegel der Moderne," in: Pieper, Ernst; Schoeps, Julius (eds.), *Bauen und Zeitgeist. Ein Längsschnitt durch das 19. und 20. Jahrhundert* (Basel et al., 1998), pp. 111–126.
95 Conder, "Remarks on architecture," pp. 3–4.

lack of competence on the part of the civil engineers: it would mean that the engineers did not perceive the essential constructive difference between the Victorian house, on the one hand, which was understood as developing from its walls, and the Japanese house, which was a skeleton structure arising from the arrangement of single vertical supports/pillars, on the other.[96] This is highly improbable in light of the lively discussions taking place at the time in Europe, where technical constructions from wrought or cast iron and glass were challenging the concepts of building and architecture. One might likewise assume that the constructive information and descriptions provided by older sources (Kaempfer, Thunberg) were perceived as sufficient to provide the necessary information. However, this seems unlikely considering the efforts taken to rebut the older evaluations.

Since civil engineering as a field of professional expertise was integrated into academic education at the same time – and not least in Japan – the lack of factual information observed here cannot be understood as coincidental. This leads to another possible explanation: disinterest. The authors did not care about the principles of Japanese architecture and construction; they did, however, wish to communicate their opinion and to express their competence as experts and their technological superiority. Since most of them owed their presence in Japan precisely to their competence in modern technologies, this position was understandable. It would have been more convincing, however, if it were not contradicted by those among their fellow advisors who did not share their easy dismissal of Japanese solutions.

The most notable of those who took a different stance was Christopher Dresser. Like his contemporary Edward William Godwin, Dresser was one of the early Japanophiles in England and was interested primarily in ornamentation. He travelled in Japan for some months in 1876 and 1877 as an expert on applied art for the Japanese government, and published his experiences in *Japan, its Architecture, Art and Art Manufactures* in 1882. The book consisted of two parts: a diary of his travels, followed by chapters with systematic information and considerations of different topics.[97] In his chapter entitled *Religion and Architecture*, Dresser addressed a number of issues regarding construction and building safety that refer conceptually to Kaempfer rather than to Brunton. Due to his professional background, this invites dismissal as

---

96 In fact, almost no-one mentioned this explicitly until the 1890s. See e.g. Stein, Ernst von, "Erdbeben und japanische Gebäude," in: *Österreichische Monatsschrift für den Orient* 19 (1893), pp. 77–79, here p. 78.

97 Dresser, *Japan*; for a more extensive treatment, see Löffler, "Thwarted," and especially Clancey, *Earthquake*.

a kind of romanticism of the traditional culture, as we already saw earlier with some of the art collectors and artists. However, his diary shows an interrelation between delight in the exploration of Japanese culture, on the one hand, and self-reflection regarding his role as a foreigner, on the other hand; both demand that his arguments be taken seriously.

Dresser's descriptions of construction principles were as brief as those in all the other sources, but he embedded them in an extended context of 'cultural logic'. His description of the Japanese house is actually the first to point out the pavilion-like characteristics of the skeleton:

> The Japanese seek shelter from the rain, and they desire houses which give shade from the sun. They also require buildings which allow of the freest circulation of air. They are a hardy people, and can stand cold, and in the warmer season lead what is practically an outdoor life. At this [warmer] period of the year, and indeed through most of the winter days, the window-like surroundings of their houses are removed, when all that remains is a roof supported on uprights.[98]

He referred to the danger of earthquakes and added:

> Japanese houses and temples are put together in a solid and simple manner, each work being complete in itself, and having an altogether independent existence. Thus a Japanese house is in no way built upon foundations, or fixed to the ground on which it rests. It stands upon a series of legs, and these legs usually rest on round-topped stones of such a height as will, during the rainy season, support the timber uprights above any water that may lie upon the ground. It is obvious that while an object fixed to the earth might, if rocked, be broken off from the ground or become strained and destroyed, that that which is loose would simply oscillate and settle down again after the cause of its vibration had ceased.[99]

Dresser saw the inhabitants not so much endangered by the collapse of the building in the event of an earthquake, but by the falling of the heavy tiles

---

[98] Dresser, *Japan*, p. 234. There are similarities to the earlier published essay of Pfoundes, Charles, "Constructive art in Japan," in: *The Builder* 37 (1879), pp. 1306–1307, 1395, but Pfoundes remained more vague.

[99] Dresser, *Japan*, p. 235.

used to cover the house for protection against fire. Hence he called for the use of organic materials such as wood and straw treated with a fire retardant.[100]

This line of thought caused little upset since it remained close not only to Kaempfer, but also to part of Lescasse's reasoning and to that of the anonymous colleague that Brunton mentioned. In addition, Dresser cautioned against the use of brick and stone since "the result of this incongruous innovation will probably be a return to the native style of building after the occurrence of some dire calamity."[101]

While this stance was indeed unusual among the western observers, it is only in subsequent pages that Dresser openly rejected received western knowledge. In a heavily didactic passage, he described first his puzzlement on observing the lavish use of wood for a pagoda, and second his learning process regarding its structural ingenuity under the tutelage of his translator Sakata Haruo. He was told about the central pillar of the pagoda and how it did not rest on the ground but remained suspended and acted like a pendulum when the ground moved, thus relocating the centre of gravity of the building. He ended this passage with a summary:

> I now understood the reason for that lavish use of timber which I had so rashly pronounced to be useless; and I see that there is a method in Japanese construction which is worthy of high appreciation. In the absence of any other instance the employment of this scientific method of keeping the pagoda upright shows how carefully the Japanese have thought out the requirements to be met.[102]

This statement includes three conceptual challenges to western architectural and engineering thought at this time. Firstly, it suggested – as with the houses – that the resilience of a somewhat flexible structure might be a viable solution for preventing damage by earthquakes, and thus contradicted Brunton's teachings on heavy and braced construction. Secondly, it connected a wooden structure with the idea of a scientific approach to construction, thus simultaneously raising this cheap, low-status material, thought worthy of use only in vernacular buildings, to the level of stone or brick (or iron); and, thirdly, it attributed to Japanese carpenters the competence to think, plan and execute a structure scientifically, as would a western architect or civil engineer.[103]

---

100 Ibid., pp. 235–236.
101 Ibid., p. 237.
102 Dresser, *Japan*, p. 238.
103 Clancey, *Earthquake*, p. 51.

It is interesting to note that Dresser himself seemed to perceive the construction of a pagoda as architecture, not engineering, favouring aesthetic pleasure over the structural achievements. Referring to experiences in England, he stated that an engineer "may be altogether unable to erect a beautiful building."[104]

Notwithstanding this somewhat disparaging description of the competencies of civil engineers, Dresser's text was well received in architectural and engineering journals in subsequent years. The book was lauded for its insights into Japanese crafts and its informative analysis of earthquake resistance. The principle of the pendulum was even mentioned as a possible method for stabilising the Statue of Liberty in New York.[105]

The information on the pagoda was also noticed in art circles, as evidenced by an essay by Victor Champier (1851–1929) in Samuel Bing's trilingual series *Artistic Japan. Illustrations and Essays*. Champier reproduced Dresser's information in his own words without referring to the source but mentioned the author later in his text.[106] The explanation of the actual function of the pagoda's flexible component lacked precision – Champier was an art critic by profession – but he conveyed Dresser's core points. These reactions showed again that the thoughts behind the Japanese construction principles were not at all incomprehensible or inapplicable in the western context. Yet they did not remain undisputed.

2.1.2   Dispute

The most significant rebuttal of Dresser's assertions came from Josiah Conder.[107] In 1883, he wrote to the editor of *The Building News and Engineering Journal* with a response to a review of Dresser's book published some months earlier. He provided a sectional drawing of an unnamed pagoda (the review had been illustrated with the view of the pagoda in front of Nikkō Tōshō-gū) and explained away any examples of 'suspended' central posts as the result of miscalculated shrinkage of the building (Figs. 3.13 and 3.14).[108] Conder

---

104   Dresser, *Japan*, p. 243.
105   "The Foundations for the Pedestal of the Statue of Liberty," in: *The American Architect and Building News* 13, 377 (1 March 1883), p. 122.
106   Champier, Victor, "Japanese architecture," in: *Artistic Japan. Illustrations and Essays* 3–4 (1888), pp. 19–42, here p. 24.
107   Clancey, *Earthquake*, pp. 50–54.
108   Conder, Josiah, "Japanese pagodas, and their construction," in: *The Building News and Engineering Journal* 44 (20 April 1883), p. 529.

THE INVISIBLE DWELLING HOUSE   111

 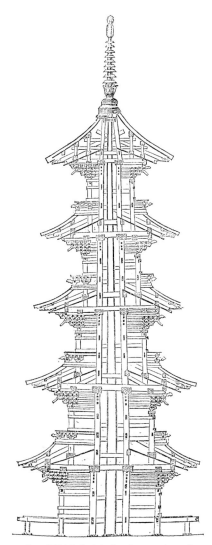

FIGURES 3.13–3.14   Christopher Dresser: depiction of the pagoda at Nikkō; Josiah Conder: section of a pagoda

invoked anonymous Japanese architects and builders as authorities to refute all of Dresser's central arguments for the application of resilient construction principles.

Dresser was nevertheless invited to give a talk before the *Architectural Association* in London. His presentation was summarised by one of the audience and described as "the first to enunciate the plan on which the Japanese pagodas were built."[109] The crucial structural information was conveyed exactly along the lines of Dresser, with a hanging core element, supplemented by the statement that no pagoda has ever been toppled by an earthquake.[110]

A parallel report on the same talk mentioned the dispute, underlining Dresser's statement of suspended posts in pagodas and the looseness of the houses' foundations.[111]

In reaction to the reports on the talk and Dresser's failure to respond, Josiah Conder's brother, Roger T. Conder, wrote to the editor of *Building News* in favour of his brother's argumentation, aiming to elicit a reply from Dresser and demonstrating the journal as a platform for public discourse.[112]

This elicited no reaction and in 1886 Josiah Conder tried again to gain the prerogative of interpretation. He submitted the essay *Further Notes on Japanese Architecture* to the Royal Institute of British Architects.[113] Conder addressed the building types of a typical Buddhist temple complex and included the pagodas. After a detailed review of their structural principles and properties, he talked about the bracing technique applied and repeated his earlier statement: the central post rested on a stone foundation as a means to stiffen the building against wind. Then he elaborated on the 'hanging' posts, arguing that "there are instances of miscalculation in which it is still an inch or two from its bearing and consequently strictly speaking suspended from the top."[114] What he omitted completely was the issue of earthquakes. He also ignored the question of how it would have been possible for the pagoda to remain permanently upright despite an artisan's supposed error, if the central post of 30 m with a diameter of 90 cm had a role in its structural setup.

What is anomalous in this essay, and would remain puzzling were it not for our knowledge of the dispute with Dresser, are Conder's disparaging comments on Japanese craftsmanship. These stand in contrast to his evaluation in the essay on *Domestic Architecture in Japan* of just a year later. There he wrote:

---

109 "Japanese Architecture and Ornament [Dresser, Christopher: "Some features of Japanese architecture and ornament"]," in: *The Builder* 47 (13 December 1884), pp. 787–788, here p. 787.
110 Ibid., p. 787.
111 "Japanese Architecture and Ornament," in: *The Building News and Engineering Journal* 47 (12 December 1884), pp. 941–942, here p. 941.
112 Conder, Roger Thomas, "Japanese Pagoda," in: *The Building News and Engineering Journal* 47 (19 December 1884), p. 1017.
113 Conder, "Further Notes."
114 Ibid., pp. 206–207.

The long retention of this material has enabled the Japanese to develop a great familiarity with its qualities, and great constructional and artistic skill in its application to building purposes.[115]

However, even then he immediately qualified this praise by presenting wooden construction as lacking sophistication, as was usual in the discourses on architecture as an art form, and by connecting its primary use to a lower stage of civilisation.[116]

With Conder's essay of 1886, the dispute reached a stalemate and subsided. Some colleagues joined the one or the other camp[117] and many later publications discussed the issue in such vague terms – if at all – that it was no longer possible to assess its key parameters in any meaningful way.

2.1.3 Dead End

It would no doubt be interesting to analyse the dispute "between a Japanophilic reformer of Britain and a British reformer of Japan"[118] with regard to the way in which positions were taken, media and professional networks utilised, and Japanese and western experts brought into the fray as supporters. It is even more interesting, however, to note what did not happen during the dispute: disclosure of data and additional on-site research.

None of the participants or discussants in the pagoda dispute named the building(s) in question, nor did they provide all of the sources of their information. None initiated additional research in the form of a building survey of pagodas, or undertook an analysis of the Japanese building manuals that had already been available for centuries at this point in time.[119] Still active as advisor after his position as a professor of architecture at the Imperial College in Tōkyō had expired, Josiah Conder would have been able to initiate a project with students and colleagues to address the issue and validate his stance.

---

115   Conder, *Domestic*, p. 104.
116   Ibid.
117   Hermann Muthesius (1861–1927), a German architect who was also active in Japan from 1887 to 1891, backed Conder's point of view. Muthesius, Hermann, "Das japanische Haus," in: *Zentralblatt der Bauverwaltung* (20 June 1903), pp. 306–307, here p. 306 and again on occasion of the Great Kantō Earthquake in 1923: id., "Der japanische Hausbau," in: *Berliner Tageblatt* 249 (13 September 1923), 1. Beiblatt.
118   Clancey, *Earthquake*, p. 50.
119   A famous example, Heinouchi Masanobu's *Shōmei* [clarification for the artisan-builder], traces back to 1608, the oldest surviving copy dates back to 1727. A reprint was published in 1971. See Coaldrake, *Carpenter*, p. 140. See also the section about *hinagatabon* later in this book.

That he did not do so can be easily explained by his position as an expert who had been hired to promote and to teach superior western technologies, not to study Japan. Nevertheless, he could have done so, not least since there was a demand with regard to the Japanese building tradition at his former department, demand which led to the inclusion of building surveys in the curriculum by his successor at about this time.[120]

After the significant destruction caused by the Mino-Owari earthquake of 1891, which affected Japanese and western buildings alike and temporarily weakened the western claim to technological superiority, this discourse intensified for a while.[121] This went as far as a letter by Sone Tatsuzō (1852–1937) to *Deutsche Bauzeitung* disagreeing with an account of the damages by the office of Berlin-based architects Böckmann & Ende.[122] No matter who was involved in the discussion, however, the only solutions sought were those which utilised modern technology. In 1899, *The Building News and Engineering Journal* reported the production of a palace for the Crown Prince of Japan by a Chicago firm, "constructed entirely of steel like a huge box, so that it cannot fall unless there should be a convulsion of sufficient force to turn it over on one side bodily."[123]

In the following years, two publications again invited a closer look at Japanese constructions, but were ignored, missing the opportunity to integrate the idea of earthquake resilience instead of resistance at an early stage. In 1907, *The Builder* imparted some critical information from the *Engineering reports on the San Francisco earthquake* of 1906, which were provided by the *American Society of Civil Engineers* and pointed towards the value of elasticity in a structure to respond to earthquake shocks.[124] And in 1921, Ōmori Fusakichi (1868–1923) provided the factual basis for the resolution of Dresser's and Conder's dispute. He sketched the historical development of the pagoda as a successive use of

---

120 Löffler, "Perpetual Other," p. 95.
121 Löffler, "Thwarted," pp. 44–46.
122 Ende and Böckmann, "Einwirkung des Erdbebens in Japan auf die dort hergestellten Massivbauten (1–2)," in: *Deutsche Bauzeitung* 65 (1894), p. 399; 80 (1894), pp. 499–500; "Japanische und deutsche Architekten," in: *Deutsche Bauzeitung* 14 (16 February 1895), pp. 84–85.
123 "The civil engineers are busy at Chicago … a steel-framed palace for the Crown Prince of Japan," in: *The Building News and Engineering Journal* 77 (24 November 1899), p. 715.
124 "Engineering reports on the San Francisco earthquake," in: *The Builder* 92 (1 June 1907), p. 656. For the full report, see "Report of Committee on Fire and Earthquake Damage to Buildings," in: *Proceedings of the American Society of Civil Engineers* 33 (1907), pp. 299–354, especially p. 325.

grounded, poised and, finally, hanging central pillars.[125] In doing so, he also deconstructed another western blind spot with regard to the Japanese building tradition: its classification as one of the 'non-historical styles', intrinsically incapable of development and thus needing to be replaced by modern solutions. We will take a closer look at this later in this chapter.

2.2 The Science and Economy of Construction

The fascinating dispute over the earthquake resistance or resilience of Japanese buildings obscured other factors that influenced engineering's stance towards Japanese construction, and that were mentioned briefly above in connection with Christopher Dresser: wood as a material for construction in general, the skeleton as fundamental construction principle, and the competence of the main actor, the carpenter. These elements were closely linked.

In terms of the use of wood as the main construction material for a building, western engineers and architects were of the same opinion: wood was understood as employable only as an auxiliary building material for roof structures, vernacular dwellings or outbuildings, and was utilised by craftsmen rather than by the scientifically trained modern engineer. In itself, wood was perceived as a building material of no consequence; but what of the skeleton structures of Japanese temples, pagodas, or houses?

In the course of the Industrial Revolution, iron had become an alternative material for some special constructions, as builders applied the structural principles familiar from wood to the new material. In addition to bridges, iron was initially used for technical infrastructures such as railway station halls, roofs for indoor markets or machine halls. The most decorative use was in conservatories and exhibition buildings, notably the *Crystal Palace* in London (1851) or the *Eiffel Tower* in Paris (1889).

However, despite the significant similarities in constructive approach between these projects and traditional Japanese techniques, none of the texts on Japanese architecture acknowledged any parallels. One is again left with the suspicion that this lack of interest was less a matter of oversight than of wilful ignorance due to fidelity to European norms. Next to a low appreciation of wood in general and scepticism with regard to Japanese construction principles, the social status of the actors involved and the concept of technological progress seem to have been significant factors as well. They refer back to the observations made above, in which it was suggested that Japanese carpenters

---

125   Omori, Fusakichi, "Measurement of Vibration of Gojunotos, or 5-Story Buddhist Stupas (Pagodas)," in: *Bulletin of the Imperial Earthquake Investigation Committee* 9.3 (1921), pp. 110–152. On Ōmori himself, see Clancey, *Earthquake*, especially pp. 177–179.

were regarded as just one group of craftsmen among many others and not equivalent to the architect in European tradition.

As the ultimate authority on a Japanese building site, however, the carpenter worked in a field of highly multivalent expertise and disciplinary delineations.

2.2.1   (Dis)Avowing the *Ars Mechanicae*: Carpenter or Engineer

The role of the traditional Japanese carpenter, the *daiku*, presented difficulty for late-nineteenth-century writers.[126] While the trade itself was often mentioned, any evaluation of its competencies remained mostly absent beyond the contexts of the artisan sketched above. The critical term 'scientific', however, which was used in some places, pointed towards a conceptional problem for western observers: how to rank the *daiku* as a professional within the realm of building? Or, more precisely, what defines an engineer?

Dresser had stated in his comments on pagodas that the "scientific method of keeping the pagoda upright"[127] demonstrated the careful thought and planning that went into Japanese building. Lowell, on the other hand, placed the Japanese artist in general on a pedestal of cultural and ethnic predestination since "his mental altitude (...) is artistic to perfection,"[128] but stressed the absence of any scientific competence. It was between these two positions that the evaluation of the carpenter as a building professional oscillated. While the actual term 'scientific' was rarely used, it is evident in the sources that some practices and procedures were perceived as appropriate for building and creating architecture in a progressive and scientific manner, and some were not.

Edward Morse expressed this when he mentioned the ability of the Japanese carpenter to successfully manage plans "drawn in ways new and strange to him"[129] and to produce objects of similar novelty. Thus he described the intellectual ability to go far beyond empirical experience alone, to reconcile abstract ideas with concrete action – as expected by academically trained western building experts – and saw the Japanese as able to act in this way.

Charles J. W. Pfoundes described the carpenters' education as a systematic application of empirical experience and inherited knowledge, including practical training, drawing instructions and generally available handbooks.[130] In addition, he addressed the hierarchy of professions:

---

126 For an extensive discussion of the term *daiku*, the overall profession and the situation during this time, see Clancey, *Earthquake*, pp. 11–12, 28–38 and in general the seminal study Coaldrake, *Carpenter*.
127 Dresser, *Japan*, p. 238.
128 Lowell, *Soul*, pp. 110–111.
129 Morse, *Homes*, p. 35.
130 Pfoundes, "Artisan," p. 540.

In Japan, the skilled workman is socially the superior of the trader, and the carpenter is foremost and the most important; in fact, he is called Dai-ku (great workman), and is architect, builder, and joiner; although for the minor branches there are special terms used, and the subdivision of labour is carried out to a greater extent than in other trades.[131]

This shows why it was difficult to classify the Japanese carpenter: while the systemic complexity of the profession was obvious, it also adhered closely to traditional practices along the lines of guilds and on-the-job training.[132] This was the background from which modern constructional competencies had grown for centuries, and it was still shaping technical education in the most technologically advanced country in the world, England.[133] Yet, it was perceived at this time as conceptually outdated by actors with academic pretensions. The disciplines in the field of engineering fought to rise from 'trades' to 'science', to distance themselves from being categorised as an *ars mechanicae,* ranking far below the traditional *artes liberales* or the recently evolved fine arts. They took institutional inspiration for a more systematised, 'scientific' education from the Higher Technical Schools (Technische Hochschulen) in Germany, for example.[134]

Consequently, the modernisation and academisation of building in Japan did not lead to further development of the competences derived from *daiku.* Building followed the emerging Euro-American concepts and became embedded into the newly founded Imperial College of Technology in Tōkyō under Principal Henry Dyer. He created a hybrid model put together from diverse existing approaches (which he suggested exporting back to England in 1880 as a means of advancing building education on home soil).[135] All of the students

---

131 Ibid., p. 540.
132 Extensively on the *daiku* in western perception in this time see Clancey, *Earthquake,* pp. 11–12, 28–38.
133 For an overview, see e.g. Kaiser, Walter; König, Wolfgang (eds.), *Geschichte des Ingenieurs. Ein Beruf in sechs Jahrtausenden* (München; Wien, 2006), in detail e.g. Allsobrook, David; Mitchell, Gordon, "Henry Dyer: Engineer and Educational Innovator," in: *Paedagogica Historica. International Journal of the History of Education* 33.2 (1997), pp. 433–457, here pp. 443–445.
134 Bartholomew, James, *The Formation of Science in Japan: Building a Research Tradition* (New Haven, 1989), p. 97.
135 Allsobrook, "Henry Dyer," pp. 442–445. Dyer, Henry, *The Education of Civil and Mechanical Engineers* (London, 1880). He sketched the situation in England and beyond in his report to the Japanese minister of public works, Ito Hirobumi (1841–1909), in 1877. Dyer, Henry (ed.), *Imperial College of Engineering (Kobu-dai-gakko) Tokei, Report by Principal and Professors, 1873–1877* ([Tōkyō,] 1877), pp. 4–20.

in the different fields of engineering shared basic classes in English, geography, mathematics, mechanics, physics, chemistry and drawing in their first two years, which were then followed by two years of specialist technical courses and two more years of practical instruction.[136] In addition, students completed internships in governmental institutions that advanced western technologies as practical training in the early stages of their education.[137] This applied to civil engineering as well as to (western) architecture, *zōka*.[138]

As a result, builders with construction tasks in Japan fell into two separate categories in terms of their profiles: those with a 'scientific' western education focused on the application of natural sciences, and those trained in the Japanese tradition of *daiku*, perpetuating and advancing established practices in a changing social context. This resonates with Conder's understanding of his vocation as expressed to the students that "an architect must be a man of culture";[139] it actually meant the emergence of two different types of 'men of culture' in Japanese building who came to shape different parts of Japan's architectural self-understanding.

The competences of the *daiku* survived primarily in religious architecture, heritage protection and housing albeit the shift in their development was significant and the profile changed over time when the field of carpentry integrated some western approaches. The professional profile, however, was never integrated into the debates concerning the profiles of construction experts but was overshadowed by the modern Japanese engineer over time. Similar phenomena apply when looking at materials and tools from an engineering perspective.

2.2.2   Tools, Practices and Material Management

The critics' observations of the Japanese building site in Philadelphia in 1876 were probably the first to bring the tools of Japanese building practices to a wider audience. Thompson Westcott noticed that the Japanese house was built "with curious tools and yet more curious manual processes. In fact, the whole work seemed to be executed upon exactly reverse methods of carpentering to those in use in this country."[140] He was not the only one to express his

---

136   Dyer, *Imperial College*, p. 27.
137   Ibid., pp. 22–24.
138   For detailed discussion of the curriculum of architecture programs, see e.g. Clancey, *Earthquake*, pp. 13–14.
139   Conder, "Remarks on architecture," p. 9.
140   Westcott, *Centennial portfolio*, p. 22.

wonderment. In 1877 an anonymous author likewise noted the differences, but primarily the competence and predicted that they "will, in fact, become formidable rivals of all kinds of Western manufactures."[141]

This uneasiness with regard to competition subsided as soon as modernisation began to have an impact on the competences and interests of Japanese artisans, most notably due to the reform of the educational system and changing economic imperatives. The tools, however, remained a topic of publication. While George Cawley was the only one to report on these more comprehensively,[142] information and/or illustration was provided by Christopher Dresser and Edward Morse as well as by a number of others such as Félix Régamey, the British artist Charles Geoffrey Holme (1887–1954), and the German railway engineer Franz Baltzer (1857–1927).[143] In many cases, the presentation of tools came with an elaboration on the different species of wood available in Japan and their respective applications.[144] Here, the discussion of the artistic or functional qualities of the material often segued into considerations of the economic importance of Japanese forestry.

This was a perspective taken not only by western observers, but also consciously exploited by the Japanese authorities. Many of the Japanese exhibitions at World's Fairs included the presentation of building material, including lists or samples of different varieties of wood.[145] The same was true of lithic materials. In 1876, the official Japanese catalogues referred both to the materials traditionally employed for plaster and other surface treatments, and to deposits of building stone such as granite or marble.[146]

Brick was another recurring topic as a building material used in Japan, but it was not a subject of closer examination in and of itself. In 1878, Cawley described the production of brick as newly imported to Japan – thus ignoring the country's long tradition in the manufacture of tiles – and saw a lack in

141 "Japanese Competition with England," p. 978.
142 Cawley, "Wood."
143 Régamey, Le Japon; Holme, Charles, Wood Carving According to the Japanese Method (London, 1899); Baltzer, Franz, Das Japanische Haus, eine bautechnische Studie (Berlin, 1903).
144 E.g. Exner, Wilhelm Franz, "Japans Holz-Industrie," in: Österreichische Monatsschrift für den Orient (1881), pp. 55–58, 82–85, 118–119. For a general overview that bridges the gaps in the sources presented here, see Coaldrake, Carpenter.
145 The catalogue for Vienna 1873 lists 169 samples of wood alone; see Catalog der kaiserlich japanischen Ausstellung (Wien, 1873), pp. 22–27. See also e.g. Commission impériale, Le Japon, 2, pp. 107–120.
146 Imperial Japanese Commission to the International Exhibition at Philadelphia, 1876, Official catalogue of the Japanese section, and descriptive notes on the industry and agriculture of Japan (Philadelphia, 1876), p. 45.

competence with regard to the firing process. This somewhat contradicts a short note in *The Building news and engineering journal* two years earlier that reported on a shortage in England remedied by importing a cargo of high-quality brick from Japan.[147] Even Josiah Conder blamed the mortar rather than the bricks for the damage done to western-style buildings by the earthquake of 1891.[148]

In summary, the field of engineering ignored Japan's structures and practitioners but for the issue of earthquake protection which was discussed by architects, not civil engineers. This contrasts with the strong parallels in wood construction between many Euro-American regions and Japan that would have invited exchange of experiences. Equating the Japanese *daiku* with the western carpenter, which did not do justice to the role of both in the overall process of building, allowed for the construction of a conceptual distinction between experience-based and academically trained practitioner and thus a hierarchy in interpretation sovereignty. Beyond that, Japan's native resources of potential building materials seemed interesting but not exciting to western observers. These materials were seen as sufficient to facilitate contemporary building practices, but they did not invite serious exploitation for trade or deeper analysis of their properties.

It might be worth considering as a further indicator of the general comprehensibility of Japanese building to the competent foreign observer, as already seen at the Philadelphia World's Fair. Thinking about this further, the non-integration of Japanese construction practices and practitioners into Euro-American knowledge systems was not a matter of conceptual incomprehension, but of deliberate exclusion, as we also already saw with the reading of architecture as an art.

3 Architecture as 'Social' Planning

Another reading of the term 'architecture' that has existed for centuries in western discourses extends far beyond the realms of fine art and engineering, with their specific interest in design and construction and individual buildings

---

147 "Japanese bricks, importation of," in: *The Building news and engineering journal* 30 (21 April 1876), p. 411.

148 Conder, Josiah, "An architect's notes on the great earthquake of October, 1891," in: *Seismological journal of Japan* 2 (1893), pp. 1–92.

or ensembles. Architecture can also be understood as the creation of a built social environment that manifests and reifies cosmological concepts, power relations, and political responsibilities, as well as ideas of education and welfare, for example.[149] Throughout history, the shifting of social and political contexts has repeatedly changed the framework of these realms of social responsibilities and created new challenges, new opportunities to apply architectural competence, and thus, not least, new ways to exercise social influence on public discussions and practices. Late nineteenth and early twentieth century discourses on Japan demonstrate how many means of addressing society and architecture are interlinked phenomena.

3.1 Urban Representation and Development

The older sources on the structure and features of Japanese cities had described sensibly-organised urban entities with comprehensible spatial configurations and conscious use of architectural representation.[150] This evaluation came under scrutiny when more and more westerners had the chance to form an opinion based on first-hand experience, primarily in Nagasaki or in Edo/Tōkyō.[151] While some of the early visitors confirmed the older sources, some came to new conclusions regarding Edo/Tōkyō and Japanese cities in general.

Heinrich Schliemann (1822–1890), German businessman and archaeologist, followed Kaempfer closely insofar as he provided facts and described what he saw without offering criticism or comments:[152]

---

149   During the twentieth century, the development of urban design and urban planning as independent fields of expertise removed some of this from the daily responsibilities of architectural planning. Yet the ideas remained part of the self-perception of an architect as a "rivale du créateur." Term quoted from Ledoux, Claude Nicolas, *L'Architecture considérée sous le rapport de l'art, des mœurs et de la législation, facsimile reproduction of the edition of 1804* (Nördlingen, 1987), p. 103.

150   See e.g. Kaempfer on Tōkyō in Kaempfer, *History of Japan*, 2, pp. 521–523.

151   One needs to keep in mind, however, that foreigners' movement remained formally restricted beyond the immediate surroundings of the few extraterritorial settlements. Exceptions were made for foreigners who had to travel in connection with their contract obligations, for health reasons or for the promotion of Japanese scholarship. Over time, however, this latitude made even extended tourism possible. Toyosawa, Nobuko, *The Cartography of Epistemology: The Production of "National" Space in Late 19th Century Japan* (Ph.D. diss., University of Illinois at Urbana-Champaign, 2008), pp. 143–146; Hockley, *Globetrotters', People*.

152   Other texts likewise adhere closely to Kaempfer's stance and were probably informed by his work, e.g. Foote, "Visit," pp. 129–137.

All the streets of Yedo are paved like the boulevards in Paris, and even the narrowest ones are no less than seven meters wide. In the business districts, the streets are at least 14 meters wide, while they are 20 to 40 meters wide in the districts of imperial palaces and palaces of the Japanese princes. (…) We passed through several of the numerous neighborhoods of the Daimios, whose palaces invariably lie in the middle of a huge, square courtyard whose length and width is between 300 and 600 meters. The courtyard is surrounded by a huge complex of two-storey wooden houses where the Daimios live with their families. But these sprawling buildings are not even enough to accommodate the entourage of these princes. Therefore, there are more apartments scattered throughout the courtyard. (…) Some of their palaces are made of stamped earth, the others only of lime-coated wood. But all are surrounded by more or less wide trenches, some also enclosed by high walls. There are more than 400 Daimios in Japan, all of which have one or more palaces in Yedo, and it is estimated that they occupy a third of the city.[153]

The information provided by an architectural journal at the time was similarly prosaic and focused on numbers and patterns. It listed "1,500,000 houses, inhabited by 6,000,000 souls."[154]

The extent of the city with its numerous and diverse inhabitants was the core topic of the accounts of Japanese cities, and was complemented by

---

153   "Alle Straßen von Yedo sind gepflastert wie die Boulevards in Paris, und selbst die schmalsten sind nicht weniger als sieben Meter breit. In den Geschäftsvierteln haben die Straßen eine Breite von mindestens 14 Meter, während sie im Bereich der kaiserlichen Paläste und der Paläste der japanischen Prinzen 20 bis 40 Meter breit sind. (…) Wir kamen durch mehrere der zahlreichen Viertel der Daimios, deren Paläste ausnahmslos mitten in einem riesigen, viereckigen Hof liegen, dessen Ausmaß in Länge und Breite 300 bis 600 Meter beträgt. Der Hof ist von einem mächtigen Gebäudekomplex aus zweistöckigen Holzhäusern, in denen die Daimios mit ihren Familien wohnen, umschlossen. Doch diese ausgedehnten Gebäude reichen nicht einmal aus, um das Gefolge dieser Fürsten aufzunehmen. Daher befinden sich über den ganzen Hof verstreut weitere Wohnungen. (…) Einige ihrer Paläste sind aus gestampfter Erde, die anderen nur aus mit Kalkmilch gestrichenem Holz. Aber alle sind von mehr oder weniger breiten Gräben umgeben, etliche außerdem von hohen Mauern eingeschlossen. Es gibt in Japan mehr als 400 Daimios, die alle einen oder mehrere Paläste in Yedo besitzen, und man schätzt, daß diese ein Drittel der Stadt einnehmen." Schliemann, Heinrich, *La Chine et le Japon au temps present* (Paris, 1867), translated from id., *Reise durch China und Japan im Jahre 1865* (Berlin, 1995), pp. 86–88.

154   "The largest city in the world …," in: *Building News and Architectural Review* 9 (5 September 1862), p. 187.

discussion of scenic features.[155] The central buildings, castles, palaces or temples were similarly embedded with reference to their position in the surrounding landscape, the width of the streets or moats surrounding them, the number of people employed, the means of transportation and so on. Within this frame, the appearance of the cities remained blurry, not least because the sights did usually not receive attention as structuring and meaningful parts of the urban environment, as mirrors of Japanese society.[156]

Rudolph Lindau (1829–1910), a German journalist and diplomat, provided similar numbers but additionally expressed aesthetic disappointment in his *Notes on the city of Yedo, the Capital of Japan*, 1864. He observed a well-ordered city but missed the "splendour and magnificence."[157] Lindau expected the importance of a nation to be expressed by an adequate spatial disposition and found the city lacking, since there were "no handsome shops, no grand establishments, no triumphal arches, no statues, no monuments"[158] to be found.

Josiah Conder told his students:

> History shows how any nation reaching a degree of civilization and power has sought to establish, dignify, and perpetuate its greatness, partly by the magnificence of its edifices. These monuments are looked upon as a part of the national wealth, dear as the soil on which they stand; and this in spite often of their unsuitability to modern requirements; and on the part of many people, of real want of Artistic appreciation.
>
> I do not lose sight of the fact that magnificence in building requires wealth, but it is wealth converted into the most solid enduring and repaying form; employing the people in some of the most intelligent industries, and thus at the same time educationally bettering a great part of the nation.[159]

---

155 See for example with regard to Shimoda: Heine, Wilhelm, *Reise um die Erde nach Japan an Bord der Expeditions-escadre unter Commodore M.C. Perry in den Jahren 1853, 1854 und 1855, unternommen im Auftrage der Regierung der Vereinigten Staaten* (Leipzig, 1856), 2, pp. 31–32.

156 With regard to Edo/Tōkyō, this might be due to the absence of the city's former landmark, the enormous main keep of the castle, which burned down in the seventeenth century and was never replaced. See e.g. Coaldrake, *Architecture*, pp. 129–137. Thomas McClatchie described the castle of Edo and the residences of the *daimyō* as disappearing phenomena of a bygone era. McClatchie, *Castle*; id., "Mansion."

157 Lindau, Rudolph, "Notes on the city of Yedo, the Capital of Japan," in: *Journal of the North China Branch of the Royal Asiatic* 1–2 (1864–1865), pp. 1–12, here p. 11.

158 Lindau, "Notes," p. 10.

159 Conder, "Remarks on architecture," pp. 3–4.

FIGURES 3.15–3.16   Entrance to the British Legation at Takanawa Tōzen-ji in Edo (Tōkyō); Felice Beato: buildings of the Tōzen-ji, 1860s

Conder contextualised the significant monuments within an overall system of the ideal reification of society: without the buildings, the city is not really there, it lacks meaning, it does not represent its cultural environment adequately. In turn, the creation of such built spaces involved society in a meaningful way and perpetuated a sense of belonging.

Meiji modernisation set out to remedy this absence of a system of urban representation which foreign visitors would have taken as a mirror of social order. On the one hand, the social reforms created administrative and governmental institutions, giving rise to public and private entities that demanded workspaces. On the other hand, the conversion of the built environment in accordance with western expectations was part of the programme of political and technological modernisation. Yet, for a number of years, social change was only occasionally made manifest in new buildings.

Rather, existing spaces were used at first: thus the western diplomatic missions re-used temple buildings during their first years in Edo, while institutions such as the Ministry of Foreign Affairs moved onto the grounds of the former *sankin kōtai* residences of the *daimyō*, which had lost their function in the course of the political change (Figs. 3.15 and 3.16).[160] While this was by

---

160   See Meid, *Einführungsprozeß*, p. 207. The policy of *sankin kōtai*, alternate attendance, had required all *daimyō* to alternate between Edo and their domain in equal measure. They

far the most momentous shift in the use of urban real estate in Edo/Tōkyō, it also occurred in other castle towns throughout the country, as the Edo period's structures of loyalty and dependence became obsolete.[161]

While the institutions eventually requested suitable buildings, this development did not have an immediate significant impact on the urban environment. This was probably not least because there were hardly any historical role models, either socially or architecturally, as the German art historian Justus Brinckmann (1843–1915) mused in the early 1880s:

> Old Japan knew as little of buildings for charitable purposes, or of assembly houses for the nobility, the citizenry or commercial guilds as it did of courthouses, hospitals, academies or public galleries or museums, there being no room or need for these in its culture. The family house is the be-all and end-all of Japan's profane architecture.[162]

The creation of modern buildings for governmental and other public functions as well as for the parallel development of infrastructural and entrepreneurial uses was one of the main tasks of the contracted foreign experts. Over time, their efforts became visible in visual media, most notably in depictions of Ginza. The Ginza area, part of the commoners' quarters east of the castle, had burned down in 1872. It was replaced by solid constructions of brick, often with neo-classical façades. The resulting novelty and modernity of the area made Ginza the symbol of modern Tōkyō for decades to come, with the first images dating from 1873.[163]

Beyond that, there were very few reports in specialist journals. The issue of urban reorganisation was addressed in only a single note on the general

---

were obliged to maintain representative residence(s) in the city in which their families and retainers remained during the lord's absence. Cybriwsky, Roman, *Tokyo. The changing Profile of an Urban Giant* (London, 1991), p. 54; Beasley, William G., *The Meiji restoration* (Stanford, 1972), p. 16; Sorensen, *Urban Japan*, pp. 16–18.

161 Gutschow, *Burgstadt*. For more detail see: Hein, Carola, "Shaping Tokyo: Land Development and Planning. Practice in the Early Modern Japanese Metropolis, in: *Journal of Urban History* 36.4 (2010), pp. 447–484.

162 "Bauten für gemeinnützige Zwecke, Versammlungshäuser des Adels, der Bürgerschaft oder gewerblicher Innungen kannte Alt-Japan ebenso wenig, wie in seiner Cultur für Gerichtshäuser, für Hospitäler, Akademien oder öffentliche Sammlungen Raum und Bedürfniß war. Das Familienhaus ist das Ein und Alles seiner profanen Baukunst." Brinckmann, Justus, *Kunst und Handwerk in Japan* (Berlin, 1889), p. 51.

163 Seidensticker, Edward, *Low City, High City. Tokyo from Edo to the Earthquake. How the Shogun's Ancient Capital Became a Great Modern City. 1867–1923* (New York, 1983), pp. 58–59; see also Brunton, "Constructive (2)," pp. 23–24.

topic of urban structure. It mentioned the recently established city of Sapporo, Hokkaidō, as one of several failed or overpriced projects aimed at infrastructural development:

> The town has been laid out with a view to its future importance, and contains a Government house, several Japanese hotels, a number of houses of superior construction, for the use of Japanese officers, and still better houses for the gentlemen of the American mission. The streets of the town are broad and well made, and there are a hospital and other edifices of a public character.[164]

This city's layout and architectural furnishing apparently fulfilled the expectations of a western observer. Its grid was created by amalgamating concepts from China, customarily employed in Japan's imperial residences such as Nara and Kyōto, and contemporary American ideas.[165]

Beyond this, glimpses into the development of Japan's cities and the application of western models of urban representation remained scarce until the end of the nineteenth century. They were afforded by only a handful of projects presented in the relevant journals: two projects by Josiah Conder in 1883 and 1884, and the designs by Böckmann & Ende for the houses of parliament and a number of ministries. All of the projects strove to transplant accepted western models of spatial organisation and the use of materials and ornamentation to Japan, and were encouraged by a Japanese government that rejected 'Japanising' proposals.[166]

To summarise, although the western experts agreed that Japanese cities needed reorganisation, they discussed neither the means nor models or methods to achieve this. It was therefore not the specialist literature that made the

---

164 "How They Manage Things in Japan," in: *The Builder* 32 (1874), p. 65.
165 Schwind, Martin, "Sapporo," in: Hammitzsch, Horst (ed.), *Japan-Handbuch. Land und Leute, Kultur und Geistesleben*, 3rd ed. (Stuttgart, 1990), cols. 238–241; id., "Siedlungsformen," in: Hammitzsch, Horst (ed.), *Japan-Handbuch. Land und Leute, Kultur und Geistesleben*, 3rd ed. (Stuttgart, 1990), cols. 244–251, here col. 251.
166 "Sale and reception rooms, kaitakushi, Tokyo," in: *The Building News and Engineering Journal* 45 (30 November 1883), p. 848; "Tokyo university, Japan," in: *The Builder* 47 (13 December 1884), p. 790; "Deutsche Baukunst in Japan," in: *Deutsche Bauzeitung* (19 February 1887), p. 92; "The Imperial law courts, Tokio," in: *The Builder* 64 (15 March 1893), p. 288 and plates; "Design for new Houses of Parliament, Tokio, Japan," in: *The Builder* 66 (13 January 1894), p. 260 and plates. – On the overall issue, see Finn, *Meiji* and in particular the project for Tōkyō Central Station.

processes of urban restructuring and the negotiation of the 'modern Japanese city' visible to European observers, but the popular media: in addition to Japanese woodblock prints depicting the urban changes that made it into European collections, the newly built environment was repeatedly addressed in travelogues. Here, the results of modernisation were discussed in widely varying ways, including the 'need' to rebuild Japan towards civilisation, on the one hand, and the steady loss of the 'real Japan' on the other. We will look at this in detail below.

3.2 The City as a Mirror of Social Order

A common characteristic of western accounts of Japanese cities at this time was the absence of reports on discord or social upheaval among residents, with the exception of references to the civil-war-like confrontations that were stoked by modernisation in general and the occasional attacks on foreigners in the early years.[167] Writers often commented on escorts and restrictions and addressed security issues,[168] but they never linked these to the overall populace or social instabilities, even though historians recorded such instabilities and Japanese newspapers reported them as well.

In his study *The Streets and Street-Names of Yedo*, William E. Griffis referred to the Japanese system of political supervision, *gonin-gumi*, and the new police force, and concluded:

> We hazard the belief that there is no other city in the world in which the public peace and order are better kept, or in which the safety of the inhabitants is better secured.[169]

In many of the commentaries, this kind of assessment was accompanied by a certain assumption: that the social order was being undermined by the ongoing modernisation process. French diplomat Charles de Chassiron (1818–1871) commented at the end of his report on Japan:

---

167 In 1861 a member of the American Legation, Hendrick Heusken (1832–1861), died after an ambush. See Hesselink, Reinier H., "The Assassination of Henry Heusken," in: *Monumenta Nipponica* 49.3 (Autumn 1994), pp. 331–351. The information on the two Tōzen-ji Incidents (British Legation) at about the same time varies with respect to the dates and the victims involved. .

168 E.g. Chassiron, Charles de, *Notes sur le Japon, la Chine et l'Inde 1858–1859–1860* (Paris, 1861), p. 17.

169 Griffis, William Elliot, "The Streets and Street-Names of Yedo," in: *Transactions of the Asiatic Society of Japan* I [1874] (reprint 1882), pp. 18–26, here p. 25.

In short, the Japanese people (…) are intelligent, gentle, and industrious; they are above all disciplined: Thus I express my sincere wish, which, I admit, is not free from doubts and regrets, that the civilization of the West, in bringing to them its enlightenment and its progress, in introducing to them enjoyments and giving to them appetites which they have not previously known, does not defile, should it fail to destroy them completely, the native and essential qualities, useful to their social equilibrium as much as to their inner repose, which it is at present impossible to overlook in them.[170]

Interestingly enough, these observations did not resonate any further in the literature. Among the many topics that arose in the context of architecture, this is the sole case in which the Japanese situation was reported but neither contextualised nor used as an educational example. The western sources contained neither suggestions to the Europeans or to the Japanese themselves for the reorganisation of Japanese cities in order to further enhance or to stabilise control, nor did they put forward any paternalistic development projects or initiatives in the context of efforts towards social reform, even in the face of the impending changes to society. This is noteworthy against the background of contemporary discourses and developments in Europe, which frequently addressed the side-effects of urbanisation. The important cities of the West were in the midst of extensive material and social reconstruction in the context of ongoing technological and economic development. The concentration of the population in working-class districts and the concurrent reordering of the socio-cultural environment due to domestic migration challenged the competences of politicians, philanthropists and planners. There was only one subtopic of this larger discourse that attracted wider interest due to its interlinked reading of society, morals and the built environment: hygiene.

3.2.1   Sewage Systems and Hygiene as a Technical and Social Issue
Within the western discourses that related to architecture, Japanese cities received attention above all in connection with the health conditions of the

---

[170] "En résumé, le peuple japonais (…) est intelligent, doux et industrieux ; il est surtout discipliné : aussi fais-je des vœux sincères, qui, je l'avoue, ne sont pas exempts de doutes et de regrets, pour que la civilisation de l'Occident, en lui apportant ses lumières et ses progrès, en l'initiant à des jouissances et eu lui donnant des appétits qu'il a ignorés jusqu'à présent, ne déflore pas, si elle n'arrive pas à les faire entièrement disparaître, les qualités natives et essentielles, utiles à son équilibre social autant qu'à son repos intérieur, que, dans l'état actuel, il est impossible de méconnaître chez lui." Chassiron, "Notes," pp. 17–18.

populace, with the prevention of diseases and epidemics, and most notably with the social practices of hygiene. Hygiene encompassed many different phenomena, including heating and ventilation methods for dwellings, the drinking water supply, toilets, and sewage disposal, and was addressed by various authors across all of the available text-based media, from travelogues to papers by experts in specialist journals. As with many other topics, this issue had already been mentioned by Kaempfer – not at all surprising considering that he was a physician – but in such a casual way that it was of no specific significance. He regarded the Japanese dwelling as superior to the European through its use of wood and the easy means of ventilation.[171]

Quite aside from Kaempfer's influence, hygiene was a common topic in the sources of the latter half of the nineteenth century. A good number of the travelogues and accounts on the built environment in Japan contained statements such as those formulated by the German artist Wilhelm Heine (1827–1885), who gave a summary of practices related to hygiene in 1856 already and linked the cleanliness of the city to its residents' individual conduct:

> Within the houses as well as on the streets, great cleanliness prevails, and the latter are even swept at least once a day, just as the residents bathe every day. The better-off have the bath in their homes, the poorer use public baths.[172]

Nearly three decades later, Johann Justus Rein commented on the issue from a primarily social angle, framing it as one of the features pervading Japanese culture.[173] However, these observations raised difficult issues when it came to social or institutional responsibilities for health care. Not the least of these concerned the challenge that Japanese practices of bathing presented to the morals of many western observers. Rein struggled with this problem:

> The unconcern with which the female members of the household use the bath in view of the men and of passers-by has caused many a European no little astonishment.

---

171 Kaempfer, *History*, 2, p. 412. Slightly changed 'quoted' by Hildreth, *Japan*, pp. 296–297.
172 "In den Häusern wie auf den Straßen herrschte eine große Reinlichkeit und selbst letztere werden alltäglich wenigstens einmal gefegt; eben so pflegen die Bewohner alltäglich zu baden. Wohlhabendere haben das Bad im Hause, Ärmere besuchen öffentliche Badeanstalten (...)." Heine, *Reise*, 2, p. 33.
173 Rein, *Travels*, p. 411.

> There are many public bath-houses for the people in every town. (...) Formerly both sexes bathed together without any concern, they are now separated by a plank partition barely one and a half metres high.[174]

Rein's uneasiness resonated with a European normative understanding of hygiene that was comparatively new in this form and not coherent in itself. It fused elements of the Christian tradition and social conduct, which included a guarded attitude towards physicality and sexuality, with an enlightened understanding of the links between sewage disposal and bodily cleanliness, while incorporating health care and disease prevention. This connected hygiene, especially bodily cleanliness, somewhat haphazardly with technological innovation and civilisation, as well as with paternalistic concepts of national education and morality.[175] The Japanese situation violated the European understanding of cause and effect, in which education and morality were seen as foundations for hygienic behaviour. Thus, Rein was unable to find a neat categorisation: his patterns of interpretation did not fit the case. Consequently, his argument was no longer consistent when he tried to come to a clear interpretation and evaluation of the observed customs:

> The Japanese, though on the whole he does not stand upon a high level of morality, did not upon such occasions indulge himself in anything that was unseemly even according to our ideas. It was only contact with Europeans that opened his eyes, and put an end to this paradisiacal simplicity. (...) Bashfulness is undoubtedly a product of social life and civilization, as was pointed out long ago by Rousseau. It is no criterion of morality, appears in different forms, and varies with the education of mankind and with the climate in which they have to live.[176]

Rein was not the only one to fall back on theories of culture and civilisation in his search for an acceptable interpretation. Some declared Japan's hygienic practices to be expressions of untainted and 'natural' moral behaviour, to be 'pre-civilised', so to speak. In other cases, those same practices were seen as just one of many intrinsic features of an 'inscrutable Japanese culture'.[177]

---

174 Ibid., p. 412.
175 Löffler, "Petrified worldviews."
176 Rein, *Travels*, p. 413.
177 Seymour, John Nicholson, "Abstract of a Lecture on the Hygienic Aspects of Japanese Dwelling-houses," in: *Transactions of the Asiatic Society of Japan XVII*, 2 (1889), pp. XVII–XXI, here p. XIX.

The background for the general interest in this issue was the critical situation in Europe. The rapid urbanisation of the leading western cities and many of the industrial hotspots had led to a dire threat of epidemics due to a lack of sufficient sanitation. A key event in this regard was the Great Stink in London in 1858, which finally triggered extensive reconstruction of the urban sewer system. Similarly, well-known urban redevelopment projects such as Georges-Eugène Haussmann's renovation of Paris from 1853–1870, or James Hobrecht's *Radialsystem* for Berlin, implemented 1873–1890, both of which addressed health risks among other issues, were still in their planning stages or were just beginning to be realised as this discussion commenced.[178]

These European undertakings explain not only the general interest, but also why the discourse on Japanese hygiene failed to move beyond simple observation and contextualisation. Western developments proceeded within a system of values in which the sophistication of technological infrastructure had become a self-evident indicator of a progressive society and promises of innovation and improvement were vigorous. Expectations for social progress saw the alleviation of poverty and disease as well as the raising of the morality of the lower classes as inevitable by-products of further industrialisation, controlled planning and education. The non-technological example of Japan contradicted this concept of directed progress. Yet the case of Japan, with its all-encompassing discipline with respect to social conduct, was a helpful model argument for social education in Europe.[179]

Interestingly enough, the topic remained visible in the sources at least until the end of the century. Edward Morse dedicated a number of pages in *Japanese Homes* to the culture of bathing and morals, and to Japanese practices and even the socio-cultural conditions of the privy.[180] American painter and writer John La Farge (1835–1910) reported his experiences in Japan in a series of essays for *The Century Magazine* and in an anthology in 1897. There are strong similarities

---

178 For an introduction to this issue, see for example Mumford, Lewis, *The City in History. Its Origins, its Transformations, and its Prospect*, 3rd ed. (London, 1966), especially chapter 15, "Paleotechnic Paradise: Coketown," pp. 446–481.

179 There were many cases of paternalistic intervention in the fields of architecture and urban planning, such as Robert Owen's settlement of New Lanark in the 1810s/1820s, or the much later settlement of Hellerau (Dresden) by Karl Schmidt, 1909. See Elsässer, Markus, *Soziale Intentionen und Reformen des Robert Owen in der Frühzeit der Industrialisierung: Analyse seines Wirkens als Unternehmer, Sozialreformer, Genossenschafter, Frühsozialist, Erzieher u. Wissenschaftler* (Berlin, 1984), pp. 124–126. On the educational ideas behind the settlement at Hellerau, see Dohrn, Wolf, *Die Gartenstadt Hellerau und weitere Schriften* (Dresden, 1992).

180 Morse, *Homes*, pp. 199–209, 231–233.

to Heine or Rein, when he noted that "(e)verything was of the cleanest – wall, floor, stairs, tables; everything was dusted, wiped, rubbed, polished."[181]

La Farge described both his own bathing preferences and his observations of a neighbouring Japanese family sharing the bath and linked the latter back to concepts of propriety and morals.[182] Again, the cultural dimension of Japanese practices served as a means of interpretation and contextualisation, and presented hygiene as likely the most lasting of all of Japan's cultural traits. Basil H. Chamberlain canonised hygiene as specifically Japanese in his standard reference *Things Japanese*:

> Cleanliness is one of the few original items of Japanese civilisation. (…) They are clean for the personal satisfaction of being clean.[183]

While he pointed to traditional Shintō practices of cleansing, to the different facilities involved, and to the role of hot baths for keeping warm, Chamberlain did not reflect any further on his observations.[184]

There is, however, another reference to this issue in his book, one which leads us into a new context in which the Japanese house did become a (small) matter of interest. After lamenting the features of the Japanese dwelling, Chamberlain concluded:

> Two things, chiefly, are to be said on the other side. First, these houses are cheap – an essential point in a poor country. Secondly, the people who live in them do not share our European ideas with regard to comfort and discomfort. … Furthermore, the physicians who have studied Japanese dwelling-houses from the point of view of hygiene, give them a clean bill of health.[185]

Having noted that the cultural dimension was a recurring topic and having covered the issue of hygiene, it is now possible to give the matter of economy closer attention.

---

181   La Farge, John, *An Artist's letters from Japan* (New York, 1897), p. 34. – A series of essays in *The Century Magazine* 39–46, later collected in a single volume.
182   La Farge, *Letters*, p. 35.
183   Chamberlain, Basil H., "Bathing," in: id., *Things Japanese. Being Notes on Various Subjects Connected with Japan* (London, 1890), pp. 43–45, here p. 43.
184   Chamberlain, "Bathing," pp. 43–45.
185   Chamberlain, "Architecture," p. 26.

3.2.2 Wooden Construction as a Socioeconomic Option

Basil H. Chamberlain was neither the first nor the only author to mention the economic advantages of the Japanese dwelling. Austrian diplomat Alexander Graf von Hübner (1811–1892) observed during his stay in Japan in 1871:

> It is the most primitive construction possible, and at the same time the most suited to the climate, and to the financial position of the nation. It resists earthquakes and typhoons infinitely better than the stone houses of the Europeans. It is more exposed to the danger of fire; but even if injured or destroyed by fire, wind, or the earth's convulsions, the evil is remedied both promptly and easily.[186]

While Hübner did not perceive these buildings as architecture and said so explicitly before and after the quote, he appreciated the pragmatic application of the material. Charles Pfoundes did so as well and mused over the use of Japanese housing concepts for colonial settlements and military quarters. "The readiness with which they can be erected, taken down, and removed, would be a strong point in their favour under some circumstances."[187]

Pfoundes was the first to explicitly characterise the Japanese house as a functional system of construction, as a building kit.[188] However, while this modular structure was addressed occasionally, it was primarily set against the background of Japan's supposed poverty, on the one hand, and the danger of fire on the other. Edward Morse addressed all three issues and urged his readers to take a Japanese viewpoint and to understand the house as affordable and suited to the actual needs instead of applying Western norms. He argued the easy and fast dismantling of dwellings and the demolition practices of the fire brigades be recognised as substitutes for unaffordable fire-proof building.[189]

The danger of conflagration was often mentioned in the western texts on Japanese building in general but was never discussed in detail.[190] This might

---

186   Hübner, Alexander Baron, *A ramble around the world, 1871* (New York, 1874), pp. 380–381.
187   Pfoundes, "Constructive art," p. 1306.
188   This technological and non-local understanding, which became of such a high relevance for housing discourses in Germany during the 1920s, remained particular to the sources of the time.
189   Morse, *Homes*, pp. 10–13. See similarly Scidmore, *Jinrikisha*, p. 59.
190   Beyond the references in travelogues, such as Dresser, *Japan*, pp. 19–20, see "Brandschutzgesetze in Japan," in: *Deutsche Bauzeitung* (1869), p. 136; "Prevention of fire," in: *The Building news and engineering journal* 16 (12 February 1869), p. 147; "Primitive Fireproof Buildings," in: *Architect and Building News* 2 (1877), p. 72; "The Fire Laws of Japan," in: *The American Architect and Building News* 7 (1880), p. 86; "The Last Great Fire in Japan,"

have been due to the equally extensive western experience with this problem throughout history, a problem which had by no means been solved at this time, as Morse pointed out as well. It might also have been due to the expectation that the danger could be reduced in the long run by the use of solid constructions, or else due to an assumption of Japan's supposed poverty.[191]

This latter issue is in fact an interesting perception, since it comes without specific context. In the sources consulted here, the term "poor" was usually used to denote a specific lack of competence with respect to architecture,[192] or to refer to the lower parts of society.[193] The summary description of Japan and the Japanese as poor is made without providing a point of reference, or at least an obvious one. Considering the observations of the previous chapters, however, the unspoken and/or assumed reference is evidently the West. The comparison is made on the basis of a normative understanding of civilisation and the prosperity of a European upper-middle-class environment, with solid and decorated houses, furniture, ball gowns, household goods, technical infrastructures and so on. The impossibility of seeing these western norms reflected in the social codes of status and wealth in Japan, together with the sense of superiority of the visitors, rendered practically all Japanese buildings poor, no matter how much artistry and expense was involved.[194]

Morse confirmed this assumption implicitly in his efforts to explain the living standard embodied in the Japanese house. Following a description of the house of a well-to-do owner of his own acquaintance, for which he gave the value of land, house building and taxes, he sketched the context for more modest housing and juxtaposed values attributed to housing conditions:

---

in: *The American Architect and Building News* 7 (1880), p. 146; "The Fireman's Journal," in: *Architect and Building News* 12 (1882), p. 166.

[191] On the Japanese side, the laws regulating the use of roof tiles are a prime example of attempts to address this issue satisfactorily. While helpful in protecting houses from flying sparks, for example, the tiles were costly and were usually used as a status symbol. Thus the legislative action was inconsistent in this respect. Coaldrake, William H., "Edo Architecture and Tokugawa Law," in: *Monumenta Nipponica* 36.3 (Fall 1981), pp. 235–284, here 253–261.

[192] E.g. "That they [, the Japanese,] should be poor, therefore, in architectural work may be only a natural consequence of living in a land of volcanoes and earthquakes." Alcock, p. 16.

[193] E.g. "These New Year devices vary, however, in character, but even the poorest of the people seem to crave after a piece of bamboo and of fir, be it ever so small, as eagerly as our poor look for a spray of holly and a bit of mistletoe at Christmas." Dresser, *Japan*, p. 34.

[194] This is one reason why buildings such as Katsura Rikyū in Kyōto were and still are perceived as very modest in western eyes.

A comfortable house, fit for the habitation of a family of four or five, may be built for a far less sum of money, and the fewness and cheapness of the articles necessary to furnish it surpass belief. In mentioning such a modest house and furnishing, the reader must not imagine that the family are constrained for want of room, or stinted in the necessary furniture; on the contrary, they are enabled to live in the most comfortable manner. Their wants are few, and their tastes are simple and refined. They live without the slightest ostentation; no false display leads them into criminal debt. The monstrous bills for carpets, curtains, furniture, silver, dishes, etc., often entailed by young house-keepers at home in any attempt at house-keeping, the premonition even of such bills often preventing marriage, are social miseries that the Japanese happily know but little about.[195]

In Morse's argumentation and this sub-chapter in general, the Japanese house played a role as a setting in which to discuss wealth and social representation within western rules and expectations. The house was seen as a material representation of a specific society and its values and norms. Thus, while Morse indicated the variety of spatial solutions available to a Japanese house owner, he did not provide examples of these for his readers. Nor did he actually explain the consequences of specific arrangements or interiors. In a way, the Japanese dwelling remained an abstract phenomenon, one that was described and occasionally depicted, but too shallowly to provide an idea of the house itself or the spatial logics (and logistics) of the life within.

Interestingly, the texts discussed the interdependency of the city and its public buildings but ignored the role of the dwelling in shaping public space.[196] However, there is still one concept of architecture still to be considered: the most general understanding of architecture as a cultural expression. Here, the relation to our topic of architecture is less obvious. Yet, it shows the ways in which tightly interwoven threads of cultural discourses embedded Japanese architecture into western knowledge systems.

---

195 Morse, *Homes*, pp. 114–115.
196 Shiga Shigetsura (1866–1936) discussed this in a series of articles in *kenchiku zasshi* in 1903 and his master thesis in architecture at the University of Illinois in 1905. Shiga, Shigetsura, "Jūka (kairyō no hōshin ni tsuite)," in: *kenchiku zasshi* 194, 196, 199, 201, 202 (February to October 1903); Shiga, Shigetsura, *Future development of Japanese dwelling houses* (unpublished thesis, University of Illinois, 1905).

4 Architecture as an Expression of Culture: Observing the Other, Defining the Self

The broadest reading of architecture does not attribute it any special significance, but instead regards it as just one among many different expressions of human life, along with customs and rites, foods and fashions, religion and language. This perspective already appeared in the sub-chapter on art, where various writers such as Louis Gonse and Basil H. Chamberlain drew connections between cultural or ethnic characteristics and artistic expression; it can also be seen in various writers' comments on hygiene and morals.

To a certain degree, it has a levelling effect on the different types of buildings and the urban environment: it is not so much the expense invested or the form chosen that makes a place or building worthy of study, but its role as part of a larger social interaction. This might still result in greater attention being paid to a place of worship or ruling power, but it means that markets, bridges and dwellings also play a vital role and are indeed indispensable to the overall picture. In consequence, spatial or architectural features are no longer discrete or self-referential in the way we saw discussed above, but become signifiers and representations of meaning in a broader context.

Travelogues and ethnographical reports contain many passages in this vein, but they are usually vague and scattered throughout the chapters. This issue, together with the patterns of description and argumentation, can be demonstrated by examining a single reference written by Hermann Maron (1820–1882), a member of the Prussian diplomatic mission to Japan – the Eulenburg expedition – between 1859 and 1862. This agricultural expert and journalist published his condensed observations, comprising fewer than 40 pages, in a national liberal journal in 1861. Maron's handling of his experience of Japan's otherness is unusual in its bluntness, and is much closer to the expert evaluations we saw earlier than to the general narrations of travelogues and ethnographical reports.

The article, entitled *Zur Charakteristik Japan's*, opened with a disclaimer in which Maron confessed to a lack of special competence due to his inability to understand the Japanese language. He referred back to Kaempfer and Thunberg, arguing for an extended stay in the country as the necessary basis for proper study and analysis, and dismissed all of the recently published books on Japan. He thus understood his own contribution as merely updating the work of Kaempfer and Thunberg and complementing it with some additional facts.

THE INVISIBLE DWELLING HOUSE 137

Maron started with the landscape and observed:

> The character of the land is peculiar, and it is difficult to pin it down. (...) It is not the magnificent, overwhelming beauty of the Alpine world, not the rugged, rocky nature of the Norwegian mountains or Abruzzo; nor is it remotely like an English or Scottish hill landscape with its green meadows and gentle slopes, and there is nothing in it of the romantic charm of the Rhine Valley. Mountains and valleys alternate continuously, but one mountain looks like the other, one valley like the next; they stand immediately next to one another; there is a lack of lush green meadows, of gentle slopes, of grazing herds; there is a lack of picturesque villages with slender towers, a lack of songbirds in the trees, a lack of scent to the flowers. What remains is nice enough, to be sure; it therefore takes a long time to realise that something is missing; and once one has noticed it, one seeks long in vain before finding what it consists of.[197]

He postulated causal links between landscape, society and general mindset and deduced his evaluation of the cultural condition of the Japanese from this point of view.[198] It is a conceptual link that is often discernible in the sources of this time, but one that leaves today's reader with considerable uneasiness due

---

[197] "Der Charakter des Landes ist eigenthümlich, und es ist schwer, ihn zu bestimmen. (...) Es ist nicht die großartige, überwältigende Schönheit der Alpenwelt, nicht der schroffe, felsig zerklüftete Charakter der norwegischen Gebirge oder der Abruzzen; es ist auch nicht entfernt einer englischen oder schottischen Hügellandschaft ähnlich mit ihren grünen Wiesen und sanften Abhängen, und es ist nichts darin von dem romantischen Zauber einer Rheinlandschaft. Berg und Thal wechseln ununterbrochen ab; aber ein Berg sieht aus wie der andere, ein Thal wie das andere; sie liegen unvermittelt nebeneinander; es fehlen die saftig grünen Wiesen, es fehlen die sanften Abhänge, die weidenden Herden, es fehlen die malerisch gelegenen Dörfer mit schlanken Thürmen, es fehlen die Singvögel in den Bäumen, es fehlt der Duft in den Blumen. Was bleibt, ist immerhin schön genug; es dauert daher eine geraume Zeit, ehe man überhaupt bemerkt, daß etwas fehlt; und wenn man es bemerkt hat, sucht man lange vergebens, ehe man findet, worin es besteht." Maron, Hermann, "Zur Charakteristik Japan's. Shanghai 18. Feb.," in: *Die Grenzboten* 20, 1, 2 (1861), pp. 265–276, here pp. 265–266.

[198] Maron, "Charakteristik Shanghai," pp. 266–267. – Later in his text, Maron arrived at a very friendly appreciation of Japanese culture, not least in comparison to China. In keeping with his Darwinist ideas, he therefore dismissed the idea of a racial relationship between the inhabitants of the two regions, but accepted the obvious impact of Chinese culture on Japan's development. Maron, Hermann, "Nachtrag zu „Charakteristik Japans" Nagasaki 7. Mai," in: *Die Grenzboten* 20, II, 3 (1861), pp. 195–199, here pp. 195–197.

to the historical consequences of some of these lines of thought throughout twentieth century, when difference often became framed as an otherness used for exclusion by culture, race or gender.

Maron's descriptions of the man-made environment likewise resonated with his understanding of Japan's social conditions:

> A peculiar spirit of calm lies over the landscape; but it is not dormant life, it is life extinguished or not yet awakened; in any case, a dark spell holds it captive. No chimney sends clouds of blue smoke in rings upward from the home fire's open hearth; the fire does not blaze here, it only glows in the form of coal in a closed cage. No heavy forge drives the steam hammer or the mill wheel, no train pulls across the plain, no lightship along the river.[199]

He went on to address the Japanese city:

> None of the sound and hubbub of the Old World. No coaches thundering over the stone pavement, no raging crowd, no dance music, no fighting, not even an angry word reaches your ear. In the open shops, half in the street, groups squat around the ever-present brazier; they smoke or they write in their books. (...) Who would seriously consider objecting to the uniformity of this way of life! However, the ideal is divine, but that is why it is not entirely human. (...) In this calm and the smooth pervasiveness of this way of life, there is something peculiar and inexplicable and thus almost uncanny.[200]

---

[199] "Ein eigener Geist der Ruhe liegt über der Landschaft; aber es ist nicht ruhendes Leben, es ist verlöschtes oder noch nicht erwachtes; jedenfalls hält ein dunkler Zauber es gefangen. Kein Schornstein sendet in Wolkenringen den blauen Rauch vom heimischen offenen Herde aufwärts; das Feuer lodert hier nicht, es glüht nur in der Form von Kohle in geschlossenem Käfig. Keine hohe Schmiedeesse treibt den Dampfhammer oder das Mühlrad, kein Eisenbahnzug braust über die Ebene dahin, kein Feuerschiff den Strom entlang." Maron, "Charakteristik Shanghai," p. 267.

[200] "Nichts von dem Geräusch und Lärm der alten Welt. Keine Karossen, die über das Steinpflaster dahin donnern, keine tobende Menschenmenge, keine Tanzmusik, keine Prügelei, nicht einmal ein zorniges Wort dringt zu deinem Ohr. In den offenen Läden, halb auf der Straße, hocken Gruppen um das nie fehlende Kohlenbecken; sie rauchen oder sie schreiben in ihren Büchern. [...] Wer wollte ernstlich einen Einwand erheben gegen diese Gleichmäßigkeit der Gesittung! Indessen – das Ideale ist zwar göttlich, aber eben darum ist es nicht ganz menschlich. [...] In dieser Stille und ununterbrochenen glatten Gesittung liegt etwas Eigenthümliches und Unerklärliches und darum fast

In Maron's observations, the dwelling was similarly linked with an understanding of a specific Japaneseness of culture as manifested in landscape and city. He discussed it only in terms of its social significance (or lack thereof):

> The Japanese girl knows exactly what fate awaits her in marriage. Whether Peter or Paul becomes her husband – it makes little difference. Peter's house looks exactly like Paul's, because all of the houses look the same in Japan; the same mats, the same paper door, the same portable hearth, the same food, the same clothes, the same duties, and the same rights.[201]

It is apparent throughout the article that Maron struggled to integrate Japan smoothly into his worldview. Yet despite his occasionally brusque comments, he confessed to harbouring a "warm, almost anxious affection for this marvellous people."[202] He ended with a strong note on the deplorable future of Japan:

> European civilisation will pour its dubious blessings upon these islands; this fate cannot be averted. What effect will it have? I do not want to burden my heart with grim speculation. Wherever the "white man" has so far set his foot, cities and churches with slender towers have arisen, trade and commerce have flourished, the idolatry of the golden calf has created new worshippers – but the happiness of the local nations? It is gradually dying, and finally the nation itself dies.[203]

Unheimliches […]." Maron, Hermann, "Zur Charakteristik Japan's. Shanghai 18. Feb," in: *Die Grenzboten* 20, 1, 2 (1861), pp. 265–276, here p. 268.

201 "Das japanische Mädchen weiß genau, welches Schicksal sie in der Ehe erwartet; ob Peter oder Paul ihr Mann wird, – der Unterschied kann nicht groß sein. Das Haus von Peter sieht genau aus wie das von Paul, denn alle Häuser sehen in Japan gleich aus; dieselben Matten, dieselbe Papierthür, derselbe transportable Feuerherd, dieselbe Nahrung, dieselbe Kleidung, dieselben Pflichten und dieselben Rechte." Maron, Hermann, "Zur Chakteristik Japan's. (Schluß)," in: *Die Grenzboten* 20, 1, 2 (1861), pp. 310–316, here p. 310.

202 Maron, "Charakteristik (Schluß)," p. 316.

203 "Die europäische Civilisation wird ihre zweifelhaften Segnungen über diese Eilande ergießen; dies Schicksal ist nicht abzuwenden. Wie sie wirken wird? Ich will mir das Herz nicht schwer durch Grübeln machen. Wohin immer bis jetzt der Fuß des „weißen Mannes" getreten ist, sind Städte und Kirchen mit schlanken Thürmen erwachsen, sind Handel und Gewerbe erblüht, hat der Götzendienst des goldenen Kalbes neue Anbeter gemacht, – aber das Glück der einheimischen Nationen? Die Geschichte lehrt: es stirbt allmälig dahin und zuletzt die Nation selbst." Maron, "Charakteristik (Schluß)," p. 316.

While Hermann Maron's article is unquestionably an interesting and very early post-isolation source from which to gain insights into the western perception of Japan, it might be not altogether obvious how it relates to our topic of architecture. Still, the quoted paragraphs frame the ways in which Japanese architecture became integrated into western knowledge systems via various tightly interwoven threads of cultural discourse.

Maron's landscape description in the first quote conveys expectations of encountering interesting and picturesque formations of nature, and the ensuing disappointment when these were not met by the places the Eulenburg expedition visited. It referred to known and well-established images of natural European landscapes such as the Alps, the Lake District and the Middle Rhine Valley.[204] While Maron did not refer to man-made sights in his text, he often linked natural and artificial places of interest, such as a bridge spanning a gorge, a royal residence on the Loire in France, or a castle overlooking a valley, such as could be found on some parts of the Rhine or in many much less well-known regions of Great Britain and Central Europe, not to mention the even more fascinating non-western regions of the world. The artificial was often seen as highlighting the natural, both in texts on Europe as well as in many touristic descriptions of Japan.

The second, third and fourth quotes from Maron address the landscape, the city and the dwelling as indicators of specific levels of technological development, and strongly contrast the situation in Japan to that of contemporary Europe with regard to the reorganisation and redesign of natural conditions, as well as the spatial and social consequences of technologisation and industrialisation.[205] Just like all of the other authors of which I am aware, and much like the experts whose comments have already been mentioned above, Maron expected the opening of Japan to have a momentous influence on its society. It is the expression of resignation in his closing paragraph that is crucial for this chapter: while predicting the modernisation and Christianisation of Japan, it also predicted the decline and final loss of the country's cultural identity.

It expresses an awareness of the differences between everyday life in the West and the situation in Japan, a feeling that Japanese society was still 'innocent' and 'pure', still 'untainted' by the chaotic and noisy irregularities of

---

204 See e.g. Withey, Lynne, *Grand Tours and Cooks' Tours: A History of Leisure Travel, 1750–1915* (London, 1997).

205 Due to the already advanced stage of urbanisation in Japan, which at times far surpassed that in Europe, this characteristic of European discourses on modern development did not play a role here.

modernisation that were already shaping the western experience and worldview at this time.[206] Against this background, Japanese customs and houses, rice paddies, shrines and rites became more than just objects of observation and study, serving instead as codes for a pre-modern, non-western imagination.

The following source materials aim to strengthen this argument with reference primarily to the building context. Before turning to them, however, it seems advisable to look more closely at the perception of landscape.

4.1 Landscape, Recreational Travel and Sight-Seeing

The places and regions of Japan travelled through and reported upon by western visitors during the latter half of the nineteenth century were extensive, especially when those visitors travelled as diplomats or as experts on behalf of the Japanese government and were thus less limited by legal restrictions.[207] Despite this, the places discussed remained limited – an issue we will address again from the visual angle in the next chapter. Aside from the natural landmark of Mount Fuji, the immediate environment of the foreign settlements and of Edo (Tōkyō) received the most attention (Fig. 3.17).

The area of Hakone, with its landscape features and hot springs, fits into this context. Rutherford Alcock described the region in 1863 with a similar approach to Maron's since he observed the deficits in comparison to common European references in the Swiss Oberland such as the Wetterhorn and Jungfrau. For Nagasaki, to mention another well-reported region, he invoked the Norwegian fiords and Swiss lakes.[208] Alcock drew explicit parallels between landscape and landscape painting and included built environments such as Edo (Tōkyō) in the discussion when he saw "some wide sweeps of landscape worthy of the pencil of a Roberts or a Stanfield" with buildings as foreground and, "giving life and movement to the scene, groups of horsemen, with pedestrians intermingled."[209]

---

206   Roy Starrs sketches this in his introduction to *Modernism and Japanese Culture*. Starrs, Roy, *Modernism and Japanese Culture* (Houndmills; Basingstoke, 2011), pp. 1–5.

207   Foreigners were subject to travel restrictions. Isabelle Bird described the situation in 1880, when settlement was only allowed in Yokohama, Nagasaki, Tōkyō, Kōbe, Ōsaka, Hakodate and Niigata and travel restricted to 25 miles around those. Bird, Isabella Lucy, *Unbeaten Tracks in Japan: an account of travels on horseback in the interior: including visits to the aborigines of Yezo and the shrines of Nikkō and Isé*, 2 vols. (London, 1880), 1, p. 8. – While many circumvented these restrictions, the absence of infrastructure remained a crucial limiting factor for tourism. Hockley, *Globetrotters', People*.

208   Alcock, *Tycoon*, 1, pp. 355, 89.

209   Ibid., p. 135. – Concerning landscape painting see for example Gilpin, William, *Three essays: on picturesque beauty; on picturesque travel; and on sketching landscape: to which is added a poem, on landscape painting* (London, 1792). For the impact on local infrastructure

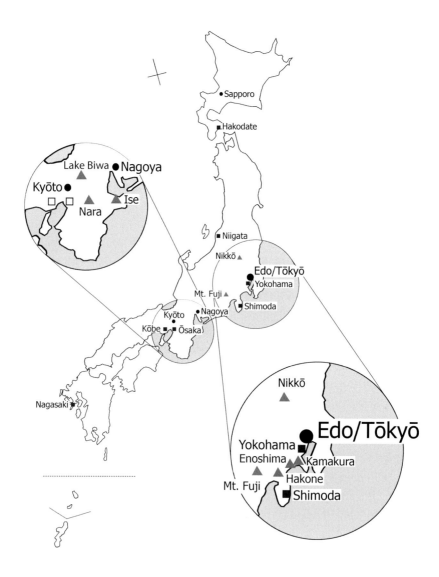

General map of Japan (omitting all of the smaller islands)

■ Exterritorial settlements ▲ Locations for recreational travel and sightseeing

FIGURE 3.17   Map of Japan with the exterritorial settlements and the locations for recreational travel and sightseeing discussed in the texts

THE INVISIBLE DWELLING HOUSE 143

Thus, landscape and city, buildings and people became part of an overall picture or even a stage set against which Japanese life was experienced and observed. Alcock even mentioned an occasion in Japan when he found himself distracted by idealising notions of a pure and simple country life "which the picture before me of agricultural life and Arcadian simplicity suggested."[210]

The cross-referencing of landscapes and their picturesque qualities was a common feature of sources of that time (as it still is in reporting on foreign regions today), and included man-made settings and the everyday environments of villages as well as acknowledged architectural sites of interest.

One of the favourite destinations for travellers in Japan was Nikkō, attractive both for its natural beauty and the architectural splendour of Tōshō-gū, the memorial to the founder of the Tokugawa dynasty, Tokugawa Ieyasu (1543–1616). Although it was a significant distance from Tōkyō and Yokohama, many westerners visited Nikkō and described the interplay of landscape and buildings there (Figs. 3.18–3.20, see colour section).

Christopher Dresser wrote in 1882:

> Nikko is a small town situated in a richly wooded dell. It has a mountain river leaping down a rocky defile, and a stream of delicious water flowing through the central street. Across the river, on the sides of a tree-covered hill, are the great shrines – the most important and the most beautiful of all the shrines of Japan – shrines as glorious in colour as the Alhambra in the days of its splendour, and yet with a thousand times the interest of that beautiful building.[211]

In 1894, the American architect Charles Thompson Mathews (1863–1934) introduced the compound in a similar way, though with a different western point of reference by describing the colours of the light and their structuring of landscape perception.[212] He ended his observations on the buildings, their measurements, and their associated rites and decorations by returning to the close relationship between architecture and landscape:

---

and tourism, see e.g. Martin, Andreas; Fröhlich-Schauseil, Anke, *Die Flusslandschaft an den Mulden. Frühe Wahrnehmungen in bildender Kunst und Reiseliteratur* (Dresden, 2012).
210   Ibid., p. 269.
211   Dresser, *Japan*, p. 198.
212   Mathews, Charles Thompson, "A Temple of the Togukawa at Nikko," in: *Architectural Record* 4 (December 1894), pp. 191–209, here p. 191.

But when everything is said, the greatest achievement of the whole mausoleum lies in the artistic distribution of the buildings. Great splashes of crimson and gold light up the dark green neutral of the mountain side, mellowed by the purples of the air, while the beauty of abstract proportion is ever present to govern and control all.[213]

John La Farge, who was already able to arrive by train when he visited Nikkō in 1886, wrote of the contrast between the artistic sophistication within the enclosure of the religious buildings and the existential purity of the sky, mountains, and plants beyond. Here he found an embodiment of the *memento mori*.[214]

The similarities among these three sources are obvious and are by no means only due to the intention of highlighting the interplay of landscape and architecture. The observations and evaluations of the building complexes in Nikkō are strikingly similar, and not only in English publications. Other texts, such as Émile Guimet's (1836–1918) extensive depictions of his multi-sensory impressions in *Promenades japonaises*, 1878, or the paragraph that German architect Wilhelm Böckmann (1832–1902) dedicated to Nikkō in 1886, followed the same pattern.[215] They all evoked an interdependence of nature, architecture and people. Böckmann, whose notes evince the same interest in a newly built iron bridge as in the buildings of Nikkō, concluded his report with an excuse for the extensive description with the argument that "the splendour of nature is equal to that of (the) mausoleum" and beyond any burial site in contemporary Europe.[216]

These reports informed the books of those aficionados who collected and appreciated Japanese art but never visited Japan themselves, such as the German scholar and collector Justus Brinckmann, who developed his understanding from sources available in Europe and through a network of personal contacts. His work and that of others like him nevertheless reinforced and multiplied the patterns of perception that were developing around places such as Nikkō by condensing and underlining the attribution of specific Japaneseness to the cultural reading of Japanese architecture.[217]

213 Mathews, "Temple," p. 209.
214 La Farge, *Letters*, p. 74.
215 Guimet, Promenades, in particular chapter XXXV, "Temples et Forêts"; Böckmann, Wilhelm, *Reise nach Japan. Aus Briefen und Tagebüchern zusammengestellt* (Berlin, 1886).
216 "(…) die Pracht der Natur giebt der (des) Mausoleums nichts nach." Böckmann, *Reise*, p. 80.
217 Here especially Brinckmann, *Kunst*, pp. 78–79. – Alfred Lichtwark (1852–1914), a similarly influential collector and educator, portrayed his friend in 1902, thereby giving a sketch of the processes of interest and collection, study and analysis that informed Brinckmann's

The sources, whether based on experience or imagination, showed an interest in the buildings and acknowledged their significant role in creating the site's impact on its visitors: the architecture was an indispensable part of Nikkō's fascination and picturesqueness, as it was for other (architectural) sights in Japan. One consequence was that architecture became tightly interwoven with western concepts of Japaneseness in general, as expressed in the sites chosen for touristic travel.

Western actors perceived, visited, discussed and appreciated Japanese architecture within this system of cultural reference; it was part of the intriguing and inspiring otherness of a non-western and (initially) pre-modern culture. This led to a gap between, on the one hand, the awareness and general basic knowledge of the buildings and places visited and the absence of dedicated research on the architectural and spatial features of those same places on the other, the reasons for which were discussed earlier. We will see, however, that this gap provided a broad space for the interpretation and negotiation of the meaning of Japanese architecture, unhindered by constricting facts. The buildings remained available to the imagination even once the processes of modernisation in Japan started to have an impact on the environment, and thereby started to recompose the 'image' of Japan.[218]

4.2 Cityscapes and the Impending Disappearance of Japaneseness

The deep-rooted historical tradition and the remoteness of the location protected the ensembles in Nikkō from destruction or obsolescence, even as other buildings and institutions became endangered by political upheaval and the ensuing attempts to devalue the landmarks of the Tokugawa dynasty, or by decisions made to foster modernisation, or simply by changing social needs and interests during the late nineteenth century. These processes impacted the whole of Japan, but are most readily traceable in the development of Edo (Tōkyō). The Kan'ei-ji in Ueno, one of the two funeral temples of the Tokugawa shōguns in the city, was largely destroyed during the Boshin War (1868–1869),[219]

---

      expertise on Japanese art, along with the named textual sources and informers and the networks and practices on which he drew. Lichtwark, Alfred, *Justus Brinckmann in seiner Zeit* (Hamburg, 1978), pp. 60–64.

218 It is important to keep in mind that the processes sketched here involved many Japanese actors behind the scenes and reflected back on the Japanese's own understandings of their culture and heritage, not least as expressed in Japanese travel guides such as two different *Nikkō meisho zue* [Illustrated guide to the famous place(s) of Nikkō]: Nakazawa, Sonō, *Nikkō meisho zue* (Tōkyō: Murakami, 1882); Ishikura, Shigetsugu, *Nikkō meisho zue* (Tōkyō: Hakubunkan, 1902).

219 Seidensticker, *Low City*, p. 27.

while many *daimyo* residences were abandoned and either re-used or fell into disrepair; at the same time, the scale of urban structures and populations changed to adapt to modern times.

The contemporary western sources reflected these changes. Thomas Russell H. McClatchie described the situation in his essay *The Feudal Mansion of Yedo*, 1879:

> The feudal system having come to an end in this country, the old yashiki are fast disappearing. Many have been destroyed by fire, others removed to afford sites for buildings in European style; some few are still retained as barracks for the soldiery, and in numerous instances the former nagaya have been portioned out into rows of small shops, etc., to be let to the townspeople.[220]

McClatchie's description of the decay and disappearance of older structures was untroubled by doubt or regret, albeit he saw their historic relevance clearly. Other authors commented in a similar way on the nearly complete disappearance of places and buildings due to the perishable nature of traditional Japanese building materials or the re-use of materials elsewhere; these were historical artefacts that gave way to change or modernisation, and they were to be remembered but not mourned given the progress that was achieved. The swiftness of such changes was a success story as far as modernisers and experts were concerned, one that could be told in the architectural context in terms of specific projects such as Ginza's brick buildings and colonnades, the projects for ministerial administration, factories or infrastructure such as railways and bridges.

Yet, while modernisation westernised central Tōkyō's sphere of self-representation, the city remained a place of interest for sightseers. They came in search of the foreign Japaneseness that Maron had struggled to grasp. These visitors told another story, one of the temples and shrines, the fortifications of the castle that now housed the emperor's court, the view of the harbour and the bay as seen from Atago-yama, the parks and gardens, the shops, crafts and many facets of street life. Again, the perception and narration of the physical place with its topography and architecture was inseparably interwoven with the explicit non-westernness of Japan.

World traveller and author Isabella Bird (1831–1904) put the perceived difference into words by describing a homogeneity encompassing bodily

---

[220] McClatchie, "Mansion," p. 186.

features, language, buildings and costumes, summing up that "everything is poor and pale, and a monotony of meanness characterises the towns."[221] This seemingly devastating evaluation, quite close to those that had led to scathing judgements among art and architecture experts, did not diminish her enthusiasm to explore northern Japan. The same went for many of the visitors whose reports were published: the foreignness of Japanese culture was sought after and appreciated by many. Thus, depending on the individual's background and interests, Japan – or, in this case, Tōkyō with its built environment and cityscape – either fulfilled expectations or left behind feelings of disappointment.

This is the very experience that American journalist Eliza Scidmore (1856–1928) reported in 1891:

> The first view of Tokio, like the first view of Yokohama, disappoints the traveller. The Ginza, or main business street, starting from the bridge opposite the station, goes straight to Nihombashi, the northern end of the Tokaido, and the recognized centre of the city, from which all distances are measured. Most of the roadway is lined with conventional houses of foreign pattern, with their curb-stones and shade-trees, while the tooting tram-car and the rattling *basha*, or light omnibus, emphasize the incongruities of the scene. This is not the Yeddo of one's dreams, nor yet is it an Occidental city. Its stucco walls, wooden columns, glaring shopwindows, and general air of tawdry imitation fairly depress one. In so large a city there are many corners, however, which the march of improvement has not reached, odd, unexpected, and Japanese enough to atone for the rest.[222]

Scidmore, informed in advance by the books of William E. Griffis, Algernon B. Freeman-Mitford, Christopher Dresser, Edward Morse, Percival Lowell, and Justus Rein, expected to find a culturally different, non-western place, and instead found a city in the process of transformation or 'westernisation'. This very transformation – which the Japanese government had initiated, western experts conceptualised and launched, and which many understood as strictly necessary in the raising of Japan's level of 'civilisation' to western standards – became the cause of her disappointment. She had to leave the areas of 'official' Tōkyō and venture into the everyday neighbourhoods to experience the cultural otherness she had been looking for.

---

221 Bird, *Tracks*, 1, pp. 7–8.
222 Scidmore, *Jinrikisha*, p. 43.

Félix Régamey found his expectations met, as he stated in his book *Le Japon pratique* in 1891:

> Contrary to the disappointment that usually follows high expectations respecting a masterpiece of art or of nature, I found on arriving at Japan only the fulfilment of my hopes. I exactly recognised the landscapes and the people the first albums reaching France had brought before my mind in 1863.[223]

This statement might seem surprising given the many years that had elapsed between 1863 and 1891, but Régamey had travelled through Japan in 1876 together with Émile Guimet, and his own books were published much later than were Guimet's *Promenades japonaises* of 1878. Thus his statement might have been reproducing the experience of bygone years, strengthened by the sketches and paintings by his own hand which he had brought back earlier.

Yet his American colleague John La Farge, who travelled Japan in 1886 with historian Henry Adams (1838–1918) and published during the 1890s, came to very similar conclusions. Looking out on Yokohama, even before having stepped off the ship, he wrote: "We are coming in; it is like the picture books. Anything that I can add will only be a filling in of detail."[224] He later specified the source of his evaluation and the background to his expectations by referring to Ueno Park and its features "which you know, having seen them on the fans and colored prints."[225]

Both artists refer to the 'images' of Japan they had gained from artefacts and visual media. Their Japan was a land of imagination, which they managed to recognise in the built environment of modernising Tōkyō. La Farge in particular often mentioned his visual sources or referred to the production of further such material (Figs. 3.21 and 3.22). On his visit to the Great Buddha in nearby Kamakura he wrote:

> We saw it first from the side through trees (...) The photographs must long have made you know it, and they also show the great base and the immense temple ornaments that stand upon it at the feet of the statue.

---

223 "Contrairement au phénomène qui se produit lorsqu'on a beaucoup présumé de la beauté d'un chef-d'oeuvre de l'art ou de la nature, je n'eus aucune déception en arrivant au Japon. Je retrouvai très exactement les paysages et les gens que les premiers albums parvenus en France m'avaient révélés en 1863." Régamey, *Le Japon*, p. 7; quoted after: id., *Art and Industry*, p. 8.
224 La Farge, *Letters*, p. 1.
225 Ibid., p. 29.

They show also the little lodge at the side, where the priest in attendance lives, and gives information, and sells photographs and takes them, and generally acts as showman. We took many photographs from new points of view, and we even removed the thatch of a penthouse so as to get nearer and under the statue to the side; and I painted also, more to get the curious gray and violet tone of the bronze than to make a faithful drawing, for that seemed impossible in the approaching afternoon.[226]

La Farge's reports show what we already knew from the emergence of Japonisme in the arts: the interlinked impact of various media. It was not only the objects and texts that created and perpetuated the idea of Japanese culture, but the images as well. We will look at this in detail in the next chapter; until then it is important to be aware that the illustrations in books and essays and the images collected in souvenir albums up to the turn of the twentieth century rarely included any reference to Japanese modernisation. The images of Japan described their non-westernness alone, a cultural totality that became known over time as 'old' or 'traditional' Japan, thus distinguishing it from the modern, westernised reality.

FIGURES 3.21–3.22   Two depictions of the Great Buddha at Kamakura

226   Ibid., pp. 225–226.

While further development strengthened Tōkyō's standing as a modern national capital, the narrative of an 'old Japan' in the city's backstreets, parks and temples survived in western publications. It integrated habits and costumes, rites and religion, culinary practices and houses, and festivals and landscapes, mixing the vernacular with high art and western interpretations of Japaneseness.[227] Additionally, it included an expectation of loss and mourning for a culture soon to disappear, as already seen in Maron's essay. Yet, this 'Sehnsuchtsort', imagined 'place of longing', inspired not only the study of Japanese architecture but also a well-read book on the Japanese dwelling house that we will address immediately. Far more than this, it influenced the formation of a modern understanding of Japanese art history and the discourse of heritage preservation. Both are connected through a tightly interwoven process of cultural exchange between Japanese and western actors.[228]

4.3   Essentialised Japaneseness: the Vernacular Dwelling House

We have already seen that the building-related professions showed very little interest in Japanese houses beyond the issues of fire prevention and earthquake resistance, and that many writers such as Maron, Heine, Brunton or Bird lamented the buildings' similarity of form and meanness of appearance. At the same time, the peculiarity of the dwellings was a constant theme in writings on Japanese culture, with topics and evaluations varying widely and addressing the size (or lack thereof) of the houses, their interior furnishing, and their comforts and shortcomings.

The most obvious topic was the lack of comfort, a cause for complaint by many a traveller or contracted expert. Typical is the commentary by Basil H. Chamberlain in *Things Japanese*, 1890:

---

227   Yoshioka, Hiroshi, "Samurai and Self-colonization in Japan," in: Pieterse, Jan N.; Parekh, Bhiku (eds.), *The Decolonization of Imagination. Culture, knowledge and power* (London, 1995), pp. 99–112.

228   This development included such heterogeneous elements as the western sale of Japanese artistic heritage, the establishment of institutions for architectural and artistic education in Japan, Japanese participation at World's Fairs, the reform of religious institutions, the abolishment of an entire social order, and the introduction of heritage surveys and protection laws. References to this are included e.g. in Löffler, "Petrified worldviews"; id., "Search, discovery, canonization and loss. Japan's Architectural Heritage as a Matter of Cultural Negotiation and Perception of Relevance in the Late Nineteenth Century," in: Bogner, Simone, et al. (eds.), *Collecting Loss* (Ilmtal-Weinstraße, 2021), pp. 80–94. – See more specifically, Foxwell, Chelsea, "Japan as Museum? Encapsulating Change and Loss in Late-Nineteenth-Century Japan," in: *Getty research Journal* 1 (2009), pp. 39–52; Wendelken, Cherie, "The Tectonics of Japanese Style. Architect and Carpenter in the Late Meiji Period," in: *Art Journal* 55.3 (1996), pp. 28–37; Tseng, *Imperial Museums*.

Japanese houses are supremely uncomfortable to ninety-nine Europeans out of a hundred. Nothing to sit on, nothing but a brazier to warm oneself by and yet abundant danger of fire, no solidity, no privacy, the deafening clatter twice daily of the opening and shutting of the outer wooden slides, draughts insidiously pouring in through innumerable chinks and crannies, darkness whenever heavy rain makes it necessary to shut up one or more sides of the house – to these and to various other enormities Japanese houses must plead guilty.[229]

John Nicholson Seymour (*1858) was unusual in offering a defence of the Japanese dwelling that went beyond its often-mentioned appropriateness to the wants and needs of Japanese culture. In a *Lecture on the Hygienic aspects of Japanese dwelling houses*, 1889, he admonished western visitors to adapt:

The general character of the house does not need alteration. But if a foreigner, in using it, retains his foreign habits, he has no right to condemn it. If he clothes himself lightly, sits on a chair, and makes a large fire in a hibachi, he has no right to find fault with the house because he suffers from headache or cold feet. If he uses a high table, he must not condemn the lighting; and if he cumbers the room with furniture, he is not justified in decrying the want of space.[230]

The challenges experienced in using these buildings were not least due to the compact arrangement of rooms in a Japanese dwelling, which presented a contrast to western codes of built representation and was another recurring topic of interest. Alexander Graf von Hübner observed the openness of the houses to the streets and the perceived absence of furniture; Eliza Scidmore introduced the houses similarly and included the Japanese in the picturesque image of a dollhouse, as did Félix Régamey.[231]

Like the majority of evaluations of the Japanese house published far into the twentieth century, these comments on specific features firmly contextualised the Japanese phenomena in an area of cultural expression, of explicit Japaneseness. This practice did not stop the authors from using the Japanese example of spatial organisation as the basis for a critique of western habits or for inspiration.

---

229   Chamberlain, "Architecture," p. 25.
230   Seymour, "Abstract," p. XIX.
231   Hübner, *Ramble*, pp. 223–224; Scidmore, *Jinrikisha*, p. 1, see p. 59 as well; Régamey, *Le Japon*, p. 5.

The description provided by American painter Theodore Wores (1859–1939) in his report *An American artist in Japan*, 1889, showed his admiration but remained restrained when he pointed to the scarcity of decorative objects and the taste in workmanship and materiality.[232]

The German architect Hermann Muthesius (1861–1927) was much less reserved some years later in his short review essay of 1903. Better known for his promotion of the English mansion and his activities in the *Deutscher Werkbund*, Muthesius worked in Japan at the beginning of his career between 1887 and 1891 at the office of Böckmann & Ende. He largely refrained from writing about its architecture, with the exception of some short paragraphs:[233]

> The treatment of the Japanese room in particular offers us a great many suggestions, not, of course, with regard to details, this being ruled out by the completely different conditions that pertain here and there, but in terms of the general aims of the formation of space. Now, if we begin by limiting the furnishings to moveable pieces only and make it our aim to create more unity and peace in the room, then the Japanese room, with its proud emptiness, provides a genuine ideal. If we no longer wish to cover our walls with good or bad pictures and aspire to clean our wall shelves of the useless bits and pieces which have been amassing there, so too do we see here in Japan the ideal state, where one puts away one's art treasures while only showing one picture in a niche provided for the purpose, and only one or two small objects on the wall boards. If we strive for a quiet, unornamented surface effect in the treatment of ceilings and walls and concentrate the decoration in just a single privileged part, then here again the Japanese room offers the best possible role model, with its elegant restraint in all of its appointments and in the single ornament of the openwork frieze. In short, especially today, in our present art movement, the Japanese room is of truly exciting interest, and a detailed demonstration of it would most forcefully help some of the healthy aspirations that have now begun with us.[234]

---

232   Wores, Theodore, "An American artist in Japan," in: *The Century Magazine* (September 1889), pp. 670–685, here 672.
233   His approach to Japan, its art and culture was analysed by Ganzer, Inga, *Hermann Muthesius und Japan: Die Rezeption und Verarbeitung japanischer Vorbilder in der deutschen Raumkunst nach 1900* (Petersberg, 2016). See also Ikeda, Yuko, "Hermann Muthesius und Japan," in: Ikeda, Yuko; Schwartz, Frederic J., et al. (eds.), *Vom Sofakissen zum Städtebau. Hermann Muthesius und der Deutsche Werkbund: Modern Design in Deutschland 1900–1927* (Kyōto, 2002), pp. 384–392.
234   "Gerade aus der Behandlung des japanischen Zimmers läßt sich für uns ungemein viel Anregung schöpfen, natürlich nicht in den Einzelheiten, das schließen schon die

Interestingly enough, this exhortation to use Japanese examples for contemporary interior designs remained largely without response within the field for more than two decades. It may have been too progressive. Even Muthesius did not use his room in a 'Japanese' way but added not only tables and chairs for easier use but also curtains and other furnishings (Figs. 3.23 and 3.24). He shifted the interior from the acclaimed Japanese disposition (Fig. 3.25) to a rather Victorian one (Fig. 3.26).

Another specific feature of the Japanese house – one that was mentioned in the very first publications and remained a matter of consternation and fascination – was its overall spatial disposition towards its environment and the subdivision of its rooms, as seen in Farsari's photograph above: "Indeed, the Japanese may be said almost to live an out-of-door life, the house being rather a floor raised above the ground with a substantial roof than a series of rooms properly enclosed by substantial side walls,"[235] wrote Christopher Dresser. "The real Japanese house does not know the idea of a protective side wall, which produces closed rooms, a warm room, protected against all the rigours of the weather and cold,"[236] commented Ernst von Stein (1857–1929).

Some authors hinted at the potential usefulness of the spatial fluidity for architectural design, and this element was to become one of the best known and most discussed characteristics of the Japanese architectural tradition

gänzlich verschiedenen Bedingungen hier und dort aus, aber in den allgemeinen Zielen der Raumbildung. Wenn wir jetzt auf Beschränkung der Ausstattung mit beweglichem Hausrat ausgehen und dem Zimmer mehr Einheit und Ruhe zu geben trachten, so ist das japanische Zimmer in seiner stolzen Leerheit hierin geradezu ein Ideal. Wenn wir unsere Wände nicht mehr so voll mit guten oder schlechten Bildern hängen und unsere Bortbretter von dem nichtsnutzigen Krimskrams säubern wollen, der sich dort eingefunden hat, so erblicken wir auch hierin in Japan den Idealzustand, wo man seine Kunstschätze wegpackt und immer nur ein Bild in der dazu vorhandenen Wandnische und nur ein oder zwei kleine Gegenstände auf dem Bortbrett zeigt. Wenn wir auf eine ruhige, ornamentlose Flächen Wirkung in der Decken- und Wandbehandlung und auf Zusammenziehung des Schmuckes auf nur einen bevorzugten Teil hinstreben, so liefert uns auch hierin das japanische Zimmer das denkbar beste Vorbild mit seiner vornehmen Zurückhaltung in allen Teilen der Ausstattung und dem einzigen Ornament des durchbrochenen Frieses. Kurz, gerade heute, in unserer gegenwärtigen Kunstbewegung, ist das japanische Zimmer von geradezu spannendem Interesse und eine ausführliche Vorführung desselben würde gewissen gesunden Bestrebungen, die sich jetzt bei uns angebahnt haben, aufs eindringlichste zu Hilfe kommen können." Muthesius, "Haus," p. 307; see also Ikeda, "Muthesius," esp. pp. 389–390.

235 Dresser, *Japan*, p. 23.
236 "Die Idee einer schützenden Seitenwand, die geschlossene Zimmerräume hervorbringt, ein warmes gegen alle Unbilden der Witterung und Kälte geschütztes Gemach kennt das eigentliche japanische Haus nicht." Stein, "Erdbeben," p. 78.

FIGURES 3.23–3.26
Two views of Hermann Muthesius' Japanese room as taken from a photo album, about 1889; Adolfo Farsari: rooms (in a Japanese house), 1886; Henry Treffry Dunn: sonnets and ballads [Gabriel Rossetti and Theodore Watts-Dunton at No. 16 Cheyne Walk], 1882

some decades later. At this moment in time, however, there was as yet no call to break up the 'box' of the Victorian-style house; this paradigm-shifting discourse would be a matter for later generations of architects.[237] For now, the spatial fluidity of Japanese dwellings was seen as more of a nuisance.

The French legal scholar Georges Hilaire Bousquet (1845–1937) described his uneasiness with these buildings' disposition in 1877:

> Temples and 'yashki' [sic], townhouses and cottages, have virtually no walls; the roof is supported by columns, connected by mobile frames. Closed, these paper-lined frames are a wall that looks murky without giving the eye real solidity and safety. Open, they let the eye wander with a kind of discomfort into a dim and indistinct interior, when the weather is bad; or allow the view to penetrate into the most intimate details of privacy, when the light floods the apartments. (...) Nobody has the right to display his life on public roads. The gods need more mystery, the people more privacy; it befits only the theatre and the promenade to be this open to all visitors.[238]

The experience of the Japanese house was an occupational hazard for the contracted foreign experts and an annoyance to recreational travellers. Thus, it merited little attention except as a source of misunderstandings, mistakes and social improprieties that shed light on the deep interconnectedness of social order and hierarchy, on the one hand, and physical space as written into the material reality of a dwelling on the other.[239]

---

237 Frank L. Wright (1867–1959) denied the influence of Japanese models on his early spatial experiments, despite his many contacts there and the sources of information that were available to him. See the extensive discussion in Nute, Kevin, *Frank Lloyd Wright and Japan. The role of traditional Japanese art and architecture in the work of Frank Lloyd Wright* (London; New York, 1993).

238 "Temples et «yashki», maisons de ville et maisons des champs, n'ont pour ainsi dire pas de murailles; la couverture est supportée par des piliers que réunissent des châssis mobiles. Fermés, ces châssis, garnis de papier, n'ont d'un mur que l'apparence maussade, sans en avoir la solidité réelle et rassurante pour l'œil; ouverts, ils laissent le regard s'enfoncer avec une sorte de malaise dans un intérieur sombre et indistinct, quand le jour est mauvais; ou pénétrer jusque dans les détails les plus intimes de la vie privée, quand la lumière inonde les appartements. (...) Nul n'a le droit d'exhiber ainsi sa vie sur la voie publique. Les dieux ont besoin de plus de mystère, les hommes de plus de réserve; il ne sied qu'au théâtre et au portique d'être ouverts à tout venant." Bousquet, Georges Hilaire, *Le Japon de Nos Jours et les Echelles de l'Extrême Orient. Ouvrage Contenant Trois Cartes*, 2 vols. (Paris, 1877), 2, pp. 138–139.

239 Interestingly, barely any of the writers even mentioned the distinctions between the 'open' houses of urban artisans and traders, on the one hand, and similarly structured residences of the higher classes, well-hidden by walls and fences, on the other hand.

This is amply illustrated by an episode recounted by Wilhelm Böckmann in which he woke a sleeping Japanese man in an inn whom he thought was a member of his group, only to discover soon after that he was a stranger, or La Farge's reflections about propriety while observing a neighbouring family of parents and children sharing the bath.[240] Both Böckmann and La Farge described experiences of a two-fold ambiguity in which both spatial and social order deviated from western expectations.

On a social level, the confrontation with an unknown Japanese actor, presumably another guest who had arrived late at the inn and was not formally acknowledged by the other guests, led to erroneous behaviour by Böckmann. The bath shared by the entire family, including the husband and his adolescent daughter, puzzled La Farge. These experiences transgressed the boundaries of appropriate social interaction, including the protection of privacy and decorum, as observed in the social order of the Victorian West, in which every individual inhabited a specific and clearly defined place in society, thus separating husband from wife, parents from children, and master from servant. On the level of the physical environment, the spatial fluidity of the interior and exterior in the Japanese house obscured the codes of social interaction, thus presenting a stark contrast to the structure of the European house of the time, in which every domestic function had its specific and clearly defined place.

Seen through the eyes of the western observers, Japanese houses appeared to function socially and spatially not in terms of an unequivocal "either/or," but as an ambiguous "both/and," allowing for the easy reshuffling and repurposing of spaces and thus the continuous re-spacing or recoding of the social order.[241]

This complex web of otherness ensured lasting interest and drove ongoing discussions, but gave rise to hardly any research. The Japanese house was discussed as entirely Japanese, as a phenomenon of its own, both structurally and socially. As such, it was one of the many expressions of Japaneseness, an

---

240 Böckmann, *Reise*, p. 79; La Farge, *Letters*, pp. 34–35. See also the paragraph on sewage systems and hygiene above.
241 See also Shiga, Shigetsura, *Future development of Japanese dwelling houses* (unpublished thesis, Urbana-Champaign, 1905), pp. 24–28. While it was mostly foreigners who were affected and commented on the lack of privacy, the change in Japanese society had an impact on Japanese living conditions as well. In 1903, Japanese architect and educator Shiga Shigetsura (1866–1936) discussed his ideas that the neglect of privacy in the schemes of houses impeded the development of self-respect within the populace in a series of articles in *kenchiku zasshi*. He referred to western publications to promote the adoption of western building patterns in order to further advance the level of civilisation in Japan. The English version, adapted to an American audience, was submitted as a Master's thesis to the University of Illinois.

integral part of the society, and was obliged to undergo modernisation. There was no question as to its future destiny. As the expression of an ultimately inferior culture – an inferiority not only asserted by western experts but also acknowledged in the government's decision to focus on modernisation – the Japanese dwelling rated no further protection or interest.

In consequence, the suggestions for improving the structure of the Japanese house that came from western observers were manifold, as indicated above. Yet, much as in the case of the discourses on the changing Japanese city, the impending demise of traditional structures was occasionally remarked with regret.

Josiah Conder, steadfast in his perspective, ridiculed efforts to conserve the 'old Japan' merely for its curiosity value, arguing that such attempts hindered Japan's advancement. Yet, he later confessed to feeling "a pang of remorse."[242]

Edward S. Morse addressed the expected losses explicitly. In his introduction to *Japanese Homes and Their Surroundings*, 1886, he declared his general fondness for Japanese culture and the apprehension of its decline. Morse explained his antiquarian intention of "(…) preserving many details of the Japanese house, some of them trivial, perhaps, which in a few decades of years may be difficult, if not impossible, to obtain. Whether this has been accomplished or not, (…) nothing can be of greater importance than the study of those nations and peoples who are passing through profound changes and readjustments as a result of their compulsory contact with the vigorous, selfish, and mercantile nations of the West, accompanied on their part by a propagandism in some respects equally mercenary and selfish."[243]

The book addressed the forms of Japanese dwellings, urban and rural, and their typical shapes and functions, from fundamental construction principles to furniture, auxiliary buildings and sewage disposal systems. It was reviewed repeatedly by architectural and art journals.

The *Building News and Engineering Journal* called it instructive and "the only reliable guide to the architecture of Japan we have seen."[244] The *British Architect* agreed, while *The Builder* was much less convinced and found nothing useful in the book but for "their manner of turning the space under the stairs to account."[245]

---

242 Conder, *Domestic*, p. 103.
243 Morse, *Homes*, pp. vii–viii.
244 "Japanese Homes and their Surroundings," in: *The Building News and Engineering Journal* 50 (5 February 1886), pp. 206–207, here p. 207.
245 "Japanese Homes and their Surroundings," in: *The Builder* 54 (26 May 1888), pp. 381–382, here 382; "The Domestic Architecture of Japan. I–III," in: *British Architect* 29.21 (25 May 1888), pp. 369–370; 29.22 (1 June 1888), pp. 389–391; 29.24 (15 June 1888), pp. 424–425, here p. 370.

While the book was initially criticised for viewing its subject "through rose-coloured spectacles,"[246] it was also appreciated within and beyond the circles of Japanese studies scholars for its detailed information on the traditional elements of Japanese culture. Morse's worries regarding the decline of Japanese culture, while expressed in a very specific context, resonated with European experiences of loss; they echoed the more general experience of cultural discontinuity due to industrialisation that had already been expressed decades earlier in, for example, the texts of Augustus W. N. Pugin (1812–1852), in parts of the Arts and Crafts movement, or in German discourses on Heimat or cultural belonging.

The Japanese house, as described by Morse and perceived by his readers, was not only an omnipresent part of the everyday Japanese environment, but simultaneously the expression of a specific Japaneseness that was distant from modernisation and change. The dwelling was as much a part of the collection of material symbols of 'old Japan' as were Mount Fuji or the shrines of Nikkō.

Due to this context of origin, and despite its numerous illustrations and wealth of information, Morse's book was much less a study of art or architecture than it was an exploration of ethnographical character. It sketched the house as a reified social sphere within a somewhat hermetic Japanese culture, while the data remained insufficient to understand the building in any depth as far as artistic expression, construction and building processes were concerned. In this regard, the information was clearly too heterogeneous and incomplete.

Basil H. Chamberlain underlined this observation in his comment on the Japanese dwelling:

> It was a true instinct that led Professor Morse to give to his charming monograph on Japanese architecture the title of "Japanese Homes," the interest of Japanese buildings lying less in the buildings themselves than in the odd domestic ways of their denizens, and in the delightful little bits of ornamentation that meet one at every turn.[247]

All these sources indicate that the Japanese house was broadly understood as an entirely cultural phenomenon, contained within the Japanese context, a built marker of Japaneseness, and without any meaning for contemporary

---

246   Chamberlain, Basil H., "Books on Japan," in: id., *Things Japanese. Being Notes on Various Subjects Connected with Japan* (London, 1890), pp. 47–55, here p. 54.
247   Chamberlain, "Architecture," p. 23.

western life beyond its enjoyable oddity.[248] It was the perceived loss of this curious otherness to the changes of modernisation that provided the incentive to study the Japanese dwelling, rather than a broader interest in learning alternative ways for humanity to address the challenges of topography and climate, of resources and social needs, by developing a suitable architectural form. This evaluation and classification was firmly in place by the end of the nineteenth century and had lasting consequences for the perception of Japanese architecture within and beyond the field when it made its way into architectural handbooks.

5 Preliminary Observations: Western Knowledge Production on Japanese Architecture up to the Turn of the Century and Its Canonisation in Handbooks

The analysis undertaken in the four sub-chapters above shows western attitudes to Japanese architecture to be a very broad and multifaceted phenomenon. It was in no way a debate within closed circles of experts, nor was it even primarily shaped by such experts, not least since the western concept of 'architectural expert' itself underwent significant reorganisation during this time. On the contrary, superficial curiosity, popular approaches to data-collection, individual hobby-horses and the odd professional in-field discourse encountered, through popular and specialist media, local actors and armchair ethnographers in a fairly random process of data collection which took place in an intellectual and disciplinary environment that we would today call multi-disciplinary.

Experiences on site in Japan were evaluated against the available information from earlier sources and against existing ideas of Japan and Japaneseness (or, for that matter, non-westernness), and the resulting conclusions were as various as the observers involved. Information on Japan was discussed by both learned men and women and a highly specialised executive elite in the light of the predominant knowledge systems created from the study of European phenomena. This might not have been a problem in itself if not for the lack of discourse and discussion of the majority of topics. Collection of data on Japan was largely just that: data was collected but rarely questioned, nor were the ensuing evaluations challenged by others except in a very small number of cases or

---

248   See in addition for example Charles Garnier's Japanese pavilion at the Exposition Universelle de Paris in 1889 and his later book: Garnier, Charles, *L'Habitation humaine* (Paris, 1892), esp. pp. 848–855.

with respect to minute differences in interpretation. Many a report or diary contained detailed observations, ambiguities, and expressions of surprise or puzzlement; and yet there is no indication that the conclusions drawn led their western writers to question the basic assumptions of their worldviews. This was in contrast to contemporary practices in Europe, both within architectural circles and on certain public issues, where elaborate and extended discourses and arguments arose around the pros and cons of approaches, processes, aims and expected outcomes.

The incoming information on Japan was slotted into the existing systems, not with the aim of integrating crucial insights and developing the knowledge system further, but as an extension of basic data in the margins. The increase in publications did not change this, since most copied or reproduced already existing data, thus confirming established convictions and doing nothing to fill the existing blanks.

What did this mean as far as architecture and the largely 'invisible' dwelling house were concerned?

As we saw above, neither buildings nor urban structures in Japan were – for a very wide range of reasons – considered architecture by a majority of western observers. They were noticed and looked at but rarely studied, either as art or (advanced modern) construction or for the sake of urban planning. If they were studied at all, it was as an expression of Japaneseness and due to their curious deviation from the western norm, their Otherness.[249] Thus, none of the fields of modern academia with an explicit interest in building felt specifically inclined to analyse, inform or teach about Japanese architecture, or to include Japanese examples in their canons of reference works. This is a significant observation, since the fields concerned – art history, architecture, civil engineering and the newly emerging urban planning – claimed scientific character in the universal and timeless validity of their approaches, evaluations and applicability: whatever the experts perceived as relevant, they perceived as being of global and eternal relevance. Everything else was assigned to the inferior levels of regional, local or time-dependent relevance alone.

While the former, the universal and global, was to be acknowledged, taught and further advanced everywhere where sufficient levels of civilisation reigned, the latter, the local issues, could only merit attention in support of national identity building or to satisfy the curiosity of recreational travellers. This is exactly where Japanese architecture ended up after the first decades of western evaluation during the late nineteenth century: firmly excluded from the

---

249   See in regard to perception biases the extended literature on *orientalism*.

realms of relevance in global architectural discourses and thus excluded from scientific research accountable to the norms and expectations of the fields of arts, architecture, construction and planning. While the artistic expressions of Japanese culture were regularly invoked as sources of inspiration, instances of original research on architectural issues remained few and far between.

Japanese architecture became a field of expertise in cultural studies. Against the background of developments in academia during the last decades of the twentieth century, notably, increasing interest from the social sciences, we can easily see this approach as a valuable complement to artefact-centred studies today and highly conducive to gaining a holistic understanding of architecture and spatial planning, its origins, developments and significances in time and space. In the historical frame, however, this concept would be misleading: to study architecture as culture was the default setting for all 'irregular' phenomena, meaning those which did not fit the normative frames of specialised scholarly analysis as seen above. To be clear, even at the risk of repetition: within the institutionalising system of scholarship and knowledge production in the late nineteenth century, all of these architectural phenomena that were excluded from the high arts and engineering fell into the domain of ethnography with its decisive focus on non-western cultures or the pre- or non-modern parts of modern western cultures;[250] ethnography (later ethnology) studied the "Other" as seen by the opinion leaders of the time, filtered through their worldviews and through the mainstream of modernisation. This had momentous consequences for the classification of Japanese architecture.

However, this did not mean that architecture did not play an interesting role in contemporary discussion of Japanese culture. We have already seen this in the sub-chapter on art where various writers such as Gonse and Chamberlain drew connections between cultural or ethnic characteristics and artistic expression. Neither does it mean that the study of Japanese culture produced no insights into Japanese architecture. The crucial point regarding knowledge production was, on the one hand, the missing link to global (western) discussion of architecture in general and, on the other, the close interlinking with reference systems of cultural hierarchies. The latter not only limited the observed phenomena to merely local relevance, but it also reduced the study of architecture to peculiarities and special cases, creating a notion of incomparability which, again, set Japan apart from the knowledge production within the West that claimed global relevance. Moreover, the study of architecture as part of cultural studies produced some data-related shortcomings due to the focus on

---

250   See e.g. Kohl, Karl-Heinz, *Ethnologie – die Wissenschaft vom kulturell Fremden: Eine Einführung, 3., rev. ed.* (München, 2012), chapter 1.

social phenomena in which material culture was often no more than a side effect, even more so for facets such as the professional expertise needed for the production and maintenance of buildings.

Yet – and this is the most stunning and disconcerting observation – beyond the general framework, which rigidly differentiated hierarchies of culture and civilisation, many evaluations of Japanese artistic and architectural phenomena were full of well-meaning and tolerant interest, thus veiling the patterns of othering and knowledge production at work and making their analysis challenging without the helpful means and possibilities of retrospective analysis.

5.1   Japan in Western Architectural Handbooks

The time period addressed in this study was one of very dynamic social change both in the West and in Japan, in which multiple dynamic processes concurrently influenced each other and impacted the matters in hand. Just a few of these processes which influenced the western view of the globalising world and the role of art and architecture within it included: industrialisation, the rise of the *ars mechanicae* to scholarly status, urbanisation, the emergence and development of modern nation states, the institutionalisation of modern academia, the crisis of the fine arts and crafts in the face of phenomena such as photography and mass production, or the emergence of high-rise building techniques that bridged the fields of engineering and artistic design.

Architectural teaching and theoretical considerations were influenced and even driven by the need to bestow significance on new architectural phenomena and to negotiate the consequences of shifting competencies, responsibilities and expectations. Here, in-field developments and external influences converged during the nineteenth century. In addition to the established practice of expressing meaning in architecture by appropriately applying the Five Architectural Orders, architectural design had not only developed specific national narratives in its attempt to emancipate itself from the dominant Italian ideals, but it also expressed social change. Fostered not least by the violent negotiations of meaning triggered during the French Revolution, the concept of progressive development was adopted into architecture from theories in biology and religious studies. These impulses, the ideas of architectural development as a mirror of social and cultural development, influenced knowledge production as summarised and structured in surveys of architectural history. Here, the expertise of art historians and architects culminated in the canonisation of forms, styles and proportions, and a conceptual understanding of architecture was negotiated and perpetuated.[251]

---

251   While the study on the emergence of architectural history surveys is still in its infancy, the discussion of the shortcomings of this kind of academic source of knowledge with

We already addressed briefly the way in which architectural books included new data on Japan. That section ended with a quote from James Fergusson's *History of Indian and Eastern Architecture*, 1876, in which he lamented the lack of knowledge regarding Japan and expressed the need for further research. We established that this did not significantly change until the end of the century and that the assessments dismissed Japanese buildings as architecturally irrelevant.[252] Since we now know how this evaluation came to pass, it is worth taking a closer look at the actual content of some of the volumes around the turn of the century, at the handbooks and surveys of architectural history, and to consider the knowledge which was thus disseminated into the field(s) of western architecture on the level of general information and teaching.

We will look at Auguste Choisy's two volumes of *Histoire de l'architecture*, 1899, at Banister Fletcher's *A history of architecture*, first published in 1896 but only relevant for this study since the enlarged fourth edition of 1901, and at the enlarged and revised second edition of James Fergusson's *History of Indian and Eastern Architecture*, 1910.[253] These books all included information on Japan, were revised and produced as new editions, and were acknowledged within the field. In contrast to the publications discussed above, in which the on-site experience and/or Japan-related competence of the authors played an

---

respect to a global, not western-centric, history of architecture is well under way. It is to be hoped that we can soon move from an understanding of the problems to a fundamental rewriting of architectural history. See e.g. Anderson, "Writing"; Bozdogan, Sibel, "Architectural History in Professional Education: Reflections on Postcolonial Challenges to the Modern Survey," in: *Journal of Architectural Education* 52.4 (May) 1999, pp. 207–215; Gürel, Meltem Ö.; Anthony, Kathryn H., "The Canon and the Void: Gender, Race, and Architectural History Texts," in: *Journal of Architectural Education* 59.3 (February 2006), pp. 66–76; Choi, "Non-Western"; Özaslan, Nuray, "The Role of Architectural History in Building Modern Turkish Architecture," in: *The Journal of International Social Research* 4.17 (Spring 2011), pp. 339–347; Zandi-Sayek, Sibel, "The Unsung of the Canon: Does a Global Architectural History Need New Landmarks?," in: *ABE Journal* 6 (2014), http://journals.openedition.org/abe/1271 [accessed 14 January 2018], s.p.; Cheng, Irene; Davis, Charles L. II; Wilson, Mabel O. (eds.), *Race and modern architecture. A critical history from the enlightenment to the present* (Pittsburgh, 2020). – See also the work of Global Architectural History Teaching Collaborative (GAHTC) and compare the efforts to write a timely overview of global architecture in the 20th and 21st edition of Banister Fletcher's handbook. Japan was covered by Eizo Inagaki and Thomas Weaver in 1996 and by Nancy Shatzman Steinhardt, Rumiko Hand and Neil Jackson in 2020.

252 The volume became part of Fergusson, James, *A history of architecture in all countries, from the earliest times to the present day: in five volumes* (London, 1893–). Volume 3 of 1899 was identical to the edition of 1876.

253 Choisy, Auguste, *Histoire de l'architecture*, 2 vols. (Paris, 1899); Fletcher, Banister; Fletcher, Banister F., *A history of architecture for the student, craftsman, and amateur: being a comparative view of historical styles from the earliest period* (London, 1896); Fergusson, James, *History of Indian and Eastern Architecture*, 2 vols., 2nd, rev. ed. (London, 1910).

important role, here there is no doubt about the compilatory character of the content: the information on Japan was embedded into an overall picture of architecture, thus enabling us to see the knowledge system of European architectural thought at work.

In his *Histoire de l'architecture*, 1899, the French civil engineer Auguste Choisy (1841–1909) positioned China and Japan among the old cultures such as Ancient Egypt and India, which he set apart from the European tradition. His eighteen pages of text on Japan and China included ten small-scaled illustrations, the latter partly referring back to William Chambers, Abel Guérineau and the Chinese manual Kong-tching-tsofa.[254] The text encompassed construction, materials and proportions, specific building parts and decorations, as well as some lines on building types such as religious buildings and dwellings. It ended with some thoughts on historical developments and the exchanges of ideas within Asia. While the information provided may have been intriguing enough to prompt readers to take a closer look at the issue by searching for further literature, in itself, the short text did not facilitate the formation of an idea either of Chinese or of Japanese architecture. The description of the dwelling actually mixed elements of both indiscriminately.[255] The reviewed and corrected edition of this volume in 1943 reproduced the information about the region identically.

The way in which Choisy's publication handled China and Japan was shared by many other such volumes:[256] if an architectural history of the time included architectural traditions which were not understood to have contributed directly to European developments, they were handled in a separate section. In Choisy's case, this segregation took place in a temporal sense that summed

---

254 Probably Chambers, William, *Designs of Chinese buildings, furniture, dresses, machines, and utensils* (London, 1757). – Abel Jean-Louis Guérineau (1841–1929) was an architecturally trained naval officer contracted by the Japanese government between 1874 and 1881. His paintings were exhibited in Paris upon his return and some drawings published in Guérineau, *Ornements*. Guérineau, Abel Jean-Louis, "Biographical sketch," in: Frédéric, Louis, *Japan encyclopaedia* (Cambridge, MA, 2002), p. 266. – Gongcheng Zuofa (Imperial Specifications for State Buildings), 1734. I am indebted to Prof. Christine Moll-Murata, Bochum, for pointing my research on this in the right direction. See also Guo, Qinghua, "Prescribing the Ideal City: Building Codes and Planning Principles in Beijing," in: Marshall, Stephen (ed.), *Urban Coding and Planning* (London, 2012), pp. 101–119; Zhu, Jianfei, et al. (eds.), *Routledge Handbook of Chinese Architecture. Social Production of Buildings and Spaces in History* (London, 2022).

255 Choisy, *Histoire*, 1, pp. 193–194.

256 An exception in structure was Mathews, Charles Thompson, *The story of architecture: an outline of the styles in all countries* (New York, 1896).

THE INVISIBLE DWELLING HOUSE 165

up ancient cultures irrespective of their locality on the globe or the actual time span observed.

Banister Fletcher's (1833–1899) *History of architecture* took a slightly different approach. The first editions concentrated exclusively on the European realm, a decision that contradicted the very first sentences in the first edition of 1896, which stated:

> The Authors' aim in writing this book has been, not only to give in clear and brief form the characteristic features of the architecture *of each people and country*, but also to consider those influences which have contributed to the formation of each special style.[257]

The volume was extended, however, in the enlarged fourth edition of 1901. The content was split into two parts: the first, entitled *The Historical Styles*, contained Europe and the cultures and regions that influenced its ancient predecessors; the second, entitled *The Non-Historical Styles*, included the traditions outside the western canon. In his introduction to the second part, Fletcher explained the structure didactically:

> The non-historical styles – Indian, Chinese and Japanese and that of Central America – are those which developed mainly on their own account and exercised little direct influence on other styles. They can thus be studied independently, and need not interrupt the story of the evolution of European Historical Architecture dealt with in Part I., which would probably be the case if they were placed in their chronological order. The position which they should occupy in a History of Architecture is, however, a matter of doubt, but it is thought that by keeping them quite separate from the historical styles, it will make for greater clearness to the student.[258]

It becomes clear that the initial aim of an all-encompassing analysis invited the extension that came some years later. Still, western architectural training was naturally embedded in western systems of reference and had no need for non-western lines of building tradition beyond their value as a source of artistic inspiration. This easily allowed for the separation. What remained unclear

---

257 Fletcher, *History of architecture* (1896), p. v. Emphasis by B. L.
258 Fletcher, Banister; Fletcher, Banister F., *A history of architecture for the student, craftsman, and amateur: being a comparative view of historical styles from the earliest period*, 4th enlarged ed. (London, 1901), p. 437.

was the choice of terminology to subsume the non-western traditions. In the general introduction, the term "historical" seems to be used to encompass epochs of known history, transmitted through writing or other means.[259] Since the long histories of China and India were already well known and studied in Europe, this reasoning would not explain the terminology.

However, there is some evidence that "non-historical" might have been used by Fletcher in a different conceptual context, in the sense of 'without (architectural) history'. The aforementioned developments in architectural theory had led to a two-fold – if not altogether frictionless – understanding of (western) architecture: there was the established artistic hierarchy with the canonical orders and Greek antiquity at its peak, on the one hand, which was by now supplemented by the notion of architecture as a field of intrinsically progressive character, thus reading its history as a process of upward development, on the other.

As we saw earlier, Japan had no part in the artistic hierarchy. In addition, there are very few references to a pattern of progression in the sources on Japanese architecture and building tradition, as we saw with the debate around the earthquake resilience of pagodas. The sources often trace the historical developments of the region, the impulses taken from China, and the changes in spatial organisation or decorative features over time. Yet, the impression remains that these were not seen as analogous to the changes from Romanesque to Gothic, Renaissance, Baroque and so on but as variations within a fixed level of cultural development alone, never to be transcended from within. This assumption was confirmed to a certain extent when Fletcher continued:

> From an architect's point of view, these non-historical styles can scarcely be so interesting as those which have progressed on the solution of constructive problems, resolutely met and overcome, as was the case in Europe from the Classic period to that of the Renaissance.[260]

Curiously, Fletcher thus legitimises the division in engineering terms and not through aesthetics, which hardly corresponds to the function of the designing architects of his time. Moreover, he indirectly erases 300 years of technological building development in Europe. It serves primarily, however, to make a distinction away from the seemingly primarily decorative characteristics of other regions, as the further text shows.

---

259   Fletcher, *History of architecture* (1896), pp. 1–2.
260   Fletcher, *History of architecture* (1901), p. 438.

Another argument for this proposed reading of the term "non-historical" and the perceived irrelevance of non-western traditions for the education of architects is an illustration which appeared as the frontispiece in the fifth edition of Fletcher's *History*, published in 1905 and included in the book up to the edition of 1954 (Fig. 3.27). It showed a stylised tree whose roots were termed "geography," "geology," "climate," "religion," "social and political" and "history." Above the root sprouted six short branches symbolising the architectural traditions of Peru, Mexico, India, China and Japan as well as certain periods in the history of Egypt and Assyria, while the main stem was labelled in ascending order with ancient Greece and Rome. Above this, two more dead-end branches dedicated to Byzantine and Saracen architecture emerged, while the tree grew on with the Romanesque and the interlinked schools of Gothic and Renaissance, before continuing upward in national traditions and "modern styles."

This illustration left no doubt about the hierarchies of architectural traditions and the role that was assigned to Japan and others with respect to the European master narrative on architecture.[261] But what about the facts? Where did Fletcher derive his information from and how did he frame it?

The information provided by the chapter on China and Japan in the edition of 1901 encompassed fifteen pages. One third of these pages comprised general information on topography, climate, history and religion, one third the illustrations (three full-page photographs on China and two full pages of detailed drawings on both countries) and the last third provided architectural data. The presentation of the various building types showed a certain hierarchical order, starting with temples, followed by imperial palaces and pagodas, and switching between religious and secular until the final entries on engineering works and cities. The information on China was dominant, the Japanese phenomena subordinate.

As a result, the overall information on Japan remained modest and, in the end, eclectic. Some information was provided twice, while other indications were missing entirely. Among the issues addressed were the prevalence of wooden construction and the "scientific ingenuity"[262] of the joinery, the wide eaves as protection from the sun, the significance of the roofs as markers of

---

261 See regarding a post-colonial approach to the handbook's later editions: Baydar Nalbantoglu, Gülsüm, "Towards Postcolonial Openings: Rereading Sir Banister Fletcher's History of Architecture," in: *Assemblage* 35 (1998), pp. 6–17; McKean, John, "Sir Banister Fletcher: pillar to post – colonial readings," in: *The Journal of Architecture* 11.2 (2006), pp. 187–204.

262 Fletcher, Banister; Fletcher, Banister F., *A History of Architecture on the Comparative Method for the Student, Craftsman and Amateur*, 5th rev., enlarged ed. (London, 1905), p. 458.

168 CHAPTER 3

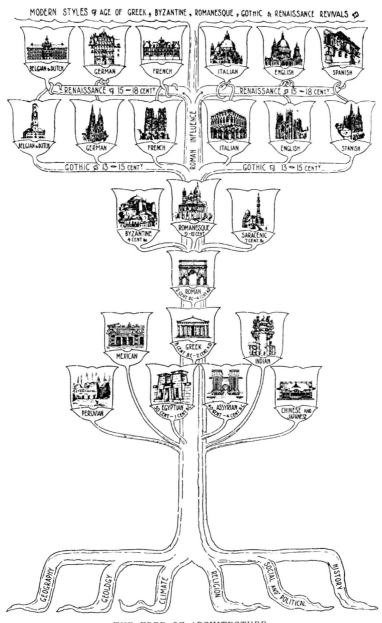

FIGURE 3.27   Banister Fletcher's Tree of Architecture, 1905

distinction, the sliding doors, the complex brackets in the temples, and the picturesque spatial arrangement of temple complexes.

The drawings were, on the one hand, as eclectic as the textual information, and on the other were very informative except for being printed exceedingly small. Likely taken predominantly from Conder, the original drawings would have been a better choice to convey an understanding of the structures than the condensed diagrams chosen for the sake of Fletcher's didactic approach.

In the initial extended edition of 1901, the difference from Choisy's *Histoire* was very slight in all but two regards. Firstly, the book gave a brief description of the system of "intercolumniation" (with an explicit reference to Conder) and mentioned the interplay between the basic measures of the ken and the tatami. The information remained very vague: just two unwieldy sentences compared to Morse's lengthy paragraph on the matter.[263] However, the book listed its references and this second original feature enabled the reader to find further information easily. In addition to five publications on China, there were five on Japan: Conder's *Notes on Japanese Architecture*, Dresser's *Japan*, Gonse's *L'Art Japonais*, Humbert's *Le Japon Illustré*, and Morse's *Japanese Homes*.

The revised and enlarged fifth edition of 1905, in which the *Tree of Architecture* first appeared, reproduced the same information and images apart from the addition of Chamberlain's *Things Japanese* to the list of references. The edition of 1919 was a reprint of the 1905 issue. The content only started to shift and extend with the revisions of the 1920s. The first Japanese references occur in 1961 with three English-language books from the 1930s by Harada Jiro (1894–1989), Minamoto Toyomune (1895–2001) and Kishida Hideto (1899–1966).[264]

The revised edition of James Fergusson's *History of Indian and Eastern Architecture* was published in 1910. Enriched by British architect Richard Phené Spiers (1838–1916), it contained – not entirely surprisingly in view of its regionally focused topic – more information on Japan than the other two overviews. The part on Japan was clearly separated from the preceding chapter on China, with four pages of general introduction, eleven pages of architectural explanations including illustrations, and seven full-page plates.[265]

---

263   Ibid., pp. 466–467, 470; see in comparison Morse, *Homes*, pp. 120–124.
264   Harada, Jiro, *The Lesson of Japanese Architecture* (London, 1936); Minamoto, Toyomune, *An Illustrated History of Japanese Art* (Kioto, 1935); Kishida, Hideto, *Japanese Architecture* (Tōkyō, 1935).
265   Fergusson, *Eastern Architecture* (1910), 2, pp. 486–502.

In his introduction, Spiers listed his sources of information, thus underlining the compilatory character of the volume. He started with a statement that was similar to others given by Burty and Godwin decades earlier:

> The principal source of information on Japanese architecture is that which is derived from photographs, but much is to be learnt from the meischos or guidebooks to the various provinces, which in Japan are largely illustrated, and from the prints by Hiro-shige, Yei-sen, and Toyo-kuni.[266]

This phrase refers to the way architecture has been and is conveyed and perceived through images, conceptually and epistemically separate from texts. We will address this issue in detail in the next chapter.

Spiers went on to refer in laudatory tones to two informants. Franz Baltzer had published *Das Japanische Haus* in 1903 to supplement Morse's well-recognised earlier work, and wrote the first western constructional analyses of Japanese religious buildings.[267] Josiah Conder's essays in RIBA publications were especially appreciated for the illustrations they included. Beyond these, he gained information from Chamberlain, Morse, Titsingh, Dresser, a recent edition of *Murray's Handbook to Japan* and Ralph A. Cram's *Impressions of Japanese Architecture and The Allied Art*, 1905.[268]

The architectural part of the chapter was structured hierarchically from religious buildings to palaces (mostly castles) and dwellings, and within each section according to historical development. Information on technical constructions such as bridges or on city planning was not addressed. General observations such as the use of raised floors were intermingled with details and special cases to form a broad picture. Yet the observations remained heterogeneous in their depth and relevance in terms of architectural understanding. As in many other accounts, the focus regularly drifted from structural or spatial considerations to decoration, detailing and colouring. We already addressed this phenomenon at the very beginning of this chapter and it is not surprising that the predilections of the specialist authors shaped the entries built upon their work.

Spiers' work also showed the consequences of gaps in information and of conflicting interpretations. His evaluation of Japanese architecture repeated

---

266 Ibid., 2, p. 487.
267 Baltzer stated in his introduction that Morse lacked technical drawings and took more the viewpoints of a layperson. Baltzer, "Haus," p. 3; Baltzer, Franz, *Die Architektur der Kultbauten Japans* (Berlin, 1907).
268 Cram, *Impressions*; Fergusson, *Eastern Architecture* (1910), 2, p. 487.

the appreciation of Japanese craftsmanship in woodwork with the simultaneous rejection of the overall construction principles. This went as far as to state that "Japanese pagodas (...) are all built in timber as being better able to resist the shock of earthquakes," only to comment some pages later that it "would be difficult, in fact, to conceive a worse system of support [in case of an earthquake] than that found in the Japanese temples."[269]

In respectful acknowledgement of the competencies shown by the compilers of the compendia discussed, the integration of non-western regions into the systems of architectural knowledge led neither to an overall increase in research nor to a conceptual breakthrough that would have changed European perceptions of the relevance of these building traditions.

To give just one example: Fiske Kimball's (1888–1955) *History of Architecture*, 1918, devoted just a single paragraph to Japan, which mentioned only temples, carvings and decorations and ended with the statement that the opening of the country had resulted in a "flood of western artistic ideas, which have tended, for the moment at least, to submerge the native art of Japan."[270] The edition of 1946 contained exactly the same information.

Yet, despite all of these critical observations, the emergence of handbooks and surveys of architectural history that looked beyond Europe changed the parameters of information dissemination. On a basic level, they allowed readers to browse the world of architecture beyond general knowledge alone and to gain glimpses of other practices and traditions, no matter how brief. A reader was able to form an image – no matter how lopsided – of the country's architecture in his or her mind enriched by authorities from within the field and occasionally supplemented by illustrations.

Beyond this, the lists of references invited readers to go deeper, to gain access to the first-hand insights of acknowledged experts, or to look for more contemporary expertise. While the lists of references were lagging behind the actual development on the book market and tended to ignore Japanese authors even in European languages,[271] some of the new publications on Japan, such as Baltzer and Cram, became part of the canon over time, most notably by way of Fletcher's *History*.

In the long run, a basic awareness of Japanese architecture made it into the knowledge systems of both learned people and field-related specialists, though it was overshadowed by a much more intense interest in Japanese applied arts.

269 Fergusson, *Eastern Architecture* (1910), 2, pp. 487 and 495.
270 Kimball, Fiske, *A History of Architecture* (New York; London, 1918).
271 Mathews was an exception here as well with the reference to Ishii Keikichi (1866–1932) and Tsumaki Yorinaka (1859–1916). Mathews, *Story*, p. x.

Compared to the interested lay audience, experts had very little additional knowledge regarding the main characteristics of Japanese architecture in general and the dwelling in particular: wooden constructions, fluid interiors with missing walls, lack of furniture, habitual sitting on the floor, and so on.

This general knowledge of Japan, its culture and architecture, built on a low level of concrete information, made the country an easily available source of western artistic inspiration and cultural imagination. At the same time, it allowed for seemingly non-contradictory readings and interpretations of Japan's architectural heritage. While as yet of no relevance at the turn of the century, this smattering of insights, canonised from handbooks, was ready to be reinterpreted and recontextualised within the worldviews of architectural modernism decades later.

CHAPTER 4

Visiting and Visualising Architecture

Buildings, Models, Images, Exoticism and the 'Esperanto' of Construction Drawing

Architectural thought and historiography are usually expressed in words. While this creates problems of its own, such as with the interpretation of Vitruvius's writings or with communication across languages, this practice makes it possible to trace and analyse arguments and to observe to a certain degree the construction of knowledge from pure data, as we did in the last chapter. Yet the world of architecture is at the same time understood and communicated through visual media, even more so in the nineteenth century when travel and the means of visualisation were much more limited than today.

This chapter addresses the ways in which the interested audience in the West was able to gain information on Japanese architecture from sources other than texts. It looks briefly at Japanese buildings and architectural models at World's Fairs and similar exhibitions. It then focuses on the illustrations in architecture-related publications, travelogues and ethnographical texts, visual material that was largely available independently of the specific location of the reader. This will be contrasted with visual sources which remained unknown or ignored or which experienced only limited distribution due to the restrictions of reproducibility or western interest. This aims to show how different layers of non-textual sources in general and of visual materials in particular had a role to play in the creation and canonisation of architectural knowledge and the degree to which visual information interlinked with textual materials.

1   Japanese Architectural Artefacts at the International Exhibitions in the West

Thanks to research on *Japonisme*, there is keen awareness of the impact Japanese art had on western artists of every kind. While many of the artefacts which triggered inspiration were imported by way of trade interests on a more local scale, the international exhibitions and World's Fairs[1] served to increase

---

1   The categorisation of these events is slightly fuzzy. For the purposes of this chapter, I use the general term 'international exhibition' to characterise these kinds of event in general and the full name respectively as well as the place and year for a particular event.

© BEATE LÖFFLER, 2025 | DOI:10.1163/9789004724174_005

attention and extend the audience. They also provided a broader audience with a convenient way to experience examples of Japanese buildings or their representations outside Japan.

There is already significant research on the historical development of international exhibitions in general: on individual events, on the networks of actors involved and on the designs chosen to represent a nation's self-perception.[2] At the same time, many an artist's biographies since the second half of the nineteenth century have contained testimony regarding the impact of such events and the overall dispositions, pavilions and objects displayed. One of the best known architectural cases is probably Frank Lloyd Wright and the World's Columbian Exposition in Chicago in 1893.[3]

Yet, while the Japanese displays were discussed in detail and the Japanese staffage gained attention, the Japanese pavilions were barely acknowledged in trans-regional journals on art or architecture and did not draw any special attention in the catalogues at the time in terms of their architectural features. Even today, after Japanese participation in international exhibitions as a means to express national identity gained significant scholarly attention from many different angles,[4] the pavilions of the nineteenth and early twentieth centuries remain unexamined but for one or two exceptions.

Extensive further research, even an entire separate volume, would be required to address this significant desideratum satisfactorily, and even more work would be needed to go beyond the dozen or so most famous and best studied events. Thus, in terms of this text, we will just sketch the character of the Japanese appearances at some international exhibitions as far as they concerned architectural issues, an approach which will primarily involve gathering images in order to gain an overview of the architectural features available

---

2 E.g. Friebe, Wolfgang, *Architektur der Weltausstellungen. 1851–1970* (Stuttgart, 1983); Sigel, Paul, *Exponiert. Deutsche Pavillons auf Weltausstellungen* (Berlin, 2000); Mattie, Erik, *Weltausstellungen* (Stuttgart et al., 1998); Kretschmer, Winfried, *Geschichte der Weltausstellungen* (Frankfurt/M. et al., 1999); Holz, Elizabeth G., *The Art of All Nations. 1850–73. The emerging role of exhibitions and critics* (Princeton, NJ, 1982); Cody, Sara (ed.), *Japan Goes to the World's Fairs. Japanese Art at the Great Expositions in Europe and the United States 1867–1904* (Los Angeles, 2005).

3 E.g. Nute, *Frank Lloyd Wright*, esp. pp. 48–72; Kirsch, Karin, *Die Neue Wohnung und das Alte Japan. Architekten planen für sich selbst* (Stuttgart, 1996); Delank, *Das imaginäre Japan*; Soros and Arbuthnott, *Godwin*.

4 Hedinger, Daniel, *Im Wettstreit mit dem Westen. Japans Zeitalter der Ausstellungen 1854–1941* (Frankfurt/M., 2011); Lockyer, Angus, *Japan at the exhibition, 1867–1970* (Ph.D. Dissertation, Stanford University, 2000); Foxwell, "Japan as Museum"; Lancaster, *Japanese influence*; Sigur, *Influence*; Odenthal, *Andere Räume*.

at this time. We will discuss the insights that might have been gained by visitors regarding the construction, spatial arrangement and design of the Japanese pavilions themselves, and the architectural information provided by the pieces on display. However, this will only skim the surface of matters and can in no way exhaust the complexity of the phenomenon.

The national displays in the general exhibition halls were usually subject to the spaces and even showcases allotted. There, architectural topics were limited to the selection and presentation of exhibits, mostly but not exclusively in the arts division.[5] The freestanding national pavilions, 'Japanese houses' or businesses of different kinds that were set up in the other areas of most of the exhibitions allowed for a conscious choice of building, design and use. These structures conveyed information about Japanese architecture to visitors not only through the buildings themselves but also through the surrounding gardens, the refreshments offered and the art objects and souvenirs on sale.[6]

1.1 London International Exhibition on Industry and Art, 1862

Japan made its first appearance at these events in 1862 at the *London International Exhibition on Industry and Art*, not on its own volition but due to initiatives by British actors. Rutherford Alcock, the British head of mission in Japan from 1858 to 1865, elaborated at length on his role in this endeavour in his introduction to *Art and Art Industries in Japan*, 1878. The objects collected and sent by Alcock spanned art, crafts and household goods as well as everyday items such as rain protection, aiming to stimulate British artisanal production of the time which was regarded as stagnant.[7] A Japanese delegation visiting England at this time took a different view. They mourned the low quality of the objects and the unfortunate impression of Japan's capabilities in this field given by this display.[8]

The *Japanese Court* was documented in a stereoscopic photograph and reproduced in *The Illustrated London News*. It shows the eclectic pieces in a picturesque arrangement within a larger hall, next to objects from Siam including a pagoda (Fig. 4.1). The Japanese delegation had already been portrayed some

---

5   Cody, *World's Fairs*, p. 10. There was for example considerable architectural content in the division of religion in Vienna.
6   Ibid., p. 11. For more detail see Tagsold, *Spaces in Translation*.
7   Alcock, *Catalogue*; Cody, *World's Fairs*, pp. 16–18. See for context e.g. Burges, William, "The international exhibition," in: *Gentleman's Magazine* 213 (July 1862), pp. 3–12.
8   Foxwell, "Japan as Museum," p. 40; Sigur, *Influence*, pp. 35–36; Kirsch, *Neue Wohnung*, pp. 48–49; Lockyer, *Japan*, p. 55, FN 41; Cody, *World's Fairs*, p. 18.

FIGURE 4.1   The International Exhibition, 1862: The Japanese Court

months earlier and with similar exotic flair, accompanied by contemporary sculpture and a western visitor in the nave of the exhibition hall.[9]

Neither the depictions nor the collection on display included architectural information. This, however, changed with Japan's next appearance in a similar context.

1.2   *Exposition universelle d'art et d'industrie de Paris, 1867*

The invitation to send objects and representatives to the *Exposition Universelle d'art et d'industrie de 1867* in Paris came at a time of turbulent political realignment in Japan. As a result, the first exhibition in which Japan intentionally participated involved not only a deputation from the reigning Tokugawa shōgunate, but a group of its political opponents as well, most notably of the *daimyō* of Satsuma.[10] Since all of the actors present invested effort and money into the objects on display, Japan's contribution of lacquerware and ceramics, fabrics and raw materials succeeded in intriguing the audience, despite

---

9   "The Japanese Ambassadors at the International Exhibition," in: *The Illustrated London News* (24 May 1862), Reprint 1997 via National Diet Library, http://www.ndl.go.jp/exposition/e/data/R/086r.html [last accessed 25 April 2024].
10   For more detail see Lockyer, *Japan*, pp. 27–29, 55–56, 58–59.

FIGURES 4.2–4.3 Exposition Universelle, 1867: The formal heterogeneity of the national displays (Japan in the middle); 'Le Kiosque Japonais' as depicted in a newspaper print

the limited space allotted and the unsuitable design of the exhibition cases (Figs. 4.2 and 4.3).[11]

At the same time, the spatial conception of the exhibition hall and the centre stage given to presentations of industrial achievements showed Japan, and for that matter other non-western countries, to be deficient in terms of technological innovation.[12] Observers drew parallels and saw a clear inferiority in fine arts as well, stating about the cultures of the Orient in general that "[t]heir architecture, although 'undoubtedly ancient', was 'essentially static'."[13] In this short evaluation, the interconnectedness of concepts of technological and cultural development and the hierarchies of civilisation in contemporary thought became more easily apparent than they were within art discourses alone. Yet, the statements echoed the analyses of Rutherford Alcock or James J. Jarves on Japanese art that we saw earlier and, like these, lack a rationale.

Parisian writers had only a limited amount of information on which to build their assessments. The park surrounding the main exhibition building provided space for additional activities by the participating nations. Among them

11 E.g. Falke, Jakob von, *Die Kunstindustrie der Gegenwart. Studien auf der Pariser Weltausstellung im Jahre 1867* (Leipzig, 1868), esp. Chapter 14, "Der Orient," pp. 237–252; Lockyer, *Japan*, pp. 58–59.
12 Lockyer, *Japan*, p. 61. On the spatial concept of the main hall see e.g. Beutler, Christian, *Weltausstellungen im 19. Jahrhundert* (München, 1973), pp. 68–70.
13 Quoted after Lockyer, *Japan*, p. 61, FN 57.

were the pavilion sent by the *daimyō* of Satsuma, of which a good photograph exists, and a 'Japanese farm', a tea house installed by the merchant Shimizu Usaburō and staffed by women from Edo's entertainment quarters, the appearance of which remains more vague.[14]

According to the official map, the buildings were in the northwestern part of the park, near Porte de Grenelle, situated between the Chinese and the Tunisian structures along a path named Japan. The key describes a circular building contour for the Japanese kiosk. Unfortunately, in a detailed bird's eye view the neighbouring buildings cover the area set aside for Japan apart from a large umbrella-like structure that might be the kiosk. An illustrated newspaper provides a more detailed map and makes a distinction between the kiosk and the hunting pavilion of Prince Satsuma further west, close to the Avenue de Suffren.[15]

The photograph of the Satsuma pavilion shows a small wooden building, elevated off the ground and covered by a projecting gabled roof with an accented ridge (Fig. 4.4). The two rooms of the pavilion were surrounded by a narrow porch, *engawa*, on three sides, the long side of the rooms open to the garden apart from three slim supports and a similarly slim beam. The small sides were formed by translucent sliding doors; the two rooms were also partially separated by opaque sliding doors. To the side of the building was a box-like structure that might have provided storage space or a toilet but probably housed the wooden shutters, *amado*, used in bad weather or to close the building during the night.

The building did not represent the complete structure of a Japanese building but a small 'cut-out' of a bigger complex, used in a way with shows similarities to a tea room or tea house.[16]

A graphic reproduction of the pavilion depicted the building in a simplified but quite similar way, except for slightly different proportions and a structural misunderstanding: the leftmost sliding door was shown in an impossible

---

14   Cody, *World's Fairs*, pp. 11, 18–20. See also the resource-rich essay by Gergely Barna: Barna, Gergely Péter, "Japanese Architectural Displays at the 1867 Paris, 1873 Vienna and 1876 Philadelphia International Exhibitions," in: Zorn, Bettina (ed.), *Archiv 65. Archiv Weltmuseum Wien* (2015), pp. 20–43.
15   "Ausstellungsgebäude für 1867, in Paris," in: *Allgemeine Bauzeitung* (1867), Plan 36; Ciceri, Eugène; Benoist, Philippe, *Vue officielle à vol d'oiseau de l'exposition universelle de 1867*, hand-colored lithograph, 68 × 98.5 cm, Library of Congress, https://www.loc.gov/pictures/item/00652015/ [last accessed 25 June 2023]; "'Jagdpavillion des Fürsten Satzumin', Die Pariser Ausstellung im Jahre 1867," in: *Über Land und Meer* 9, 17, 22 (February 1867), pp. 344, 352–354, here p. 353.
16   Barna, "Architectural Displays," pp. 24–25.

VISITING AND VISUALISING ARCHITECTURE 179

FIGURES 4.4–4.5   Exposition Universelle, 1867: Satsuma Pavillon, and 'Kiosque du Japon'

position, beyond the structural frame of the building's core and the sliding rails (Fig. 4.5).

The 'Japanese farm', an "amusement house," *mizuchaya*, translocated from Yokohama, was documented in a view from a bridged creek and surrounded by visitors.[17] The structure, with a straw-covered hipped roof and eaves hung with lanterns, was shown as part of a larger group of heterogeneous buildings. The arrangement of the building components of the 'farm' itself remained unclear (Fig. 4.6).

Neither the illustrations nor the textual descriptions of the time were specific enough to make it clear to readers that there were actually two buildings in the area, the Satsuma pavilion and the 'farm'. Beyond the different types of supposed roof covering, only the historical accounts of the various Japanese actors provide evidence in this respect. The confusion is increased by the fact that the three women residing at the 'farm' were depicted as inhabiting the Satsuma pavilion.[18]

17 Ibid., p. 25.
18 Lockyer, *Japan*, pp. 63–64; Duchesne de Bellecour, P., "Exposition chinoise et japonaise au Champ de Mars," in: *Revue des deux-Mondes* (1 August 1867), pp. 710–742, here p. 726; Bellet, P., "Les Costumes populaires du Japon," in: *L'Exposition universelle de 1867 illustrée*, vol. 1, pp. 363–365. – See also "The Japanese Women in the late Paris International Exhibition," in: *The Illustrated London News* 51, Issue 1455 (Paris International Exhibition (Supplement)) (16 November 1867), p. 541; "Japon. Intérieur de la maison du gouverneur de Satzouma," in: *Le monde illustré* 11, 546 (1867), p. 197.

FIGURE 4.6 Exposition Universelle, 1867: General view of the 'Japanese farm', the Japanese women in the centre of the image

Consequentially, the spatial and material information and, of course, the sensual perception of the buildings from Japan remained limited to actual visitors and did not translate into the reports with their meagre images and descriptions.

There was, however, another source of architectural information: architectural models. A contemporary author noted in the context of Chinese and Japanese exhibits among others:

> In addition to the house in the park, the Champ de Mars also offers models for various other types of dwellings, which are richer and more spacious. First, there is the house of a wealthy citizen of Yedo or Yokohama. It has two floors; a wooden staircase leads from the interior of the first room to the upper floor where the family lives. In front of the entrance is a porch; around it a courtyard with the outbuildings.[19]

---

19 "Outre la maison du parc, le Champ de Mars nous offre des réductions de diverses autres genres d'habitations, celles-ci, plus riches et plus spacieuses. Voici d'abord la demeure d'un bourgeois aisé de Yédo ou de Yokohama. Elle a deux étages, un escalier de bois monte de l'intérieur de la première pièce à l'étage supérieur, où loge la famille. Devant

The text mentioned the sole use of wood and the unfurnished interior of the house and alluded to a depiction of Edo's castle area.

In general, there is even less information on these models than the full-sized Japanese buildings. There are some visual hints in illustrations of Japanese displays in the main exhibition hall, and since many of the exhibits were usually sold after international exhibitions, one or the other of the models might have survived in private collections but there is no evidence of this.[20]

The buildings and architectural models on display in Paris during the *Exposition universelle* of 1867 certainly provided authentic Japanese constructions and spatial dispositions, in contrast to the environment to be found in the main exhibition hall. This would have allowed construction principles, materials and details to be studied during the exhibition itself. However, there is no indication of this in any of the textual or visual sources. On the contrary: the drawings available show flaws with respect to the visual rendering of the buildings. The depictions of Japanese buildings in Paris therefore helped to circulate the basic features of Japanese architecture, while their inherent architectural information – if it was even perceived as such – was not transferred in the discourses traceable through the trans-regional publications.

1.3 Weltausstellung Wien, 1873

The *Weltausstellung 1873* in Vienna saw the first Japanese presentation as an emerging nation-state under the Imperial Meiji government. As far as architecture was concerned, the initial situation was largely the same as in Paris in 1867: Japan shared a marginal space with China and Siam on the fringes of the main exhibition hall. The building was once again designed by the hosts, albeit without the ethnicising interior seen in Paris. In addition to this, however, the country was represented twice, both in an individual commercial and an official context, in the many other larger and smaller, variously themed pavilions in the surrounding park.

The Austrian photographer and entrepreneur Baron Raimund von Stillfried (1839–1911) had applied to have a Japanese tea house included in the official exhibition programme. Having worked in Japan for some years, he intended to sell curios and his photographs along with the tea. Since the Japanese

---

l'entrée, une vérandah; une cour à l'entour avec des communs." Duchesne de Bellecour, "Exposition," p. 727. See also: Salacroup-Buchard, Agnès, "Le Japonisme en architecture, 2000," via https://laurent-buchard.alwaysdata.net/index.html/Japonisme/index.html [last accessed 29 April 2024].

20 Barna, "Architectural Displays," p. 26.

FIGURE 4.7 Weltausstellung Wien, 1873: The Egyptian Palace and the Japanese Garden

delegation opposed the idea strongly, the building was erected outside the exhibition grounds as part of the larger entertainment district.[21]

The official Japanese contribution, an area containing a Japanese garden with an arched bridge, a Shintō shrine and a hall for ritual Shintō dance and music, was situated between the palace of the Khedive of Egypt to the north and the *K. und K. Gartenbaugesellschaft* (Imperial and Royal Horticultural Society) to the south. Master carpenter Matsuo Ihei was responsible for the construction work (Fig. 4.7).[22]

---

21 F. St., "Das japanische Theehaus im Vauxhallgarten des Praters," in: *Illustrirte Zeitung* 1581 (8 October 1873), pp. 287–290; see especially the elaboration on the ambivalent understanding of the term Tea house, p. 290. Barna, "Architectural Displays," p. 29 FN; Gartlan, Luke, "Changing Views: The Early Topographical Photographs of Stillfried & Company," in: Rousmaniere, *Reflecting Truth*, pp. 40–65, here p. 57; Bennett, *Photography*, pp. 133–141, esp. p. 139.

22 Barna, "Architectural Displays," pp. 28–29. See also National Diet Library Tōkyō, Reader Services and Collections Department, "Expositions. Where the modern technology of the times was exhibited," here http://www.ndl.go.jp/exposition/e/s1/1873.html [accessed 9 September 2023] and the information on the building team in Sakamoto, Hisako,

The south-oriented planning document of the area shows an axial concept of spaces aligned with the focus of the area, the shrine (Figs. 4.8 and 4.9). The entrance was marked by a *torii* gate, signifying a Shintō precinct. The path leading from it was flanked by display stands and plant borders on both sides, guiding visitors towards the shrine. After passing the stands, the path widened to an open space, equipped with a pole with Japan's flag on the left-hand side and the *kagura-den*, the stage for Shintō dances, on the right hand. A small bridge, part of the garden area, extended the path towards the shrine, behind which a hidden exit led to a botanic garden of Japanese specimens.

The focal point of the area, the small shrine, resembled in size and proportions many of the wayside Shintō shrines seen in Japan or the subordinate shrines within larger compounds. The building, arguably a wooden construction, was raised off the ground, and the main room was surrounded by a railed veranda (Figs. 4.10, 4.11, 4.14, 4.15).

It was accessed by some steps in the centre of the long side; the high-hipped saddle roof extended down on this side to protect the stairs. The walls were formed by sturdy supports and beams, filled in partly by boarding, partly with lattice work. The roof was the defining feature of the small building. While the material of the covering remains obscure in the images, the ridge was marked and weighted down by an additional beam and adorned by *chigi* and *katsuogi*, the signifying elements typical of the shrines of Ise and their branches, thus connecting the building with the dynastic legitimation of the imperial dynasty.

The garden surrounding the shrine was composed mainly of a small pond, shrubs, trees and rocks. The illustrations are not consistent in terms of the architectural elements beyond the arched bridge. While the photographs documented the use of stone lanterns, the drawings showed some of them entirely out of proportion and in various positions (Figs. 4.12–4.15).

The *kagura* stage is best seen in the foreground of a photograph that shows the shrine, the garden and a stone lantern (Fig. 4.14). It forms part of the background to another illustration of the garden and the centrepiece of a drawing depicting the process of building the 'Japanese village', which shows it, rather unconvincingly, as a busy scene. The stage is easily recognisable from its roof with its slight inward curve (Figs. 4.15 and 4.16).

There is only limited visual evidence for the buildings flanking the path between the *torii* and the shrine. The slightly raised longitunal constructions

---

"Relationship between the Japanese Exhibits at the Philadelphia International Exhibition of 1876 and the Vienna World Exhibition of 1873," in: *Proceedings of the 54th Annual Conference of JSSD* (2007), s.p.

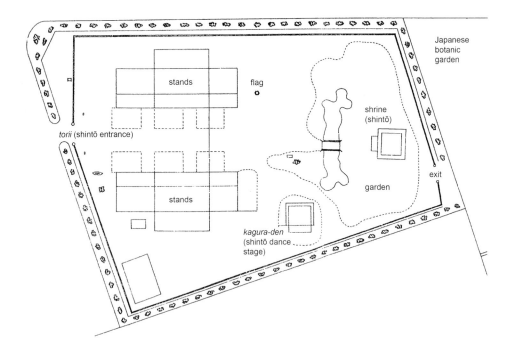

FIGURES 4.8–4.9 Weltausstellung Wien, 1873: Map of Japanese Garden (reworked and annotated from original scan); View from just behind the *torii* towards the Japanese garden and shrine

FIGURES 4.10–4.11　　Weltausstellung Wien, 1873: two views of the Japanese garden and shrine

FIGURES 4.12–4.13   Weltausstellung Wien, 1873: Two views of the Japanese garden; the right hand scene depicting the opening visit by the Austrian Emperor Franz Joseph I and Empress Elisabeth

had porches along the entire frontage; the separate roofs of these were braced by a row of supports. The rooms behind opened with *shōji* (Fig. 4.9).

A contemporary impression of a similar structure was provided by a sketch of Stillfried's tea-house in operation. While probably less elaborate in design, it showed the same spatial disposition of roof and porch (Fig. 4.17). The box for the weather shutters, the *amado*, is easily recognisable on the right, while the position of the lanterns that lined the porch roof was arguably misunderstood (compare to Fig. 4.9). The tree trunk with the bowl on the left with the non-specific element above might have indicated the washbasin and accompanying towel of a toilet.

The design of the whole official complex as well as the selection of the industrial exhibits had been developed under the advice of Gottfried Wagener (1831–1892) and Heinrich von Siebold (1852–1908), and intentionally focused on the exotic flair and artistic taste of Japanese tradition to catch the audience's fancy. This approach succeeded and drew not only the interest of the Imperial couple Franz Joseph I and Elisabeth, who visited the area, but also led a British trading company to purchase all of the buildings and garden components to be re-arranged as the 'Japanese Village' in the park of Alexandra Palace, an entertainment venue in London.[23] It was announced as such in *The British Architect* in 1874, including "a residence, a temple, and a bazaar," the

---

23   Historic England, "Listing 1001253: Alexandra Palace," https://historicengland.org.uk/listing/the-list/list-entry/1001253 [accessed 15 July 2023]; National Diet Library, "Expositions," http://www.ndl.go.jp/exposition/e/s1/1873-2.html [accessed 15 July 2023].

VISITING AND VISUALISING ARCHITECTURE 187

FIGURES 4.14 – 4.15   Weltausstellung Wien, 1873: Views of the Japanese garden with lanterns, shrine and *kagura* stage

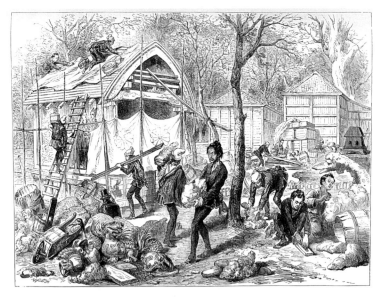

FIGURE 4.16   Weltausstellung Wien, 1873: Japanese workmen building a Japanese village

FIGURE 4.17   Vienna, 1873: Stillfried's Japanese Tea-house outside the exhibition area

latter to sell authenticated Japanese products to the visitors. The group of buildings remained on site until destroyed by fire in 1897.[24]

An even more permanent existence was foreseen for some architecture-related exhibits and models presented at the *Weltausstellung*. The exhibits were listed and detailed in both the general and the Japanese catalogue in at least four different categories: specimens of wood, stone and earth; models of fire-resistant warehouses and an aqueduct; models of urban and rural dwellings of different classes including all interior fittings; drawings and models of shrine and temple buildings; and architectural details such as the fish-shaped acroterion made from gilt copper sheeting that adorned Nagoya castle.[25]

The latter was documented in a photograph held by the Tōkyō National Museum before transportation to Vienna with two men provided for scale, presented against the backdrop of a garden that was barren but for the plants covered against snow and frost damage. In the exhibition, the acroterion was placed in a central position in Japan's section of the main hall, as evidenced by two interior views (Figs. 4.18 and 4.19). Other interiors evidence the position of further architectural models from various categories within the exhibition. One view shows a group of houses, the foremost with a thatched hip-and-gable roof and a strongly accentuated ridge in the left part of the picture, and a five-storied pagoda in the right margin (Fig. 4.20).

The pagoda, a replica of the pagoda in Yanaka, Tōkyō,[26] was documented by Michael Moser (1853–1912) before shipping in the same garden as the acroterion

---

24   "Alexandra Palace [Architectural, Engineering, and Local Public Works]," in: *British architect* 1 (15 May 1874), p. 315; Historic England, "Alexandra Palace."

25   *Welt-Ausstellung 1873 in Wien. Officieller General-Catalog* (Wien, 1873), p. 767. See also *Catalog der kaiserlich japanischen Ausstellung* (Wien, 1873). – The information on the material was provided by Lorenz, Reinhold, *Japan und Mitteleuropa. Von Solferino bis zur Wiener Weltausstellung (1859–73)* (Brünn; München; Wien, 1944), p. 161. Beyond some factual data such as this, the book's content is a study of cultural cliché and nationalism. – The *acroterion* was depicted by Katsushika Hokusai (1760–1849) as one of the *Fugaku hyakkei* [One Hundred Views of Mount Fuji] in 1834–1835 and by Utagawa Hiroshige II (1826–1869) in 1859 as *True View of Nagoya in Owari Province* in *One Hundred Views of Famous Places in the Provinces*, but it did not come out in western publications on architecture until later. For a much smaller sample see Détain, C., "La couver ture en tuiles au Japon," in: *Revue générale de l'architecture et des travaux public* 44 (1887), cols. 111–117, 152–161, plate 39. For an illustration taken from the Vienna exhibit see Reed, Edward James, *Japan. Its History, Traditions, and Religions* (London, 1880), vol. 2, p. 261, and for a reproduction of the original print see Strange, Edward Fairbrother, "Architecture in Japan," in: *The architectural review for artist and craftsman: a magazine of architecture and decoration* 1 (1896/1897), pp. 126–135, here p. 135.

26   Cody, *World's Fairs*, pp. 22–24. – The original building was lost in a suicide fire in 1957. Waley, Paul, "Who Cares about the Past in Today's Tokyo?," in: Brumann, Christoph;

FIGURES 4.18–4.19   Weltausstellung Wien, 1873: Two interior views of the Japanese exhibition

FIGURE 4.20   Weltausstellung Wien, 1873: The so-called 'Japanese Gallery'

dwelling"[33] in the official catalogue, the model depicts a section of the residence of a *daimyō*, a feudal lord of the Tokugawa period (1603–1867).[34] The model shows only a small part of the spatial programme: the very representative gate system with two guard houses, which marks the complex hidden behind walls as the residence of a high ranking person/family; a watchtower; reception rooms and a *nō*-stage, as well as some residential rooms (Fig. 4.31, see colour section).[35] Often spreading over hundreds of square metres, these representative residences, *yashiki*, also included fortifications and barracks, servants' quarters and utility rooms, family quarters and ceremonial rooms, interspersed with courtyards and gardens.

Both the farmstead replica and the *daimyō* residency elements were created at the Musashiya workshop located in Tōkyō-Asakusa. Dating back to the 1820s, the workshop employed master craftsmen from various fields to create luxury toys. During the 1870s and early 1880s, the head of the workshop was Musashiya Kamakichi who contributed to several exhibitions both within Japan and overseas. His successor, Musashiya Yonekichi, continued this tradition up until 1900.[36]

The model was damaged during its time in storage and needed extensive restoration, which was completed in the laboratories at the Weltmuseum with support from scholars from other places and institutions (Figs. 4.28–4.30, 4.31–4.32, see colour section).[37] This made it possible to study the model, starting from the choice of material and extending to the conceptual understanding of 'architectural model' in Japan at the time, and also allowed the architectural information the model was supposed to convey to be unearthed.[38] One

---

33 "Modell eines städtischen Wohnhauses," *Catalog der kaiserlich japanischen Ausstellung* (Wien, 1873), s.p.; *Welt-Ausstellung 1873 in Wien*, p. 767.

34 Coaldrake, "Beyond Mimesis," pp. 202–203; Barna, "Architectural Displays," pp. 31–36.

35 See also Coaldrake, "Beyond mimesis," pp. 203, 209. – On the social function of nō stages in Tokugawa society, see Shigeta, Michi, "The Nō Stage of the Buke Hinagata. The Historical Context and Background of its Production," in: Zorn, Bettina (ed.), *Archiv 65. Archiv Weltmuseum Wien* (2015), pp. 110–117.

36 Barna, Gergely Peter; Shimizu, Shigeatsu; Ishida, Jun'ichiro; Li, Chang Wei, "Intercultural Transmission of Architectural Elements. A Case Study of 19th-Century Japanese Architectural Models," in: S. Xu, Subin; Aoki, Nobuo; Vieira Amaro, Bébio (eds.), *East Asian Architecture in Globalization. Values, Inheritance and Dissemination*, corrected publication (Cham, 2022), pp. 541–551, here p. 547; Barna, "Architectural Displays," pp. 31–36, here p. 32; Mamba (Musashiya), Masayuki; Huber, Michael (transl.), "The model of a Daimyō Residence *yashiki* and Musashiya Kamakichi," in: Zorn, Bettina (ed.), *Archiv 65. Archiv Weltmuseum Wien* (2015), pp. 77–83.

37 Zorn, *Archiv 65*.

38 Coaldrake, "Beyond Mimesis"; Coaldrake, "Vienna"; Zwerger, "Präsentation."

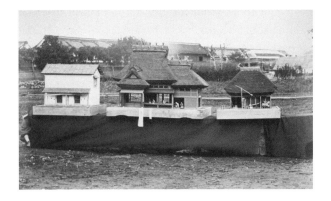

FIGURES 4.23–4.24
Weltausstellung Wien, 1873: Architectural models of rural and urban dwellings

FIGURE 4.25   Weltausstellung Wien, 1873: Architectural models of shrines of the Ise type

This corresponds not only to the textual information, but also to other photographs from Moser's album, kept by the Austrian National Library.[29] One photograph shows three supposedly rural buildings (from left to right): a fire-resistant storehouse, *kura*; the dwelling from the exhibition with the thatched hip-and-gable roof, consisting of different building parts; and another, much simpler thatched building with a draw well to the front (Fig. 4.23).

A similar display shows urban dwellings (from left to right): a building for commercial use such as an artisan's workshop, merchant's shop or inn; an elaborate fire-resistant storehouse, *kura*; and a detached dwelling of an affluent owner. The same album included some urban scenes in Japan and another model that strongly resembles the spatial composition of the shrine complex in Ise, again corresponding to the information provided by the catalogues (Figs. 4.24 and 4.25).[30]

The fate of some of the models is unknown, but two groups of them survived in the depths of Viennese museum collections: they have been restored and examined in detail recently. Today, they are in the care of the *Weltmuseum* in Vienna.[31]

First, there is the farmhouse with its outbuildings as documented in the exhibition and in Moser's photographs (Figs. 4.20, 4.23, see also 4.26, 4.27 in colour section).[32]

Much more spectacular is a model measuring about 3 by 4.5 metres with a maximum height of 1.5 metres. Inconspicuously named "model of an urban

---

29 On Moser see Bennett, *Photography*, pp. 150–152; Moser, Alfred, "My Grandfather Michael Moser (1853–1912)," in: Zorn, Bettina (ed.), *Archiv 65. Archiv Weltmuseum Wien* (2015), pp. 12–19.

30 A publication of 1989 focusing on the Weltausstellung seems to mention an additional building or model in the exhibition halls, a temple from Kyōto. This reference turns out to be misleading when checked against its original source which explicitly mentioned the park grounds and the Ise shrine and thus referred to the life-sized shrine structure and its famous template. See Pemsel, Jutta, *Die Wiener Weltausstellung von 1873* (Wien; Köln, 1989), pp. 49–50; Lorenz, *Japan und Mitteleuropa*, pp. 162–163.

31 Coaldrake, "Vienna"; Zwerger, Klaus, "Präsentation japanischer Baukultur im Wien des 19. Jahrhunderts," in: *Archiv für Völkerkunde* 57–58 (2007–2008), pp. 185–220; "Vienna museum to restore daimyo mansion model from 19th century," in: *The Japan Times*, online edition (26 March 2015), https://www.japantimes.co.jp/news/2013/03/26/national/vienna-museum-to-restore-daimyo-mansion-model-from-19th-century/#.XG1q2rgxmbg [accessed 20 February 2019]. – On this matter, see the extensive material in: Zorn, Bettina (ed.), *Archiv 65. Archiv Weltmuseum Wien* (2015).

32 Coaldrake, William, "Beyond Mimesis: Japanese architectural models at the Vienna Exhibition and 1910 Japan British Exhibition," in: Cox, Rupert, *The Culture of Copying in Japan. Critical and Historical Perspectives* (London, 2007), pp. 199–212, here pp. 203–204; Barna, "Architectural Displays," pp. 36–37.

FIGURES 4.21–4.22   Weltausstellung Wien, 1873: Architectural model of a pagoda, and its (Chinois) depiction as part of the 'Japanese Gallery'

and became – now more *chinois* in proportion and design – the focus in one of the many illustrations communicating the events at the *Weltausstellung* to the readers of *Illustrirte Zeitung* (Figs. 4.21 and 4.22). The model, built by Muramatsu Kichizō, was sold to England after the exhibition closed.[27]

The arrangement of objects makes it possible to conclude that there were more architectural models in the exhibition than were seen in the earlier photograph alone. Coaldrake traced them in the exhibition plan and Barna in the photograph of the 'Japanese Gallery'.[28]

Schulz, Evelyn (eds.), *Urban Spaces in Japan: Cultural and Social Perspectives* (London et al., 2012), pp. 148–166, here p. 158. The University Library in Nagasaki holds two contemporary photographs of the building. Nagasaki University Library, "Metadata Database of Japanese Old Photographs in Bakumatsu-Meiji Period," http://oldphoto.lb.nagasaki-u.ac.jp/en/about.html [accessed 15 July 2023].

27   Barna, "Architectural Displays," p. 40.
28   Coaldrake, William H., "Japan at Vienna. The Discovery of Meiji Architectural Models from the 1873 Vienna Exhibition," in: *Archiv für Völkerkunde* 53 (2003), pp. 27–43, here pp. 28, 30; Barna, "Architectural Displays," p. 32.

important indicator regarding the latter was the phrase *buke hinagata* with which the model was labeled. This contains a reference to *buke*, the class of warriors usually known as samurai, and thus marked the dwelling as belonging to a specific stratum of Japanese society. The term *hinagata* carries a double meaning in this context.[39]

Firstly, it is an abbreviation of the term *hinagatabon*, a genre of handbooks or pattern-books on planning and construction which go back to at least the sixteenth century but which were largely kept in secret by master carpenters' families. By the mid-seventeenth century, the increasing need for a qualified workforce for large-scale building projects overwhelmed the established practices of professional training and led to the broader publication of manuals discussing proportions and measurements, the overall layout of building complexes, and structural or decorative detailing. These books did not teach carpentry itself but the application of the carpenter's manual competences to the design and realisation of building projects. One genre of such pattern books that went through many editions up to the latter half of the nineteenth century was named *buke hinagata*, pattern-book of samurai architecture.[40]

Secondly, the term *hinagata* can indicate "[a] miniature or a scaled-down model of a planned work of art. It is usually identical in form and proportion to the final work, and is often made to serve as a preparatory model which was then enlarged."[41] Hinagata had been used in Japan since the sixth and seventh centuries and examples of such were part of Japan's displays at international exhibitions.[42]

Hence, while the model in Vienna is neither a pattern-book nor a planning model, its character is close to both definitions. As William Coaldrake explains, it presents a generic example of a specific building type, the 'idea' behind it, but not the image of an existing building. The same holds for the model of the farmhouse. Neither building shows markers of regional or familial specifics. They do, however, show features which signify status, such as the gate of the *daimyō* residence or the extended layout of the farmhouse, which was intended to receive and entertain high-ranking guests.[43]

The attention to detail in both models underscores the expertise inherent to the Musashiya workshop. Such precision enabled visitors in 1873 to distinguish

---

39   For the general use of such terms as *hinagata* and *yashiki* see JAANUS. Japanese architecture and art net users system, http://www.aisf.or.jp/~jaanus/ [accessed 8 August 2023].
40   Coaldrake, "Beyond Mimesis," p. 203; Coaldrake, *Carpenter*, pp. 38–40, 139–140.
41   *hinagata*, in: JAANUS, here http://www.aisf.or.jp/~jaanus/deta/h/hinagata.htm [accessed 8 August 2023].
42   Barna, "Architectural Displays," pp. 25, 29–30.
43   Coaldrake, "Beyond Mimesis," p. 203.

primary construction elements from secondary features, such as the walls and partitions shaping the interior space, and the elements used as decoration. It thus provided a window into the general principles of Japanese architecture, highlighting its similarities and contrasts to Central European practices. However, what might have eluded the uninformed observer were the architectural codes of status, taste and luxury embedded within these miniaturised representations.[44]

1.4 Centennial International Exhibition in Philadelphia, 1876

The *Centennial International Exhibition* of 1876 in Philadelphia was the next large event at which Japan was represented. It was the only Asian country with a national pavilion, underlining its claim to significance in international negotiations of power.[45]

Much as in Paris in 1867, it is difficult to reconstruct the shape and position of the buildings, despite the contemporary reports, since maps and illustrations are limited.[46]

First, there was the 'Japanese dwelling' or 'Japanese pavilion' (Figs. 4.33 and 4.35), again built by Matsuo Ihei and sent by a rich merchant from Kanazawa.[47]

The two-storied building, with a hipped tiled roof and surrounded by a simple fence, stood to the northwest of the central *Machinery Building* among the pavilions of other countries and the American states. The construction of the ground floor was hidden by a slightly projecting lattice work, similar to a bay window, protected by a separate roof. The walls of the upper floor were set back, making a wraparound porch possible. Here, the structure of the walls was visible: it was made from supports and beams and had a partial plaster in-fill with some sliding windows. There is evidence of the use of fabric or natural fibre hangings, *sudare*, suspended from the eaves to provide additional protection from the sun. In addition, the upper floor was equipped with wooden shutters in case of bad weather, *amado*; two of the storage boxes for these were visible in a photographic detail showing the entrance (Fig. 4.34). The latter featured a sloping gabled roof, *hafu*, with elaborate carvings, positioned off-centre on the main façade.[48]

---

44   See further Zorn, Bettina, "The History of the Daimyō House Model in the Collection of the Weltmuseum Wien and its traces in Vienna," in: id. (ed.), *Archiv 65. Archiv Weltmuseum Wien* (2015), pp. 44–55, esp. pp. 49–50.
45   Sigur, *Influence*, p. 41.
46   Sadly, Christian Tagsold's seminal work muddies the water on his account. Tagsold, *Spaces in Translation*, p. 55.
47   Barna, "Architectural Displays," p. 42.
48   The *hafu* was a building detail which had 'migrated' from *daimyō* residences and temples into "formal" use. Barna, "Architectural Displays," p. 42.

FIGURES 4.33–4.35
Centennial International Exhibition, 1876: two photographs and an engraving of the 'Japanese dwelling'

The textual sources reported the building had a U-shaped floorplan and an interior courtyard formed by the wings and some outbuildings, an unusual composition for traditional Japanese dwellings and a Meiji-era phenomenon of formal hybridity.[49] Visual evidence for this plan is largely lacking among the known views, not least due to the prevalent use of a very low perspective; an exception is a hint at a longer side façade given in one of them. An unpublished sheet with four sketches of the Japanese buildings by the architect Benjamin Linfoot (1840–1912), however, documented the rear view of the 'Japanese dwelling' with secondary structures (Fig. 4.36).

There is disagreement between this and the other illustrations regarding the size and proportions of the buildings, not least since often none of the neighbouring structures were part of the views. While some of the illustrations seem to have used the same initial drawing or photograph, the use of staffage personnel of different sizes changed the overall impression of the building, occasionally suggesting a palace-sized construction with high ceilings. Linfoot's

---

49 See for example Lancaster, Clay, "Japanese Buildings in the United States before 1900: Their Influence upon American Domestic Architecture," in: *Art Bulletin* 35 (1953), pp. 217–224, here p. 218; Barna, "Architectural Displays," p. 42.

FIGURE 4.36   Centennial International Exhibition, 1876: Rear view of the 'Japanese dwelling' by Benjamin Linfoot

sketches were vague on that point as well and suggested a much loftier upper floor than did the photographs, an indication of how much the unfamiliar structure may have challenged the perception and comprehension of observers, even those trained as architects, at that time.

There is an illustration showing the *Interior of the Japanese Quarters, Fairmont Park, Philadelphia* (Fig. 4.37, see colour section). However, it leaves reason for some doubt. The interior shows only western furniture and a spatial organisation which is in strong contrast to the exterior structure of the building that supposedly served as a dwelling for the Japanese delegation, despite the stylistic changes of Meiji architecture.[50] In addition, the remaining examples of Japanese buildings of this era, which provided a communal living space for the workforce, found other ways to accommodate larger groups, as seen in the house of the Aoyama family in Sapporo's architectural museum (Figs. 4.38 to 4.40, see colour section).

The second complex of Japanese buildings was the 'Japanese Bazaar' by the same builder in the centre of the overall exhibition area, between the House of Public Comfort and the Swedish School-house. This single-storey building with a tiled gabled roof on a U-shaped plan was depicted from three different angles, one of them a bird's-eye view, thus making it possible to reconstruct its exterior spatial arrangement. The three wings of the building formed an open

---

50   Barna points out that it was also used to entertain important customers. Barna, "Architectural Displays," p. 42.

FIGURES 4.41–4.42   Centennial International Exhibition, 1876: Japanese bazaar

courtyard; the resulting impression of invitation to the audience was underlined by wide porches and a garden (Figs. 4.41 and 4.42).[51]

The bazaar complex was enriched by a garden to the south of the building.[52] Utilising a triangle of land between two pathways, it combined Japanese elements such as fences made from lattice work or brushwood and a tall stone lantern with western flowerbeds. Some sources mentioned a tea house in relation to the garden, which would lead today's Japanophilic reader to expect a small building or part of a building for *chadō*, the way of the tea. Here it most

---

51   Westcott, Thompson, *Portfolio. A Souvenir of the International Exhibition at Philadelphia, Comprising Lithographic Views of Fifty of its Principal Buildings* (Philadelphia, 1876), pp. 22, 55; Cf. Kirsch, *Neue Wohnung*, p. 54.
52   See also Tagsold, *Spaces in Translation*, pp. 55–56.

probably indicated a shop selling refreshments, as visible to the rear of the garden (Fig. 4.43).[53]

The two buildings had a significant impact on American building discourses, just as the Japanese art objects near the northwestern corner of the main exhibition hall had on interior design and art production.[54] An interior view of the hall showed the shelves of porcelain and bronzes on display. A photograph of another part of the exhibition showed carvings, bronzes and a miniature building similar to a wayside shrine or temple.[55] This, however, is the sole visual example of an object at this exhibition that might have been an architectural model (Figs. 4.44–4.45).

Seen from the perspective of architectural knowledge transfer, however, the Philadelphia exhibition is of special interest, not for its pavilions or its models, but for the descriptions and depictions of Japanese builders that it generated. We already offered a critical view of the exoticisation of Japanese building practices in the introduction to the sub-chapter on *Architecture as a Field of Engineering*. Yet, while the descriptions in the *American Architect and Building News* were full of cultural clichés, they did provide information. The same holds true for two plates published at the same time, being among the first to convey Japanese building practices to a western audience apart from a more idealistic scene in Humbert's *Le Japon illustré* in 1870 and the scene from Vienna of 1873 (see Fig. 4.16).[56]

One of these plates illustrated the laying of a foundation using a ram, while the other summarised glimpses of the daily life of the Japanese workmen as well as details of the use of tools and planning documents (Figs. 4.46, 4.47). The latter's central illustration depicted the *Erecting of the Japanese dwelling house*, showing the structural skeleton. However, the illustrations have to be taken with a pinch of salt. Firstly, the buildings were initially erected in Japan, then dismantled and shipped to Philadelphia.[57] The actual erection would therefore have been a very swift process of assembly, barely necessitating the use of saw or adze, except possibly for the outbuildings. Secondly, the position of the supports that supposedly formed the structure of the dwelling is doubtful. The distribution of the supports seems more picturesque than rational: this is most apparent with regard to the illustration on the centre left side of

---

53 Sigur, *Influence*, p. 42.
54 Lancaster, "Japanese Buildings," pp. 218–219; Cody, *World's Fairs*, pp. 30, 40–45.
55 In contradiction to its listing on https://libwww.freelibrary.org, the building is not a pagoda. – On the objects on display, see also Cody, *World's Fairs*, pp. 28–36.
56 Humbert, *Japon*, 2, p. 349. The English edition was published in London in 1874 without this illustration.
57 Sigur, *Influence*, p. 42.

VISITING AND VISUALISING ARCHITECTURE 201

FIGURE 4.43   Centennial International Exhibition, 1876: Japan Pavilion (Bazaar)

FIGURES 4.44–4.45   Centennial International Exhibition, 1876: Two views of the Japanese exhibition

FIGURE 4.46   Centennial International Exhibition, 1876: Japanese workmen laying the foundation of the Japanese building

the drawing, where the workman is partially hiding a floating support, the role of which in the overall scheme remains obscure.

Whether this was because the audience was accustomed to the widespread use of wood as a primary building material or because of the Japanese presentation choices, the Philadelphia exhibition made Japanese building practices visible and accessible to the public even before its official launch.[58] Beyond that, the architectural impact remained limited to vague ideas and general notions of form.

---

58   Cf. Sakamoto, "Relationship."

FIGURE 4.47   Centennial International Exhibition, 1876: erection of the Japanese buildings on the centennial grounds in Fairmount Park

1.5 *Exposition universelle de Paris, 1878*

While *Japonisme* was well under way, Japan's appearance at the *Exposition universelle* in Paris in 1878 provides heterogeneous architectural information.[59] The country had a presence both on the *Street of Nations* and with a cottage building in the park around the Trocadéro.

Since the structure of the entrances along the *Street of Nations* was determined by the exhibition halls beyond, the scope for the respective national designs was limited. Japan chose a rather shallow façade with a disposition of colours and structures that created a Neo-Renaissance appearance.

It was set back relative to China and Italy on either side, thus making it possible to accentuate the entrance with a bold gate that underlined – at least in the traditional role of Japanese gate buildings as architectural signifiers of social status[60] – the importance of the national exhibition within (Figs. 4.48–4.50). Built from one of the best Japanese woods, *keyaki* (zelkova serrata),[61] the gate itself seemed to consist of four basic parts: first, the roofed frame around the door of the exhibition hall; second, two wooden walls leading towards it from the promenade; third, two huge wooden pillars protruding farthest from the façade and serving as gateposts and 'joints' for the entire construction; and, fourth, two perpendicular wings oriented parallel to the main façade.

Japanese architectural history is full of gate buildings of different sizes and significance, and the carpenter's manuals of the eighteenth and early nineteenth centuries included many forms, but this construction did not fit the canon. The entire ensemble of façade and gate on the *Street of Nations* was – much more obviously than was the pavilion in Philadelphia two years earlier – a hybridisation of architectural ideas taken from both Japanese and western practices, and thus was part of the negotiation of meaning that was ubiquitous in Japan during the Meiji era, not only in art and architecture.

The architectural features of the cottage, which was set up with a fenced garden near the Trocadéro, were a marked contrast to the section of façade on the *Street of Nations*: a smallish building without grandeur, it was seemingly cobbled together with different roofs, some of them gabled, some pent. The roof covering remained indistinct in a contemporary photograph and the engravings of the time show a broad variety of interpretations, including

---

59 Kirsch, *Neue Wohnung*, p. 54.
60 On this point, see for example Coaldrake, *Architecture and Authority*, esp. chapter 8, "Shogunal and Daimyo Gateways. The Intersecting Spheres of Arbitrary Will and Technical Necessity," pp. 193–207.
61 Cody, *World's Fairs*, p. 38.

FIGURE 4.48 Exposition Universelle, 1878: Rue des nations (section including the neighbouring nations)

different kinds of marked main ridge common for vernacular houses, most notably in rural areas (Figs. 4.51–4.54).[62]

Some of the views suggested arrangements of furniture and people in the garden, which resembled those of tea houses at scenic viewpoints or sights in Japan, while they did not agree on the size and number of trees and parasols involved.[63]

At least two interiors were published, which make it possible to gain some architectural information (Figs. 4.55, 4.56). A view from the garden showed part of the building's construction and the wooden detailing, as well as a view of the interior furniture and proportions. In both cases, the overall appearance was Japanese in the somewhat 'condensed' way often seen in *Japonisme*: the rooms were stuffed with ceramics and fans, shelving and pillows, arguably acting as the bazaar depicted in one of the exteriors as well. In addition, there were some other details, which did not easily accord with the functions and forms of a supposed farmer's house, such as the tiles in the foreground of the garden view. This invites the conclusion that this pavilion was set up based on Japan's building tradition as far as its construction in general was concerned,

---

62 Cf. "Bazar Giapponese," in: *L'Illustration, Journal Universel 1841*, Volume LXXI (8 June 1878), p. 264; "La ferme Japonaise," in: *L'Univers illustré* (29 June 1878), p. 414; (31 August 1878), p. 549.

63 On the plants, see Commission impériale, *Le Japon*, 2, 188, and on the garden, see Tagsold, *Spaces in Translation*, pp. 57–58.

FIGURES 4.49–4.50
Exposition Universelle, 1878: Pavillon du Japon in a photograph and, with closed gate, in an advertisement

but that it was no less a hybrid design than was the façade on the *Street of Nations*.

It is also necessary to mention that the two men in the interior scene were too large for the overall proportions of the building. This made the frequently mentioned diminutiveness of the Japanese houses even more apparent. We will look at this issue later in this chapter in the excursus on transfer errors.

There was something to be learned in an architectural sense from the building, but the reports of the time were brief in this respect, just as the depictions of the area conveyed impressions rather than concrete information.[64] One

---

64   See for example "China and Japan at the Paris exhibition," in: *The Builder* 16 (1 June 1878), pp. 552–553; Burty, Philippe, "Exposition universelle de 1878: Le Japon ancien et le Japon moderne," in: *L'art: revue hebdomadaire illustrée* 4 (1878), pp. 241–264.

FIGURES 4.51–4.53   Exposition Universelle, 1878: three depictions of the 'Japanese Pavilion' on the Trocadero and the Japanese garden

year later, however, Philippe Burty's *Notes sur l'architecture au Japon* incorporated architectural details from the same compound: these included two gates, one of them heavily ornamented with carvings (Fig. 4.56).[65] The latter was documented in a photograph during the exhibition, while precise visual evidence for the second is lacking other than showing it on the right-hand side of the same photograph (Fig. 4.57).

65   Burty, "Notes."

FIGURE 4.54   Exposition Universelle, 1878: external view of the 'maison japonaise au Trocadéro'

The 1878 *Exposition universelle* in Paris provided a fragmented glimpse into the architecture of Japan, revealing its various facets. While it drew attention, Japan was no more than a minor presence among others at these international exhibitions where both time and space were limited, and any experience of a specific culture or phenomenon could easily be eclipsed by many other fascinating attractions. There were, however, other ways to acquaint western audiences with Japan and its architecture over an extended period of time or without spatial restrictions.

FIGURES 4.55–4.56 Exposition Universelle, 1878: interior view of the 'Japanese farm' or 'maison japonaise'

FIGURES 4.57–4.58   Exposition universelle, 1878: the gates of the Japanese area at Trocadéro

EXCURSUS: THE *JAPANESE NATIVE VILLAGE*, LONDON, 1885–1887

At the same time as official appearances at the various international exhibitions, Japan and its architecture were also presented to a western audience through other activities, such as by theatre companies and entertainment enterprises. The former, and their depiction of Japan in the popular media, is a topic in itself, and will only be mentioned here for the sake of completing the picture. The latter, which was hinted at already in connection with the buildings in Vienna that were sold and translocated to London, will be covered using a single example, the Japanese Village in London, 1885–1887.

More than anything else, at this time, it was the operetta *The Mikado* by William S. Gilbert (1836–1911) und Arthur Sullivan (1842–1900) that brought dramatic scenes of Japan to life for a broader audience.[66] The stage design by Hawes Craven (1837–1910) for the Savoy Theatre, 1885, showed a representative building to the right which succeeded in conveying an East Asian or even Japanese impression, but made no sense in terms of its structural and decorative features (Fig. 4.59, see colour section). The *Mikado* was restaged many times afterwards and deep into the twentieth and twenty-first centuries, with many different stage sets.[67] The Castanet Club in Montreal staged the operetta as early as 1886 with an imposing design, most likely pieced together from souvenir photographs (Fig. 4.60). A much later stage set for a high school performance of 1924 showed a significantly more abstracted version, in which Mount Fuji served as the key feature to underline the Japanese setting instead of the architecture.

At the same time as this popular operetta, at least one Japanese theatre company staged Japanese stories around the turn of the century, before Puccini's *Madama Butterfly* outshone everything else after its

---

[66] Further see Cortazzi, Sir Hugh, *Japan in Late Victorian London. The Japanese Native Village in Knightsbridge and The Mikado, 1885* (Norwich, 2009), esp. chapter 4, "Japan as Reflected in the Theatre: The Mikado," pp. 59–72.

[67] Among these was a German version of a children's paper theatre in 1890 by the Schreiber-Verlag, Esslingen. The stage designs are an overwhelmingly condensed compilation of formal references to Japan and China. They were re-edited in recent years by Benno Mitschka (Multum in Parvo Papiertheaters) and used for a performance at the Chair of Modern Japanese Studies at Düsseldorf University. See Scherer, Elisabeth, "Ausstellungseröffnung und Papiertheater-Performance," in: *Blog Modernes Japan*, 02.10.2018, http://www.phil-fak.uni-duesseldorf.de/oasien/blog/?p=18513 [accessed 12 August 2023].

FIGURE 4.60   The Mikado, performed by the Castanet Club, Montreal, QC, composite, 1886

first performance in 1904. The company of Kawakami Otojiro (1864–1911) and its star, Otojiro's wife Sada Yacco (1871–1946), travelled both North America and Europe.[68] The available photographs of their performances show the stage setting with three different architectural environments: an urban scene in an entertainment area with establishments such as tea houses lining the street; an arrangement of detached buildings in the park-like environment of a high-ranking residence or a temple compound; and a highly ornamented gate (Figs. 4.61, 4.62).

While the first two settings showed a certain artificiality of proportions or perspectives, the last came close to depicting an actual structure,

---

68   Cortazzi, *Late Victorian London*, p. 96, FN 144. – See the extensive discussion by Anderson, Joseph L., *Enter a Samurai. Kawakami Otojiro and Japanese Theatre in the West* (Tucson, AZ, 2011). – In terms of dance and Sada Yacco, see also: *Pardee School of Global Studies* (Center for the Study of Asia), https://www.asiaworldsfairs.org/ [accessed 12 August 2023] or Downer, Lesley, *Madame Sadayakko. The geisha who bewitched the West* (New York and London, 2003). – A contemporary account with a similar stage scene including the Karamon of Tōshō-gū in Nikkō can be found in Holmes, Elias Burton, "The Paris Exposition," in: *The Burton Holmes Lectures. With Illustrations from Photographs by the Author*, 10 vols. (Battle Creek, MI, 1901), 2, pp. 115–336, here pp. 246–250.

FIGURES 4.61–4.62   Two stage scenes with Sada Yacco and Otojiro Kawakami in front of different settings

albeit removed from its original context with the neighbouring buildings: the *karamon* of the Tōshō-gū in Nikkō, one of the most famous Japanese architectural structures (Fig. 4.63). It marks the entrance to the halls of prayer and worship, the final stages in the drama of Tōshō-gū's spatial disposition. The use of such settings and elaborate buildings was well suited to meeting the expectations of the western audience, not least because Nikkō's ornamentality and colourfulness made it one of the most recognised Japanese buildings in the West at the time.

In contrast to the ephemeral experience of a theatre performance, the *Japanese Native Village* in London was intended to last (Fig. 4.64, see colour section). The enterprise was envisaged by Tannaker Buhicrosan (1839–1894) and installed in 1885 in Humphrey's Hall, a building complex originally set up for roller skating and subsequently extended and used for exhibitions.[69] This show, supposedly "a working replica of a Japanese village centre, inhabited by Japanese craftsmen and artists and their families,"[70] opened at a time when the 'Japan craze' was at its peak. In consequence, many newspapers and magazines reported it, as did the architectural journals of the time, between them providing some useful information on materials, techniques, buildings and spatial disposition. In addition, many Japanophile British actors such as Sir Rutherford

---

69   "Knightsbridge Green Area: Scotch Corner and the High Road," in: *British History Online, Survey of London*, https://www.british-history.ac.uk/search/series/survey-london, here https://www.british-history.ac.uk/survey-london/vol45/pp79-88#h3-0006 [accessed 12 August 2023]; Cortazzi, *Late Victorian London*, pp. 9–11.

70   "The Japanese Native Village," in: *British History Online, Survey of London*, https://www.british-history.ac.uk/search/series/survey-london, here https://www.british-history.ac.uk/survey-london/vol45/pp79-88#h3-0007 [accessed 12 August 2023], s.p.

FIGURE 4.63   A photograph of the elaborately decorated gate, the Karamon of Tōshō-gū in Nikkō, with the Haiden visible beyond, that served as a template for one of the stage settings

Alcock, Christopher Dresser or Charles Holme visited and/or commented on the event.[71]

The village, populated by around a hundred residents during the day, featured a main street flanked by various side streets. These streets were lined with houses, the front areas of which served as workshops. Additional structures included a temple, theatre, tea house, and garden. Though the backdrop was artfully painted, an author from the times emphasised that the structures were "not mere painted fronts but well-built apartments of varied appearance, each with its own characteristic ornamentation of parti-coloured bamboo, on solid panels, with

---

71   McLaughlin, Joseph, "'The Japanese Village' and the Metropolitan Construction of Modernity," in: *Romanticism and Victorianism on the Net*, Issue 48 (November 2007), s.p.; "A Japanese Village in London," in: *British architect* 23.2 (9 January 1885), p. 15; "A Japanese village," in: *The Building news and engineering journal* 48 (16 January 1885), pp. 77–78; For more detail, see Cortazzi, *Late Victorian London*, pp. 3–5.

FIGURES 4.65–4.66   The Japanese village at Knightsbridge: the theatre, and one of the streets

shingled or thatched roof, and with sliding trellis-shutters and translucent paper screens to serve as a substitute for glass in cold weather."[72]

Despite this wide coverage, there are only a small number of visual information sources for the material specifics of the village, including its architectural features. The advertisements targeted the imagination, as did the sketches published in illustrated media such as *The Graphic*, *The Illustrated Sporting and Dramatic News* and – of course – *The Illustrated London News*. However, the latter made it possible to gain some ideas beyond the textual descriptions. One scene showed the theatre surrounded by other buildings. Another detailed a street, showing elevated wooden structures of different sizes, their eaves hung with paper lanterns (Figs. 4.65, 4.66).

A third scene depicted visitors taking tea (Fig. 4.67). Here, the cultural differences of everyday practices (beyond the regional specifics of the tea ritual[73]) became visible: the guests were seated 'western style' on the right-hand side, while a Japanese woman in the centre proffered a serving tray while standing on the raised floor of the Japanese-style building fitted with *tatami*, panels of flooring from compacted rice straw. This platform would have been the seating area for a Japanese audience. Yet, the sketch depicted another Japanese woman and her child with a western table and chair on top of the *tatami*. Around this time, furniture was often seen on the *tatami* in the context of westerners using Japanese houses. The point load applied by the legs of tables and by chairs with people sitting

72   "A Japanese village in London," in: *The Times* (10 January 1885), p. 6.
73   For the Japanese tea tradition and modern adaptations see Surak, Kristin, *Making Tea, Making Japan: Cultural Nationalism in Practice* (Stanford, CA, 2013).

FIGURE 4.67   Afternoon tea at the Japanese village

on them, however, would have caused serious damage to the structure of the flooring and was to be avoided, as is still the case today.[74]

Beyond this interesting scene, the most architecturally detailed depiction of the Japanese village showed the area around the temple, as published in *The Building News and Engineering Journal*. It showed the building with a gabled roof and a portico under which some steps led towards the interior (Fig. 4.68). On its right was a two-storied dwelling with sliding doors and a porch on the upper floor. The drawing included two women to indicate scale; they were too small compared to the structure of the dwelling, however, and made the buildings seem bigger and distinctly vertical. It is to be assumed that this sketch did not exactly mirror the situation on site.

There is some evidence for this in a different drawing of similar building parts and a photograph published by Cortazzi that showed the garden

---

[74]   The impact of the load can be reduced in part by adapting the design of the furniture's legs and in part by placing carpeting on top of the *tatami*. Historical buildings in use today, such as Kitaichi-jo Catholic Church in Sapporo, protect the *tatami* flooring in this way.

FIGURE 4.68
Temple, &c., at the Japanese village, 1885

with a stone lantern and a bridge as well as the built environment beyond (Fig. 4.69).[75]

The detached building in the middle ground of the drawing has significant markers: the (half-)hipped roof with the two layers of either main roof, or main roof and *mokoshi*, as well as the curved *karahafu* gable covering the entrance. Assuming that this building was the temple, the difference in proportion between the earlier drawing and the actual building on site was significant. However, there is one caveat: the entire village burned down in May 1885 and was rebuilt by the end of the year along the same lines but with some modifications, including the addition of the garden bridge, as reported in *The Times* newspaper.[76]

As a result, the two drawings and the photograph possibly depicted the two different versions of the village. However, the later drawing and photograph showed architectural features which were indeed close to those documented by photographs from Japan at the same time, underlining the statements on which the advertisements, visitors with experience of Japan, and later scholars agreed: the buildings were built by Japanese

75 Cortazzi, *Late Victorian London*, plate 6.
76 Ibid., pp. 39–42; "The Japanese village," in: *The Times* (2 December 1885), p. 6.

FIGURE 4.69   The new Japanese village at Knightsbridge. The temple and the sleeping quarters

with Japanese materials and according to Japanese practice.[77] Thus, it is to be concluded that the earlier drawing focused on other material, to the detriment of the architectural features, or else fell short of grasping the crucial elements, as seen in Philadelphia.

For the contemporary architect or interested lay people, the Japanese village in London would have provided ample opportunity to study Japanese architecture, to discuss its specifics and to compare it with English solutions. Yet, the articles and notes in the journals and newspapers failed to do this: they described some specifics elements of the buildings, as we saw already concerning the buildings at the international exhibitions, but went no further, much as travellers to Japan had largely already been doing for 30 years. Again, the architecture served as a mere setting to indulge Japonisme's primary interest in crafts and décors.

There is reason to expect similar results from the analysis of the Japanese villages displayed in Berlin in 1885 and in Boston in 1886, but this would far exceed the aims of this excursus.[78] Suffice to say, the

---

77 Cortazzi, *Late Victorian London*, pp. 9–13; Dresser, Christopher, "A Japanese village," in: *The Building news and engineering journal* 48 (30 January 1885), p. 189.
78 See for example Wellnau, Rudolf, *Die Japanische Ausstellung in Berlin 1885* (Berlin, 1885); Rees, Jochen, "Menzel Meets Meiji: Die „Japanische Ausstellung" von 1885 im

Berlin village – set up by the personnel from London during the reconstruction of Humphrey's Hall – was documented in a similar way to the arrangement in London with illustrations such as the full-page plate in *Leipziger Illustrirte Zeitung*, a collage-like arrangement of peoples' activities and partially incorrect architectural features.[79]

We have already seen that the Japanese buildings at the early international exhibitions were not formally or stylistically homogeneous, not even among those sent by the Meiji government. In addition, design decisions were sometimes subordinate to the overall fabric of the exhibitions. Next to buildings of traditional form and use transplanted to foreign soil, this created architectural designs which aimed to fulfil the new functions and representations of a modernising society, such as the bazaars. Adding enterprises such as Tannaker Buhicrosan's village and the travelling troupes of entertainers and actors with their stories and stage settings narrating the 'vernacular' Japan, the samples of full-sized Japanese architecture experienced in the West not only documented Japanese buildings but, unbeknownst to the majority of the western audience, simultaneously represented the discourses on cultural identity occurring during the decades of most virulent modernisation.[80]

1.6   *Exposition Universelle de Paris, 1889*

The Exposition Universelle in Paris, 1889, continued with this official line and also added another kind of Japanese architecture, as we will see shortly.[81]

Werk von Adolph Menzel," in: Bergmann, Annegret (ed.), *Elegante Zusammenkunft im Gelehrtengarten* (Weimar, 2015), pp. 210–217; *A veritable Japanese village under the sanction of the Imperial Japanese Gouvernement. Souvenir booklet for exhibitions of the Japanese Village Company held at Horticultural Halls in Boston, 1886* (Boston, 1886).

79   Koch, C., "Aus der Japanischen Ausstellung in Berlin," in: *Leipziger Illustrirte Zeitung* 2194 (18 July 1885), p. 58. – There was in parallel an echo among caricaturists who made fun of the 'Japan craze'. Cortazzi, *Late Victorian London*, pp. 18–20. For Berlin, see the full-page caricature *Japan in Berlin*, in: *Kladderadatsch* 38, 31 (5 July 1885), supplement; and for the context, see Wagner, Wolf-Rüdiger, "Japanische Bettschirme, die große Weltpolitik und die Moral," https://roman-als-zeitbild.blog/2017/07/05/effis-interesse-an-einem-japanischen-bettschirm-und-die-grose-weltpolitik/ [last accessed 27 April 2024].

80   For an introduction, see for example Coaldrake, *Authority*, esp. chapter 9; Finn, *Meiji*; Meid, *Einführungsprozeß*; Tseng, "Styling" and Vogel Chevroulet, "Architecture."

81   However, in regard to Japonisme and Japan's appearances at the international exhibitions, this event was skipped by many studies in favour of the subsequent events in Chicago 1893 and Paris 1900.

In general, the distribution of Japanese exhibits and buildings was similar to the majority of the earlier events, and, again, the information on the kind of Japanese architecture the visitors might have been able to experience remained limited. The usual illustrations of the official exhibition depicted interior scenes with ceramics, furniture and bronze objects, for example.[82] There is no visual evidence of exhibits of an architectural character, such as photographs of historical buildings displayed in the context of education. The same holds for *Un ville Japonaise* which was mentioned several times in the more lengthy overviews of the exhibition but only once in any detail, in a description of it as a privately financed museum on two levels showing life and manners of Japan.[83]

Some more can be said about the architecture framing Japan's display within the central hall(s) on the one hand, and a building with a garden near the Trocadéro on the other.

Situated parallel to the northeastern exterior wall of the central exhibition building, the Japanese section included a significant part of the hall's exterior façade, similar to the *Street of Nations* some years earlier. It was designed as a row of houses with different heights, roof shapes and surface materials, and created a picturesque experience for the visitors. For the main entrance, the skeleton structure of the hall was filled with half-timbering of carved wood, tile patterns and lattices (Figs. 4.70–4.72).[84]

The official overviews of the exhibition provided very little textual information on the garden near the Trocadéro. The illustrations of the time, as summed up by Hervé Duplessis's article on the garden, also touched on the accompanying building only briefly: a very lofty construction of some slim uprights,

---

82   See *L'Exposition chez soi 1889. Exposition universelle de 1889*, 2 vols. (Paris, 1889), 1, pp. 697, 704; Monod, Émile, *L'Exposition universelle de 1889: grand ouvrage illustré, historique, encyclopédique, descriptif*, 4 vols. (Paris, 1890), 3, pp. 57, 61; *Les merveilles de l'exposition de 1889. Historie, construction, inauguration, description détaillée des palais, des annexes et des parcs, les chefs-d'oeuvre de l'art de tous les pays, les machines, les arts industriels, les produits manufacturés, les expositions spéciales, la Tour Eiffel, Paris* [1889], pp. 507–511. – For an evaluation of the art objects see for example Falke, Jacob von, "Die Pariser Weltausstellung," in: *Mittheilungen des k.k. oesterreichischen Museums für Kunst und Industrie* 48 (1889), pp. 488–504, here 498.

83   Michel, Émile, "Le Japon à l'Exposition universelle," in: *L'art: revue hebdomadaire illustrée* 15.2 (1889), pp. 217–224, here p. 218; *Les merveilles* (1889), p. 494.

84   *L'Exposition chez soi 1889*, 1, p. 695; *Les merveilles* (1889), p. 507.

VISITING AND VISUALISING ARCHITECTURE

FIGURES 4.70–4.71   Exposition Universelle, 1889: Façade of the Japanese section and entrance to the Japanese exhibition

FIGURE 4.72
Exposition Universelle, 1889: Japanese joiners

FIGURES 4.73–4.74   Exposition Universelle, 1889: Two Views of the Japanese garden at Trocadéro

FIGURE 4.75
Exposition Universelle, 1889:
the Japanese Garden

partially made from unworked trunks and boughs, with a shallow saddle roof in one part and a pent roof in another part (Figs. 4.73–4.75).[85]

Some walls were closed by *shōji*, translucent sliding doors, while some appeared to be made from boards or interlacing fibres or were completely absent. The overall impression given was one of the utmost ephemerality, as though the building had grown from the trees and shrubs themselves, in clear

---

85 Andre, Ed., "Le Jardin japonais au Trocadero," in: *Journal d'agriculture pratique, de jardinage & d'économique* 53.2 (December 1889), pp. 239–243; *Les merveilles* (1889), pp. 454–457; Duplessis, Hervé, "Un lis japonais au Trocadéro," 12.05.2017 via https://blogpourmemoire.wordpress.com/2017/05/12/un-lis-japonais-au-trocadero/ [accessed 10 August 2023].

contrast to the neatly ordered building and garden area of 1878.[86] The planted areas also seemed much more overgrown with various plants than they had been eleven years earlier.

From an architectural perspective, it was neither the façades of the exhibition hall nor the pavilion in the garden, which was interesting in Paris in 1889. The most acknowledged and depicted 'Japanese' building was the *Japanese house* in the exhibition of *L'histoire de l'habitation humaine* along the banks of the Seine. Charles Garnier (1825–1898) designed the 44 buildings with the objective of presenting examples of the historical development of culture(s) according to the contemporary (hierarchical) understanding of the concept. The houses were divided into three groups: prehistoric dwellings, those created by (European) culture (from ancient Egypt to the Renaissance), and finally those of indigenous peoples or otherwise which did not concur with the contemporary understanding of cultural and architectural development. The latter category included buildings of China and Japan.[87]

Garnier supposedly aimed for authenticity and based his designs on received materials, where these were available, or on his own imagination, where they were not.[88] For Japan, he designed a two-storied structure, raised off the ground by about one metre, with a largely wraparound porch on the ground floor and a partial porch above (Figs. 4.76 and 4.77, see colour section). The hipped roof had widely projecting eaves. White walls and a black roof dominated the colouring with black detailing on the window frames and railings, and white and golden decoration along the underside of the roof. While the building did not look at all Japanese compared to the depictions available in contemporary sources on Japan, the floor plan in fact showed a pavilion-like skeleton structure. Four large uprights formed the corners of the main room, while four smaller ones at the corners of the porch supported its roof and bold

---

86 The very rustic character of the building invites today's observer to understand the building as a tea-house, set apart for *chadō*. However, one would expect a highly artistic building such as this to have been positioned much more centrally in the Japanese self-representation at the exhibition and accompanied by explanations from the Japanese side, as was the case with the small *Shintō* shrine in Vienna, 1873. In addition, the western interest in Japanese gardens started at about this time, while *chadō* and, for that matter, Zen Buddhism, started to become of interest in the West during the first decades of the twentieth century. On gardens in cultural exchange, see Tagsold, *Spaces in Translation*.

87 Wörner, Martin, *Vergnügung und Belehrung. Volkskultur auf den Weltausstellungen 1851–1900* (Münster, 1999), pp. 67–68. – For a contemporary account, see Falke, "Weltausstellung," pp. 499–500.

88 Wörner, *Vergnügung*, p. 68; Labat, Alexandre, "Charles Garnier et l'exposition de 1889. L'histoire de l'habitation," in: *1889. La Tour Eiffel et l'Exposition Universelle* (Paris, 1989), pp. 130–147, here pp. 142–146.

cantilevers the main roof's eaves. There was a massive wall in the back but nearly all of the other 'walls' did not carry weight and were supposed to be moveable but for a fixed part with a window on the left side of the main façade on the ground floor, and another on the right-hand side of the upper floor. The doors of Garnier's design seemed inspired by *shōji*, while the lattice of the fixed windows was too symmetrical to accord easily with traditional Japanese patterns.

The subsequent depictions of these buildings – a photograph, a number of engravings, postcards and such – showed a range of (re-)interpretations of their proportions and forms, including the depiction of the neighbouring *Chinese house* instead (Figs. 4.78–4.81).[89]

The *Japanese house* at the *Exposition Universelle* in 1889 was relevant for western knowledge production on Japanese architecture in two ways. Firstly, it was probably one of the first 'Japanese' structures to be built by a western architect since the times of Chinoiserie during earlier centuries. As with Cram's house for Arthur M. Knapp, which was completed in the same year,[90] the design was developed second-hand from textual and visual sources such as Morse's *Japanese homes* and arguably from observations made of Japanese art objects in private collections.

Such 'built Japonisms' remained much rarer than interiors or single rooms fitted out to showcase *Japonica*, but came to be part of Japan-related architectural discourses during the ensuing decades, in addition to the 'traditional Japanese' and 'modern Japanese' buildings of the Meiji era.[91] This was due not least to their much more immediate communication and perception among colleagues and to their conception as long-term structures, which outlasted the ephemeral character of most of the exhibition pavilions.

Secondly, the conceptual position of both the *Japanese* and the *Chinese houses* and, for that matter, all houses in this category mirrored and underlined the discourses and judgements on the systematisation of cultures in general and of non-western cultures in particular.[92] The buildings served as material evidence for the hierarchical understanding of civilisation, with Europe at its

---

89 See *Les sections Ètrangeres. – Le Pavillon Japonais*. Monod, *L'Exposition 1889*, 2, p. 585.
90 Locher, Mira, "Introduction," in: Cram, Ralph Adams, *Impressions of Japanese architecture* (North Clarendon, VT, 2011), pp. 11–21, here p. 16.
91 This, again, is an issue that merits closer analysis. Clay Lancaster collected the American examples, and Karin Kirsch gathered later European approaches, but there is more to be done. Lancaster, *Japanese Influence*; Kirsch, *Neue Wohnung*.
92 Wörner, *Vergnügung*, p. 69.

VISITING AND VISUALISING ARCHITECTURE

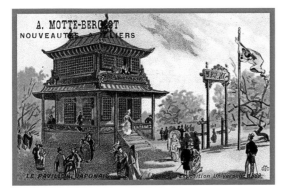

FIGURES 4.78–4.81   Exposition Universelle, 1889: Histoire de l'habitation humaine, photograph of the Japanese (left) and the Chinese house (right), two depictions of the front and rear of the Japanese house and an interpretation in an advertising card

apex. This ran in parallel with the evaluations summarised in the architectural handbooks towards the end of the century, as we already saw earlier, making field-specific evaluations known to the broader public.[93]

1.7 World's Columbian Exhibition in Chicago, 1893

Japan's contribution to the World's Columbian Exhibition in Chicago in 1893 was arguably the most significant in terms of the western experience, perception and discussion of Japanese architecture during the late nineteenth century. The pavilion was the first actual Japanese building in the West to be noticed beyond a few short lines in field-related texts, and it was remembered and visited for decades by American architects.[94] It was the first Japanese pavilion for which technical drawings were published in a field-related journal, even accompanied by illustrations of the pavilion's 900-year-old model building. Finally, it was documented in numerous photographs – including bird's-eye views and scenes from the building process.

The Japanese commissioner Kuki Ryuichi (1852–1931), director of the Tōkyō National Museum, successfully negotiated a prime piece of real estate on the exhibition grounds, placing the pavilion on the wooded island in the centre of the exhibition (Figs. 4.82, 4.83). It was not the only architectural exhibit sent from Japan but it outshone everything else, including a tea house, a bazaar and a home interior, as well as some architectural models.[95]

The conception, design and erection of the pavilion, named Hō-ō-den (Phoenix Palace), was a joint effort by numerous actors both Japanese and American. Members of the official Japanese commission, such as western-trained architect Kuru Masamichi (1855–1914) and the commissioner himself, overlapped with the cross-cultural networks of the 'Boston Orientalists', Japanophile art collectors and theoreticians such as Edward Morse. Okakura Kakuzō, the official art director of the endeavour, and Ernest F. Fenollosa (1853–1908), who picked the art submissions, bridged the two interest groups

---

93   See in more detail Garnier's book on that matter: Garnier, Charles, *L'Habitation humaine* (Paris, 1892), esp. pp. 848–855.

94   Lancaster, *Japanese Influence*, esp. pp. 76–83; Finn, *Meiji Revisited*, p. 168; Nute, *Frank Lloyd Wright*, esp. pp. 48–72; Conant, Ellen P., "Japan 'Abroad' at the Chicago Exposition, 1893," in: id. (ed.), *Challenging Past And Present: The Metamorphosis of Nineteenth-Century Japanese Art* (Honolulu, 2006), pp. 254–280.

95   Nute, *Frank Lloyd Wright*, p. 31 FN 59; Cody, *World's Fairs*, p. 72. Sigur, *Influence*, p. 47; Hatta, Yoko, "The Japanese Position in the Chicago World's Columbian Exposition of 1893," in: *Bulletin of the faculty of language and literature* 12.1 (1998), pp. 35–79, here p. 52. Conant, "Japan." For the latter, see the photograph in Tōkyō National Museum, et al. (eds.), *Arts of East and West from World Exhibitions. 1855–1900: Paris, Vienna and Chicago. Commemorating the 2005 World Exposition, Aichi, Japan* (Tōkyō, 2004), p. 92.

FIGURES 4.82–4.83   World's Columbian Exhibition, 1893: the exhibition site with the Hō-ō-den once on the island in the left and in the centre on the right

with Okakura as the charismatic leader. The latter wrote an illustrated guidebook of the Hō-ō-den, its furnishings and displays, which was reprinted in an abbreviated version in an interior-design journal.[96]

---

96   Kuru graduated from Josiah Conder's class in 1883 and joined the ministry of education before working as an architect later. Coaldrake, *Architecture and Authority*, p. 241. On Okakura see for example Mizuta, Noriko (ed.), "Beyond Tenshin: Okakura Kakuzo's

A photograph by Charles Dudley Arnold (1844–1927) depicts Okakura sitting proudly on the steps of the pavilion with both the Japanese builders and exhibition officials (Fig. 4.84).[97]

This was not the only depiction of the Japanese workmen with their ornamental coats. There are also some images of the builders posing in padded winter wear with elements of the prefabricated building material, while an impression done by an artist included some instructive information on the building's structure (Figs. 4.85, 4.86). The carpenters, however, were neither using their tools in a serious manner (see the man sitting on the left who is toying with his plane), nor are the men on the porch, *engawa*, shown in scale with the structure of the wall behind them. Apart from these images, some of the photographs of the opening ceremony also included the builders.

The building in question, a central hall connected on either side via roofed corridors to two accompanying pavilions, was situated on the northern end of the wooded island and consisted of a raised, single-storey complex with large, slightly curved half-hipped roofs (Figs. 4.87 and 4.88). Unlike the designs at preceding international exhibitions, this design was not a contemporary artistic invention but a reference to an important historical building, the Hō-ō-dō (Phoenix Hall) of the Byōdō-in in Uji near Kyōto (Fig. 4.89, see colour section). Initially built as a residence, the mid-eleventh century structure was later converted to a temple hall. Okakura explained: "The Hō-ō-Den now exhibited is substantially a replica of the edifice at Uji, somewhat smaller in size and modified to adapt it for secular use."[98]

In fact, the differences between the buildings went beyond interior changes and scale: the original temple's floor plan is Y-shaped, its parts supposedly resembling the mythical phoenix with the central hall as the body and the corridors and pavilions as wings, reaching out as if to embrace the garden and pond in front of the hall; the auxiliary tract pointing in the opposite direction represented the phoenix's tail. In contrast, the building in Chicago was basically designed around a central axis running through the halls. This made sense in terms of the position of the complex on the island, but gave it a more rigid appearance.

Multiple Legacies," in: *Review of Japanese Culture and Society* 24, special edition (December 2012); Sigur, *Influence*, pp. 71–73; Nute, *Frank Lloyd Wright*, pp. 49–51. Okakura, Kakudzo [Okakura, Kakuzo], "The Decoration of the Ho-o-den," in: *The Decorator and Furnisher* 23.5 (February 1894), pp. 181–182.

97 Sigur, *Influence*, p. 72.
98 Okakura, Kakuzo, *The Hō-ō-den. An illustrated Description of the Building erected by the Japanese Government at the World's Columbian Exhibition* (Jackson Park; Chicago; Tōkyō, 1893), pp. 13, 9–10.

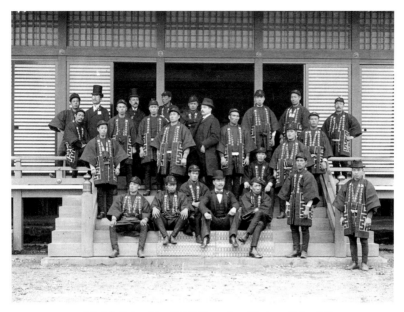

FIGURE 4.84   World's Columbian Exhibition, 1893: Okakura Kakuzō (lower group, centre) on the steps of the Hō-ō-den

FIGURE 4.85   World's Columbian Exhibition, 1893: constructing the Japanese Pavilion Hō-ō-den at the World's Columbian Exposition, Chicago, 1893

FIGURE 4.86   World's Columbian Exhibition, 1893: at work on the Japanese building, by T. Dart Walker

Both buildings shared characteristics of *shinden zukuri*, the forms used for aristocratic residences during the Heian era (794–1185). While already a Japanese adaptation of the Chinese original model, the *shinden* complexes were designed to impress.[99] In consequence, the elegant Hō-ō-dō in Uji has an inviting and inconspicuous appearance when viewed from a distance, but significantly exceeds the human scale when entered. (See the small figure with the arms clad in white at the top of the stairs in Fig. 4.89, see colour section.)

In contrast, the Hō-ō-den was closer to the more comfortable proportions of later times, if not in its strict floorplan. This became visible in the photograph with Okakura and the builders, in which the horizontal beam above the doors, *kamoi*, was safely above the heads of the standing men but not extremely so. It was higher than today's door frames but not by much, especially considering the difference in height between the surface of the porch and the sill of the hall's framing (see Figs. 4.84 and 4.90).

---

99   For an introduction, see for example Locher; Kuma; Simmons, *Traditional Japanese Architecture*, especially pp. 17–28, or Nishi, Kazuo; Hozumi, Kazuo, *What is Japanese Architecture?* (New York, 2012), pp. 64–67 and 18–19; for a more extensive contextualisation, see Paine, Robert T.; Soper, Alexander, *The Art and Architecture of Japan* (Harmondsworth, 1974), pp. 206–207.

FIGURES 4.87–4.88   World's Columbian Exhibition, 1893: view and depiction of the Hō-ō-den

Beyond these significant features, the two buildings differed in many more architectural details, such as the use of hinged or sliding doors, or the application and shape of gables, dormers, brackets and eaves. However, these were of scant relevance compared to the minimal western knowledge of Japan's architecture in general, and to the didactic programme of the pavilion in particular. In addition to affording an opportunity to experience the building, it clearly aimed to communicate and teach the basics of Japanese (art) history to its audience.[100] The building provided not only the decorative frame to do so, but also substantial architectural information.

Among the surviving photographs are many of a more general character, which focused on the appearance of the whole building complex. Others showed parts of it in a way that made it evident how much architectural

---

100   Cf. Conant, "Japan," pp. 263–265.

FIGURE 4.90
World's Columbian Exhibition, 1893: dedication ceremony of the Japanese building

information it was possible to gain from the study of the Hō-ō-den, albeit large parts of the inner workings of the structural systems, most notably those of the foundations and the roof, remained hidden behind ornamental panelling and similar. A photograph of the dedication ceremony in Chicago documented the Japanese workmen once more, but also showed a number of constructional features of the pavilion: the grid of the overall structure, the infills comprising sliding doors and lattices, the widely projecting eaves, and the complex ridgelines and roof tiling of the main hall. Other photographs made it possible to observe differences between the structural elements of the pavilion, while at the same time demonstrating a harmonious interplay of variations on Japanese detailing and infills. Further photographs made it possible to see the roof's under-construction, with the whitened end faces of the rafters above plastered wall sections, the pillars of the connecting corridors, and even the under-construction of the wraparound porch and the hall itself (Figs. 4.91 and 4.92).

For those with a more technical interest, a plate in the *Inland Architect* provided further clarity. It showed technical drawings of the uprights and joint details, annotated in Japanese and supplemented with English explanations (Fig. 4.93).

The variations between the front and rear views of the central hall as well as between the former and the wing pavilions might have been due to front/rear

FIGURES 4.91–4.92   World's Columbian Exhibition, 1893: views of the central hall and the north wing of the Hō-ō-den

considerations, but they correspond to the floor plans published at this time, which showed differing uses of space in the different halls.

The variations in outer form arguably resembled the intentional interior design decisions which Okakura explained in his text. Not a building expert himself but interested in the fine arts, Okakura dedicated the majority of his attention to the art objects and furniture displayed within the pavilion. However, his explanation of the architectural features was crucial to understanding the context of the overall concept.

One wing was designed to follow the interior of the Heian era's *shinden zukuri*, the period in which the original Hō-ō-dō was designed. The floor plan (Figs. 4.95, right, and 4.96) shows "the pillars round instead of square as they were usually made at a later period. (…) The sliding doors being a later invention, protection to the room is afforded by means of vertical shutters (…)."[101] The same was true of other features of the Japanese building tradition which were not yet common, such as *tokonoma* and *tatami* flooring, as Okakura explained to his readers.[102]

The second wing's interior reproduced the spatial dispositions of the Ashikaga or Muromachi period (1338–1573), copying the library and tea room of Kyōto's Ginkaku-ji (1585–1490).[103] (Figs. 4.95, left, and 4.97, 4.98) The model building had initially been erected for residential purposes and was turned

101   Okakura, "Hō-ō-den," p. 14.
102   Ibid., pp. 14, 19.
103   Ibid., pp. 20, 23.

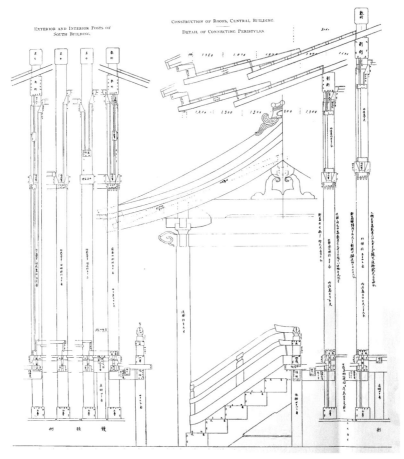

FIGURE 4.93   World's Columbian Exhibition, 1893: construction details of the Hō-ō-den (section)

into a religious institution later, as was the historical Hō-ō-dō.[104] The development of residences from the representative forms of *shinden zukuri* towards the more human-scaled, even cosy *shoin zukuri* becomes apparent here.

Evolving from the eponymous 'writing room' of the Zen-Buddhist abbot's quarters, the spatial and formal concept came to mean a formal reception room-cum-studio. It featured many of the characteristics perceived as

---

104   Nute, *Frank Lloyd Wright*, p. 57. For an introduction, see also Nishi, *Japanese Architecture*, pp. 30–31.

FIGURES 4.94–4.95   World's Columbian Exhibition, 1893: east side elevation and floor plan of the Hō-ō-den, adjusted to west

'traditionally Japanese' in the late nineteenth century and still today, such as the sliding doors, *shōji*, and the *tokonoma*, the decorative wall recess.[105]

The central hall of the Hō-ō-den was set up to represent the perfecting of interiors during the reign of the shōguns of the Tokugawa dynasty (1603–1868).[106] Here, the model was one of the rooms of Edo Castle, the *jodan-no-ma*, "the furthermost and highest apartment of a suite of two or three rooms, used as a sitting room for the prince, [which] is raised above that where the attendants were in waiting" (Fig. 4.99).[107]

In the closing paragraph of his description of the building, its interior and exhibits, Okakura Kakuzō underlined the overall aim of Japan's self-representation in Chicago:

> The buildings of the Hō-ō-den are built of unpainted wood, and the principles of Japanese construction and proportion are wholly adopted. The roofs are covered with sheet copper according to the Japanese method.

---

105   Okakura, "Hō-ō-den," p. 20. – For an introduction, see for example Locher; Kuma; Simmons, *Traditional Japanese Architecture*, pp. 28–29, or Nishi, *Japanese Architecture*, pp. 74–75.
106   Okakura, "Hō-ō-den," p. 24.
107   Ibid., p. 24.

The work of interior decoration was undertaken by the Tokyo Art Academy, and the furniture and art works in the exhibition are selected by the Imperial Museum. All represent the three epochs to which they belong. The principal design of the buildngs [sic] was made by Masamichi Kuru, the Government Architect of Japan, and the builders are Okura & Co., who have sent a number of their workmen to Chicago.[108]

The statement and the narrative of the description itself embedded Japan, its history and its acclaimed art products – both the traditional objects displayed within the pavilion and the modern products in the industrial exhibition, and for that matter probably the objects sold at the Japanese bazaar as well – within a larger picture of Japanese culture and development.[109]

It is sufficient to point out here that Okakura explained and contextualised the Hō-ō-den in a way comprehensible to an educated western audience: he named the decision-makers and actors according to common western art canons and explained a historical development towards a perfection of ornamental and spatial design.[110] He sketched Japan's awareness of its own history and development, thus implying an awareness of Japan's further progress as well. As a result, Okakura laid out Japan's claim to acknowledgement among the leading civilised nations of the time, using the established interest in Japanese art and crafts as his means.[111]

This was of even greater significance given that the pavilion was understood as a gift to the city of Chicago, and was thus to remain on site after the end of the exposition – which it did until it burned down in 1946.[112]

---

108   Ibid., p. 40.
109   For a deeper analysis see Conant, "Japan"; Tseng, *Imperial Museums*, and Satō, *Modern Japanese Art*.
110   Despite his efforts, not all of the multipliers internalised Okakura's information. As the team around Catherine Yeh of the Pardee School of Global Studies (Center for the Study of Asia) points out, some authors saw Kyōto's Kinkaku-ji as the original model of the pavilion; https://www.asiaworldsfairs.org/, here https://www.asiaworldsfairs.org/architecture-room-2. See for example Flinn, John J., *The best things to be seen at the world's fair* (Chicago, [1893]), pp. 127–128.
111   At the same time, Josiah Conder gave a paper at the Convention of the American Institute of Architects in Chicago and drew a line between the architectural needs of modern Japan and the traditional competencies in building. Conder, Josiah, "The condition of architecture in Japan," in: *Proceedings of the twenty-seventh Annual Convention of the American Institute of Architects* (Chicago, 1893), pp. 365–381.
112   Sigur, *Influence*, p. 47; Kirsch, *Neue Wohnung*, p. 59.

FIGURE 4.96
World's Columbian Exhibition, 1893: interior of left wing [*shinden zukuri*]

FIGURES 4.97–4.98 World's Columbian Exhibition, 1893: library in right wing of the Hō-ō-den and tea room in right wing of the Hō-ō-den [*shoin zukuri*]

FIGURE 4.99
World's Columbian Exhibition, 1893: the Jodan-no-ma, or Central hall of the Hō-ō-den at the World's Columbian Exposition

The extent to which Japan's other 'architectural' contributions in Chicago had a part in Okakura's overall scheme is unclear. He did not mention any of them in his text, but they drew enough attention to invite visual documentation.

The tea house was positioned farther north on the wooded island with the Hō-ō-den, on the shore of the waterway connecting the Lagoon and the Northern Pond. As with other tea houses at previous international exhibitions, both the building's structure, furniture and equipment and its staff were brought from Japan.[113]

The photographs, often taken from the water side, show a loosely arranged group of single-storey buildings with largely pragmatic hipped roofs. These were mostly just roofs on uprights, the walls omitted but for hangings comprised of striped fabric or thin boarding. While this ephemeral appearance fits with the surrounding vegetation, it was in strong contrast to the massive structures of the exhibition's main buildings as seen in the background of some of the photographs and, for that matter, in contrast to the sturdy construction of the Hō-ō-den (Figs. 4.100, 4.101).

One of the tea-house buildings was of note due to its more complex construction and roof. While this roof was significantly less elaborate than those of the Hō-ō-den or the main exhibition pavilion, its half-hipped structure had marked and ornamented ridges. The height of the room and the auxiliary roofs underline the building's leading role within the small compound. The garden design underscored the overall arrangement of the interconnected structures.

Apart from the two complexes of the Hō-ō-den and the tea house, the industrial exhibition was located in the relevant halls. Discussions surrounding it mirrored previous exhibitions, ranging from evaluations of the quality, innovativeness and/or decline of Japanese art production, to debates about Japan's broader progress. Some departments were framed by pavilion-like architectural settings, such as Japan's main exhibition and its contribution in forestry. The former was an impressive fusion of representative gate architecture and plate-glass display cases (Figs. 4.102, 4.103).[114] The photograph of the entrance to Japan's art exhibition provides evidence of the ongoing involvement of architectural models, with a five-storied pagoda in a prominent position (Fig. 4.104). An additional architectural contribution was the living room of a Japanese lady as part of the Woman's Building. Similar to the interiors of

---

113   National Diet Library, "Expositions," http://www.ndl.go.jp/exposition/e/s1/1893-1.html [accessed 2 May 2019].
114   See Conant, "Japan," pp. 261–262 who points to Kubota Beisen's (1852–1906) published sketches, which broaden the visual documentation of Japan.

FIGURE 4.100   World's Columbian Exhibition, 1893: Japanese tea garden complex

FIGURE 4.101   World's Columbian Exhibition, 1893: view of the Japanese tea house

FIGURES 4.102–4.104   World's Columbian Exhibition, 1893: the façade of the Japanese department, Japan's pavilion in the hall for forestry and the entrance to Japan's department within the art section

the Hō-ō-den, the room was not only an exhibit in its own right, but at the same time a display case for related items such as furniture and art.

The final Japanese exhibit with a specific architectural setting was the Japanese Bazaar in the middle of Midway Plaisance. It consisted of a group of buildings around a two-storied gate in a half-timbered construction, with lanterns adorning its upper lintel. Compared to the Hō-ō-den, it gave an impression of being built from plywood and cardboard with just enough 'Japaneseness' to allow for easy recognition (Figs. 4.105, 4.106).

FIGURES 4.105–4.106   World's Columbian Exhibition, 1893: Japanese Bazaar – Midway Plaisance

The World's Columbian Exposition in Chicago of 1893 was without doubt the key event for the western experience of Japanese architecture during the later nineteenth century. This was due not only to the architectural quality of the Hō-ō-den, but also to the skilful propagation of the building in field-related journals and the Japanophile networks that embedded the building and its artefacts in contemporary American narratives. Its legacy was further amplified by its alleged lasting impact on architectural icons such as Adolf Loos (1870–1933) and Frank L. Wright. Whether they shared their encounters firsthand or were the subjects of others' writings, their experiences and insights continued to reverberate well into the twentieth century.[115]

In the context of knowledge production of Japanese architecture in the Euro-American sphere, the Hō-ō-den and its contemporary conception was likewise of relevance in terms of the question of genuineness. Some secondary sources discussing the pavilion specifically underline its authenticity.[116] Sadly, the context of these statements remains unclear. They might see the historical origin of the model building, the Hō-ō-dō in Uji, as an indicator of the specific authenticity of real historical Japaneseness compared to the earlier pavilions, which expressed contemporary Japanese architectural ideas and were thus often of an apparently hybrid character. In the light of the overall elaboration of this sub-chapter, any such reading would fall short of doing justice to the different expressions of architectural Japaneseness we have seen so far by

---

115   See for example Kirsch, *Neue Wohnung*, pp. 8–10, 58 and Loos, Claire, *Adolf Loos privat* (Wien, 1936), p. 104.
116   National Diet Library, "Expositions," http://www.ndl.go.jp/exposition/e/s1/1893-1.html [accessed 17 August 2023]; Cody, *World's Fairs*, p. 11; and with some caveats Kirsch, *Neue Wohnung*, p. 58 in context with an extended quote from Lancaster, *Japanese Influence*.

restricting architectural authenticity only to the buildings of eras before the arrival of Perry's fleet in 1853. This would make the authenticity of Japanese architecture an exclusively historical phenomenon, drawing an impenetrable line between the past and present of Japanese architecture.

It is thus essentially important that we not end the narration of Japanese architectural objects in the West at this point. It would mean leaving the storyline with the notion of increasing mutual understanding and comprehension between Japan and the Euro-American nations concerning architecture. This, however, would be an underestimation of the actual complexity of the cultural contacts between the two spheres in general and the architecture-related knowledge production in particular. We will see this with the Exposition Universelle in Paris in 1900, where what was probably the most lasting architectural catalyst of Japaneseness was not provided by Japan's contribution.

1.8 Exposition Universelle de Paris, 1900

The Exposition Universelle in Paris in 1900 saw the continuation of an artistic Japanese self-representation that challenged western concepts of hegemony. The discourses of cultural self-determination, which had accompanied the entire modernisation process, found expressions in art and architecture and were communicated strongly with Japan's self-confidence in the wake of its military triumph over China and the end of the *Unequal Treaties* just the year before.[117] The commissioner Hayashi Tadamasa (1851–1906) had already come to Paris as a translator for the *exposition* in 1878 and had opened an art trade business about twenty years later, catering to the western interest in Japanese arts, much as Fenollosa and Okakura did, but with a different, less traditional angle, which made him less known than the former.[118]

His handling of matters shifted Japan's artistic contributions from a presentation of art production into a statement on art history, cultural heritage and national identity. While pieces of historical Japanese art had already been part of a larger art exhibition in the Trocadéro in 1878 and were a significant part of the staging of Hō-ō-den in 1893, it was only in 1900 that a comprehensive collection of such objects was set up and caused a new stir among art aficionados.[119]

---

117 See e.g. Kirsch, *Neue Wohnung*, pp. 60–61. See also Yoshioka, "Samurai"; Tseng, *Imperial Museums*; Satō, *Japanese Art*. – Contemporary sources also commented on this issue: *Paris Exposition 1900. Guide pratique du visiteur de Paris et de l'exposition* (Paris, 1900), pp. 357–358.

118 Sigur, *Influence*, pp. 75–77.

119 See Kirsch, *Neue Wohnung*, pp. 60–61; Baumuck, Bodo, "Japan auf den Weltausstellungen 1862–1933," in: *Japan und Europa 1543–1929. Essays* (Berlin, 1993), pp. 44–49, here

As a result, Parisian discourses on the fine and applied arts assigned only secondary importance to the architectural contributions as they had done on similar occasions previously, a phenomenon that stood in strong contrast to the framing of Japan's artistic contributions in Chicago in 1893 and, for that matter, some years later in St. Louis. This did not mean that the audience did not note and comment upon the pavilion, but the information remained shallow and contradictory in comparison.

The 'Japanese village' was positioned in the most northeasterly part of the Trocadéro area, close to the river banks, and contained a garden, facilities for consuming tea and sake, a bazaar and the main pavilion, dedicated to the display of traditional Japanese art.[120] The original model is supposed to have been the Golden Hall of the Hōryū-ji in Ikaruga near Nara.[121] Yet there is some rumour, notably on the World Wide Web, that sees the Kinkaku-ji (Golden Pavilion) or Ginkaku-ji (Silver Pavilion) in Kyōto as the main inspiration. The confusion might be due in part to apparent similarities in name or to inaccurate transliterations, but the stylistic characteristics of the four buildings involved explain a great deal as well.

The photographs of the pavilion in Paris show a two-storied building of about 18 × 24 metres on a massive foundation (Figs. 4.107–4.110).[122] The structure's ground floor consisted of eight by six bays formed by pillars of half-timbering covered by a hipped or half-hipped roof with curved eaves. The upper level was largely set back to six by four bays, but with an irregularity on one side (see Fig. 4.113 in the colour section). This part had a curved hipped roof and a wraparound veranda.

Beyond this, its doors and windows dominated the building's appearance. The photographs show the door in the central *intercolumnium* of the short façade, allowing the assumption that there were three doors in the central *intercolumnia* in the long façade. All of the remaining spaces were filled with

---

p. 48; Nōshōmushō (ed.), *1900nen Pari Bankoku Hakurankai Rinji Hakuraikai Jimukyoku Hōkoku* 1 (Tōkyō: Nōshōmushō, 1902), p. 836, "Summary on Tokyo Research Institute for Cultural Properties (Tōbunken): Exhibition catalogue of the 1st and 2nd special exhibition (combined) Tokyo Imperial Museum," *List of the works of the Exhibition of Japanese Art held at the Paris World Exposition in 1900*, https://www.tobunken.go.jp/~joho/japanese/collection/paris/paris-e.html [accessed 18 August 2023]; Cody, *World's Fairs*, pp. 42–44, 91; Ministère de la Culture et la Communication (ed.), *Le japonisme, catalogue* (Paris, 1988), pp. 116–117.

120 *Paris 1900. Guide pratique*, pp. 358–359.
121 Nōshōmushō, *1900nen Pari*, pp. 879–880, "Summary on Tokyo Research, Exposition in 1900"; *Paris 1900. Guide pratique*, p. 358.
122 Nōshōmushō, *1900nen Pari*, plan past p. 830.

FIGURES 4.107–4.110   Exposition Universelle, 1900: the Japanese pavilion, tea house and garden

bell-shaped windows, *katōmado*, with plate-glass set in a rectangular grid. A plain area of façade above the doors and windows marked the transition towards the bracket system for the roof on the lower floor, while on the upper floor the bracketing started immediately above the horizontal beam. The photographs only hint at the form of the bracketing and its extension along the eaves.

None of these features accord easily with the supposed original model. The Golden Hall of the Hōryū-ji is a Buddha hall of the seventh century, which may have burned down, and was replaced by 711 at the latest.[123] The sturdy single-storey hall rests on a stone clad earthen pedestal of about 18 × 15 metres and is introverted in character. The two layers of the main roof dominate its appearance, half-hipped on top, hipped below. The corridor circling the sanctuary, *mokoshi*, was added later and obscures the view of the building's windowless façade and many of its structural parameters (Figs. 4.111 and 4.112 in colour section).

A reconstruction of the original building shows the basic structure of five by four bays, the interior space primarily shaped by ten massive wooden pillars on the ground floor, and the central position of the doors on the long side, while the door in the short side is off-centre. The (inaccessible) upper part of the hall is set back and has a more decorative structural solution that does not necessarily correspond to the structure below.[124] The differences between the two buildings are also evident in the light of a floor plan of the Paris pavilion published in 1902 (Fig. 4.113 in colour section). The basic concept shares some traits, such as the pavilion's position on its foundation, the points of access, and the external and internal rows of columns, but the design of the pavilion forsook both the reduced *intercolumnium* at the corners of the older building and some of the attempts at symmetry. It did so in favour of a representative staircase at the southern longitudinal wall. The latter explains the irregularities in the wraparound veranda on the upper floor. This invites a search for alternative explanations for the pavilion's design, most notably due to the domineering feature of the bell-shaped windows. This comparatively recent decorative element found its way from its original context in the monasteries

---

123   The complex is part of Japan's World Heritage sites. For an overview of the architecture and art as well as the fire, see Mizuno, Seiichi, *Asuka Buddhist Art: Horyu-Ji* (New York, 1974), and for a visual analysis Nishioka, Tsunekazu; Miyakami, Shigetaka; Hozumi, Kazuo, *Hōryūji. Sekai saiko no mokuzō kenchiku* [Hōryūji. How the Japanese made buildings] (Tōkyō: Sōshisha, 1990).
124   Nishioka; Miyakami; Hozumi, *Hōryūji*, pp. 54–55.

of Zen-Buddhism into a variety of uses from sixteenth century onwards.[125] Against this background, it actually makes sense to look at the two famous Kyōto buildings, the Ginkaku-ji and the Kinkaku-ji. This might even have been done in 1900. There is an illustration of the building in question that showed it literally as 'Golden Pavilion' (Fig. 4.114, see colour section). Another depiction coloured roofs and timber elements in bold red (Fig. 4.115, see colour section). While vermilion finish is well known for shrine gates and temple architecture, Japanese roof tiles are usually dark grey or black while the colour of the organic coverings ranges through different shades of brown and grey. Nevertheless, one text mentioned the use of copper sheets for this building.[126]

The two buildings in question are of a more delicate and less symmetrical appearance than either the much older Golden Hall of the Hōryū-ji or the Japanese pavilion in Paris (Figs. 4.116 and 4.117, see colour section). This is due on the one hand to the chosen construction principles, which did not use pillars but slim square uprights, and on the other to the buildings' origins in the residential *shoin zukuri* of later times. They carry traces of the symmetrical design patterns of earlier times in the upper façades but not in the main floors. Both buildings are functionally multi-storied with similar tent roofs covered with shingles or similar material. Thus, the buildings in Kyōto are neither structurally nor formally closer to the Paris pavilion, except for the decorative windows.

Beyond these difficulties, the sources seemed to agree that the materials needed for the buildings were purchased in France, but it is unclear whether the workforce completing the construction originated in Europe or Japan. Not even the Japaneseness of the building's character was undisputed. While Elias Burton Holmes (1870–1958), an American traveller and photographer, was as disappointed by the complex as was the writer of a French guidebook, a German report noted the convincing similarity between the building and the known images of architecture from Japan.[127]

Despite all this, the pavilion did not provoke any further discussion. This might have been due to the limited access to the building, for which the majority of visitors had to purchase tickets.[128] As a result, it was not the pavilion that prompted more prolonged desire in Paris for western knowledge of Japanese architecture, but a book and another building project.

---

125 For the origin of this type of window, see *katoumado*, in: JAANUS, here http://www.aisf.or.jp/~jaanus/deta/k/katoumado.htm [accessed 15 July 2019].

126 Malkowsky, Georg (ed.), *Die Pariser Weltausstellung in Wort und Bild* (Berlin, 1900), p. 168.

127 Holmes, "Paris Exposition," p. 257; *Paris 1900. Guide pratique*, pp. 357–358; Malkowsky, *Pariser Weltausstellung*, p. 167; Ministère, *Le japonisme*, pp. 116–117; "Tokyo Research, Exposition in 1900."

128 "Tokyo Research, Exposition in 1900."

FIGURES 4.118–4.119   Exposition Universelle, 1900: title page and example plate of the volume *Histoire de l'art du Japon*

During the exhibition, the Imperial Commission of Japan for the Exposition Universelle de Paris presented a volume of 280 pages entitled *Histoire de l'art du Japon*. Subdivided by epochs, the book provided a chronological and richly illustrated overview of painting, sculpture, architecture and the applied arts against the background of the general sociocultural development of Japan from prehistoric times to the Tokugawa period. This volume was probably among the first ever to tell a nation's art history in a comprehensive and systematic manner (Figs. 4.118 and 4.119).[129] While the initial edition of 1900 provided only a few photographs as far as architecture was concerned, later editions contained drawings, floor plans, sections and detailing alike, inviting a cross-cultural professional discourse on constructive features between western and Japanese builders. Regrettably, this discourse did not come to fruition at this time and the authors of Euro-American handbooks such Bannister Fletcher ignored the volume.

---

129   Fukuchi, Mataichi; Kino, Toshio; Mabuchi, Akiko, *Japan. Rinji Hakurankai Jimukyoku, Tōkyō Teishitsu Hakubutsukan: Histoire de l'art du Japon. Ouvrage publié par la Commission Impériale du Japon à l'Exposition universelle de Paris, 1900* (Paris, 1900). – Rémi Labrusse argues that Louis Gonse wrote the first of such with his *L'Art japonais*, 1882. I do not agree with this stance, not least due to Gonse's imbalanced handling of architecture. Labrusse, Remi, "GONSE, Louis, 03.11.2008," in: Sénéchal, Philippe; Barbillon, Claire (eds.), *Dictionnaire critique des historiens de l'art actifs en France de la Révolution à la Première Guerre mondiale*, via Institut national d'histoire de l'art, https://www.inha.fr/fr/ressources/publications/publications-numeriques/dictionnaire-critique-des-historiens-de-l-art/gonse-louis.html [accessed 18 August 2023].

FIGURE 4.120
Exposition Universelle, 1900: le tour du monde, Alexandre Marcel, 1900

The second lasting architectural impulse came from a source much less portable than the book and not at all Japanese but part of one of the many entertainments, the *Tour du Monde*. Initiated by Louis-Jules Dumoulin (1860–1924), the French passenger steamship line *Compagnie des Messageries maritimes* financed the project and Parisian architect Alexandre Marcel (1860–1928) drew the designs. The building aimed to bring the cultures of Asia together in one place and to allow the visitor to experience its architecture on the outside and its people and customs on the inside. Architectural elements from diverse backgrounds mingled with practical functions such as restaurants. The immense structure itself must have drawn the eye,[130] as did some singular elements in its façade, such as the six-storied pagoda painted in red. The effect was probably heightened still further by the bold letters of the advertisement for *Brasserie Vetzel* (Figs. 4.120–4.122).

The American traveller Elias Burton Holmes, who had complained about the lack of Japaneseness in the Japanese pavilion, wrote in this regard: "The pagoda and the entrance-gate carved in Japan bear the stamp of genuineness. It remained for this money-making enterprise to introduce into Paris the

130 Malkowsky, *Pariser Weltausstellung*, p. 28; *Paris 1900. Guide pratique*, p. 264; Clericuzio, Peter, "The Shifting Meanings and Uses of the Japanese Tower at Laeken," paper given at "The Object and Beyond", Third Annual Graduate Conference of the Pennsylvania State University Graduate Student Association for Visual Culture, University Park, PA, March 2011 via https://www.academia.edu/2606248/The_Shifting_Meanings_and_Uses_of_the_Japanese_Tower_at_Laeken [downloaded 6 May 2019], p. 4.

VISITING AND VISUALISING ARCHITECTURE 249

FIGURES 4.121–4.122
Exposition Universelle,
1900: views of the 'Tour
du Monde'

only worthy examples of the architecture of Japan." He went on to praise the "atmosphere of Dai Nippon" in the interior.[131]

The *Tour du Monde* was demolished after the end of the exhibition but the pagoda experienced a 'rebirth' within a few years. King Leopold II of Belgium (1835–1909) had been inspired by the *Exposition Universelle* in Paris in 1900 in

---

131 Holmes, "Paris Exposition," pp. 299 and 302–303.

general and by the *Tour du Monde* in particular. He commissioned Alexandre Marcel to recreate the pagoda as part of a planned display of exotic buildings in Brussels in the area of the Royal Park in Laeken (Figs. 4.123–4.125, see colour section). Over time it was joined by other buildings such as a Chinese pavilion, and the entire group of buildings was subsequently converted into a museum of East Asian art.[132] With its position allowing it to be viewed from the Royal Greenhouses, the brilliant red tower remains a landmark to the present day (Figs. 4.126 and 4.127, see colour section). The building's history and artistic expression are shrouded in layers of commentary around its genuineness and authenticity. As with the Japanese gate of the *Tour du Monde* in Paris, which had supposedly been erected by Japanese carpenters, part of the work for the pagoda was said to have been done in Japan. It was understood by some to be Japan's national pavilion, translocated from the Paris exhibition, or by others to be a replica of a Japanese pagoda, such as that of Asakusa Sensō-ji in Tōkyō.[133]

The pagoda in Laeken with its contradicting claims and ensuing assumptions provides a fitting end point for the discussion in this sub-chapter. While it was neither designed, made, nor commissioned by Japanese actors – in contrast to many of the buildings, models and depictions discussed before – it was supposed to appear as such. Both Kozyreff and Clericuzio underline in their writing the very limited knowledge concerning Japanese architecture in Europe at this time, an evaluation that dovetails with our observations made regarding Garnier's *Japanese House* in Paris in 1889 and, for that matter, Ralph A. Cram's *Knapp House*.[134]

From the point of view of knowledge production, this is a sad evaluation after about 35 years of Japanese architectural appearances at international fairs, many of them within travelling distance of Brussels. It is even sadder in light of Europe's interest in all things artistically Japanese in this period, as well as the many levels of the art trade with East Asia beyond the exhibitions.

---

132   Clericuzio, "Shifting Meanings"; Vandenbreeden, Jos; Bastin, Christine, *Vom Klassizismus zum Jugendstil. Das 19. Jahrhundert in Belgien – Architektur und Interieurs* (Eupen, 1996), pp. 32–33.

133   See for a much more extensive treatment Kozyreff, Chantal, *The Oriental Dream: Leopold II's Japanese Tower and Chinese Pavilion at Laeken* (Antwerp, 2001), esp. pp. 41–42; Clericuzio, "Shifting Meanings," pp. 6, 11; Ministère, *Le japonisme*, p. 116; *Paris 1900. Guide pratique*, p. 264.

134   Kozyreff, *Oriental Dream*, p. 41; Clericuzio, "Shifting Meanings," p. 11. See for the latter e.g. Locher, "Introduction," p. 16; Lancaster, *Japanese Influence*, pp. 64–75. See also Demeulenaere-Douyère, Christiane, "Japan at the World's Fairs: A Reflection," in: *Journal of Japonisme* 5.2 (2020), pp. 129–151.

However, this evaluation is similar to some observations from the earlier textual analysis: Books, albums, collections and exhibitions of the time include a broad interest in Japan, its art and culture, with the resulting accumulation of materials and information, among which architecture itself was less a matter of intellectual study than one of curiosity and aesthetic pleasure.

But what have we seen in this brief overview of Japanese architecture at the exhibitions? The aim was to provide an overview of the architectural features available to western audiences at these events in Europe and North America until the end of the nineteenth century and to guess at the insights that might have been gained by visitors regarding construction, spatial arrangement and design of the Japanese pavilions themselves and the information provided by the pieces on display.

First of all, there was an overwhelming focus on Japanese applied art in contemporary publications as there is in today's research. Yet, this was more obvious in the texts and the art collections of the time than it was in the depictions of Japan's appearances at the international exhibitions. The latter contained examples of displays with a particular emphasis on art but at the same time documented the buildings themselves or the interiors used to frame Japan's contributions. As a result, it is possible to trace Japanese architecture through the World's Fairs since Paris 1867 in the form of buildings, façades, interior designs or exhibition objects in the narrower sense of architectural models, tools, handbooks or drawings.[135]

However, the Japanese buildings at the exhibitions did not present a consistent narrative of architectural Japaneseness but mirrored national changes in approaching one's own culture as well as international discourses on cultural identity.[136] There were vernacular buildings such as elsewhere in Japan as well as highly artificial inventions; contemporary designs as well as reproductions aiming at historical authenticity.

There is some evidence for a shift in Japanese policy which can be seen in the choice of buildings alone. The attention given to the 'historical' pavilions and their artistic exhibits in Chicago in 1893 and Paris in 1900 hints at a policy of double-tracked self-representation: in these years Japan was shown both as a rapidly modernising nation in the industrial displays and as a nation of enduring and accomplished culture in its national pavilions.

---

135 The less famous international exhibitions such as Sydney, 1879, Melbourne, 1880, or Barcelona, 1888, are a different story: basic data about the participants and visitors, the specific focus and so on is available, but a lot of additional work is still needed.

136 Regarding the national Japanese exhibitions see e.g. Hedinger, *Wettstreit*; Cody, *World's Fairs*.

Yet, despite the broad variety of building types, the life-sized architectural contributions shared a number of traits, which were even evident in part in the Parisian façades, such as those on the *Street of Nations*: the buildings were wooden constructions based on the established Japanese patterns of the trade, with the exception of occasional contemporary adaptations in design. The work on site was done by Japanese workmen with pre-fabricated materials, usually brought from Japan. As a result, the pavilions, tea houses and bazaars at the international exhibitions showed the basic characteristics of Japanese building practice again and again: half-timbered skeletons, surfaces suited to the characteristics of the materials, and a nearly endless variety of spatial dispositions and detailing. It would have been easy for the western observers to understand the structure and to compare it with either the textual and visual reports from Japan, such as Morse's *Homes*, or the western practices of wooden construction.

Much as in the textual sources, however, the perception of the Japanese buildings and the discussion of their architectural characteristics barely extended beyond an appreciation of the buildings' non-western-ness and never shifted into a broader analytical engagement with the matter or the spatial solutions.

However, there is no doubt about the tremendous influence of Japan's contributions to the international exhibitions on the overall development of western art and on the development of specific artists. This included some architects whose work and writings multiplied the impulses of their late-nineteenth-century experiences into the awareness, design and discourse of the first decades of the twentieth century. This also included some surviving buildings, genuinely Japanese or 'built Japonisms', models, photographs and such, which were added to books and essays to inspire architectural thought for the challenges of the new century. It is the images that we need to look at next in order to round off our observations on knowledge transfer and the building of canons, on imagination and knowledge.

2   Japanese Architecture Visualised: Books, Woodblock Prints and Souvenir Photographs

It is reasonable to assume that images of Japanese architecture left the greatest impact on western discussants. These certainly had a greater impact than texts alone and lasted longer than the ephemeral impulses provided by the architectural displays at events such as the international exhibitions, despite the unquestionable relevance of the physical experience of visiting an actual building.

This chapter looks at the kinds of illustrations available, their content and their influence on the production and dissemination of architectural knowledge of Japan. It addresses these questions primarily in terms of illustrations published more generally, such as those appearing in books or journals, and focuses on mainstream discourses rather than the in-field discussions among small groups of Japanophile architects and designers. Yet, it is important to look at other groups of contemporary visual media as well: firstly, because they did in fact influence the process of knowledge production by being limited to elite circles, by being kept in archives without publication, or by being altogether ignored; and secondly, because today's processes of digitisation make it possible to gain a constantly improving overview of these visual sources and invite speculation on whether they would have changed western understandings of Japanese architecture if only they had been recognised in time. Thus, we will have a look at printed media first, followed by visual material of limited dissemination, and finally, material which was available but remained unknown to western audiences.

2.1 *Illustrations in Western Books and Periodicals*

The nineteenth century saw a tremendous change in publication practices due to a shift towards the industrial production of books and periodicals and the attraction of a mass audience to lending libraries, encyclopaedias and cheap print media.

Prior to that, line drawings to accompany the text had been incorporated into printing plates without difficulty. It was, however, much more challenging to include nuanced illustrations – not to mention coloured ones – and doing so meant an enormous increase in effort and cost. Now, in a process that saw the parallel development of different innovative techniques, new types of original prints and reprography made it possible to reproduce illustrations at reasonable costs.[137] This resulted in a price reduction in terms of illustration, most notably through increasingly popular illustrated magazines such as *The Illustrated London News* (1842–2003). The authenticity of the depicted matter depended not only on the available visual information, but on the practices of journalism as well as the means of print production. The images in magazines were "processed images that did not bear a resemblance to reality in

---

137 Janzin, Marion; Güntner, Joachim, *Das Buch vom Buch. 5000 Jahre Buchgeschichte* (Hannover, 1995), pp. 329–334.

the modern sense. To 'increase the level of reality' they were enriched with characteristic details in a more or less 'atmospheric' way."[138] Similarly, after the mid-1880s the precision of reproduction of visual information made it possible even to include photographs, thus approaching real life depictions as well.[139]

This was a process which developed during the decades examined here, influencing the number, type and character of illustrations used in publications up to the turn of the twentieth century. It certainly influenced the ways in which images and visual information in general were disseminated. However, it probably did not influence the topics chosen for the illustrations we are interested in, since architecture in its technical sense is traditionally communicated by means of line drawings.

The current far-reaching availability of digitised publications in the public domain allowed this project to systematically extract, index and systematise illustrations and to analyse these on their own as visual sources which convey meaning and information independently of their textual context.[140] For the purposes of this study, illustrations were taken from the same publications which informed the textual analysis: art and in-field architectural essays and monographs, and ethnographical publications and travelogues, most notably those mentioned above. This frame was checked against and slightly extended by the work completed in Nichibunken's project *Images of Japan in Non-Japanese Sources*,[141] which captures the years 1854 to 1890.

---

138   Es „waren bearbeitete Bilder, die keine Wirklichkeitstreue im heutigen Sinne besaßen. Zur ‚Steigerung des Wirklichkeits-wertes' hatte man sie mehr oder weniger ‚stimmungsvoll' mit charakteristischen Details angereichert." Janzin, *Buch*, p. 329.

139   For much more detail concerning the intricacies of technology, affordability, visual expectation and the mobility of visual motives, see for example Bann, Stephen, "The Photographic Album as a Cultural Accumulator," in: id. (ed.), *Art and the early photographic album* (New Haven, CT; London, 2011), pp. 7–30 and id., "The Past in Print: Ancient Buildings Represented by Engraving, Etching and Lithography in Early-Nineteenth-Century England," in: Hvattum, Mari; Hultzsch, Anne (eds.), *The printed and the built. Architecture, print culture, and public debate in the Nineteenth Century* (London; New York; Oxford; New Delhi; Sydney, 2018), pp. 51–72 or Bergdoll, Barry, "Architecture and Print Culture in the Nineteenth Century: 'The Public Square of the Modern Age': Architecture and the Rise of the Illustrated Press in the Early Nineteenth Century," in: Hvattum, Mari; Hultzsch, Anne (eds.), *The printed and the built. Architecture, print culture, and public debate in the Nineteenth Century* (London; New York; Oxford; New Delhi; Sydney, 2018), pp. 27–50.

140   Google's initiative in this regard was extremely helpful. Sadly, the attempts to save data storage occasionally resulted in a lamentable quality of illustrations which was sufficient to understand their content, but insufficient to recognise satisfactorily some of the detailing or the process of copying between versions and editions.

141   International Research Center for Japanese studies (nichibunken), *Images of Japan in Non-Japanese Sources*, 5 vols., https://www.nichibun.ac.jp/en/publications/data/gaiz/ [accessed 29 July 2023].

The visual material covers the same broad understanding of 'architecture' as delineated earlier, ranging from technical details to views of specific buildings, street scenes and staffage buildings in the depiction of Japanese manners and customs, sights, and places for recreational travel. Collectively, the illustrations which relate to or include Japanese architecture up until 1900 amount to approx. 3,900 images, spanning from small vignettes to full-sized plates of technical drawings, with some illustrations published only once, while others have been reproduced many times.

Within the general framework of research on architecture-related knowledge production, we will answer some core questions. What characterised the illustrations which were published for western audiences? Did differences of content occur according to the different types of audience addressed? Did experts use different pictures from travellers? What kind of information on architectural issues in the broadest sense was communicated, and what was missing when seen through the lens of today's understanding of architectural history?

As we will see, the experts' publications used different topics and types of illustrations to accompany architectural issues compared to the publications conveying general knowledge of Japan. The two realms were very distinct, with the exception of one publication whose images bridged the clear delineation: Edward Sylvester Morse's *Japanese Homes and Their Surroundings*, 1885.[142]

2.1.1   Publications on Artistic or Architectural Topics

The architectural experts, ranging from art collectors and art historians, to architectural practitioners and civil engineers, did not necessarily use illustrations at all. The more than 30 authors in these fields whose texts and images contributed to this study jointly published about 500 images, or one eighth of the total body of 'architectural' illustrations in this analysis. If they did use images, the vast majority of them showed parts or segments of the overall story: individual buildings out of context, parts of buildings such as gates or ceilings, or decorative details such as carvings, fastenings or tiles.[143] The most spectacular among the latter were the systems of brackets which primarily adorned temples and temple gates and transmitted the roof's load to the vertical supports and the overall structure. Their complicated three-dimensional puzzle of elements challenged even trained artists and draughtsmen. Christopher

---

142   Morse, *Homes*.
143   This largely corresponds to the common architectural photographic practice of the time in France at least. Bressani, Martin; Sealy, Peter, "The Opera Disseminated: Charles Garnier's Le Nouvel Opera de Paris (1875–1881)," in: Bann, Stephen (ed.), *Art and the early photographic album* (New Haven, CT; London, 2011), pp. 195–220, here 203–205.

Dresser commented on commissioning photographers and draughtsmen and added in a footnote:

> Accompanying the drawings which I ultimately received from this latter artist was a coloured model of a complicated bracket of which I wished to have a drawing. To my question why this model was made, the answer came that – owing to his imperfect knowledge of perspective he could not draw this elaborate work, and that he had consequently made a model instead.[144]

After all this effort, the illustration in the book was somewhat disappointing (Fig. 4.128, see colour section). It showed the decorative complexity of the element on a very small scale without a real explanation of its intrinsic logic or constructive function. A similar bracket system was depicted in an illustration on the following page, and a frontal view appeared some pages later (Figs. 4.129 and 4.130, see colour section). Another detail of bracketing was counted among the select group of coloured reproductions of architecture. It was painted by Abel Guérineau and published in 1886 as an accompaniment to César Daly's *Les temples japonais* (Fig. 4.131, see colour section).[145]

The two smaller illustrations are interesting in their similarly decorative approach to architectural issues and make it possible to address their different handling of references as well. In most cases, architectural details were given without any reference to the place or building depicted as the majority were of vernacular buildings of whatever kind. Only in the case of larger sections, usually taken from famous building complexes such as temples or shrines, were the names of the complexes mentioned. Even then, however, it would have been quite a challenge to relate the drawing to the corresponding part of the building upon visiting.

In Dresser's case – and for that matter Guérineau's – the origin of the illustrations is comparatively clear, particularly since there were no other visual sources similar to his previously, as far as we know. In addition, he offered a

---

144 Dresser, *Japan*, p. 147 FN.
145 Guérineau, a contracted foreign expert between 1874 and 1880, taught drawing and designed buildings in Japan. Upon his return to Europe, he exhibited his painstakingly detailed paintings at the Salon in 1881. Hayashi, Yoji, "Japanese Experience of Abel Guérineau, Hired French Architect. The Imperial Japanese Army academy and the French architectural education institutions," in: *Journal of Architecture and Planning (Transactions of AIJ)* 80, 709 (2015), pp. 709–715; Frédéric, *Encyclopedia*, p. 266. Daly, "Temples japonais."

rare explanation of the source material in his introduction and this provides an insight into the amount of data being collected behind the scenes for this book. He reported the acquisition of about 1,000 photographs and numerous coloured drawings during his visits to a hundred temples and shrines. He also described commissioning the prints for his book.[146] In the end, Dresser's book showed a remarkably homogeneous pattern of visual content, even if the style of portrayal did vary, ranging from reduced 'technical' drawings, through detailed depictions, to some 'impressions' of larger architectural contexts, such as a temple gate in Kyōto or the shrines at Ise. In addition, Dresser included a selection of Japanese sources to illustrate building trades and tools.

Experts without the benefit of on-site experience in Japan, with less training in drawing or with fewer resources, assembled the illustrations they needed from a range of sources and created many-faceted impressions of Japanese architecture. In Louis Gonse's *L'art Japonais* the depiction of a bracket was taken from a Japanese illustration of the life of Satō Tadanobu, a medieval warrior (Fig. 4.132). Thus, the hero's crouched body jumping from a building to surprise his master's enemies and the architectural detail shared space on the page, conveying somewhat confusing information as far as Japanese architecture was concerned. The later English version of the book in 1891 reduced the number of illustrations to about a quarter of the original and removed this element together with many others, thus creating a much more standardised layout.[147]

While Gonse chose an alternative illustration for the bracketing, he took some of his architectural illustrations from Dresser and referred to the latter's work in the text. Interestingly, he attributed an interior view and a fountain to Josiah Conder directly in the caption, but refrained from doing so with Dresser. Carl von Lützow referred back to Gonse but did not even mention the original source due to not having this information, while Justus Brinckmann mentioned Dresser in his text, but not in connection with the images, while copying them and their captions. As a result, there are four copies of the same illustration in different books and different languages, from the original *The*

---

146 Dresser, *Japan*, pp. vi–vii. – The engraver was probably George Pearson (1850–1910), while the illustrator might have been Philip Hundley, to whom the British Museum attributes a working period of between 1863 and 1880. The British Museum, collection database, https://www.britishmuseum.org/research/search_the_collection_database/term_details.aspx?bioId=120365 [accessed 1 August 2023].

147 Gonse, *L'Art*, p. 12; Gonse, *Art*.

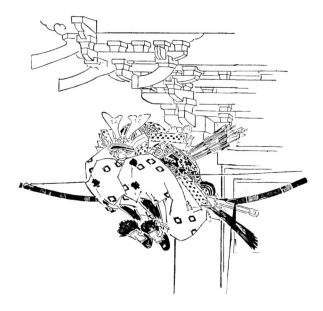

FIGURE 4.132
The bracket system as illustrated in the story about Satō Tadanobu

Water-Tank at Shiba in Dresser's book of 1882 to Gonse's English edition in 1891 (Figs. 4.133–4.137).[148]

The same architectural context was shown in some editions of Alexander Graf von Hübner's travel reports, but from a different angle (Figs. 4.138, 4.139). Both Dresser's and Hübner's were detailing based on photographs. In the case of Hübner, the Nagasaki University Library has a photographic print by Felice Beato, which shows exactly the same situation, but for two human figures placed discreetly to the right, providing a measure of scale. Another photograph of the same building by Kusakabe Kimbei (1841–1932) comes close to the cut-out chosen by Dresser (Figs. 4.140, 4.141). Such souvenir photographs were easily obtainable by well-off travellers in Japan at this time – a matter we will discuss in more detail later – further strengthening the argument that templates such as these informed many of the engravings.

While Dresser's 'migrating images' serve as helpful examples of the production and dissemination of illustrations, they do not allow the use of images to be generalised. Only a small proportion of the nearly 70 architectural illustrations from Dresser's book was re-used elsewhere. Yet, his influence was

---

148 Lützow, Carl von, "Die Japanische Kunst," in: *Österreichische Monatsschrift für den Orient* (1884), pp. 1–6, 44–49, 73–78, 97–103, here p. 1, Brinckmann, *Kunst* – The depicted courtyard was part of the grounds of Zōjō-ji in Tōkyō, which served as a burial ground for some of the shōgun of the Tokugawa dynasty. It was largely destroyed in 1945.

VISITING AND VISUALISING ARCHITECTURE

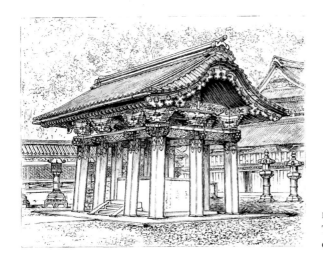

FIGURE 4.133
The water tank at Shiba as depicted by Dresser

FIGURES 4.134–4.137   Four reproductions of the water tank in Shiba in the books of Gonse, Lützow and Brinckmann

FIGURES 4.138–4.141
Courtyard of a mausoleum in Shiba in Hübner's books; Felice Beato: Tombs Of Taikuns – At Shiba Near Yeddo, and Kusakabe Kinbei: basins of bunshoin's burial ground at Shiba Zōjō-ji temple

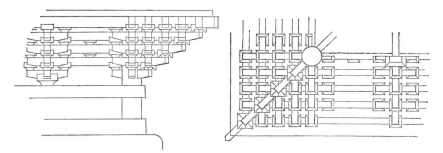

FIGURE 4.142   System of brackets

considerable as his work quickly became available in several European languages with the help of Gonse and Brinckmann.

Some much more technical illustrations were also being published at the same time. Josiah Conder communicated his insights on Japanese building traditions to his fellows at the Royal Institute of British Architects (RIBA) in that professional body's periodicals.[149] While his initial text of 1878 included two plates with impressions and details similar to Dresser's, he later changed the style of his illustrations. He provided details in a manner that even made it possible to trace the governing principles. Looking at the brackets mentioned above, Conder's drawings were abstract delineations, in strong contrast to Dresser's. Furthermore, Conder presented floor plans, views and sections of different secular building types without any embellishment or staffage. Among the experts' publications, only his go substantially beyond the picturesque Japaneseness that was prevalent in the books (Figs. 4.142, 4.143).

Yet, Conder's impulses did not change the prevailing pattern of architectural illustrations at the time for a number of reasons. Firstly, there were only a few of his drawings, and secondly, they were published only in the *Transactions of the Royal Institute of British Architects*, while abstracts of his talks also appeared elsewhere. While this publication undoubtedly had some readers beyond the membership of RIBA, it nevertheless had only limited impact on larger discourses around art and architecture in general, and Japan in particular.[150]

---

149   This paragraph's reasoning includes two essays on Japanese architecture written by Roger Thomas Conder (d. 1906). They follow the same patterns and are arguably built on information provided by his brother. There is no indication that Roger Thomas ever visited Japan. Conder, "Mausoleum"; id., "A Japanese Gentleman's House at Tokio," in: *J.R.I.B.A. Transactions* (2. Series), vol. III (1886/1887), pp. 181–184.
150   Baltzer confirmed this in his introduction to *Das Japanische Haus*. Baltzer, *Haus*, p. 3.

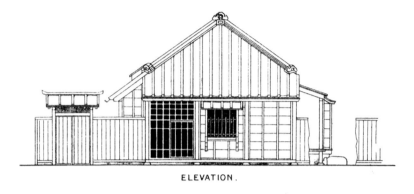

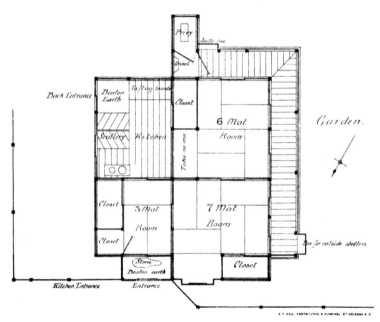

FIGURE 4.143   Middle-class Japanese dwelling

The third and arguably the crucial factor, however, was a general lack in interest in Japanese architecture among the experts involved and addressed.

The choice of illustrations generated, provided and distributed showed a focus on decorative inspiration and an almost complete disinterest in patterns of housing, construction, and the spatial arrangements of actual buildings beyond the picturesque pleasure of a general disposition. The illustrations were chosen to provide applicable aesthetic impulses against the background of the creative crisis in the European arts at the time. They aimed neither at collecting encyclopaedic knowledge on Japanese architecture, nor at

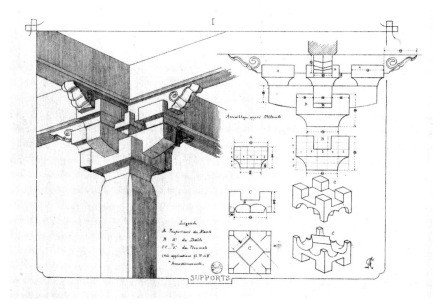

FIGURE 4.144   Supports depicted by Guérineau

gleaning conceptual impulses on architectural design and building technologies. Consequently, information on urban environments, domestic arrangements or functions, or structural solutions beyond joinery remained largely absent, as did references to many other building types and tasks; even the information provided on religious architecture remained largely incomplete.

In later publications such as Guérineau's *Ornements japonais* or Franz Baltzer's *Das Japanische Haus*, there was a considerable increase in the volume of visual material while the pattern was maintained: many images of details were included, while only a few, seemingly arbitrarily chosen and often disconnected technical drawings were provided.[151] Even Guérineau's stunning plates showing the character of the bracket systems in minute detail and multiple variations do not change this conclusion. However, some of them are included here for the enjoyment of the perfect beaux-arts tradition of drawing (Figs. 4.144–4.146).

Despite all this, it was and still is impossible to construct mentally a sound Japanese structure based on the available textual and visual materials provided in the course of the experts' exploration of Japan's architecture up to the end of the nineteenth century.

---

151   Guérineau, *Ornements*; Baltzer, *Haus*.

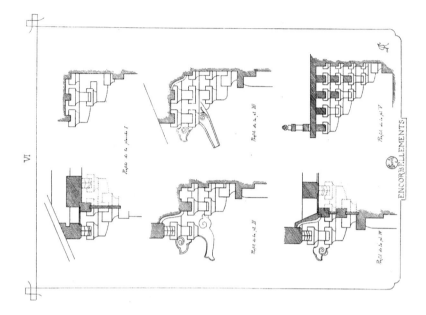

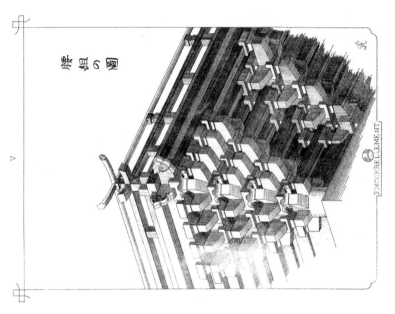

FIGURES 4.145–4.146   Corbels by Guérineau

This leaves the question of the remaining bulk of the 3,400 illustrations containing architectural information on Japan. In this context, architectural information was not provided for its own sake but was embedded in a broader narrative on Japan, its history and traditions, its topography and manners.

2.1.2   Edward S. Morse's *Japanese Homes and Their Surroundings*

The most 'architectural' publication among those providing a broader narrative of Japanese culture was Edward Sylvester Morse's *Japanese Homes and Their Surroundings*. It was very special due to its impact on the western perception of the Japanese dwelling. Inspired by a notion of impending loss of the traditional Japanese house due to the changes of modernisation, Morse had collected all available information and prepared an ethnographical account of the various types of building, domestic functions and practical solutions.

The 180 illustrations were largely his own, and comprised relatively small line drawings which allowed for good three-dimensional impressions due to the deft use of shading and perspective. About half of the motifs were details of a constructive, functional and decorative nature. The other half consisted in about equal parts of exterior views, interior views and technical drawings, such as construction principles and floor plans.

In an architectural sense, these illustrations were often much more informative than those provided by Dresser and the other 'architectural' experts with their strong interest in ornamentation. In contrast, Morse's details often captured vernacular phenomena of a non-artistic character such as fire places, bathrooms and the roofs of farmhouses (Figs. 4.147–4.150). While his interiors of living rooms focused exclusively on the representative, the book nevertheless provided impressions of everyday architectural arrangements which considerably broadened the available information. Yet, the information was not sufficient to provide the data needed for a convincing construction of a Japanese-style house, as we have already seen.

FIGURES 4.147–4.148   Ridge of thatched roof at Kabutoyama, Musashi, and bamboo-ridge of thatched roof in Musashi

 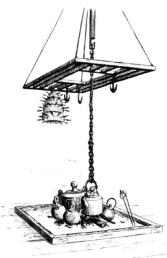

FIGURES 4.149–4.150   Kitchen in old farmhouse at Kabutoyama, and fireplace in country house

It is interesting to note that despite the early appreciation of this volume for its all-encompassing attention to everyday Japanese culture, the illustrations were only rarely copied and re-used by others. This might have been due to their small size and lack of graphic representativeness, or to the ordinariness of the content of the image.

2.1.3   Publications on Japanese Culture in General

In other publications of a more or less ethnographic character, the number of illustrations ranged from a single frontispiece plate to several hundred images, depending on the author's interest and the publisher's capacities. Occasionally, different issues of the same book used different illustrations, or even entirely different styles of illustration.

In this group of publications, the creation, use and re-use of visual material is much more common and obvious than seen above. Bearing in mind that only 'architectural' illustrations have been included in this analysis, there were four main sources of this type of illustration: Philipp Franz von Siebold's *Nippon*; the reports on the travels of Commodore Matthew Perry, documented in the drawings and prints of Wilhelm Heine and Eliphalet M. Brown (1816–1886) and retold numerous times by different authors; the publications of Swiss diplomat Aimé Humbert (1819–1900); and, finally, Japanese drawings and prints.

Siebold's encyclopaedic approach to all things Japanese did not pay any particular attention to buildings as such, apart from their role in the overall story. Thus, his plates which included architecture – some dwellings already introduced at the beginning of chapter 3 and some exterior and interior views of temples and shrines – were pragmatic and free of embellishment, as were many of Conder's plates some years later. The exact origin of the plates is a matter of ongoing research but there is significant evidence that the plates of houses were prepared in the Netherlands, based on more than twenty architectural models which Siebold had brought from Japan.[152]

Interestingly, apart from some of the early ethnographic reports and travelogues, none of the architectural texts borrowed from Siebold's architectural plates. The garden view of his *Heerenhuis* had already been reproduced in 1850 by Adolphe Philibert Dubois de Jancigny (1795–1860), in the compilatory volume *Die Nippon-Fahrer*, 1861, in Gustav Spieß' report on the *Preußische Expedition nach Ostasien*, 1864, and in Oscar Mothes' *Illustrirtes Bau-Lexikon*, 1866 (see Fig. 3.2).[153] The same books also used his plates of a small Buddhist temple and of a revolving storage unit for *sutra*s, Buddhist scriptures (Figs. 4.151, 4.152). The template of the latter was itself taken from a Japanese source, namely Katsushika Hokusai's *Manga*. It can be assumed that it was inspired or informed by the *rinzō* of the Kamakura Hase-dera (Figs. 4.153, 4.154).[154]

In this interrelation of 'migrating images', it was not only the garden view of Siebold's *Heerenhuis* that was copied. The street view found its way into another group of publications as well, albeit not as an exact copy of the former but in a more picturesque way, augmented with foliage and staffage figures (Figs. 4.155, 4.156).[155] No matter who took from whom, however, none of the secondary users referred back to Siebold (just as he did not refer to Hokusai), despite the general acknowledgement of his expertise by other authors and the encyclopaedias at the time.

---

152 The models are kept at the National Museum of Ethnology (Rijksmuseum voor Volkenkunde) in Leiden and are currently being studied by Noguchi Kenji, both on their own merit and concerning Siebold's plates. See for example Noguchi, Kenji; Hatano, Jun, "Characteristics of the townhouse model of the National Museum of Ethnology, Leiden collections," in: *Journal of architecture and planning: Transactions of AIJ (Nihon-Kenchiku-Gakkai-keikakukei-ronbunshū)* 82, 733 (2017), pp. 757–766.

153 Dubois de Jancigny, *Japon*, plate 13; Steger, Friedrich; Wagner, Hermann, *Die Nippon-Fahrer, oder, Das wiedererschlossene Japan in Schilderungen der bekanntesten älteren und neueren Reisen insbesondere der amerikanischen Expedition unter Führung des Commodore M. C. Perry in den Jahren 1852 bis 1854* (Leipzig, 1861), p. 169; Spieß, Gustav, *Die Preußische Expedition nach Ostasien während der Jahre 1860–1862: Reiseskizzen aus Japan, China, Siam und der indischen Inselwelt* (Berlin, 1864); Mothes, *Bau-Lexikon*, p. 307.

154 Hokusai, Katsushika, *Manga*, 15 vols. (s.l., 1814–1837). – Regarding Hokusai's depictions of architecture, see Cluzel, Jean-Sébastien; Marquet, Christophe; Nishida, Masatsugu, *Hokusai, le vieux fou d'architecture* (Paris, 2014).

155 Macfarlane, *Japan*; Steinmetz, Andrew, *Japan and her people* (London, 1859).

FIGURES 4.151–4.152   Buddhist temple, and Rin-Zoo in Siebold's book

In terms of the pattern of secondary use, the identical copy and the edited illustration were common among the publications analysed for this study. The same is true of the referencing. This was even more obvious in the second group of illustrations that provided architectural information: the reports on the travels of Commodore Matthew C. Perry (1794–1858).

Having made a significant contribution to the end of Japan's isolationist policy, Perry's legations to Japan in 1853 and 1854 were also pivotal for western knowledge production on Japan. The official report compiled in 1856 by Francis L. Hawks was illustrated with images based on the work done by two members of the expedition, Eliphalet M. Brown and Wilhelm Heine, as stated with gratitude in the prefatory note:

> The Commodore, unwilling to appropriate what may belong to others, desires here to acknowledge the use of (…) the services of Mr. Portman, Dutch interpreter, and of the artists, Mr. W. Heine and Mr. E. Brown, jr. (…) Nor would he pass by without notice minor contributions from any under his command; to all he would render due credit and thanks.[156]

---

156   Hawks; Perry, *Narrative*, p. iv, FN. – For more context see for example Dower, John, "Black ships and Samurai II. Commodore Perry and the Opening of Japan (1853–1854)," online resource, *MIT Visualizing culture*, https://visualizingcultures.mit.edu/black_ships_and_samurai_02/index.html [accessed 8 March 2019]; Baxley, George C., "Eliphalet M. Brown, Jr. Daguerreotypist and Artist for the Perry Expedition To Japan," http://www.baxleystamps.com, here http://www.baxleystamps.com/litho/brown.shtml [accessed 1 August 2023]; Bennett, *Photography*, pp. 27–29; "People: Peter Bernhard Wilhelm Heine,"

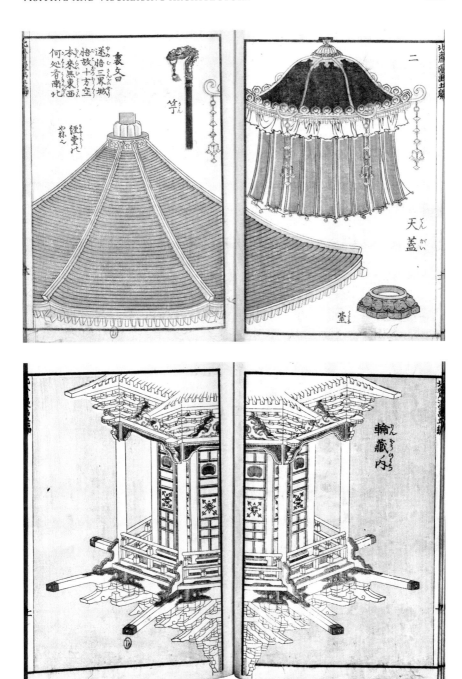

FIGURES 4.153–4.154   Elements of a *rinzō* by Katsushika Hokusai

FIGURES 4.155–4.156   Siebold's manor and Steinmetz' country house version

Together with other publications on the expedition, Heine's own publications, and re-told stories by other authors, some images were published and reproduced repeatedly, sometimes with Siebold's material.[157] Interestingly, even a member of the Prussian Eulenburg expedition of 1859–1862, which generated its own photographs and drawings, used these sources in a publication.[158]

To give just one example of such re-use, there was an in-text woodblock illustration in Hawks' narration depicting a *Farm Yard, Yokuhama*. Since the

"Perry In Japan: A Visual History," A joint project of Brown University Library and the Department of American Studies, online resource, https://library.brown.edu/cds/perry/about.html, here https://library.brown.edu/cds/perry/people_Heine.html [accessed 1 August 2023]. – See also Erickson, Bruce T., "Eliphalet M. Brown, Jr. An early expedition photographer," in: *The Daguerreian Annual* (1990), pp. 145–156.

157   Perry, Matthew Calbraith; Tomes, Robert, *Japan and the Japanese: a narrative of the U.S. government expedition to Japan, under Commodore Perry* (New York, 1857); id., *The Americans in Japan: an abridgment of the government narrative of the U.S. expedition to Japan, under Commodore Perry* (New York, 1859); Heine, Wilhelm, *Graphic Scenes of the Japan Expedition by Wm Heine, Artist of the Expedition* (New York, 1856); id., *Reise um die Erde nach Japan an Bord der Expeditions-escadre unter Commodore M.C. Perry in den Jahren 1853, 1854 und 1855, unternommen im Auftrage der Regierung der Vereinigten Staaten*, 2 vols. (Leipzig, 1856); id., *Die Expedition in die Seen von China, Japan und Ochotsk*, 3 vols. (Leipzig, 1858), id., *Japan: Beiträge zur Kenntniss des Landes und seiner Bewohner* (Berlin, 1875); Religious Tract Society, *Japan Opened: Compiled Chiefly from the Narrative of the American Expedition to Japan, in the years 1852-3-4* (London, 1858); Steger; Wagner, *Nippon-Fahrer* (1861), and extended 2nd ed. (1869), and newly edited Hintze, Eduard; Wagner, Hermann, *Das alte und das neue Japan, oder, Die Nippon-Fahrer: In Schilderungen der bekanntesten älteren und neueren Reisen*, 3rd ed. (Leipzig, 1874); Knox, Thomas Wallace, *The boy travellers in the Far East, part first: adventures of two youths in a journey to Japan and China* (New York, 1879).

158   See Spieß, *Preußische Expedition*.

FIGURE 4.157 Farm Yard, Yokuhama, in Hawks' book

book listed all illustrations with title, page, means of printing and artist, the origin of the template is clear, even if Heine never used this motif in one of his own publications. In addition, the signature in the lower left corner is discernible (Fig. 4.157).

The scene shows an open space against the background and framing of buildings, behind which the treeline of a wooded area is visible. While two men pound rice, others carry loads or load horses. The building on the left-hand side is a fire-resistant storehouse, *kura*, with plastered walls and a tiled saddle roof. It is set apart from the other buildings and only loosely connected to other structures, which would be separated easily in the event of a fire. The other buildings in the centre and on the right-hand side are made from wood with different types of panelling. The roofs, largely hipped, are thatched or shingled. The different features of the buildings and spatial arrangements are comprehensible, showing a variability of forms and materials in this apparently rural context.

The next year, a cut-out was used in another publication on the Perry expedition, with a different block and without any information regarding the topic or artist. It omitted one third of the image on the left-hand side in addition to some of the foreground, sky and right-hand margin, enhancing the depth effect (Fig. 4.158). It appeared again two years later.[159]

In 1858, the entire scene, minus some of the sky, was reproduced with yet another new block. While the name of the original artist was missing, the image was titled *Japanese Farmyard*. Here, the trees are given more branches and the active personnel have been changed: a kneeling woman behind the right-hand rice pounder has vanished and two people have appeared in front of the shrubs in the left-hand corner. Some details of the architecture have been simplified, above all the eaves and roof-ridges (Fig. 4.159).

A fourth block was produced in 1861 for *Die Nippon-Fahrer* and re-used in subsequent editions. In this case, the cut-out focused on the activities in the centre of the image by reducing the right-hand and left-hand margins and thus changing the framing role of the buildings around the workspace in the centre. The title *Hof eines japanischen Landguts* uses an ennobling term for farm – 'estate' – thus contextualising the scene in a different way compared to the initial title. The edition of 1874 even referred to Perry in the caption (Fig. 4.160).[160]

The final copy among the publications in this analysis used the original print block including the signature, except for the caption that read *A village on the Tokaido*. This renaming was another slight reframing of the image's supposed content.[161]

The extent to which the changes in image section and caption influenced the perception of contemporary readers remains an open question. Would it have made a difference to be introduced to Japan and its built environment with the information that the image depicted an entire village, and thus to understand that the daily work was done on the street – and indeed on the most important trade route in Japan, the Tōkaidō, at that? Would an architect have evaluated Japanese architecture differently based on the information that this scene showed an estate, and not just the workspace of a regular farm?

In general, of the 'architectural' illustrations in the publications surrounding Perry's expedition, just eight out of 72 in the official report, and about 30 more in Heine's later publications, had a strong spatial component. The depth of space became immediately apparent through interiors and exteriors, close-ups or wide-angle views, while the architectural information of décor, detail and construction remained vague. The three-dimensionality of buildings and building complexes, gardens and landscapes was most dominant in Heine's

---

159   Perry, *Japan and the Japanese*, p. 258.
160   Hintze, *Nippon-Fahrer*, p. 61.
161   Knox, *Boy travellers*, p. 157.

VISITING AND VISUALISING ARCHITECTURE 273

FIGURES 4.158–4.160
Japanese farmyard in
the books of Perry, the
Religious Tract Society
and Steger

illustrations, especially in his later plates from 1875.[162] Some places were even depicted as natural and cultural sights, unlike the majority of illustrations in this group, which rarely identified their subjects as specific places but referred to them simply as a city or village.

Yet, the members of the Perry expedition were limited in their time on shore and their overall mobility in exploring Japan, as were many of those who reported during the early years of renewed western contact with Japan. This started to change in subsequent years. Not only was the ability to create illustrations and to obtain Japanese drawings and prints broadened in the course of the longer stays of resident westerners, but the rapid establishment of photography in Japan led to an overall rise in the material available. We will look at this later.

Aimé Humbert, dispatched to Japan during 1863–1864 in his capacity as the Swiss ambassador, was another influential figure in the dissemination of architectural visual content. Leveraging his diplomatic standing, Humbert embarked on an extensive tour, as highlighted in the celebratory, albeit anonymous, preface to the condensed English edition of his works. This preface painted vivid vignettes of Humbert's methodical data collection process: sketching landscapes with the aid of an unspecified assistant, indulging in photography, and finally culminating with a description of the graphics, "in the way of engravings, Indian-ink sketches, and coloured pictures," procured from Tōkyō's bustling printing offices.[163] This multifaceted approach to information gathering by Humbert arguably surpassed even the comprehensive techniques employed by Dresser.

Humbert's own introduction acknowledged the works of Kaempfer and Siebold and expressed the aim of adding to the existing material through his collection of illustrations. He placed the illustrations of photographs and of the sketches of both Charles Wirgmann (1832–1891), the correspondent of the *Illustrated London News* in Yokohama, and Alfred Roussin, a member of the French navy, next to the material of Japanese origin – to which he saw the need to "apply the control and advanced processes of Western art" to achieve the resemblance deemed necessary.[164] He was thus hopeful that he could present

---

162 Heine, *Japan*.
163 Humbert, *Japan*, p. v–vi. – In fact, the proportion of depictions of Tōkyō increased significantly after his publication, not least due to his 'migrating' images.
164 "(…) appliquer le contrôle et les procédés perfectionnés de l'art occidental." Humbert, *Le Japon*, 1, p. 11.

the "most complete and picturesque array of institutions, customs and morals of the Japanese people."[165]

The two volumes of *Le Japon illustré*, 1870, included 480 illustrations in total, among which 200 contained architectural information in its widest sense, from architectural details in the background, to interiors and social scenes, and landscape views with architectural elements. Beyond the original French version, an abbreviated English publication came out some years later, as did shorter essays in two other languages, all of them including some of the images of the original edition.

The latter's origin is traceable thanks to a list of illustrations in the appendix, which is comparable in detail to Hawks' *Narrative*. After stating the subject matter, the engraver of the print plate was named, as was the original source, be it a Japanese print, a photograph or a drawing by one of the other foreign residents. This meticulous work was not reproduced in the English edition, where the list was reduced to the images alone.

To give an example as we did above, we will look at a view of Tōkyō's harbour (Fig. 4.161). It shows a channel somewhere in the wide area where the Sumida river flows into the bay, occupied on both sides by warehouses. In the background is a fragile bridge arching high above the water. The view, angled downward from the height of the houses' roof-ridges, suggests a uniformity or sameness in the height and structure of the buildings extending far beyond the area immediately depicted, while hinting at some slightly higher and somehow different buildings at the same time.

The caption read *View of a canal in the trader's quarter of Edo, at midday*; the index of illustrations added the information that the design was provided by E. Thérond after a photograph. The plate found its way into at least five more publications during the next twelve years, with changing captions and without references to the original source. While one was reprinted without information, and another was titled *Noon scene on a Japanese canal* without giving the name of the city, the other three provided the image with the name of the city and even added the city district.[166]

---

165   "(...) le tableau le plus complet et le plus pittoresque qui se soit fait des institutions, des usages et des mœurs du peuple japonais." Humbert, *Le Japon*, 1, p. 11.

166   E.g. Mossman, Samuel, *Japan* (London, 1880), after p. 28; Taylor, Bayard, *Japan in our day* (New York, 1872), past p. 104. The book went through many later prints and editions, for example in 1882, 1883, 1892, 1893 and 1903; Villetard, Edmond, *Le Japon* (Paris, 1879), p. 35; Hübner, *Spaziergang* (1882), p. 195. – The name of the part of the city to which Hübner referred changed in his books due to the different transliteration of the sounds: *soto-siro*, *soto-jiro*, *soto-djiro*.

FIGURE 4.161   View of a canal in the trader's quarter of Edo

While the original template of the print block is unknown, there are photographs with later dates, which back up the information in the illustration. The Widener Library at Harvard University holds a view across a channel similar to that seen above, titled *River band at Tokio* (Fig. 4.162). Similar scenes appeared elsewhere in the following years, reproducing the urban impression as a print and a drawing, for example by Australian painter Mortimer Menpes (1855–1938) (Figs. 4.163, 4.164).

In general, Humbert's illustrations themselves used architecture to assist as background scenery for social life, as can be seen in some more examples from his book (Figs. 4.165–4.168). They helped to create a two-fold narrative of Japan and its architecture: firstly, there was the focus on a decidedly non-western Japan, not least since the changing, modernising Japan took a while to manifest substantially in architecture beyond the trading settlements. Secondly, and unsurprisingly in the context of the source genre, architectural Japan, in the sense of a depiction of built environments, was not portrayed in any analytical way, with the aim of understanding the interplay between volumes, codes, signs and materials. Architecture merely supported and strengthened the narrative of Japanese culture as entirely Japanese and distinct from western models.

VISITING AND VISUALISING ARCHITECTURE 277

FIGURES 4.162–4.164   A photograph titled 'River band at Tokio', ca. 1880; a depiction of a canal in Tokio; and a scene in the harbour by Menpes

The fourth group of illustrations which provided readers of western publications with information on Japanese architecture were Japanese drawings and prints. While many were rendered more or less to inform western prints, such as those we saw above, just as many became objects of art collections, as we will see in the next sub-chapter. In addition to these two dominant phenomena in the use of images, there are two more we would like to address briefly: on the one hand, woodblock prints with architectural information which were

FIGURES 4.165–4.168 The shrine on Atango-yama; the American legation in Edo, a shrine area, and a tea house

largely reproduced as illustrations without editing, and on the other, illustrations in translations of Japanese texts for a western audience.

A small group of illustrations with architectural information appeared first in Laurence Oliphant's (1829–1888) *Narrative of the Earl of Elgin's Mission to China and Japan*, 1859, and then repeatedly until the end of the century.[167] It drew attention in this analysis due to the unusual perspective and – beyond the picturesque general composition – unclear image content: some tiled roofs and among them a long, towering ladder with a bell at the top; the finial, *sōrin*, of a pagoda; a rooftop platform with possibly a piece of astronomical equipment and other elements (Figs. 4.169–4.171). The formal similarity among the illustrations suggests a common source, and the common denominator appearing in all of them, Mount Fuji, points to their origin in the context of Katsushika Hokusai's (1760–1849) *Thirty-six Views of Mount Fuji*. Indeed, a much less famous series by the same artist, the *Hundred views of Mount Fuji*, was the source of all these and some more views of Fuji as well, which were common in the books of the time.[168]

The rooftop scene with the astronomers was recreated or rather reinvented in 1861 for a German compilation of Japan-related information.[169] The initial roofscape was not only shifted from day to night but was extended in the middle ground by the addition of the upper part of a temple roof and a tower-like building resembling the chinoiserie model of a pagoda depicted in the context of the *Weltausstellung* in Vienna in 1873 (Fig. 4.172).

The second group of Japanese drawings and prints for a broader western audience came to the West in a belletrist context,[170] largely with either western novels set in Japan or translations of Japanese texts. This included illustrated books retelling Japanese fairy tales, myths or historical accounts, such as the story of the *47 Ronin* who avenged their master's disgrace and death. While Freeman-Mitford's *Tales of Old Japan* used this means of illustration for

---

167 Compare Oliphant, Laurence, *Narrative of the Earl of Elgin's Mission to China and Japan in the years 1857, '58, '59*, 2 vols. (London, 1859) and Griffis, William Elliot, *The Mikado's Empire*, 8th extended ed. (New York, 1895).
168 King, James, *Beyond "The Great Wave": The Japanese Landscape Print, 1727–1960* (Bern, 2010), pp. 22–29, 71–77; Katsushika Hokusai, *Fugaku Hyakkei* [Hundred views of Mount Fuji], 3 vols. (1834–1835).
169 Steger; Wagner, *Nippon-Fahrer*, 1861.
170 Western novels set in Japan and their illustrations are a topic all their own; to address them any further would far exceed the aims of this study.

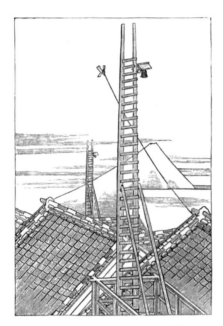 

FIGURES 4.169–4.170   A Fire-Ladder; Finial of a Japanese Temple in Oliphant's book

FIGURES 4.171–4.172   Japanese Astronomers and Japanische Astronomen as depicted in Oliphant's book and reinvented by Steger

years in the many editions of his book,[171] the 1880s saw a group of publications, which tripled the number of interiors (Figs. 4.173–4.176, see colour section).

The prints shared the characteristics of spatial description known from Japanese visual media but showed among them many stylistic differences. Despite some exterior scenes, the majority depicted the interiors of dwellings with typical elements of furniture and decoration such as portable fireplaces. Often, the rooms were marked as studies or representative spaces for receiving and entertaining guests by the inclusion of a *tokonoma* recess and/or *chigaidana* shelving. In terms of architectural information, these illustrations provided few constructive ideas or indications of large-scale spatial arrangements, but did offer a multitude of insights into interior arrangements and decoration. They added significantly to the small body of interior views already available based on Japanese templates and Morse's sketches.

By end of the nineteenth century, the available visual information in western publications therefore added up to a broad range of forms of representations and topics. Architectural information was provided through drawings, photographs and prints, of both Japanese and western origin, in various forms of adaptations and editions. Apart from some materials primarily intended to provide information about Japanese architecture itself, most of the visual material was available in the context of describing Japan and its culture in a broader sense.

Thus, the knowledge collection and knowledge transfer regarding architecture was not so much a rational set of academic documentation as a narrative in an aesthetic sense. Many stories of experiencing a foreign culture were told through architectural artefacts and sights such as houses, temples or street scenes, coincidentally conveying characteristics of a built environment perceived as typically Japanese.

In general, the architecture-related topics were manifold as we saw above, ranging from constructional or ornamental details to cityscapes. There was, however, a certain narrowness of interest which became more significant over time. While the visualizations of building types such as shrines, temples, tea houses or dwellings remained vague and often repeated what was known from earlier publications, perhaps adopting a slightly different angle or showing another building of the same type, some places and buildings were depicted over and over again. As we saw earlier, this was in part due to the limited travel opportunities available to foreigners in Japan during this period and the routes

---

171   Freeman-Mitford, Algernon Bertram, *Tales of Old Japan* (London, 1871) and (among others) 1876, 1883, 1888, 1894, 1910.

chosen for recreational tourism in particular. In addition, it showed pragmatism in the use of available templates and print blocks. Yet, there is evidence for a subsequent 'canonisation' of visual topics as well, most notably in regard to sights: reports, such as those about Nikkō, drew more visitors who in turn wrote more reports and so on.

In the scheme of 'architectural' illustrations for which location information existed or is assignable retrospectively – comprising less than half of the illustrations in this overall analysis – around a dozen places came to dominate the available information and thus the 'image' of Japan.

Initially, during the years of treaty negotiations and the establishment of the first foreign settlements, the places depicted varied greatly and reflected the limited time and mobility ashore: coastlines and harbours, harbour cities and bay-side temples. Over time, the places and topics changed and while some sites became irrelevant, others became tourist destinations.

The harbour cities of Shimoda and Hakodate, which had provided the first urban impressions, were no longer depicted while the long-serving commercial harbour of Nagasaki remained moderately relevant. The hot springs and landscape of Hakone gained constant attention over the years but these rural views were clearly overshadowed by the picturesque qualities of Kamakura.

About 20 kilometres southwest of the foreign settlement of Yokohama, Kamakura was within easy reach for many of the western residents and visitors, who were drawn by the *daibutsu*, the bronze statue of Amida Buddha of Kōtoku-in (Figs. 4.177–4.181).

Having lost its protecting hall to a tsunami in the fifteenth century, the huge statue came to sit in the open, accompanied only by the much lower buildings housing the temple offices.[172] Its significant form soon became one of the visual abbreviations for Japan. While the city had a long tradition of Zen Buddhism, its Buddhist temples were rarely depicted; rather, the Tsurugaoka Hachiman-gū, a Shintō shrine in the centre of Kamakura appeared regularly in publications. Both the painter Wilhelm Heine and the photographer Felice Beato documented the buildings. The latter's pictures of a Buddhist pagoda on the shrine grounds and the ensuing prints in some publications became a historical document of architectural history within just a few years: the pagoda was demolished during the 1870s in the course of Meiji era's policy of

---

172   Scheid, Bernhard, "Der Große Buddha von Kamakura," in: *Religion in Japan. Ein Web-Handbuch*, https://www.univie.ac.at/rel_jap/an/Religion-in-Japan, here https://religion-in-japan.univie.ac.at/an/Essays/Daibutsu_Statuen#Der_Gro.C3.9Fe_Buddha_von_Kamakura [last accessed 27 April 2024].

FIGURES 4.177–4.178   The Daibutsu in Kamakura in the books of Jephson and Humbert

separating Shintoist and Buddhist institutions, *shinbutsu bunri* (Figs. 4.182 and 4.183, see also 4.184 and 4.185).[173]

However, these places played but a minor role within the overall body of illustrations and were clearly eclipsed by Nikkō as the most dominant architecture-related sight, along with the cities of Ōsaka, Yokohama, Kyōto and Edo/Tōkyō.

---

173 Scheid, Bernhard, "Shinbutsu bunri. Trennung von kami und Buddhas," in: *Religion in Japan. Ein Web-Handbuch*, https://www.univie.ac.at/rel_jap/an/Religion-in-Japan, here https://religion-in-japan.univie.ac.at/an/Geschichte/Staatsshinto/Shinbutsu_bunri [last accessed 27 April 2024]; "Kamakura, temple Tsurugaoka Hachiman-gū, Pagode tahōtō en cours de destruction" (Musée national des arts asiatiques – Guimet, Paris, département Photographie, Japon, albums de photographies, https://www.guimet-photo-japon.fr/index.php, here: http://www.guimet-photo-japon.fr/notices/notice.php?id=245 [accessed 10 July 2019]). The Musée Guimet attributes the photograph to Raimund Stillfried (1839–1911). The collection of the New York Public Library attributes it to Felice Beato (1832–1909) (New York Public Library, The Miriam and Ira D. Wallach Division of Art, Prints and Photographs: Photography Collection, https://digitalcollections.nypl.org/divisions/the-miriam-and-ira-d-wallach-division-of-art-prints-and-photographs-photography, here https://digitalcollections.nypl.org/items/510d47d9-c581-a3d9-e040-e00a18064a99 [accessed 10 July 2019]).

FIGURES 4.179–4.181 The Daibutsu in Kamakura in the books of Gardiner, Dixon and Mortimer

We have already spoken about Nikkō in the context of Japaneseness and recreational travel. Thus, it should suffice to add that half of the approximately 160 images assignable to this place were dedicated to the Tōshō-gū alone, the burial grounds of the first shōgun of the Tokugawa dynasty. Here, the focus was on the overall disposition of the buildings and the ornamental character of the gates and architectural details.

While the views of the more touristic places soon entered the canon, the visual material of the four cities which gained the most attention within the

VISITING AND VISUALISING ARCHITECTURE

FIGURES 4.182–4.183
Felice Beato: two photographs of the pagoda of Tsurugaoka Hachiman-gū, 1867–1868, and with the finial already missing, 1870s

FIGURES 4.184–4.185   The pagoda of Tsurugaoka Hachiman-gū in publications of Jephson and Humbert, with a difference in proportion in the case of Humbert's engraving (below)

observed time period was much more heterogeneous. Ōsaka was depicted showing the castle and street scenes, and Yokohama through its harbour and the streetscapes of the western and Japanese parts of the settlement, which only grew to significance during these decades. There were also plans, maps and bird's-eye views from the cliffs of *The Bluff*, sketching the city's overall urban development.

Kyōto was present in a significant number of illustrations depicting Japan's past: temples, such as Kiyomizu-dera, Kinkaku-ji and Nishi Hongan-ji, the urban grid and the buildings and gardens of the Imperial residence. The number and variety – only surpassed by Edo/Tōkyō – conceals the fact that there was little interest in Kyōto as far as the books are concerned. While local travel guides such as Yamamoto's *Guide to the celebrated places in Kiyoto and the surrounding places* catered to foreign visitors as early as 1873 and provided a significant number of the overall available images here, these efforts seem to have had only minimal impact at the time.[174] The large majority of the images of Kyōto's sights that were to become 'classics' of the western perception of Japan were only published from the late 1880s onwards.

When it comes to the overall picture of 'architectural' Japan, Edo/Tōkyō was the dominant and most manifold source of visual information in western publications. Bridges, the harbour and street scenes including the Yoshiwara entertainment district were depicted alongside the western legations and some sights. These included the castle, Mount Atago and its shrine, the Kameido Tenjin Shrine with its moon bridge and wisteria trellis, Asakusa Sensō-ji, Ueno Park and Shiba Park with the Zōjō-ji, the latter two entailing the sites of graves of the replaced Tokugawa dynasty.

Overall, the approximately 3,900 'architectural' images of Japan provided in the publications for a western audience up to the turn of the twentieth century communicated impressions of Japan's built environment that included the vernacular as well as the highly artistic, the contemporary as well as the old or even ancient. Architecture was rarely depicted as a matter of professional relevance for design and construction but as an integrated expression of Japanese culture with manifold expressions: holistic, not encyclopaedic. It is safe to assume that this phenomenon of information transfer and the ensuing knowledge production had a strong influence on the perception of Japanese architecture at the time and in the decades to come.

---

174   Yamamoto, *Guide*.

However, images in publications for a broader audience were not the only source of visual information that was available; they were merely the most easily accessible. We will look at two more groups of visual material which was less widely disseminated for various reasons. Before that, however, we should include an excursus on some side effects of knowledge transfer: the transfer errors.

EXCURSUS: TRANSFER ERRORS AND UNINTENDED KNOWLEDGE PRODUCTION

The production and reproduction of textual and visual information always entails the risk of errors, no matter where and when it occurs. However, the transfer of information between different languages and cultures demands a level of (re-)interpretation of meaning that may lead to creative insights and inspiration, but also to disorientation and to the unintended creation of misinformation. We already saw some indication of this above, with the image of a Japanese farmyard, which was reproduced with manipulated image content as well as with differing captions, thus shifting the image's initial meaning. This excursus introduces more such phenomena, starting with an altogether non-architectural example.

Aimé Humbert' book *Le Japon illustré* included among its many other illustrations a sketch of a small, furry animal from the class of the mustelids. It sits halfway up a slightly tilted bamboo stem. The stylistic features and the accompanying characters on the right side point to an East Asian origin for the motif, and the table of illustrations confirms it as a facsimile of a Japanese engraving (Fig. 4.186).

The illustration was re-used several times over the following years, once as an identical copy and twice in a more creative way. The English edition of Humbert's book flipped the image vertically, thus making the caption unreadable and turning the bamboo's leaves into grass. A second American publication seems to have taken this version, cropped the caption and straightened the bamboo stem without editing the 'grass' around its root (Figs. 4.187 and 4.188).

These interferences with an initial motif were a very basic feature of the creative use of visual media, as a second example shows. In his report on the American North Pacific Exploring and Surveying Expedition, 1858, Wilhelm Heine included a plate of a woman with her daughter in front of

FIGURES 4.186–4.188   Original calligraphy of a mustelid and reversed and edited copies by Humbert and Greey

an entrance with a carved lintel. The illustration clearly aimed to outline features of traditional Japanese costume; the attending architecture was but staffage. Yet, this scene makes it possible to trace the 'migration' of visual elements (Fig. 4.189).

In the same year, the two women re-appeared in mirror image, with the same attention to clothing yet still including the architectural details. In a publication of 1861, the girl was part of an interior scene with a different woman sitting on a platform next to a low table, and in yet another scene published in 1875, mother and daughter turn towards each other in front of faded, wallpaper-like architectural features (Fig. 4.190).[175]

While these variations are extremely easily discernible here, it is necessary to assume that similar processes also happened elsewhere in the production of illustrations of Japan, and that they may have had an impact on the architectural information. We saw some evidence for this in the Japanese buildings at the international exhibition in Philadelphia in 1876, where the architecturally trained and experienced draughtsmen struggled to depict the unfamiliar structures and the resulting

---

175   Religious Tract Society, *Japan*, p. 203. It is reasonable to assume that this illustration was created mostly from the imagination, drawing on texts for information about Japanese interiors for which the visual sources were still scarce. It was reproduced in Spieß, *Preußische*, p. 145; Steger; Wagner, *Die Nippon-Fahrer* (1861), p. 183.

FIGURES 4.189–4.190 Mother and daughter from Shimoda by Heine and the ensuing re-configuration by Oliphant

drawings diverged in terms of their proportions from the documentary photographs.

Some of the 'architectural' illustrations of Japan were arguably derived from the imagination, such as the supposed view of Mount Fuji appearing on the front page of a publication as early as 1861 (Fig. 4.191). It showed a colonnade or pergola comprised of stone pillars about six meters high, which opened onto a view of the landscape and a mountain in the distance. The setting had a strong Mediterranean touch, conflicting with both the caption and the intention of the book.

A much less obvious 'westernism' was concealed in the depiction of an archer from the Tokugawa forces kneeling next to a wall made up of rectangular blocks of stone (Fig. 4.192). While the archer's armour meets expectations, the wall was not one to be found easily in Tokugawa Japan. Although masonry was used occasionally, e.g. for stone lanterns and wells, and although fortifications rested on mounds reinforced by stone, the walkways along the battlements were plastered wooden constructions (Fig. 4.193). One can assume that the photograph that informed the engraving only included the soldier, and that the wall was added as an enhancement to the imagined situation.

FIGURE 4.191   View of Mount Fuji

In other cases, the 'westernisms' seemed to have emerged during the process of reproduction due to unfamiliarity with the circumstances on site. A very illustrative example is the depiction of a Japanese funeral in Shimoda. The original lithograph by Wilhelm Heine carefully characterised the houses that lined the street (Fig. 4.194, see colour section).[176] A reproduction in *Nippon-Fahrer* simplified the architectural features to bring them closer to western ideas (Fig. 4.195, see colour section).

A similar process happened with a funeral published in Laurence Oliphant's *Narrative*, 1859. While generally more imaginative than architecturally precise, it showed a very accurate depiction of part of a fireproof storehouse, *kura*, with its thickly plastered shutters for the small window.[177] The motif was reinterpreted in mirror image and was extended and architecturally 'westernised' in *Nippon-Fahrer*, the different editions of which made it a major source of such phenomena among the Japan-related publications (Figs. 4.196 and 4.197, see colour section).[178]

176   His own publication of the scene in 1875 simplified some architectural elements and changed the personage of the cortège. Heine, *Japan*.
177   Oliphant, *Narrative*.
178   See Steger; Wagner, *Nippon-Fahrer* (1861 and 1869), and Hintze, *Nippon-Fahrer* (1874).

FIGURES 4.192–4.193   E. Thérond: Japanese archer, and the stone surfaces of the walls of Kumamoto Castle, 2009

One more case in which the inattentive treatment of architecture in visual storytelling of Japan was evident, was the dramatic depiction of Alexander Graf von Hübner's attempt to enter the Imperial palace area in Kyōto. The scene, supposed to be created from sketches by Hübner himself, is dramaturgically reminiscent of European historical paintings of battle scenes with rearing horses and fleeing infantry or civilians, and with a multitude of bodies, motions and poses (Fig. 4.198). The depiction of the palace's wall and gate, however, reproduced a mixture of western assumptions and chinoiserie in stark contrast to the architectural features of walled residences in Japan. Hübner's gate complex had neither the spatial depth nor the elaborate design customary for such an elevated building component, while the walls lacked their rain-shedding tiling. The inaccuracies are even more striking when compared to two more sketches of Hübner's, which also lack precision but resemble actual buildings much more closely (Figs. 4.199 and 4.200).

Unlike its appearance today, the Imperial palace area might have been in less than perfect condition due to the political changes of the time when Hübner visited; yet the differences compared to a current photograph of a similar gate are too significant to be explained away by any

FIGURE 4.198
Baron Hübner in front of the Imperial palace in Kyōto

state of preservation (Fig. 4.201).[179] It is more plausible to assume that the gate's architecture was inspired by a chinoiserie source or drawn in a simplified way after textual descriptions, ignoring Hübner's other material for the sake of providing an appropriate setting for the scene.

It is more difficult to detect formal 'Sinoism' than 'westernism' among the illustrations due to China's role in Japan's architectural development over time.[180] Elements of earlier chinoiserie are more easily traceable in architectural contexts since their two-dimensional origin and inspiration did not usually translate convincingly into architecture, as corresponding buildings in western parks and gardens showed and still show. However, there are few landscape scenes with chinoiserie among the illustrations to hand, while some interiors showed 'Sinoism' in interpretation (Figs. 4.202 and 4.203).

The two examples shown here used "Chinese" costumes for the personnel and an eclectic ornamentation, but the most telling factor was the ignorance with respect to the 'zoning' of floors within a Japanese building and the practice of sitting on the floor: the supposed *tatami* flooring was depicted as furniture, not as a room's basic feature.

---

179   The photographic material created during the Jinshin Survey of 1872 underlines this. See *Visual Material without Dissemination in the West* later in this chapter.

180   In addition, the author's own European background and training – even after years of work on Japan – results in an ineluctable deficit of subtlety and depth compared to her competences on western traditions of architecture.

FIGURES 4.199–4.201
Hübner's sketches of the Sun gate and the Kitchen gate, and the Kenshun gate of the Kyōto Imperial palace in 2016

FIGURES 4.202–4.203   'Sinoisms': the tea-party; family worship by Steinmetz

Obvious 'westernisms' and 'Sinoisms' in architectural illustrations of Japan were a significant feature up to the 1860s due to the overall lack of visual material of a documentary character. This changed in the wake of Siebold's publications and the high number of original Japanese visual media such as the famous wood cuts, as well as the use of photography as we will see shortly. Yet, some of these illustrations remained in use until the end of the nineteenth century in later editions of earlier publications, such as the 1874 edition of *Nippon-Fahrer*, or the archer, who went on to illustrate the many editions of William E. Griffis' *Mikado's Empire* up to 1895.[181]

Beyond the transfer errors we have seen so far, there are two more phenomena to look at: images which raise doubt in terms of proportions, and various versions of conflicting or erroneous captions.

The issue of proportions in visual representations of architecture is a longstanding and familiar one in the field, and is not limited to cultural transfer. It depends on techniques of portrayal, for example, or is due to intentional representation. An early case regarding Japan was the audience hall illustrating Engelbert Kaempfer's *History of Japan*, 1727–1729 (Fig. 4.204).

---

181   Griffis, William Elliot, *The Mikado's Empire* (New York, 1876); in the 8th edition, p. 226.

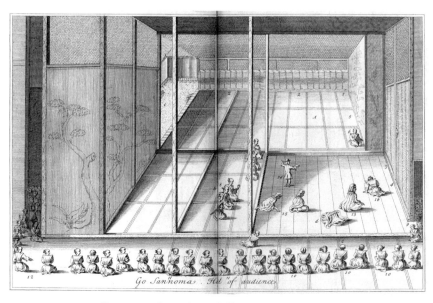

FIGURE 4.204   Engelbert Kaempfer: audience hall

Here, the situation was clear in terms of architecture: the construction shown was impossible and the spatial disposition unreasonable, but both served to describe a room of exceptional structural character and large size. There were and still are large and high rooms in Japanese temples, not to mention the Imperial palace or the shōgunal residence on the grounds of Nijō Castle in Kyōto, or even in vernacular dwellings.[182] Yet, a number of western interior depictions of the late nineteenth century showed residential interiors which did not adhere to Japanese custom in terms of their proportions.

Two contemporary photographs will serve to underline this and to provide pointers for estimating likely spatial dimensions – even more necessary given the lack of familiar furniture as an indication of scale. They show a contemporary living room in a traditional construction, opened up entirely for use during summer, and an interior view of the audience hall, ōhiroma, in Ninomaru-goten of the Nijō-jō in Kyōto, 1624–1626 (Figs. 4.205 and 4.206, see colour section). There is a significant difference in size between the rooms. The living room is of a regular size of about eight to ten mats (approx. 360 × 360/450 cm), while the raised area

---

182   See for example the communal fishermen's quarters for 60 men, House Aoyama, Historical Village of Hokkaidō (Kaitaku-no Mura) Sapporo in Figs. 4.38–4.40, see colour section.

of the audience hall alone is more than twice as large. Yet, both interiors have the same structural features which became systemised during the Tokugawa shōgunate (1603–1868): a skeleton of uprights at regular intervals braced with beams. The beam usually acts as a head jamb, *kamoi*, for the sliding doors, and the height of the ceiling is negotiated by the upper part of the wall in proportion to the size of the room.

Embedded into a systemic interplay of fixed measurements and rules of proportion, the head jamb was at a height of about 175–180 cm.[183] Regular dwellings of traditional build largely remained close to the suggestions of the design patterns which were seen as most balanced and appropriate. This resulted in a broad variety of adaptable spatial dispositions of human scale which nevertheless shared many characteristics. Larger residences used the same rules of design but abandoned the fixed patterns if necessary to make possible representative rooms. Starting from this shared adherence to human scale, some illustrations from the late nineteenth century raise doubts, as in the following examples.

The lady depicted at the imperial court is very small compared to the overall structure, even though a European observer, used to the magnificent halls of baroque palaces, may not have noticed this. Yet, this depiction of the rooms comes close to 'westernism' (Fig. 4.207). However, since some of the imperial buildings used different patterns of proportions for representative reasons at times, this illustration might have only slightly exaggerated the actual spatial proportions of its interior.

The same cannot be said about an interior view of the residence of the *daimyō* of Satsuma (Fig. 4.208). Compared to the structure of the walls, the people in the room are far too small. The room has the structural features of a dwelling but the dimensions of a temple hall. The latter, however, used different rules of design to achieve breadth and monumentality and omitted many basic considerations relevant for residential buildings.[184]

Another depiction of a dwelling shows a room that is much too large and high, and ignores the internal variations in flooring between compacted earth, wooden flooring and flooring made from rice straw, *tatami*

---

183 On the means of designing and building, often subsumed under the term *kiwari*, see introductory Engel, Heino, *The Japanese House: A tradition for contemporary architecture* (Ruthland, VT; Tōkyō, 1964).
184 The successive differentiation of imported Chinese building forms into separate solutions for religious (Buddhist) architecture on the one hand, and residential architecture on the other, is one of the core developments in Japanese architectural history.

FIGURE 4.207
A lady at the court in Kyōto by Humbert

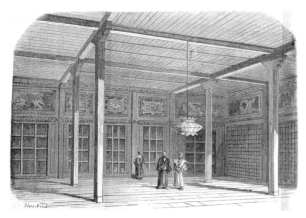

FIGURE 4.208
Main hall in the Satsuma residency, out of scale, depicted by Paris

(Fig. 4.209). Steps such as shown here would usually denote the sales area of a shop or the entrance of a (residential) building, both less spacious in area (see Fig. 4.210). The sliding doors to the rear, supposed to be less than 1.80 metres high, support this observation compared to the size of the actors in the scene.

In the case of the interior scene of a dining group, the height of the room as indicated by the sliding doors on both sides is similarly doubtful compared to the size of the diners (Fig. 4.211). The static structure of the wall at the rear – usually discernible in dwellings – has been omitted in favour of an ornamentation which resembles East Asian fabrics. In addition, the wall hanging is positioned centrally in contrast to the asymmetric Japanese composition of decorative recesses (see e.g. Figs. 4.173 and 4.174 in colour section).

VISITING AND VISUALISING ARCHITECTURE

FIGURES 4.209–4.210
Interior of Japanese dwelling as depicted in Converse's book, and the *genkan* of a historic business building

FIGURE 4.211   A Japanese dinner, out of size, depicted in Glass' book

The proportions of rooms remained a pictorial challenge in many western illustrations for many years after the first decades in which only limited information was available. They often remained interlinked with 'westernisms' or 'Sinoisms'. They point to the contemporary challenges of depicting spatial arrangements which differed from western patterns of human scale and representation.

Similar problems were caused by Japanese gardens. They were mentioned regularly as an integral part of the dwellings, but were portrayed much less often before Josiah Conder published his richly illustrated *Landscape gardening in Japan* in 1893.[185]

Even before the many photographs in Conder's book, most of the illustrations of gardens provided helpful information, with a small number of exceptions. Andrew Steinmetz' Japanese garden with its lake, trees and shrubbery, for example, was by no means Japanese except for the slight curve of the tempietto's roof and the exotic staffage personnel in the foreground (Fig. 4.212). A small group of other illustrations was similarly close to western parks in terms of plants and the arrangement of water, but not with respect to ornamental architectural details. A few geometrical elements were arranged around the shore of a pond near which two men pause in conversation. Some of these resemble abstract pavilions, some low tambours. The arrangements changed between the subsequent

---

185   Conder, Josiah; Ogawa, Kazumasa, *Landscape gardening in Japan. Supplement* (Tōkyō, 1893).

FIGURES 4.212–4.213
Japanese garden by Steimetz and Tronson

reproductions up to the mid-1870s, but the relative proportions of the landscape elements, architectural details and human figures remained unrealistic, especially given the supposed motif, the Japanese tea garden (Figs. 4.213–4.215).

Some years later, another engraving of a *Japanese temple garden* came much closer to the actual arrangement and proportions of elements (Fig. 4.216, see colour section). It allows us to guess at the reasons for

FIGURES 4.214–4.215   Japanese tea gardens by Ainsworth and Bæckström

some of the proportional incongruities seen before, which were similar to some of the illustrations of the Japanese garden at the *Weltausstellung* in Vienna in 1873 discussed above. There, the tremendous size of some of the stone lanterns seemed to pose a challenge to the artists when it came to appropriately reproducing distances and sizes. Here again, the lanterns were depicted as being as high as a man or even higher, becoming landmarks within the artificial landscape. Yet, despite the convincing overall composition, there remains some doubt as to the proportions.

Were the Japanese gardens used for boating, or is this a 'westernism'? Would the pond depicted even have been large or deep enough for such activity? There are two contemporary photographs of the *Hotta Garden* in Tōkyō, which may have informed the illustration. They confirm the proportions of lanterns, personnel, bridge and lake, but neither the caption's attribution to a temple complex nor the practice of boating on the pond (Figs. 4.217 and 4.218, see colour section).

There were, however, plenty of illustrations of boats of different sizes and functions in books on Japan, including leisure boats such as those included in the illustration. Since these illustrations were not part of the selection that informs this analysis, the visual example for the boats in question was taken from a woodblock print from the late Tokugawa period, depicting fireworks in Edo's harbour area (Fig. 4.219, see colour section).

This brief list of visual transfer errors and inconsistencies aims to point towards the unintentional creation of imperfect knowledge with respect to architectural Japan. It occurred less in the visual material illustrating architectural expertise but was largely a phenomenon found in ethnographical publications. Here, facets of Japanese culture were condensed, reassembled and occasionally even invented to compensate for the lack of appropriate visual material. Yet, these processes have to be taken into consideration for the overall understanding of information transfers due to the ongoing interlinking and cross-referencing between these two genres of publications: the aim of the ethnographic publications was to describe a unique, essentially Japanese 'image' of Japan which reflected on the discourses on art and architecture.

Beyond the largely creative transfer errors discussed above, there are two more groups that merit attention: conflicting or erroneous captions and incorrect image content.

As we already saw with the 'migrating' images, both the shift in ascription and the reinterpretation of image content occurred repeatedly. The cases here are more specific inasmuch as the precise information given with the illustrations conflicted with other examples of the same motif. There was, for example, Heine's depiction of a funeral in Shimoda that we looked at already with respect to 'westernisms' (see Fig. 4.194 in colour section). The scene was reprinted without change in 1859 but was entitled *A Japanese Funeral Procession, Nagasaki*.[186]

Something similar happened with a depiction of Nagoya castle, the building whose huge gilded acroterion was exhibited at Vienna in 1873. The illustrations published during the 1880s, of which there were at least four, were most probably based on the same photographic image, but their captions differed.[187] While two were identified by the city, Nagoya, and one by the province, Owari, the image from Samuel Mossman's book *Japan*, 1880, called it *Ehmidge castle, Kioto* (Figs. 4.220–4.223). Further complicating matters in this latter case is the fact that the book mentions the two different castles from Ōsaka and Yodo on the page where the illustration appears, while the shōgunal castle of Kyōto is not mentioned until two pages later.[188] Neither of the castles from Ōsaka or Yodo is depicted at all.

Among the examples of incorrect image content are three interesting cases, all supposedly depicting Japanese dwellings. James McCabe used the Japanese pavilion from the Centennial Exhibition in Philadelphia 1876 to represent this type of building (Fig. 4.224, compare to Figs. 4.33, 4.35). This was not altogether wrong, since the building was in fact used as a

---

186 Cornwallis, Kinahan, *Two Journeys to Japan, 1856–7*, 2 vols. (London, 1859), 2, p. 254.
187 The Nagasaki University Library holds a large collection of such photographs, albeit none that are identical to these ones. Nagasaki University Library, Metadata Database.
188 Mossman, *Japan*, pp. 21, 23.

FIGURES 4.220–4.223   Tower of Nagoya castle as found in the books of Reed, Mossman, Greey and Maclay

dwelling during the exhibition. However, the building itself was unique and by no means representative of Japanese vernacular architecture. This was also true of the image chosen for Annie Butler's *Stories about Japan*, 1888, namely the Golden Pavilion of the Rokuon-ji in Kyōto, better known as Kinkaku-ji (Fig. 4.225, see also Fig. 4.116 in colour section). The building was part of a residential complex before it was bequeathed to be used as Buddhist temple. Thus, the caption *A Japanese mansion* was simultaneously accurate and misleading.

There are no mitigating circumstances with the third case. The buildings identified as *Japanese dwellings* in Wilson's *Letters from the orient*, 1890, are actually a pagoda and other Buddhist edifices belonging to the area of Tsurugaoka Hachiman-gū in Kamakura, as already seen above (Fig. 4.226, see also Fig. 4.185).

Due to the significance of the affected buildings and the large number of indexed images, it was possible to compare and to detect these

FIGURES 4.224–4.225   A Japanese dwelling house as depicted by McCabe, and the Japanese mansion in Butler's book

FIGURE 4.226   Japanese dwellings in Wilson's book

inconsistencies. However, in terms the main question of this chapter, how Japan's architecture was depicted in western publications, these transfer errors did not change the overall story. This is principally due to the fact that they remained largely limited to the general accounts of Japan and did not directly impact the more architectural sources. Arguably, the (partial) absence of other visual material had greater consequences for knowledge production.

2.2   *Visual Material with Limited Dissemination in the West*
The visual material depicting Japan available during the latter half of the nineteenth century was by no means limited to the illustrations published in books

and essays. However, in contrast to the latter, a significant part and perhaps even the majority of Japanese visual material that found its way into the West reached a limited audience. Many pieces were kept in private collections: they were seen and discussed by the collectors themselves as well as by others interested in trade or discourse, but were not available to the public. We know about some of these collections from biographical accounts, through documents of the art trade, or through references made in many of the books on Japan, and, of course, from the in-depth work of generations of scholars on *Japonisme* and related fields of cultural studies.[189]

In addition, there are sample cases that allow us to gain an overview of the kinds of visual materials assembled, regardless of the specific character of each collection, not least since some of these collections became (part of) public institutions over time, such as the Museum of Fine Arts in Boston and the Musée Guimet in Paris.[190]

There were different genres involved in these chancy transfers of visual information, but as far as architecture is concerned, we will focus on just two of them, woodblock prints and souvenir photographs. This choice is primarily based on their significant numbers and known impact; secondly, they represented two distinctly different media and two different perspectives on architecture in Japan. A third factor is the ongoing digitisation of both, which today allows for a broader overview beyond the pieces previously selected for publication elsewhere.

---

189   The collection and display of artefacts from western and non-western cultures has received increased scholarly attention in recent years, not only in the context of discourses on provenance and postcolonial studies, but also in connection with efforts to establish a global history of art and architecture. A prime example for the complexity of such efforts was the conference *Changing Global Hierarchies of Value? Museums, Artifacts, Frames, and Flows* in Copenhagen in August 2018. It included keynote papers and case studies drawn from every continent, and underlined the common challenge involved in communicating art from different parts of the world on equal terms.

190   See e.g. the concise summary of such collections at the New York Metropolitan Museum of Art, in Meech-Pekarik, Julia, "Early Collectors of Japanese Prints and the Metropolitan Museum of Art," *Metropolitan Museum Journal* 17 (1982), pp. 93–118. – For an introduction, see Museum of Fine Arts, Boston, https://www.mfa.org/news/japan [accessed 15 May 2019], resp. Musée national des arts asiatiques – Guimet, Paris, http://www.guimet.fr/musee-guimet/histoire-du-musee-guimet-2/ [accessed 15 May 2019]. For the broader context, see Weston, Victoria, *East Meets West. Isabella Stewart Gardner and Okakura Kakuzō* (Boston, 1993); Omoto, Keiko, *Quand le Japon s'ouvrit au monde: Émile Guimet et les arts d'Asie* (Paris, 2001).

2.2.1　Japanese Woodblock Prints

The Japanese woodblock print was a flourishing genre of the urban culture of the Edo period (1603–1867), a popular means to comment on everyday occurrences. While the importance of the genre declined over time, the technique of the woodblock print remained in use during the decades of modernisation. It expanded on topics and developed new modes of presentation deep into the twentieth century in parallel with reinvigorated western developments in woodblock prints and the technique remains deeply embedded in discourses on Japan's artistic identity.[191]

Woodblock printing's impact on and embeddedness in European art history has led to an immense number of publications, both academic and popular in scope. In line with the pictorial themes most popular among collectors and the artistic issues prevalent during the heyday of *Japonisme*, the primary focus in collections, exhibitions and publications was and still is the depictions of Japanese life in the prints themselves, or issues of the aesthetics and/or craftsmanship related to their production.[192]

This entire development largely ignored the role of architectural motifs; attention to them and secondary literature on them is lacking in western languages. To be precise: the depiction of architectural structures was not a primary aim of the visual stories, and is absent most notably from works of the best-known sub-genre of *ukiyo-e*, the transient world of pleasure quarters and theatre streets. Yet, there were many woodblock prints with scenes set in interiors or the urban environment, reproducing temples, shrines, dwellings, businesses and inns and, interestingly enough, bridges.

Preserved print collections of western aficionados such as Claude Monet (1840–1926) and Vincent van Gogh (1853–1890) and knowledge of collectors such as Frank Lloyd Wright show which topics were collected. The resultant overview confirms the above observations: architecture was conceptually secondary in character in the fundamental orientation of the visual narratives, and frequently occurred as a background or a stage set.[193] Yet, it is not the sup-

---

191　See e.g. Satō, *Meiji State*.
192　The exhibition "Yokohama 1868–1912. Als die Bilder leuchten lernten" ["Yokohama 1868–1912. When Pictures Learned to Shine"] at the *Museum für Angewandte Kunst* in Frankfurt am Main, 08.10.2016–28.05.2017, was a prime example: While architectural topics were present throughout the well-curated exhibition, the catalogue did not discuss them.
193　On the 231 prints collected by Monet, see Aitken, Geneviève; Delafond Marianne, *La Collection D'estampes Japonaises de Claude Monet à Giverny* (Lausanne, 2003); on Wright's collecting and trading activities, see Meech, Julia, *Frank Lloyd Wright and the Art of Japan: The Architect's Other Passion* (New York, 2001).

porting role of the architecture alone, which has led to the lack of research so far, but also, and above all, the scholarly perspective taken on these prints. This can be seen, for example, in the online repository of more than 600 prints from Van Gogh's collection maintained by the Van Gogh Museum in Amsterdam. The prints are indexed using various criteria, such as artist, type or genre.[194] Among the latter are *female beauty* (*bijinga*), *actor print* (*yakusha-e*) or *landscape* (*fūkeiga*);[195] tags delve into nuances like seasons, fauna, flora, and weather phenomena, and they also highlight spatial elements such as Mount Fuji, or the historical Tōkaidō route. Interestingly, while *interior* is a noted term, exterior views of dwellings or temples are conspicuously absent from the Japanese print tags. Although tags like *street scene*, for example, do exist, they seem to be overlooked, regardless of their apparent and sometimes prominent presence in the prints (Figs. 4.227 and 4.228, see colour section). The examples chosen for purposes of illustration here – admittedly among the most architectural of the collection – were tagged with the subject categories *landscape* (*fūkeiga*), *Tōkaidō*, and *night*.

This observation is relevant in terms of knowledge systems in general and the study of architectural information on Japan based on the rich source of woodblock prints in particular: the prints found their way into western art canons as pictorial art, embedded into a reference system defined by artist, period and genre. Beyond these, the actual image content is of marginal relevance and as a result is neglected. Even the digitised material thus merely reproduces the established patterns of referencing and indexing. It remains to be seen whether changes in image recognition and digital archiving will be able to overcome this pattern and move towards the cross-referencing of image content in a more neutral way.[196]

So far, the study of architectural information in these Japanese woodblock prints is limited primarily by the heterogeneous nature of the source; despite significant improvements in ease of use in the course of digitisation, the tracing of architectural content is still a manual process of sorting through collections, and is thus fundamentally dependent on the researcher's prior willingness to

---

194   Van Gogh Museum Amsterdam, "Van Gogh Collects: Japanese Prints," here https://www.vangoghmuseum.nl/en/collection?q= [accessed 2 August 2023].
195   The choices of genre terminology vary, for example, between those applied to the collection of the Van Gogh Museum Amsterdam, and the data sets used in the specialised dictionary JAANUS.
196   About some challenges with the meta text of digitized material see, for example, Löffler, Beate; Mager, Tino, "Minor politics, major consequences – Epistemic challenges of metadata and the contribution of image recognition," in: *Digital Culture & Society: The Politics of Metadata* 6.2 (2021): 221–238.

'read' the material against the grain of a specific canon of knowledge in art history.

However, despite all of these conceptual and methodological considerations, there is still the question of architectural information in Japanese woodblock prints: is there anything to be learned from studying the buildings depicted?

Apart from the very famous *Manga* of Katsushika Hokusai, which was mentioned already as an inspiration for William Goodwin's understanding of Japanese architecture and as a source of information for Philipp Franz von Siebold's illustrations, there were at least three groups of prints that included significant architectural information in such a way as to provide valuable insights. Firstly, there are the different image series of *Famous Views*, examples of which we have already seen above. The most famous of them were coloured, but some were black and white.[197] The genre was closely related to a group of travel guides, the *meisho zue*, or *illustrated guides to famous places*. They were also woodblock prints, but were published as books in black and white with varying weighting between texts and images.

The third group are *yokohama-e*, *Yokohama pictures*, a late sub-genre of *ukiyo-e* that emerged between about 1859 and the 1880s.[198] The name referred to the developing harbour and foreign settlement just south of Edo/Tōkyō, in which foreign lifestyles and buildings soon became a matter of interest, before the scenes shifted location to Tōkyō following the installation of the Meiji government in 1868.[199] As a result, the cultural and architectural information in these prints depicted not just Japan but the peculiarities of the western impact on Japan, including habits, costumes and the changing environment. Starting

---

197   See, for example, the comment earlier in this chapter on Katsushika Hokusai's (1760–1849) thirty-six and hundred views of Mount Fuji respectively.

198   *Yokohama-e*, in: JAANUS, here http://www.aisf.or.jp/~jaanus/deta/y/yokohamae.htm [accessed 15 May 2019].

199   Suzuki, Keiko, "Yokohama-e and kaika-e prints: Japanese Interpretations of Self and Other from 1860 Through the 1880s," in: Hardacre, Helen; Kern, Adam Lewis (eds.), *New Directions in the Study of Meiji Japan* (Leiden et al., 1996), pp. 676–687, here pp. 677, 682–683. – On this genre's historical emergence and its interconnectedness with other phenomena, see the more extensive treatment in Wakita, Mio, "Sites of 'Disconnectedness': The Port City of Yokohama, Souvenir Photography, and its Audience," in: *Transcultural Studies* 2 (2013), s.p., http://dx.doi.org/10.11588/ts.2013.2.11067 [accessed 3 June 2019]; Dower, John W., "Yokohama Boomtown. Foreigners in Treaty-Port Japan (1859–1872)," online resource, 2008, https://visualizingcultures.mit.edu/yokohama/index.html [last accessed 28 April 2024]. See also Dower, John W., "Throwing Off Asia I. Woodblock Prints of Domestic 'Westernization' (1868–1912), 2008," on: *Visualizing culture*, here https://visualizingcultures.mit.edu/throwing_off_asia_01/toa_essay02.html [accessed 5 June 2019].

FIGURES 4.229–4.230   Utagawa Hiroshige III: View of Foreign Residences and the Catholic Church in Yokohama, 1870; Yokohama Catholic church, Prudent Girard, 1862

with the 'Black Ships' of Perry's fleet in 1853 and 1854, and proceeding via the western-style houses, churches and carriages in the exterritorial settlements, to the early buildings of modern Japan, these images captured changes in the built environment and infrastructure and mirrored the curiosity of the western observers and their souvenir photographs.

The buildings in these prints, such as the Catholic church in Yokohama, flanked by businesses, or Mitsui House, a bank building in Tōkyō, showed abbreviated structural features and were more of a stage setting for the busy scenes of people and activities around them. Despite this subordination, they depicted architectural information such as perforated façades with rustication, balconies, arched windows and folding shutters, thus capturing the transient and soon-lost architectural dispositions of a changing society (Figs. 4.229 and 4.230).

The three-aisled basilica constructed of plastered wood in Yokohama's foreign settlement was designed by Father Prudent Girard in 1862. Comparing the woodblock print and a contemporary western engraving demonstrates both the differences in the modes of depiction, such as the creation of depth effects, and the recording of the church's characteristic features, such as the porch and the ridge turret (Figs. 4.229 and 4.230).

Similarly, the Mitsui bank building in Tōkyō was depicted in its urban environment in both woodblock prints and photographs, thus making it possible to compare the available information. The building was designed and erected by Shimizu Kisuke II in around 1873 and demolished in 1890.[200]

The compact three-storied building seemed to have had a roughly square ground plan, although some prints hinted at additional building parts which may indicate a less symmetrical layout (Figs. 4.231–4.233, see colour section). The building's first impression is of very symmetrical façades with rectangular windows, and central entrances framed by porticos and topped by verandas. The uppermost floor was set back. Its tent roof was crowned by a pedestal-like ridge turret and a large bronze dolphin, similar to the creatures adorning Nagoya castle. However, closer attention and a detailed reconstruction of one side façade by Dallas Finn show that this level of symmetry – traditional for temples and shrines but very unusual in secular contexts – was probably only realised on the main façade.[201]

Comparison with contemporary photographs shows the building to be more cubic, as depicted in the print.[202] It also shows that some prints simplified the architectural detailing of both Japanese and western façades. Beyond that, however, all depictions underlined the formal contrast between Mitsui House and the surrounding urban neighbourhood, with larger businesses along the road, built with elements of thickly plastered fireproof *kura*, and small-scale houses at the back. The narrative rather than primarily documentary character

---

200 Finn, *Meiji*, p. 17; Tamai, Tetsuo; Ishiguro Keishō, *Yomigaeru Meiji no Tōkyō: Tōkyō jūgoku shashinshū* [Revival of Tōkyō in the Meiji Era. A photo collection of Tōkyō's 15 wards] (Tōkyō: Kadokawa Shoten, 1992), pp. 95–97. – The text dates it to 1874, but at least one print is dated 1873.
201 Finn, *Meiji Revisited*, p. 17.
202 For more examples see Tamai; Ishiguro, *Yomigaeru*, pp. 95–97.

of the prints can be seen in the way in which Mount Fuji was depicted in the prints, changing its position relative to the house (see Figs. 4.231 and 4.232 in the colour section, as well as Fig. 4.238).

The *yokohama-e* with architectural content seem comparatively rare in western art collections, probably due to their motifs, which did not aim to capture the 'traditional Japan' appreciated by most of the western audience. They do, however, represent a valuable resource for understanding the development of Japan's built environment during the decades of the Meiji era, a period from which the vast majority of buildings have been lost over time.

In the overall scheme of architectural information on Japan, the yokohama-e are probably of more interest to scholars today than they were of relevance to the western perception of Japanese architecture in the late nineteenth century, even though some of their contemporaries would have noticed the rapid changes taking place in the built environment and the speed at which this was happening. Utagawa Sadahide's many views of Yokohama's foreign settlement and Japanese quarters, to give just one more example, chronicled these changes for years, tracing the subsequent extension of streets and buildings inland from the shore line (Fig. 4.234, see colour section).[203]

Somewhat in contrast to the *yokohama-e* but actually overlapping in terms of motifs, the illustrations relating to *meisho zue*, the *illustrated guides to famous places*, were an omnipresent but probably still underrated source of visual information.

The *meisho zue* were a very popular genre of publication during the Tokugawa Era. They started their triumphal march with Akisato Ritō's (active 1780–1814) *Miyako meisho zue* in 1780, which addressed the sights of the Imperial capital of Kyōto.[204] While there had been and still were other volumes containing such travel information, and much more handy ones at that, the publication set a new standard of interplay between scholarly information and illustration. It can be assumed that many of the recreational journeys of western visitors during the late nineteenth century were inspired and/or informed by these books, since they listed the must-see places and sites, even if they lacked practical information.[205]

---

203   The numbers of the issued prints alone were astonishing: "[M]ore than five hundred separate designs by thirty-one artists were issued by fifty or more publishers from 1859 to 1862" alone. Yonemura, Ann, *Yokohama: Prints from Nineteenth-Century Japan* (Washington, DC, 1991), p. 31.
204   Akisato, Ritō, *Miyako meisho zue* [Kyōto 1780].
205   Goree, Robert, "Meisho Zue and the Mapping of Prosperity in Late Tokugawa Japan," in: *Cross-Currents. East-Asian History and Culture Review* 23 (June 2017), https://doi.org/10.1353/ach.2017.0023, pp. 73–107, esp. p. 77; see also id., *Fantasies of the Real: Meisho*

In consequence, a number of western writers made reference to these books, as we saw earlier: Satow listed *Ise Sangu Meisho Zue*, McClatchie the *Edo Meisho Zue*, and Burty various unspecified "géographies illustrées";[206] and Yamamoto's *Guide* was a clear 'translation' of such *meisho zue* to accommodate western visitors.

The *meisho zue* showed a preference for very three-dimensional, generally bird's-eye views of topography and the environment, with some 'zoom-in' scenes providing details from a similar perspective (Figs. 4.235–4.238). Here, the use of linear perspective with clear vanishing lines was common to communicate the spatial disposition.[207] At the same time, the depiction was also abstracted, at times seeming to reduce complexity for the sake of the overall comprehension of the situation and the staging of the social activities in question.[208] The close-ups had a higher level of architectural information but used 'abbreviations' of building types, constructions and detailing; these were arguably sufficient to activate the (Japanese) reader's existing cultural knowledge, but insufficient to satisfy a (westerner's) search for architectural information beyond the very general.

The third group of images addressed in this part of analysis, the series of woodblock prints of famous sights inspired by the *meisho zue*, addressed many of the same places and followed the same pattern in terms of architectural information. Yet, they showed more variation.

An example is provided by a collection of prints from the first volume of *Edo meisho zue* which depict the same scene as in Figures 4.231 to 4.233, see colour section, and Fig. 4.238: namely, the neighbourhood of Suruga-chō in Edo/Tōkyō, in which the shops of the Mitsui family flourished and Mitsui's bank house was eventually built (Figs. 4.239–4.244, see colour section).[209]

---

zue in Early Modern Japan (unpubl. dissertation, Yale University, 2010); Wieczorek; Sui, *Kirschblüte*.

206 Burty, "Notes," cols. 56–57.
207 On the use of perspective in Japanese architectural drawing, see Coaldrake, William H., "From Customary Practice to Conscious Design. The Emergence of the Architect in Tokugawa Japan 1608–1638," in: *Fabrications* 11.2 (2001), pp. 46–59, here esp. pp. 53–54.
208 For a playful approach to Edo/Tōkyō and its sights, see e.g. National Diet Library, "The Landmarks of Edo in Colour Woodblock Prints," https://www.ndl.go.jp/landmarks/e/ [accessed 21 May 2019].
209 A very, very similar scene shows a street in Yokohama. However, there were some flowering cherry trees and the street was lined not only with the shops of the Mitsui family, but with those of some competitors as well. The crest or trademark, *yagōmon*, of Mitsui is seen on the indigo curtains, *noren*, of the stores on the left side. Utagawa (Gountei) Sadahide (1807–1878/79), "The Newly Opened Port of Yokohama in Kanagawa Prefecture, 1860" (New York Metropolitan Museum of Art, Bequest of William S. Lieberman, 2005,

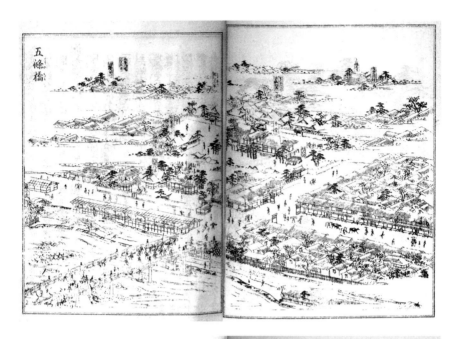

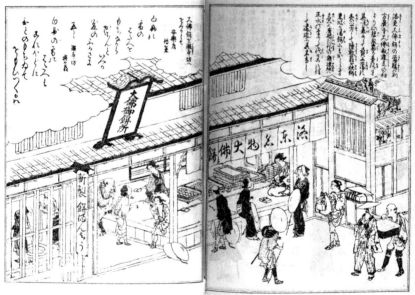

FIGURES 4.235–4.236   *Miyako meisho zue*: View of the area of Gojō-bashi in Kyōto; Shop selling sweets near Kyōto Daibutsu (Hōkō-ji)

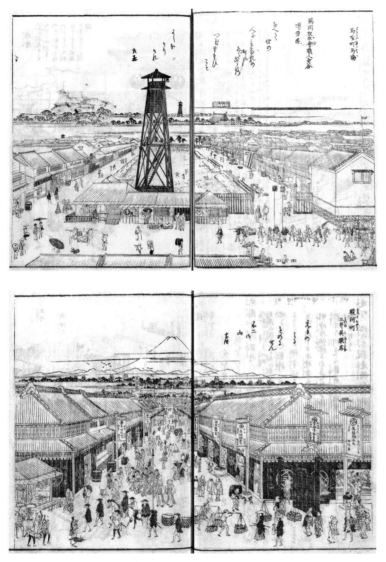

FIGURES 4.237–4.238 *Edo meisho zue*: Houses and fire-watch tower in Edo's Baba-chō; Street scene with businesses in Edo's Sugura-chō

Three of the six prints, shown here chronologically over a period of about five decades, were completed by Utagawa Hiroshige (1797–1858), and three were by other artists. While there are two bird's-eye perspectives among them, most of the views are at eye level or even zoom in on a particular scene. The means of perspective preferred heavily cropped settings but played around with different angles. Just as before, Mount Fuji played an important role in staging the views. The architecture was abstracted to mere lines and volumes in the wide-angle views and was provided with detailing in the close-up compositions (Figs. 4.240 respective 4.241, see colour section).[210]

Close-up views can be found in other prints of famous places as well, such as the pagoda of the Zōjō-ji and the gate of Sensō-ji: here architectural elements in the foreground received detailed attention (Figs. 4.245 and 4.246). The elements were depicted correctly as far as the exterior was concerned but served a picturesque purpose in the end, and were not intended to transfer information on architecture. They therefore certainly did not shed any light on any of structure of the building in question.

As a general rule, these guides and views conveyed architecture and the built environment in a largely correct but abstracted way that did not allow viewers to 'read' the structural characteristics. Yet, there may have been an exception to this: bridges. There were quite a few depictions of large bridges both among the *meisho zue* and the series of views of famous places (see Figs. 4.235, 4.245, and 4.247 in the colour section). While many seemed to address buildings in Edo/Tōkyō such as Nihon bashi, others showed bridges in Kyōto, some along the Tōkaidō road, and specific images from all over the country, such as those appearing in Katsushika Hokusai's *Shokoku meikyō kiran*, Remarkable Views of Bridges in Various Provinces, ca. 1830.

To be precise, bridges frequently served as a small element in the pictorial story. In some instances, however, the bridges took centre stage as massive structures of beams and trusses, landmarks in their environment; examples include the boat scene beyond Ryōgoku Bridge in Edo/Tōkyō, discussed earlier in this chapter, and the depiction of the station of Okazaki on Tōkaidō (Figs. 4.219 and 4.248, see colour section). In the latter print, the detailed depiction of the bridge contrasts with the extreme simplification of the structure

---

https://images.metmuseum.org/CRDImages/as/original/DP147960.jpg [accessed 28 May 2019]).

210 See also Yonemura, *Yokohama*, pp. 84–85.

FIGURES 4.245–4.246   Utagawa Hiroshige: The Pagoda of Zōjō-ji Temple and Akabane, 1857, and Kinryūzan Temple in Asakusa (One Hundred Famous Views of Edo), 1856

in the right middle ground, denoting a castle. The roof adornments, while entirely out of proportion, arguably referred to the nearby castle of Nagoya.[211]

Yet, the apparent precision of the bridge structures may have been misleading. A comparison between different depictions of the Yahagi Bridge near Okazaki – including one of Siebold's – during the earlier nineteenth century shows various constructions with different curvatures (Figs. 4.248–4.252, see colour section). Structural loss and replacement may have been involved, but caution in interpretation is required, nevertheless.

Again, these bridges were part of an overall story and not the story itself. Their shapes and sizes might have been exaggerated, their proportions adapted to fit aesthetic aims. Still, it would have been possible to gain an understanding of Japanese approaches to bridgework from woodblock prints as well as from the many bridges reproduced in publications on Japan; yet there was no

---

211   Note the adornments on the castle's ridge, the cousins of the famous fish shown at the Vienna World's Fair in 1873.

discussion on Japanese bridges and their construction in western in-field discourse at this time at all.[212]

The very many woodblock prints that made their way into western trade networks and collections provided an ambiguous source of architectural information in general, with each case depending on the specific prints assembled by the respective collector and their accessibility. On the one hand, the architectural information was largely subordinate to the narrative and aesthetic aims of the prints. On the other, they provided a great deal of fragmentary information on urban environments, building types, spatial arrangements and detailing. However, an existing background knowledge of Japanese architecture would have been required to gain additional information from the prints, a knowledge that very few western observers could have had at that time.

2.2.2 Souvenir Photographs

The situation with souvenir photographs was similarly problematic in the context of this study as far as the erratic pattern of dissemination was concerned. Photographs are much more difficult to work with since reliable metadata on photographer and date is very often absent. This absence of metadata has certainly hindered deeper research into their production, marketing and collection, but it has not reduced interest in them, their omnipresence in publications on Japan, or their subsequent digitisation.[213]

Photography came to Japan as a novel technology during the latter years of the Tokugawa Era via the Dutch outpost on Deshima (Nagasaki).[214] The

---

212   The illustrations in western publications showed a number of different bridges, among which a cable pull inspired by an image in Hokusai's *Manga* was probably the single most copied example. It appeared first in Aimé Humbert's *Japan. De Aarde en haar Volken* in 1867, and in at least eight more publications up to 1883. Hokusai, *Manga*, 13, s.p.

213   See e.g. Wieczorek, *Kirschblüte*; Kühn, Christine (ed.), *Zartrosa und Lichtblau. Japanische Fotografie der Meiji-Zeit (1868–1912)* (Berlin, 2015).

214   Himeno, Junichi, "Encounters with Foreign Photographers. The Introduction and Spread of Photography in Kyūshū," in: Rousmaniere, Nicole C.; Hirayama, Mikiko (eds.), *Reflecting Truth. Japanese Photography in the Nineteenth Century* (Amsterdam, 2004), pp. 18–29. – The history of early Japanese photography is comparatively well-studied as far as the main actors and issues of orientalism are concerned. See e.g. Delank, *Japan in der Kunst*; Bennett, Terry, *Early Japanese images* (Rutland, VT et al., 1996); Gartlan, Luke, "Photography in Nineteenth-Century Japan," in: *History of Photography* 33.2 (May 2009, theme issue); Gartlan, Luke, *A Career of Japan: Baron Raimund von Stillfried and Early Yokohama Photography* (Leiden, 2016); Harvard, "Early Photography." – For a broader look at photographic orientalism, see Pratt, Mary Louise, *Imperial Eyes: Travel Writing and Transculturation* (London, 1992); Gartlan, Luke; Behdad, Ali, *Photography's Orientalism: New Essays on Colonial Representation* (Los Angeles, 2013).

first photographs to find their way to the West some years later were taken by foreigners attached to the expeditions and embassies, but soon resident photographers set up shop in Nagasaki and Yokohama and provided a range of services including portrait photography. This was the situation in 1863, when Italian-British war photographer Felice Beato (1832–1908) arrived and established a business. Staying in Japan for two decades, his work became associated with many of the people and developments within and outside the settlements and shaped the photographic perception of Japan. Beato trained influential photographers and was one of those who provided the 'blueprints' for both the souvenir photographs of Japan and the souvenir albums created to present and protect them.[215]

This specific sub-genre of photography informed some illustrations in western publications, but beyond that it was largely kept in private collections, as the woodblock prints had been. Photographs were collected with a different purpose, however: they were travelling souvenirs and/or collections of individual visual memories of extended stays in Japan. They were also often selected from the collections of one or more professional photographers and assembled in customised albums in one of the foreign settlements in Japan, notably Yokohama or Nagasaki. While they may have started out with different materials, shapes and designs, the albums became standardised over time to encompass largely 50 pages between lacquer covers of two sizes, about 30 × 40 centimetres or 13 × 18 centimetres.[216] In the end, the albums became part of an 'industrialised' tourist circuit as expressions of individual experiences and narratives.[217]

The same was true of the photographs themselves. The body of available motifs developed in a competitive atmosphere among a dozen or so photographers, both western and Japanese, and covered issues of touristic interest:[218] there were beautiful women and famous sights, everyday landscapes, and trades and customs (Figs. 4.253–4.256, see colour section).

---

215   Hockley, Allen, "Felice Beato's Japan: Places. An album by the pioneer foreign photographer in Yokohama," online resource, 2008, https://visualizingcultures.mit.edu/beato_places/index.html [accessed 3 June 2019]; Wakita, "Disconnectedness"; Wilson, Alona C., "Felice Beato's Japan: People. An album by the pioneer foreign photographer in Yokohama," online resource, 2010, https://visualizingcultures.mit.edu/beato_people/index.html [accessed 3 June 2019].
216   Hockley, *Globetrotters', Places*, p. 41.
217   Ibid., p. 48.
218   For an extensive introductory treatment of the entire context, see Hockley, "Felice Beato's Japan."

In terms of the architectural information provided by these photographs, three different sources contributed to the analysis in this study: the collection of around 2,200 digitised souvenir photographs hosted by the Nagasaki University Library; a number of individual albums kept in Yokohama at the city's digital archive *Yokohama's Memory*, as well as those at Harvard University Library, the National Library of Australia, and the New York Public Library,[219] all of which show the specific character of each album; and about a dozen thematic albums edited by the Japanese photographer and publisher Ogawa Kazumasa (1860–1929) on his own, or in cooperation with other editors.[220] The materials differ in character but they make possible a larger-scale comparison of the topics and images of souvenir photographs of Japan during the latter half of the nineteenth century.

In general, there are genre scenes, on the one hand, and sights and landscapes on the other. The relative proportions of these two groups of images vary, the genre scene category representing one third to one half of the photographs in the Nagasaki University Library as well as in the individual albums, while Ogawa's albums were monothematic.

In terms of architecture, the two large groups were of very different relevance. The genre scenes largely showed close-ups of individual people or small groups, set within a building or in the immediate environment of a house, such as the garden or the street in front of the gate. As a result, the images tended to show architectural details such as walls and flooring, lighting and heating fixtures or furniture (Figs. 4.257–4.259).

However, the staging of interiors often involved adaptations and props which might, on occasion, have been misleading to observers, similar to the

---

219   Nagasaki, Bakumatsu; City of Yokohama, library, digital archive, https://www.city.yokohama.lg.jp.e.sj.hp.transer.com/kurashi/kyodo-manabi/library/shuroku/digitalarchive.html; Harvard University Library, here https://curiosity.lib.harvard.edu/early-photography-of-japan; National Library of Australia, catalogue.nla.gov.au, here e.g. https://catalogue.nla.gov.au/Record/5565388; New York Public Library, digital collections, Photographs of Japan, https://digitalcollections.nypl.org/collections/photographs-of-japan#/?tab=about [all accessed 21 August 2023]. – Among others, the collections contain works by Anthonius Franciscus Bauduin (1820–1885), Felice Beato (1832–1909), Enami Nobukuni (1859–1929), Adolfo Farsari (1841–1898), Kajima Seibei (1866–1924), Kusakabe Kimbei (1841–1934), Ogawa Kazumasa (1860–1929), Shimooka Renjo (1823–1914), Raimund von Stillfried (1839–1911), Suzuki Shinichi (1855–1912), Tamamura Kozaburo (1856–1923?), Tomishige Rihei (1837–1922), Uchida Kuichi (ca. 1844–1875), Ueno Hikoma (1838–1904) and Usui Shuzaburo.

220   Leaving aside his famous photographs and publications of Geishas and Flowers as irrelevant to the focus of this research, there were at least seven albums with content of at least indirect architectural interest between the early 1890s and 1912. Please see the bibliography.

FIGURES 4.257–4.259
Genre scenes with architectural information: Tamamura Kozaburo: woman in rickshaw, with two drivers, and woman carrying an infant on her back, probably 1880s; Ogawa Kazumasa: Japanese women playing go, ca. 1887

visual transfer errors discussed earlier. In one album, two sliding door elements, *shōji*, reappear again and again and the staged quality becomes even more obvious with the sudden end of the 'wall' in the upper margins of one of the photographs (Figs. 4.260–4.262, esp. 4.260).

The other group of souvenir photographs consists of sights, including landscapes, street scenes and general views of villages and cities, and buildings of specific interest such as temples, shrines, castles, palaces and bridges.[221]

---

221 On the shifts in places of interest across the decades, see e.g. Wakita, "Disconnectedness."

FIGURES 4.260–4.262
Recurring architectural details, here *shōji*, in genre scenes

FIGURES 4.263–4.264
Felice Beato: American legation,
Yedo, and Yokohama, ca. 1867

Here, interiors are in fact absent with a few exceptions and details of the *haiden/honden* complexes in Nikkō's Tōshō-gū and Taiyu-in.

As with the genre scenes, the earliest of these photographs were black-and-white only, but later they were nearly all colourised by the studios. Some of the views took the perspective of an ordinary passer-by, but a slightly elevated position was chosen for the majority that allowed the spatial depth of the depicted area to unfold in a manner similar to the way the *meisho zue* introduced urban neighbourhoods and temple complexes (Figs. 4.263–4.264, 4.265–4.268, see colour section, and Figs. 4.269–4.271).

FIGURE 4.269
Funeral procession on city street in Japan, ca. 1870–ca. 1890

FIGURES 4.270–4.271
Tamamura Kozaburo: Tonosawa Onsen, and women relaxing on veranda of teahouse, ca. 1870–ca. 1890

The places depicted in the photographs show a much broader variety of places in Japan than the woodblock prints, with their strong roots in the urban culture of Edo. The earlier observation that western image preferences paralleled the development of foreign settlements and the emergence of recreational travel applies here as well.[222] However, due to the unspecific dates of many of the images, it is difficult to trace the change in regional preferences in greater detail.

As with the illustrations in the western publications, a significant number of images lack information about the places or buildings depicted – most notably the vernacular scenes. Where the information is given or deducible, Edo/Tōkyō, Yokohama and the immediate environment once again make up a large part of the source material. Nikkō and Kamakura are common as well, to name only two of the sightseeing spots of architectural character discussed already. In contrast, there is a significant increase in the rate of appearance of Kyōto among the souvenir photographs towards the end of the century.

To summarise, souvenir photographs portrayed significant buildings, sightseeing spots and vernacular urban environments dominated by traditional Japanese structures. It is arguable that this was not entirely due to the prevalence of such buildings in Japan at this time, or to the lack of photographs of modern, western-style constructions. It was a choice made by those who selected the images for the albums. This is underlined both by source collections of Meiji era photographs containing many images of new buildings in Tōkyō, for example, and by the images on picture postcards that emerged just a few years later. Among the latter, modern structures played a role equal to that of traditional images, as far as preliminary research has been able to show.[223]

Western-style structures appeared in the albums only rarely, and when they did appear it was only in specific contexts, often centred around Tōkyō. At first, it was streets in foreign settlements such as Yokohama and hotels catering to foreigners that were the focus of attention (Figs. 4.272 and 4.273).

---

222   In addition, see Wakita, "Disconnectedness."
223   See e.g. Tamai; Ishiguro, *Yomigaeru*. – Picture postcards were used in Japan from the last years of the 1890s onwards. While they are collected and traded globally today, picture postcards are even more underrated than many other historical visual sources and are often just as insufficiently provided with meta-text. With respect to Japan, there are some platforms which contextualise individual pieces, such as the East Asia Image Collection of Lafayette College, https://dss.lafayette.edu/collections/east-asia-image-collection, https://www.oldtokyo.com/, or https://oldphotosjapan.com/ [all accessed 21 August 2023]; however, the genre is entirely underrated as a visual source in the context of museum or library collections due their vernacular character. – See also Satō, Kenji, "Postcards in Japan. A Historical Sociology of a Forgotten Culture," in: *International Journal of Japanese Sociology* 11 (2002), pp. 35–55.

FIGURES 4.272–4.273
Tamamura Kozaburo:
Honmachi-dori, Yokohama,
ca. 1870–ca. 1883 and Fujiya Hotel in
Hakone, ca. 1870–ca. 1890

This might also explain the appearance of the first Tōkyō Imperial Hotel, 1890, by Watanabe Yuzuru (1855–1930) in one of the albums (Fig. 4.274).[224] Further modern structures chosen as images were Ginza, the model case of western building practices in Tōkyō, and the entertainment district of Yoshiwara (Figs. 4.275 and 4.276).

What kinds of architectural information did these souvenir photographs contain? What could have been learned by looking at them, if photographs were

---

224 Meid, *Einführungsprozeß*, pp. 273–274.

FIGURE 4.274 Tōkyō Imperial Hotel, Watanabe Yuzuru, 1890, ca. 1892

the "principal source of information on Japanese architecture,"[225] as James Fergusson's handbook stated in 1910?

The images provided strong impressions of urban environments in terms of their scale and extent; they also offered views of infrastructure such as streets, bridges and means of transportation, and made it possible to guess at the uses of some of the structures. The genre scenes provided glimpses into interiors and showed building details such as gates and fences. Specific buildings singled out for their architectural or historical relevance, such as shrines and temple halls, bell towers, pagodas, or *torii*, were depicted with a focus on the picturesque. On occasion, staffage personnel was positioned to give a sense of scale and/or to enhance the Japaneseness of the situation.

Dwellings were not included among the buildings portrayed, apart from some rare exceptions. Even Ogawa Kazumasa's thematic album *A model Japanese villa* adhered to this pattern. The nineteen images with their very restrained colouring focused not on the house but the garden and a flower show. The building itself was shown once from the garden and once from the

---

225 Fergusson, *Eastern Architecture* (1910), 2, p. 487.

FIGURES 4.275–4.276
View of main street, Tōkyō
[Ginza], after 1873; Yoshiwara,
Tōkyō, ca. 1873–ca. 1890

driveway. In addition, three interior views depicted two different reception rooms.[226]

As a result, the information on Japanese architecture, which could have travelled to the West by way of souvenir photographs, was limited. The topics and non-topics of the images were very similar to those discussed in connection with textual descriptions and in the illustrations of Japan-related publications. The broad field of architecture and construction was omitted or was lost between the minute detail of artistic fancy at one extreme and the overall

---

226   Ogawa, *Japanese villa*.

disposition of building complexes and cities at the other. Against this background of information, it is easy to understand how the 'built Japonisms' that appeared in the West and the western experts' interpretations of Japanese architecture came to take on the character they did.

What remains to be discussed is the question of whether western observers could have found better visual materials with which to judge Japanese architecture: materials they did not know about, or which they failed to notice or to take seriously. We will see shortly that such visual sources existed, and will consider briefly whether these could have been of consequence for western processes of knowledge production about Japan.

2.3 *Visual Material Not Disseminated in the West*

The previous sub-chapter focused on two bodies of visual material that clearly informed western discourses on Japan, namely woodblock prints and photographs. We will now look at further material which remained largely unknown in the West during the late nineteenth century – material, the lack of which has affected Japan-related western research and knowledge up to the present day: documentary photography of architecture, exemplified by the photographs taken during the *Jinshin Survey* of 1872, and the Japanese building manuals known as *hinagatabon*.

2.3.1   Documentary Photography

As mentioned above, photography was immediately successful in Japan and became a means to accompany and comment on Japanese life and the changes occurring in the course of modernisation during the latter half of the nineteenth century. There were photographs that informed the illustrations created for newspapers in Japan and abroad, photographs that documented disasters, and photographs that aided in collecting data on national heritage.[227] Of these documentary materials, only a small proportion made its way to the West.[228]

The material created in the course of the *Jinshin Survey* of 1872 did not reach the West at all. The survey was among the first research efforts by the newly inaugurated Tōkyō National Museum and combined information gathering with heritage protection. It was, on the one hand, part of the process by which

---

[227] In addition to the literature mentioned above, see e.g. the material in Mainichi Shimbun (ed.), *Nihon no hyaku nen. Shashin de miru fuzoku bunkashi. 1860–1959* [A hundred years in Japan · History of customs and culture seen in pictures] (Tōkyō: Mainichi Shimbun, 1960) and the body of photographs by Kusakabe Kinbei on the Great Nobi Earthquake, 1891, and the damage caused by a typhoon that hit Kōbe; see Nagasaki, Bakumatsu.

[228] See e.g. Japanese Photographic Association, *A Century of Japanese Photography* (New York, 1980).

exhibits were selected for display at the Vienna international exhibition in 1873 and, on the other, an aspect of governmental attempts to prevent the sale of Japan's artistic heritage to foreign countries. At this time, the tremendous western interest in such items coincided with a Japanese disinterest in the 'remnants' of the former political and cultural system, resulting on occasion in the abandonment of buildings and objects being left to decay.[229] To counter this, the government issued a preservation edict and initiated a research project under the leadership of Machida Hisanari (1838–1879) to gather information on traditional artefacts. Over four months, a group of officials accompanied by the photographer Yokoyama Matsusaburo (1838–1884), three painters and a naturalist, travelled the Kansai area around Kyōto, Ōsaka, Nara and beyond. The depth of the visits, even those to sites of major importance, was limited due to time constraints imposed by ongoing decision-making in the capital. Nevertheless, the materials gathered in drawings and photographs were a treasure trove of information on Japanese art.[230]

While it focused on portable artefacts, the documentation included some drawings of architectural details and – most importantly – photographic depictions of the building complexes visited by the officials, such as the Imperial palace in Kyōto, the shrines of Ise, the Tōdai-ji in Nara and nearby Hōryū-ji, and many more (Figs. 4.277–4.280).[231] This material was kept at the museum and was later labelled Important Cultural Property; yet it was never published until its digitisation a few years ago. The visual material has therefore remained largely unknown except for single examples of Yokoyama's photographs, which found their way into western collections in the latter part of his career.[232]

---

229 For a brief summary, see also Dower, "Throwing off." – Finally, the development of Japanese heritage protection strategies has its roots in these years of change and reorganisation and the experience or fear of loss of cultural identity. Löffler, "Search."

230 Tōkyō National Museum, "History," https://www.tnm.jp/modules/r_free_page/index.php?id=147 [accessed 21 August 2023]; Tanaka, Stefan, *New Times in Modern Japan* (Princeton, NJ, 2004), pp. 31–32.

231 National Museums of Japan, e-Museum, Jinshin Survey related materials and photographs, https://emuseum.nich.go.jp/detail?langId=en&webView=&content_base_id=100815&content_part_id=0&content_pict_id=0; https://emuseum.nich.go.jp/detail?langId=en&webView=&content_base_id=100817&content_part_id=0&content_pict_id=0 [accessed 21 August 2023]. – Compare also Yokoyama's series on the castle of Edo/Tōkyō, National Museums of Japan, e-Museum, Photograph Album of the former Edo Castle, https://emuseum.nich.go.jp/detail?langId=en&webView=&content_base_id=100813&content_part_id=0&content_pict_id=0 [accessed 21 August 2023].

232 See also e.g. Kühn, "Zartrosa und Lichtblau. Japanische Fotografie der Meiji-Zeit," in: id. (ed.), *Zartrosa und Lichtblau. Japanische Fotografie der Meiji-Zeit (1868–1912)* (Berlin, 2015), pp. 9–23, here esp. p. 15.

Did this gap in information transfer have any impact on the western knowledge system? Did these images convey information that was not included in the souvenir photographs? Could the learning process have unfolded differently if this had been part of western architectural discourses on Japan?

Unlike the photographs in most souvenir albums, those comprising the Jinshin Survey remained black-and-white. While the entire set included a handful of genre-like scenes, the architectural images were largely free of staffage personnel, except for the occasional person included for scale. In general, the buildings were depicted axially or crosswise, an angle of approach similar to that chosen for the souvenir photographs. However, while there were some close-ups and even few interiors, most of the survey photographs adopted a very wide angle that embedded the buildings into their broader environments while omitting any detailed information.

These differences would not be significant enough to merit mentioning a comparatively small group of unpublished photographs, were it not for the choice of topics: the survey documented many sites which attracted hardly any western attention during these first decades of intensified information transfer and were not (yet) the destinations of recreational journeys. Thus, they remained largely unknown to western audiences until the end of the nineteenth century or even later.

Among them were many photographs of buildings in Nara or its environs and more than 70 images being taken within the complex of the Kyōto Imperial palace alone. There were even images of Katsura Rikyū, the Imperial villa near Kyōto (Figs. 4.281, 4.282).[233]

One can assume that the publication of these images would have had extended western knowledge, particularly if had they been accompanied by detailed captions on the historical relevance of the sites, as was the case with Felice Beato's annotated albums.[234] Alternatively, they could have illustrated, for example, some of the historical information provided in Griffis' *The Mikado's Empire*.[235] However, since hardly any of the visitors at this time expressed any interest in learning about temples and shrines beyond their basic religious functions and their visually pleasing picturesqueness, the images would probably have made no difference in this regard.

---

233   The building did not appear in the visual material available to western observers and was largely unknown until Bruno Taut's writings made the complex a reference work for architectural modernism during the 1930s.
234   Hockley, "Felice Beato's Japan."
235   Griffis, *Empire* (1876).

常御殿

法隆寺金堂

FIGURES 4.277–4.280   Photographs of the Jinshin Survey of 1872 by Yokoyama Matsusaburo: Kyōto Imperial palace, Tsunegoten; Main Hall of Hōryūji Temple; Nara, Shōshōin (storage building), and Ise, Naiko (Inner Shrine), 1872

FIGURES 4.281–4.282   Yokoyama Matsusaburo: two views of Katsura Rikyū (Katsura Imperial Villa), stereo photographs, 1872

That said, publication of the survey and the related material could have been utilised to initiate communication of Japan's architectural heritage and heritage sites that would have gone far beyond the actions taken by the Japanese government and by individuals interested in cultural transfer alone. Public acknowledgement of this rich heritage at such an early stage of the modernisation process would have underlined Japan's awareness of its historical evolution and, in turn, might have accelerated western recognition of that trajectory, at least if the latter had been willing to listen, which, regrettably, remains uncertain.

The same could also be said of the second body of sample material that was not disseminated, the *hinagatabon*, but most of the other parameters were different.

2.3.2   *Hinagatabon*

The history of Japanese architectural thought, design and planning was passed on using a number of tools and means of information transfer, such as models, drawings and texts; these were practices which in part dated back to the introduction of Buddhist architecture via Korea during the Asuka period (sixth and seventh centuries).[236]

---

236   *hinagata*, in: JAANUS, here http://www.aisf.or.jp/~jaanus/deta/h/hinagata.htm [accessed 21 August 2023]. – For a general overview of the profession, see Hein, Carola, "Baumeister

Among them were different kinds of records relating to building practices, both texts and drawings. Some of these were initially handwritten, and were passed down within the builders' family businesses alone. By the early seventeenth century, the characteristics of the different records had started to intermingle. In the course of the century, some of them were published in print and took on some of the characteristics of handbooks, as the profession changed to adapt to the building policy of the Tokugawa shōgunate.[237] In the ensuing centuries, different versions and many editions of such *hinagatabon*[238] were developed. From the late nineteenth century onwards, new editions addressed western forms of building and decoration as well.

These books are usually called 'pattern books' and/or 'design manuals' in English, a terminology which probably fails to express the books' functions and contents appropriately.[239] A look at the *hinagatabon* digitised by the Architectural Institute of Japan alone is enough to reveal the significance of the material as a source of architectural thought. Some *hinagatabon* provided numerous patterns for the decorative details of brackets, shelf arrangements, sliding doors, *shōji*, or transoms, *ranma*, to name just a few examples (Figs. 4.283–4.284).[240] Others discussed, among other things, the proportions of pagodas or the appropriate curvature of rafters (Figs. 4.285 and 4.286). The books clearly did not teach carpentry but seemed to discuss specific issues in largely non-vernacular building projects.[241] There is significant evidence that the *hinagatabon* played a part in Japanese discourses on the theory of architecture. They negotiated critical questions of architectural meaning, such as the dispositions of buildings in relation to cosmological or anthropological

---

und Architekten in Japan," in: Winfried Nerdinger (ed.), *Der Architekt. Geschichte und Gegenwart eines Berufsstandes* 1 (Munich; London; New York, 2012), pp. 258–277; but compare this with Coaldrake, "Customary Practice."

237 Coaldrake, "Customary Practice," esp. p. 49. See, also, the paragraph on the architectural models displayed at the international exhibition in Vienna, 1873, earlier in this chapter.

238 The term literally means "miniature stamped book" and is used not only for architecture but for the fabric patterns of kimonos as well, see *hinagatabon*, in: JAANUS, here https://www.aisf.or.jp/~jaanus/deta/h/hinagatabon.htm [accessed 21 August 2023].

239 The entire topic is vastly understudied in western languages. Only Coaldrake wrote more than two sentences on the matter, while voluminous editions exist in Japanese. Coaldrake, *Carpenter*, pp. 38–40, 139–140.

240 The AIJ provides a collection of digitised *hinagatabon* between 1700 and 1914. The Architectural Institute of Japan, *hinagatabon*, https://www.aij.or.jp/da1/hinagata/kizou.html [accessed 21 August 2023].

241 While some seem to discuss proportions, the parts of building elements, scaling and such, there are no step-by-step instructions in the drawings. There are later publications, however, which teach in this fashion. See e.g. Saito, Heijirō, *Nihon kaoku kōzō* [Japanese house structures] (Tōkyō: Shin'yudō, 1904).

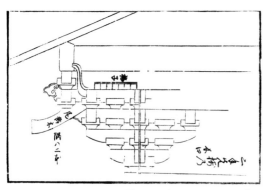
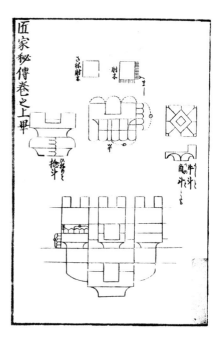

FIGURES 4.283–4.284   *Hinagatabon*, 1727: view and details of a bracketing system

systems of reference. They provided information about the appropriate architectural expression of social status as it relates to best-practice aesthetic solutions.[242]

However, although some examples were part of Japan's displays at international exhibitions during the late nineteenth century, none of these volumes or their individual drawings were referred to in western publications on architecture in Japan.[243] While it is reasonable to assume that some of Abel Guérineau's depictions of brackets, for example, might have profited from such templates,

---

242 The most famous *hinagatabon* is the *shomei* of the Heinouchi family, the "official master carpenter's family for the construction department of the Edo bakufu," which dates back to 1608. It contains five volumes on varying topics such as gates and fences, shrines, temples and palaces, See *shoumei*, in: JAANUS, here http://www.aisf.or.jp/~jaanus/deta/s/shoumei.htm [accessed 21 August 2023]. For a reprint, see Ōta Hirotarō; Itō Yōtarō, *Shōmei*, edited reprint (Tōkyō: Kajima Shuppankai, 1971) and later editions. For further edited material, see Kawata, Katsuhiro (ed.), *Kinsei kenchikusho – dōmiya hinagata* [Source books of Japanese temple and shrine design] (Kyōto: Tairyūdō Shoten, 1988); Wakayama, Shigeru; Fumoto, Kazuyoshi (eds.), *Kinsei kenchikusho – kōhō hinagata* [Sourcebooks of Japanese building construction] (Kyōto: Tairyūdō Shoten, 1993) and Togashi, Shinzo, *Daiku miyahinagata: Ikken'yashiro kara haiden torii made* (Tōkyō: Omusha, 2011); id., *Daiku terahinagata: Hondo mon kara gojunoto made* (Tōkyō: Omusha, 2011); id., *Daiku mon hinagata: Sukiyamon kara yotsuashimon koraimon made* (Tōkyō: Omusha, 2018).

243 Barna, "Architectural Displays," pp. 25, 29–30.

VISITING AND VISUALISING ARCHITECTURE

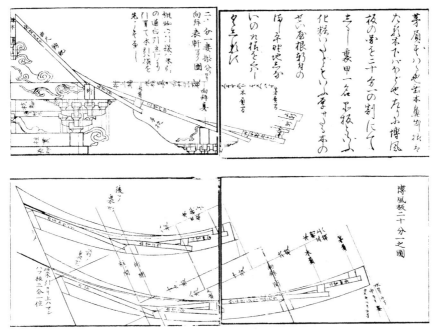

FIGURES 4.285–4.286 *Hinagatabon*, 1812: position of rafters and eave laths with respect to the curvature of the roofing

this observation remains speculative (compare Figs. 4.128–4.131 in the colour section to Figs. 4.284–4.285).

Had they been acknowledged and discussed by the western experts, such a large amount of advanced technical information and visualisation could have influenced the relationship between Japanese and western traditions in architecture early on. This seems even more likely if we keep in mind that the documents discussed here represent only a fairly mundane level of professional visual communication, and not the high end of the art as represented by the plans for Edo castle, for example.[244] Unfortunately, until a contemporary source is found which discusses this apparent oversight, the reasons for it must remain a topic of speculation.

Beyond these general observations regarding an unmentioned genre of architecture-related writings, the *hinagatabon* are relevant to this study for another reason: they provided technical illustrations such as views, sections, floor plans or constructional and decorative details (e.g. Figs. 4.287–4.289).

---

244 Coaldrake, "Customary Practice."

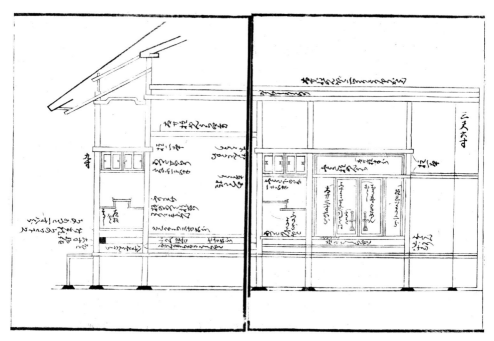

FIGURE 4.287 *Hinagatabon*, 1851: section of a dwelling with interior fittings

These drawings stood in strong contrast to all of the visual information addressed above, with the exception of a few examples mentioned in connection with Josiah Conder's publications. The drawings were anything but depictions and/or visualisations of architecture as experienced in daily life, as provided by photographs and woodblock prints; rather, they visualised architectural phenomena at a very high level of abstraction, thus limiting the audience which could benefit from them to readers with some technical training themselves. In this sense, the visual material of the *hinagatabon* paralleled the visual(ised) communication seen in contemporary European sources such as treatises on construction or the theory of architecture.

In retrospect, the *hinagatabon* genre might represent one of the most significant failures in architectural information transfer to have occurred in the late nineteenth century. Arguably, this absence of acknowledgement was due neither to the scarcity of such publications at this time, nor to any lack of awareness of their existence among Japanese builders. Rather, it was likely a result of western perceptions of their irrelevance. Based on the observations made throughout this research project, it must be assumed, until proven otherwise, that the books were ignored due to their 'empirical tradition' and 'lack'

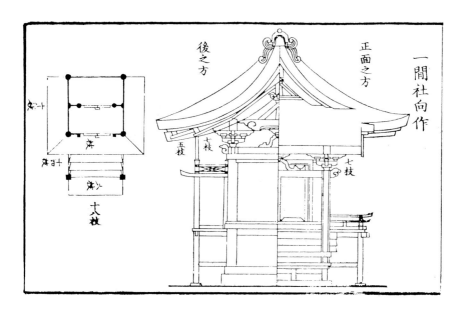

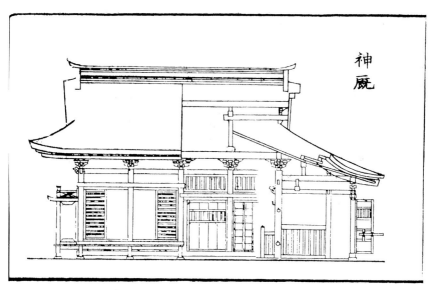

FIGURES 4.288–4.289   *Hinagatabon*, 1866: view, section and floor plan of a very small shrine; View and section of a larger shrine building

of scientific character, and thus due to wilful ignorance of the significant parallels they offered to western practices in architectural publication, discourse and teaching.[245]

The failure to acknowledge and integrate material such as documentary photography or *hinagatabon* into western discourses on Japanese architecture may have contributed significantly to the imbalance in evaluations and knowledge production observed among textual sources and 'built Japonisms'. However, it is important to remember that there were mitigating circumstances for the absence in western circles of material of entirely native Japanese origin: namely, the language barrier and the unavailability of these materials outside Japan. While this did not hinder travellers and art collectors at this time from accessing many materials, as we saw earlier, it was an important factor and needs to be considered in any subsequent analysis.

In the course of this chapter, we looked at illustrations that appeared in publications and were thus available to many interested readers in the West, and at woodblock prints and photographs that belonged to individual collections and were often acquired as souvenirs. Finally, we learned about some media for the transmission of architectural information which remained unknown at the time. In summary, the visual material that found its way to the West and that informed western audiences about Japanese architecture was both manifold and biased.[246]

It included sketches and photographs by westerners and Japanese alike as well as woodblock prints of different kinds, some primarily informative in character, some more aesthetic. Yet the image content chosen for sketches and photographs or for illustrations in western books was delimited by a frame of (professional) interest and expectation, which in turn was connected to western perceptions of Japan and its culture in general.[247]

Architectural motifs were very common but were usually embedded in established patterns of the picturesque, which favoured aesthetic and/or exotic impressions. At the same time, architectural experts concentrated on

---

245   See also Clancey, *Earthquake*, p. 31.
246   The chapter has ignored the architectural information that might have been provided by collectibles of Japanese origin such as ceramics, lacquer ware or picture scrolls, *kakemono*. While there are architectural elements to be found on occasion, they are very rare and to my knowledge entirely subsumed in the design ideas of the object.
247   See for example the analysis in Delank, *Japan in der Kunst*, and id., "Die Weltausstellungen in Paris, Wien und Chicago sowie das neue Printmedium der Fotografie als Vermittler japanischer Kunst und Kultur im Westen," in: Ehmcke, Franziska (ed.), *Kunst und Kunsthandwerk Japans im interkulturellen Dialog* (Munich, 2008), pp. 19–48.

images which were understood to be of interest to the designing architect at home: spatial arrangements of buildings in the landscape, on the one hand, and decorative or functional details on the other. The choice of motifs drawn from the Japanese built environment was evidently not driven by a scholarly interest in encyclopaedic depiction or in-depth analysis of building concepts, but reflected a desire to capture eclectic elements of fascination/inspiration.

As a result, the visual material used to communicate buildings to a Euro-American audience across various publications and visual sources tended to foster and perpetuate interest, but lacked the complexity and depth necessary to generate an even remotely comprehensible 'image' of Japanese architecture. Ignorance of (or disregard for) material that did not accord with narrative and visual expectations, such as documentary photography and building manuals, led to an unbalanced, fragmentary and incomplete transfer of information on architecture.

In addition, what was initially a broad approach to Japanese culture, as evidenced in text and images, became selective, condensed and essentialised over time, until western images came to underline and strengthen narrative expectations of difference between Japan and the Euro-American world. In terms of architecture, this meant underlining the characteristics of 'traditional Japan', while largely ignoring contemporary developments in technological modernisation. Sadly, it did not mean actually studying 'traditional Japan', but only preserving a superficial 'image' frozen in time.[248]

This visual idea of Japanese architecture as communicated through picturesque images of castles, tea houses and shrines became included in western systems of cultural knowledge alongside conceptions of other world regions and cultures. Built on a foundation of visual materials largely selected according to western expectations and patterns, it reflected a joyful interest in artistic inspiration and cultural imagination that overshadowed knowledge production on architecture for years to come.

---

248 This western idea of 'traditional Japan', its art and architecture did not necessarily concur with the Japanese point of view, as the discussion about the art collection at the Exposition Universelle in Paris, 1900, showed earlier.

CHAPTER 5

Conclusions and Further Questions

The collection, evaluation, and canonisation of western knowledge of Japanese architecture during the late nineteenth century was a complex interplay of reading, collecting, rewriting, expanding, and at times, discarding existing data. This intricate process took place alongside the broader endeavour to position architecture within the realms of modern western academia. It was part of a far broader process of knowledge production in a rapidly globalising world and characterised by the biographical coincidences of the actors involved, the possibilities of the available media, the existing concepts of culture, scholarship and technological development, and not least, by the western claim to prerogatives of interpretation.

As a result, the information that was generated and became canonised in architectural handbooks some decades later fell considerably short of being balanced, complete and truthful. Rather, it mirrored the shortcomings of the data gathering on site, the inner-western negotiations of society and nationhood, cultural identity and modernisation, and the hegemonic worldviews and ideas of cultural superiority on a global scale.

The number of westerners who visited Japan or who came to reside there during the period in question was significant. However, the number who actually involved themselves in public discussion of Japan by giving presentations at home or writing essays and books was comparatively small. This was particularly the case for architecture.

There were only about a dozen writers, whose stays in Japan were usually a matter of biographical coincidence, who gained architectural insights locally. About the same number formed their opinions from afar, many of them involved in *Japonisme* by collecting and trading Japonica or by discussing the transfer of Japanese impulses into western art canons. They were all largely learned men and modern engineering experts with the most diverse backgrounds and interests. While monographs remained few and far between, essays and notes were published widely across the available print media, from arts journals to the periodicals of ethnographic societies.

It was through such channels that information on Japanese phenomena of an artistic or architectural nature reached a broad audience. Still, this information was merely fragmentary: a description of a shrine here, a decorative solution there, often without any illustration or only with a few line drawings. The general cultural reference and explanatory context were provided through different means. The fragments were understood only because they were embedded within an informational environment created by other fields and genres.

Firstly, there were dozens of travelogues and ethnographic reports which included Japan or focused exclusively on the country. While many of their authors based their information not on personal observation alone, but on other sources as well, and mixed this information with attribution and myth, their publications served as a background without which the writings on architecture would have been incomprehensible, appearing as random pieces of unrelated information. These publications provided synthesising impressions of landscapes and cities, houses and shrines, temples and streets, not only in text form but often in plates as well.

Secondly, architectural information was contextualised by western publications on Japanese art. Written by collectors and art historians, many without any personal experience of East Asia, they aimed to provide an overview of the fine and applied arts in Japan, of the artistic schools and their characteristics, and of the circumstances of manual work and art production. Here, Japanese architecture had a place, even if only in a short sub-chapter or in a few short sentences asserting the absence in Japan of anything at all that could be described as architecture. Here, the legitimation for studying Japanese architecture derived from its established role within the western system of art production, collection and trade.

In addition, art discourse depended on the depiction of objects and sought to find modern means to illustrate art studies and collection catalogues. Soon, publications on Japanese art profited from such developments. The overall discourse, the published material, and the wide-ranging exhibitions of art, including woodblock prints and the like, helped to create a second layer of reference through which to address Japanese architecture, despite its marginal role in the greater scheme of things.

Thirdly, the international exhibitions provided a platform where this information and imagery could be extended, disseminated and strengthened in settings that were as Japanese as was possible outside of Japan.

Collection of information and the discussion of Japanese architecture up to the turn of the twentieth century was therefore not a matter of expert discourse within the regulated realms of academia or learned societies;[1] there was neither an opinion leader nor a dominant medium for publication. Rather,

---

1 It would be worth checking this in more detail against Ludwik Fleck's (1896–1961) theories of thought, especially his concept of the *thought collective*. He underlines the interconnectedness of 'closed' groups of experts and general discourses in society. Fleck, Ludwik, *Entstehung*

engagement with Japanese architecture took place across a range of media and genre, and included impressions and assumptions as naturally as it did scientific arguments. While the authority of the actors played an important role as soon as actual discourse arose, it was not necessarily rooted in specific expertise or social background alone. On-site experience in East Asia and language competence had a part to play as well, while source critique or methodological approach were largely irrelevant.

As far as knowledge production on Japan was concerned, this heterogeneous process of creation, evaluation and dissemination was double-edged. It was holistic but superficial; it was very helpful for exploring and defining the field, but too incomplete for the consistent development and creation of complex insights. It remains uncertain whether the later diversification into specific fields was in part a reaction to this, or – as seems more likely – was a by-product of general disciplinary delineations in modern western academia at that time. By the end of the century, however, it led to an 'expertification' of the discussion of architectural topics. Some topics, such as earthquake-resistant construction and railways, experienced a slight consolidation of interest in engineering journals, while others disappeared altogether. An issue that emerged subsequently, but did not develop fully before the turn of the century, was a certain awareness of the historical epochs of Japan's architectural history.[2]

Given these unfavourable conditions of knowledge production, it is even more relevant to understand how the western experts in building-related fields made sense of the data they collected themselves or received from others.

Put briefly, the attribution of meaning to the observed phenomena of Japan's architecture was as heterogeneous as its collection and distribution had been before. It was determined by both the comprehensibility of the phenomena within the western system of general knowledge and by western perceptions of its relevance to contemporary social challenges. It was for this reason that *Japonisme* in the arts became so significant: impressions of Japanese culture and art gained from images and artefacts slotted into the already existing framework of Chinoiseries. They were able to jump the language barrier and provide both economic revenue for the art trade and inspiration for the supposedly ailing European field of art production.

---

und Entwicklung einer wissenschaftlichen Tatsache. Einführung in die Lehre vom Denkstil und Denkkollektiv (Frankfurt a.M., 1980), esp. pp. 135–145 and 148–151.

2 This awareness was initially limited to just a few actors on the western side. However, its emergence was probably connected to the development of a national cultural identity in Japan that found expression in 1900 in *Histoire de l'art du Japon*, see chapter 4.1.

CONCLUSIONS AND FURTHER QUESTIONS 345

With respect to architecture that was much less easy to transport, understand, interpret and explain, there were three ways of translating and integrating incoming information into western knowledge systems.

A lot of self-explanatory information merged into existing structures without difficulty and later re-emerged in literature without exciting any discussion or triggering explicit evaluation. This applied to technical data and additions to existing knowledge systems for the sake of completeness, such as measurements and specific terms for buildings, tools or materials, or lists of woods and other building-related materials. It also applied to information on Japanese building law and fire prevention, as well as news about the ceremonies marking the start or completion of work on modern large-scale projects in Japan or the involvement of western actors in such projects. It applied as well to terms for generic building types such as castles, bridges or dwellings.

Specific building types and many other phenomena related to architecture in the widest sense, such as customs around the use of public space and interior rooms, hygiene practices or the layouts of shrine and temple areas, fell into another category: they required additional context to understand the pertinence of the information provided. In some travelogues and ethnographical reports, the contextualisation served to explain and underline the specific Japaneseness of a phenomenon. This not only contrasted Japan with the European mainstream through storytelling and/or tourism marketing, but also helped to create, piece by piece, a notion of Japan as a decidedly non-western culture.

In other cases, most of them in the context of in-field communication, the information deviated from acknowledged patterns and evaluation became necessary, as is usual in research contexts. Often, the additional context was used merely to find an uncomplicated way of mediating and reconciling the deviating bodies of information: the *kura* was defined by its function as a fire-resistant warehouse and its material features; the role of the public bath-house was explained by its infrastructural context and the hygiene customs in Japan.[3] Usually, the contextualising information did not enhance the architectural understanding but rather that of the cultural content provided.

The vast majority of contextualised technical information on Japanese architecture went unchallenged, not least due to the comparatively small number of contributions on such topics and the even smaller number of actors prepared

---

3 The contextualisation of the term *tea-house* was of a more delicate character, since the western simplification subsumed meanings such as premises providing food and drink in every price category with institutions of exclusive entertainment and brothels. See e.g. F. St., "Theehaus," here p. 290.

to offer opinions. A significant, if singular example of an actual exchange of positions and arguments was the dispute about the earthquake-resistant quality of traditional Japanese constructions. Here, the extensive explanations given for the seemingly extravagant and irrational use of wood for roofs and large structures, such as temple halls and pagodas, was evidently much too far outside contemporary teachings and too challenging in its implications for some western readers even to consider. It did, however, lead to a clash of conflicting interpretative patterns: that of historically developed empirical competence versus that of the mathematical model. This clash was entirely internal to the western discourse, where the Japanese case served merely as a peg on which to hang claims to the superiority of scientifically based modern architecture over the traditional experience of the building trades.

This dispute shifts this case into the third category of integration of information into western knowledge systems, involving the group of phenomena that were in such conflict with established western norms as to require extensive explanation and legitimation.

Most of these cases were of an aesthetic, ethical or moral nature. Solutions typically involved subtly readjusting western patterns of interpretation to accommodate Japanese instances at the periphery. This did not challenge the western prerogative of interpretation or its perceived superior position in the hierarchy of cultural achievements. On occasion, this led to arguments marked by internal contradictions[4] or over-simplifications. This was the case, for example, with the wholesale rejection of a genuine Japanese architecture due to its perceived Chinese roots or by examining it through the lens European criteria of architecture as a form of fine art. Here, Japanese otherness was both the issue and the answer: all incomprehensible or uncomfortable differences between western norms and Japanese examples were explained away with reference to a distinct Japaneseness. This separation served as the default position where a conclusive explanation would have been challenging for existing systems of reference.

In the end, the acculturation of Japanese architecture into western systems of knowledge largely followed just two paths: the integration of unquestioned information, on the one hand, and on the other, the 'quarantining' of challenging or conflicting information in a newly created field defined and kept apart

---

4 There are famous historical examples of these in other fields as well: a case in point are the complicated formulas developed to describe astronomical observations before Johannes Kepler and Galileo Galilei. See the entire storyline on astronomy or, more briefly, Nikolaus Copernicus' problems with the orbits, in Cohen, Floris, *Die zweite Erschaffung der Welt. Wie die moderne Naturwissenschaft entstand* (Bonn, 2011), pp. 84–87.

by otherness and incommensurability. Here, information was collected but not integrated.

The actors involved in evaluating the incoming information evidently strove to maintain existing worldviews and knowledge systems. In this respect, they succeeded. They failed in a scholarly sense, however, by being unable or unwilling to expand the limits of the 'thinkable' set out by their fields, their disciplines and not least their general worldviews.[5] They failed to allow for the potential value of knowledge beyond their 'comfort zones'. In fact, they failed to actually learn.[6]

However, unlike the actors involved in art production, those taking part in architectural discourses did have the freedom to decide whether they wanted to learn or not learn: there was no crisis in architecture apart from the struggle to keep civil engineering at bay. The modern nation states had a broad need for architectural self-representation, and economic growth and urbanisation kept architects and building companies busy and creative. Industrialisation and social change had not yet called the role of the architect into question. There was as yet no immediate need to reform or renew architectural thought. And, sadly, there was evidently not yet enough interest among most architects, even those residing and working in Japan, in studying Japanese architecture merely for the sake of extending their own knowledge.

To be clear, knowledge production on Japanese architecture during the late nineteenth century was entirely in tune with contemporary practices and expectations. As citizens of the leading nations of the world, western architects or engineers would not have seen the need to acknowledge Japan's cultural expressions as equal and relevant. Therefore, nearly all uses of and discourse around Japanese architecture remained immediately utilitarian. While this was entirely professional, it nevertheless fell short of the self-image of architects as learned men that prevailed at that time and is even more prevalent today.

In the end, western knowledge systems of Japanese architecture comprised an almost incidental combination of fact, attribution, imagination and ignorance, barely vetted by enquiry or discourse. Yet, this was the foundation on which later discourses based their assumptions and questions. It remains a

---

5 This case shows parallels to the arguments about Gregor Mendel's (1822–1884) studies of inheritance made by Michel Foucault (1926–1984) in his inaugural lecture at the Collège de France. Foucault, Michel, *Die Ordnung des Diskurses*, extended ed. (Frankfurt a.M., 1993), pp. 22–25.
6 On a certain level, this stands in contrast to the processes observable in the arts at the same time, where Japanese impulses may not have changed the hegemonic claims of western discourses, but led at least to actual involvement in new experiences of design.

subject of further study to determine why later generations shifted their stance from disinterest to appreciation, and how the protagonists of architectural modernism came by their fascination with the Japanese dwelling. There was, after all, a significant difference between, on the one hand, Basil H. Chamberlain's description of the Japanese house as an inexpensive and healthy commodity and, on the other, the enthusiasm expressed by Walter Gropius (1883–1969) on a picture postcard to Le Corbusier (1887–1965) in 1954:

> Dear Corbu, all what we have been fighting for has its parallel in old Japanese culture. (…) The Japanese house is the best and most modern that I know of and really prefabricated.[7]

In addition to this intriguing shift in perception, which strengthens the resolve to continue research, there are further consequences to be drawn from the results of this study.

A number of observations invite comparison with developments in other world regions, most notably China, India and the Ottoman Empire. Like Japan, these regions had long traditions of cultural exchange with the West which ensured western interest in their arts and culture during the nineteenth century. Did research of their architecture show the same patterns and result in the same evaluations? Were these cultural histories told in the same way as was Japan's, i.e. were they split into two distinct narratives of tradition and modernity?[8] Or were there even more such splits, and if so, what were the crucial arguments that led to divergence?

In terms of knowledge production and the management of knowledge of Japanese architecture, filling in the gaps remains a significant challenge. It would already be a big step forward if scholars were able to accumulate and interlink the existing architecture-related knowledge published in western languages that is scattered across different fields such as ethnology, religious and Japanese studies, art history, and urban (history) studies. This cross-disciplinary borrowing and exchange became an established practice in western architectural history and most notably in urban history decades ago. With regard to Japan's architecture, it is used by many scholars as a stop-gap solution to compensate for a lack of publications that integrate the diverse approaches from the start. Combined with translations of major publications

---

7 Francesco Dal Co, "La princesse est modeste," in Ponciroli, Virginia; Isozaki Arata (eds.), *Katsura Imperial Villa* (Milan, 2005), pp. 386–389, here 388–389.
8 There is some evidence for this on a more general level, for example in popular travel marketing, where places are increasingly labelled as concurrently modern and traditional.

from Japanese into English (or, for that matter, into French or German), this approach should succeed in laying a reasonable foundation for further work towards a comprehensive understanding of Japanese architecture in the past and present.

In addition, this would provide a framework for a critical discussion of the clichés which surround modern Japanese design and architecture. The aim of such a discussion would certainly not be to undermine the creative processes emerging from cultural exchanges and transfers; rather, it would be to raise awareness of the inspiring as well as the occasionally questionable potential of 'creative misunderstandings' across cultures and to encourage study of the hows and whys of this phenomenon.

Glossary of Technical Terms

amado   Architectural element: wooden shutters used to close up a dwelling during the night or in bad weather and otherwise stored away in designated boxes.

bakufu   Shōgunate administration. Term for the military government first established by Minamoto no Yoritomo at the end of the 12th century. The three *bakufu* of Minamoto, Ashikaga and Tokugawa ruled intermittently on the authority of the imperial court until the onset of the Meiji Restoration.

bakumatsu period   The final years of the Tokugawa shōgunate, between the arrival of Matthew C. Perry's first expedition in 1853 and the resignation of the 15th shōgun Tokugawa Yoshinobu (1837–1913).

buke (or *bushi*; in western texts usually *samurai*)   Social class of Japanese military nobility existing from the Middle Ages until its abolition during the Meiji period.

chadō   'the way of the tea'. Practice of preparing tea and receiving and entertaining guests. The practice does not necessarily include specific utensils or settings such as dedicated tea-houses and gardens, but is usually discussed with reference to these in art and architecture.

chigaidana   Staggered shelves, element of the interior design of *shoin*, usually together with *tokonoma*.

chigi   Architectural element: forked finials. A common element of shrine buildings, but together with *katsuogi* a typical marker of the shrines of the Ise tradition.

daiku   master craftsman, here: lead carpenter, principal designer and coordinator of the whole process of constructing and equipping the building.

daimyō   Feudal lord, member of the military nobility, *buke*. Since the Tokugawa period, the designation for the members of the sword nobility, initially almost 300 strong, who had an annual income of more than 10,000 *koku* of rice.

Deshima   Island in the harbour of Nagasaki (today silted up). Guarded, lone outpost of Dutch East India Company (VOC) in Japan during the more than 200 years of the Japanese isolationist policy during the Tokugawa shōgunate.

Edo (today Tōkyō)   Medieval castle town and later seat of power of the Tokugawa *bakufu*.

Edo period   Era between 1603 and 1867 in which the Tokugawa family ruled Japan, named after the seat of power, Edo = Tokugawa period.

engawa   Architectural element: boarded flooring (in contrast to an area with tatami flooring) in a Japanese dwelling; today denoting a veranda.

fusuma   Architectural detail: sliding doors between rooms, made from wooden frames covered with opaque paper. See *shōji*.

futon   Bedding consisting of a mattress and a duvet that is stored in a closet during the day and spread out on the *tatami* floor at night.

genkan   Architectural element: initially, a vestibule in the sacred environment over an antechamber in a stately residence, then developing over several centuries into the porch-like entrance of a residential building. The *genkan* mediates between the soil or stone floor of the public outdoor space and the wooden floor of the private interior, with a low step usually marking the transition. The shift to the interior is accompanied by the removal of the shoes.

gonin-gumi   Neighbourhood groups of five families, part of the system of administration and supervision during the Tokugawa period.

hinagata   Architectural term: "A miniature or a scaled-down model of a planned work of art."[1]

hinagatabon   Architectural term: small-format woodblock-print books "containing architectural drawings of models, design techniques, and sample plans."[2]

hondō   Main hall of worship of a (Buddhist) temple.

jodan-no-ma   Architectural element: room containing an area of raised floor on which the person of highest rank is positioned, specifically when receiving visitors.

kagura-den   Architectural structure: stage for *shintō* dance within the shrine precinct.

kakemono   "A hanging scroll. A work of calligraphy or a painting which is mounted and hung in an alcove or on a wall."[3]

kamoi   Architectural element: head jamb, structural detail embedded in the considerations and rules of *kiwari*.

karahafu   Architectural element: undulating bargeboard. A decorative element of representative gates and entrances, often with elaborate carvings and/or colouring.[4]

katōmado   Architectural element: "A window with a special curvilinear top part (...). [It] has an ogee-type pointed top with a series of S-like curves on either side of the peak."[5]

katsuogi   Architectural element: wooden billet, weighing down the roof ridge. A largely decorative element of residences and shrines; together with *chigi*, a typical marker of shrines of the Ise tradition.

---

1 *Hinagata*, in: JAANUS, here http://www.aisf.or.jp/~jaanus/deta/h/hinagata.htm [accessed 15 July 2019].
2 *Hinagatabon*, in: JAANUS, here http://www.aisf.or.jp/~jaanus/deta/h/hinagatabon.htm [accessed 15 July 2019].
3 *Kakemono*, in: JAANUS, here http://www.aisf.or.jp/~jaanus/deta/k/kakemono.htm [accessed 15 July 2019].
4 *Karahafu*, in: JAANUS, here http://www.aisf.or.jp/~jaanus/deta/k/karahafu.htm [accessed 15 July 2019].
5 *Katōmado*, in: JAANUS, here http://www.aisf.or.jp/~jaanus/deta/k/katoumado.htm [accessed 15 July 2019].

GLOSSARY OF TECHNICAL TERMS 353

keyaki   Wood of *zelkova serrata* from the Ulmaceae family. One of the best Japanese woods for architectural construction.

kiwari   Architectural term: set of rules and adaptions to dimension structural elements in the process of carpentering.[6]

koku   Measure of volume, especially for rice, approx. 180 L. One *koku* corresponded to the annual rice requirement for an adult.

kura   Architectural structure: fire-resistant store-house. The building's wooden skeleton was covered with a thick cover comprised of numerous layers of plaster; it was structurally disconnected from the surrounding buildings, such as shops and dwellings.

Meiji period   Reign of Emperor Mutsuhito (1852–1912) from 1868 to 1912.

meisho zue   Genre of literature consisting of illustrated guides to places or landscapes in Japan that emerged during the Edo period.

mokoshi   Architectural element: a "pent roof enclosure usually one bay deep. Its structure may extend from the aisles (…) on one to four sides [or may] surround the core (…) of a building directly."[7]

nō-stage   Architectural structure: roofed stage for performances, with a main stage of about 5.70 by 5.70 metres and auxiliary parts such as places for musicians and passageways for actors.

noren   Cloth hangings "suspended from the eaves or in the openings (especially entrances) of a building as protection from either sunlight or wind" that came to function as a shop sign in urban contexts.[8]

ōhiroma   Architectural element: audience hall.

o-yatoi gaikokujin   Foreign contract expert, hired by the Japanese government or private clients to transfer knowledge and promote modernization, mainly during the Meiji period.

rangaku   "Dutch studies." Field of scholarship in Japan, mainly during the Tokugawa era. While Japanese-western contact was limited due to the isolationist policy, knowledge transfer was facilitated through the Dutch settlement on Deshima island in Nagasaki.

rinzō   Architectural detail: revolving shelf. Storage for Buddhist writings, *sutras*.

---

6   *Kiwari*, in: JAANUS, here http://www.aisf.or.jp/~jaanus/deta/k/kiwari.htm [accessed 15 July 2019], see also Engel, Heino, *The Japanese House: A tradition for contemporary architecture* (Ruthland, VT; Tōkyō, 1964), pp. 57–66.

7   *Mokoshi*, in: JAANUS, here http://www.aisf.or.jp/~jaanus/deta/m/mokoshi.htm [accessed 15 July 2019].

8   *Noren*, in: JAANUS, here https://www.aisf.or.jp/~jaanus/deta/n/noren [accessed 28 August 2023].

Samurai   'one who serves'. In general, every member of the warrior class; more precisely the armed henchman of a *daimyō*. See *buke*.

sankin kōtai   'alternate attendance'. Periodically required residency of *daimyō* in Edo, important part of the system of political control during the Tokugawa period.

shachihoko   Architectural detail: fish-shaped roof ornament.

shinbutsu bunri   Meiji era's policy of separating Shintoist and Buddhist institutions during the 1870s.

shinden zukuri   Architectural term: "shinden style" (of building). Set of characteristics typical of walled aristocratic residences in the Imperial capital of Heiankyō (today Kyōto) in the mid-10th century. Inspired by palatial structures in China, the complexes were arranged symmetrically along a north-south axis. The main building, *shinden*, was accompanied by subsidiary buildings towards the east and the west and connected to these by corridors. The overall ensemble of buildings formed a south-facing courtyard completed by a landscaped garden surrounding a pond. The primary building within the complex consisted of a core room formed by round supports and surrounded by aisles. Except for a walled area used for sleeping and the storage of valuables, the interior was not divided, but could be configured using movable partitions such as folding screens or textile hangings.[9]

shintō   'way of the gods'. Initially, an indigenous Japanese religion in which forces of nature or higher beings which take up temporary residence in objects, plants, or specific places are worshipped. Following the introduction of Buddhism to Japan during the 6th century, these two main religions came to influence each other considerably. Today, the majority of Japanese observe both Shintoist and Buddhist practices of worship.

shitomi   Architectural detail: "timber shutters or doors that generally have vertical and horizontal lattices."[10]

Shōgun (*seii taishōgun*)   Military title: from 1192–1868, the hereditary office of the military leader of Japan. While theoretically appointed by the emperor, the shōgun and his administration, *bakufu*, acted autocratically.

shoin zukuri   Architectural term: "shoin style" (of building). A set of characteristics typical of residential buildings starting in about the 15th century. Departing from the strict and ritually regulated arrangements of *shinden*, the residential parts became much less symmetrical and more compact: the round supports were replaced by square ones thanks to the development of carpenter's tools,

---

9   *Shinden zukuri*, in: JAANUS, here http://www.aisf.or.jp/~jaanus/deta/s/shindenzukuri.htm [accessed 15 July 2019].

10   *Shitomi*, in: JAANUS, here http://www.aisf.or.jp/~jaanus/deta/s/shitomi.htm [accessed 18 July 2019].

thus making it possible to join rooms directly and to divide the interiors of large spatial units using sliding doors of different kinds. This went along with the use of wall-to-wall *tatami* flooring in the living area and the furnishing of the main reception room, *shoin*, with functional and decorative elements such as *tokonoma, chigaidana* and a built-in desk.[11]

shōji   Architectural detail: sliding doors made from a wooden lattice covered with translucent rice paper. Historically, the term encompassed a much broader meaning that included diverse types of partitions and covering materials. Today, Western literature largely distingushes between *shōji*, used towards the aisles and the exterior of the house to take advantage of natural light, and opaque *fusuma*, used between rooms or for closets.

Shrine (*jinja, jingu*)   Sanctuary of *shintō* worship.

sōrin   Architectural element: the finial of a pagoda.

sudare   Architectural detail: blinds made from the stems of plants such as bamboo. They protect the house interior from the sun while ensuring high air permeability.

sukiya zukuri   Architectural term: "sukiya style" (of building). A set of characteristics typical of residential buildings as of the beginning of the Edo period in the 17th century. The overall idea was derived from *shoin zukuri* but was applied with a greater freedom of design and use of materials. It is assumed that *sukiya zukuri* was influenced by, among other things, the architecture of rooms and buildings for *chadō*.[12]

sutra   Buddhist writing.

Taishō period   Reign of Emperor Yoshihito (1879–1926) from 1912 to 1926.

tatami   Architectural detail: floor panel made from rice straw in the size of an adult's sleeping area. The compacted rice straw of the panel is covered by tightly woven grass and bordered with strips of fabric. While the dimensions vary regionally and historically, a standard measure is about 1.80 m by 0.90 m by 0.05 m. The arrangement of *tatami* within the room, the quality of the covering, the types and colours of the cloth border and many more factors were historically dependent on local practices and social status.

Temple (*tera*)   Sanctuary and/or monastery of Buddhist worship.

tennō   Designation for the Japanese emperor, dynastic ruler of Japan.

tōkaidō   Most important trade street/highway route in Japan, connecting Edo/Tōkyō with Kyōto.

---

11   *Shoin zukuri*, in: JAANUS, here http://www.aisf.or.jp/~jaanus/deta/s/shoinzukuri.htm [accessed 15 July 2019].

12   See the extensive entry on *sukiya zukuri*, in: JAANUS, here http://www.aisf.or.jp/~jaanus/deta/s/sukiyazukuri.htm [accessed 15 July 2019].

tokonoma   Alcove, element of the interior design of *shoin*, often together with *chigaidana*.

Tokugawa period   Era between 1603 and 1867 in which the Tokugawa family ruled Japan = Edo period.

torii   Architectural element: gate signifying a *shintō* precinct.

ukiyo-e   'pictures of the floating world'. "Paintings and woodblock prints of genre themes developed from the mid-Edo to early Meiji periods, supported by the people in the middle class of society (…) mainly in the city of Edo."[13]

yashiki   Architectural structure: habitation of a *daimyō* in the time of obligatory residence in Edo, *sankin kōtai*, during the Tokugawa reign.

yagōmon   Abstract sign or symbol denoting the shop name or firm similar to a crest or logo.

yokohama-e   'Yokohama pictures', a sub-genre of *ukiyo-e* addressing phenomena that arose around the foreign settlement.

---

13   *Ukiyo-e*, in: JAANUS, here https://www.aisf.or.jp/%7Ejaanus/deta/u/ukiyoe.htm [accessed 28 August 2023].

Glossary of Persons

Adams, Henry   (1838–1918). American historian.
Adams, William   (1564–1620). English navigator in Service of a Dutch East India company.
Alcock, Rutherford   (1809–1897). British physician and diplomat in East Asia, serving in Japan from 1858 to 1865.
Arnold, Charles Dudley   (1844–1927). American photographer.
Audsley, George Ashdown   (1838–1925). Scottish architect and artist, author and co-author of books about Japanese art.
Ayrton, William Edward   (1847–1908). British physicist, contracted expert, among others at the Imperial College of Engineering.
Baltzer, Franz   (1857–1927). German railway engineer, hired foreign expert between 1898 and 1903.
Bauduin, Anthonius Franciscus   (1820–1885). Dutch physician, active primarily in Nagasaki for several years during the 1860s.
Beato, Felice   (1832–1909). Photographer, born in Italy, resident in Japan between 1863 and 1884.
Bing, Samuel   (1838–1905). German-French art expert and art dealer.
Bishop, Isabelle   (born Bird; 1831–1904). World traveller and author visiting Japan during the 1870s and again in the 1890s.
Böckmann, Wilhelm   (1832–1902). German architect, partner of the office Böckmann & Ende, visiting Japan in 1886 in the course of negotiations concerning designs for Tōkyō's government district.
Bousquet, Georges Hilaire   (1845–1937). French legal scholar.
Bowes, James Lord   (1834–1899). British businessman, art collector and author.
Brandt, Max von   (1835–1920). German diplomat, member of the Prussian expedition to Japan in 1859–1861.
Brinckmann, Justus   (1843–1915). German art historian and museum director.
Brown, Eliphalet M.   (1816–1886). US-American artist, member of the Perry expedition to Japan.
Brown, Samuel R.   (1810–1880). US-American missionary, initially responsible for the American legislation, later with other activities and interests in Japan; formative member of the Asiatic Society of Japan.
Brunton, Richard Henry   (1841–1901). Scottish civil engineer hired by the Japanese government as a foreign expert.
Burges, William   (1927–1831). British architect.
Burty, Philippe   (1830–1890). French art critic, art collector, and graphic artist said to have coined the term *Japonisme*.

Cawley, George (1848–1927). English civil and mechanical engineer, instructor at the Imperial College of Engineering in Tōkyō 1873–1878.
Chamberlain, Basil Hall (1850–1935). British Japanologist.
Champier, Victor (1851–1929). French art critic and educator.
Chassiron, Charles de (1818–1871). French diplomat.
Choisy, Auguste (1841–1909). French civil engineer.
Conder, Josiah (1852–1920). English architect and founding professor of the Chair of (Western) Architecture at the Imperial College of Engineering in Tōkyō in 1876/77.
Cram, Ralph A. (1863–1942). American architect, major representative of neo-Gothic architecture and theory at the turn of the 20th century.
Craven, Hawes (1837–1910). English scene painter and designer for a number of theatres.
Daidōji Yūzan (1639–1730). 大道寺友山. Japanese military strategist and author.
Daly, César (1811–1894). French architect and writer.
Demmin, August (1817–1898). German art historian and collector.
Doeff, Hendrik (1764–1837). Dutch commissioner of Dejima, the Dutch trading colony in Nagasaki.
Dooman, Isaac (1857–1931). Persian born American, missionary of the American Episcopal Mission for more than 30 years.
Dresser, Christopher (1834–1904). English designer, travelling Japan in 1876–1877 as an official British emissary in terms of Japanese art.
Dubard, Maurice (1845–1929). French naval officer.
Dumoulin, Louis-Jules (1860–1924). French artist and traveller.
Enami Nobukuni (1859–1929). 江南信國. Japanese photographer.
Farsari, Adolfo (1841–1898). Italian publisher and, later, photographer based in Yokohama between 1873 and 1890.
Fenollosa, Ernest F. (1853–1908). American philosopher and orientalist with much impact on the discourses on Japanese art.
Fergusson, James (1808–1886). British architect and architectural writer with a focus on Indian architecture.
Fletcher, Sir Banister (1833–1899). English architect and writer.
Foote, Andrew Hull (1806–1863). Member of the US Navy, commanding officer in the East India Squadron during the Second Opium War.
Freeman-Mitford, Algernon B. (1837–1916). British diplomat and writer.
Fróis, Luís (1532–1597). Portuguese missionary.
Garnier, Charles (1825–1898). French architect.
Gilbert, William S. (1836–1911). English dramatist, often cooperating with Arthur Sullivan.

GLOSSARY OF PERSONS 359

Godwin, Edward William (1833–1886). English architect and early admirer of Japanese art.
Gogh, Vincent van (1853–1890). Dutch painter, formative figure in the development of modern expression of European art.
Golownin, Wassili Michailowitsch (1776–1831). Russian navigator and high-ranking naval officer.
Gonse, Louis (1846–1921). French art historian, writer and early expert in Japanese art.
Griffis, William Elliot (1843–1928). American orientalist and writer.
Gropius, Walter (1883–1969). German-American architect, primary representative of the Modern Movement in architecture; founder and director of the Bauhaus school in Weimar and Dessau (1919–1928).
Guérineau, Abel Jean-Louis (1841–1929). French architect and naval officer, contracted by the Japanese government between 1874 and 1889.
Guimet, Émile (1836–1918). French collector, travelling Japan with Félix Régamey.
Harada, Jiro (1878–1963). 原田治郎. Japanese author, contributed to English-language information on Japanese art in the early 20th century.
Hasegawa Settan (1778–1843). 長谷川雪旦. Japanese artist.
Haussmann, Georges-Eugène (1809–1891). French official, responsible for the renovation of Paris from 1853 to 1870.
Hawks, Francis L. (1798–1866). American writer and historian, member of Matthew C. Perry's expedition to Japan.
Hayashi Tadamasa (1851–1906). 林忠正. Japanese art dealer in Europe.
Heine, Wilhelm (1827–1885). German artist, member of the Perry expedition.
Hepburn, James Curtis (1815–1911). American missionary and linguist, known for his system of Romanization.
Heusken, Hendrick (1832–1861). Dutch born member of the American Legation in Japan who died after an ambush in 1861.
Hildreth, Richard (1807–1865). American writer.
Hobrecht, James (1825–1902). Prussian architect and public employee in the field of urban planning in Berlin.
Hogarth, William (1697–1764). English artist and art writer.
Holme, Charles (1848–1923). British journalist and collector, founder of the journal *The Studio*.
Holmes, Elias Burton (1870–1958). American traveller and photographer.
Hübner, Alexander Graf von (1811–1892). Austrian diplomat and early visitor to Japan.
Humbert, Aimé (1819–1900). Swiss politician and diplomat, posted to Japan in 1863–1864.

Ishida Saijirō / Ishida Kyokuzan (1847–1926). 石田, 才治郎 / 石田旭山. Japanese printmaker and publisher.
Ishii Keikichi (1866–1932). 石井敬吉. Japanese architect.
Jancigny, Adolphe Philibert Dubois de (1795–1860). French explorer and diplomat serving in India and China during the First Opium War.
Jarves, James Jackson (1818–1888). American art historian and collector.
Jaucourt, Louis de (1704–1779). French physician and scholar.
Kaempfer, Engelbert (1651–1716). German physician under contract with the Dutch East India Company (VOC), served at the Dutch settlement in Nagasaki between 1690 and 1692.
Kajima Seibei (1866–1924). 鹿島清兵衛. Japanese photographer.
Karow, Otto (1913–1992). German Japanologist.
Katsushika Hokusai (1760–1849). 葛飾北斎. Japanese *ukiyo-e* artist, among the most influential representatives of the genre.
Kawakami Otojiro (1864–1911). 川上音二郎. Japanese actor and leader of theatre company.
Kawakami Sada Yacco (1871–1946). 川上貞奴. Japanese *geisha*, actress and dancer travelling the world with the theatrical company of Kawakami Otojiro.
Kimball, Fiske (1888–1955). American architect and architectural historian.
Kishida Hideto (1899–1966). 岸田日出刀. Japanese architect and writer.
Klaproth, Heinrich Julius (1783–1835). German Orientalist, expert in languages.
Kobayashi Kiyochika (1847–1915). 小林清親. Japanese *ukiyo-e* artist.
Kubota Beisen (1852–1906). 久保田米僊. Japanese artist, art instructor and picture reporter.
Kuki Ryuichi (1852–1931). Japanese commissioner director of the Tōkyō National Museum.
Kuru Masamichi (1855–1914). 久留正道. Western-trained Japanese architect.
Kusakabe Kimbei (1841–1934). 日下部金兵衛. Japanese photographer primarily famous for his souvenir albums including reprints of other colleagues.
La Farge, John (1835–1910). American painter and writer.
Le Corbusier (Charles-Édouard Jeanneret; 1887–1965). Swiss-French architect and theoretician, main protagonist of architectural modernism in France and Western Europe.
Leighton, John (1822–1912). English artist.
Leopold II of Belgium (1835–1909). King of the Belgians (1865–1909).
Lescasse, Jules (1842–1901). French civil engineer and architect, realising a number of projects in Japan between 1871 and 1892.
Lévi, Édouard (Edward) named Montefiore (1826–1906/7). Engineer, resident in Paris and employed at the finance house Cahen d'Anvers et Compagnie.

GLOSSARY OF PERSONS 361

Levieux, Fernand   (1870–1896). Belgian jurist and traveller.
Lichtwark, Alfred   (1852–1914). German art historian and educator.
Lindau, Rudolph   (1829–1910). German journalist and diplomat.
Linfoot, Benjamin   (1840–1912). English-born US-American architect and lithographer.
Loos, Adolf   (1870–1933). Austrian architect and critic, leading representative of modernism in Austria.
Lowell, Percival L.   (1855–1916). American astronomer, diplomat and author.
Machida Hisanari   (1838–1879). 町田久成. Public employee at the Japanese Ministry of Education and leader of the Jinshin Survey in 1872.
Marcel, Alexandre   (1860–1928). French architect.
Maron, Hermann   (1820–1882). German agriculturist and journalist, member of the Prussian diplomatic mission to Japan 1859–1862.
Mathews, Charles Thompson   (1863–1934). American architect.
Matsuo, Ihei   (dates unknown). 松尾伊兵衛. Japanese master carpenter, responsible for the national pavilions at the World's Fairs in Vienna and Philadelphia.
McClatchie, Thomas Russell Hillier   (1852–1886). British member of the Consular Service in Japan since 1870.
McVean, Colin Alexander   (1838–1912). Scottish civil engineer, initially member of Brunton's lighthouse team and serving in Japan between 1868 and 1876.
Meijlan, Germain Felix   (1785–1831). Dutch civil servant at Batavia and later head of Dutch Trade in Japan.
Menpes, Mortimer   (1855–1938). Australian painter.
Mies van der Rohe, Ludwig   (1886–1969). German-American architect, one of the primary representatives of the Modern Movement.
Milne, John   (1850–1913). British geologist, Founding Professor of mining and geology at the Imperial College of Engineering, seismologist.
Minamoto Toyomune   (1895–2001). 源豊宗. Japanese art historian.
Monet, Claude   (1840–1926). French painter, formative figure of Impressionism.
Montanus, Albertus   (1625–1683). Dutch theologian, historian and writer.
Mori Arinori   (1847–1889). 森有礼. Japanese government official and diplomat.
Morse, Edward Sylvester   (1838–1925). American zoologist and archaeologist, residing in Japan first between 1877 and 1880.
Moser, Michael   (1853–1912). Austrian photographer, largely resident in Japan between 1869 and 1877, and travelling for Japan in the course of the World's Fairs in Vienna and Philadelphia.
Mothes, Oskar   (1828–1903). German architect and art historian.
Münsterberg, Oskar   (1865–1920). German manufacturer and art historian.
Muramatsu Kichizō   (dates unknown). 村松吉蔵. Japanese model builder.

Musashiya Kamakichi/Manba Kamakichi (dates unknown). 武蔵屋鎌吉/万場鎌. Japanese model builder, head of the workshop Musashiya, gaining recognition with objects submitted to the World's Fairs in Vienna and Paris (1876).

Musashiya Yonekichi (dates unknown). 武蔵屋米吉. Japanese model builder, head of the workshop Musashiya, submitting price winning objects to the World's Fairs in Chicago and Paris (1900).

Muthesius, Hermann (1861–1927). German architect, employee of Böckmann & Ende in Tōkyō (1887–1891).

Neumann, Karl Friedrich (1793–1870). German orientalist and Sinologist, collector of the largest collection of Chinese books at this time.

Nicholson, Peter (1765–1844). Scottish architect.

Niijima Jō/Neesima, Joseph Hardy (1843–1890). 新島襄. Japanese educator, founder of a Christian college in Kyōto that became the Doshisha University over time.

Niijima Yae (born Yamamoto; 1845–1932). 新島八重. Japanese educator, school founder and nurse.

Niwa Keisuke (1856–1941). 丹羽圭介. Japanese merchant and director of the Kyōto Commercial Museum.

Ogawa Kazumasa (1860–1929). 小川一眞. Japanese photographer, collotypist and publisher.

Ogawa Sashichi (†1909). 小川佐七. Japanese photographer with a studio in Yokohama.

Okakura Kakuzō (1863–1913). 岡倉覚三. Japanese art critic, educator and writer.

Oliphant, Laurence (1829–1888). South African-born British author, traveller and diplomat.

Ōmori Fusakichi (1868–1923). 大森房吉. Japanese physicist and seismologist, formative figure in the development of the field.

Ōno Hiroki (1788–1841). 大野広城. Japanese author of books about the life and functions of *bushi*.

Overmeer-Fisscher, Johannes Gerhard Frederik van (1800–1848). Dutch employee at the Deshima trading post (Nagasaki).

Parker, Peter (1804–1888). American physician and a missionary serving in China.

Parkes, Sir Harry Smith (1828–1885). British diplomat serving in Japan between 1865 and 1883.

Perry, John (1850–1920). Irish engineer and physicist teaching at the Imperial College of Engineering in Tōkyō between 1875 and 1879; influential in the emerging field of seismology.

Perry, Matthew C. (1794–1858). US naval officer heading the 1853–1854 expedition that forced Japan to end its isolationist policy and to enter into trade and diplomatic relations with the West.

GLOSSARY OF PERSONS

Pfoundes, Charles James William   (1840–1907). Irish born in the service of the Australian navy when first arriving in Japan in 1863. Active throughout his life as a translator and mediator between Japanese and western actors and institutions.

Pugin, Augustus W. N.   (1812–1852). English architect, theoretician and publicist; protagonist of Gothic Revival.

Rai San'yo   (1780–1832). 頼山陽. Japanese author of the Nihon Gu'aishi 日本外史, 1836–1837.

Ramée, Daniel   (1806–1887). French architect and art historian.

Régamey, Félix   (1844–1907). French artist, travelling Japan with Émile Guimet.

Rein, Johannes Justus   (1835–1881). German geographer and Japanologist.

Rosny, Léon de   (1837–1914). French ethnologist and orientalist.

Ruskin, John   (1819–1900). English writer, philosopher and art critic; formative figure in the theory of heritage conservation.

Saitō (Gesshin) Yukinari   (1804–1878). 藤月岑. Japanese author.

Sakata Haruo   (1849–1915). 坂田春雄. Japanese translator and government official involved in cultural exchange.

Satow, Ernest Mason   (1843–1929). British diplomat serving in Japan initially between 1862 and 1884 and as minister plenipotentiary from 1895 to 1900.

Schliemann, Heinrich   (1822–1890). German businessman and archaeologist; travelled Asia and the Americas in 1865.

Scidmore, Eliza   (1856–1928). American journalist, repeatedly visiting Japan from the mid-1880s onwards.

Seckel, Dietrich   (1910–2007). German art historian, formative figure in the establishment of East Asian art history in German academia.

Shiga Shigetsura   (1866–1936). Japanese architect, trained at the University of Illinois, university teacher and author involved in housing reform debates.

Shimizu Kisuke II   (1815–1881). 清水喜助. Japanese carpenter blending architectural forms of Japanese and western traditions.

Shimizu Usaburō   (1829–1910). 清水卯三郎. Japanese merchant involved in cultural exchange.

Shimooka Renjo   (1823–1914). 下岡蓮杖. Japanese artist and photographer.

Siebold, Heinrich von   (1852–1908). German, entering the Service of the Austrian legislation in Tōkyō in 1871 and spending most of his life in Japan as a translator, collector and writer.

Siebold, Philipp Franz von   (1796–1866). German physician and naturalist serving with the VOC in Nagasaki between 1823 and 1829 and returning to Japan 1859 and 1863.

Smith, Thomas Roger   (1830–1903). English architect.

Sone Tatsuzō   (1852–1937). 曽禰達蔵. Japanese architect, graduate of the first cohort trained at the Imperial College of Engineering in Tōkyō.

Spiers, Richard Phené (1838–1916). British architect.
Stein, Ernst Ludwig von (1858–1929). German economist, visiting Japan 1887–1888 on behalf of his father Lorenz von Stein (1815–1890), a German economist who advised the Japanese government.
Stillfried, Baron Raimund von (1839–1911). Austrian photographer and entrepreneur.
Strahan, Edward (Earl Shinn; 1837–1886). American art historian and art writer.
Strange, Edward F. (1862–1926). Curator at the Victoria and Albert Museum in London.
Sullivan, Arthur (1842–1900). English composer, often cooperating with William S. Gilbert.
Suzuki Shin'ichi (1855–1912). 鈴木真一. Japanese photographer.
Syle, Edward W. (1817–1890). American missionary, pastor of the British consulate at Yokohama 1872–1874 and later teaching on behalf of the Japanese government until 1879.
Symonds, John Addington (1840–1893). English writer and art historian.
Taine, Hippolyte (1828–1893). French philosopher and historian.
Tamamura Kozaburo (1856–1923?). 玉村康三郎. Japanese photographer with influential studios in Tōkyō and Yokohama.
Terajima Ryōan (*1654). 寺島良安. Japanese scholar, editor of the encyclopaedia Wakan Sansai Zue 和漢三才図会.
Thunberg, Carl Peter (1743–1828). Swedish naturalist residing in the Dutch trading post of Deshima in 1775–1776.
Titsingh, Isaac (1745–1812). Dutch commissioner of Dejima, the Dutch trading colony in Nagasaki.
Tokugawa Ieyasu (1543–1616). 徳川家康. Daimyō and commander; third of the three unifiers of the Japanese empire and founder of the Tokugawa shōgunate.
Tokugawa A family that traced its origins to Emperor Seiwa (9th c.) and the Minamoto family. After Tokugawa Ieyasu's victory in the Battle of Sekigahara in 1600, they established a dynasty of shōgun and ruled until 1868. The seat of power was Edo (today Tōkyō).
Tomishige Rihei (1837–1922). 富重利平. Japanese photographer with centre of work in Kyūshū.
Tsumaki Yorinaka (1859–1916). 妻木頼黄. Japanese architect trained at the Imperial College of Engineering, in the US and Germany.
Uchida Kuichi (ca. 1844–1875). 内田九一. Japanese photographer with studios in Osaka, Yokohama and Tōkyō.
Ueno Hikoma (1838–1904). 上野彦馬. Pioneering Japanese photographer with centre of work in Nagasaki.
Usui Shuzaburo (dates unknown). 臼井秀三郎. Japanese photographer during the Meiji era.

GLOSSARY OF PERSONS

Utagawa (Gountei) Sadahide (1807–1878/79). 歌川貞秀. Japanese *ukiyo-e* artist.
Utagawa Hiroshige (1797–1858). 歌川広重. Japanese artist, master of *ukiyo-e*.
Utagawa Hiroshige III (1842–1894). 三代歌川広重. Japanese *ukiyo-e* artist.
Utagawa Kuniteru II (1830–1874). 二代歌川国輝. Japanese print designer, painter and book illustrator.
Utagawa Kunitsuna (dates unknown). 歌川国綱. Japanese *ukiyo-e* artist during Edo period.
Wagener, Gottfried (1831–1892). German naturalist, contracted in different contexts by firms and governmental bodies in Japan, consultant of the Japanese government for the World Exhibition in Vienna.
Watanabe Yuzuru (1855–1930). 渡辺譲. Japanese architect and educator.
Waters, Thomas James (1842–1898). Irish civil engineer, contracted in different contexts by firms and governmental bodies in Japan between 1865 and 1875.
Westcott, Thompson (1820–1888). American editor.
Williams, Samuel Wells (1812–1884). Missionary of the American Board Mission, member of the Perry expedition to Japan.
Wores, Theodore (1859–1939). American painter.
Wright, Frank L. (1867–1959). American architect and educator, most prominent US-architect of the 20th century, especially renowned for his residential buildings; collector of Japanese woodblock prints and active in Japan between 1917 and 1922.
Yamagata Daini (1725–1767). 山縣大貳. Japanese scholar and critic of the Tokugawa shōgunate.
Yamamoto Kakuma (1828–1892). 山本覺馬. Japanese scholar, social reformer and promotor of western knowledge.
Yokoyama Matsusaburo (1838–1884). 横山松三郎. Japanese photographer, participant in the Jinshin Survey in 1872.

Bibliography

Periodicals That Were Subjected to Systematic Analysis

(Das) Werk (1914–1976).
American Architect and Building News (1876–1938, analysed 1876–1909).
Architectural Record (1891–, analysed 1891–1924).
Centralblatt der Bauverwaltung (1881–1931).
Deutsche Bauzeitung (1867–, analysed 1867–1923).
Deutsche Kunst und Dekoration (1897–1932).
Die Gartenlaube (1853–1984, analysed 1853–1908).
Die Kunst für Alle (1885–1943).
Gazette des beaux-arts (1859–1925), L'art (1875–1907).
Journal asiatique (1822–, analysed 1855–1940).
Journal of the North China Branch of the Royal Asiatic Society (1858–1948, analysed 1858–1922).
L'architecture (1888–1939).
L'architecture d'aujourd'hui (1930–, analysed 1930–1940).
La construction moderne (1885–, analysed 1885–1938).
L'Esprit nouveau (1920–1925).
Mitteilungen der deutschen Gesellschaft für Natur- und Völkerkunde Ostasiens (1873–, analysed 1873–1979).
Nachrichten der OAG (1926–, analysed 1926–1985).
Österreichische Monatsschrift für den Orient (1875–1918).
Revue française du Japon (1892–1897).
Revue orientale et américainee (1859–1900, analysed 1859–1875).
RIBA Journal (1884–, analysed 1884–1893).
Schweizerische Bauzeitung (1883–1978).
Studio: International Art (1893–1925).
The Art Journal (1839–1912, evaluated 1849–1912).
The British Architect and Northern Engineer (1875–1919).
The Builder. A Journal for the Architect & Constructor (1842–, analysed 1851–1926 via indexes).
The Building News and Engineering Journal (1854–1926, analysed 1860–1926, partially via indexes).
The Chinese and Japanese Repository (1863–1865).
Transactions and Proceedings of the Japan Society, London (1892–1941, analysed 1892–1928).

Transactions of the Asiatic Society of Japan (1874–, analysed 1874–1910).
Über Land und Meer (1858–1923, analysed 1860–1911).
Ver Sacrum (1896–1903).
Zeitschrift der Deutschen Morgenländischen Gesellschaft (1847–).
Zeitschrift für Bauwesen (1851–1931, analysed 1851–1900).

Digital Resources

Abel, Laszlo, "Thomas Russell Hillier McClatchie (1852–1886)," http://www.aikidojournal.com/article?articleID=710 [Download 17 July 2013].
Asia at the World's Fairs, Pardee School of Global Studies (Center for the Study of Asia), https://www.asiaworldsfairs.org/ [accessed 21 August 2023].
Baxley, George C., "Eliphalet M. Brown, Jr. Daguerreotypist and Artist for the Perry Expedition To Japan," http://www.baxleystamps.com, here http://www.baxleystamps.com/litho/brown.shtml [accessed 21 August 2023].
Boston Museum of Fine Arts, William S. and John T. Spaulding Collection, https://collections.mfa.org/collections/ [21.08.2023].
Bridgeman Images, https://www.bridgemanimages.com/de/ [accessed 21 August 2023].
British History Online, *Survey of London*, online-resource, https://www.british-history.ac.uk/search/series/survey-london [accessed 21 August 2023], here esp. "Knightsbridge Green Area: Scotch Corner and the High Road," on: British History Online, *Survey of London*, https://www.british-history.ac.uk/survey-london/vol45/pp79-88#h3-0006 [accessed 15 April 2018].
"The Japanese Native Village," on: British History Online, *Survey of London*, https://www.british-history.ac.uk/survey-london/vol45/pp79-88#h3-0006 [accessed 15 April 2018], s.p.
Campbell-Dollaghan, Kelsey, "Beautiful Pieces of the 1893 World's Fair Discovered In Storage In Chicago," on: https://gizmodo.com/beautiful-pieces-of-the-1893-worlds-fair-discovered-in-1726922526 [accessed 30 April 2019].
City of Yokohama, library, digital archive, https://www.city.yokohama.lg.jp.e.sj.hp.transer.com/kurashi/kyodo-manabi/library/shuroku/digitalarchive.html [accessed 21 August 2023].
Clericuzio, Peter, "The Shifting Meanings and Uses of the Japanese Tower at Laeken, paper given at 'The Object and Beyond,'" Third Annual Graduate Conference of the Pennsylvania State University Graduate Student Association for Visual Culture, University Park, PA, March 2011 via https://www.academia.edu/2606248/The_Shifting_Meanings_and_Uses_of_the_Japanese_Tower_at_Laeken [accessed 6 May 2019].

Downer, Lesley, "Sadayakko in London, 14.03.2017," via The History Girls, http://the-history-girls.blogspot.com/2017/03/sadayakko-in-london-by-lesley-downer.html [accessed 21 August 2023].

Duplessis, Hervé, "Un lis japonais au Trocadéro," 12 May 2017, on: https://blogpourmemoire.wordpress.com/2017/05/12/un-lis-japonais-au-trocadero/ [accessed 1 August 2023].

Free Library of Philadelphia, Digital Collections, https://libwww.freelibrary.org/digital/ [accessed 21 August 2023], here esp. "Centennial Exhibition 1876 Philadelphia Scrapbook," on: Free Library of Philadelphia, Digital Collections, https://libwww.freelibrary.org/digital/ [accessed 2 July 2019].

Getty Images International, https://www.gettyimages.de/ [21 August 2023].

Harvard College Library, "Early photography of Japan," online-resource, https://curiosity.lib.harvard.edu/early-photography-of-japan [accessed 19 July 2023].

Harvard University, Widener Library, E. G. Stillman photograph albums of Japan and Korea, ca. 1870–ca. 1900, http://id.lib.harvard.edu/alma/990074672500203941/catalog [accessed 21 August 2023].

Historic England, online resource, https://historicengland.org.uk [accessed 1 July 2019], here esp. "Alexandra Palace," on: Historic England, Listing 1001253: https://historicengland.org.uk/listing/the-list/list-entry/1001253 [accessed 1 July 2019].

International Research Center for Japanese studies (nichibunken), *Images of Japan in Non-Japanese Sources*, 5 vols., https://www.nichibun.ac.jp/en/publications/data/gaiz/ [accessed 29 July 2023].

JAANUS. Japanese architecture and art net users system, hosted by Atsumi International Foundation, http://www.aisf.or.jp/~jaanus/ [accessed 21 August 2023].

Library of congress, https://www.loc.gov/, here esp. Ciceri, Eugène; Benoist, Philippe, "Vue officielle a vol d'oiseau de l'exposition universelle de 1867," hand-coloured lithograph, 68 × 98.5 cm, 1867, Library of Congress, https://www.loc.gov/pictures/item/00652015/ [accessed 25 June 2022].

Lafayette College Easton, Pen., East Asia Image Collection, https://dss.lafayette.edu/collections/east-asia-image-collection [accessed 21 August 2023].

Lepach, Bernd: Meiji Portraits, online resource, http://meiji-portraits.de/ [last accessed 15 May 2024].

Massachusetts Institute of Technology: Visualizing Cultures – Image-Driven Scholarship, online-resource, https://visualizingcultures.mit.edu/home/index.html [accessed 21 August 2023].

Musée national des arts asiatiques – Guimet, Paris, département Photographie, Japon, albums de photographies, https://www.guimet-photo-japon.fr/index.php [accessed 21 August 2023].

Museum für angewandte Kunst Wien, https://sammlung.mak.at/ [accessed 21 August 2023].

Nagasaki University Library, Metadata Database of Japanese Old Photographs in Bakumatsu-Meiji Period, http://oldphoto.lb.nagasaki-u.ac.jp/en/about.html [accessed 21 August 2023].

National Diet Library Tokyo, https://www.ndl.go.jp/en/index.html, here esp. "Expositions. Where the modern technology of the times was exhibited." http://www.ndl.go.jp/exposition/e/s1/1873.html [accessed 9 August 2023]; "The Landmarks of Edo in Colour Woodblock Prints," https://www.ndl.go.jp/landmarks/e/ [accessed 21 August 2023]; "Second London International Exposition of 1862. First international exposition seen by Japanese," web presentation, http://www.ndl.go.jp/exposition/e/s1/1862-1.html [accessed 26 April 2018].

National Library of Australia, https://catalogue.nla.gov.au/ [accessed 21 August 2023].

New York Metropolitan Museum of Art, https://www.metmuseum.org/ [accessed 21 August 2023].

New York Public Library, digital collections, The Miriam and Ira D. Wallach Division of Art, Prints and Photographs: Photography Collection, https://digitalcollections.nypl.org/divisions/the-miriam-and-ira-d-wallach-division-of-art-prints-and-photographs-photography [accessed 21 August 2023].

Nihon Minka-en, Japan Open-Air Folk House Museum, in Kawasaki, https://www.nihonminkaen.jp/index_english.html [accessed 21 August 08.2023].

Old Photos of Japan, photo blog, https://oldphotosjapan.com [accessed 21 August 2023].

"Perry In Japan: A Visual History," A joint project of Brown University Library and the Department of American Studies, online resource, https://library.brown.edu/cds/perry/about.html [accessed 21 August 2023].

Petit, Pierre; Bisson (jeune); Michelez, Charles-Louis, *Exposition universelle*. 1867. Paris (album with 100 photographs, Bibliothèque Historique de la Ville de Paris, 2-ALB-0042).

Scheid, Bernhard, *Religion in Japan. Ein Web-Handbuch*, https://www.univie.ac.at/rel_jap/an/Religion-in-Japan [accessed 21 August 2023], here esp. "Der Große Buddha von Kamakura," https://www.univie.ac.at/rel_jap/an/Essays/Daibutsu_Statuen#Der_Gro.C3.9Fe_Buddha_von_Kamakura [accessed 10 July 2019]; "Shinbutsu bunri. Trennung von kami und Buddhas," https://www.univie.ac.at/rel_jap/an/Geschichte/Staatsshinto/Shinbutsu_bunri [accessed 10 July 2019].

Sénéchal, Philippe; Barbillon, Claire (ed.), *Dictionnaire critique des historiens de l'art actifs en France de la Révolution à la Première Guerre mondiale*, via Institut national d'histoire de l'art, https://www.inha.fr/fr/ressources/publications/publications-numeriques/dictionnaire-critique-des-historiens-de-l-art/gonse-louis.html [accessed 18 August 2023].

Sundberg, Steve, "Old Tokyo. Vintage Japanese Postcard Museum. 1900–1960," https://www.oldtokyo.com/ [accessed 21 August 2023].

The Architectural Institute of Japan, *hinagatabon*, https://www.aij.or.jp/da1/hinagata/kizou.html [accessed 21 August 2023].

The British Museum, collection database, https://www.britishmuseum.org/collection [accessed 21 August 2023].

Tōkyō National Museum, https://www.tnm.jp/, e-Museum, since September 2020 partially via https://colbase.nich.go.jp [last accessed 20 May 2024], here esp. "Jinshin Survey related photographs," https://emuseum.nich.go.jp/detail?langId=en&webView=&content_base_id=100817&content_part_id=0&content_pict_id=0 [accessed 21 August 2023]; "Jinshin Survey related materials," https://emuseum.nich.go.jp/detail?langId=en&webView=&content_base_id=100815&content_part_id=0&content_pict_id=0 [accessed 21 August 2023]; "Photograph Album of the former Edo Castle," https://emuseum.nich.go.jp/detail?langId=en&webView=&content_base_id=100813&content_part_id=0&content_pict_id=0 [accessed 21 August 2023]; "Tokyo National Museum, History of the TNM," https://www.tnm.jp/modules/r_free_page/index.php?id=143 [accessed 21 August 2023].

Tokyo Research Institute for Cultural Properties (Tōbunken), "Exhibition catalogue of the 1st and 2nd special exhibition (combined) Tokyo Imperial Museum, List of the works of the Exhibition of Japanese Art held at the Paris World Exposition in 1900," https://www.tobunken.go.jp/~joho/japanese/collection/paris/paris-e.html [18.08.2023].

Van Gogh Museum Amsterdam, Collection, https://www.vangoghmuseum.nl/en/collection [accessed 21 August 2023].

Weltmuseum Wien, https://www.weltmuseumwien.at/onlinesammlung/ [accessed 21 August 2023].

Printed Matter

"A Japanese Village in London," in: *British architect* 23.2 (9 January 1885), p. 15.

"A Japanese village in London," in: *The Times* (10 January 1885), p. 6.

"A Japanese village," in: *The Building news and engineering journal* 48 (16 January 1885), pp. 77–78.

A veritable Japanese village under the sanction of the Imperial Japanese Government. Souvenir booklet for exhibitions of the Japanese Village Company held at Horticultural Halls in Boston, 1886 (Boston, 1886).

Ainsworth, William, *All around the world. An illustrated record of voyages, travels, and adventures in all parts of the globe*, 2 vols. (London and Glasgow, 1866).

Aitken, Geneviève; Delafond, Marianne, *La Collection D'estampes Japonaises de Claude Monet à Giverny* (Lausanne, 2003).

Akisato, Ritō, *Miyako meisho zue* [Guide to Famous Places in Kyōto] [Kyōto, 1780].
Alcock, Rutherford, *Art and Art Industries in Japan* (London, 1878).
Alcock, Rutherford, *Catalogue of works of industry and art*, sent from Japan. International Exhibition, 1862 (London, 1862).
Alcock, Rutherford, "Japanese Art," in: *Art Journal* (1875), pp. 101–105, 201–206, 333–334; (1876), pp. 41–44, 113–116; (1877), pp. 41–44, 97–99, 161–163; (1878), pp. 1–3, 137–140.
Alcock, Rutherford, *The capital of the tycoon. A narrative of a three years' residence in Japan*, 2 vols. (London, 1863).
"Alexandra Palace [Architectural, Engineering, and Local Public Works]," in: *British architect* 1 (15 May 1874), p. 315.
Allsobrook, David; Mitchell, Gordon, "Henry Dyer: Engineer and Educational Innovator," in: *Paedagogica Historica. International Journal of the History of Education* 33.2 (1997), pp. 433–457.
Anderson, Christy, "Writing the Architectural Survey. Collective Authorities and Competing Approaches," in: *Journal of the Society of Architectural Historians* 58.3, Architectural History 1999/2000 (Sept. 1999), pp. 350–355.
Anderson, Joseph L., *Enter a Samurai. Kawakami Otojiro and Japanese Theatre in the West* (Tucson, AZ, 2011).
Anderson, William, *The pictorial arts of Japan. With a brief historical sketch of the associated arts, and some remarks upon the pictorial art of the Chinese and Koreans*, 2 vols. (London, 1886).
Andre, Ed., "Le Jardin japonais au Trocadero," in: *Journal d'agriculture pratique, de jardinage & d'économique* 53.2 (December 1889), pp. 239–243.
Arnold, Charles D.; Higinbotham, H. D., *Official Views Of The World's Columbian Exposition* ([Chicago], 1893).
Asiatic Society of Japan. *Catalogue of the books and manuscripts in the library of the Asiatic society of Japan* (Tōkyō, 1888).
Asiatic Society of Japan. "List of members," in: *Transactions of the Asiatic Society of Japan* 8 (1880), pp. xxii–xxv.
Asiatic Society of Japan. "Report," in: *Transactions of the Asiatic Society of Japan* 1 (1874) (Reprint 1882), pp. v–ix.
Aslin, Elisabeth, *E. W. Godwin. Furniture and Interior decoration* (London, 1986).
Audsley, George Ashdown; Bowes, James Lord, *Keramic Art of Japan* (London, 1875).
"Ausstellungsgebäude für 1867, in Paris," in: *Allgemeine Bauzeitung* 1867, Plan 36.
Aviler, Augustin-Charles d', *Dictionnaire d'architecture civile et hydraulique et des arts qui en dépendent: comme la maçon-nerie, la charpenterie, la menuiserie ...* [Reprod.] (Paris, 1755).
Bachmann-Medick, Doris, "Kulturanthropologie," in: Nünning, Ansgar; Nünning, Vera (eds.), *Konzepte der Kulturwissenschaften* (Stuttgart, Weimar, 2003), pp. 86–107.

Bæckström, Anton, *Ett besök I Japan och Kina jemte bilder från vägen dit öfver Goda-Hoppsudden, Bourbon, Nya Kaledonien, Manilla och Kokinkina: anteckningar och minnen från en treårig tjenstgöring I franska flottan* (1871) (Stockholm, 1871).

Baltzer, Franz, *Das Japanische Haus, eine bautechnische Studie* (Berlin, 1903).

Baltzer, Franz, *Die Architektur der Kultbauten Japans* (Berlin, 1907).

Baltzer, Franz, "Die Tempelanlage von Horiuji bei Nara in Japan," in: *Centralblatt der Bauverwaltung* (1902), 83: pp. 507–510; 89: pp. 545–547; 91: pp. 559–160.

Bann, Stephen, *Distinguished images. Prints in the visual economy of nineteenth-century France* (New Haven and London, 2013).

Bann, Stephen, "The Past in Print: Ancient Buildings Represented by Engraving, Etching and Lithography in Early-Nineteenth-Century England," in: Hvattum, Mari; Hultzsch, Anne (eds.), *The printed and the built. Architecture, print culture, and public debate in the Nineteenth Century* (London; New York; Oxford; New Delhi; Sydney, 2018), pp. 51–72.

Bann, Stephen, "The Photographic Album as a Cultural Accumulator," in: id. (ed.), *Art and the early photographic album* (New Haven, CT; London, 2011), pp. 7–30.

Barna, Gergely Péter, "Japanese Architectural Displays at the 1867 Paris, 1873 Vienna and 1876 Philadelphia International Exhibitions," in: Zorn, Bettina (ed.), *Archiv 65. Archiv Weltmuseum Wien* (2015), pp. 20–43.

Barna, Gergely Péter; Shimizu, Shigeatsu; Ishida, Jun'ichiro; Li, Chang Wei, "Intercultural Transmission of Architectural Elements. A Case Study of 19th-Century Japanese Architectural Models," in: S. Xu, Subin; Aoki, Nobuo; Vieira Amaro, Bébio (eds.), *East Asian Architecture in Globalization. Values, Inheritance and Dissemination*, corrected publication (Cham, 2022), pp. 541–551.

Bartholomew, James, *The Formation of Science in Japan: Building a Research Tradition* (New Haven, 1989).

Baschet, René (ed.), *Le Panorama: Exposition universelle 1900* (Paris, 1900).

Baumuck, Bodo, "Japan auf den Weltausstellungen 1862–1933," in: *Japan und Europa 1543–1929. Essays* (Berlin, 1993), pp. 44–49.

Baydar Nalbantoglu, Gülsüm, "Towards Postcolonial Openings: Rereading Sir Banister Fletcher's History of Architecture," in: *Assemblage* 35 (1998), pp. 6–17.

Beasley, William G., *The Meiji restoration* (Stanford, 1972).

Beauchamp, Edward R. (ed.), *Brunton, Richard Henry: Schoolmaster to an Empire, 1868–1876* (New York; Westport, CT; London, 1991).

Bellet, Paul, "Les Costumes populaires du Japon," in: *L'Exposition universelle de 1867 illustrée*, vol. 1, pp. 363–365.

Bennett, Terry, *Early Japanese images* (Rutland, VT; Tōkyō, 1996).

Bennett, Terry, *Photography in Japan. 1853–1912* (Rutland, VT, 2006).

Bergdoll, Barry, "Architecture and Print Culture in the Nineteenth Century: 'The Public Square of the Modern Age': Architecture and the Rise of the Illustrated Press in the

Early Nineteenth Century," in: Hvattum, Mari; Hultzsch, Anne (eds.), *The printed and the built. Architecture, print culture, and public debate in the Nineteenth Century* (London; New York; Oxford; New Delhi; Sydney, 2018), pp. 27–50.

Bersihand, Roger, *Geschichte Japans von den Anfängen bis zur Gegenwart* (Stuttgart, 1963).

Beutler, Christian, *Weltausstellungen im 19. Jahrhundert* (München, 1973).

Bhabha, Homi K., *The location of Culture* (London; New York, 1994).

Bird, Isabella Lucy, *Unbeaten Tracks in Japan: an account of travels on horseback in the interior: including visits to the aborigines of Yezo and the shrines of Nikkō and Isé*, 2 vols. (London, 1880).

Black, Alexandra; Murata, Noboru, *Japanische Häuser. Architektur und Interieurs* (Köln, 2001).

Blaser, Werner, *Tempel und Teehaus in Japan* (Olten; Lausanne, 1955).

Blaser, Werner, *West Meets East. Mies van der Rohe* (Basel; Boston; Berlin, 1996).

Bocking, Brian, "Flagging up Buddhism: Charles Pfoundes (Omoie Tetzunostuke) among the International Congresses and Expositions, 1893–1905," in: *Contemporary Buddhism* 14.1 (2013), pp. 17–37.

Bocking, Brian; Cox, Laurence; Yoshinaga Shin'ichi, "The First Buddhist Mission to the West: Charles Pfoundes and the London Buddhist mission of 1889–1892," in: *Diskus. The Journal of the British Association for the Study of Religions* (16 March 2014), pp. 1–33.

Böckmann, Wilhelm, *Reise nach Japan. Aus Briefen und Tagebüchern zusammengestellt* (Berlin, 1886).

Bousquet, Georges Hilaire, *Le Japon de Nos Jours et les Echelles de l'Extreme Orient. Ouvrage Contenant Trois Cartes*, 2 vols. (Paris, 1877).

Bozdogan, Sibel, "Architectural History in Professional Education: Reflections on Postcolonial Challenges to the Modern Survey," in: *Journal of Architectural Education* 52.4 (May 1999), pp. 207–215.

Brailey, N. J., "Satow, Sir Ernest Mason (1843–1929)," in: *Oxford Dictionary of National Biography* (Oxford University Press, 2004); online resource, Jan 2008, http://www.oxforddnb.com/view/article/35955 [accessed 12 February 2015].

"Brandschutzgesetze in Japan," in: *Deutsche Bauzeitung* (1869), p. 136.

Bremner, Alex, *Building Greater Britain: Architecture, Imperialism, and the Edwardian Baroque Revival, c.1885–1920* (New Haven; London, 2022).

Bressani, Martin; Sealy, Peter, "The Opera Disseminated: Charles Garnier's Le Nouvel Opera de Paris (1875–1881)," in: Bann, Stephen (ed.), *Art and the early photographic album* (New Haven, CT; London, 2011), pp. 195–220.

Brinckmann, Justus, *Kunst und Handwerk in Japan* (Berlin, 1889).

Brinkley, Frank; Okakura, Kakuzo, *Japan, Described and Illustrated by the Japanese, Written By Eminent Japanese Authorities and Scholars*, 10 vols. (Boston; Tōkyō, 1897).

Brouwer, Petra, "An illustrated comparison of 'true styles'. James Fergusson's The illustrated handbook of architecture (1855)," in: Burioni, Matteo (ed.), *Weltgeschichten der Architektur. Ursprünge, Narrative, Bilder 1700–2016* (Passau, 2016), pp. 42–44.

Brouwer, Petra, "Das niederländische Architekturhandbuch im 19. Jahrhundert. Motor der Erneuerung," in: Hassler, Uta (ed.), *Der Lehrbuchdiskurs über das Bauen* (Zürich, 2015), pp. 152–167.

Brown, Azby, *The Japanese Dream House. How technology and tradition are shaping new house design* (New York et al., 2001).

Brumann, Christoph; Schulz, Evelyn (eds.), *Urban Spaces in Japan. Cultural and Social Perspectives* (London; New York, 2012).

Brunton, Richard Henry, *Building Japan 1868–1876* (Sandgate; Folkestone; Kent, 1991).

Brunton, Richard Henry, "Constructive Art in Japan (1)," in: *Transactions of the Asiatic Society of Japan II* (1874), pp. 64–86.

Brunton, Richard Henry, "Constructive Art in Japan (2)," in: *Transactions of the Asiatic Society of Japan III* (1875), pp. 20–30.

Buchanan, David, "Japan," in: *The Encyclopaedia Britannica, or, Dictionary of arts, sciences, and general literature, 12: Hydrodynamics – Kyreeghur*, 7th ed., with preliminary dissertations on the history of the sciences, and other extensive improvements and additions; including the late supplement, a general index, and numerous engravings (Edinburgh, 1842), pp. 510–522.

Buel, James William, *The magic city: a massive portfolio of original photographic views of the great world's fair and its treasures of art, including a vivid representation of the famous Midway Plaisance* (Chicago, 1894).

Buntrock, Dana, *Japanese Architecture as a Collaborative Process. Opportunities in a flexible construction culture* (London et al., 2002).

Buntrock, Dana, *Materials and meaning in contemporary Japanese architecture: tradition and today* (London, 2010).

Burges, William, "The international exhibition," in: *Gentleman's Magazine* 213 (July 1862), pp. 3–12.

Burioni, Matteo (ed.), *Weltgeschichten der Architektur. Ursprünge, Narrative, Bilder. 1700–2016* (Passau, 2016).

Burty, Philippe, "Exposition universelle de 1878: Le Japon ancien et le Japon moderne," in: *L'art: revue hebdomadaire illustrée* 4.4 (1878), pp. 241–264.

Burty, Philippe, "Japonisme," in: *L'art: revue hebdomadaire illustrée* 2 (1876), part 2: pp. 49–58 (les femmes de qualité), pp. 277–282 (yébis et daï-kokou), part 3: pp. 150–155 (yébis et daï-kokou) as well as *Japonisme: conférences de M. Burty* 3 (1877), part 2: p. 116.

Burty, Philippe, "Le mobilier modern," in: *Gazette des beaux-arts: la doyenne des revues d'art* 24 (1868), pp. 26–45.

Burty, Philippe, "Notes Sur L'architecture Au Japon. A Propos De L'exposition Universelle De 1878," in: *Revue De L'architecture Et Des Travaux Publics* 35 (1878), cols. 55–63, 103–111, 153–163.

Butler, Annie R., *Stories about Japan* (London, 1888).

C., F. R., "Japanese art," in: *Art Journal* (1872), pp. 293–295.

Carver, Norman F. Jr., *Japanese Folkhouses* (Kalamazoo, MI, 1984).

Castelluccio, Stéphane, "La réception de l'architecture japonaise en France aux xviie et xviiie siècles. Un rendez-vous impossible," in: Cluzel, Jean-Sébastien (ed.), *Le japonisme architectural en France, 1550–1930* (Dijon, 2018), pp. 89–95.

Catalog der kaiserlich japanischen Ausstellung (Wien, 1873).

Cawley, George, "Some remarks on Construction in Brick and Wood, and their relative suitability for Japan," in: *Transactions of the Asiatic Society of Japan VI* (1878), pp. 291–317.

Cawley, George, *Vehicle to be used in electric traction on railways*. Patent US 708462 A, 1902.

Cawley, George, "Wood, and its Application to Japanese Artistic and Industrial Design," in: *Transactions and proceedings of the Japan Society* 2 (1895), pp. 194–223.

Chamberlain, Basil H., "Architecture," in: id., *Things Japanese. Being Notes of Various Subjects Connected with Japan*, London 1890, pp. 22–31.

Chamberlain, Basil H., "Bathing," in: id.: *Things Japanese. Being Notes of Various Subjects Connected with Japan*, London 1890, pp. 43–45.

Chamberlain, Basil H., "Books on Japan," in: id.: *Things Japanese. Being Notes of Various Subjects Connected with Japan*, London 1890, pp. 47–55.

Chambers, Ephraim, *Cyclopaedia, or, An Universal Dictionary of Arts and Sciences: Containing the Definitions of the Terms ...*, vol. 2 (London, 1728).

Chambers, Ephraim, *Cyclopaedia, or, An Universal Dictionary of Arts and Sciences: Containing the Definitions of the Terms ...*, Supplement 1 (London, 1753).

Chambers, Ephraim; Rees, Abraham, *Cyclopaedia, or, An universal dictionary of arts and sciences ...* (London, 1786).

Chambers, William, *Designs of Chinese buildings, furniture, dresses, machines, and utensils* (London, 1757).

Champier, Victor, "Japanese architecture," in: *Artistic Japan. Illustrations and Essays* 3–4 (1888), pp. 19–42.

Chaplin, Winfield S., "An Examination of the Earthquakes Recorded at the Meteorological Observatory, Tôkiyô," in: *Transactions of the Asiatic Society of Japan VI* (1878), pp. 352–356.

Charlevoix, Pierre François-Xavier de, *Histoire et description générale du Japon*, 9 vols. (1736).

Chassiron, Charles de, *Notes sur le Japon, la Chine et l'Inde 1858–1859–1860* (Paris, 1861).

Checkland, Olive, *Japan and Britain after 1859: Creating Cultural Bridges* (New York; London, 2003).

Checkland, Olive, "Richard Henry Brunton and the Japan Lights 1868–1876, a brilliant and abrasive engineer," in: *Transactions of the Newcomen Society* 63.1 (1991), pp. 217–228.

Cheng, Irene, "Structural Racialism in Modern Architectural Theory," in: Cheng, Irene; Davis, Charles L. II; Wilson, Mabel O. (eds.), *Race and modern architecture. A critical history from the enlightenment to the present* (Pittsburgh, 2020), pp. 134–152.

Chevallier, Paul; Bing, S., *Objets d'art japonais provenant du cabinet de monsieur E.-L. M***[Montefiore] qui seront vendus a Paris a l'hotel des commissaires-priseurs 9, Rue Drouot, Salle N 7 du Jendi 17 au Samedi 19 et le Lundi 21 Mai 1894 à deux heures précises*, 1894.

"China and Japan at the Paris exhibition," in: *The Builder* 16 (1 June 1878), pp. 552–553.

Choi, Don, "Non-Western Architecture and the Roles of the History Survey," in: *Fresh Air. Proceedings of the 95th ACSA Annual Meeting* (2007), pp. 745–750.

Choisy, Auguste, *Histoire de l'architecture*, 2 vols. (Paris, 1899).

Clancey, Gregory, *Earthquake Nation. The cultural politics of Japanese Seismicity, 1868–1930* (Berkeley; Los Angeles; London, 2006).

Clowney, David, "A Third System of the Arts? An Exploration of Some Ideas from Larry Shiner's The Invention of Art: A Cultural History," in: *Contemporary Aesthetics* 6 (2008), https://digitalcommons.risd.edu/liberalarts_contempaesthetics/vol6/iss1/4/ [last accessed 30 April 2024], s.p.

Cluzel, Jean-Sébastien (ed.), *Le japonisme architectural en France, 1550–1930* (Dijon, 2018).

Cluzel, Jean-Sébastien, *Architecture éternelle du Japon. De l'histoire aux mythes* (Dijon, 2008).

Cluzel, Jean-Sébastien; Gautier, Marion; Nishida, Masatsugu, "Maquettes d'architecture japonaise. 1840–1937. La collection du musée du Quai Branly," in: Cluzel, Jean-Sébastien (ed.), *Le japonisme architectural en France, 1550–1930* (Dijon, 2018), pp. 138–141.

Cluzel, Jean-Sébastien; Marquet, Christophe; Nishida, Masatsugu, *Hokusai, le vieux fou d'architecture* (Paris, 2014).

Coaldrake, William H., *Architecture and Authority in Japan* (New York, London, 1996).

Coaldrake, William H., "Beyond Mimesis: Japanese architectural models at the Vienna Exhibition and 1910 Japan British Exhibition," in: Cox, Rupert, *The Culture of Copying in Japan. Critical and Historical Perspectives* (London, 2007), pp. 199–212.

Coaldrake, William H., "Edo Architecture and Tokugawa Law," in: *Monumenta Nipponica* 36.3 (Fall 1981), pp. 235–284.

Coaldrake, William H., "From Customary Practice to Conscious Design. The Emergence of the Architect in Tokugawa Japan 1608–1638," in: *Fabrications: The Journal of the Society of Architectural Historians, Australia and New Zealand* 11.2 (2001), pp. 46–59.

Coaldrake, William H., "Japan at Vienna. The Discovery of Meiji Architectural Models from the 1873 Vienna Exhibition," in: *Archiv für Völkerkunde* 53 (2003), pp. 27–43.

Coaldrake, William H., "Review of Nishi, Kazuo; Hozumi, Kazuo: What is Japanese architecture?, Tokyo (Kodansha) 1983," in: *Monumenta Nipponica* 41.3 (1986), pp. 374–376.

Coaldrake, William H., *The Way of the Carpenter. Tools and Japanese Architecture* (Tōkyō; New York, 1990).

Codell, Julie F., "Holme, Charles (1848–1923)," in: *Oxford Dictionary of National Biography* (Oxford University Press, 2004); online edn, May 2008, http://www.oxforddnb.com/view/article/33950] [accessed 14 January 2016].

Cody, Sara (ed.), *Japan Goes to the World's Fairs. Japanese Art at the Great Expositions in Europe and the United States 1867–1904* (Los Angeles, 2005).

Cohen, Floris, *Die zweite Erschaffung der Welt. Wie die moderne Naturwissenschaft entstand* (Bonn, 2011).

Commission impériale japonaise à l'Exposition universelle de Paris, 1878 (ed.), *Le Japon à l'Exposition universelle de 1878*, 2 vols. (Paris, 1878).

Conant, Ellen P., "Japan 'Abroad' at the Chicago Exposition, 1893," in: Conant, Ellen P. (ed.), *Challenging Past And Present: The Metamorphosis of Nineteenth-Century Japanese Art* (Honolulu, 2006), pp. 254–280.

Conant, Ellen P., "Refractions of the Rising Sun. Japan's participation in international exhibitions 1862–1910," in: Sato, Tomoko; Watanabe, Toshio (ed.), *Japan and Britain. An aesthetic dialogue 1850–1930* (London, 1991), pp. 79–92.

Conder, Josiah, "A few remarks on architecture (Lecture upon Architecture. Addressed to the architectural students. Kobudaigakko, Tokei, Japan), [Tokyo 1878]," archival material, Royal Institute of British Architects (RIBA, 72(042) // CON).

Conder, Josiah, "An architect's notes on the great earthquake of October, 1891," in: *Seismological journal of Japan* 2 (1893), pp. 1–92.

Conder, Josiah, "Architecture," in: *Imperial College of Engineering (Kobu-dai-gakku), Tokei. Class reports by the professors for the period 1873–77* ([Tōkyō,] 1877), pp. 63–65.

Conder, Josiah, "Domestic Architecture in Japan," in: *Transactions of the Royal Institute of British Architects* 3 (2nd Ser.) (1886–1887), pp. 103–127.

Conder, Josiah, "Further Notes on Japanese Architecture," in: *Transactions of the Royal Institute of British Architects* 2 (2. Ser.) (1886), pp. 185–214.

Conder, Josiah, "Japanese pagodas, and their construction," in: *The Building News and Engineering Journal* 44 (20 April 1883), p. 529.

Conder, Josiah, "Notes on Japanese architecture," in: *Transactions of the Royal Institute of British Architects* 28 (1877/1878), pp. 179–192, 209–212.

Conder, Josiah, "The condition of architecture in Japan," in: *Proceedings of the twenty-seventh Annual Convention of the American Institute of Architects* (Chicago, 1893), pp. 365–381.

Conder, Josiah, "Theatres in Japan," in: *The Builder* (5 April 1879), pp. 368–376.
Conder, Josiah; Ogawa, Kazumasa, *Landscape gardening in Japan*. Supplement (Tōkyō, 1893).
Conder, Roger Thomas, "A Japanese Gentleman's House at Tokio," in: *Transactions of the Royal Institute of British Architects 3* (2nd series) (1886/1887), pp. 181–184.
Conder, Roger Thomas, "Japanese Pagoda," in: *The Building News and Engineering Journal* 47 (19 December 1884), p. 1017.
Conder, Roger Thomas, "The Mausoleum at Nikko," in: *Transactions of the Royal Institute of British Architects* 2 (2. series) (1885/1886), pp. 209–214.
Conrad, Sebastian; Eckert, Andreas; Freitag, Ulrike (eds.), *Globalgeschichte. Theorien, Ansätze, Themen* (Frankfurt/M., 2007).
Converse, Loring, *Notes of what I saw, and how I saw it. A tour around the world, including California, Japan, China, Malacca, Ceylon, India, Arabia, Europe, Cuba, and Mexico* (Bucyrus, OH, 1882).
Cornwallis, Kinahan, *Two Journeys to Japan, 1856-7*, 2 vols. (London, 1859).
Cortazzi, Sir Hugh, *Japan in Late Victorian London. The Japanese Native Village in Knightsbridge and The Mikado, 1885* (Norwich, 2009).
Cram, Ralph Adams, *Impressions of Japanese Architecture and The Allied Arts* (New York, 1905).
Crook, J. Mordaunt, "Josiah Conder in England. Education, training and background," in: Conder, Josiah; Kawanabe, Kusumi; Suzuki, Hiroyuki, *Rokumeikan no kenchikuka josaia kondoru ten* (Tōkyō: Higashinihon tetsudō bunkazai dan, 1997), pp. 22–24.
Cupers, Kenny, "The Invention of Indigenous Architectur," in: Cheng, Irene; Davis, Charles L. II; Wilson, Mabel O. (eds.), *Race and modern architecture. A critical history from the enlightenment to the present* (Pittsburgh, 2020), pp. 187–202.
Cybriwsky, Roman, *Tokyo. The changing Profile of an Urban Giant* (London, 1991).
Dal Co, Francesco, "La princesse est modeste," in: Ponciroli, Virginia; Isozaki Arata (eds.), *Katsura Imperial Villa* (Milan, 2005), pp. 386–389.
Dale, Peter N., "On Identity as Difference," in: id., *The Myth of Japanese Uniqueness* (London, 1990), pp. 201–227.
Daly, César Denis, "Les temples bouddhistes du Japon," in: *Revue générale de l'architecture et des travaux publics* 43 (1886), cols. 97–107, 193–198, plates 16–26 and 44 (1887), cols. 7–18.
Daly, César Denis, "Les temples japonais," in: *Revue générale de l'architecture et des travaux publics* 43 (1886), cols. 50–51.
D'Amat, Roman, "Burty (Philippe)," in: Balteau, Jules (ed.), *Dictionnaire de biographie française*, vol. 7 *Bournonville – Cayrol* (Paris: Librairie Letouzey et Ané, 1956), p. 707.
Das Kaiserreich Japan, nach den besten vorhandenen Quellen geschildert von einem Vereine Gelehrter; nach den besten vorhandenen Quellen herausgegeben von einem Vereine Gelehrter (Karlsruhe, 1860).

Delank, Claudia, *Das imaginäre Japan in der Kunst. „Japanbilder" vom Jugendstil bis zum Bauhaus* (Munich, 1996).

Delank, Claudia, "Die Weltausstellungen in Paris, Wien und Chicago sowie das neue Printmedium der Fotografie als Vermittler japanischer Kunst und Kultur im Westen," in: Ehmcke, Franziska (ed.), *Kunst und Kunsthandwerk Japans im interkulturellen Dialog* (Munich, 2008), pp. 19–48.

"Deluge," in: *The Encyclopaedia Britannica, or, Dictionary of arts, sciences, and general literature* 7: *Clodius – Dialling*, 7th ed., with preliminary dissertations on the history of the sciences, and other extensive improvements and additions; including the late supplement, a general index, and numerous engravings (Edinburgh, 1842), pp. 690–703.

Demeulenaere-Douyère, Christiane, "Japan at the World's Fairs: A Reflection," in: *Journal of Japonisme* 5.2 (2020), pp. 129–151.

Demmin, August, *Encyclopédie historique, archéologique, biographique, chronologique et monogrammatique des Beaux-Arts plastiques, architecture et mosaïque, céramique, sculpture, peinture et gravure* (Paris, 1873–1874).

Dening, Walter, *Japan in days of yore*, 2 vols., 2nd ed. (Tōkyō, 1904).

"Der Pavillon des Deutschen Reiches an der internationalen Ausstellung Barcelona 1929," in: *(Das) Werk* 16.11 (1929), pp. 350–351.

"Design for new Houses of Parliament, Tokio, Japan," in: *The Builder* 66 (13 October 1894), p. 260.

Détain, C., "La couverture en tuiles au Japon," in: *Revue générale de l'architecture et des travaux public* 44 (1887), cols. 111–117, 152–161, plate 39.

Dettmer, Hans A., *Grundzüge der Geschichte Japans* (Darmstadt, 1992).

"Deutsche Baukunst in Japan," in: *Deutsche Bauzeitung* (19 February 1887), p. 92.

Dictionnaire D'Architecture ou Explication De Tous Les Termes, dont on se sert dans L'Architecture (etc.) / 1693.

Diderot, Denis, "Japonois, Philosophie des," in: Diderot, Denis; d'Alembert, Jean le Rond (eds.), *Encyclopédie ou Dictionnaire raisonné des sciences, des arts et des métiers* (Paris, 1765), vol. 8, pp. 455–458, accessed via: University of Chicago, ARTFL Encyclopédie Project (Spring 2013 Edition), Robert Morrissey (ed.), http://encyclopedie.uchicago.edu/ [accessed 9 March 2015].

"Die Pariser Ausstellung im Jahre 1867," in: *Über Land und Meer* 9, 17, 22 (February 1867), pp. 344, 352–354.

Divers, Edward, "Notes on the Amount of Sulphuretted Hydrogen in the Hot Springs of Kusatsu," in: *Transactions of the Asiatic Society of Japan* VI (1878), pp. 346–348.

Dixon, William Gray, *The land of the morning. An account of Japan and its people, based on a four years' residence in that country Including travels into the remotest parts of the interior* (Edinburgh, 1882).

Dobson, Sebastian, "Photography and the Prussian Expedition to Japan, 1860–61," in: *History of Photography* 33.2 (2009), pp. 112–131.

Doeff, Hendrik, *Herinneringen uit Japan* (Haarlem, 1833).
Dohrn, Wolf, *Die Gartenstadt Hellerau und weitere Schriften* (Dresden, 1992).
Dooman, Isaac, "The influence of Greco-Persian art on Japanese arts," in: *Transactions of the Asiatic Society of Japan* 24 (1896), pp. 137–175.
Dower, John W., "Throwing Off Asia I. Woodblock Prints of Domestic 'Westernization' (1868–1912), 2008," on: *Visualizing culture*, here https://visualizingcultures.mit.edu/throwing_off_asia_01/toa_essay02.html [accessed 5 June 2019].
Dower, John W., "Yokohama Boomtown. Foreigners in Treaty-Port Japan (1859–1872), 2008," on: *Visualizing culture*, here https://visualizingcultures.mit.edu/yokohama/index.html [last accessed 28 April 2024].
Dower, John W., "Black ships and Samurai II. Commodore Perry and the Opening of Japan (1853–1854), 2008," on: *Visualizing culture*, here https://visualizingcultures.mit.edu/black_ships_and_samurai_02/index.html [accessed 8 March 2019].
Downer, Lesley, *Madame Sadayakko. The geisha who bewitched the West* (New York and London, 2003).
Draffin, Nicholas, "An Enthusiastic Amateur of the Arts: Eliezer Levi Montefiore in Melbourne 1853–71," in: *Art journal of the National Gallery of Victoria* 28 (1987), online resource, https://www.ngv.vic.gov.au/essay/an-enthusiastic-amateur-of-the-arts-eliezer-levi-montefiore-in-melbourne-1853-71/ [accessed 29 August 2017].
Dreesbach, Anne, "Colonial Exhibitions, 'Völkerschauen' and the Display of the 'Other'," *European History Online* (Mainz: Institute of European History, 2012), http://www.ieg-ego.eu/dreesbacha-2012-en [accessed 30 May 2023].
Dresser, Christopher, "A Japanese village," in: *The Building news and engineering journal* 48 (30 January 1885), p. 189.
Dresser, Christopher, *Japan, its Architecture, Art and Art Manufactures* (London and New York, 1882).
"Dubard, Louis François Maurice," in: *Archives Biographiques Françaises* (*ABF*) via http://db.saur.de/WBIS/basicSearch.jsf, [accessed 26 November 2014].
Dubard, Maurice, *Le Japon pittoresque* (Paris, 1879).
Dubard, Maurice, *Japanese Life, Love, and Legend: A Visit to the Empire of the 'Rising Sun'* (London, 1886).
Dubois de Jancigny, Adolphe Philibert, *Japon, Indo-Chine, Empire Birman (ou Ava), Siam, Annam (ou Cochinchine), Péninsule Malaise, etc., Ceylan*, (= *L'univers: histoire et description de tous les peuples; C, Asie; 8*) (Paris, 1850).
Duchesne de Bellecour, P., "Exposition chinoise et japonaise au Champ de Mars," in: *Revue des deux-Mondes* (1 August 1867), pp. 710–742.
Duke, Benjamin C., *The History of Modern Japanese Education: Constructing the National School System, 1872–1890* (New Brunswick, NJ, 2009).
Duret, Théodore, *Voyage en Asie: Le Japon, La Chine, La Mongolie, Java, Ceylan, l'Inde* (Paris, 1874).

Dyer, Henry (ed.), *Imperial College of Engineering (Kobu-dai-gakko) Tokei, Report by Principal and Professors, 1873–1877* (Tōkyō, 1877).

Dyer, Henry, *Dai Nippon: a study in national evolution* (London, 1904).

Dyer, Henry, *The Education of Civil and Mechanical Engineers* (London, 1880).

Elsässer, Markus, *Soziale Intentionen und Reformen des Robert Owen in der Frühzeit der Industrialisierung: Analyse seines Wirkens als Unternehmer, Sozialreformer, Genossenschafter, Frühsozialist, Erzieher u. Wissenschaftler* (Berlin, 1984).

Ende and Böckmann, "Einwirkung des Erdbebens in Japan auf die dort hergestellten Massivbauten (1–2)," in: *Deutsche Bauzeitung* 65 (1894), p. 399; 80 (1894), pp. 499–500.

Enders, Siegfried, *Japanische Wohnformen und ihre Veränderung* (Hamburg, 1979).

Enders, Siegfried; Gutschow, Niels (eds.), *Hozon. Architectural and Urban Conservation in Japan* (Stuttgart; London, 1998).

Engel, Heino, *The Japanese House: A tradition for contemporary architecture* (Ruthland, VT; Tōkyō, 1964).

"Engineering reports on the San Francisco earthquake," in: *The Builder* 92 (1 June 1907), p. 656.

Erickson, Bruce T., "Eliphalet M. Brown, Jr. An early expedition photographer," in: *The Daguerreian Annual* (1990), pp. 145–156.

Exner, Wilhelm Franz, "Japans Holz-Industrie," in: *Österreichische Monatsschrift für den Orient* (1881), pp. 55–58, 82–85, 118–119.

F. St., "Das japanische Theehaus im Vauxhallgarten des Praters," in: *Illustrirte Zeitung* 1581 (8 October 1873), pp. 287–290.

Falke, Jakob von, *Die Kunstindustrie der Gegenwart. Studien auf der Pariser Weltausstellung im Jahre 1867* (Leipzig, 1868).

Falke, Jakob von, "Die Pariser Weltausstellung," in: *Mittheilungen des k.k. oesterreichischen Museums für Kunst und Industrie* 48 (1889), pp. 488–504.

Farrington, Anthony, "The Asiatic Society of Japan – Its Formative Years," in: *Historical English Studies in Japan* 9 (1976), pp. 81–91.

Fergusson, James, *A history of architecture in all countries, from the earliest times to the present day: in five volumes* (London, 1893).

Fergusson, James, *History of Indian and Eastern Architecture*, 2 vols., 2nd, rev. ed. (London, 1910).

Fergusson, James, *History of Indian and Eastern Architecture* (London, 1876).

Fergusson, James, *The illustrated handbook of architecture. Being a concise and popular account of the different styles of architecture prevailing in all ages and all countries*, 2 vols. (London, 1855).

Fiévé, Nicolas, *Atlas historique de Kyōto. Analyse spatiale des systèmes de mémoire d'une ville, de son architecture et de son paysage urbain* (Paris, 2008).

Fiévé, Nicolas, "Kyoto's Famous Places. Collective Memory and 'Monuments' in Tokugawa Period," in: Fiévé, Nicolas; Waley, Paul (eds.), *Japanese capitals in historical perspective: place, power and memory in Kyoto, Edo and Tokyo* (London, 2003), pp. 153–171.

Fiévé, Nicolas, *L'architecture et la ville du Japon ancien: espace architectural de la ville de Kyōto et des résidences shōgunales aux XIVᵉ et XVᵉ siècles* (Paris, 1996).

Fiévé, Nicolas, *Pratique architecturale et naissance de l'histoire de l'architecture au Japon* (Paris, 1999).

Fiévé, Nicolas; Waley, Paul (eds.), *Japanese Capitals in Historical Perspective: Place, power and memory in Kyoto, Edo and Tokyo* (London, 2003).

Finn, Dallas, "Josiah Conder (1852–1920) and Meiji Architecture," in: Cortazzi, Hugh; Daniels, Gordon (eds.), *Britain and Japan 1859–1991: themes and personalities*; published on the occasion of the centenary of the Japan Society 1891–1991 (London, 1991), pp. 86–106.

Finn, Dallas, *Meiji Revisited. The Sites of Victorian Japan* (New York, 1995).

Fleck, Ludwik, *Entstehung und Entwicklung einer wissenschaftlichen Tatsache. Einführung in die Lehre vom Denkstil und Denkkollektiv* (Frankfurt a.M., 1980).

Fletcher, Banister; Fletcher, Banister F., *A history of architecture for the student, craftsman, and amateur: being a comparative view of historical styles from the earliest period*, 4. enlarged ed. (London, 1901).

Fletcher, Banister; Fletcher, Banister F., *A History of Architecture on the Comparative Method for the Student, Craftsman and Amateur*, 5. rev., enlarge. ed. (London, 1905).

Fletcher, Banister; Fletcher, Banister F., *A history of architecture for the student, craftsman, and amateur: being a comparative view of historical styles from the earliest period* (London, 1896).

Fletcher, Banister; Fraser, Murray; Gregg, Catherine (eds.), *Sir Banister Fletcher's global history of architecture*, 2 vols., 21 edn. (London; New York; Oxford; New Delhi; Sydney, 2020).

Fletcher, Sir Banister; Cruickshank, Dan (eds.), *Sir Banister Fletcher's a history of architecture* (Oxford, 1996).

Flinn, John J., *The Best Things to be Seen at the World's Fair* (Chicago, 1893).

Foote, Andrew Hull, "Visit to Simoda and Hakodai in Japan," in: *Journal of the North China Branch of the Royal Asiatic Society* 1 (1858), pp. 129–137.

Foucault, Michel, *Die Ordnung des Diskurses*, extended ed. (Frankfurt a.M., 1993).

Foxwell, Chelsea, "Japan as Museum? Encapsulating Change and Loss in Late-Nineteenth-Century Japan," in: *Getty research Journal* 1 (2009), pp. 39–52.

Frédéric, Louis, *Japan Encyclopedia* (Cambridge; London, 2002).

Freeman-Mitford, Algernon Bertram (Baron Redesale), *Tales of Old Japan* (London, 1871).

Friebe, Wolfgang, *Architektur der Weltausstellungen. 1851–1970* (Stuttgart, 1983).

Froís, Luís, *Brevis Iapaniae Insvlae Descriptio, Ac Rervm Qvarvndam In Ea Mirabilium, à Patribus Societatis Iesv nuper gestarum, succincta narratio: Item, Insigne Qvoddam Martyrium, quod in Aphrica quidam pro Christiana religione Catholica inuicta constantia subijt* (Coloniae Agrippinae, 1582).

Fujimori, Terunobu, "Josiah Conder and Japan," in: Conder, Josiah; Suzuki, Hiroyuki; Fujimori, Terunobu; Hara Tokuzō (eds.), *Josiah Conder: A Victorian Architect in Japan, Catalogue/Rokumeikan no kenchikuka josaia kondoru ten*, revised edition ([Tōkyō]: Kenchiku Gahōsha, 2009), pp. 13–17.

Fujitsuka, Mitsumasa; Koshihara, Mikio, *Japan's Wooden Heritage: A Journey Through a Thousand Years of Architecture* (Tōkyō, 2017).

Fukuchi, Mataichi; Kino, Toshio; Mabuchi, Akiko, *Japan. Rinji Hakurankai Jimukyoku, Tōkyō Teishitsu Hakubutsukan,* [*Hayashi, Tadamasa; Universal Exposition Commission Impériale du Japon*]: *Histoire de l'art du Japon. Ouvrage publié par la Commission Impériale du Japon à l'Exposition universelle de Paris, 1900* (Paris, 1900).

Ganzer, Inga, *Hermann Muthesius und Japan: Die Rezeption und Verarbeitung japanischer Vorbilder in der deutschen Raumkunst nach 1900* (Petersberg, 2016).

Gardiner, Robert Septimus, *Japan as we saw it* (Boston, 1892).

Garnier, Charles, *L'Habitation humaine* (Paris, 1892).

Gartlan, Luke, *A Career of Japan: Baron Raimund von Stillfried and Early Yokohama Photography* (Leiden, 2016).

Gartlan, Luke, "Changing Views: The Early Topographical Photographs of Stillfried & Company," in: Rousmaniere, Nicole C.; Hirayama, Mikiko (eds.), *Reflecting Truth. Japanese Photography in the Nineteenth Century* (Amsterdam, 2004), pp. 40–65.

Gartlan, Luke, "Photography in Nineteenth-Century Japan," in: *History of Photography* 33.2 (May 2009, theme issue).

Gartlan, Luke; Behdad, Ali, *Photography's Orientalism: New Essays on Colonial Representation* (Los Angeles, 2013).

Geertz, Clifford, *Dichte Beschreibung. Beiträge zum Verstehen kultureller Systeme* (Frankfurt/M., 1983).

Gerabek, Werner E., "Siebold, Philipp Franz Balthasar," in: *Neue Deutsche Biographie* 24 (2010), pp. 329–330 [Onlinefassung]; http://www.deutsche-biographie.de/ppn 118613960.html [accessed 29 August 2017].

Gilpin, William, *Three essays: on picturesque beauty; on picturesque travel; and on sketching landscape: to which is added a poem, on landscape painting* (London, 1792).

Girveau, Bruni, *Charles Garnier. Un architecte pour un empire* (Paris, 2010).

Glass, Chester, *The world. Round it and over it* (Toronto, 1881).

Glimpses of the World's Fair: A Selection of Gems of the White City Seen Through a Camera (Chicago, 1893).

Godwin, Edward William, "Japanese Building," in: *The British Architect and Northern Engineer* (30 August 1878), p. 85.

Godwin, Edward William, "Japanese wood construction v–vi," in: *Building News and Engineering Journal* (12 February 1875), pp. 173–174; (19 February 1875), pp. 200–201, 214.

Goff, Lieutenant Colonel, *A walk through Japan, 1877* (London, 1878).

Golownin, Wassili Michailowitsch, *Begebenheiten des Capitains von der russisch-kaiserlichen Marine Golownin in der Gefangenschaft bei den Japanern in den Jahren 1811, 1812 und 1813 nebst seinen Bemerkungen über das japanische Reich und Volk und einem Anhange des Capitains Rikord*, 2 vols. (Leipzig, 1817–1818).

Gonse, Louis, *Japanese art* (Chicago, 1891).

Gonse, Louis, *L'Art Japonais* (Paris, 1883).

Goree, Robert, *Fantasies of the Real: Meisho zue in Early Modern Japan*, unpublished dissertation (Yale University, 2010).

Goree, Robert, "*Meisho Zue* and the Mapping of Prosperity in Late Tokugawa Japan," in: *Cross-Currents. East-Asian History and Culture Review* 23 (June 2017), https://doi.org/10.1353/ach.2017.0023 [last accessed 29 April 2024], pp. 73–107.

Grand album de l'Exposition Universelle 1867 (Paris, 1868).

Greey, Edward, *The wonderful city of Tokio, or, Further adventures of the Jewett family and their friend Oto Nambo* (Boston, 1883).

Greey, Edward, *Young Americans in Japan or the adventures of the Jewett family and their friend Oto Nambo* (Boston, 1882).

Griesecke, Birgit, *Japan dicht beschreiben. Produktive Fiktionalität in der ethnographischen Forschung* (München, 2001).

Griffis, William Elliot, *The Mikado's Empire* (New York, 1876).

Griffis, William Elliot, *The Mikado's Empire*, 8th extended ed. (New York, 1895).

Griffis, William Elliot, "The Streets and Street-Names of Yedo," in: *Transactions of the Asiatic Society of Japan I* [1874] (reprint 1882), pp. 18–26.

Guérineau, Abel Jean-Louis, "Biographical sketch," in: Frédéric, Louis, *Japan encyclopedia* (Cambridge, MA, 2002), p. 266.

Guérineau, Abel, *Ornements japonais* (s.l. 1889).

Guimet, Émile, *Promenades Japonais. Tokio-Nikko* (Paris, 1878).

Guo, Qinghua, "Prescribing the Ideal City: Building Codes and Planning Principles in Beijing," in: Marshall, Stephen (ed.), *Urban Coding and Planning* (London, 2011), pp. 101–119.

Gürel, Meltem Ö.; Anthony, Kathryn H., "The Canon and the Void: Gender, Race, and Architectural History Texts," in: *Journal of Architectural Education* 59.3 (February 2006), pp. 66–76.

Gutschow, Niels, *Die japanische Burgstadt* (Paderborn, 1976).

Hall, John Whitney (ed.), *Das Japanische Kaiserreich*, 13th ed. (Frankfurt/M. et al., 2002).

Handa, Rumiko, "Japan, 1334–1868," in: Fraser, Murray (ed.), *Sir Banister Fletcher's Global History of Architecture*, 21st ed. (London; New York; Oxford; New Delhi; Sydney, 2020), pp. 391–405.

Harada, Jiro, *The Lesson of Japanese Architecture* (London, 1936).

Hardacre, Helen; Kern, Adam Lewis (eds.), *New Directions in the Study of Meiji Japan* (Leiden et al., 1997).

Harris, Neil, "All the World a Melting-pot? Japan at American World Fairs, 1876–1904," in: Iriye, Akira (ed.), *Mutual Images. Essays in American-Japanese Relations* (Cambridge, MA, and London, 1975), pp. 24–54.

Hatta, Yoko, "The Japanese Position in the Chicago World's Columbian Exposition of 1893," in: *Bulletin of the faculty of language and literature* 12.1 (1998), pp. 35–79.

Hattori, I., "Destructive Earthquakes in Japan," in: *Transactions of the Asiatic Society of Japan VI* (1878), pp. 249–275.

Hawks, Francis L.; Perry, Matthew Calbraith, *Narrative of the expedition of an American squadron to the China seas and Japan, performed in the years 1852, 1853, and 1854, under the command of Commodore M. C. Perry, United States Navy, by order of the government of the United States. Compiled from the original notes and journals of Commodore Perry and his officers, at his request and under his supervision* (Washington, 1856).

Hayashi, Yoji, "Japanese Experience of Abel Guérineau, Hired French Architect. The Imperial Japanese Army academy and the French architectural education institutions," in: *Journal of Architecture and Planning (Transactions of AIJ)* 80.709 (2015), pp. 709–715.

Hedinger, Daniel, *Im Wettstreit mit dem Westen. Japans Zeitalter der Ausstellungen 1854–1941* (Frankfurt/M., 2011).

Hein, Carola, "Baumeister und Architekten in Japan," in: Winfried Nerdinger (ed.), *Der Architekt. Geschichte und Gegenwart eines Berufsstandes* 1 (Munich; London; New York, 2012), pp. 258–277.

Hein, Carola, "Shaping Tokyo: Land Development and Planning. Practice in the Early Modern Japanese Metropolis," in: *Journal of Urban History* 36.4 (2010), pp. 447–484.

Hein, Carola; Diefendorf, Jeffry M.; Ishida, Yorifusa (eds.), *Rebuilding Urban Japan after 1945* (Houndmills; Basingstoke; Hampshire, 2003).

Heine, Wilhelm, *Die Expedition in die Seen von China, Japan und Ochotsk*, 3 vols. (Leipzig, 1858).

Heine, Wilhelm, *Graphic Scenes of the Japan Expedition by Wm Heine, Artist of the Expedition* (New York, 1856).

Heine, Wilhelm, *Japan. Beiträge zur Kenntniss des Landes und seiner Bewohner* (Berlin, 1875).

Heine, Wilhelm, *Reise um die Erde nach Japan an Bord der Expeditions-Escadre unter Commodore M.C. Perry in den Jahren 1853, 1854 und 1855, unternommen im Auftrage der Regierung der Vereinigten Staaten*, 2 vols. (Leipzig, 1856).

Hesselink, Reinier H., "The Assassination of Henry Heusken," in: *Monumenta Nipponica* 49.3 (Autumn 1994), pp. 331–351.

Higinbotham, H. D., *Official views of the World's Columbian Exposition* (Chicago, 1893).

Hijiya-Kirschnereit, Irmela, *Das Ende der Exotik: Zur japanischen Kultur und Gesellschaft der Gegenwart* (Frankfurt/M., 1988).

Hildreth, Richard, *Japan. As it was and is* (Boston, 1855).

Himeno, Junichi, "Encounters with Foreign Photographers. The Introduction and Spread of Photography in Kyūshū," in: Rousmaniere, Nicole C.; Hirayama, Mikiko (eds.), *Reflecting Truth. Japanese Photography in the Nineteenth Century*, (Amsterdam, 2004), pp. 18–29.

Hintze, Eduard; Wagner, Hermann, *Das alte und das neue Japan, oder, Die Nippon-Fahrer: In Schilderungen der bekanntesten älteren und neueren Reisen* (ursprünglich bearbeitet von Friedrich Steger und Hermann Wagner), 3rd ed. (Leipzig, 1874).

Hirai, Kiyoshi, *Feudal Architecture of Japan* (New York, 1973).

Hockley, Allen, "Felice Beato's Japan: Places. An album by the pioneer foreign photographer in Yokohama, 2008," on: *Visualizing culture*, here https://visualizingcultures.mit.edu/beato_places/index.html [accessed 3 June 2019].

Hockley, Allen, "Globetrotters' Japan: People. Foreigners on the tourist circuit in Meiji Japan, 2008," on: *Visualizing culture*, here https://visualizingcultures.mit.edu/gt_japan_people/index.html [accessed 15 July 2019].

Hockley, Allen, "Globetrotters' Japan: Places. Foreigners on the tourist circuit in Meiji Japan, 2008," on: *Visualizing culture*, here https://visualizingcultures.mit.edu/gt_japan_places/index.html [accessed 3 June 2019].

Hogarth, William, *The Analysis of Beauty* (London, 1753).

Hokusai, Katsushika, *Fugaku Hyakkei* [Hundred views of Mount Fuji], 3 vols. (1834–1835).

Hokusai, Katsushika, *Manga*, 15 vols. (s.l., 1814–1837).

Hollingworth, William, "West's first Buddhist mission was in London," in: *Japan Times* (18 March 2015), here https://www.japantimes.co.jp/news/2015/03/18/national/wests-first-buddhist-mission-was-in-london/#.XRsKbI9CSUk [accessed 2 July 2019].

Holme, Charles, *A Course of Instruction in Wood Carving According to the Japanese Method* (London, 1899).

Holme, Charles; Huberman, Toni (eds.), *The diary of Charles Holme's 1889 visit to Japan and North America with Mrs Lasenby Liberty's "Japan: a pictorial record"* (Folkestone, UK, 2008).

Holmes, Elias Burton, "The Paris Exposition," in: id., *The Burton Holmes Lectures. With Illustrations from Photographs by the Author*, 10 vols. (Battle Creek, MI, 1901), 2, pp. 115–336.

Holz, Elizabeth B. G., *The Art of All Nations. 1850–73. The emerging role of exhibitions and critics* (Princeton, NJ, 1982).

Horiguchi, Sutemi; Harada, Jiro; Sato, Tatsuzo, *The Katsura Imperial Villa* (Tōkyō: Mainichi, 1952).

Horiuchi, Masaaki, "Die Beziehungen der Berliner Baufirma Ende & Böckmann zu Japan," in: Krebs, Gerhard (ed.), *Japan und Preussen* (München, 2002), pp. 319–342.

"How They Manage Things in Japan," in: *The Builder* 32 (1874), p. 65.

Hübner, Alexander Baron, *A ramble around the world, 1871* (New York, 1874).

Hübner, Alexander Graf von, *Ein Spaziergang um die Welt*, 4th ed. (Leipzig, 1882).

Hübner, Alexander Graf von, *Ein Spaziergang um die Welt* (Paris, 1872).

Hübner, Alexander Graf von, *Promenade autour du monde*, 7th ed., 2 vols. (Paris, 1881).

Hübner, Alexander Graf von, *Promenade autour du monde* (Paris, 1872).

Hudson, Hugh, "A Jewish Philanthropist in Colonial Australia: Eliezer Levi Montefiore's Papers in the Autograph Collection of the State Library of Victoria," in: *Australian Jewish Historical Society Journal* XX.3 (2011), pp. 349–394.

Huish, Marcus B., *Japan and its Art* (London, 1889).

Humbert, Aimé, *Japan. De Aarde en haar Volken* (Haarlem, 1867).

Humbert, Aimé, *Japan and the Japanese illustrated* (London, 1874).

Humbert, Aimé, *Le Japon illustré*, 2 vols. (Paris, 1870).

Ikeda, Yuko, "Hermann Muthesius und Japan," in: Ikeda, Yuko; Schwartz, Frederic J., et al. (eds.), *Vom Sofakissen zum Städtebau. Hermann Muthesius und der Deutsche Werkbund: Modern Design in Deutschland 1900–1927* (Kyōto, 2002), pp. 384–392.

Ikeda, Yuko; Schwartz, Frederic J., et al. (eds.), *Vom Sofakissen zum Städtebau. Hermann Muthesius und der Deutsche Werkbund: Modern Design in Deutschland 1900–1927* (Kyōto, 2002).

Imperial Government Railways; Ogawa, Kazumasa, *Sights and Scenes in Fair Japan* (Tōkyō, [1910?]).

Imperial Japanese Commission to the International Exhibition at Philadelphia 1876, *Official catalogue of the Japanese section, and descriptive notes on the industry and agriculture of Japan* (Philadelphia, 1876).

Inagaki, Eizo, "Japan and Korea [Meiji]," in: Cruickshank, Dan (ed.), *Sir Banister Fletcher's a history of architecture*, 20th ed. (Oxford, 1996), pp. 1238–1245.

Inagaki, Eizo, "Japan and Korea," in: Cruickshank, Dan (ed.), *Sir Banister Fletcher's a history of architecture*, 20th ed. (Oxford, 1996), pp. 716–746.

Inoue, Kiyoshi, *Geschichte Japans*, 3rd ed. (Frankfurt; New York, 2003).

Inoue, Mitsuo, *Space in Japanese Architecture* (= *Nihon kenchiku no kūkan*) (New York; Tōkyō, 1985).

Institute of British Architects, *Questions upon various subjects connected with architecture: suggested for the direction of correspondents and travellers, and for the purpose of eliciting uniformity of observation and intelligence in their communications to the Institute* (London, 1835).

Irvine, Gregory, *Japonisme and the Rise of the Modern Art Movement: The Arts of the Meiji Period* (London, 2013).

Ishida, Aritoshi, *Kioto meishiyo fifty kei* [Kyōto's Famous Places: 50 Views] ([Kyōto,] 1890).

Ishikura, Shigetsugu, *Nikkō meisho zue* [Guide to Famous Places in Nikkō] (Tōkyō: Hakubunkan, 1902).

Isozaki, Arata; Ishimoto, Yasuhiro, *Katsura. Raum und Form* (Stuttgart, 1987).

Itō, Teiji; Futagawa, Yukio, *Alte Häuser in Japan* (= *Nihon-no-minka*) (Stuttgart, 1984).

Itoh, Teiji; Arai, Masao; Ogawa, Taisuke, *Katsura, A Quintessential Representative of the Sukiya Style of Architecture* (Tōkyō, 1983).

Ives, Colta Feller, *The Great Wave: The Influence of Japanese Woodcuts on French Prints* (New York, 1974).

Jackson, Anna, "Imagining Japan: The Victorian Perception and Acquisition of Japanese culture," in: *Journal of Design History* 5.4 (1992), pp. 245–256.

Jackson, Neil, *Japan and the West. An architectural dialogue* (London, 2019).

Jackson, Neil, "Japan, 1853–1945," in: Fraser, Murray (ed.), *Sir Banister Fletcher's Global History of Architecture* (London; New York; Oxford; New Delhi; Sydney, 2020), pp. 747–762.

Jackson, Neil, "Japan, 1945–Present Day," in: Fraser, Murray (ed.), *Sir Banister Fletcher's Global History of Architecture*, 21st ed. (London; New York; Oxford; New Delhi; Sydney, 2020), pp. 1148–1164.

Jansen, Marius B.; Rozman, Gilbert (eds.), *Japan in Transition. From Tokugawa to Meiji* (Princeton, 1986).

Janzin, Marion; Güntner, Joachim, *Das Buch vom Buch. 5000 Jahre Buchgeschichte* (Hannover, 1995).

"Japan and its building trades and appliances," in: *The Building News and Engineering Journal* 48 (6 March 1885), pp. 353–354.

"Japan in Berlin," in: *Kladderadatsch* 38.31 (5 July 1885), supplement.

"Japan," in: *Allgemeine Deutsche Real-Encyklopädie für die gebildeten Stände. Conversations-Lexikon*, 7. *Heim bis Juwelen*, 9., Originalaufl. (Leipzig, 1845), pp. 621–626.

"Japan," in: *Allgemeine Deutsche Real-Encyklopädie für die gebildeten Stände*, 8. *Höfken – Kirchenbann*, 10., verb. und verm. Aufl. (Leipzig, 1853), pp. 418–423.

"Japan," in: Meyer, Joseph (ed.), *Das große Conversations-Lexicon für die gebildeten Stände: dieser Encyclopädie des menschlichen Wissens sind beigegeben: die Bildnisse der bedeutendsten Menschen aller Zeiten, die Ansichten der merkwürdigsten Orte, die*

Pläne der größten Städte, 100 Karten für alte und neue Erdbeschreibung, für Statistik, Geschichte und Religion ... / 1,16: Hügel – Johann (Geogr.) (Hildburghausen, 1850), pp. 1167–1186.

"Japanese architecture (extract from Alcock's essay in The Art Journal)," in: *The Builder* 33 (17 April 1875), p. 357.

"Japanese Architecture and Ornament [Dresser, Christopher: "Some features of Japanese architecture and ornament"]," in: *The Builder* 47 (13 December 1884), pp. 787–788.

"Japanese Architecture and Ornament," in: *The Building News and Engineering Journal* 47 (12 December 1884), pp. 941–942.

"Japanese Architecture," in: *American Architect and Building News* 1 (1876), p. 136.

"Japanese bricks, importation of," in: *The Building News and Engineering Journal* 30 (21 April 1876), p. 411.

"Japanese Competition with England," in: *The Builder* 35 (1877), p. 978.

"Japanese Homes and their Surroundings," in: *The Builder* 54 (26 May 1888), pp. 381–382.

"Japanese Homes and their Surroundings," in: *The Building News and Engineering Journal* 50 (05 February 1886), pp. 206–207.

"Japanese Houses," in: *American Architect and Building News* 1 (1876), pp. 26–27.

Japanese Photographic Association, *A Century of Japanese Photography* (New York, 1980).

"Japanese work at the Centennial grounds," in: *American Architect and Building News* 1 (1876), pp. 55–56.

"Japanische und deutsche Architekten," in: *Deutsche Bauzeitung* 14 (16 February 1895), pp. 84–85.

"Japon," in: Mellado, Francisco de Paula, *Enciclopedia Moderna. Diccionario universal de literatura, ciencia, arte, agricultura, industria y comercio* (Madrid; Paris, 1851–1855), vol. 25, cols. 135–141, resp. 141–143.

"Japon. Intérieur de la maison du gouverneur de Satzouma," in: *Le monde illustré* 11, 546 (1867), p. 197.

"Jarves, James Jackson," in: *Dictionary of Art Historians. A Biographical Dictionary of Historic Scholars, Museum Professionals and Academic Historians of Art*, Online-Resource, https://arthistorians.info/jarvesj/ [last accessed 29 April 2024].

Jarves, James Jackson, *A Glimpse at the Art of Japan* (New York, 1876).

Jaucourt, Louis de, "Japan, le," in: Diderot, Denis; d'Alembert, Jean le Rond (eds.), *Encyclopédie ou Dictionnaire raisonné des sciences, des arts et des métiers* (Paris, 1765), vol. 8, pp. 453–455, cited from: The Encyclopedia of Diderot & d'Alembert Collaborative Translation Project. Translated by Jennifer Rappaport (Ann Arbor: Michigan Publishing, University of Michigan Library, 2013), http://hdl.handle.net/2027/spo.did2222.0002.634 [accessed 9 March 2015].

Jaucourt, Louis de, "Temples des Japonois," in: Diderot, Denis; d'Alembert, Jean le Rond (eds.), *Encyclopédie ou Dictionnaire raisonné des sciences, des arts et des métiers* (Paris, 1765), vol. 16, pp. 83–84, accessed via: University of Chicago: ARTFL Encyclopédie Project (Spring 2013 Edition), Robert Morrissey (ed.), http://encyclopedie.uchicago.edu/ [accessed 9 March 2015].

Jephson, R. Mounteney; Elmhirst, Edward Pennell, *Our life in Japan* (London, 1869).

J-N. C., "Japan," in: *The Encyclopaedia Britannica, or Dictionary of Arts, Sciences, and General Literature* / 12: Hum – Jom, 8th ed., with extensive improvements and additions, and numerous engravings (Edinburgh, 1856), pp. 688–699.

Jones, Hazel J., *Live Machines. Hired Foreigners and Meiji Japan* (Tenterden, Kent/Vancouver, 1980).

Juneja, Monica, "Kunstgeschichte und kulturelle Differenz – Erweiterung oder Paradigmenwechsel," in: Juneja, Monica; Bruhn, Matthias; Werner, Elke (eds.), *Die Universalität der Kunstgeschichte?*, in: *Kritische Berichte* 2 (2012), pp. 6–12.

Kaempfer, Engelbert, *The History of Japan, Giving an Account of the Ancient and Present State and Government of that Empire: of its Temples, Palaces, Castles and Other Buildings, of its Metals, Minerals, Trees, Plants, Animals, Birds and Fishes, of the Chronology and Succession of the Emperors, Ecclesiastical and Secular, of the Original Descent, Religions, Customs, and Manufactures of the Natives, and of their Trade and Commerce with the Dutch and Chinese: Together with a Description of the Kingdom of Siam*, 2 vols. (London, 1727–1729).

Kaiser, Walter; König, Wolfgang (eds.), *Geschichte des Ingenieurs. Ein Beruf in sechs Jahrtausenden* (München; Wien, 2006).

Katahira, Miyuki, "Ōbei ni okeru nihon teienz ō no keisei to harada jiro nō The Gardens of Japan" [The formation of the image of Japanese gardens in the West and Jiro Harada's "The Gardens of Japan"], in: *Nihon kenkyū* 34.3 (2007), pp. 179–208.

Kawashima, Chūji, *Japan's Folk Architecture. Traditional thatched farmhouses* (Tōkyō, 1986).

Kawashima, Chūji, *Minka. Traditional houses of rural Japan* (Tōkyō; New York, 1986).

Kawata, Katsuhiro (ed.), *Kinsei kenchikusho – dōmiya hinagata* [Source books of Japanese temple and shrine design] (Kyōto: Tairyūdō Shoten, 1988).

Kawazoe, Noboru (ed.), *Metaborizumu senkyūhyakurokujū: toshi e no teian/ Metabolism: the proposals for new urbanism* ([Tōkyō]: Bijutu Syuppan Sha, 1960).

Keane, Augustus. H., *Asia* (London, 1882).

Kenrick, Douglas Moore, *A century of western studies of Japan: the first hundred years of the Asiatic Society of Japan 1872–1972* (= The transactions of the Asiatic Society of Japan: Ser. 3; 14) (Tōkyō, 1978).

Kimball, Fiske, *A History of Architecture* (New York; London, 1918).

Kinchin, Juliet; Stirton, Paul, *Is Mr. Ruskin living too long?* (Oxford, 2005).

King, James, *Beyond "The Great Wave": The Japanese Landscape Print, 1727–1960* (Bern, 2010).

Kirsch, Karin, *Die Neue Wohnung und das Alte Japan. Architekten planen für sich selbst* (Stuttgart, 1996).

Kishida, Hideto, *Japanese Architecture* (Tōkyō, 1935).

Klaproth, Heinrich Julius, *Annales des empereurs du Japon* (*Nihon Ōdai Ichiran*) (Paris, 1834).

Knox, Thomas Wallace, *The boy travellers in the Far East, part first: adventures of two youths in a journey to Japan and China* (New York, 1879).

Koch, C., "Aus der Japanischen Ausstellung in Berlin," in: *Leipziger Illustrirte Zeitung* 2194 (18 July 1885), p. 58.

Kohl, Karl-Heinz, *Ethnologie – die Wissenschaft vom kulturell Fremden: Eine Einführung*, 3, rev. ed. (Munich, 2012).

Koppelkamm, Stefan, *Der imaginäre Orient. Exotische Bauten des 18. und 19. Jahrhunderts in Europa* (Berlin, 1987).

Kornhauser, David, *Urban Japan. Its Foundations and Growth* (London et al., 1976).

Kornicki, Peter F. "Ernest Mason Satow (1843–1929)," in: Cortazzi, Hugh; Daniels, Gordon (eds.), *Britain and Japan 1859–1991: themes and personalities* (London, 1991), pp. 76–87.

Köth, Anke, et al. (eds.), *Building America 1. Die Erschaffung einer neuen Welt* (Dresden, 2005).

Köth, Anke, et al. (eds.), *Building America 2. Migration der Bilder* (Dresden, 2007).

Köth, Anke, et al. (eds.), *Building America 3. Eine große Erzählung* (Dresden, 2008).

Kozyreff, Chantal, *The Oriental Dream: Leopold II's Japanese Tower and Chinese Pavilion at Laeken* (Antwerp, 2001).

Krauskopf, Kai; Lippert, Hans-Georg; Zaschke, Kerstin (eds.), *Neue Tradition 1. Konzepte einer antimodernen Moderne in Deutschland von 1920 bis 1960* (Dresden, 2009).

Krauskopf, Kai; Lippert, Hans-Georg; Zaschke, Kerstin (eds.), *Neue Tradition 2. Vorbilder, Mechanismen und Ideen* (Dresden, 2012).

Krauskopf, Kai; Lippert, Hans-Georg; Zaschke, Kerstin (eds.), *Neue Tradition 3. Europäische Architektur im Zeichen von Traditionalismus und Regionalismus* (Dresden, 2012).

Kreitner, G. R. von, *Im fernen Osten: Reisen des Grafen Bela Széchenyí in Indien, Japan, China, Cibet und Birma in den Jahren 1877–1880* (Wien, 1881).

Kretschmer, Winfried, *Geschichte der Weltausstellungen* (Frankfurt/M. et al., 1999).

Kühn, Christine (ed.), *Zartrosa und Lichtblau. Japanische Fotografie der Meiji-Zeit (1868–1912)* (Berlin, 2015).

Kühn, Christine, "Zartrosa und Lichtblau. Japanische Fotografie der Meiji-Zeit," in: id. (ed.), *Zartrosa und Lichtblau. Japanische Fotografie der Meiji-Zeit (1868–1912)* (Berlin, 2015), pp. 9–23.

L'Exposition Universelle de 1867 Illustré, 1867.

La Farge, John, *An Artist's letters from Japan* (New York, 1897).

Labarthe, Charles de, "Le Catalogue des palais des souverains-pontifes japonais," in: *Revue orientale et américainee*, t. VIII (1863), suppl., pp. 65–69.

Labat, Alexandre, "Charles Garnier et l'exposition de 1889. L'histoire de l'habitation," in: *1889. La Tour Eiffel et l'Exposition Universelle* (Paris, 1989), pp. 130–147.

Labrusse, Remi, "GONSE, Louis," in: Sénéchal, Philippe; Barbillon, Claire (eds.), *Dictionnaire critique des historiens de l'art actifs en France de la Révolution à la Première Guerre mondiale*, via Institut national d'histoire de l'art, 3 November 2008, https://www.inha.fr/fr/ressources/publications/publications-numeriques/dictionnaire-critique-des-historiens-de-l-art/gonse-louis.html [last accessed 18 August 2023].

Lacroix, A., "Fernand Levieux," in: l'Institut Royal Colonial Belge (ed.), *Biographie Coloniale Belge IV* (1955), cols. 520–521.

Lagarde-Fouquet, Annie, "Contribution d'ingénieurs et architectes français à la construction de Yokohama (Japon) entre 1860 et 1900," in: Bertoncello, Brigitte, *"Les Acteurs de la composition urbaine (édition électronique)", 137ᵉ Congrès national des sociétés historiques et scientifiques, Tours, 2012* (Paris: Éditions du CTHS, 2014), pp. 56–69.

Lambourne, Lionel, *Japonisme: Cultural Crossings Between Japan and the West* (New York, 2007).

Lancaster, Clay, "Japanese Buildings in the United States before 1900: Their Influence upon American Domestic Architecture," in: *Art Bulletin* 35 (1953), pp. 217–224.

Lancaster, Clay, *The Japanese influence in America* (New York, 1963).

Landau, Georg, "Der Hausbau," in: *Beilagen z. Correspondenz-Blatt des Gesangvereins der deutschen Geschichts- und Alterthumsvereine*, 1857–1862.

Lane-Poole, Stanley; Dickins, Frederick Victor; Parkes, Harry Smith Sir K. C. B., *The Life of Sir Harry Parkes, K. C. B., G. C. M. G., sometime Her Majesty's Minister to China & Japan*, 2 vols. (London, 1894).

Larsen, Knut Einar, *Architectural Preservation in Japan* (Trondheim, 1994).

Ledoux, Claude Nicolas, *L'Architecture considérée sous le rapport de l'art, des mœurs et de la législation, facsimile reproduction of the edition of 1804* (Nördlingen, 1987).

Lemoine, Bernadette (ed.), *Regards et discours européens sur le Japon et l'Inde au XIXᵉ siècle* (Limoges, 2000).

Lepach, Bernd, "Cawley, George [Cauley]," in: *Meiji-Portraits*, online resource, http://www.meiji-portraits.de/meiji_portraits_c.html [last accessed 26 April 2024].

Lepach, Bernd, "Lescasse, Jules," in: *Meiji-Portraits*, online resource, http://www.meiji-portraits.de/meiji_portraits_l.html [last accessed 26 April 2024].

Les merveilles de l'exposition de 1889. Historie, construction, inauguration, description détaillée des palais, des annexes et des parcs, les chefs-d'œuvre de l'art de tous les pays, les machines, les arts industriels, les produits manufacturés, les expositions spéciales, la Tour Eiffel, Paris [1889].

Lescasse, Jules, *Étude sur les constructions japonaises et sur les constructions en général, au point de vue des tremblements de terre, et description d'un système destiné à donner une grande sécurité aux constructions en maçonnerie* (Paris, 1877).

Lescasse, M. J., "Earthquakes and Buildings" (serialised in four parts), *Japan Gazette* (2 March to 15 March 1877).

Lescasse, M. J., "Étude sur les Constructions Japonaises, &c.," in: *Memoires de la Societé des Ingénieurs Civils* (6 April 1877), pp. 211–218 (meeting and discussion), pp. 451–458 (text).

Levieux, Fernand, "Essai sur l'architecture japonaise," in: *Extrait du Bulletin de la Société Royale Belge de Géographie* 19.3 (1895), pp. 229–250.

L'Exposition chez soi 1889. Exposition universelle de 1889, 2 vols. (Paris, 1889).

Lichtwark, Alfred, *Justus Brinckmann in seiner Zeit* (Hamburg, 1978).

Lindau, Rudolph, "Notes on the city of Yedo, the Capital of Japan," in: *Journal of the North China Branch of the Royal Asiatic* 1–2 (1864–1865), pp. 1–12.

Lippert, Hans-Georg, "Die Kunst des guten Bauens. Architekturtraktate als Handreichung für den Wohnhausbau," in: Onnen, Elke; Spohn, Thomas (eds.), *Die neuen Häuser in den neuen Städten und Dörfern. Neuerungen im Hausbau unter dem Einfluss der Landesherren und ihrer Baumeister zwischen 1650 und 1830* (Petersberg, 2019), pp. 59–66.

Lippert, Hans-Georg, "Systematik und Sehnsuchtsbild. Der Beitrag der frühen Hausforschung zum traditionellen Bauen im 20. Jahrhundert," in: Krauskopf, Kai; Lippert, Hans-Georg; Zaschke, Kerstin (eds.), *Neue Tradition. Vorbilder, Mechanismen und Ideen* (Dresden, 2012), pp. 13–40.

Locher, Mira, "Introduction," in: Cram, Ralph Adams, *Impressions of Japanese architecture* (North Clarendon, VT, 2011), pp. 11–21.

Locher, Mira; Kuma, Kengo; Simmons, Ben, *Traditional Japanese Architecture. An exploration of elements and forms* (Tōkyō, 2010).

Lockyer, Angus, *Japan at the exhibition, 1867–1970*, Ph.D. dissertation (Stanford University, 2000).

Löffler, Beate, "Designing a global city: Tokyo," in: Exenberger, Andreas, et al. (eds.), *Globalization and the City: Two Connected Phenomena in Past and Present* (Innsbruck, 2013), pp. 191–206.

Löffler, Beate, "From teaching 'progress' to learning 'tradition'? Tokyo's built environment as a mirror of ideas of modernity in German-language discourses of architecture (1900–1940)," in: Mori, Takahito; Liedtke, Rainer; Schmidtpott, Katja (eds.), *Towards a Transnational Urban History of Japan and Europe: Organized Modernity and Governance (1900s–1940s)* (Stuttgart, 2023), pp. 71–103.

Löffler, Beate, "Petrified worldviews. Eurocentric legacy in architectural knowledge bases on Japan," in: *InterDisciplines* 8.2 (2017), pp. 69–95.

Löffler, Beate, "Search, discovery, canonization and loss. Japan's Architectural Heritage as a Matter of Cultural Negotiation and Perception of Relevance in the Late Nineteenth Century," in: Bogner, Simone, et al. (eds.), *Collecting Loss* (Ilmtal-Weinstraße, 2021), pp. 80–94.

Löffler, Beate, "The Perpetual Other. The Japanese architecture in western imagination," in: *International Journal for History, Culture and Modernity* 3.3 (2015), pp. 83–112.

Löffler, Beate, "Thwarted Innovation: The discourse on earthquake resistance in Japanese architecture – a historical review," in: *Construction History* 34.2 (2019), pp. 35–52.

Löffler, Beate; Hein, Carola; Mager, Tino, "Searching for Meiji-Tokyo: Heterogeneous Visual Media and the Turn to Global Urban History, Digitalization, and Deep Learning," in: *Global Urban History* [Blog], 20 March 2018, https://globalurbanhistory.com/2018/03/20/searching-for-meiji-tokyo-heterogeneous-visual-media-and-the-turn-to-global-urban-history-digitalization-and-deep-learning/ [last accessed 15 May 2019].

Löffler, Beate; Mager, Tino, "Minor politics, major consequences – Epistemic challenges of metadata and the contribution of image recognition," in: *Digital Culture & Society: The Politics of Metadata* 6.2 (2021), pp. 221–238.

Long, Basil S., "William Payne, water-colour painter working 1776–1830," in: *Walker's Quarterly* 6 (January 1922), pp. 3–35.

Loos, Claire, *Adolf Loos privat* (Wien, 1936).

Lorenz, Reinhold, *Japan und Mitteleuropa. Von Solferino bis zur Wiener Weltausstellung (1859–73)* (Brünn; München; Wien, 1944).

Lowell, Percival, *The soul of the Far East* (Boston and New York, 1888), pp. 110–111.

Lowen, Lenore, *One Foot in the Past, One Foot in the Future: Japanese Cultural Identity and Preservation Law 1868–1950*, Ph.D. thesis (Los Angeles: University of Southern California, 2013).

Lützow, Carl von, "Die Japanische Kunst," in: *Österreichische Monatsschrift für den Orient* (1884), pp. 1–6, 44–49, 73–78, 97–103.

Mabuchi, Akiko, *Japanese art and Japonisme. Part 1, Early English writings (John La Farge; James Jackson Jarves; Marcus Bourne Huish; Christopher Dresser)* (Bristol, 1999).

Macfarlane, Charles, *Japan. An account, geographical and historical, from the earliest period at which the islands composing this empire were known to Europeans, down to the present time, and the expedition fitted out in the United States, etc.* (New York; London, 1852).

Maclay, Arthur Collins, *Budget letters from Japan* (New York, 1886).

Mae, Michiko; Scherer, Elisabeth (eds.), *Nipponspiration: Japonismus und japanische Populärkultur im deutschsprachigen Raum* (Cologne; Weimar; Vienna, 2013).

Mainichi Shimbun (ed.), *Nihon no hyaku nen. Shashin de miru fuzoku bunkashi. 1860–1959* [A hundred years in Japan · History of customs and culture seen in pictures] (Tōkyō: Mainichi Shimbun, 1960).

Malkowsky, Georg (ed.), *Die Pariser Weltausstellung in Wort und Bild* (Berlin, 1900).

Mamba (Musashiya), Masayuki; Huber, Michael (transl.), "The model of a Daimyō Residence yashiki 屋敷 and Musashiya Kamakichi 武蔵屋鎌吉," in: Zorn, Bettina (ed.), *Archiv 65. Archiv Weltmuseum Wien* (2015), pp. 77–83.

Manners and customs of the Japanese, in the nineteenth century; from the accounts of Dutch residents in Japan and from the German work of Dr. Philipp Franz von Siebold (London, 1841).

Maron, Hermann, "Nachtrag zu 'Charakteristik Japans' Nagasaki 7. Mai," in: *Die Grenzboten* 20, II, 3 (1861), pp. 195–199.

Maron, Hermann, "Zur Charakteristik Japan's. (Schluß)," in: *Die Grenzboten* 20, I, 2 (1861), pp. 310–316.

Maron, Hermann, "Zur Charakteristik Japan's. Shanghai 18. Feb.," in: *Die Grenzboten* 20, I, 2 (1861), pp. 265–276.

Marshall, D. H., "Notes on some of the Volcanic Mountains in Japan," in: *Transactions of the Asiatic Society of Japan* VI (1878), pp. 321–345.

Martin, Andreas; Fröhlich-Schauseil, Anke, *Die Flusslandschaft an den Mulden. Frühe Wahrnehmungen in bildender Kunst und Reiseliteratur* (Dresden, 2012).

Massa-Gille, Geneviève, *Journal d'Hippolyte Fortoul: Ministre de l'instruction publique et des cultes (1811–1856), Tome 2, 1er Juillet 1855–4 Juillet 1856* (Genève, 1989).

Mathews, Charles Thompson, "A Temple of the Togukawa at Nikko," in: *Architectural Record* 4 (December 1894), pp. 191–209.

Mathews, Charles Thompson, *The story of architecture; An outline of the styles in all countries* (New York, 1896).

Mattie, Erik, *Weltausstellungen* (Stuttgart et al., 1998).

Maxwell, Anne, *Colonial Photography and Exhibitions. Representations of the 'Native' and the Making of European Identities* (London et al., 1999).

May, Ekkehard; Schmitt-Weigand, John; Köhn, Stephan, et al. (eds.), *Edo bunko. Die Edo Bibliothek. Ausführlich annotierte Bibliographie der Blockdruckbücher im Besitz der Japanologie der J. W. Goethe-Universität Frankfurt am Main als kleine Bücherkunde und Einführung in die Verlagskultur der Edo-Zeit* (= Bunken. Studien und Materialien zur japanischen Literatur, Band 8) (Wiesbaden, 2003).

McCabe, James Dabney, *A tour around the world by General Grant. Being a narrative of the incidents and events of his journey* (Philadelphia; Chicago [etc.], 1879).

McClatchie, Thomas R. H., "The Castle of Yedo," in: *Transactions of the Asiatic Society of Japan* VI (1878), pp. 119–150.

McClatchie, Thomas R. H., "The Feudal Mansions of Yedo," in: *Transactions of the Asiatic Society of Japan* VII 3 (1879), pp. 157–186.

McKean, John, "Sir Banister Fletcher: pillar to post-colonial readings," in: *The Journal of Architecture* 11.2 (2006), pp. 187–204.

McLaughlin, Joseph, "'The Japanese Village' and the Metropolitan Construction of Modernity," in: *Romanticism and Victorianism on the Net* 48 (November 2007), s.p.

Meech, Julia, *Frank Lloyd Wright and the Art of Japan: The Architect's Other Passion* (New York, 2001).

Meech-Pekarik, Julia, "Early Collectors of Japanese Prints and the Metropolitan Museum of Art," in: *Metropolitan Museum Journal* 17 (1982), pp. 93–118.

Meid, Michiko, *Der Einführungsprozeß der europäischen und nordamerikanischen Architektur in Japan seit 1542* (Cologne, 1977).

Meier-Lemgo, Karl, "Kaempfer, Engelbert," in: *Neue Deutsche Biographie* 10 (1974), pp. 729–730, online resource, http://www.deutsche-biographie.de/ppn118559168.html [accessed 29 August 2017].

Mémoires de la Société d'ethnographie de Paris. Mémoires et documents originaux Société d'ethnographie de Paris, Section D'ethnographie Descriptive, Séance Du 7 Juin 1869, pp. 259–260.

Menpes, Mortimer, "A letter from Japan," in: *Studio: international art* (December 1898), pp. 21–26.

Meyer, Eva-Maria, "The Guide to the Celebrated Places in Kiyoto," blog entry, February 2014, http://www.meyer-sensei.de/post/77373183755/the-guide-to-the-celebrated-places-in-kiyoto [last accessed 26 April 2024].

Meylan [Meijlan], Germain Felix, *Japan. Voorgesteld in schetsen over de zeden en gebruiken van dat ryk, byzonder over de ingezetenen der stad Nagasaky* (Amsterdam, 1830).

Michel, Émile, "Le Japon à l'Exposition universelle," in: *L'art: revue hebdomadaire illustrée* 15.2 (1889), pp. 217–224.

Milne, John, *Earthquakes and other Earth Movements* (New York, 1886).

Milne, John, "On Construction in Earthquake Countries," in: *Minutes of the Proceedings of the Institution of Civil Engineers* 83, session 1885–86, part I, paper 2108, pp. 278–295.

Milne, John, *Seismology* (London, 1898).

Milne, John; Burton, William K.; Ogawa, Kazumasa, *The Great Earthquake in Japan, 1891* (Yokohama, 1891).

Minamoto, Toyomune, *An Illustrated History of Japanese Art* (Kioto, 1935).

Ministère de la Culture et la Communication (ed.), *Le japonisme*, catalogue (Paris, 1988).

Mizuno, Seiichi, *Asuka Buddhist Art: Horyu-Ji* (The Heibonsha Survey of Japanese Art 4) (New York, 1974).

Monod, Émile, *L'Exposition universelle de 1889: grand ouvrage illustré, historique, encyclopédique, descriptif*, 4 vols. (Paris, 1890).

Montanus, Arnoldus; Ogilby, John, *Atlas Japannensis: being remarkable addresses by way of embassy from the East-India company of the United Provinces, to the emperor of Japan. Containing a description of their several territories, cities, temples, and fortresses; their religions, laws, and customs; their prodigious wealth, and gorgeous habits; the nature of their soil, plants, beasts, hills, rivers, and fountains. With the character of the ancient and modern Japanners* (London, 1670).

Montefiore, Edouard Levi, "Les temples au Japon avec une eau-forte," in: *Mémoires de l'Athénée oriental fondé en 1864* (1871), pp. 95–100.

Mori Art Museum (ed.), *Japan in Architecture. Genealogies of its Transformation* (Tōkyō: Echelle, 2018).

Morris, John, *Advance Japan. A nation thoroughly in earnest* (London, 1895).

Morse, Edward Sylvester, *Japanese Homes and Their Surroundings* (Boston; New York; London, 1885).

Mortimer, Favell Lee, *Far off, or, Asia described*. With anecdotes and numerous illustrations, new, revised ed. (London, 1890).

Moser, Alfred, "My Grandfather Michael Moser (1853–1912)," in: Zorn, Bettina (ed.), *Archiv 65. Archiv Weltmuseum Wien* (2015), pp. 12–19.

Mossman, Samuel, *Japan* (London, 1880).

Mothes, Oscar (ed.), *Allgemeines deutsches Bauwörterbuch, das ist Encyclopädie der Baukunst für Alle, die mit dem Hochbau, Flachbau, Bergbau, Maschinenbau etc. zu thun haben*, 2 vols. (Leipzig, 1858–1859).

Mothes, Oscar (ed.), *Illustrirtes Bau-Lexikon: praktisches Hülfs- und Nachschlagebuch im Gebiete des Hoch- und Flachbaues, Land- u. Wasserbaues, Mühlen- u. Bergbaues, der Schiffs- und Kriegsbaukunst, sowie der Mythologie, Ikonographie, Symbolik, Heraldik, Botanik und Mineralogie, so weit solche mit dem Bauwesen in Verbindung kommen; für Architekten und Ingenieure ...*, 2 vols. (Leipzig, 1863–1866).

Mumford, Lewis, *The City in History. Its Origins, its Transformations, and its Prospects*, 3rd ed. (London, 1966).

Münsterberg, Oskar, *Japanische Kunst und das japanische Land. Ein Beitrag zur Kunstwissenschaft* (Berlin, 1896).

Murai, Noriko, "Beyond Tenshin: Okakura Kakuzo's Multiple Legacies," in: *Review of Japanese Culture and Society* 24, special edition (December 2012), pp. 70–93.

Muthesius, Hermann, "Das japanische Haus," in: *Zentralblatt der Bauverwaltung* (20 June 1903), pp. 306–307.

Muthesius, Hermann, "Der japanische Hausbau," in: *Berliner Tageblatt* 249, (13 September 1923), 1. Beiblatt.

"Nachrichten aus den Missionen. Japan," in: *Die katholischen Missionen* (May 1876), pp. 104–107.

Naito, Akira, *Edo, the City that Became Tokyo. An illustrated history* (Tōkyō: Kodansha, 2003).

Naito, Akira; Nishikawa, Takeshi, *Katsura. A Princely Retreat* (New York, 1977).

Nakamori, Yasufumi, *Katsura. Picturing modernism in Japanese architecture* (New Haven; London, 2010).

Nakazawa, Sonō, *Nikkō meisho zue* [Guide to Famous Places in Nikkō] (Tōkyō: Murakami, 1882).

Nansouty, Max de, "L'Empire du Japon à l'Exposition universelle de 1889," in: *La Nature* 846 (17 September 1889), pp. 177–179.

Nerdinger, Winfried (ed.), *Der Architekt – Geschichte und Gegenwart eines Berufsstandes*, 2 vols. (München; London; New York, 2012).

Neumann, Karl Friedrich, "Japan," in: Ersch, Johann Samuel; Gruber, Johann Gottfried (eds.), *Allgemeine Encyclopädie der Wissenschaften und Künste: mit Kupfern und Charten* (Leipzig, 1818–1889), vol. 14 (1937), pp. 366–378.

Nicholson, Peter, *Encyclopedia of architecture. A dictionary of the science and practice of architecture, building, carpentry, etc., from the earliest ages to the present time, forming a comprehensive work of reference for the use of architects, builders, carpenters, masons, engineers, students, professional men, and amateurs*, 2 vols. (New York, 1852).

Nihon Rekishi Gakkai (ed.), *Meiji Ishin Jinmei Jiten* (Yoshikawa Kōbunkan, 1981).

Nishi, Kazuo; Hozumi, Kazuo, *What is Japanese Architecture?* (New York, 2012).

Nishi, Kazuo; Hozumi, Kazuo, *What is Japanese architecture?* (Tōkyō: Kodansha, 1983).

Nishibori, Akira, "Meiji jidai no kōzan kankei furansuhito ni tsuite (1)" [French involved in mining during the Meiji period. The government-run Ikuno mine], in: *Yokohama keiei kenkyū. Yokohama business review* 12.3 (1991), pp. 61–72.

Nishioka, Tsunekazu; Miyakami, Shigetaka; Hozumi, Kazuo, *Hōryūji. Sekai saiko no mokuzō kenchiku* [Hōryūji. How the Japanese made buildings] (Tōkyō: Sōshisha, 1990).

Nitschke, Günter, *From Shinto to Ando. Studies in Architectural Anthropology in Japan* (London; Berlin, 1993).

Noguchi, Kenji; Hatano, Jun, "Characteristics of the townhouse model of the National Museum of Ethnology, Leiden collections," in: *Journal of architecture and planning: Transactions of AIJ* (*Nihon-Kenchiku-Gakkai-keikakukei-ronbunshū*) 82.733 (2017), pp. 757–766.

Norton, Frank H.; Leslie, Frank, *Frank Leslie's historical register of the United States Centennial Exposition, 1876. Embellished with nearly eight hundred illustrations drawn expressly for this work by the most eminent artists in America. Including illustrations and descriptions of all previous International exhibitions* (New York, 1877).

Nōshōmushō (ed.), *1900nen Pari Bankoku Hakurankai Rinji Hakuraikai Jimukyoku Hōkoku 1* [Report of the Secretariat of the Extraordinary Exhibition of the 1900th Paris World's Fair] (Tōkyō: Nōshōmushō, 1902).

Nute, Kevin, *Frank Lloyd Wright and Japan. The role of traditional Japanese art and architecture in the work of Frank Lloyd Wright* (London; New York, 1993).

Nute, Kevin, *The Constructed Other: Japanese Architecture in the Western Mind* (London; New York, 2021).

"Obituary for George Cawley," in: *Proceedings of the Institution of Mechanical Engineers 1* (1927), p. 579.

"Obituary to Thomas R. H. McClatchie," in: *Japan Weekly Mail* 5.9 (27 February 1886), p. 195.

Odenthal, Julia, *Andere Räume – Räume der Anderen. Die Rezeptionsgeschichte der japanischen Architektur in der deutschen und japanischen Kunst- und Architekturgeschichte (1850–1950)* (Munich, 2015).

Ogawa, Kazumasa, *A model Japanese villa* (Tōkyō, [1898?]).

Ogawa, Kazumasa, *Famous Castles and Temples of Japan* (Yokohama; Hong Kong; Shanghai and Singapore, 1898).

Ogawa, Kazumasa, *Japanese Life* (Yokohama, [1892?]).

Ogawa, Kazumasa, *Matsushima. One of the Three Most Famous Views of Japan* (s.l., 1895).

Ogawa, Kazumasa, *Scenes in Nikko and Vicinity = Temples of Nikko* (s.l., 1893).

Ogawa, Kazumasa, *Souvenirs de Yézo* (s.l., 1897).

Ogawa, Kazumasa, *The Nikko District* (Tōkyō, 1912).

Ogawa, Kazumasa; Enami, T.; Tamamura, K., *Fuji San* (Tōkyō, 1912).

Okakura, Kakudzo [Okakura, Kakuzo], "The Decoration of the Ho-o-den," in: *The Decorator and Furnisher* 23.5 (February 1894), pp. 181–182.

Okakura, Kakudzo [Okakura, Kakuzo], *The Ho-o-den. An illustrated Description of the Building erected by the Japanese Government at the World's Columbian Exhibition, Jackson Park, Chicago* (Tōkyō, 1893).

Oliphant, Laurence, *Le Japon, raconté par Laurence Oliphant. Traduction publiée par M. Guizot* (Paris, 1875).

Oliphant, Laurence, *Narrative of the Earl of Elgin's Mission to China and Japan in the years 1857, '58, '59*, 2 vols. (London, 1859).

Omori, Fusakichi, "Measurement of Vibration of Gojunotos, or 5-Story Buddhist Stupas (Pagodas)," in: *Bulletin of the Imperial Earthquake Investigation Committee* 9.3 (1921), pp. 110–152.

Omoto, Keiko, *Quand le Japon s'ouvrit au monde: Émile Guimet et les arts d'Asie* (Paris, 2001).

"Orientalische Literatur," in: *Allgemeine Deutsche Real-Encyklopädie für die gebildeten Stände. Conversations-Lexikon*, 10. *Moskau bis Patricier*, 9. Originalaufl. (Leipzig, 1846), pp. 509–511.

Oshima, Ken Tadashi, *Constructed natures of modern architecture in Japan, 1920–1940. Yamada Mamoru, Horiguchi Sutemi, and Antonin Raymond*, Ph.D. thesis (New York: Columbia University, 2003).

Oshima, Ken Tadashi, *International Architecture in Interwar Japan. Constructing Kokusai Kenchiku* (Seattle, 2009).

Ōta, Hirotarō; Itō Yōtarō, *Shōmei*, edited reprint (Tōkyō: Kajima Shuppankai, 1971).

Ōta, Hirotarō (ed.), *Nihon kenchikushi kiso shiryō shūsei* [History of Japanese building basics document collection], 21 vols. (Tōkyō: Chūō Kōron Bijutsu Shuppan, 1971–2006).

Overmeer Fisscher, Johannes Frederik van, *Bijdrage tot de kennis van het Japansche Rijk; Met platen* (Amsterdam, 1833).

Özaslan, Nuray, "The Role of Architectural History in Building Modern Turkish Architecture," in: *The Journal of International Social Research* 4.17 (Spring 2011), pp. 339–347.

Paine, Robert Treat; Soper, Alexander Coburn, *The Art and Architecture of Japan* (Harmondsworth, 1974).

Paine, Robert Treat; Soper, Alexander Coburn, *The Art and Architecture of Japan* (Baltimore, 1955).

Paris Exposition 1900. Guide pratique du visiteur de Paris et de l'exposition (Paris, 1900), pp. 357–358.

Paris, A., *Une excursion a Kioto, capitale du Japon* (Paris, 1869).

Parker, Peter, *Journal of an expedition from Sincapore to Japan, with a visit to Loo-Choo; descriptive of these islands and their inhabitants; in an attempt with the aid of natives educated in England, to create an opening for missionary labours in Japan* (London, 1838).

Payne, Alina, *From Ornament to Object. Genealogies of Architectural Modernism* (New Haven, CT; London, 2012).

Pemsel, Jutta, *Die Wiener Weltausstellung von 1873* (Wien; Köln, 1989).

Perry, Matthew Calbraith; Tomes, Robert, *Japan and the Japanese: a narrative of the U.S. government expedition to Japan, under Commodore Perry* (New York, 1857).

Perry, Matthew Calbraith; Tomes, Robert, *The Americans in Japan: an abridgment of the government narrative of the U.S. expedition to Japan, under Commodore Perry* (New York, 1857).

Pezeu-Massabuau, Jacques, *La maison japonaise* (Paris, 1981).

Pfoundes, Charles, "Constructive art in Japan," in: *The Builder* 37 (1879), pp. 1306–1307, 1395.

[Pfoundes, Charles,] "Something more about Japanese theatres," in: *The Builder* 37 (24 May 1879), p. 583.

[Pfoundes, Charles,] "The Artisan of Japan and his Work," in: *The Builder* (17 May 1879), p. 540.

Piggott, Francis Taylor, "Some notes on Japanese architecture," in: *The Builder* 64 (8 April 1893), pp. 262–263; (15 April 1893), pp. 280–282.

Pohl, Manfred, *Geschichte Japans* (Munich, 2002).

Ponciroli, Virginia; Isozaki, Arata, *Katsura. La villa imperiale* (Milan, 2004).

Pratt, Mary Louise, *Imperial Eyes: Travel Writing and Transculturation* (London, 1992).

"Prevention of fire," in: *The Building News and Engineering Journal* 16 (12 February 1869), p. 147.

"Primitive Fireproof Buildings," in: *Architect and Building News* 2 (1877), p. 72.

"Proposed importation of Carpenters," in: *The Building News and Engineering Journal* 34 (18 January 1878), p. 73.

Quatremère de Quincy, Antoine, *Encyclopédie méthodique. Architecture*, 4 vols. (1788–1825).

Ramée, Daniel, *Dictionnaire général des Termes d'Architecture en français, allemand, anglais et italien* (Paris, 1868).

Reed, Edward James, *Japan. Its History, Traditions, and Religions*, 2 vols. (London, 1880).

Rees, Jochen, "Menzel Meets Meiji: Die „Japanische Ausstellung" von 1885 im Werk von Adolph Menzel," in: Bergmann, Annegret (ed.), *Elegante Zusammenkunft im Gelehrtengarten* (Weimar, 2015), pp. 210–217.

Régamey, Félix, *Japan in Art and Industry with a Glance at Japanese Manners and Customs* (New York, 1892).

Régamey, Félix, *Le Japon pratique* (Paris, 1891).

Rein, Johann Justus, "Das japanische Kunstgewerbe," in: *Österreichische Monatsschrift für den Orient* (1882), pp. 1–7, 20–24, 52–58, 58–70, 88–93, 100–106.

Rein, Johannes Justus, *Japan. Nach Reisen und Studien im Auftrage der Königlich Preussischen Regierung*, 2 vols. (Leipzig, 1881–1886).

Rein, Johannes Justus, *Japan. Travels and Researches. Undertaken at the cost of the Prussian Government*, 2nd ed. (London, 1888).

Religious Tract Society, *Japan Opened: Compiled Chiefly from the Narrative of the American Expedition to Japan, in the years 1852-3-4* (London, 1858).

"Report of Committee on Fire and Earthquake Damage to Buildings," in: *Proceedings of the American Society of Civil Engineers* 33 (1907), pp. 299–354.

Rogala, Jozef, *A Collector's Guide to Books on Japan in English: An Annotated List of Over 2500 Titles with Subject Index* (Abingdon, 2004).

Rohan, Kieran M., "Lighthouses and the Yatoi Experience of R. H. Brunton," in: *Monumenta Nipponica* 20.1–2 (1965), pp. 64–80.

Rosny, Léon de, *Notice ethnographique de l'encyclopédie japonaise Wa-kan-san-saï-dzou-yé* (Paris, 1861).

Rothfels, Nigel, *Savages and Beasts. The Birth of the Modern Zoo* (Baltimore, 2002).

Rousmaniere, Nicole C.; Hirayama, Mikiko (eds.), *Reflecting Truth. Japanese Photography in the Nineteenth Century* (Amsterdam, 2004).

Royal Institute of British Architects, *How to observe: architecture: or, questions upon various subjects connected therewith, suggested for the direction of correspondents and travellers, and for the purpose of eliciting uniformity of observation and intelligence in their communications to the Institute* (London, 1842).

Rujivacharakul, Vimalin, "Asia in World Architecture and World Cartography," in: Rujivacharakul, Vimalin; Hahn, H. Hazel; Oshima, Ken Tadashi; Christensen, Peter (eds.), *Architecturalized Asia. Mapping a Continent through History* (Honolulu, 2013), pp. 17–34.

Rundall, Thomas, *Memorials of the empire of Japan in the XVI and XVII centuries* (London, 1850).

Ruprechter, Walter, *Passagen. Studien zum Kulturaustausch zwischen Japan und dem Westen* (Munich, 2015).

Ruskin, John, *Laws of Fésole* (Sunnyside; Orpington; Kent, 1877).

Saaler, Sven; Szpilman, Christopher W. A. (ed.), *Routledge Handbook of Modern Japanese History* (Abingdon; New York, 2018).

Sachsenmaier, Dominic; Eisenstadt, Shmuel; Riedel, Jens (eds.), *Reflections on Multiple Modernities. European, Chinese, and Other Approaches* (Leiden, 2002).

Said, Edward, *Orientalism* (New York, 1978).

Saito, Heijirō, *Nihon kaoku kōzō* [Japanese house structures] (Tōkyō: Shin'yudō, 1904).

Saitō, Yukio; Hasegawa, Settan, *Edo meisho zue* [Guide to Famous Places in Edo], 20 vols. (Edo, 1834–1836).

Sakamoto, Hisako, "Nihon no shuppin ni miru Firaderufia Bankokuhakurankai to Uīn Bankokuhakurankai no kanren [Relationship between the Japanese Exhibits at the Philadelphia International Exhibition of 1876 and the Vienna World Exhibition of 1873]," in: *Proceedings of the 54th Annual Conference of JSSD* (2007), s.p.

Salacroup-Buchard, Agnès, "Le Japonisme en architecture, 1993/2000," on: https://laurent-buchard.alwaysdata.net/index.html/Japonisme/index.html [last accessed 29 April 2024].

"Sale and reception rooms, kaitakushi, Tokyo," in: *The Building News and Engineering Journal* 45 (30 November 1883), p. 848.

Salz, Jonah, "Intercultural Pioneers: Otojiro Kawakami and Sada Yakko," in: *The journal of intercultural studies* 20 (1993), pp. 25–74.

Sand, Jordan, *House and Home in Modern Japan. Architecture, Domestic Space, and Bourgeois Culture, 1880–1930* (Cambridge, MA; London, 2005).

Satō, Dōshin, *Modern Japanese Art and the Meiji State: The Politics of Beauty* (Los Angeles, 2011).

Satō, Kenji, "Postcards in Japan. A Historical Sociology of a Forgotten Culture," in: *International Journal of Japanese Sociology* 11 (2002), pp. 35–55.

Satow, Ernest Mason, *A Guide Book to Nikkō* (Reprint in: Collected Works, pt. 1, vol. 4) (Yokohama, 1875).

Satow, Ernest Mason, "The Shin-tau Temples of Ise," in: *Transactions of the Asiatic Society of Japan* II (1874), pp. 113–139.

Satow, Ernest Mason; Hawes, A. G. S., *A handbook for travellers in central & northern Japan, being a guide to Tōkiō, Kiōto, Ōzaka, Hakodate, Nagasaki, and other cities, the most interesting parts of the main island; ascents of the principal mountains; descriptions of temples; and historical notes and legends* (Yokohama, 1881).

Schaefer, Carl, *Die Holzarchitektur Deutschlands vom XIV. bis XVII. Jahrhundert* (Berlin, 1883–1888).

Schäfer, Dietrich, *Das Bauernhaus im deutschen Reich und seinen Grenzgebieten* (Dresden, 1906).

Scharabi, Mohamed, *Einfluss der Pariser École des Beaux-Arts auf die Berliner Architektur in der 2. Hälfte des 19. Jahrhunderts. Nachgewiesen anhand von Entwürfen in d. Plansammlung d. Fakultät f. Architektur an der Technischen Universität Berlin* (Berlin, 1967).

Scherer, Elisabeth, "Ausstellungseröffnung und Papiertheater-Performance," on: *Blog Modernes Japan*, 2 October 2018, http://www.phil-fak.uni-duesseldorf.de/oasien/blog/?p=18513 [accessed 1 July 2019].

Schliemann, Heinrich, *La Chine et le Japon au temps present* (Paris, 1867).

Schliemann, Heinrich, *Reise durch China und Japan im Jahre 1865* (Berlin, 1995).

Schulz, Evelyn, *Stadt-Diskurse in den "Aufzeichnungen über das Prosperieren von Tōkyō" (Tōkyō hanjō ki). Eine Gattung der topographischen Literatur Japans und ihre Bilder von Tōkyō (1832–1958)* (Munich, 2004).

Schwind, Martin, "Sapporo," in: Hammitzsch, Horst (ed.), *Japan-Handbuch. Land und Leute, Kultur und Geistesleben*, 3rd ed. (Stuttgart, 1990), cols. 238–241.

Schwind, Martin, "Siedlungsformen," in: Hammitzsch, Horst (ed.), *Japan-Handbuch. Land und Leute, Kultur und Geistesleben*, 3rd ed. (Stuttgart, 1990), cols. 244–251.

Scidmore, Eliza Ruhamah, *Jinrikisha days in Japan* (New York, 1891).

Seckel, Dietrich; Karow, Otto, "Der Ursprung des Torii," in: *Mitteilungen der deutschen Gesellschaft für Natur- und Völkerkunde Ostasiens XXXIII* (1942–1943), Teil B, pp. B1–B86.

Seidensticker, Edward, *Low City, High City. Tokyo from Edo to the Earthquake. How the Shogun's Ancient Capital Became a Great Modern City. 1867–1923* (New York, 1983).

Seymour, John Nicholson, "Abstract of a Lecture on the Hygienic Aspects of Japanese Dwelling-houses," in: *Transactions of the Asiatic Society of Japan XVII*, 2 (1889), pp. XVII–XXI.

Shatzman Steinhardt, Nancy, "Japan, 538–1333," in: Fraser, Murray (ed.), *Sir Banister Fletcher's Global History of Architecture*, 21st ed. (London; New York; Oxford; New Delhi; Sydney, 2020), pp. 799–819.

Shiga, Shigetsura, *Future development of Japanese dwelling houses*, unpublished thesis (Urbana-Champaign, 1905).

Shiga, Shigetsura, "Jūka (kairyō no hōshin ni tsuite)," in: *kenchiku zasshi* 194, 196, 199, 201, 202 (February to October 1903).

Shigeta, Michi, "The Nō Stage of the Buke Hinagata. The Historical Context and Background of its Production," in: Zorn, Bettina (ed.), *Archiv 65. Archiv Weltmuseum Wien* (2015), pp. 110–117.

Shimada, Takau, "The authorship and date of Harl. ms. 6249, ff. 106v–110," in: *The British Library journal* 16 (1990), pp. 187–191.

Shiner, Larry, *The invention of art. A cultural history* (Chicago, 2001).

Shugio, H.; Ogawa, Kazumasa; Tamura, T., *Japanese Art Folio*, issued in twelve monthly parts (s.l., 1898–1899).

Siebold, Philipp Franz von, *Nippon. Archiv zur Beschreibung von Japan und dessen Neben- und Schutzländern Jezo mit den südlichen Kurilen, Sachalin, Korea und den Liukiu-Inseln*, 7 vols. (text), 5 vols. (plates) (Leiden, 1832–1852).

Sigel, Paul, *Exponiert. Deutsche Pavillons auf Weltausstellungen* (Berlin, 2000).

Sigur, Hannah, *The Influence of Japanese Art on Design* (Salt Lake City et al., 2008).

Sorensen, André, *The Making of Urban Japan: Cities and planning from Edo to the twenty-first century* (London, 2002).

Soros, Susan Weber, "Godwin, Edward William (1833–1886)," in: *Oxford Dictionary of National Biography* (Oxford University Press, 2004), http://www.oxforddnb.com/view/article/10889 [accessed 12 February 2015].

Soros, Susan Weber, "The Furniture of E. W. Godwin," in: Soros, Susan Weber; Arbuthnott, Catherine, *E.W. Godwin: Aesthetic Movement Architect and Designer* (Yale, 1999), pp. 225–261.

Soros, Susan Weber; Arbuthnott, Catherine, *E. W. Godwin: Aesthetic Movement Architect and Designer* (Yale, 1999).

Spang, Christian W.; Wippich, Rolf-Harald; Saaler, Sven, *Die OAG. Die Geschichte der Deutschen Gesellschaft für Natur- und Völkerkunde Ostasiens 1873–1979* (München, 2024).

Speidel, Manfred (ed.), *Bruno Taut in Japan. Das Tagebuch*, 3 vols. (Berlin, 2016).

Speidel, Manfred (ed.), *Ex Oriente lux. Die Wirklichkeit einer Idee. Eine Sammlung von Schriften 1914–1938* (Berlin, 2007).

Spiers, R. Phene, "The French Diplōme d'Architecture and the German System of Architectural Education," in: *Transactions of the Royal Institute of British Architects of London* 5 (1883–1884), pp. 121–132.

Spieß, Gustav, *Die Preußische Expedition nach Ostasien während der Jahre 1860–1862: Reiseskizzen aus Japan, China, Siam und der indischen Inselwelt* (Berlin, 1864).

Starrs, Roy, *Modernism and Japanese Culture* (Houndmills; Basingstoke, 2011).

Stavros, Matthew, *Kyoto. An Urban History of Japan's Premodern Capital* (Honolulu, 2014).

Steger, Friedrich; Wagner, Hermann, *Die Nippon-Fahrer, oder, Das wiedererschlossene Japan: In Schilderungen der bekanntesten älteren und neueren Reisen insbesondere* der amerikanischen Expedition unter Führung des Commodore M. C. Perry in den Jahren 1852 bis 1854 (Leipzig, 1861).

Stein, Ernst von, "Erdbeben und japanische Gebäude," in: *Österreichische Monatsschrift für den Orient* 19 (1893), pp. 77–79.

Steinmetz, Andrew, *Japan and her people* (London, 1859).

Stillfried, Raimund von; Beato, Felice, et al., *Japonais*, 5 vols. (s.l.: Stillfried & Andersen, 1878) (Gallica/BnF).

Strahan, Edward, *The Masterpieces of the Centennial International Exhibition (Philadelphia) 1: Fine Art* (Philadelphia, 1876).

Strange, Edward Fairbrother, "Architecture in Japan," in: *The architectural review for artist and craftsman: a magazine of architecture and decoration* 1 (1896/1897), pp. 126–135.

Suleski, Ronald, "Japanese Studies in the East: The Asiatic Society of Japan," in: *Tsūshin* 4.1 (1998), pp. 15–16.

Surak, Kristin, *Making Tea, Making Japan: Cultural Nationalism in Practice* (Stanford, CA, 2013).

Suzuki, Keiko, "Yokohama-e and kaika-e prints: Japanese Interpretations of Self and Other from 1860 Through the 1880s," in: Hardacre, Helen; Kern, Adam Lewis (eds.), *New Directions in the Study of Meiji Japan* (Leiden et al., 1997), pp. 676–687.

Symonds, John Addington, *Miscellanies* (London, 1871).

Tagsold, Christian, *Spaces in Translation. Japanese Gardens and the West* (Philadelphia, 2017).

Taine, Hippolyte, *The philosophy of art* (New York, 1873).

Takahashi, Yasuo, et al. (eds.), *Zushū Nihon toshishi* [An illustrated history of Japanese cities] (Tōkyō: Tōkyō Daigaku Shuppankai, 1993).

Takai, Kiyoshi, *Minka: The Quintessential Japanese House* (Tōkyō, 1998).

Takashima, Suteta; Ogawa, Kazumasa, *Illustrations of Japanese Life* (Tōkyō, 1896).

Takizawa, Bakin; Régamey, Félix, *Okoma* (Paris, 1883).

Tamai, Tetsuo; Ishiguro, Keishō, *Yomigaeru Meiji no Tōkyō: Tōkyō jūgoku shashinshū* [Revival of Tōkyō in the Meiji Era. A photo collection of Tōkyō's 15 wards] (Tōkyō: Kadokawa Shoten, 1992).

Tamenaga, Shunshō, *The loyal ronins, an historical romance*, translated from the Japanese of Tamenage Shunsui by Shiuichiro Saito and Edward Greey. Illustrated by Kei-sai Yei-sen, of Yedo (New York, 1880).

Tanaka, Stefan, *New Times in Modern Japan* (Princeton, NJ, 2004).

Tange, Kenzo; Gropius, Walter; Ishimoto, Yasuhiro, *Katsura. Tradition and Creation in Japanese Architecture* (New Haven; London, 1960).

Taut, Bruno, *Das japanische Haus und sein Leben* (= *Houses and People of Japan*, 1938) (Berlin, 1997).

Taut, Bruno, *Ich liebe die japanische Kultur. Kleine Schriften über Japan* (Berlin, 2003).

Taylor, Bayard, *Japan in our day* (New York, 1872).

Technologisches Wörterbuch: Deutsch-Englisch-Französisch: Gewerbe, Civil- & Militär-Baukunst, Artillerie, Maschinenbau, Eisenbahnwesen, Strassen- und Wasserbau, Schiffbau und Schiffahrt [...] (Wiesbaden; Paris; London), 2., revised ed., 1869 (vol. 1, German), resp. 1870 (vol. 2, English).

Tegethoff, Wolf, "Vom Landhaus zur 'Wohnmaschine'. Der Wandel des Lebensumfeldes im Spiegel der Moderne," in: Piper, Ernst; Schoeps, Julius (eds.), *Bauen und Zeitgeist. Ein Längsschnitt durch das 19. und 20. Jahrhundert* (Basel et al., 1998), pp. 111–126.

"The civil engineers are busy at Chicago ... a steel-framed palace for the Crown Prince of Japan," in: *The Building News and Engineering Journal* 77 (24 November 1899), p. 715.

"The Domestic Architecture of Japan. I–III," in: *British Architect* 29.21 (25 May 1888), pp. 369–370; 29.22 (1 June 1888), pp. 389–391; 29.24 (15 June 1888), pp. 424–425.

The Far East. A monthly illustrated journey 6.3 (September 1874).

"The Fire Laws of Japan," in: *The American Architect and Building News* 7 (1880), p. 86.

"The Fireman's Journal," in: *Architect and Building News* 12 (1882), p. 166.

"The Foundations for the Pedestal of the Statue of Liberty," in: *The American Architect and Building News* 13.377 (1 March 1883), p. 122.

The Heibonsha Survey of Japanese Art, 30 vols. (Tōkyō: Heibonsha, 1972–1979).

"The Imperial law courts, Tokio," in: *The Builder* 64 (15 April 1893), p. 288.

"The Japanese Ambassadors at the International Exhibition," in: *The Illustrated London News* (24 May 1862), Reprint 1997 via National Diet Library, http://www.ndl.go.jp/exposition/e/data/R/o86r.html [accessed 6 February 2019].

"The Japanese Court in the International exhibition," in: *The Illustrated London News* 41, Issue 1165 (20 September 1862), pp. 318–320.

"The Japanese village," in: *The Times* (2 December 1885), p. 6.

"The Japanese Women in the late Paris International Exhibition," in: *The Illustrated London News* 51, Issue 1455 (Paris International Exhibition (Supplement)), (16 November 1867), p. 541.

"The largest city in the world ...," in: *Building News and Architectural Review* 9 (5 September 1862), p. 187.

"The Last Great Fire in Japan," in: *The American Architect and Building News* (1880), p. 146.

Thunberg, Carl Peter, *Karl Peter Thunbergs ... Reise durch einen Theil von Europa, Afrika und Asien, hauptsächlich in Japan, in den Jahren 1770 bis 1779. Aus dem Schwedischen frey übers. von Christian Heinrich Groskurd*, 2 vols. (Berlin, 1792–1794).

Thunberg, Carl Peter, *Travels in Europe, Africa, and Asia, made between the years 1770 and 1779*, 3 vols., London 1795.

Titsingh, Isaac, *Illustrations of Japan; consisting of Private Memoirs and Anecdotes of the reigning dynasty of The Djogouns, or Sovereigns of Japan; a description of the Feasts and Ceremonies observed throughout the year at their Court; and of the Ceremonies customary at Marriages and Funerals: to which are subjoined, observations on the legal suicide of the Japanese, remarks on their poetry, an explanation of their mode of reckoning time, particulars respecting the Dosia powder, the preface of a work by Confoutzee on filial piety, &c. &c. by M. Titsingh formerly Chief Agent to the Dutch East India Company at Nangasaki. Translated from the French, by Frederic Shoberl with coloured plates, faithfully copied from Japanese original designs* (London, 1822).

Todd, Pamela, *Pre-Raphaelites at Home* (London, 2003).

Togashi, Shinzo, *Daiku miyahinagata: Ikken'yashiro kara haiden torii made* [Explanations for the builder of Shrines. From the One-bay Shrine to the Worship Hall and Torii] (Tōkyō: Omusha, 2011).

Togashi, Shinzo, *Daiku monhinagata: Sukiyamon kara yotsuashimon koraimon made* [Explanations for the builder of gate systems. From the Sukiya to the Yotsuashi and Kōrai gates] (Tōkyō: Omusha, 2018).

Togashi, Shinzo, *Daiku terahinagata: Hondo mon kara gojunoto made* [Explanations for the builder of temples. From the main hall and gate to the five-story pagoda] (Tōkyō: Omusha, 2011).

Tōkyō National Museum, et al. (eds.), *Arts of East and West from World Exhibitions. 1855–1900: Paris, Vienna and Chicago. Commemorating the 2005 World Exposition, Aichi, Japan* (Tōkyō, 2004).

"Tokyo university, Japan," in: *The Builder* 47 (13 December 1884), p. 790.

Toyosawa, Nobuko, *The Cartography of Epistemology: The Production of "National" Space in Late 19th Century Japan*, Ph.D. dissertation (University of Illinois at Urbana-Champaign, 2008). Courtesy of the author.

Tronson, John M., *Personal narrative of a voyage to Japan, Kamtschatka, Siberia, Tartary, and various parts of coast of China; in H. M. S. Barracouta with charts and views* (London, 1859).

Tseng, Alice Y., "Styling Japan: The Case of Josiah Conder and the Museum at Ueno, Tokyo," in: *Journal of the Society of Architectural Historians* 63.4 (December 2004), pp. 472–497.

Tseng, Alice Y., *The Imperial Museums of Meiji Japan. Architecture and the Art of the Nation* (Seattle, WA; London, 2008).

Turner, Alicia; Cox, Laurence; Bocking, Brian, "A Buddhist Crossroads: Pioneer European Buddhists and Globalizing Asian Networks 1860–1960," in: *Contemporary Buddhism* 14.1 (May 2013), pp. 1–14.

Ueda, Mōshin; Watanabe, Kazan, *Nikkōsan shi*, 5 vols. (Edo: Suharaya Ihachi, 1837).

Union Centrale des Arts Décoratifs (ed.), *Le Livre des expositions universelles, 1851–1989* (Paris, 1983).

Unsere Weltausstellung. Eine Beschreibung der Columbischen Welt (Chicago, 1894).

Vandenbreeden, Jos; Bastin, Christine, *Vom Klassizismus zum Jugendstil. Das 19. Jahrhundert in Belgien – Architektur und Interieurs* (Eupen, 1996).

Vandières, Simon de, *L'exposition universelle de 1878 illustrée: quatre-vingt-sept belles gravures sur bois* (Paris, 1879).

"Vienna museum to restore daimyo mansion model from 19th century," in: *The Japan Times*, online edition, 26 March 2015, https://www.japantimes.co.jp/news/2013/03/26/national/vienna-museum-to-restore-daimyo-mansion-model-from-19th-century/#.XG1q2rgxmbg [accessed 20 February 2019].

Villetard, Edmond, *Le Japon* (Paris, 1879).

Viollet-le-Duc, Eugène, "Maison," in: *Dictionnaire raisonné de l'architecture française du XIe au XVIe siècle* (Paris, 1854–1868), vol. 6, pp. 214–300.

Vogel Chevroulet, Irène, *La création d'une japonité moderne (1870–1940) ou le regard des architectes européens sur le Japon: Josiah Conder, Robert Mallet-Stevens, Bruno Taut et Charlotte Perriand* (Saarbrücken, 2010).

Vogel Chevroulet, Irène, "The Architecture of Japan: Discovery, Assimilation and Creation – Josiah Conder opens the Way," in: Müller, Simone; Itō, Tōru; Rehm, Robin (eds.), *Wort-Bild Assimilationen Japan und die Moderne*, Berlin 2016, pp. 68–93.

Wada, Masanori, *Engineering Education and the Spirit of Samurai at the Imperial College of Engineering in Tokyo, 1871–1886*, Master thesis (Blacksburg, VA: Virginia Polytechnic Institute and State University, 2007).

Wagner, Wolf-Rüdiger, "Japanische Bettschirme, die große Weltpolitik und die Moral," on: https://roman-als-zeitbild.blog/2017/07/05/effis-interesse-an-einem-japanischen-bettschirm-und-die-grose-weltpolitik/ [17 April 2019].

Wakayama, Shigeru; Fumoto, Kazuyoshi (eds.), *Kinsei kenchikusho – kōhō hinagata* [Sourcebooks of Japanese building construction] (Kyōto: Tairyūdō Shoten, 1993).

Wakita, Mio, "Sites of '"Disconnectedness": The Port City of Yokohama, Souvenir Photography, and its Audience," in: *Transcultural Studies* 2 (2013), s.p., http://dx.doi.org/10.11588/ts.2013.2.11067 [03 June 2019].

Waley, Paul, "Who Cares about the Past in Today's Tokyo?," in: Brumann, Christoph; Schulz, Evelyn (eds.), *Urban Spaces in Japan: Cultural and Social Perspectives* (London et al., 2012), pp. 148–166.

Walravens, Hartmut, "Kunstbeziehungen zwischen Preußen und Japan," in: Krebs, Gerhard (ed.), *Japan und Preussen* (Munich, 2002), pp. 249–266.

Watts, Talbot, *Japan and the Japanese. From the most authentic and reliable sources, with illustrations of their manners, costumes, religious ceremonies &c* (New York, 1852).

Weaver, Thomas, "Japan and Korea [postwar]," in: Cruickshank, Dan (ed.), *Sir Banister Fletcher's a history of architecture*, 20th ed. (Oxford, 1996), pp. 1572–1593.

Weisberg, Gabriel P., "Burty, Philippe," in: *Allgemeines Künstlerlexikon – Internationale Künstlerdatenbank – Online*, originally: Beyer, Andreas; Savoy, Bénédicte; Tegethoff, Wolf (eds.), *Allgemeines Künstlerlexikon (AKL). Die Bildenden Künstler aller Zeiten und Völker* 15, p. 289.

Wellnau, Rudolf, *Die Japanische Ausstellung in Berlin 1885* (Berlin, 1885).

Welsch, Wolfgang, "Was ist eigentlich Transkulturalität?," in: Darowska, Lucyna; Lüttenberg, Thomas; Machold, Claudia (eds.), *Hochschule als transkultureller Raum? Kultur, Bildung und Differenz in der Universität* (Bielefeld, 2010), pp. 39–66.

Welt-Ausstellung 1873 in Wien. Officieller General-Catalog (Wien, 1873).

Wendelken, Cherie, "The Tectonics of Japanese Style. Architect and Carpenter in the Late Meiji Period," in: *Art Journal* 55.3 (1996), pp. 28–37.

Wendelken-Mortensen, Cherie, *Living with the Past: Preservation and Development in Japanese Architecture and Town Planning*, Ph.D. Thesis (Cambridge: Massachusetts Institute of Technology, 1994).

Wertheimber, Louis, *A Muramasa blade: a story of feudalism in old Japan* (Boston, 1887).

Westcott, Thompson, *Centennial portfolio: a souvenir of the international exhibition at Philadelphia, comprising lithographic views of fifty of its principal buildings* (Philadelphia, 1876).

Weston, Victoria, *East Meets West. Isabella Stewart Gardner and Okakura Kakuzō* (Boston, 1993).

White, William H., "A Brief Review of the Education and Position of Architects in France Since the Year 1671," in: *Transactions of the Royal Institute of British Architects of London* 5 (1883–84), pp. 93–120.

Wichmann, Siegfried; Whittall, Mary, *Japonisme: The Japanese Influence on Western Art Since 1858* (London, 1999).

Wieczorek, Alfried; Sui, Claude W. (eds.), *Ins Land der Kirschblüte. Japanische Reisefotografie aus dem 19. Jahrhundert* (Heidelberg, 2011).

Wight, P. B., "Japanese architecture at Chicago," in: *Inland Architect and News Record* XX, 5 and 6 (December 1892 and January 1893), plates 5 and 6.

Wilkinson, Hugh, *Sunny lands and seas: a voyage in the ss. "Ceylon"* (London, 1883).

Wilkinson, Nancy B., "E. W. Godwin and Japonisme in England," in: Soros, Susan Weber; Arbuthnott, Catherine, *E. W. Godwin: Aesthetic Movement Architect and Designer* (Yale, 1999), pp. 71–91.

Wilkinson, Nancy B., *Edward William Godwin and Japonisme in England*, unpublished Ph.D. thesis (Los Angeles: University of California at Los Angeles, 1987).

Wilson, A. W., *Letters from the Orient to her daughters at home* (Nashville, TN, 1890).

Wilson, Alona C., "Felice Beato's Japan: People. An album by the pioneer foreign photographer in Yokohama, 2010," on: *Visualizing culture*, here https://visualizingcultures.mit.edu/beato_people/index.html [accessed 3 June 2019].

Wilson, Joseph Miller, *The Masterpieces of the Centennial International Exhibition (Philadelphia)* (Philadelphia, 1876).

Withey, Lynne, *Grand Tours and Cooks' Tours: A History of Leisure Travel, 1750–1915* (London, 1997).

Wores, Theodore, "An American artist in Japan," in: *The Century Magazine* (September 1889), pp. 670–685.

Wörner, Martin, *Vergnügung und Belehrung. Volkskultur auf den Weltausstellungen 1851–1900* (Münster, 1999).

Yamamoto, Kakuma, *Guide to the celebrated places in Kiyoto and the surrounding places for the foreign visitors* (Kyōto: Niwa Keisuke, 1873).

Yarnall, James L., "John La Farge and Henry Adams in Japan," in: *The American Art Journal* 21.1 (1989), pp. 40–77.

Yokohama Kaiko Shiryokan (ed.), *Felice Beato shashinshu 1. Bakumatsu Nihon no fūkei to hitobito* [Felix Beato's Photograph Collection: Landscapes and People of Bakumatsu Japan] (Akashi Shoten, 2006).

Yonemura, Ann, *Yokohama: Prints from Nineteenth-Century Japan* (Washington, DC, 1991).

Yoshii, Tsunetaro, *Illustrated guide to Kyoto & its suburbs: with map, an entirely new work* (Osaka, 1890).

Yoshioka, Hiroshi, "Samurai and Self-colonization in Japan," in: Pieterse, Jan N.; Parekh, Bhiku (eds.), *The Decolonization of Imagination. Culture, knowledge and power* (London, 1995), pp. 99–112.

Young, Michiko, et al., *Introduction to Japanese architecture* (Hong Kong, 2004).

Young, Michiko, et al., *The Art of Japanese Architecture* (Tōkyō; Rutland, VT, 2007).

Yu, Lina; Koiwa, Masaki, "A Typological Study on Rinzō of Japan and China – On the base of examples and architectural technic books," in: *Journal of Architecture and Planning (Transactions of AIJ)* 82.740 (2017), pp. 2701–2711.

Zandi-Sayek, Sibel, "The Unsung of the Canon: Does a Global Architectural History Need New Landmarks?," in: *ABE Journal* 6 (2014), http://journals.openedition.org/abe/1271 [accessed 14 January 2018], s.p.

Zhu, Jianfei, et al. (eds.), *Routledge Handbook of Chinese Architecture. Social Production of Buildings and Spaces in History* (London, 2022).

Zöllner, Reinhard, *Geschichte Japans. Von 1800 bis zur Gegenwart* (Paderborn, 2006).

Zorn, Bettina (ed.), *Archiv 65. Archiv Weltmuseum Wien* (2015).

Zorn, Bettina, "The History of the Daimyō House Model in the Collection of the Weltmuseum Wien and its traces in Vienna," in: id. (ed.), *Archiv 65. Archiv Weltmuseum Wien* (2015), pp. 44–55.

Zwerger, Klaus, "Präsentation japanischer Baukultur im Wien des 19. Jahrhunderts," in: *Archiv für Völkerkunde* 57–58 (2007–2008), pp. 185–220.

Zwerger, Klaus, "Recognizing the Similar and Thus Accepting the Other: The European and Japanese Traditions of Building With Wood," in: *Journal of Traditional Building, Architecture and Urbanism* 2 (2021), pp. 305–317.

Figures: Colour Section

FIGURES 3.18–3.20
Ogawa Sashichi: Temple front of Nikkō Tōshō-gū with the pagoda to the left, before 1888; Tamamura Kozaburo: Store house for treasure at Nikkō Tōshō-gū, 1880s?; Buildings in the second courtyard of Nikkō Tōshō-gū, 1880s?

FIGURES 4.26–4.27   Architectural model of a rural outbuilding, belonging to the group of rural building models prepared for the Weltausstellung in Vienna in 1873, here during its restoration

FIGURES 4.28–4.30
Details of the architectural model of a daimyō residence prepared for the Weltausstellung in Vienna in 1873 during restoration

FIGURES: COLOUR SECTION 413

FIGURES 4.31–4.32   Overall view and detail of the architectural model of a daimyō residence prepared for the Weltausstellung in Vienna in 1873 after restoration

FIGURE 4.37
Centennial International Exhibition, 1876: Interior of the Japanese Quarters, Fairmont Park, Philadelphia

FIGURES 4.38–4.40
Communal fishermen's quarters for 60 men, House Aoyama, Historical Village of Hokkaidō (Kaitaku-no Mura) Sapporo

FIGURES: COLOUR SECTION 415

FIGURE 4.59   Stage set for Gilbert & Sullivan's The Mikado by Hawes Craven (1837–1910), 1885

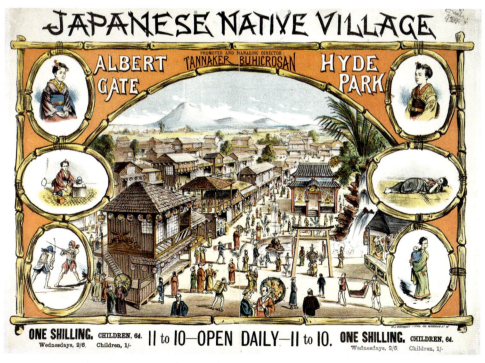

FIGURE 4.64   Advertisement poster for Tannaker's Japanese Native Village

FIGURES 4.76–4.77   Exposition Universelle, 1889: Charles Garnier, *Histoire de l'habitation humaine*, main façade and floor plan of the Japanese house

FIGURE 4.89   Byōdō-in's Phoenix Hall in Uji

FIGURES: COLOUR SECTION 417

FIGURE 4.111
Golden Hall of the Hōryū-ji, north façade

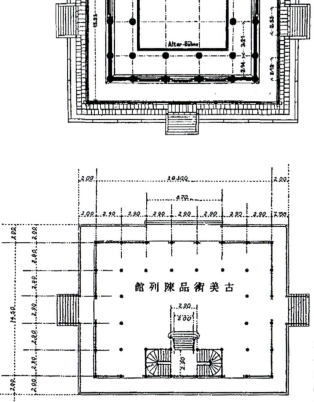

FIGURES 4.112–4.113
Golden Hall of Hōryū-ji, floor plan, and Exposition Universelle, 1900: Exhibition Hall of Japanese traditional art

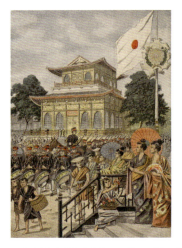

FIGURES 4.114–4.115 Exposition Universelle, 1900: two depictions of the Japanese pavilion

FIGURES 4.116–4.117
Kinkaku-ji (formally: Shari-den of Rokuon-ji, Kyōto, originally 1398, here reconstruction of 1955 after loss due to arson in 1950) and Ginkaku-ji (formally: Kannon-den of Jishō-ji, Kyōto, 1482–1490)

FIGURES: COLOUR SECTION

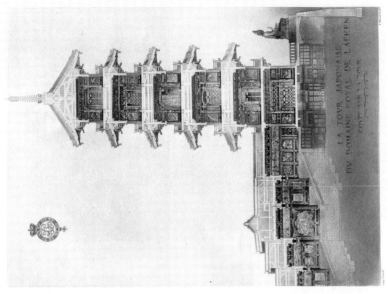

FIGURES 4.123–4.124   Alexandre Marcel, design for the Japanese Tower in Laeken with auxiliary structures

FIGURE 4.125   Alexandre Marcel, design for the Japanese Tower in Laeken with auxiliary structures

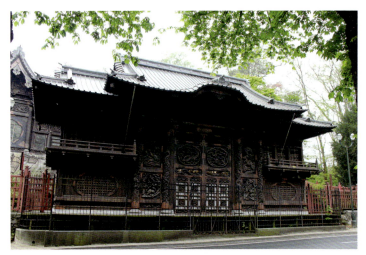

FIGURES 4.126–4.127
The Pagoda in Laeken, seen from the site of the Chinese pavilion, and the entrance pavilion

FIGURES: COLOUR SECTION

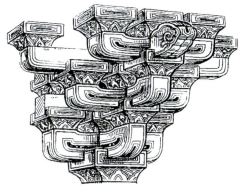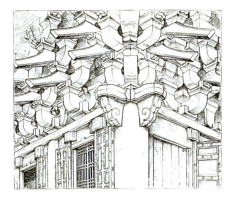

FIGURES 4.128–4.129   Compound bracket, and bracketing supporting roof of temple-gate, Chionjin, Kioto [Chion-in]

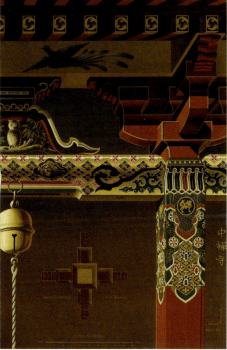

FIGURES 4.130–4.131   Column and tie-beams from the Chion-in in Kyōto and the polychrome work of the Chūzen-ji in Nikkō

FIGURES 4.173–4.174
Interior scenes of dwellings, both with *tokonoma* on the right side

FIGURES 4.175–4.176   The entrance of a business and an interior, probably a tea room

FIGURES: COLOUR SECTION 423

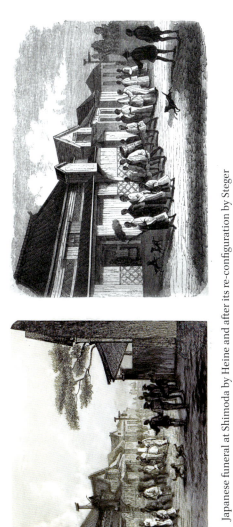

FIGURES 4.194–4.195   Japanese funeral at Shimoda by Heine and after its re-configuration by Steger

FIGURES 4.196–4.197   Japanese funeral as depicted by Oliphant and Steger

FIGURES 4.205–4.206 Living room with bamboo hangings, *sudare*; and the Audience Hall of Ninomaru Gōten of the Nijō-jō in Kyōto

FIGURES: COLOUR SECTION 425

FIGURE 4.216
Temple garden in Tōkyō published by Kreitner

FIGURES 4.217–4.218
Photographs of the Hotta family garden by Kusakabe Kimbei and Esaki Reiji in the mid-1880s

FIGURE 4.219   Utagawa Hiroshige I (1797–1858): Fireworks in the cool of the evening at Ryōgoku Bridge, about 1840

FIGURES 4.227–4.228   Utagawa Hiroshige: Ishibe (Fifty-Three Stations along the Tōkaidō), 1855; Utagawa Hiroshige: Goyu (The Tōkaidō: The Fifty-Three Stations), 1847–1850

FIGURE 4.231   Utagawa Kuniteru II: Mitsui Group's Western-Style Three-Story House at Surugachō, Tōkyō, 1873

FIGURE 4.232   Utagawa Yoshitora: An accurate picture of the Mitsui Building at Suruga-chō, 1874

FIGURE 4.233   Mitsui House in Suruga-chō, Tōkyō

FIGURES: COLOUR SECTION 429

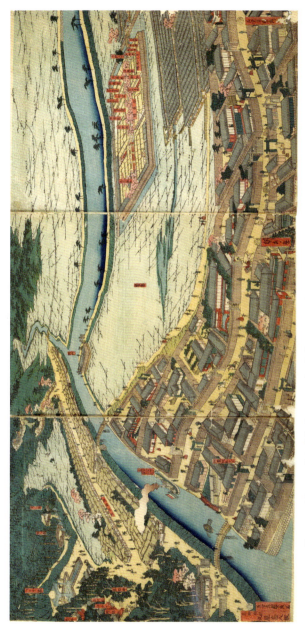

FIGURE 4.234　Utagawa (Gountei) Sadahide: Revised Yokohama Landscape (section), 1861

FIGURE 4.239
Utagawa Hiroshige I: View of Suruga-chō (Tōto meisho), about 1832–1838

FIGURES 4.240–4.241   Utagawa Hiroshige: Suruga-cho (Meisho Edo hyakkei), 1856, and View of Mt. Fuji from Suruga-chō (Thirty-six Views of Fuji), 1858

FIGURES: COLOUR SECTION

FIGURES 4.242–4.243
Shōsai Ikkei: Suruga-chō (Thirty-six Views of Tōkyō), 1871; Kobayashi Kiyochika: Snow in Suruga-chō, 1879

FIGURE 4.244   Utagawa Hiroshige III: The Mitsui store in Suruga-chō (Tōkyō meisho), 1881

FIGURE 4.247   Utagawa Sadahide: View of a daimyo procession at Nihonbashi (Famous views of Edo), 1863

FIGURES 4.248–4.249
Utagawa Hiroshige: Okazaki (Yahagi no bashi) (The Tōkaidō: The Fifty-Three Stations), 1833–1835; Katsushika Hokusai: Yahagi Bridge at Okazaki on the Tōkaidō (Shokoku meikyō kiran), ca. 1833–1834

FIGURES: COLOUR SECTION

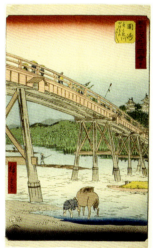

FIGURES 4.250–4.252   Further depictions of the Yahagi Bridge in Okazaki: the bridge in Yahaki as depicted by Siebold; Utagawa Hiroshige: Okazaki, Yahagi Bridge (53 Stations of the Tōkaidō), ca. 1840, and Yahagi Bridge on the Yahagi River near Okazaki, 1855

FIGURES 4.253–4.256 Examples of souvenir photographs: Ogawa Kazumasa: Girls having afternoon tea; Fujigawa river and Mt. Fuji from Iwabuchi, Tōkaidō; Omizusha, a basin, at Nikkō Tōshō-gū Shrine; A vegetable vendor

FIGURES: COLOUR SECTION   435

FIGURES 4.265–4.266   Tamamura Kozaburo: Kintai Bridge on Nishiki River at Iwakuni; Shinto shrine, somewhere in Japan, ca. 1870s

FIGURES 4.267–4.268   Uchida Kuichi: Kodaiji temple at Nagasaki; Kusakabe Kimbei: Buddhist temple at Asakusa, Tokio, ca. 1870–ca. 1888

Index

acroterions   189, **190**, 303
Adams, Henry   148
Adams, William   24
Ainsworth, William   302
Akisato, Ritō   312
Alcock, Rutherford   52–53
  on Japanese architecture   32, 80–81
  on Japanese art   79
  on Japanese landscapes   141
  on Japanese vs. English craftsmen   91–92
  objects on display at London Exhibition   175–176, **176**
  references to works of   53
  on simple country life   143
  sources use by   53, 54
  mention of   48
  See also under names of specific works
Alexandra Palace (London)   186, 189
Allgemeine Encyclopädie der Wissenschaften und Künste   27
Allgemeines deutsches Bauwörterbuch (Mothes)   34
amado (wooden shutters)   178, **179**, 186, **188**, 196, **197**
American Architect and Building News (journal)   52, 98–101, 200
American expeditions (Perry) (1853–1854)   23, 28–29
  See also Narrative of the expedition of an American squadron to the China seas and Japan
American legation (Tōkyō)   278, 323
American Society of Civil Engineers   114
"An American artist in Japan" (Wores)   152
Anderson, William   53, 63
archers   290, **292**, 295
Architectural Association (London)   111–112
architectural models, Japanese
  in general   180–181, 189
  of *daimyō* residences   192, 194–195, **412**, **413**
  of dwelling houses, Japanese   **193**
  of farmhouses   190, 192, **193**, 195, 412
  of pagodas   191, **191**, 238, 240
  of shrines   **193**

Architectural Museum (Sapporo)   198, **414**
architecture
  in China   164, 348
  in Europe. *See* architecture, Western
  as expression of culture   136
  in India   348
  in Japan. *See* architecture, Japanese
  national narratives and   162
  in Ottoman Empire   348
  periodicals about. *See* periodicals
  reference books about   27–28, 34, 161–172
    See also under names of specific reference books
  as social planning   120–121
  in USA. *See* architecture, Western
architecture, Japanese
  in general   1–2
  arts and
    in general   343
    combined survey of   33
    craftsmen / craftsmanship   91–97
    decorative details   86–90
    disconnection between   32
    at International Exhibitions   32–33, 95
  authenticity of   241–242
  building process in   64, 95, 98–101, 226
  construction principles. *See* construction principles
  earthquake-resistant construction. *See* earthquake-resistant construction
  fireproofing   64
  influences on Western architecture   174, 200, 252
  information transfer of   334–335
    See also hinagatabon
  at International Exhibitions. *See* International Exhibitions
  perishable nature of   49–50
  political upheavals and   124, 145–146
  in stage settings of operas   211–213, **212**, **213**
  study of   161–162
  two categories of Japanese builders and   118

INDEX 437

architecture, Japanese (*cont.*)
　Western artistic values and
　　frame of reference　80–85
　　othering and　84, 346–347
　　See also artistic values, Western
　Western knowledge of. *See* knowledge /
　　knowledge production, Western
　Western views on. *See* Westerners
architecture, Western
　concept of　70
　hierarchy in　82, 166–167
　influences of Japanese architecture on
　　174, 200, 252
　three different concepts of　23
Arnold, Charles D.　228
ars mechanicae　117, 162
Art and Art Industries in Japan (Alcock)　32,
　　53, 79, 91, 175
art history, books on Japanese　247, **247**
L'Art Japonais (Gonse)　32, 57, 83–84, 89–90,
　　169, 257
The Art Journal　40, 53, 77–78, 80
art periodicals. *See* periodicals
"The artisan of Japan and his work"
　　(Pfoundes)　64
artisans. *See* craftsmen / craftsmanship
Artistic Japan. Illustrations and Essays (Bing)
　　110
artistic values, Western
　architectural hierarchy in　224, 226
　Cram on　85–86n43
　Japanese architecture and
　　frame of reference　80–85
　　othering and　84, 346–347
　Japanese art and　79–80
　Japanese craftsman and　93
　superiority of　346
art(s), American. *See* art(s), Western
art(s), Japanese
　in general　77–78
　architecture and
　　in general　343
　　combined survey of　33
　　craftsmen / craftsmanship　91–97
　　decorative details　86–90
　　disconnection between　32
　　at International Exhibitions　32–33,
　　　95

　books on　32–33, 38, 247, **247**
　essays on　54, 61, 78
　history of　150
　influence on Western art of　77, 86, 200
　at International Exhibitions　243, 251
　modernisation and decline of　92
　Westerners on
　　inferiority of　18–19, 22, 79–81, 177
　　Western artistic values and　79–80
　woodblock prints. *See* woodblock prints
art(s), Western
　architecture and　97–98
　artistic values in. *See* artistic values,
　　Western
　canonical order in　78
　high vs. low　79
　influences of Japanese art on　77, 86
Ashikaga / Muromachi period　233
Asiatic Society of Japan　67–68
　focus of　67
　Japanese construction principles and
　　102
　lecture at　60
　members of　47, 49, 53, 56, 58, 61, 67
　socio-cultural structure of　68
　mention of　66
astronomers　279, 280
authenticity　223, 241–242
Ayrton, William E.　61, 106

Baba-chō neighbourhood (Tōkyō)　**315**
Bæckström, Anton　302
Baltzer, Franz　119, 170, 263
Barcelona, International Exhibition at　42
Barna, Gergely P.　191
bath-houses　130, 345
bathing practices, Japanese　129–130, 131,
　　132
Beato, Felice　34, 44, **124**, 258, **260**, 282, **285**,
　　319, **323**, 331
Berlin　131, 218–219
Bing, Samuel　110
Bird, Isabella　146–147
Blaser, Werner　13, 51–52n118
boats / boating　302
Böckmann, Wilhelm　144, 156
Böckmann & Ende architects　55, 114, 126,
　　152

books / monographs
    Japanese architecture in
        in general   32, 38, 342–343
        books on architecture   27–28, 34, 38, 161–172, 254–258, 263, **263**
        books on art   32–33, 38
        encyclopaedias   18–24
        illustrations of. *See* illustrations, Japanese; illustrations, Western
        travelogues   29–31
        See also periodicals
Boshin War (1868–1869)   145
Bousquet, Georges H.   62, 155
bracket systems
    Conder's illustrations of   261, **261**
    Guérineau's illustrations of   263, **264**
    in *hinagatabon*   **336**
    as illustrated in story about Satō Tadanobu   257, **258**
    intricacy of   255–256, **421**
Brandt, Max von   50
Brasserie Vetzel (Paris International Exhibition, 1900)   248, **248**, **249**
Brevis Iapaniae Insvlae Descriptio (Fróis)   38
brick   55, 60, 109, 119–120, 125, 146
bridges
    souvenir photographs of   **435**
    woodblock prints of   316–318, **432**–**433**
Brinckmann, Justus   50, 125, 144, 257, **259**, 261
The British Architect and Northern Engineer (journal)   51, 157, 186
British Legation (Tōkyō)   **124**
British Library   52
Brockhaus Enzyklopädie (1843–1848)   22
Brown, Eliphalet M.   266, 268
Brown, Samuel R.   50
Brunton, Henry R.   47–48
    in general   31, 65
    on dwelling houses   71
    on earthquake-resistant construction   104–106
    on Japanese carpenters   95–96
    references to   48, 62
    See also under names of specific works
Buddhism   63
Buddhist monasteries   45
Buddhist temples. *See* temples / shrines

Buhicrosan, Tannaker   213
The Builder (journal)   53, 64, 114, 157
building materials
    brick   55, 60, 109, 119–120, 125, 146
    Japanese
        cedar wood   21
        at International Exhibitions   119, 246
        Westerners on   119–120
The Building News and Engineering Journal   51, 95–96, 110, 112, 114, 120, 157, 216
building process, Japanese
    International Exhibitions and   95, 98–101, 226
    Pfoundes on   64
building tools, Japanese   118–119
building types, survey of   57
Burges, William   55
Burty, Philippe   45, 48, 61–63, 207, 313
Butler, Annie   304, **305**

Cahen, Emma   43
Cahen d'Anvers et Compagnie   43
carpenters, Japanese (*daiku*)
    Westerners on
        in general   64, 94–97
        evaluation of   116–118
        intellectual ability   116
        status of   117
    See also craftsmen / craftsmanship
carvings   87, 90, 207, 210
Castanet Club (Montreal)   211, **212**
"The Castle of Yedo" (McClatchie)   31, 59
"Catalogue des palais des souverains-pontifes japonais" (Labarthe)   45
Cawley, George   60–61
    on earthquake-resistant construction   106
    on Japanese building materials   119–120
    on Japanese carpenters   96–97
    on Japanese tools   119
    See also under names of specific works
cedar wood   21
Centennial International Exhibition (1876) (Philadelphia). *See* International Exhibition (1876) (Philadelphia)
The Century Magazine   131
Cernuschi, Henri   63

INDEX 439

Chamberlain, Basil H.
   in general   48, 50
   on economy of Japanese buildings   132, 348
   on Japanese building vs. decorations   84–85
   on Japanese dwellings   158
   on Japanese hygiene   132
   on lack of comfort   150–151
   references to works of   169, 170
   sources used by   57, 61
   See also under names of specific works
Chambers, Ephraim   18
Chambers, William   164
Champier, Victor   110
Charlevoix, Pierre François-Xavier de   62
Chassiron, Charles de   127
Chicago. *See* International Exhibition (1893)
chigaidana shelving   281, **422**
China, architecture in   164, 348
Chinoiserie   11, 27, 292, 293
Choisy, Auguste   163–165, 169
cities, Japanese
   urban reorganisation of   124–127, 128
   Westerners on
      in general   121–123
      hygiene   129–130, 132
      lack of grandeur   123
      on Nagasaki   141
      on Nikkō   50, 62, 84, 85, 87–88, **111**, 143–144
      othering and   138
      social order in   127–128
      urban reorganisation   126
      on Yokohama   148
cities, Western   21, 128, 131
Clericuzio, Peter   250
Coaldrake, William H.   2, 7, 11, 191, 195
codes / norms. *See* norms / codes
collections / collectors   44, 63
comfort, lack of   150–151
Commission Impériale du Japon   32
Compagnie des Messageries maritimes (steamship line)   248
Conder, Josiah   55–58
   in general   32, 42
   building projects of   126
   comments on   64
   on decline of Japanese culture   157
   on decorative details   87, **88**
   detailed illustrations by   261, **261, 262**
   on dwelling houses   71
   on earthquake-resistant construction   110–111, 112
   illustrations of gardens in book of   300
   on Japanese building materials   120
   lectures of   236*n*111
   on monuments   123–124
   references to works of   57–58, 169, 170, 257
   sections of a pagoda   **111**
   sources of   59
   on substantiality   81–82, 106
   See also under names of specific works
Conder, Roger T.   31–32, 50, 112, 261
"The condition of architecture in Japan" (Conder)   236*n*111
"The Conditions of Life of the Japanese Artisan and his Work" (Jarves)   91
"Construction" (Godwin)   51
construction principles, Japanese
   earthquake frequency and   21, 24, 29, 102–104
      See also earthquake-resistant construction
   of pagodas   109–112, **111**, 114–115
   Western disinterest in   107, 115
   Western exclusion of   120
   Westerners on   55, 98–102, 171
   See also iron constructions; wooden constructions
"Constructive Art in Japan" (Brunton)   31, 47–48, 62, 104–106
"Constructive Art in Japan" (Pfoundes)   64
Converse, Loring   299
craftsmen, Western   91–92, 94
craftsmen / craftsmanship, Japanese
   at International Exhibitions
      in general   252
      Chicago (1893)   **229–230**, 232
      Paris (1889)   **221**
      Philadelphia (1876)   99–100, 200, 202, **202, 203**
   training of   64
   Westerners on
      in general   112–113, 116

craftsmen Westerners on (*cont.*)
  appreciation of   171
  carpenters   64, 94–97, 116–118
  modernisation and   92
  vs. Western   91–92, 94
  work ethics of   93
Cram, Ralph Adams   85–86*n*43, 170, 224, 250
Craven, Hawes   211
Crystal Palace (London)   115
cultural journals   39–40
culture, Japanese
  Japanese architecture and   161
  loss of   139, 140, 150
  othering and   84, 85, 137–139, 161
culture, Western   158
culture(s), systematisation of   224
Cyclopedia (Chambers)   18

Daibutsu (Kamakura)   282, **283**, 284
daiku. See carpenters, Japanese
daimyō residences
  in general   124, 146
  architectural models of   192, 194–195, **412**, **413**
d'Alembert, Jean le Rond   18
Daly, César D.   31, 62, 89, 256
David and Thomas Stevenson (Edinburgh)   47
decorative details, Japanese
  in Western illustrations   262–263
  Westerners on   86–90, **88**, **89**, **90**
Demmin, August   35
Deshima   26, 318–319
  See also Nagasaki
Deutsche Bauzeitung (periodical)   114
Deutsche Gesellschaft für Natur- und Völkerkunde Ostasiens (OAG)   66, 67
Deutscher Werkbund   152
Dickins, Frederick V.   62
Dictionnaire général des Termes d'Architecture en français, allemand, anglais et italien (Ramée)   35
Diderot, Denis   18, 27
diplomatic personnel
  as knowledge mediators   47–48, 52–54, 58–59
  restrictions on   42–43, 141

disinterest, of Westerners
  in Japanese architecture   161, 174, 262, 347–348
  in Japanese construction principles   107, 115
Dixon, William G.   **284**
documentary photography, of Jinshin Survey   329–331, **332–334**, 334
Doeff, Hendrik   25
"Domestic Architecture in Japan" (Conder)   59, 112–113
Dooman, Isaac   39, 82
Doshisha English School (Kyōto)   46
Dresser, Christopher
  in general   32, 42, 107–108
  on brackets   255–256
  on decorative details   87–89, **89**
  on earthquake-resistant construction   108–109
  on Japanese dwellings   153
  on Japanese craftsmen   92–93
  on Japanese tools   119
  on Nikkō   87–88, **111**, 143
  on pagodas   110–112, **111**, 116
  on pavilion-like characteristics of dwellings   108
  presentations of   111–112
  references to works of   110, 169, 170, 257
  sources used by   50
  for illustrations   256–258, **259**, **260**
  See also Japan, its Architecture, Art and Art Manufactures
Dubard, Maurice   103
Dubois de Jancigny, Adolphe P.   267
Dumoulin, Louis-Jules   248
Dunn, Henry T.   **154**
Duplessis, Hervé   220
Duret, Théodore   62
Dutch East India Company (*Vereenigde Oostindische Compagnie*, VOC)   25
dwelling houses, Japanese
  architectural models of   **193**
  construction principles. *See* construction principles
  designed by Westerners   223–224, **225**, 250, **416**
  earthquake-resistant construction of. *See* earthquake-resistant construction

dwelling houses (*cont.*)
  fire-proofing of   64
  interior fittings of   338
  at International Exhibitions
    Paris (1889)   223–224, **225**, 250, **416**
    Philadelphia (1876)   95, 196–198, **197**, **198**
  Westerners on
    in general   21
    complete descriptions of   71–73
    as cultural phenomenon   151, 156–157, 158–159
    demise of   157
    economy of   133
    errors in spatial dimensions   295–298, **296**, **297**, **298**, **299**, **300**, **300**, **424**
    floor coverings of   72
    hygiene   132
    illustrations of   73, **74**, **75**, 77, 266–267, **268**, **270**
    incomplete descriptions of   71
    inferiority of   156–157
    interior design of   74–**75**, **75**, 152–153, **154**
    irrelevance of   69–70
    lack of comfort of   150–151
    partitioning of   71–72, **75**
    pavilion-like characteristics of   108
    spatial fluidity   153, **154**, 155–156
Dyer, Henry   117–118

earthquake frequency, construction principles and   21, 24, 29, 36, 102–104
earthquake-resistant construction, Japanese
  Westerners on
    in general   42, 61, 102–104
    disinterest in   107
    Dresser-Conder dispute on   110–112, 113
    Lacasse on   54–55
    lack of additional research   113–114
    negative statements on   104–106
    positive statements on   108–109
    value of elasticity in   114
    Western accepted models and   48, 106–107
"Earthquakes and Buildings" (Lescasse)   54–55

eave laths   337
École d'Arts et Métiers (Paris)   80
École des Beaux-Arts (Paris)   41, 80–81
École des Ponts et Chaussées (Paris)   80
École Polytechnique (Paris)   80
Edo. *See* Tōkyō
Edo Castle (Tōkyō)   235
Edo Meisho Zue (*Pictorial guide to the celebrated localities of Edo*)   59, 313, **315**, **427–428**
Eiffel Tower (Paris)   115
elasticity, in construction   114
Elisabeth, Empress consort of Austria   186, **186**
Enciclopedia Moderna (1851–1855)   23–24
Encyclopædia Britannica (1842)   20–22
Encyclopaedia Britannica (1852–1860)   24
encyclopaedias   18–26
  See also under names of individual encyclopaedias
Encyclopédie historique, archéologique, biographique, chronologique et monogrammatique des Beaux-Arts plastiques, architecture et mosaïque, céramique, sculpture, peinture et gravure (Demmin)   35–36
Encyclopédie méthodique. Architecture, 4 vols. (1788–1825)   27
Encyclópedie ou Dictionnaire raisonné des sciences, des arts et des métiers (Diderot & d'Alembert)   18, 27
engagement, reciprocal   348–349
engineering
  in general   97–98
  training in   117–118
  Western concept of   117
  See also construction principles
"Engineering reports on the San Francisco earthquake" (American Society of Civil Engineers)   114
entrepreneurs / traders   43–45
errors in knowledge transfer
  about Japanese architecture
    in book illustrations   288–289, **289**, **290**, **291**, **292**, **293**, **294**, 295–298, **295**, **296**, **298**, **299**, **300**, 300–305, **300**, **301**, **302**, **426**
    in souvenir photographs   321, **322**
Esaki, Reiji   **425**

"Essai sur l'architecture japonais" (Levieux) 57
essays
  on Japanese architecture
    in general 31–32
    by Alcock 53
    by Brunton 47–48
    by Burty 62
    by Cawley 60
    by Conder 56–57
    by Godwin 51–52
    by Lescasse 54–55
    by McClatchie 59
    by Milne 55
    by Montefiore 44–45
    by Pfoundes 64
    by Satow 49–50
    by Yamamoto 46–47
  on Japanese art
    in general 78
    by Burty 61
    by Jarvis 54
  See also under names of specific essays
ethnographic reports 38
ethnography / ethnology 161
"Étude sur les Constructions Japonaises" (Lescasse) 55
Eulenburg expedition (1859–1862) 270
"Exposition universelle de 1878: Le Japon ancien et le Japon moderne" (Burty) 61
Exposition Universelles (Paris). *See* International Exhibitions (Paris)

façades
  of Japanese pavilions at International Exhibitions 243, 245
  of Japanese sections on International Exhibitions 204, **205**, **206**, 221, **222**, 240
  in Tōkyō 310, 311, 427–428
fairy tales, Japanese 279
Far East (journal) 62
farmhouses, Japanese
  architectural models of 190, 192, **193**, 195, **412**
  farmyards and 271–272, **271**, 288
  interiors of 266
  at International Exhibitions 204–206, 207, **208**, **209**
  roofs of **267**
farmyards, Japanese 271–272, **271**, 288
Farsari, Adolfo 153, **154**
Fenollosa, Ernest F. 226
Fergusson, James 14–15, 28, 36, 163, 169–170, 327
  See also under names of specific works
"The Feudal Mansion of Yedo" (McClatchie) 59, 146
The Fifty-three Stations of the Tōkaidō Road (Hiroshige) 75, **76**, 77
Finn, Dallas 311
fire-ladders 280
fireproofing, of buildings 64
fires / conflagrations 133–134
The Firste Booke of Relations of Moderne States (Harleian Mss. 6249) 24
Five Architectural Orders 162
Fletcher, Banister
  on architecture of China 167
  on architecture of Japan 167, 169
  on non-historical styles 165–167
  sources of 58, 169
  tree of architecture 167, **168**
  See also A history of architecture
floor coverings 72
  See also tatami flooring
floor plans
  Conder's 261, **262**
  of Golden Hall of Hōryū-ji (Ikaruga) 245, **417**
  of Japanese pavilion (Paris, 1900) 245, **417**
  of small shrine **339**
folding screens 21
Foote, Andrew H. 29–30, 103
foreign settlements 141, **142**, 282, 319, 325
Franz Joseph I, Emperor of Austria 186, **186**
Freeman-Mitford, Algernon B., Baron Redesdale 279, 281
Fróis, Luís 38
Fuji, Mount 211, 279, 290, **291**, 312, 316, 430
Fujiya Hotel (Hakone) 326
funerals, Japanese 291, 303, **324**, **423**

INDEX 443

"Further Notes on Japanese Architecture" (Conder) 112

gardens, Japanese
   at International Exhibitions
      Paris (1889) 220, 222–223, **222**
      Philadelphia (1876) 199–200, **201**
      Vienna (1873) 182, **182**, **184**, **185**, **186**, **187**
   Western illustrations of
      skewed proportions in 301–302, **425**
      westernisms in 300, **301**, **302**
   Western photographs of **425**
   See also tea gardens
Gardiner, Robert S. 284
Garnier, Charles 223–224, 250
Die Gartenlaube (magazine) 39
gates, Japanese
   in general 204, 207, **210**
   of *daimyō* residence 183, 194, 195, **413**
   of Imperial Palace (Kyōto) 292, **293**, **294**
   of Street of Nations 204, **206**
   of Tōshō-gū (Nikkō) **214**
Gazette des beaux-arts (journal) 40
general-interest magazines 39–40
genkan (entryways) **299**
Geographical Society (London) 67
German East Asiatic Society (Deutsche Gesellschaft für Natur- und Völkerkunde Ostasiens, OAG) 66, 67
Gilbert, William S. 211
Ginkaku-ji (Silver Pavilion) (Kyōto) 233, 243, 246, **418**
Ginza district (Tōkyō) 125, 146, 326, **328**
Girard, Prudent **310**, 311
Glass, Chester **299**
A Glimpse at the Art of Japan (Jarves) 32, 53–54, 79–80, 81, 91
Godwin, Edward W. 31, 51–52, 82–83
Goff, Lieutenant Colonel 62
Gogh, Vincent van 307–308
Golownin, Wassili Michailowitsch 26, 42
Gonse, Louis
   in general 79, 136, 161, 247*n*129
   on decorative details 89–90
   on Japanese architecture 32, 83–84

references to works of 169, 257
sources used by 57
   for illustrations 257, **259**
See also under names of specific works
Goodwin, William 309
Great Buddha (Kamakura) 148–149, **149**
Great Stink (London) 131
Greey, Edward 289, 304
Griffis, William E. 59, 62, 127, 295
Gropius, Walter 348
Guérineau, Abel J.-L. 89, **90**, 164, 256, 263, **263**, **264**, 336
Guide Book to Nikkō (Satow) 31, 49
Guide to the celebrated places in Kiyoto and the surrounding places for the foreign visitors (Yamamoto) 31, 46, 287, 313
Guimet, Émile 89, 144, 148

Hakodate 141*n*207, 282
Hakone 141, 282, **326**
Handbook of Architecture (Fergusson) 28, 36
Harada, Jiro 41, 169
Haruo, Sakata 109
Hasegawa, Settan 59
Haussmann, Georges-Eugène 131
Hawks, Francis L. 24, 268, 270–271, **271**, 275
Hayashi, Tadamasa 242
Heine, Wilhelm 129, 266, 268, 270–271, 272, 274, 282, 288–289, **290**, 291, 303, **423**
Hepburn, James C. 50
hierarchy, in Western architecture 82, 166–167
Hildreth, Richard 29, 103
hinagata, use of term 195
hinagatabon (pattern books)
   in general 195, 335
   technical illustrations in **336**, 337–338, **337**, **338**
   on theory of architecture 335–336
   unknown to Westerners 336–337, 338–339
hipped roofs
   curved 243
   half 217, 228, **231**, 238, 243
   with projecting eaves 223
   saddled 183
   straw-covered 179, **180**
   tiled 196

Hirata, Atsutane   50
Hiroshige. *See* Utagawa, Hiroshige
Histoire de l'architecture (Choisy)   163, 164, 169
Histoire de l'art du Japon (Imperial Commission of Japan for the Exposition Universelle de Paris)   32, 247, **247**
L'histoire de l'habitation humaine (exhibition) (Paris)   223–224, **225**, **416**
historical styles, vs. non-historical styles   165–167
A history of architecture (Fletcher)   14–15, 58, 163–164, 165–167, **168**, 169, 171
   See also Fletcher, Banister
A history of architecture in all countries (Fergusson)   36
History of Architecture (Kimball)   171
History of Indian and Eastern Architecture (Fergusson)   36, 163, 169–171
The History of Japan (Kaempfer)   25, 29, 33, 59, 102–103, 121, 136, 274 295, **296**
   See also Kaempfer, Engelbert
Hobrecht, James   131
Hokusai. *See* Katsushika, Hokusai
Holme, Charles   41, 214
Holme, Charles G.   119
Holmes, Elias B.   246, 248–249
Honmachi-dori (Yokohama)   **326**
Hō-ō-den (Phoenix Palace) (Chicago International Exhibition)   32–33, 226–228, **227**, **229**, 230
Hō-ō-dō (Phoenix Hall) (Uji)   32, 228, 230, **416**
Hōryū-ji Temple (Ikaruga)   246, **332**
hotels   325–326, **326**
Hotta Garden (Tōkyō)   301, **425**
houses. *See* dwelling houses
Hozumi, Kazuo   2
Hübner, Alexander Graf von   62, 133, 151, 258, 260, 292–293, **293**
Humbert, Aimé   51, 169, 266, 274–275, **286**, **298**
   See also Le Japon illustré
Hundred views of Mount Fuji (Hokusai)   279
hygiene, in Japan   128–130, 132

The Illustrated London News (magazine)   175, **176**, 215, 253, 274

illustrations, Japanese
   of Japanese architecture
      used in Western publications   267, **269**, 277, 278–279, **280**, **281**, **422**
   woodblock prints. *See* woodblock prints
illustrations, Western
   of Japanese architecture
      in general   305–306, 340–341
      in architectural books   254–258, **259**, 260, 263, **263**, **264**, 265–266, **265**, **266**, **421**
      in architectural periodicals   256, 257, **259**, 261, **261**, **262**, **421**
      in books about Japanese culture   266–268, **268**, **269**, 270–272, **270**, **271**, **273**, 274–277, **276**, **277**, **278**
      canonisation of visual topics in   282–284, 287
      focus on decorative aspects   262–263
      imagination and   290, **291**
      incorrect captions by   303–305, **304**, **305**
      Japanese sources for   267, **269**, 277, 278–279, **280**, **281**, **422**
      in literary works   279, **280**, **281**, **422**
      re-use of   257–258, **259**, 260, 267–268, 270–272, 275, 279
      Sinoisms in   293, 295, **295**
      skewed proportions in   295–298, **296**, **299**–300, **300**
      source material for   256–257, 266, 267, 275
      transfer errors in   288–289, **289**, **290**
      westernisms in   290–293, **292**, **293**, **423**
   of Japanese gardens
      skewed proportions in   301–302
      westernisms in   300, **301**, **302**
Illustrations of Japan (Titsingh)   74, **75**
Illustrirte Zeitung (magazine)   191, 219
Illustrirtes Bau-Lexikon (Mothes)   35, 267
Images of Japan in Non-Japanese Sources (Nichibunken project)   254
Imperial College of Engineering (Tokyo)   56, 60

INDEX 445

Imperial College of Technology (Tōkyō)   117–118
Imperial Commission of Japan for the Exposition Universelle de Paris   247
Impressions of Japanese Architecture and The Allied Art (Cram)   170
indexing, of woodblock prints   308–309
India, architecture in   348
industrialisation   128, 131, 140, 158
"The influence of Greco-Persian art on Japanese arts" (Dooman)   39
Inland Architect (journal)   233
inns, interiors of   74–75, **76**, 77
Institute of British Architects   27
   See also Royal Institute of British Architects (RIBA)
intercolumnium   169, 243, 245
interiors / interior design, Japanese
   at Architectural Museum (Sapporo)   414
   of dwelling houses   73, 74, 152–153, **154**, 281, **422**
   of farmhouses   266
   of inns   74–75, **76**, 77
   at International Exhibitions
      Chicago (1893)   237
      Paris (1878)   205–206, 209
      Philadelphia (1876)   193, **413**
   in Western illustrations
      in general   266
      skewed proportions in   298, **299**–300, **300**
International Exhibition (1862) (London)   175–176, **176**
International Exhibition (1867) (Paris)   176–181
   Japanese displays at   176–177, **177**
   pavilion of *daimyō* of Satsuma at   178–179, **179**
   tea house / Japanese farm   178, 179, **179**, 180
International Exhibition (1873) (Vienna)   181–196
   Japanese complex bought by trading company   52, 186, 189
   Japanese exhibits / models at   181–182, 189, **190**, 190–191, 191–192, **191**, 193, 194–196, 330, **412**, **413**
   Japanese garden at   182, **182**, **184**, **185**, 186, **187**
   kagura stage at   183, **187**
   Shintō shrine at   182, **184**, **185**, 186, **187**
   tea houses at   181–182, 186, **188**
International Exhibition (1876) (Philadelphia)   196–203
   Japanese Bazaar at   198–199, **199**
   Japanese construction at   98
   Japanese dwelling at   95, 196–198, **197**, **198**
   Japanese exhibits / models at   200, **201**
   Japanese garden at   199–200, **201**
   Japanese interior at   198, **413**
   Japanese workmen at   99–100, 200, 202, **202**, **203**
   preparations for   63
International Exhibition (1878) (Paris)   204–210
   catalogue of   62–63
   Japanese farmhouse at   204–205, **207**, **208**, **209**
   Japanese interior at   205–206, 209
   Japanese pavilion at   204, **205**, **206**
International Exhibition (1889) (Paris)   219–226
   exterior façade of Japanese section   220, **221**
   Japanese dwelling at   223–224, **225**, 250, **416**
   Japanese exhibits / models at   220
   Japanese garden at   220, 222–223, **222**
   Japanese workmen at   221
   tea houses at   222–223
International Exhibition (1893) (Chicago)   226–242
   Hō-ō-den at
      compared to Hō-ō-dō   228, **229**, 230, 231, **232**, **416**
      dedication ceremony at   232, **232**
      floor plan of   235
      half-hipped roofs of   228
      Jodan-no-ma   235, **237**
      as joint effort   226–227
      library and tea room at   233, **237**
      Okakura's booklet on   32–33, 227, 228, 233, 235–236

International Exhibition Hō-ō-den (*cont.*)
    structural elements of   **231**, **232**, **233**, **234**
  Japanese Bazaar at   240, **241**
  Japanese exhibition site at   **226**, **227**
  Japanese exhibits / models at   238, 240, **240**
  Japanese interiors at   **237**
  Japanese workmen at   **229**–**230**, **232**
  tea house / *mizuchaya* at   238, **239**
International Exhibition (1900) (Paris)   242–252
  art book presented at   247, **247**
  Japanese exposition site at   243
  Japanese pavilion at   244, **418**
    building material for   246
    compared to Ginkaku-ji / Kinkaku-ji (Kyōto)   243, 246
    compared to Golden Hall of Hōryū-ji (Ikaruga)   243, 245, **417**
    description of   243
    Japanese self-representation at   242
  Tour du Monde at   248–249, **248**
  See also Japanese Tower
International Exhibition (1929) (Barcelona)   42
International Exhibitions
  German architecture at, Barcelona (1929)   42
  Japanese architectural models at   180–181, 189, 190, 191–192, **191**, **193**, 194–196, 238, 240, **412**, **413**
  Japanese architecture at
    in general   173–175, 343
    authenticity and   241–242
    Chicago (1893)   226–242
    disinterest in   174
    influence on Western architecture   174, 250, 252
    Paris (1867)   176–181
    Paris (1878)   204–210
    Paris (1889)   219–226
    Paris (1900)   242–252
    Philadelphia (1876)   196–203
    Vienna (1873)   181–196
    Western knowledge / knowledge transfer   200, 224, 231, 241–242, 246, 250–252
  Japanese art at   251
  Japanese building materials at   119
  Japanese exhibits / models at   200, **201**
  Japanese policies towards   251
  Japan's self-representation at   223n86, 235–236, 242
iron constructions   115
  See also wooden constructions
Ise, shrines at   44, 49–50, 183, **333**
Ise Sangu Meisho Zue   50, 313
Ishida, Saijirō   46
Iwakuni   **435**

Japan
  landscapes of. *See* landscapes
  map of   **142**
  Meiji modernisation programme   4, 29, 124
  political upheavals in   145
  recreational sights in. *See* recreational sights
  research on   5
  tourist travel in   30–31
  use of term   41–42
  Western knowledge of. *See* knowledge / knowledge production, Western
  Westerners on. *See* Westerners
Japan (Mossman)   303
Japan, its Architecture, Art and Art Manufactures (Dresser)   32, 92, 107–110, 169, 256, **421**
  See also Dresser, Christopher
Japan. As it was and is (Hildreth)   29, 103
Japan Gazette (journal)   54–55
Japan Society (London)   41, 49, 53, 56, 60, 66
The Japan Weekly Mail (newspaper)   56
Japanese, use of term   41–42
"Japanese architecture" (Champier)   110
"Japanese Art" (Alcock)   80
The Japanese Bazaar (Strahan)   95
"Japanese Building" (Godwin)   51, 82–83
The Japanese Dwelling (Westcott)   95
Japanese Homes and Their Surroundings (Morse)
  in general   32, 48, 69–70, 255, 265
  criticism of   158
  illustrations in   265–266, **265**, **266**
  references to   169

INDEX 447

Japanese Homes (cont.)
    reviews of   157, 158
    See also Morse, Edward S.
Japanese temples and Tea-Houses (Blaser)   51–52n118
Japanese Tower (Laeken, Belgium)   250, **419, 420**
Japanese Village (Berlin)   218–219
Japanese Village (London)
    in general   186, 189, 211, 213–214, 218
    description of   214–215
    sleeping quarters at   218
    streets at   215
    taking tea at   215–216, **216**
    temple at   216–217, **217**, 218
    theatre at   215
"Japanese wood construction" (Godwin)   31
Japaneseness
    dwelling houses and   151, 156–157, 158–159
    use of term   41, 42
Das Japanische Haus (Baltzer)   170, 263
"Die Japanische Kunst" (Lützow)   257, **259**
Le Japon illustré (Humbert)   51, 169, 200, 275–276, **278**, **283**, **286**, **288**, **289**, **298**
    See also Humbert, Aimé
Le Japon pratique (Régamey)   147
Japonica   6, 44, 224, 342
Japonisme
    academic studies on   12
    architecture and   2–3, 6, 224, 329
    in art periodicals   40–41
    Burty and   61, 63
    Godwin and   52
    influence on Western art   77, 149, 173–174
Jarves, James J.   32, 53–54, 79–80, 81, 91
Jaucourt, Louis de   18–19, 27
Jeanneret, Charles-Édouard   348
Jephson, R. Mounteney   **283**, 286
Jinshin Survey (1872)   329–330, **332–334**, 334

Kaempfer, Engelbert
    in general   25, 42
    on building safety   102–103, 107
    on Japanese dwellings   129
    references to   25, 29, 53, 59, 103, 121, 136, 274
    See also *The History of Japan*

kagura stages   183, **187**
Kamakura   148–149, **149**, 282, **283**
Kami temple (Ise shrine)   44
kamoi (head jambs)   296–297
Kan'ei-ji (Tōkyō-Ueno)   87, 88, 145
karahafu gable   217, **217**, 218
karamon (decorated gate)   213, **214**
Karow, Otto   38
katōmado (bell-shaped windows)   **244**, 245
Katsushika, Hokusai   51, 267, **269**, 279, 309, 316, **432**
Kawakami, Otojiro   212–213, **213**
Kawakami, Sadayakko   213
ken (basic measure)   169
keyaki (zelkova serrata)   204
Kimball, Fiske   171
Kingo, Tatsuno   56
Kinkaku-ji (Golden Pavilion) (Kyōto)   236n110, 243, 246, 304, **418**
Kinryūzan Temple (Tōkyō)   **317**
Kintai Bridge (Iwakuni)   **435**
Kishida, Hideto   169
Klaproth, Heinrich Julius   26, 62
Knapp, Arthur M.   224
Knapp House   224, 250
knowledge / knowledge production, Western
    about Japan
        in general   17–18, 343
        in encyclopaedias   18–26
        heterogeneity of   344
        mediators of. See knowledge mediators
        in popular media   211–212, **212**
        in travelogues   29–31
    about Japanese architecture
        in general   3–4, 171–172, 281, 287–288, 302–303, 342, 343, 348–349
        in architectural books   27–28, 34, 38, 161–172, 254–258, 263, **263**
        in art books   32–33, 38
        attribution of meaning to   344–345
        data collecting and   159–160
        deficiencies in   1–2
        through documentary photography. See documentary photography
        in encyclopaedias   18–24
        in essays. See essays
        in ethnographical reports   39–40

knowledge about Japanese (*cont.*)
    in illustrations. *See* illustrations, Western
    through International Exhibitions   200, 224, 231, 241–242, 246, 250–252. *See also* International Exhibitions
    through Japanese Villages. *See* Japanese Villages
    mediators of. *See* knowledge mediators
    in periodicals   39–40
    through souvenir photographs. *See* souvenir photographs
    transfer errors in   288–293, **290**, **291**, **292**, **293**, **294**, 295–298, **295**, **296**, **298**, **299**, 300–305, **300**, **301**, **302**, **426**
    in travelogues   29–31
    visual sources and   33–34
    See also knowledge systems, Western; Westerners
knowledge mediators
    in general   65–66
    architects working in Japan as   54–58
    art historians as   53–54
    diplomatic personnel as   47–48, 52–54, 58–59
    engineers working in Japan as   60
    English architects as   51–52
    entrepreneurs / traders as   43–45
    foreign advisors / teachers as   43, 47–48, 66
    Japanese administrators as   46–47
    military / navy personnel as   63–65
    networks and   42–43, 66
    restrictions on   42–43
    topics addressed by   66
    See also under specific knowledge mediators
knowledge systems, Western   79–80, 120, 140, 345–346
Kobayashi, Kiyochika   **431**
Kōbe   141*n*207
Kodaiji temple (Nagasaki)   **435**
Kojiki-den (Norinaga)   50
Kondō (Golden Hall) of Hōryū-ji (Ikaruga)   243, 245, **417**
Kong-tching-tsofa   164

Koshi seibun (Hirata)   50
Kozyreff, Chantal   250
Kreitner, G. R. von   **425**
Kuki, Ryuichi   226
Kunst und Handwerk in Japan (Brinckmann)   257, **259**
kura (fire-resistant storehouses)   271, 291, 345, **423**
Kuril Islands   26
Kuru, Masamichi   226, 236
Kusakabe, Kimbei (also Kinbei)   258, **260**, **425**, **434**, **435**
Kyōto
    Gojō-bashi area in   **314**
    Imperial palace in   292, **293**, **294**, 332
    Imperial Villa in   **333**
    industrial exhibitions in   46
    Nijō Castle   296, **424**
    Satsuma residence in   297, **298**
    as source of visual information   283, 287

La Farge, John   131–132, 144, 148–149, 156
Labarthe, Charles de   45
Landscape Gardening in Japan (Conder)   300
landscape painting   141
landscapes
    of Japan
        Westerners on   137–138
        See also recreational sights
    picturesqueness of   143
    Western appreciation of   140
Le Corbusier   348
"Lecture on the Hygienic aspects of Japanese dwelling houses" (Seymour)   151
"A Lecture upon Architecture" (Conder)   56, 57
Leipziger Illustrirte Zeitung (magazine)   191, 219
Leopold II, King of Belgium   249–250
Lescasse, Jules   54–55, 106
Letters from the Orient (Wilson)   304, **305**
Levieux, Fernand   57
libraries / library rooms   67, 233, **237**
lighthouses   47
Lindau, Rudolph   123
Linfoot, Benjamin   197, **198**
lithic materials   119

INDEX

living standards, Japanese   134–135
London. *See* International Exhibition (1862)
Lowell, Percival L.   94
Lützow, Carl von   257, **259**

Machida, Hisanari   330
Maclay, Arthur C.   **304**
Madama Butterfly (opera) (Puccini)   211–213
Manga (Hokusai)   51, 267, 309
Manners and customs of the Japanese (ed. unknown)   26
Marcel, Alexandre   248, **248**, **249**, 250, **419**, **420**
Maron, Hermann   136–140
marriage, Japanese   139
Mathews, Charles Thompson   143–144
Matsuo, Ihei   182, 196
"The Mausoleum at Nikko" (Conder)   31
McCabe, Jame   303
McClatchie, Thomas R. H.   31, 57, 58–59, 123n156, 146, 313
McVean, Colin A.   64
Meijlan, Felix   25
meisho zue (illustrated travel guides)   309, 312–313, **314**
Mellado, Francisco de Paula   23–24
Memoires de la Societé des Ingénieurs (journal)   55
Memorials of the Empire of Japan (Rundall)   24
Menpes, Mortimer   276, **277**
metal fittings   87
Meyers Conversations-Lexicon   22, 23, 25–26
The Mikado (opera) (Gilbert & Sullivan)   211, **212**, **415**
The Mikado's Empire (Griffis)   59, 62, 295
military / navy personnel   29, 43, 63–66
Milne, John   48, 55
Minamoto, Toyomune   169
Ministry of Foreign Affairs (Japan)   124
Mino-Owari earthquake   114
missionaries   29, 43
   See also Brown, Samuel R.; Dooman, Isaac; Fróis, Luís; Hepburn, James C.; Syle, Edward W.
Mitsui bank building (Tōkyō)   310–311, **427**, **428**

Miyako meisho zue (Akisato)   31, 46–47, 312, **314**
mizuchaya. See tea houses / *mizuchaya*
A Model Japanese Villa (Ogawa)   327–328
modernisation
   decline in Japanese craftsmanship and   92
   Meiji programme of   4, 29, 124
mokoshi (enclosures)   217, **217**, 218, 245, **418**
monasteries   45, 245–246
Monet, Claude   307
monographs. *See* books / monographs
Montanus, Arnoldus   26
Montefiore, Édouard [Edward] Lévi   43–45, 62
monumental buildings   123–124
morality   130–131
Mori, Arinori   50
Morse, Edward S.
   in general   48
   on decline of Japanese culture   157
   on decorative details   89
   on economy of Japanese buildings   133
   on Japanese carpenters   96, 116
   on Japanese hygiene   131
   on Japanese living standards   134–135
   on Japanese tools   119
   references to   169, 170
   sources of   50, 57, 59, 61
   See also Japanese Homes and Their Surroundings
Mortimer, Favell L.   **284**
Moser, Michael   189, 192, **193**
Mossman, Samuel   303, **304**
Mothes, Oscar   34–35, 267
Muramatsu, Kichizō   191
Murray's Handbook to Japan   170
Musashiya, Kamakichi   194
Musashiya, Yonekichi   194
Musashiya workshop (Tōkyō)   194
Muthesius, Hermann   152

Nagasaki
   Dutch settlement in   25–26
   harbour of   282
   Kodaiji temple at   **435**
   photographers in   318–319
   Westerners on   141

449

450   INDEX

Nagasaki University Library   191n26, 258,
    303n187, 320
Nagoya castle   189, 303, **304**, 311
Naiko (Inner Shrine) (Ise)   **333**
Nara (city)   **333**
*Narrative of the Earl of Elgin's Mission to
    China and Japan* (Oliphant)   279, 280
*Narrative of the expedition of an American
    squadron to the China seas and Japan*
    (Hawks)
    in general   24, 266
    illustrations from   268, 270–272, **271**,
        273, 274
National Library of Australia   320
National Museum (Tōkyō)   189, 329–330
networks, knowledge mediators and   42–43,
    66
Neumann, Karl F.   27
New York Public Library   320
Niijima, Jō   46
Niijima, Yae   46
Nikkō
    in general   145
    as source of visual information   283
    Westerners on   50, 62, 84, 85, 87–88, **111**,
        143–144
    See also Tōshō-gū
Nippon (Von Siebold)
    in general   25
    illustrations in
        in general   33, 35, 73
        manor houses   **74**, 270
        origins of   266–267
        temples   **268**
        Yahagi Bridge   317, **433**
Die Nippon-Fahrer (Steger a.o.)   267, 272,
    273, 280, **423**
Nishi, Kazuo   2
Niwa, Keisuke   46
non-historical styles, vs. historical styles
    165–167
Norinaga, Motoori   50
norms / codes, of built representations   151,
    160
"Notes on Japanese architecture" (Conder)
    56–57, 87, 169
"Notes on Japanese architecture" (Dresser)
    88

"Notes on the city of Yedo, the Capital of
    Japan" (Lindau)   123
"Notes sur L'architecture au Japon. A Propos
    de L'exposition Universelle de 1878"
    (Burty)   45, 48, 62, 207
novels, Japanese   279

Ogawa, Kazumasa   320, **321**, 327–328, **434**
ōhiroma (audience halls)   296, **296**, **424**
Okakura, Kakuzō   32–33, 226–227, 228, **229**,
    233, 235–236
Okazaki   316, **432**
Oliphant, Laurence   279, 291, **423**
Ōmori, Fusakichi   114
"On a Neglected Principle that may be
    Employed in Earthquake Measurement"
    (Ayrton & Perry)   61
"On Construction in Earthquake Countries"
    (Milne)   55
"On structures in earthquake countries"
    (Ayrton & Perry)   61
One Hundred Famous Views of Edo
    (Hiroshige)   47
opera   211–213, **212**, **213**
Ornements japonais (Guérineau)   89, **90**,
    263
Ōsaka   35, 141n207, 283, 287, 303
Österreichische Monatsschrift für den Orient
    (journal)   40
othering, Japanese culture and   84, 85,
    137–139, 161
Ottoman Empire, architecture in   348
Overmeer Fisscher, J. Frederik van   25

pagodas
    architectural models of   191, **191**, 238,
        240
    construction principles of   109–112, **111**,
        114–115
    Japanese Tower (Laeken, Belgium)   250,
        419, **420**
    See also under specific pagodas
Paris
    art schools in   41, 80–81
    International Exhibition (1867) at
        176–181
    International Exhibition (1878) at
        62–63, 204–210

INDEX 451

Paris (cont.)
    International Exhibition (1889)
        at   219–226, **416**
    International Exhibition (1900) at
        242–252, **417, 418**
    renovations of   131
    See also International Exhibitions
Paris, A.   298
Parker, Peter   26
Parkes, Harry S.   48, 50, 58
partitioning, of dwelling houses   71–72
pattern books. *See hinagatabon*
periodicals
    Japanese architecture in
        in general   342–343
        architectural journals   41–42
        art journals   40–41
        cultural journals / general-interest
            magazines   39–40
        illustrations in. *See* illustrations,
            Japanese; illustrations, Western
    See also books / monographs; essays;
        under specific names of periodicals
Perry, John   61, 106
Perry, Matthew C.   23, 28–29, 266, 268
Pfoundes, Charles J. W.   57, 63–66, 116–117, 133
Philadelphia. *See* International Exhibition (1876)
Philadelphia Times (newspaper)   98–100
The philosophy of art (Taine)   54
photography
    in Japan
        in general   318–319
        of Jinshin Survey   329–331, **332–334**, 334
    See also souvenir photographs
The pictorial arts of Japan (Anderson)   63
Pictorial guide to the celebrated localities of Edo (issued by Saitō)   59, 313, **315, 427–428**
picturesqueness   143
popular media   211–213, **213**
poverty   21
Preußische Expedition nach Ostasien (Spieß) 267
privacy, lack of   155, 156
production, knowledge   348–349

Promenades japonaises (Guimet)   89, 144, 148

Questions upon various subjects connected with architecture (Institute of British Architects)   27–28

rafters   **337**
Ramée, Daniel   35
rangaku (Dutch learning)   46
recreational sights, of Japan   141, **142**, 143–144
    See also landscapes; tourist travel
Reed, Edward J.   **304**
referencing by authors
    in general   65, 171, 343
    to Alcock   53
    to Baltzer   170
    to Brunton   48, 62
    to Burty   63
    to Cawley   61
    to Chamberlain   169, 170
    to Conder   57–58, 169, 170, 257
    to Cram   170
    to Dresser   110, 169, 170, 257
    to Godwin   52
    to Gonse   169, 257
    to Humbert   51, 169
    to individuals in VOC service   25–26
    to Japanese sources   45, 50, 51, 59, 169
    to Jarvis   54
    to Kaempfer   25, 29, 59, 103, 121, 136, 274
    to de Labarthe   45
    lack of   268
    to Lescasse   55
    to McClatchie   57, 59
    to *meisho zue* guides   313
    to Morse   169, 170
    to Pfoundes   64
    to de Rosny   45
    to Satow   50
    to Von Siebold   25, 29, 267, 270, 274
    to Titsingh   170
    to travelogues   62–63
Régamey, Félix   104, 119, 147, 151
Rein, Johannes J.   103–104, 129–130
religions. *See* temples / shrines
"Remarks on Architecture" (Conder)   81–82

Renjo, Shimooka   34
Revue de l'architecture et des travaux publics (journal)   62
rinzō (storage unit for *sutra*)   267, **268**, **269**
Rohe, Ludwig Mies van der   42
roofs
    hipped. *See* hipped roofs
    ridged   **265**
    thatched   **265**
Rosny, Léon de   45
Rossetti, D. Gabriel   **154**
Roussin, Alfred   274
Royal Asiatic Society (London)   67
Royal Courts of Justice (London)   95–96
Royal Institute of British Architects (RIBA)   112, 261
    See also Institute of British Architects
Rundall, Thomas   24
Ryōgoku Bridge (Tōkyō)   316, **426**
Ryukyu Islands   26

Sada Yacco   212–213, **213**
Saitō, Yukinari   59
sanitation   131
Sapporo   126, 216*n*74
Satō, Tadanobu   257
Satow, Ernest M.   31, 48–52, 313
Satsuma residence (Kyōto)   297, **298**
Schliemann, Heinrich   121–122
Schweizerischer Werkbund   42
Scidmore, Eliza   147, 151
sciences   22, 118
Seckel, Dietrich   38
self-representation, Japanese
    at International Exhibitions   223*n*86, 235–236, 242
        See also under specific International Exhibitions
    at Tōkyō   146
Senso-ji temple (Tōkyō)   250, 316, **317**, **435**
sewer systems   131
Seymour, John N.   151
Shiba   85, **259**–260
Shimizu, Kisuke II   311
Shimizu, Usaburō   178
Shimoda   29–30, 282, 291, 303, **423**
Shimonoseki Campaign (1864)   44
shinden zukuri   230, 233, 234, **237**, 246

Shinn, Earl (Edward Strahan)   95
"The Shin-tau Temples of Ise" (Satow)   31, 49–50
Shintō shrines. *See* temples / shrines
shōji (sliding doors)   222, 234, 321, **322**
Shokoku meikyō kiran (Hokusai)   316
Shōsai, Ikkei   **431**
Shōshōin (Nara)   **333**
Siebold, Heinrich von   186
Siebold, Philipp Franz von
    in general   25, 42, 317
    references to works of   25, 29, 53, 267, 270, 274
    sources used by   309
    See also Nippon
sight-Seeing. *See* recreational sights; tourist travel
Sinoism, in illustrations   293, 295, **295**
Sixty-nine Stations of the Kisokaidō (Hiroshige)   74, **76**
Smith, T. Roger   55
social norms   155–156
Société d'Ethnographie Americaine et Orientale (Paris)   44
"Some remarks on Construction in Brick and Wood, and their relative suitability for Japan" (Cawley)   60
Sone, Tatsuzō   114
The soul of the Far East (Lowell)   94
souvenir albums   319, 320
souvenir photographs
    in general   34, 318
    architectural information in
        in general   320, 325, 327–329, 340–341
        of interiors   320–321, **322**, **434**
        lack of information on   325
        of sights / landscapes   321, 323, **324**, 325, **435**
        Western-style structures in   325–326, **326**, **327**
    collecting / collections of   319, 320
spatial dimensions, errors in   295–298, **296**, 297, 298, 299, 300, **300**, **424**
spatial fluidity   153, **154**, 155–156
Spiers, Richard Phené   169–170
Spieß, Gustav   267
staffage personnel   197, 300, 327, 331
Steger, Friedrich   **423**

INDEX 453

Stein, Ernst von   153
Steinmetz, Andrew   295, 300, 301
Stevenson, David   47
Stevenson, Thomas   47
Stillfried, Baron Raimund von   181–182, 186, 188
Stories about Japan (Butler)   304, 305
Strahan, Edward (Earl Shinn)   95
Strange, Edward F.   48, 82
"The Streets and Street-Names of Yedo" (Griffis)   127
Studio: international art (journal)   40–41
substantiality   81–82, 106
Sullivan, Arthur   211
Suruga-chō neighbourhood (Tōkyō)   313, 315, 427–428, 430
suspended posts   110–112
Syle, Edward W.   50

Taine, Hippolyte   54
Tales of Old Japan (Freeman-Mitford)   279, 281
Tamamura, Kozaburo   321, 324, 326, 434, 435
tatami (basic measure)   169
tatami flooring   215, 216, 233
tea gardens   239, 301, 302
tea houses / *mizuchaya*
    book illustrations of   278
    at Chicago Exhibition (1893)   238, 239
    at Paris Exhibition (1867)   179, 179, 180
    at Paris Exhibition (1889)   222–223
    at Vienna Exhibition (1873)   181–182, 186, 188
tea rooms, at International Exhibitions   233, 237
Technologisches Wörterbuch: Deutsch-Englisch-Französisch: Gewerbe, Civil- & Militär-Baukunst, Artillerie, Maschinenbau, Eisenbahnwesen, Strassenund Wasserbau, Schiffbau und Schiffahrt   35
temples / shrines (Shintō & Buddhist)
    architectural models of   193
    book illustrations of   267, 268, 278, 422
    Hōryū-ji Temple (Ikaruga)   332
    at International Exhibitions   182, 184, 185, 186, 187
    irrelevance in architectural discourse   70
    at Ise   44, 49–50, 183, 333
    at Japanese Village (London)   216–217, 217, 218
    Kinryūzan Temple (Tōkyō)   317
    Kodaiji temple (Nagasaki)   435
    photographs of   435
    section and floor plans for   339
    Senso-ji (Tōkyō)   250, 316, 317, 435
    Tozen-ji temple (Tōkyō)   124
    Tsurugaoka Hachiman-gū (Kamakura)   282, 285–286, 304, 305
    Westerners on   19–20, 21, 44
    in Yamamoto's guide   46
    Zōjō-ji temple (Tōkyō)   258, 259, 260, 316, 317
"Les temples au Japon avec une eau-forte" (Montefiore)   44, 62
"Les temples japonais" (Daly)   31, 89, 256, 421
Terajima, Ryōan   45
"Theatres in Japan" (Conder)   56, 57
Thérond, E.   275, 292
Things Japanese (Chamberlain)   57, 61, 84, 132, 150–151, 169
Thirty-six Views of Mount Fuji (Hokusai)   279
Thunberg, Carl P.   25–26, 71–73
The Times (newspaper)   217
Titsingh, Isaac   25, 62, 74, 75, 170
tokonoma (recessed alcove)   233, 234, 281, 422
Tokugawa shogunate
    burial site. *See* Zōjō-ji temple
    changing building policies of   335
    memorial sites. *See* Nikkō; Shiba
    See also daimyō residences
Tōkyō (Edo)
    Baba-chō neighbourhood in   315
    destruction of buildings in   145–146
    Edo Castle   235
    façades in   310, 311, 427–428
    foreign residences /settlements in   124, 141n207, 278, 323
    Ginza district   125, 146, 326, 328
    harbour of   275, 276, 277
    hotels in   326, 327
    Hotta Garden in   301, 425
    Kinryūzan Temple in   317

Tōkyō (Edo) (*cont.*)
    Mitsui bank building in   310–311, **427**, 428
    Musashiya workshop   194
    National Museum   189, 329–330
    Ryōgoku Bridge in   316, **426**
    Senso-ji temple at   250, 316, **317**, **435**
    as source of visual information   283, 287
    Suruga-chō neighbourhood in   313, **315**, **427**–**428**, **430**
    tourist travel to   146
    Tozen-ji temple   124
    urban reorganisation of   124–125, **124**
    Western descriptions of   122–123, 147
    westernisation of   146, 147
    Yoshiwara district in   328
    Zōjō-ji temple   316, **317**
Tōkyō Imperial Hotel   326, **327**
tools. *See* building tools, Japanese
Tōshō-gū (Nikkō)   50, 143, 213, **214**, 284
tourist travel
    noteworthy sites   30–31, **142**, 282
    souvenir photographs and. *See* souvenir photographs
    to Tōkyō   146
    to Yokohama   148
    See also recreational sights
towns. *See* cities
Tozen-ji temple (Tōkyō)   124
Transactions of the Asiatic Society of Japan   47, 49, 59, 61, 67
Transactions of the Royal Institute of British Architects   56, 261
travelogues
    early examples of   29–30
    increase in   38
    noteworthy sites in   30–31
Travels in Europe, Africa and Asia, made between the years 1770 and 1779 (Thunberg)   71–73
Tronson, John M.   301
Tsumaki Yorinaka   55
Tsurugaoka Hachiman-gū (Shintō shrine, Kamakura)   282, **285**–**286**, 304, **305**

Über Land und Meer (magazine)   39
Uchida, Kuichi   **434**, **435**

ukiyo-e (woodblock prints genre). *See* woodblock prints
urbanisation   124–127, 128, 131
Der Ursprung des Torii (Seckel & Karow)   38
Utagawa, Hiroshige   46, 47, 74–75, **76**, 77, 316, **317**, **426**, **430**, **432**, **433**
Utagawa, Hiroshige III   310, **431**
Utagawa, Kuniteru II   427
Utagawa, Sadahide   312, **429**, **432**
Utagawa, Yoshitora   427
Utagawa Hiroshige. *See* Hiroshige, Utagawa

Van Gogh Museum (Amsterdam)   308
Vereenigde Oostindische Compagnie (VOC)   25
Vienna. *See* International Exhibition (1873)
Visit to Simoda and Hakodai in Japan (Foote)   29–30
visual materials. *See* illustrations, Japanese; illustrations, Western
Vogel Chevroulet, Irène   58

Wagener, Gottfried   186
Wakan Sansai Zue (Terajima)   45
A walk through Japan (Goff)   62
walls   291, **292**
Watanabe, Yuzuru   326, **327**
Waters, Thomas James   64
Water-Tank at Shiba   258
Watts-Dunton, Theodore   **154**
wedding ceremony   75
Weltausstellung (1873) (Vienna). *See* International Exhibition (1873) (Vienna)
Weltmuseum (Vienna)   192
Das Werk (journal of the Schweizerischer Werkbund)   42
Westcott, Thompson   95, 118
Westerners
    designing Japanese dwellings   223–224, **225**, **416**
    on Japan
        homogeneity   146–147
        influence of the West on   139, 140, 150
        landscapes of   137–138
        as poor   134–135
        recreational sights   141, 143–144, 146–148

INDEX

Westerners (*cont.*)
  on Japanese architecture
    building materials   119–120
    building process   64, 95, 98–101
    building tools   118–119
    cities. *See under* cities, Japanese
    construction principles   55, 98–102, 171
    craftsmen. *See under* craftsmen / craftsmenship
    decorative details   86–90, **88, 89, 90**
    denial of creative spark   81
    disinterest in   161, 174, 262, 347–348
    dwelling houses. *See* dwelling houses, Japanese
    earthquake-resistant construction. *See* earthquake-resistant construction
    heterogeneous observations   170–171
    historical development of   166
    inferiority of   177
    irrelevance of   32, 36–37, 54, 60–61, 80, 101, 160–161, 166
    lack of knowledge of   36, 163
    perishable nature of   49–50
    similarity to Chinese   35
    substantiality and   81–82
    survey of building types   57
    temples / shrines   19–20, 21, 44
    Western artistic values and   80–82
    wooden constructions   60, 101, 104, 109, 115, 133
  on Japanese art
    inferiority of   18–19, 22, 79–80, 177
    Western artistic values and   79–80
  on Japanese landscapes   137–138
  See also knowledge / knowledge production, Western
westernisms, in illustrations   290–293, **292, 293,** 423
Wilson, A. W.   304, **305**
windows, bell-shaped   244, **245**
Wirgmann, Charles   274
women
  Japanese
    at International Exhibitions   179, **180, 181**
    in photographs   321, **322, 324**

Western
  Asiatic Society of Japan and   68
  as authors   65
"Wood, and its Application to Japanese Artistic and Industrial Design"(Cawley)   96–97
wood, varieties of   119
woodblock prints (*ukiyo-e*)
  in general   307
  architectural information in
    in general   74–75, **76,** 77, 307–309, 318, 340–341
    of bridges   316–318, **432–433**
    of famous sites   313, 316
    in *meisho zue*   312–313, **314**
    three genres of   309
    used in Western publications   277, 278–279, **280,** 281, 422
    yokohama-e   309–312, **310,** 427, **428**
  indexing of   308–309
  Western collectors of   307–309
wooden constructions
  parallels between iron and   115
  Westerners on
    economy of   133
    negative statements on   60, 101, 104, 115
    positive statements on   109
Wores, Theodore   152
workmen. *See* craftsmen / craftsmanship, Japanese
World's Columbian Exhibition (1893) (Chicago). *See* International Exhibition (1893) (Chicago)
World's Fairs. *See* International Exhibitions
worship practices   20
Wright, Frank Lloyd   174, 307

Yahagi Bridge (Okazaki)   316–317, **432, 433**
Yamamoto, Kakuma   31, 46–47, 287, 313
Yeh, Catherine   236*n*110
Yokohama
  in general   141*n*207, 283
  Catholic Church in   310–311, **310**
  Honmachi-dori in   **326**
  as source of visual information   283, 287

Yokohama (*cont.*)
   souvenir photographs of   **323**
   Westerners on   148
   woodblock prints   309, 312, **429**
Yokohama City Central Library   320

yokohama-e (woodblock prints genre)
   309–312, **427**
Yokoyama, Matsusaburo   330, **332**–**334**

Zōjō-ji temple (Tōkyō)   258, **259**, **260**, 316, **317**
"Zur Charakteristik Japan's" (Maron)   136–139